The Duchess of Windsor

Previous Works by Charles Higham

History and Politics
Trading with the Enemy
American Swastika
Rose: The Life Rose Kennedy
Howard Hughes: The Secret Life

Film and Theatre
Kate: The Life of Katharine Hepburn
Bette: The Life of Bette Davis
Errol Flynn: The Untold Story
Marlene Dietrich
The Art of the American Film
Hollywood in the Forties (with Joel Greenberg)
The Celluloid Muse (with Joel Greenberg)
The Films of Orson Welles
Orson Welles: The Rise and Fall of an American Genius

Plays (New York and Los Angeles)
His Majesty, Mr. Kean
Murder by Moonlight
Fighting the Gorilla
The Triumph of Eros

Literature
The Adventures of Conan Doyle

Poetry
A Distant Star
Spring and Death
The Earthbound and Other Poems
Noonday Country
The Voyage to Brindisi

The Duchess of Windsor

The Secret Life

REVISED AND UPDATED EDITION

Charles Higham

WILEY

John Wiley & Sons, Inc.

Published by John Wiley & Sons, Inc., Hoboken, New Jersey
Published simultaneously in Canada

Illustration credits: pages 239, 241–248 (top), 250, 252–253, 255–257 (top), 258, and 260–261 courtesy of Hulton Archive/Getty Images; pages 240 and 248 (bottom) courtesy of Hulton-Deutsch Collection/Corbis; page 249 courtesy of David E. Scherman/Time Life Pictures/Getty Images; pages 251, 254 (top), and 259 courtesy of Bettman/Corbis; page 254 (bottom) courtesy of Loomis Dean/Time Life Pictures/Getty Images; page 257 (bottom) courtesy of Corbis; page 262 (top) courtesy of Tim Graham/Corbis; and page 262 (bottom) courtesy of Popperfoto/Retrofile.com.

For general information about our other products and services, please contact our Customer Care Department within the United States at (800) 762-2974, outside the United States at (317) 572-3993 or fax (317) 572-4002.

Wiley also publishes its books in a variety of electronic formats. Some content that appears in print may not be available in electronic books. For more information about Wiley products, visit our web site at www.wiley.com.

ISBN 0-471-48523-3

10 9 8 7 6 5 4 3 2 1

For Richard V. Palafox
and Dorris Halsey

Special acknowledgment
to
Dr. Gerald Turbow

Contents

Photographs follow page 238

Author's Note

I have been fascinated by the Windsors from the age of 5 when, as the precocious child of Sir Charles Higham, the advertising tycoon and a member of Parliament (who would die when I was 7 and who had married, like Henry VIII, six times), I was brought from the nursery by my German nanny to the elegant drawing room of The Mount, our family home, to attend what I was informed was to be a momentous occasion. The men were in black tie, wreathed in clouds of smoke from expensive cigars; the women were in backless evening gowns, their shoulders vanishing in explosions of ruffles.

The combination of perfume and tobacco smoke made me feel ill; the decor of red, plush furniture and Chinese carpets swarming with dragons and exotic birds made me feel even worse. I sat on the edge of a Victorian chair, having been told that I must fix my attention on a speckled walnut cabinet that stood under a gothic landscape painting. The cabinet was the family shrine: a radiogramophone.

Father turned on the switch, and everyone at last stopped talking. We heard a voice announce the advent of the king. I understood nothing of what he said, in an American cockney voice adopted partly from his ladylove and partly from a succession of nannies. (Some fifty years later, I discovered that the only language he spoke with a perfect modulation was German.)

When the speech was over, the abdication speech which would become one of the half-dozen most famous broadcasts in history, there was a murmur of conversation. I am told that my godfather, the bestselling novelist Gilbert Frankau, broke into tears, that the staff was sobbing in the background, and that more than one visiting European aristocrat had mist on his monocle. I had no idea what "abdication" meant. I was probably thinking about my pet goldfish, whether my father would continue to keep me a kidnap victim (I had been snatched

from Mother in a Silver Ghost Rolls-Royce, hidden and almost smoth-
ered under a heavy sable rug), or whether I would be able to finish, under the bedcovers, unraveling a stubborn tennis ball with a penknife.

For years I have thought of writing about the Windsors. Every
book is a new adventure; my three visits to England in ten months in
1987 to research the first edition of this book were as much an exile's
journey of rediscovery as they were voyages of investigation. The England I had fled long ago had disappeared, to be replaced by a kinder,
warmer, and more appealing country. Along with its empire, Britain
had lost its stiffness and its stern, heartless formality. I was rewarded by
examples of kindness that made me feel as much at home as though I
had never left. I enjoyed lunch with Laura, Duchess of Marlborough,
and dinner with the legendary Margaret, Duchess of Argyll, as well as
country visits to Sir Dudley Forwood, former equerry and secretary to
King Edward VIII, and his fascinating wife, and to Adrian Liddell
Hart, son of the London *Times* military correspondent Basil Liddell
Hart. Sadly, by 2004 all have died. I had pleasant days at the home of
Hugo Vickers, who showed me evidence of the Windsors' charm in a
recording made of them in London, read this book for accuracy, and
gave me valuable advice. In France I had a memorable afternoon with
Pierre Laval's son-in-law, Comte René de Chambrun, at his offices,
the Cabinet Chambrun, at 25 Avenue des Champs-Elysées, and I
stayed at the Windsors' favorite French hotel, the Meurice, where the
staff showed me their suite. I also lunched with the late Lady Diana
Mosley at the Temple de la Gloire.

In the United States, I shall not forget visiting Alfred de Marigny
(falsely accused and acquitted of the murder of Sir Harry Oakes) and
his enchanting wife Mary at their home in secret-filled, luxurious
River Oaks, Houston, Texas. Among others who helped in America, I
must single out James P. ("Jay") Maloney, who in Washington, D.C.,
spent countless hours exploring obscure documents, struggling against
the restrictions of the Freedom of Information Act, and poring over
shipping lists of the Dollar Lines, the Royal Canadian Pacific Lines,
the Cunard Lines, naval intelligence files, passport files, immigration
records from Seattle and New York, and thousands more abstruse documentary sources that no other biographer or historian had examined.
Simultaneously, I spent sometimes frustrating but more often exciting
months at the University of California Research Library and the Von

Kleinsmid Library of the University of Southern California, as well as the Glendale and Pasadena Public Libraries, reading through scores of old magazines and examining such abstruse items as the 1924 guest lists of the Astor House Hotel, Shanghai, issues of the *South China Morning Post* and *Hong Kong Telegraph*, and reports on the Prince of Wales's Ball at San Diego's Hotel del Coronado sixty-five years ago.

In San Diego I had a series of enjoyable meetings with Mrs. Dale St. Dennis, charming granddaughter of Wallis Simpson's cousin and friend Corinne Montague Mustin Murray, who gave me first access to letters in which the duchess gave a vivid account of her life. Her father, Vice Admiral Lloyd Mustin, had found them. The Maryland Historical Society and Radcliffe College came up with more letters, the latter supplying the correspondence of Mary Kirk Raffray, Wallis's school friend, who later married Wallis's second husband, Ernest Simpson. Sir John Colville, former secretary to Sir Winston Churchill, and now sadly deceased, was a mine of information. So too was the late John Costello; Nigel West (Rupert Allason) proved to be informative on the intelligence background. The late Charles Bedaux, Jr., loyally did his best to soften my judgments upon his late father, who had committed suicide in 1944 following charges of treason and who had been the duke and duchess's host at the Château de Candé when they were married in 1937. Robert Barnes of Baltimore was very good on the genealogical background. The late John Ball helped me with the Sir Harry Oakes murder case, and I was further assisted by Dr. Joseph Choi, a forensic expert, and by Sergeant Louis Danoff. Richard A. Best did some early research.

A special acknowledgment must go to Dr. Gerald Turbow. Herbert Bigelow, Rabbi Abraham Cooper, Boris Celovsky, the late Richard Coe, Jim Christy, Mrs. Evelyn Cherfak, the Earl of Crawford, Alain Deniel, the late Kenneth de Courcy, Todd Andrew Dorsett, the late Tony Duquette, Hutton Wilkinson, the late Count Dino Grandi, Barbara Goldsmith, Martin Gilbert, Betty Hanley, Lord Hardinge, Kirk Hollingsworth, John Hope, Lord Ironside, Anna Irwin, Michael Kriz, Mrs. Milton E. Miles, Philippe Mora, Lady Mosley, the Duchess of Normanby, Donatella Ortona, Chapman Pincher, Peter Quennell, Daniel Re'em, Kenneth Rose, Jill Spalding, Rudolph Stoiber, Roberta Stitch, Mrs. Beatrice Tremain, John Vincent, and Frederick Winterbotham all gave of their help. And the excellent physical training methods of Richard M. Finnegan, the fine typing of Victoria Shellin, the great help and cooperation of Ann Craig, the expert copyediting of Susan Gottfried, and, in London, of Gillian Paul, and the very skilled editing and warm encouragement of Thomas W. Miller in New York and Robert Smith in London were indispensable in 1987–1988.

For assistance in obtaining the information for the new edition I am especially grateful to my Washington researcher Jill Cairns-Gallimore, who worked long and gallantly to find obscure records not seen outside of the National Archives in decades; to John Taylor, wise and illustrious head of the Modern Military branch of the same archives, colleague, supporter and friend; Dorris Halsey, incomparable literary agent, sage adviser; Bob O'Hara, diligent London researcher, and Jessica Gerger in the same city; Eleanor Davies Tydings Ditzen, in her late nineties a fount of information; Scott Libson and Tanya Chebotareff; Michael Neal in Paris, notable bookstore manager, good historian; Chi-Chi Barthelemy, French friend and contact; Andrea Lynn, indispensable source of the vanished diaries of Constance Coolidge; Martin Allen, excellent and incorruptible author; Aline, Countess of Romanones; Professor Jonathan Petropoulos; Herbert Reginbogen; Joel Greenberg; Jane Singer; and Michael Sutherland of Occidental College, Los Angeles; Margaret Shannon; Madgid Madgidi; Dr. Mildred de Riggi; Carolyn Ugolini; Heidi Sugden; Chapman Pincher; Nigel West; Fulton Oursler, Jr., and Harry Cooper of Sharkhunters. And it was a pleasure to work again with my original editor, Thomas Ward Miller, and with new editors in London, Emma Marriott and Jacqui Butler, as well as with the fine theater director Michael Clark Haney, and Udana Powers, master of word processing. My thanks also go to Kellam Ayres and Hope Breeman at John Wiley & Sons and to the copy editor of this revised edition, Roland Ottewell.

In the year 2003, after an interval of sixteen years, I was approached by American and British publishers to write an enlarged edition— hence the present, considerably enhanced reprint. The publication of the collected papers of Joseph P. Kennedy, former ambassador to London, and father of the later president, in 2002, with unprecedented details of royal reactions to the Windsors, rendered such a publication mandatory; and my chance discovery of Andrea Lynn's excellent *Shadow Lovers*, about the love affairs of H. G. Wells, led me to the unpublished diary of Constance Coolidge, which in turn revealed the existence of an astonishing story of attempted blackmail and extortion, set in Paris in the troubled March of 1938, that took me months to unravel.

In addition, at the suggestion of a friend, I contacted the remarkable Eleanor Davies Ditzen, daughter of U.S. ambassador to Russia Joseph E. Davies, who told me of the Duchess of Windsor's prolonged and unknown affair with William Christian Bullitt, Davies's replacement as emissary to Moscow and the famous ambassador to France from 1936 to 1940, who new documents show was a Nazi collaborator. In the course of researching this unknown romance, I found in Washington, through Jill Cairns-Gallimore, the massive FBI files on Elsa Schiaparelli, the great Italian dress designer, whose salon the duchess and the ambassador used for their liaison.

Other leads brought me to the previously unavailable files of Kenneth de Courcy, Duke de Grantmesnil, at the Hoover Institution on War, Revolution and Peace at Stanford University, which confirmed the existence of the much argued-over China dossier in which King George V and Prime Minister Stanley Baldwin explored the duchess's activities as prostitute and drug dealer in China in 1924; and I was led by complicated threads to the little-known archives of Russian émigrés at the Bakhmeteff Archive at Columbia University, courtesy Tanya Chebotarev, where one remarkable letter from the Queen of England attacking the Windsors had survived generations of weeders in England, and where the highly explosive letters of the Duke of Kent to Prince Paul of Yugoslavia have been preserved. Through the British historian Martin Allen, a leading authority on the subject, I learned of the confession of the assassination of the Duke of Kent by Squadron Leader Frederick Winterbotham of the British Secret Intelligence Service in 1942.

In June 2003, I stumbled on a forgotten memoir housed in the labyrinthine stacks of the Doheny Library of the University of California. Princess Viktoria Luise, the Duchess of Brunswick, daughter of Kaiser Wilhelm II of Germany, illuminated for me, as nobody else could have done, that Hitler and King George V's approved choice of wife for the future King Edward VIII was Viktoria's daughter, Princess Friederike of Prussia and Hanover. Had that wedding taken place, and Wallis Simpson been royal mistress, the course of history might have been changed. How could England declare war on Germany when the granddaughter of its former ruler, and the choice of Hitler and King George V, was on the English throne? That the British royal family had forgiven their cousin the kaiser by 1935 is clear from the flood of German members who appeared at the Silver Jubilee of King George V that summer and the following January at his funeral, not to mention the flood of royal congratulations sent to his Dutch place of exile on the occasion of his eightieth birthday in 1939.

Of my many intriguing experiences exploring sites of the events during a visit to Paris and London in October 2003, the most curious was a visit to 36 Boulevard Emile Augier, scene of the 1938 blackmail plot against the Duke and Duchess of Windsor described on pages 275–281. This once elegant street had become a litter-strewn anomaly, the area gloomy and unkempt under threatening black clouds and bursts of rain.

Next to the badly painted apartment house where once Wallis's friend Constance Coolidge had a strange assignation with an Italian adventuress, stood a mysterious abandoned building, a prison perhaps, or a reform school, with high beetling black walls; and on the other side of the street, protected by black-painted iron railings, a desolate chasm, filled with enormously tall weeds, some as high as thirty feet, and beneath their sinister proliferating, sickly yellow, orange, and purple growths, the indications of an abandoned railway siding, the tracks of the long-vanished La Muette (the woman who does not speak), a railroad station long since abandoned after the Metro, the underground system, replaced it sometime in the 1950s. No more melodramatic a mise-en-scène could be imagined by a biographer who had not previously seen the site of a dark and unknown chapter in the perilous lives of the Windsors.

From this book, and from associative chronicles by royal figures of that era, I obtained a deeper understanding than hitherto of a powerful motive that drove both the Duke and Duchess of Windsor—to preserve and enhance the royal connections through Hitler that would result in the destruction of the Soviet Union, itself the destroyer of Czar Nicholas and his wife, Alexandra, blood kindred of Windsor himself.

It was after this a complicated journey to learning of the Nazi connection, of which I was not aware in 1988, between the Duke of Windsor, his brother the Duke of Kent, and their cousin Queen Victoria's great-grandson Prince Philipp of Hesse, the basis of the aforementioned blackmail plot of 1938. Philipp was the favorite and emissary of Hitler; his wedding to Princess Mafalda, daughter of King Victor Emmanuel III of Italy, with Mussolini presiding over the civil ceremony, provided the support of the Hitler-Mussolini alliance of which the Windsors and the Kents were so much a part. This royal tapestry of pro-Fascist loyalties provided much of my new text, and seemed to make a new edition eminently worthwhile.

I

A Baltimore Childhood

Tʜe world into which Bessie Wallis Warfield was born, out of wedlock, on June 19, 1895,* was without airplanes, television, radio, movies, automobiles, income tax, chain stores, supermarkets, cafeterias, ice cream sundaes, crossword puzzles, or bathing trunks. Almost everyone attended church on Sundays. Mail deliveries were made by horse and buggy, and blacksmiths still hammered out horseshoes; America had less than 75 million people, and much of the nation breathed the atmosphere of the frontier.

The United States was recovering painfully from a disastrous depression. The once buoyant and brash New World had long been stifled under a shroud of gloom. The chief causes of the panic of 1893, in which millions liquidated their stockholdings and banks collapsed by the dozen, were overexpansion, excessive confidence, and the unbridled investments of the robber barons. President Grover Cleveland was unable to find a salve, much less a solution; the Treasury had to fight to stop the constant drain on gold.

Yet the shabby-genteel backwater of Baltimore, in which Wallis's family lived, showed few obvious signs of distress. The Warfields were housed at 34 East Preston Street, a four-story, narrow row house fashioned of gray Maryland brick. The kitchen was in the basement; the parlor, hidden from prying eyes by handmade Irish-lace draw curtains and rich, dark red satin drapes, was on the main floor; at the back there was a dining room flanked by African mahogany sideboards; the library

---

*Not 1896, as given in most sources.

was on the second floor; the family rooms were on the third floor and the servants' quarters on the fourth, or top, floor of the house.

The matriarch of the clan was Anna Emory, the widow Warfield. She was in her sixties, and her hair was snow white, piled high and fixed at the back by a black lacquered Chinese ivory comb. Her sole companion, other than her overworked and harshly disciplined cook, maids, and butler, was her bachelor son Solomon Davies Warfield. Three other boys had moved away: two of them, Emory and Henry, to get married, and one, Teackle, to set up in a small apartment.

Solomon Warfield's households, which included his handsome farms Manor Glen, where he shot game, Mount Eyrie, and Mount Prospect, and his 109-acre Parker-Watters Place, with its aviary of 100 rare birds, still had slave quarters, where blacks were maintained in substandard conditions. Solomon Warfield was to all appearances a pillar of rectitude, with his close-cropped, carefully parted black hair, his square-cut, neatly mustachioed face, imposing physique, and erect bearing, his handsome suits and chamois gloves; he was cold, haughty, and disdainful in the Warfield tradition. Yet it was whispered that this smart Baltimore gentleman was a lecher in private, and there were few women, married or not, on whom his cool eye lit who escaped his villainous advances. His list of actress and opera singer mistresses in New York, where he retained a hideaway apartment on Fifth Avenue, was an open scandal.

Anna Warfield's youngest son (she also had two married daughters living in Baltimore) was Teackle Wallis. Teackle was an anomaly in the clan. Not a black sheep—the Warfields could have stood that, and sent him off to Canada or California—but something unforgivably un-American: he was a physical weakling who had no athletic ability and even had to leave college because of his ill health. The normally robust strain of Warfield genetics had faltered when a failing Henry Mactier, at the age of 62, had fathered this ill-fated child.

At 18, Teackle suffered from consumption. Instead of sending the boy to an expensive sanatorium, his brother Sol insisted he learn the banking business from the ground up. He was forced to toil as a clerk, with green eyeshade and leather sleeve protectors, at the Continental Trust, while his brothers were already insurance executives, working for Uncle Henry Mactier Warfield.

Tubercular patients were forbidden to cohabit with women. The benign family physician, Dr. Leonard E. Neale, must surely have given advice in the matter of celibacy to the young man. But at 25 Teackle made the mistake of falling in love; sometime in the early 1890s, he met the pretty, golden-haired, lively, and adorable 24-year-old Alice Montague, whose ancestry, like the Warfields', went back to the Normans at the time of William the Conqueror. She always claimed that both families' knights were in the army that invaded England. She was the daughter of William and Mary Anne Montague, an insurance man and his wife, of 711 St. Paul Street.

When even a kiss from a tuberculosis sufferer was considered dangerous, possibly even a cause of death, Alice needed all her young courage to enter into a romantic liaison with her lover. He seems to have given no thought to the consequences to her, but in fact she did not contract the disease. Somehow, in cheap hotels or parks at night, they escaped the watchful eyes of their families and consummated their relationship. Horror of horrors, Alice became pregnant. Dr. Neale reached that conclusion two months after the conception.

In an Episcopalian family, birth out of wedlock was a disaster. It meant potential disgrace, social ruin, and possible expulsion. The Warfields or the Montagues would risk exposure to such a scandal. The baby must not be born in Baltimore, nor would the official family history of the Warfields, then being written (and published finally in 1905), include the names of father, mother, or child. Nor would Dr. Neale preside over the birth or cousin Mactier, also a physician, be involved.

In the early months of 1895, the young couple left for Blue Ridge Summit, a popular resort high in the mountains that straddle the Pennsylvania-Maryland border. The excuse for this ignominious exile was that the resort was said to be good for consumptives. Warfield money ensured there would be no mention of Alice's pregnancy or the child's birth in the Blue Ridge or Baltimore papers. Alice would remain indoors for the entire length of the stay.

On June 19, 1895,* Alice was seized by the first contractions. Dr. Lewis Miles Allen, a postgraduate student of Dr. Neale, arrived by train from Baltimore to ensure a safe delivery and no scandal. On seeing the baby, Dr. Allen said, "It's all right. Let her cry. It'll do her good." He

---

*The date is documented in the census report on the Warfield household taken in 1900. No birth certificate exists.

did not say, and he spent much of his life saying he did not say, "She's fit for a king."

Not only was the birth the only Warfield or Montague advent that was never featured anywhere in print, but the baby, named Bessie Wallis* Warfield, was the first Warfield not to be baptized. The family's Episcopalian advisers reached the decision not to permit baptism; birth out of wedlock was sufficient reason, Baltimorean church authorities confirm, for this grave verdict.

When Wallis came to be confirmed at Christ Church, Baltimore, on April 17, 1910, the baptismal record was falsified in order to secure her confirmation, and as a result of her unbaptized state, two of her three marriages, including her marriage in 1937 to the Duke of Windsor, were religiously invalid. In the eyes of the church she would suffer eternal damnation as an unbaptized person.

A marriage was finally arranged for Teackle and Alice seventeen months after Wallis's birth. It could not in any circumstances take place in a church. This in itself was a disgrace: no Warfield or Montague marrying for the first time had ever been denied a church wedding, nor could there be a dowry, or a trousseau, or even a municipal office wedding or a ceremony in either the Montague or Warfield family home.

The solution was to have the nuptials performed in the rectory living room of the Episcopalian minister, the Reverend Ernest Smith, who suspended his finer feelings in order to perform his disagreeable task. The wedding took place on November 19, 1896. Alice wore a green, sable-trimmed silk afternoon dress, with hat and gloves to match, and she carried a small posy of violets; the groom wore a plain gray suit. No family members were present; there was no best man or matron of honor, and nobody to give the bride away. There was neither wedding party nor honeymoon.

The unhappy couple moved first to the husband's digs at 28 Hopkins Place and thence to the Brexton Residential Hotel, a faded family hostelry on Park Avenue with rooms rented out at $1.50 a week. There, the enfeebled boy, often prostrated, debilitated, and flushed in the grip of fevers, no doubt brought anxious glances from the other boarders.

How Alice must have felt is beyond comprehension. Caring for a

---

*Not Bessiewallis, as given in most sources.

baby, with a husband whose days were numbered and whose coughing could ensure her own and her child's death, she faced every day with fear and anxiety that not even her stubbornly cheerful and optimistic nature could quell.

The Warfield ranks closed; the decision was made that parents and child should travel, presumably incognito, to Teackle's mother's house at 34 East Preston Street, which they did as soon as Alice was sufficiently recovered from postnatal complications to take the train.

Teackle lasted only six months; he died on November 15, 1897. Just before he passed away, he asked to see Wallis's baby picture—he was not permitted to touch her or kiss her. He was only 26.

Anna Emory Warfield never went without her brooches and rings set with black enamel; corseted and starched, brooding over her substantial landholdings, she remained a despot. By the time Wallis was 5, the child was up with the family at dawn for prayers. Breakfast was announced at eight each morning by the banging of a brass Indian gong. Immediately afterward, Mrs. Warfield summoned her staff of six bonneted and aproned maids and instructed them in the business of the household. Mrs. Warfield carried with her a chatelaine of keys; when a maid wished to take linen from a closet or fetch the season's preserves, the servant had to apply formally for the use of the key. Each night at precisely the same hour Uncle Solomon would return and would inspect the rooms for dust, disorder, or other evidence of the incompetence of the help. Sometimes Uncle Henry and his wife Aunt Rebecca would visit from next door to look at the child with her large, violet, eager eyes.

Wallis was an outgoing, mischievous, and buoyant child. Alice adored her; she had her photographed week by week as she grew, so that by 1900 more than 300 pictures of the little girl filled her room. She called them the "Wallis Collection," after the name of the London gallery. Wallis was a Warfield: a born snob. According to the writer Cleveland Amory, she named her first dolls after Mrs. Astor and Mrs. Vanderbilt, the reigning queens of New York City society. Her first reading was of magazines of fashion, the theater, and the fashionable world and of English kings and queens. She behaved royally from the first: instead of saying "Mama," she said "Me Me."

The atmosphere at 34 East Preston Street was tense and unpleasant for Alice Montague Warfield. Uncle Sol never ceased to make her aware that she was living on charity, but at the same time he was casting lecherous glances over her voluptuous young body. In 1901 Alice moved out, taking Wallis with her, and checked back into the Brexton Residential Hotel.

Uncle Sol's meager allowance did not meet the hotel bills, so Alice had to work. She could not type or bookkeep; her only skill was as a dressmaker. She joined the Women's Exchange, a charitable organization, altering children's clothes at a small weekly fee. At least she could make Wallis's dresses on the Exchange's sewing machine during her lunch hours.

In 1902, Alice's sister Bessie came to the rescue. Warm, sweet, plump Bessie had been widowed recently when her husband, auctioneer David B. Merryman, died suddenly from pneumonia at the age of 43 in 1901. Lonely in her big brick house at 9 West Chase Street, she adored Alice and Wallis and made a cozy home for them.

That same year Wallis became a pupil at Miss Ada O'Donnell's kindergarten at 2812 Elliott Street. It was there that the child's character began to emerge. She was determined to be first in everything. She was 7 years old when Miss O'Donnell asked the class, "Who tried to blow up the houses of Parliament in London?" A boy seated at a desk behind Wallis jumped up and yelled, "Guy Fawkes!"—just as she was about to give the same correct answer. Furious, she smacked him hard over the head with her wooden pencil box.

Ninety-four-year-old Mrs. Edward D. Whitman, formerly Susan Waters White, daughter of a distillery owner, in 1987 remembered Wallis at Miss O'Donnell's:

She was as busy as a cartload of monkeys. Oh! She was bright, brighter than all of us. She made up her mind to go to the head of the class and she *did*. She was poor, mind you. The Warfields had nothing. Servants? Anyone could afford those. But she had no pocket money, not a penny. She loved the country. She would stay with us at our estates, Robinswood and Knowle, both are still standing, and she would have a great time with us—we were *eleven* children. She *loved* to play Jacks. At night, she'd get excited over the fireflies. She loved a story we would tell: how an English Lord came to stay and said, "Oh look at all the lights, where do they come from?" And grandfather would say, "Don't you have any more mint juleps!"

In 1906, Alice was back at East Preston Street; she left Wallis in the care of Bessie as surrogate mother. In 1908 she moved, with Wallis, into the Preston Apartments, and began letting back rooms, an unthinkable disgrace in Baltimore society, especially since she let them to young and good-looking male students, including, for a time, her Montague cousins. She was lax in collecting rents, so much so that she had difficulty in paying her own; she too generously gave her tenants such expensive meals as terrapin à la Maryland or lobster cardinal free of charge.

She taught Wallis to cook; the antic, prattling little girl was able to manage a Lady Baltimore cake or a pecan pie at the age of 10—and heaven help anyone who stood in her way or failed to smack lips over her efforts.

At 10 Wallis attended the fashionable Arundell School for Girls, just four houses away from her maternal grandparents, at 714 St. Paul Street. When pupils laughed at her because her mother took in boarders, she would hit them with her heavy walking shoes.

Miss Carroll was the head teacher at Arundell. Wallis often defied her authority; she was known as impertinent and haughty. She also used bad language, to the stupefaction of her teachers. She was spanked at school and at home, but remained proud, stubborn, and unregenerate. She was maddeningly hardworking at everything from basketball to needlework to cooking to history lessons. Though she was not pretty, and was subject to theatrical headaches and fainting spells when attention strayed from her, she was popular because of her enthusiasm, vitality, and charm. With her angular, efficient body, her boyish shoulders, her "Indian" hair and face, and her jutting chin, she was, according to one fellow pupil, different from the other girls: "special." She was always immaculately groomed; she knew that a slackening of deportment would earn her a hairbrush smacking or a plunge in an icy bath. Her pencils were sharpened to fine points. She was never seen harboring gum or half-eaten apples. Her middy blouses and pleated skirts were always ironed immaculately.

2

A Stubborn Young Lady

Wallis was fiercely angry when her mother, after eleven years of widowhood, took a lover in 1907. John Freeman Rasin was the ne'er-do-well, 37-year-old eldest son of the leader of the Baltimore Democratic party. He had not married before and was the worst possible prospect as a husband: a big, moon-faced, portly alcoholic who liked to lie in bed all day reading the comic sections and drinking beer. His excessive love of the bottle had given him kidney and liver ailments. But he had been kind and generous to Alice and Wallis, and her offered Alice, who still carried the stigma of her first marriage, a chance for a proper home and a father for her child.

During the courtship, which Wallis treated with sulks and fainting fits as she saw her exclusive domain invaded, Alice moved to a better address, 212 Biddle Street. There, in defiance of all conventions, she spent the nights with Rasin in the guest bedroom, just a thin wall away from her 11-year-old daughter. When Alice announced that Rasin would be her husband, Wallis flew into a tantrum, screaming hysterically. It was quite obvious to her that the world had come to an end. She announced she would boycott the wedding—until Aunt Bessie Merryman talked her into going. Aunt Bessie could talk Wallis into anything.

The nuptials took place at 3 p.m. on June 20, 1908, at 212 Biddle; once more, there could be no question of a church wedding. On this occasion the Warfields and the Montagues did attend. But Wallis could not bring herself to see her mother married. When nobody noticed her display of sulks, she left the parlor during the ceremony and began tearing the wedding cake to pieces. She was determined to steal the traditional ring, thimble, and newly minted dime that were contained within it. She was surprised at her task just as she located these elusive treasures. The whole wedding party burst into laughter at the sight of her.

She had behaved better at the wedding of her favorite cousin, the gorgeous blue-eyed blonde Corinne De Forest Montague, in 1907—a glamorous affair because Corinne was marrying the ruggedly handsome 33-year-old Henry Croskey Mustin, a pioneer Navy flier. There was a full white-uniformed honor guard. Wallis vowed that when she was wed she would have a similar husband, and an even grander wedding.

At 12 Wallis was a rebel and a tomboy. She was almost too bright to be bearable. With her sharp voice, constant question asking, air of confidence and boldness, and theatrical sickness attacks, she was considered a handful. She dutifully endured the religious practices of the Episcopalian Warfields and Montagues, who made sure she was confirmed even though she had, of course, never been baptized. She struggled through the endless round of prayers at morning, noon, and night and the irritating advice of ministers led by the Reverend Francis Xavier Brady, who had no more idea of the feverish romantic daydreams that went on in a young girl's head than would the man in the moon. At a time when young girls were supposed to think of nothing but sewing, cooking, preparing menus, dressing, and playing basketball, Wallis was already pursuing boys (who were used to doing the pursuing themselves) and planning a future as a doctor, scientist, or explorer.

She liked many things passionately: riding the back roads on her donkey cart, dressing in smart new shirtwaists, wearing lace-up boots. Above all, she loved the taste, the smell, the feel of wealth. She was addicted to her richer, prettier cousins: Lelia, whose home was the big Wakefield Manor in Virginia, with its Ionic, four-pillared portico; and Corinne, now settled in a nice house in Washington and soon to go to Florida. Wallis liked fine Irish linen, lace doilies, solid silver napkin rings, Waterford crystal, Crown Derby plates, orchids, tapestries, chandeliers, jewels—diamonds, emeralds, rubies—money.

In 1911 Wallis went to the exclusive and snobbish Burrland, at Middleburg, Virginia, a family country property turned into a summer camp. While there, enjoying the antebellum mansion and its 1,000 acres of grounds, she fell in love for the first time. The object of her crush—or "pash" as it was then called—was the teenage Lloyd Tabb, a slim, dark, athletic, good-looking heir to a fortune. The other girls at Arundell and Burrland were jealous of her prize catch. They asked each other how she, the least pretty of them all, had managed to hook the handsomest boy they knew.

Her secret was that she researched her prey. She, who had no interest in football, found out every school score Tabb had made. She knew in how many minutes he had swum to victory at meets, what kind of ice cream he liked, and that he enjoyed skating in winter. His friends secretly helped her in her conspiracy of seduction.

She knew how to praise, how to build the adolescent male's ego. Although it was thought immodest, she boldly felt biceps. Lloyd had a bright red Lagonda sporting roadster Wallis loved to go out in. The first night he took her for a spin in it, she said, as he kissed her on her Biddle Street doorstep, "Ah, the leader of the younger set honors me with his presence!" and she threw back her head and laughed. Lloyd never forgot those words—or Wallis.

Later in 1911 Wallis went to Oldfields, the most expensive girls' school in Maryland. Uncle Sol had to dig deep into his pockets to send her there. But she figured he could afford it as president of the Seaboard Air Line Railway and (by now) six other railroads. The school was housed in an eighteenth-century white-clapboard farm building on 200 acres on the banks of the Gunpowder River. It had been founded in 1867 by the Reverend Duncan McCulloch and his wife Anna, whose family owned the farm. Anna, known as Miss Nan, was the principal when Wallis was enrolled.

There were "rags" and dances and going-away showers and graduate parties, and, of course, dashing Lloyd Tabb in his red Lagonda and Wallis's second-best beau, rangy young Tom Shyrock, who went horseback riding with her. Tom said later:

> Wallis took the highest jumps without batting an eyelash. There was something regal about the way she sat on a horse. I was rightly proud of my riding, but I had to take my hat off to Wallis.

Like millions of young girls, Wallis had a crush on the legendary Prince of Wales, the 17-year-old, golden-haired heir to the British throne. She had dozens of pictures of him in her room, cut out clippings of articles about him, and followed his movements incessantly. Lloyd and Tom took this schoolgirl silliness in their stride.

In 1914 Wallis left Oldfields, and Alice, who had lost her husband and was much aged, took an apartment at 16 Earl Court, Baltimore, on Warfield-haunted Preston Street. At 19, Wallis now had to make her society debut, which would—custom required it—be followed as soon as possible by marriage to a rich and attractive young man from an old Baltimore family. First, she would, she insisted, go to the Princeton Ball with her cousin Lelia of Wakefield Manor as the date of Lelia's frail but good-looking brother Basil Gordon. Basil, who was dating another girl, said the idea was out of the question. Wallis ranted and raved until Basil arranged for his best friend to break a date and take Wallis to the prom. Wallis changed from tantrums to ecstasy. She and Alice fussed for hours over what she would wear. Wallis favored blue organdy; Alice preferred pink. Wallis won by discovering that she would be the only girl at the dance wearing blue.

Now came a greater challenge: the major event of the year for any young woman in Baltimore.

3

Running Up the Ladder

The Bachelors Cotillon was the summit: admittance to the ball ensured a girl's place in society. Only 49 young women out of 500 could be admitted to this occasion, which traditionally took place at the Lyric Theater on the first Thursday in December.

At last the great morning arrived, and Wallis tore open the invitation. She had to somehow obtain a wardrobe, a family member as escort, and a corsage.

She had to sweet-talk old Uncle Sol into backing her to the limit. She sallied forth in the family Pierce-Arrow to the crucial appointment at his offices at "Solomon's Temple," the rebuilt, handsome Continental Trust Building. She sat like a princess, gazing out from the sumptuous auto as the chauffeur in gray livery drove her to her destination. Money! Was there anything like it?

Uncle Sol received her pompously and listened to her pleas. He knew as well as she did there was no way a Warfield girl would not make a splash at the Cotillon. He gave her the incredible sum of $20—enough to buy at least thirty dresses! She made her way to Maggie O'Connor, Baltimore modiste, and invested her entire, newly acquired fortune in one dress and one alone.

It was an exact copy of a white satin Worth gown made in Paris for the famous society dancer Irene Castle. Wallis stood for hours while it was fitted to her angular form. She spent more hours learning the one-step and the newly sensational tango. She greatly improved her waltzes. Her mother waltzed with her at home; various beaux led by Lloyd

Tabb whirled her across country club dance floors until she fancied she was as proficient as Irene Castle herself.

Of course, she must, she simply must have the best possible escort on the big night. It was traditional to have an uncle or an older cousin dance with the debutantes. But Wallis would have none of that. She would have her handsomest, most dashing, and youngest relative, her rugged, 27-year-old cousin Henry Warfield, who was already half in love with her anyway. That settled, there were weeks of predebut teas and lunches and dances and meetings and hour-long phone calls with Alice going mad because she couldn't use the telephone.

Finally, December 7 came around. Wallis, after prolonged fussing and spinning around in front of mirrors, was at last satisfied that she looked like a dream. At the appointed hour Cousin Henry, looking like a million dollars in white tie and tails, roared up to 212 Biddle in Uncle Sol's Pierce-Arrow.

At the Lyric Theater, she was danced off her feet for hours. Each time a new partner joined her, she gave him her absolute and undivided attention, never talking about herself. As a result, the young men came back to her again and again. Though she was probably among the least pretty debs in the place, she was bright and bewitching and she knew it.

In the wake of that glorious night, Wallis now considered herself a woman. Alice acted as her chaperone on date after date. Wallis was man-mad; she risked tongue-wagging by having a bewildering succession of romances. Asked to sum her up in one word, a contemporary says, "Fast." She especially liked uniformed men—and in 1915, with war in Europe, and after the *Lusitania* went down from a German torpedo, more and more boys in the social set were at Annapolis or West Point.

After Grandma Anna died, Wallis found that she had been left $4,000 in the will. She was beside herself, and in no mood to stay in mourning for months on end. Worse, her beau, Carter Osburn, whom she had almost made up her mind to marry, was posted to Mexico with General Pershing's army to fight Pancho Villa. Wallis made a theatrical farewell with tears and fluttering handkerchief as his train pulled out of the depot.

She filled the months of family mourning for Anna by writing love letters to Osburn, which he read by the light of hurricane lamps in lonely Mexican encampments after days of scouting or skirmishes. But it irritated her that she couldn't date or go to dances. Even learning contract bridge was no consolation.

At last, she found an opportunity to get out of town. On January 20, 1914, her cousin Corinne's husband, Lieutenant Commander Henry C. Mustin, had sailed into Pensacola, Florida, as master of the battleship USS *Mississippi*. He had been appointed to help establish a naval aeronautic center for flight and ground training for defense operations as America lumbered toward war. Corinne had written Wallis often about life at the newly formed base: the first in American history just a few years after the Wright Brothers made their pioneer flight at Kitty Hawk. In November 1915 Corinne reported excitedly that Mustin had been the first man to be catapulted from a ship—in the AB-2 flying boat, off the rolling deck of the USS *North Carolina*.

Wallis, with her mania for servicemen and her addiction to the Army-Navy game, was excited by Corinne's news and still more so when Corinne asked her to come to Pensacola and stay with her. Wallis begged her depressing family to let her go. A family meeting was held, with Aunt Bessie and Alice pleading her cause to stern, black-clad Uncles Sol, Henry, Emory, and cousin Mactier. The women won. Pensacola it would be. And Uncle Sol owned part of the railroad that would take her southwest to the Florida panhandle; that would ensure her a free first-class ticket.

In Pensacola, Corinne met her at the Gregory Street depot and drove her to the white-painted wooden house, part of a long row of similar bungalows, overlooking the huge, landlocked, palm-fringed bay and the aeronautic station with its hangars, slipways, derricks, and machine shops. Wallis was in her element. Pensacola, the major Gulf town of the northeast Florida panhandle, with 100 miles of unspoiled, snowy-white beaches to east and west, was predominantly Spanish in flavor.

Wallis very much liked Henry Mustin. Older than Corinne, he was 42, wrinkled and dark from years on an open fuselage in the tropical sun. His infectious grin and strong voice were pleasing, and he looked impressive in his flying helmet and goggles. He was having problems with the Navy Department that caused an angry exchange of letters between him and Washington. His chief quarrel was with Captain Mark L. Bristol, director of naval aeronautics. Mustin wanted more autonomy and better operational management from the capital. It was an uphill fight every day.

Wallis stayed with the Mustins and their three children, occupying a big, sunny guest room and helping Corinne with the cooking and housework. On Saturday nights she went with the Mustins to the San Carlos Hotel, where there were dances to a palm court orchestra in the big Spanish-style dining room. Once again she attracted many beaux through her expert one-stepping and tangoing, and focusing on their interests to the exclusion of her own.

Early in May, after weeks of sunbathing, swimming in clear, clean water, picnicking, moviegoing, and dancing, Wallis was asked by Corinne to stay in for lunch to meet three young airmen. They were coming to the house as a special favor. Wallis, on the porch, saw the officers in starched white uniforms stride up. She was excited, they were all good-looking, but one of the three was riveting and irresistible.

Mustin introduced him to Wallis as Earl Winfield Spencer. She wrote later, "He was laughing, but there was a suggestion of inner force and vitality that struck me instantly." At lunch, when most of the discussion about aeronautics matters went right over her head, Wallis couldn't take her eyes off him. As she looked at his shoulders and their gold braid, he made it clear, by the merest indication in his eyes, that he knew what she felt about him; she hung on every word he was saying, and he noted that, too. She wanted to know all about flying.

His close-cropped black hair stood *en brosse* above a high forehead; his piercing, bold, arrogant eyes, sharp nose, and firm, jutting jaw were very attractive; his expression was proud, challenging, and fierce. There was a slight suggestion of the simian in him. His body was tanned, lithe, and muscular, and his posture was erect and assured. His demeanor did not suggest gentleness, courtesy, or ingratiating charm. He appealed to Wallis; he went to her head like champagne. She was always drawn to tigers.

After lunch Spencer sauntered up to her the instant they were alone and asked her to dinner the next night. He brushed aside her demurs and told her he would be calling on her, then he left. The casual, almost contemptuous arrogance of the young man left her breathless. She was in a daze; she felt no warning signals.

Spencer was born in a small town in Kansas on September 20, 1888. His father was a Chicago stockbroker, whose American antecedents, like Wallis's, went back to the early 1600s. Big, brawling Earl Senior was formerly on the Ithaca, New York, baseball team and had been a big-game hunter in his day, bagging buffalo, wolves, deer, and antelope, whose heads bristled from the walls of the family home at 109 Wade Street, Highland Park, Illinois.

Winfield was his eldest child. The others were Gladys, Ethel, Egbert, Dumaresq, and Frederick. Win was the bad seed in the family, though Wallis did not know it then. Enlisting in the naval academy at Annapolis in 1905, he had earned a long list of demerits in his conduct record for, among other things, dirty shoes and uniform, room dirty and badly swept, bathing trunks falling down at a swim meet, lateness at meals and drill and choir practice, skylarking in corridors, rowdyism, and moving furniture without authorization. Yet he was popular, especially in naval academy vaudeville shows, in which he excelled in drag. He was a good athlete at football, and he was cheerleader and head of the Christmas parade; "a merry devil, a singer nicknamed Caruse," said the naval academy magazine. He was a secret bisexual whose predilection, if discovered, would have resulted in expulsion.

His face stares out at us from the group photograph of the class of 1910: moody, dark, petulant among all the open, fresh faces, his jug ears standing out almost at right angles from the head and slightly undercutting the primitive, threatening, somewhat simian handsomeness of the whole.

Fond though Wallis was of Corinne, with her innocent, china-doll eyes and flow of bright tittle-tattle, she was glad to escape with Win, unchaperoned, whenever possible, for blameless romantic trysts at night.

Given the restrictions of the time, and the disaster of her mother's indiscretion with Teackle Warfield, there could be no question of her going "all the way" with him, no matter how urgent his pleadings. Finally, he proposed, as she had hoped he would, on the country club porch late at night after the last picture show. She told him she must think about it and discuss it with her mother and Uncle Sol. He told her—he did not ask her—not to keep him waiting too long.

She went home in June. He saw her off with a lingering kiss that made her blush and flee into the train. Back at the Baltimore apartment, Alice was full of predictable warnings. But Wallis was set on her path and nothing would stand in her way. She had a persuasive argument: Win's family was rich and socially prominent; Win could ensure her a future. She won.

In August Win took Wallis by train to Illinois to meet his family:

big, imposing, big-game-hunting Earl Senior, his mousy British wife Agnes, and their five other children. They approved of Wallis at once; the Warfields were not unknown in Chicago. Win bought Wallis a diamond engagement ring, and the announcement of their intentions appeared in the Baltimore papers on September 25, 1916. The wedding date was set for November 8. How would Wallis sleep until then?

4

A Stylish Marriage

W allis decided the wedding should take place romantically
after dark at the Christ Episcopal Church. The beautiful
building was lit by beeswax candles according to Wallis's
instructions; she would have nothing as parvenu as tallow. The lighted
tapers and annunciation lilies, the bower of white chrysanthemums and
roses created an appealing atmosphere as Wallis entered, to the organ
strains, on the arm of Uncle Sol. She was followed by the matron of
honor, Ellen Yuille, a friend from Oldfields, and by the bridesmaids,
Mary Kirk, Lelia Barnett, Renée du Pont, Ethel Spencer (Win's sister),
and two others, all in pink and blue. Win was accompanied by a Navy
honor guard, including his friends, in full-dress uniform; his youngest
brother, Dumaresq Spencer, the family favorite and its handsomest
member, was best man.

The Reverend Edmund Niver made Wallis and Win man and wife.
The couple ran down the steps to a shower of rice and then made their
way by automobile to the Hotel Stafford for the reception. Wallis gave
gold rings to each of the bridesmaids; they later used them as teething
rings for their children. As the couple took off for their honeymoon,
Wallis threw her bouquet at Mary Kirk and the guests showered the
couple with white rose petals.

The newlyweds traveled via the Shoreham Hotel in Washington
and the Shenandoah Valley Inn to the newly built and lavish Greenbriar Hotel at White Sulphur Springs in the mountains of West Virginia, where Wallis had spent many a childhood vacation and which

she had visited just the year before.* It was a spectacular train journey uphill to the expensive and exclusive hostelry.

They were shown into Room 528 on the top floor, which commanded an unobstructed view of oaks, maples, and fir-clad mountain slopes wreathed in mist. It was already time for dinner and they changed at once. She wrote later that Win, impatient on discovering that West Virginia was a dry state, dragged a bottle of gin from his suitcase. But he had been in West Virginia before.

His alcoholism was an established fact. There is no doubt that he drank heavily on the honeymoon, both at the Greenbriar and in New York, where they saw Wallis's favorite Army-Navy game and the Ziegfeld Follies, and in Atlantic City, where the widowed Alice still had her little cottage. They took a train back to Pensacola in December, and once again Corinne met the express and drove them to the San Carlos Hotel. They stayed there a few days and then moved to the Widow Covington's house at Baylen and Gonzalez until the repairs of a recent hurricane's damage were partly finished at Number Six, "Admiralty Row"—a wooden bungalow just a few houses down from the Mustins' home, and of almost identical design, with a view of the ocean and a small veranda.

Always correct, neat, disciplined, and proud, Wallis found that Win's behavior started to grate on her. He stored water in gin bottles to upset Henry Mustin when Mustin, who kept a dry base, made the Saturday morning inspections. He caused excitement at the San Carlos Saturday night dances by performing impromptu in a straw boater, carrying a cane, as an amateur song-and-dance man, fronting the orchestra in an imitation of George M. Cohan. He liked to dress up on off-duty days in loud checked knickerbockers, lurid sweaters, and brogues. He constantly swilled beer. He would use the excuse of toasting the flag before a flight; then he would have another drink to boost his courage, and a third afterward "to settle down." Martinis before lunch and dinner were concealed in open Campbell's soup cans and served in cups and bowls.

Wallis hated the drinking and feared that Win would crash. When two ensigns collided in midair in a drunken daredevil stunt, she panicked.

---

*In her memoirs Wallis said she told Win Spencer she scarcely remembered the place. But her name in the 1915 register belies the statement.

Every time Win went up on a practice flight, she felt worse. Corinne was her chief consolation, but on January 31, 1917, much to her despair, Henry was fired and transferred to Washington to be executive officer of the USS *North Dakota*, and Corinne went with him. Wallis found herself very much alone in the long, empty, sun-drenched, humid days.

One afternoon Wallis returned home to learn that Spencer had crashed his plane and had been fished, almost unharmed, out of the bay. She was learning the pain and stress of a difficult marriage. Wallis already hated flying and for the rest of her life she was to loathe the idea of war.

On April 6, 1917, America entered the world conflict. Win applied at once for active duty in France. It was a shock to Wallis that he would want to leave her, but he had a fierce desire to get into the fight. His brother, beloved Dumaresq, was already in the Lafayette Escadrille, and Egbert and Frederick were on their way to join the American Army Expeditionary Force for service in the trenches.

Win was refused permission to go overseas, probably because of his conduct record as an alcoholic. The Navy wanted its image in Europe untarnished. Win was furious and took his rages out on Wallis; he grumbled when, on May 8, he was directed to leave Pensacola and travel to Boston to train recruits at the newly formed naval militia station at Squantum. He was promoted to lieutenant junior grade, and his salary was increased.

After a brief visit to Oldfields School for the fiftieth anniversary celebrations on May 2 and 3, Wallis and Win took a flat at the Mulberry Apartments near the Boston Common. The Squantum experience was short-lived. Wallis filled the time going to museums and attending criminal trials. She drove Win to the base every morning and picked him up at night. Because of drunken driving incidents, he was forbidden a license.

By October someone in the Navy Department realized belatedly that the late fall and winter climate of Boston would make it unsafe to train fliers there, so the recruit operation was shifted overnight to Hampton Roads, Virginia. Wallis was pleased; she would be close again to Lelia and Corinne and her mother. But instead the Navy ordered Win to San Diego in faraway California.

He was placed in charge of training cadets at North Island. This new appointment of Win's was almost certainly a relief as well as an irritation to Wallis; Win would not be sent to a probable death on the war front. She began packing for the long journey west.

The trip, which started on November 3, 1917, involved a change of trains in Chicago—from the Baltimore and Ohio to the Santa Fe Chief—and a night stopover at the Blackstone Hotel. At long last, the Spencers arrived in Los Angeles and then took another train on November 8, 1917, to San Diego, a pleasant, sleepy town of 100,000 people with a paradisiacal winter climate, on the edge of the blue-gray Pacific. Wallis and Win moved into the rambling Hotel del Coronado, a hodgepodge of Victorian gingerbread with rich African mahogany fixtures and a driver-equipped Otis cage elevator of ancient vintage.

While Win spent his days at offices downtown, Wallis looked for an apartment. Eventually, she found 104, the Palomar, 536 Maple Street, with a fine view of an imitation Spanish fountain patio* and Balboa Park, which still had many signs of the big 1915 Exposition. Number 104 was one of only two apartments with a view and one of the very few with a separate bedroom.

Win was busy in those months, setting up the training school at the newly commissioned naval air station on North Island. He trained not only pilots but mechanics. He soon added Marine and military personnel and raw recruits out of Los Angeles. For a while he cut out drinking, but news of the death of his brother Dumaresq in an aerial dogfight in France on January 16, 1918, drove him into depression and a guilty feeling of inadequacy that he had not served with his sibling. He began to drink again.

Win and Wallis moved often—an indication that they were restless and unhappy. They went back to the Hotel del Coronado, the second floor of which was commandeered as officer quarters by the Navy, and then to Pine Cottage, later renamed Redwood Cottage, at 1115 Flora Avenue. With its tiny, twelve-foot-long living room, sun porch, and minuscule bedrooms, and its quaint, gabled exterior, it was like a witch's house in a Grimms' fairy tale.

They went on to the slightly larger 1029 Encino Row and then to 1143 Alameda Street, their home for over three years. Wallis celebrated her twenty-second birthday on June 19, 1917. She cannot have felt much

---

*The apartment didn't have its own patio, as described in her memoirs.

happiness in the event. Win was subject to rages, sulks, and deep, brooding silences; were his bisexual impulses plaguing him? As for Wallis, she did not want to have children despite the fact that all the Montague women she so envied, and whom she had emulated by "marrying Navy," had families, as did several of Win's siblings. A man in the service wanted sons; Win's disappointment was gnawing and lasting. Wallis's flirtatiousness with any man in uniform vexed Win greatly; at a mere 28, he was already growing coarse and plump, his face that of a man fifteen years older, his once-proud chin buried in fat. Drink cost him his looks and his figure. San Diego was a backwater; Wallis was tired of making her clothes on a Singer sewing machine. She was lost; there seemed to be no escape. She fell out of love.

In June 1918 Wallis traveled to New York City to be a bridesmaid at the wedding of her school friend Mary Kirk to the French commercial and military delegate Captain Jacques Achille Raffray. The trip cheered her up; when she returned, she began to make friends in San Diego, including Katherine Bigelow, whose husband had been killed in action in France; Rhoda Fullam, daughter of a naval officer later a rear admiral; Mrs. Claus Spreckels, rich in land and sugar interests; young Marianna Sands; and Grace Flood Robert.

On November 11, 1918, the *San Diego Union* was delivered, along with the milk bottle, to the doorstep of Wallis's house. She picked it up and read the news that the war had ended in Europe. Hundreds of San Diegans ran from their homes in night attire, screaming and yelling.

After that great day, Win was more grim and depressed than ever. His drinking grounded him now; there was no war on, so his job at North Island seemed pointless; he was insulting to Wallis when they went out to parties, and made snide remarks about her cooking when they were at home. A clumsy dancer, he was furious when men came over to their table at various Navy parties, whisking flirtatious Wallis across the floor to the new, popular numbers by Irving Berlin and Jerome Kern. He charged Wallis with adultery; to be sure that she didn't visit or entertain other men, he often locked her in the house for the day.

On December 8, 1919, Mustin took command of the local air detachment of the Pacific Fleet. He had moved to Coronado ahead of Corinne, who followed in mid-January 1920. Wallis rejoiced in Corinne's presence in Coronado.

On April 7, 1920, a big event took place. The Prince of Wales was in San Diego with his cousin Louis Mountbatten on his way to Australia aboard the battle cruiser *Renown*. He arrived early in the morning and received the San Diego mayor, L. J. Wilde, and the governor of California, William E. Stephens, along with the press, on the boat deck. Addressed by Wilde as "Your Royal Highness," he told him to "cut out that stuff," in an odd, half-American, half-Cockney accent he had developed because he hated the plummy diction of the British upper classes.

Wallis must have been galled by the fact that she was not invited to the elaborate luncheon held on board the battleship *New Mexico* in honor of the prince, followed by receptions aboard the *Aroostook* and the HMS *Renown*. The guests were taken out to the vessels by minesweeper. The Towerses, Corinne and Henry Mustin, and their friends the Charlie Masons and the Pete Mitschers were included. Why were the Spencers not? It is inconceivable that Wallis would have missed out on such an opportunity. It is probable that Win's drinking and misbehavior and his clashes with the authorities had resulted in this example of cruel social punishment.

Slim, short, golden-haired, charming, and informal, the young prince conquered San Diego at once. He came ashore with Mountbatten at 2:30 p.m., shook hands with the war veterans, and addressed some 25,000 people at the Stadium, while close to 70,000 thronged the sidewalks to watch him in the motorcade.

Wallis was in attendance with Win that night at the Hotel del Coronado for the mayoral ball. But in another major blow to her pride, she was not included on the banquet guest list. She and the Mustins were among the thousand guests who thronged the ballroom, which was hung with native California wildflowers and the British and American flags. The band of the USS *New Mexico* played current hits; a local adagio dance team performed exhibition waltzes and "the Whirlwind One-Step," and the men in full-dress uniforms and girls in expensive gowns soon joined them on the floor, forming, according to the *San Diego Union*'s somewhat overwrought society correspondent, "a scene of kaleidoscopic gaiety."

Wallis only saw the prince far off, in Royal Navy tropical whites, shaking hundreds of hands. He left early, to go, according to some eyewitnesses, to Tijuana to sample the local pleasures. That was typical of him; he hated receptions and banquets and wanted only to enjoy life.

Although it must have been exciting for Wallis to catch a glimpse of her girlhood idol, the episode was swallowed up in the darkness of her marriage. In May, Alice came out to visit Wallis. She found her in tears; Win was staying out all night and frequently broke up furniture when he came home. One afternoon Alice arrived at their house to find Win shaking Wallis; they had been arguing because Wallis was not in a mood to join him at a game of golf. He announced he was going back to Florida, saying that he was in love with a girl there. Wallis begged him to stay; but by November he had obtained his transfer and left.

Wallis suffered through four months without a word from Win. Then, in the spring of 1921, he was appointed to the Navy Department in Washington under Rear Admiral William A. Moffett. Win asked her to come and join him; she agreed. Henry Mustin had finally made it into the department, and she wanted to see Corinne again. Alice was working now at the Chevy Chase Country Club as a social hostess and was dating a legal clerk, Charles Gordon Allen.

Wallis moved with Win into the Brighton Apartment Hotel on California Avenue. She soon regretted the decision. Win's screaming fits were unendurable and woke up the hotel at night; he locked her in the bathroom and left her there for hours; he fell down drunk; he had affairs with other women and, it is alleged, with men. Finally, it was obvious to her that she had to obtain a divorce.

There had never been such a scandal in either the Montague or the Warfield families. Alice and Aunt Bessie were shocked. They tried to talk her out of her decision. The Episcopalian Church would countenance no such thing. But Wallis's mind was made up. Just because nobody divorced in her family was no reason for her to be bound for the rest of her life to a man she hated.

She went to see Uncle Sol, now the biggest railroad baron in the South, in his offices at the Continental Trust. He was furious, horrified; he screamed, "I will not let you bring this disgrace upon us!" Then he softened a little and asked her to try again.

She did, but it was hopeless. She would prepare a dinner as carefully and expertly as she could, and Win would not turn up for it.

On June 19, 1922, Win told Wallis he was moving out, to the Army and Navy Club. Wallis called Alice; her mother came to the hotel, and Wallis tearfully showed her the closets empty of Win's clothing. Alice stayed overnight. The next day Wallis called the club. The reply was, "Commander Spencer will not care to talk to you." Alice waited an hour; then she called him herself. She urged him to come and have a family conference. Win said, "It's useless to talk about my returning. I have made up my mind to live my own life as I see fit."

Anguished, deeply disappointed, and depressed, Wallis moved in with her mother, at 2301 Connecticut Avenue. Win moved to Rauscher's Hotel. That fall Alice asked Win to come to her apartment for a chat. There, he told Alice flatly that he was in love with another woman. "I'm far happier away from Wallis," he said. Then he left, declining Alice's invitation to stay for dinner.

He drank more heavily than ever. In February 1923 his extramarital affair collapsed. Win quarreled constantly with the Navy and, like Henry Mustin before him, was grounded: he was transferred to warship service, as master of the *Pampanga*, of the South China Patrol of the Asiatic Fleet.

Wallis made the best of the separation. The fact that her husband was on active service and that China was too dangerous a place for a young woman made her position more acceptable than that of a would-be divorcée; she met many old friends again and through two of them from San Diego, Marianna Sands and Ethel Noyes, she entered diplomatic society. Although she would deny it at a crucial stage later on, she spoke fairly good German, having studied it at Oldfields; and she had a smattering of French.

At a reception at the Italian embassy Wallis set her cap for, and won, the attractive Italian ambassador himself. The 45-year-old Prince Gelasio Caetani had at least two popes and two cardinals in his family. He was the son of Prince Teamo and the American Ada Bootle Wilbraham. He graduated in civil engineering from the University of Rome in 1901; he became a geologist and mining authority and in 1910 based an engineering firm, Burch, Caetani and Hearsley, in San Francisco.

In World War I he served in the Italian army and won several decorations. A convinced nationalist, he was a passionate supporter of fascism and participated in the march on Rome in 1922. He was appointed to Washington; Mussolini saw in him the ideal person who could succeed in winning the interest and sympathy of the American ruling classes: he had a vast network of connections in eastern cultural and money circles.

He worked hard on the extinction of the Italian war debt and establishment of strong relations with the Italo-American military and navy. He built a new embassy with Mussolini money, an ornate imitation of a Renaissance palace.

There is no question that it was Caetani who first and most deeply involved Wallis in an interest in his Italian dictator master and in the Italian system of government; exercising such influence was his main purpose in becoming involved with her, apart from the strong sexual bond between them. He knew she moved through every level of Washington society; that she could purvey the Fascist doctrine, albeit in a somewhat superficial manner, wherever she went. Such is confirmed by a reliable source in Rome who was a close friend and associate of Caetani's.

The affair didn't last; Wallis soon settled for friendship.

5

China

Felipe Espil, an Argentinian diplomat Wallis dated, met and fell in love with the society beauty Courtney Letta Stilwell, of the famous political and military family. When she found out, Wallis was furious. In an excess of jealousy she attacked Espil, clawing his cheeks until they bled. He dropped her at once; she decided to give up Washington, where her defeat had made her a laughingstock.

There is a substantial documentary file on her at the time, preserved at the State Department, which shows that she moved in with Captain Luke McNamee, the chief of naval intelligence, and his wife, the painter Dorothy McNamee, at their Georgetown house, a typical preliminary move to test confidentiality and to be briefed in secrecy. Harry W. Smith, chief clerk at the naval intelligence headquarters, examined her carefully on July 9, 1923. That month she sailed to France and England aboard the *President Garfield*, accompanied by Corinne Mustin. In Paris she made contact with William E. Eberle and Gerald Green, both intelligence liaisons for the U.S. Navy at the embassy; she proceeded to London and Rome.

It was a custom of the time to use trusted Navy wives, briefed at headquarters, as unofficial couriers carrying classified documents to Europe and the Orient. Couriers were necessary because all telegraph messages transmitted to the U.S. Navy in China were intercepted and read, and the cyphers were broken; all radio messages were transmitted from a central tower in Manila and again could be read. Thus, the only way to transmit information was by trusted immediate family members of naval personnel. On her return from Europe, Wallis was seconded to link up with Win Spencer in China. Captain Henry R. Hough, who had taken over from Captain McNamee as chief when the latter was put in charge of intelligence at the Panama Canal, personally signed the papers that authorized the trip. Meantime, Spencer was appointed a naval intelligence officer of the South China Patrol, combining his job of gunboat captain of the *Pampanga* with that more important office. His headquarters at Shameen Legation Island, Canton, were crucially situated since both Sun Yat-sen and the Communists were constantly attacking missionaries and annexing American properties in the region. Win was to join Wallis in Hong Kong on September 8; she would link up there with Mary Sadler, wife of the intelligence officer Rear Admiral Frank H. Sadler of the USS *Sacramento*. The two women would then proceed to Shanghai, where American interests were endangered by Russian-controlled warlords in the civil war.

Wallis was given another intelligence clearance, and put aboard the troop carrier *Chaumont*, a former double-ended Hog Island ferry, carrying 1,200 enlisted men to Pearl Harbor, Guam, and Cavite.

The voyage into Pearl Harbor, Hawaii, was tricky, involving the navigation of a dangerous coral reef in a violent, gusty squall. Wallis stayed one week in Honolulu; the vessel sailed on August 13. At Guam, Governor Henry B. Price received her and the other wives with the *Chaumont's* officers at an official reception; three days later Price was piped aboard the vessel to make the rest of the journey to Cavite.

After weeks of stifling, monotonous voyaging, the vessel at last made landfall off San Miguel Light and Manila Bay on August 30, 1924. Wallis had to be billeted at naval headquarters because she was one of the few wives continuing to Hong Kong; there had been riots along the wharves following student demonstrations the week before. She was sent aboard the *Empress of Canada*, the famous "jinx ship" of the Canadian Pacific Line, on the fourth of September.

The week Wallis arrived in Hong Kong, civil war, which had been threatened for several months, exploded in full force across China. There were constant outbreaks of violence in the Crown Colony. When Wallis arrived, typhoid was raging and there was record heat. With fire and gunshot surrounding her, Wallis moved into the Repulse Bay Hotel and then, reconciled with Win, into a Navy-owned Kowloon apartment that came equipped with cook and maid. Win was busy during that stopover of a few weeks. He had to have the *Pampanga* coaled, provisioned, patched up, and ready for emergency sailing orders, and that was at least a sixteen-hour-a-day job.

On October 16, 1924, the sailing orders arrived. It must have been painful for Wallis, after managing to patch up her shattered marriage, to realize that Win was traveling into conditions of extreme danger. He had been seconded back to Canton. That tormented city was plunged into terror and bloodshed.

In a shambles of violence, famine, and disease, the *Pampanga* docked at the militarily protected Shameen Legation Island, its three-pounder and one-pounder guns ready to shell the shore. Three British gunboats followed the ship into the docks, and Wallis was stubbornly on board one of them, probably the *Bee*. She was not to be left behind. She joined Win at the naval quarters in the British-American settlement, the only billet available to Navy wives at the time. The island was closed to foreign civilians. The air was acrid and full of cinders, and both water and food were in very short supply. She became ill from a kidney disorder brought on by the toxic water and was evacuated to Hong Kong on October 28.

With missionaries and evacuee doctors and nurses aboard, the *Pampanga* returned to Hong Kong on November 3 for provisioning before sailing to Kongmoon on the thirtieth to protect American interests and to ship Standard Oil in the region. Something curious took place that month. According to a dossier prepared on Prime Minister Stanley Baldwin's orders by the Secret Intelligence Service (MI6) for King George V and Queen Mary in 1935 (when it became crucial to prevent Wallis's becoming Queen of England), Wallis was introduced by Win to the "singing houses" of the Crown Colony, run by an American woman, Gracie Hale, who, with her peroxided hair, false eyelashes, heavily rouged cheeks, and plump but attractive figure, was still going in the 1930s, when she gave an interview to the Dutch author Hendrik de Leeuw for his book *Cities of Sin* (London: Noel Douglas, 1934) describing her earlier career when Wallis was in Hong Kong.

The singing houses were luxurious brothels; the inmates, recruited from the Chinese seaboard, were trained from their early teens in the arts of love. The client was entertained with stringed instruments, delicately erotic songs, and dances of rare beauty.

There were two kinds of singing (or "singsong," as they were sometimes known) houses. The best-known were the "purple mansions."

The only one of these establishments which admitted foreign women was in Repulse Bay. As the visitor entered, a smiling male slave in a blue cotton robe would appear, bowing deeply. He would usher the arrival into an immense, exactly square room with green and white draperies covering the walls.

Beyond the entrance hall there was a long corridor that led to another hall surrounded by sumptuously upholstered chairs and settees. Both doors and walls were decorated with latticework and scrolls in Chinese. There were cabinets fashioned of expensive mahogany and containing shelves of valuable china ornaments. The girls were customarily dressed in blue or red silk. The upper floor consisted of a series of tiny but elegantly furnished rooms where the prostitutes awaited their customers. Some houses had individual names, such as "Fields of Glittering Flowers" or "Club of the Ducks of the Mandarins."

Other houses of prostitution were known as *Hoa Thing*, or "flower boats," and were moored or floated in the harbor. The boats were sixty to eighty feet long and fifteen feet wide; inside they were lavishly carpeted and furnished, and crystal lamps dangled from the ceilings. It was customary for an individual to hire the entire boat for the evening and to begin with a multicourse dinner at 9 p.m. When the dinner was over, the guest would take his companion of the night across a small wooden platform to one of a series of boats that was attached by ropes to the mother vessel.

According to witnesses of the China dossier, Wallis was taught "perverse practices" in these houses of prostitution. The practices can only mean lesbian displays and the art of Fang Chung. This skill, practiced for centuries, involved relaxation of the male partner through a prolonged and carefully modulated massage of the nipples, stomach, thighs, and, after a deliberately protracted delay, the genitals. The exponent of Fang Chung was taught the nerve centers of the body so that the brushing movement of the fingers had the effect of arousing even the most moribund of men. Fang Chung was especially helpful in cases of premature ejaculation. By the application of a firm, specific touch between the urethra and the anus, climax could be delayed. Masseuses delayed intromission as long as possible to remove the fear of failure in intercourse that afflicted men suffering from dysfunction.

According to a close friend of Wallis's, she had no sooner had an opportunity to apply this technique than she received a shock. Win left her in order to share an apartment with a handsome young painter whose looks and talent had earned him much attention in the Crown Colony. By November 21 she was on her way, no doubt in great distress, to Shanghai aboard the *Empress of Russia* with the charming, 42-year-old Mrs. F. H. (Mary) Sadler, wife of Admiral Sadler, commanding officer of the USS *Saratoga* and head of naval intelligence (as arranged long ago in Washington).

On arrival, Wallis and Mrs. Sadler undertook the short trip to the fashionable Astor House Hotel; with civil war raging, soldiers and police stopped them every few yards to examine their passports. Shanghai was an amazing spectacle in the grip of war. Each day there were skirmishes and killings. Although the international settlement was protected by U.S. and British marines so that the old, privileged life could continue, there were bursts of gunfire less than a block from the Astor House.

Behind the walls and the bristling lines of infantry, the British and American tradesmen and the colonial officers defiantly enjoyed a life of luxury and ease at the Eiwo Racetack and the clubs and hotels *thés dansants* while opposing forces fought for possession of the sprawling native quarters of the metropolis. Local newspapers show Wallis attending many race meets that season.

A report on Wallis's activities at the time, issued just one day before Pearl Harbor, turned up in the FBI files, declassified on appeal to the associate attorney general, after seven years of waiting, on April 30, 1987. Although the informant was confused about Commander Spencer's rank and location, the report is intriguing in other respects; the long time during which it had to be considered and reconsidered for possible release by one committee after another indicates that it was not regarded as the work of a mere gossip or aggrieved crank:

FBI, December 6, 1941:

Confidential. Memorandum for D. M. Ladd by P. J. Wacks of the Bureau (Washington).

On September 26, 1941, at 2:30 p.m., (blank) contacted the writer in the latter's office concerning the Duchess of Windsor. (Blank) advised that the first husband was a midshipman [*sic*] of the United States Navy whom the Duchess met in San Diego, California; that the midshipman was subsequently ordered to Singapore [*sic*]; that the Duchess followed him to that city where she frequented various night clubs and contacted various naval officers of both the United States and British navies; that the British authorities received information that the Duchess was attempting to obtain information concerning Naval secrets from the British officers she met; that as a result of her activities her husband . . . was transferred from that port of duty.

Was this mere idle gossip? The informant was a person who must have known something. But what? If Wallis was spying for some enemy power, it could only have been Russia, which was America and Britain's opponent in China. John Costello, author of *The Pacific War* and an able historian, says that Foreign Office rumors, recently confirmed by a reliable source in London, state that Wallis was used by the Soviets during her sojourn. It is all a fascinating subject of conjecture, impossible to authenticate at this stage.

The American-born biographer, historian, and editor Leslie Field, who had recently been working at Buckingham Palace in consultation with Her Majesty the Queen on a book on the subject of the royal jewels, stated in 1987 that the China dossier, which, she said, people she knew had examined in detail, contains still further damaging information about Wallis. Mrs. Field said that Wallis was involved in extensive drug peddling at the time and that her activities in drug dealings were not determined until years later when, on royal instructions, Hong Kong authorities managed to obtain the facts from various individuals in China who were aware of them. Also, Mrs. Field revealed to me, Wallis was backed by wealthy men as a high roller at the gambling tables. In view of the fact that gambling at the time in China was totally corrupt and very often the "right" people were allowed to win at the tables, it is not surprising that she succeeded in winning substantial sums at baccarat, roulette, and blackjack. Mrs. Field said that Wallis was notoriously a kept woman and that even during her marriage to Win she was bedded by rich men, including a Chinese general.

Wallis and Mary Sadler went to Peking on December 4, 1924; no travel by American women to the capital was permitted at the time except on official business.

The railroad tracks were so badly broken by warring forces that the famous Blue Express could no longer make its way from Shanghai to Peking. Wallis and Mary Sadler had to take the SS *Shuntien*, a 1,200-

ton vessel of the B. and S. Company, under the command of Captain Einar Christiensen, to Tientsin via Weiheiwei and Chifoo; at Tientsin they would change to a train for the rest of the journey.

Mary Sadler fell ill with stomach trouble and returned to Shanghai. Wallis reached the Tientsin Central National Railway Station on the morning of the eleventh. The ramshackle depot was an infernal spectacle of typhoid and famine victims, rabble soldiery, hysterically crying children, and exhausted women fighting for seats. Wallis had been given a special military authorization and still carried a special intelligence-authorized naval passport. When she boarded the eight-coach Inter-Allied train, reserved for official or military personnel, at 12:10 p.m., she was subjected to a close examination, and at Pei-Tsang station, the first whistle-stop, she was again questioned as Chang's troops came aboard, marching up and down the corridors.

Long before the train chugged a day late into Peking, Wallis could see the lines of Marshal Chang Tso-lin's machine guns along the tracks. When she finally arrived, she was met in the clanging darkness of the station, which was in the grip of a power failure, by Commander Louis M. Little of the Marines. She must have been carrying very important documents; it was a rule that a commanding officer was never to leave a major military post in civil war without some pressing reason, such as contacting a courier.

As Little's gray armored Navy car drove through the plaza and the Hatamen Gate to the protected Legation Quarter, the first thing Wallis would have seen was a line of heads stuck on thirty-foot bamboo poles: signals by General Feng, who was now camped in the western hills awaiting possible battle with Marshal Chang and Sun Yat-sen, that he would brook no rebelliousness in the city.

Peking was overcome with a thunderous sense of terror. When Wallis checked into the Grand Hôtel, a riot of chinoiserie, the papers were reporting that Feng's enemies were being dragged into the parks and decapitated by sword without benefit of trial. Day by day, a tense and anxious British and American population awaited word of Sun Yat-sen's imminent arrival and a full-scale outburst of Communist activity against all foreigners. Suspense hung over the ancient city with its walled cities within the city, its vast gateways and yellow and blue roofs, its cruelly cold, dusty winds from the plain, its dominating color of recently dried blood.

While in Peking, Wallis became romantically entangled with Alberto da Zara, the suavely handsome, blond, 35-year-old naval attaché to the Italian embassy. Da Zara descended from a long line of cavalry officers, from whom he inherited his valiant and gallant manners as well as a deep knowledge and love of horses. She first met him at the embassy compound at an open house which took place every Friday evening.

Well educated and with a grasp of several languages, he was in youth sent abroad every summer, where he built up a number of international contacts. In 1907 he fulfilled an adolescent dream and entered the Annapolis naval academy, where he met and became acquainted with Earl Winfield Spencer.

In May 1922 he was assigned command of a ship, the *Carlotto*, berthed at Hankow, China; he sailed on to Shanghai in November of that year. His memoirs, *La Pelle di un Ammiraglio (Admiral's Skin)* (Mondadori, 1949), contain vivid descriptions of military missions along the Yangtze River and of the social life of China at the time.

He took up his post of naval attaché in Peking a few months before Wallis arrived, in the spring of 1924. He observed in his book: "The prospect of commanding a barracks and to carry out the role of naval, military and aviation attaché in a country without a navy or aviation, and with an army of feudal militia, did not appeal."

Da Zara's passion was horses. Wallis joined him enthusiastically at the racetrack. She had no real interest in horses; as usual, she knew what she was doing. He wrote in his memoirs:

The winter of 1924–1925 was a great season for Italian participants in the Peking Horse Shows . . . without distinction of age or sex, of profession or social status, everyone cheered for someone: a horse or rider, an athlete or team, a club or city; ministers and consuls, customs officers, bank directors, industrialists, great dames and young beauties.

He added gallantly:

Among these, one of the most frequently present fans was Mrs. Wallis Spencer. In those days she wore a classical hairdo which fit the beauty of her forehead and eyes, with her hair, as the Americans say, off the face, stroked, as I would say, to which she has kept faithful until the present day. Already then she expressed a fondness for the color which would become famous as Wallis blue. It matched her eyes.

Wallis became deeply fascinated by da Zara. He was a poet, an addict of d'Annunzio, to whose works he introduced her. Authoritative as a commander, he was discreet and generous. Wallis loved his proud, independent, untamed spirit. His aide in China, Lieutenant Giuseppe Pighini (later an admiral), remembered da Zara's affair with Wallis vividly:

> Mrs. Simpson and da Zara had a very close relationship which from love developed into lasting friendship. Da Zara used to say about her that although she was not beautiful she was extremely attractive and had very refined and cultivated tastes. Her conversation was brilliant and she had the capacity of bringing up the right subject of conversation with anyone she came in contact with and entertaining them on that subject. This quality of conversation and her great knowledge and love of horses were things which she had in common with da Zara.

Soon the affair cooled, but Wallis remained friendly with da Zara.

Pighini remembered that for years da Zara carried an autographed photograph of Wallis wherever he went; it was signed, "To You, Wally." In 1938, when da Zara's ship the *Montecuccoli* was docked in Melbourne, a reporter found the picture by snooping in the cabin and published a story about it in the Melbourne *Age* the next day. Da Zara was furious.

Alberto da Zara undoubtedly cemented Wallis's love of Italy and conviction of the value of fascism as the only possible block to communism, views which would, in turn, soon cement her to the Prince of Wales.

Wallis discovered the Imperial Yellow City, the Forbidden Violet City, and the fairy-tale beauty of the sea palaces built on icy lakes spanned by marble bridges and dotted with frosted lotus leaves. She had letters of introduction to French intelligence and German officials combating Soviet influences in the region and to the elegant aesthete and architect George Sebastian. One night, Wallis saw a familiar face among the other dancing couples at the Grand Hotel: Katherine Bigelow, now Katherine Rogers, a young widow who had befriended Wallis in Coronado, southern California, just six years before. Katherine's husband, Herman Rogers, was a U.S. intelligence officer attached to the local embassy. (His family confirms this fact.) He liaised with Lieutenant Colonel J. H. Barnard, U.S. military attaché, and Dr. Jacob Gould Sherman, American minister to Peking. Rogers was a classic example of the man who had everything; his only flaw was that he was a very un-convincing novelist. He was the son of the millionaire railroad tycoon Archibald Rogers, whose estate, Crumwold Hall, was two houses away from Franklin D. Roosevelt's at Hyde Park, New York. Tall, handsome, athletic, Rogers was educated at Groton and Yale. He had retired at the age of 35, and after his marriage to Katherine, whom he had met orig-inally in France during World War I, had decided to devote the rest of his life to travel, leisure, trying to write the "great American novel," and the acquisition of culture.

In the normal tradition of intelligence contacts, the Rogerses bil-leted Wallis with them at their house, 4 Shih Chia Huting, in the Lega-tion Quarter. They did everything possible to make her feel at home; she had her own rickshaw driver and her own maid. On weekends, Herman and Katherine drove her to their rented Buddhist temple in the foothills of the mountains that doubled as lookout post on General Feng's army. Wallis joined them in horseback riding and in playing poker, contract bridge, and the inevitable mah-jongg. However, the circumstances of her stay were not nearly as idyllic as she later claimed.

According to a friend of Wallis's, she entered into a bizarre ménage à trois with Herman and Katherine. This created great tension and dif-ferences, followed by quarrels; the mutual jealousies and conflicts of feeling deeply upset her. The atmosphere in the house became charged. There was much gossip among the servants.

When Wallis returned to Hong Kong by train on March 21, Win had just left the *Pampanga* and was about to command the *Whipple* at harbor in Shanghai and then en route to the United States. They tried to patch up their relationship once more and took a busman's honey-moon aboard the *President Grant* to Shanghai on March 23.

That she was under special orders from Real Admiral C. V. McVay of the South China Patrol is clear from the fact that Navy wives, along with all other civilians, were forbidden entry to Shanghai at that time. Much of the city had been occupied after a violent conflict in which Marshal Chi-hsieh-yuan defeated the army of Marshal Chang and drove 12,000 of his followers out of the city or into the International Settlement. As the Shanghai Volunteer Corps clashed with the Chi militia, the gutters ran once more with blood, and the journey from the wharf to the quarters where Wallis and Ernest were billeted was exceedingly dangerous. The next weeks were perilous for any American in Shanghai.

Wallis left for that city again in May. By now Win had sailed to the United States as commander of the *Whipple*, while Wallis was stranded in Shanghai, unable to sail for weeks and subject, as a courier, to being kidnapped and murdered by militant Communists at any time.

While in Shanghai, Wallis met and became involved romantically with another handsome Fascist, the dark, moody, proud 21-year-old Count Galeazzo Ciano, a keen supporter of Mussolini. Fascinated by China, the count was on a reconnaissance trip to Peking. At the time he was a student in Rome; later, in 1927, he would be vice-consul.

According to Mrs. Milton E. Miles, whose husband was an officer on the *Pampanga* and later became an admiral:

> Wallis went up the coast to Qunhuangdao, the beautiful summer resort where the Great Wall of China meets the sea. Ciano came down from Peking to spend a lot of time with her there. It was the gossip among us Navy wives in Hong Kong; it was an open scandal.

Mrs. Miles said that Wallis became pregnant by Ciano. Since she was still married to Win, giving birth to a child out of wedlock would have destroyed her chances of getting an equitable divorce and could have been so great a disgrace that it might have caused Win's cashiering from the Navy. According to Mrs. Miles, Wallis attempted an abortion which destroyed her chances of ever having a child and caused her severe gynecological problems that dogged her the rest of her life. Mrs. Miles remembered that when she arrived in Hong Kong on September 7 to join her husband, he told her that Wallis had been in the gynecological ward of the Women's Hospital on August 20.

Wallis returned to Shanghai on the *Empress of Canada* to recover. The strike was continuing, although American ships were allowed in and out of the harbor. In a severe rainstorm on August 29, Wallis sailed, in very poor health, in a first-class cabin aboard the Dollar Lines' *President McKinley* via Kobe, Yokohama, and Honolulu to Seattle. When she arrived, after a rough trip, on September 8, she was immediately hospitalized.

Win had meanwhile left his command of the *Whipple* and was

about to assume command of the USS *Wright* at Hampton Roads, leading a torpedo boat squadron. Wallis remained in touch with him; concerned about her health, though apparently not knowing the cause of her illness, he met with her in Chicago, and they made an attempt at a reconciliation. They returned to Washington by train together in mid-September; soon he was transferred to the *Wright*. They remained good friends.

Win, like Wallis, had established strong connections with the Mussolini administration in Italy. That fall he entertained the Italian soldier and pioneer air ace Italo Balbo, the early Fascist leader and Ciano associate who was building up the Mussolini air force at the time and who would eventually become air minister. Balbo had been in charge of the Blackshirt militia, and with Ciano's father he had been a leader of the march on Rome. His friendship with Win continued until his death; he was shot down in 1940 due to an error by an Italian artillery post at Tobruk. In 1936, Win was awarded the high decoration of Cavalier of the Order of the Crown of Italy for his assistance to Mussolini in matters concerning the Italian air force.

Wallis stayed with her mother in the capital for three weeks, slowly recuperating from her illness. From time to time she traveled to Wakefield Manor, Front Royal, which was scarcely changed from the days of her childhood. Her cousin Lelia was living there with her husband, General George Barnett, who had just retired after eleven years in San Francisco as commandant of the U.S. Marines in the Pacific. The Barnetts took Wallis under their wing; they put her in touch with their able attorney, Aubrey "Kingfish" Weaver, of Weaver and Armstrong, Front Royal.

Weaver told Wallis that at Warrenton, across the Blue Ridge Mountains in Fauquier County, Virginia, divorces could easily be obtained on the basis of the husband's desertion. It would be a simple matter to have Win write a letter backdated to June 1924, stating that he would not live with her again. The letter would be headed "USS *Pampanga*."

She would have to establish residence in Warrenton for at least a year and she must not leave the town for longer than a few weeks. Wallis listened carefully, but surprisingly she had a fit of nostalgia and made yet another effort to patch up the marriage. She wrote to Win on the USS *Wright*; he met her at Aubrey Weaver's office at Front Royal. He told Wallis he wanted to be free.

In a spirit of resignation, Wallis traveled to Warrenton on October 3, 1925. The town was close to Middleburg, where she had been at Burrland, and it was in the heart of fox-hunting country. Horse shows were the focus of all the major social events of the community. Conversation hinged upon the studbook and the saddle.

At Christmas 1926, Wallis answered an invitation from her old friend Mary Raffray and Mary's husband Jacques to stay with them in New York at their "Henry Jamesian" townhouse in Washington Square. Her decision to travel there resulted in a meeting that was to change her life and propel her on her most dangerous adventure so far.

6

Ernest

Late on the afternoon of Christmas day, Jacques, Mary, and their friends and relatives were gathered around the tree when the doorbell rang and Jacques went to answer it. Two men walked in; one of them made so little impression on Wallis that within days she had forgotten his name or what he did for a living. But the other man had the same strong effect on her as Winfield Spencer had some ten years earlier. Jacques introduced him as Ernest Aldrich Simpson; he had a fake British accent and a slightly haughty manner. His brown hair was lightly flecked with gold. He had mild, sympathetic, dark blue eyes, pink cheeks, and a square jaw. Like Win, he had a dark mustache. Well-built, he walked with a cocky, confident military swagger. He was 29 years old.

As the Christmas evening went on, and presents were unwrapped and dinner served, Wallis became intrigued. Simpson had a polished, suave manner, an air of good breeding and intellect, and a well-balanced disposition that lacked the underlying sense of danger that had un-wisely drawn her to Win. The chief problem was that he was married, to the former Dorothea Parsons Dechert, daughter and granddaughter of well-known Massachusetts Supreme Court judges, and the couple had a young daughter, Audrey.

Ernest Simpson was a partner in Simpson, Spence and Young, a company that bought and sold ships. The firm had extensive dealings on both sides of the Atlantic and had offices in the City of London and agents in Hamburg, Germany, where it worked in close alliance with the Hamburg-American Line, and in Italy, where it made deals with

Mussolini's government. Simpson had left Harvard without graduating to follow the impulse of an intense love of England; both his parents came from the British Isles. He joined the cadet battalion of the Coldstream Guards. Then, at the end of World War I, he was compelled, due to his father's negligent management, to surrender his commission and take up the reins of the company. But he remained ultra-British in New York: he walked the avenues in bowler hat, Guards tie, and plain, dark suit, carrying a tightly rolled umbrella as if he were in Mayfair.

This impeccably dapper and correct young American gentleman had a secret, so carefully kept that not even his own daughter knew it. He was Jewish. His father had changed the family name from Solomons because he feared, not without reason, that the business world would close its doors to a new and struggling Jewish company. Because both he and his father were fair of complexion and the masquerade could be sustained, Ernest neglected to tell his first wife, and he joined several clubs that never admitted Jewish members. He was especially careful to conceal the truth in Germany, where anti-Semitism was even more pervasive than it was in the ruling and commercial classes of Manhattan and London.

Wallis had no inkling of Ernest's racial background. Throughout her life her attitude toward Jews was ambiguous and changeable; she would eventually be close to members of the two richest (and interrelated) Jewish families, the Sassoons and the Rothschilds, yet she could, according to Stephen Birmingham, scream out about "kikes." In this she was typical of her time; Cecil Beaton was equally known for using that term; in 1938 he scandalized the world by using it in a notorious cartoon.

Wallis should have returned to Warrenton to sustain the residency requirement called for by the divorce, but instead she boldly embarked on a liaison with Ernest, despite the fact that Dorothea Simpson was present at his East 68th Street townhouse. Wallis and he had much in common. Both enjoyed good books (he was better read than she); both liked to collect figurines and knickknacks; both knew a great deal about silver and china. Ernest was an expert in many fields, including painting, poetry, and music. He was representative of a now-endangered species: the businessman of culture. He took Wallis to museums, galleries, bookstores, libraries; she learned all he had to teach her.

He had other advantages. He appeared to be financially secure. He had perfect manners and knew how to order wines and food. It was true he smoked—she hated smoking—but he liked only the finest pipe tobacco, Havana cigars, and Sobranie or Turkish cigarettes. He had a couple of expensive touring cars. He was respectful, even subservient, and Wallis had never been able to release the dominating side of her personality in the way she wanted.

Their relationship began to develop through bridge and poker and a trip to the Army-Navy football game. But Wallis felt it was a dead end. Ernest refused to consider a divorce. There was the presence of his child. Wallis broke with him for a time. First, she moved from the Raffrays' house to a tiny room at the quasi-British New Weston Hotel. Then she tried to sell an article to *Vogue*; it was rejected. She enlisted with a secretarial school but rapidly withdrew. She was beginning to feel sorry for herself.

She was partly consoled by meeting an old friend from San Diego days, the ugly but charming Benjamin Thaw, who was in charge of the Latin American Division of the State Department and was married to Consuelo Morgan, elder sister of the famous twins Gloria Vanderbilt and Thelma Furness. Consuelo, Gloria, and Thelma were gorgeous, the spoiled and willful children of an American diplomat, Harry Hays Morgan.

In 1923, Consuelo married Benjamin Thaw; the Thaws were one of the reigning families of Pittsburgh. Soon afterward, Gloria's child, Little Gloria, was born. In 1925 Reggie Vanderbilt died of drink; Thelma married Lord (Marmaduke) Furness, owner of the Furness-Withy shipping line that ran cruise vessels from New York to Bermuda. Benny Thaw arranged for Wallis to stay in Pittsburgh with his cousin, the immensely rich, 85-year-old Mary Copley Thaw; at the same time he was talking about Wallis with some other friends, the Morgan Schillers, who were looking for attractive women to work for them, improbably selling construction elevators. Staying with Mary Thaw had its pleasant aspects but also its problems. Mary's mansion, Oak-lawn, was an immense gothic pile, filled with antiques, gloomy land-scape paintings, and a collection of Corots. There were seventy rooms, a dozen live-in servants, and a Paris chef. Mary was deeply troubled. She was suing her grandson for $600,000 she claimed he had extorted from her. She was being blackmailed for some alleged shady business dealings. Above all, she was tortured by the manic presence on the scene of her dissolute son Harry K. Thaw, who in 1906 had shot and killed New York's most prominent architect, Stanford White, on the Madison Square Garden roof over the famous showgirl Evelyn Nesbit Thaw.

While Wallis was at Oaklawn, Thaw, who had been saved from the electric chair by Mary's money and influence, and had served years in a mental asylum, kept arriving without warning in hysterical, terrifying rages. He would take off to New York, where his ex-wife, Evelyn Nesbit, had a nightclub; storming into the club, he would knock all the bottles and tables to the floor and stamp on the broken glass.

Wallis was unable to get a job with the architects Morgan Schiller because of her poor grasp of mathematics, necessary in dealing with specifications, and she returned via New York to Warrenton. Depressed during that spring of 1927, she was consoled when Aunt Bessie, who was now acting as paid companion to Mary B. Adams, owner of the *Washington Evening Star*, offered her a free trip to Europe. Just before sailing, on June 16, Wallis made her official divorce application through her Front Royal lawyers.

The European trip was meaningless and bland. In Paris, in late October, Wallis heard that her Uncle Sol had died of heart failure in Baltimore. He had been very annoyed by her divorce proposal, and he had been severely depressed by the $3 million worth of damage to his railroads caused by the Florida hurricane in July that year. The constant struggle with rival railroad interests and his exhausting lobbying in the Florida cities had worn him out. At first, Wallis, who owed so much to him, was sorry that she had not been available to attend the funeral. But she was greatly displeased by the will when it was read a few days later. Uncle Sol had left her only the interest from $15,000 worth of shares in his railroad companies and in the related Alleghany Company and the Texas Company. She had expected a slice of his $5 million, and she furiously began a lawsuit against the trustees of the estate, in the form of a caveat. Using her proxy, Josephine Warfield, granddaughter of her Uncle Henry, she charged that Warfield was mentally incompetent and emotionally disturbed at the time he made the will and that his signature was forged.

In December 1927 Judge George Latham Fletcher granted her divorce in Warrenton; among the depositions by her mother and others was the letter Win was supposed to have sent from China, complete with American postage stamps, a detail that the judge chose to overlook.

There is no question that this was a collusive divorce, since Wallis's statement that she had not seen Win in four years was contradicted by the evidence and she had omitted any mention of China from her deposition, thereby perjuring herself.

Now that Wallis was free, she turned her mind back to Ernest Simpson and returned to New York to resume her affair with him. Dorothea learned of this while she was ailing at the American Hospital in Paris and filed divorce proceedings there. Prematurely gray-haired and frail, this Massachusetts gentlewoman years later allowed herself to say to Cleveland Amory, "Wallis was very smart. She stole my husband while I was ill." Later in 1928 Ernest decided he would take up the managing directorship of his company in London; his father was increasingly negligent and was involved in a somewhat questionable liaison with a woman in Paris.

Wallis needed time; she was fond of Ernest, but she wasn't in love with him. The Rogerses came to the rescue; they had moved from Peking back to their ancient haunted villa, Lou Viei, in Cannes, in the exotic hillside suburb known as Californie, and, past conflicts and emotional complications forgotten, invited her to stay with them. The villa had been partly remodeled by Barry Dierks, a talented American architect.

Wallis arrived in perfect winter weather; Californie was a riot of hibiscus, frangipani, and coral trees, and at night the scent of flowering jasmine filled the air. The villa was festooned with creepers and had a striking view of the Mediterranean. Herman and Katherine took Wallis out, with various eligible bachelors, dancing at the Palm Beach Club or sailing on chartered yachts under the stars. The Riviera was dreamlike in its charm and tropical loveliness, and Wallis again bathed in the luxury of great wealth.

She discussed with Herman and Katherine whether she should marry Ernest. They urged her to follow her own instincts. It didn't take long for her to make up her mind. Ernest offered freedom from want and a safe haven. Word that his divorce had been granted meant that he was free. She had no money. He was up and coming in British financial circles. She cabled her acceptance of his long-standing proposal and left for London in late June 1928.

Her timing, as always, was perfect. Just as she had arrived in China in the midst of civil war, so she reached London in time for the height of the social season, which officially began on July 1. It was a dazzling month. The Prince of Wales, who continued to fascinate Wallis, and whom she had not seen since that crowded night seven and a half years earlier in San Diego, had just launched a series of parties at York House, his grace-and-favor home at St. James's Palace. He was busy shattering the pomp and circumstance of court life by featuring at these fancy shindigs a dance orchestra, a vaudeville, and cabaret dancers, and by inviting oceans of the "gilded youth" of London.

Born while his great-grandmother Queen Victoria was still on the throne, the prince was obsessed with empire; he knew that one day he would be the ruler of one-third of the world and of millions of people for whom the monarch was almost a divinity.

The Prince of Wales was fond of Austria and Germany; he much regretted the divisions in the royal family that had preceded World War I. So did his mother, the German, but London-born Princess of Teck. George V's cousin and godfather, Czar Nicholas, had been murdered by the Bolsheviks at Ekaterinburg; he never forgot that, and he was committed from the beginning to wiping out communism. Another cousin of his father's, the kaiser, fascinated him; he became very friendly with the kaiser's family, spoke German, and spent much of his youth in Germany. His favorite cousin was the Eton-educated Charles, Duke of Saxe-Coburg-Gotha, who would one day play a sinister role in his life.

In the 1920s, the prince undertook his famous empire tours. No royal figure before him or after him covered so much territory or shook so many thousands of hands. His small, slim figure with its golden crown of hair became the world's symbol of the promise of youth.

He was the most sought-after eligible bachelor of his age, surpassing even Valentino in the immensity of his popularity among young women of all nations. In January 1923 it was announced on the front page of the *New York Times* that he would marry Lady Elizabeth Bowes-Lyon, whose face, under a chaplet of spring flowers, stared prettily out of an ornamental oval next to the announcement. A week later her engagement to his brother Albert was announced; later she was of course the Queen Mother. The following year Queen Marie of Romania tried to match the prince with her daughter, the Princess Ileana. In 1926 Lady Alexandra Curzon, who would soon marry his equerry Edward

"Fruity" Metcalfe, was named as being engaged to him; in fact, she was said to have been enamored of the Duke of Kent. That same year he was linked to the Infanta Beatriz of Spain and in 1928 to Princess Ingrid of Sweden.

By the time Wallis came to London, the prince was in his early thirties. He was willful, spoiled, charming, furious when crossed. He was decades ahead of his time in his obsession with fitness, a trim waist, and a well-toned, carefully trained physique.

The prince had recently been in Paris, where he had been involved in a steamy affair with the notorious Marguerite Laurent, the Princess Fahmy Bey, an exotic beauty who, on the third floor of the Savoy Hotel, on the night of July 9, 1923, at the height of a gothic thunderstorm, had shot and killed her husband, a voluptuous Egyptian, in a fit of jealousy brought on by his apparent interest in another woman.

At the same time he was involved, after many years, with Mrs. Freda Dudley Ward, who in 1918, despite the fact that she was married to a Liberal whip of the House of Commons and had two children, allowed herself to enter into a prolonged liaison with the prince. She was introduced to him, oddly enough, by Ernest Simpson's sister, Maud Kerr-Smiley. More gossip again averred that the prince was bisexual and that he had enjoyed a romantic liaison on an empire tour with his celebrated cousin, Louis Mountbatten, while Edwina Mountbatten found consolation with an odd assortment of partners including the famous black nightclub pianist Leslie "Hutch" Hutchinson. Such gossip cannot be substantiated today.

During an Australasian tour in 1920, Lord Louis Mountbatten's diaries reveal, the prince indulged in some odd, infantile, and sexually peculiar games: he rode in a perambulator, disguised in a diaper as a baby; he fought with Rear Admiral Sir Lionel Halsey disguised as a woman. On one occasion, he sat on the head of the handsome Lord Claud Hamilton of the Grenadier Guards and stripped him naked. At another party, the prince again assumed infant clothes and was rushed at headlong speed around the room in his baby carriage.

On June 10, 1930, in a letter to Dora Carrington, the homosexual author Lytton Strachey would write of a visit to the Tate Gallery:

> I went yesterday to see the Duveen room. . . . There was a black-haired tart marching round in india-rubber boots, and longing to be picked up.

We both lingered in the strangest manner in front of various master-pieces—wandering from room to room. Then on looking around I saw a more attractive tart—fair-haired this time—bright yellow and thick hair—a pink face—and plenty of vitality. So I transferred my attentions, and began to move in his direction when on looking more closely I observed that it was the Prince of Wales—no doubt at all. . . . I fled—perhaps foolishly—perhaps it might have been the beginning of a really entertaining affair.

This, of course, indicates no more than the feverish imaginings of a brilliant flibbertigibbet. Was there anything in all this? The truth prob-ably is that the sexually ambivalent prince at that time had not had an actual homosexual experience; that he was considerably lacking in viril-ity, despite his romantic image in the eyes of millions of women; and that even by the late 1920s he was what the French call a *demivierge*. Uncertain and insecure, he was an unsatisfactory lover, and his homo-sexual leanings, deeply repressed, were revealed in what became an al-most hysterical aversion to anyone homosexual. Nevertheless, gay figures of society continued to weave daydreams around his golden head and slim, perfectly proportioned figure. He was the very stuff of salon gos-sip when Wallis Spencer began to make her way in London society. Ernest Simpson might not be exciting, but at least he had entry to the middle levels of that society when Wallis, who was tired of wandering, weary of struggle, married him, after a very brief engagement, not out of love but out of apathy. The marriage took place at the Chelsea Reg-istry Office on July 21, 1928.

Throughout the honeymoon, which began in Paris and continued all over France and Spain, Ernest continued to teach Wallis much about art and architecture. He walked her off her feet combing through gal-leries and museums and palaces. She tried to seem interested.

Back in London the Simpsons found a house at 12 Upper Berkeley Street. This was a pleasant address, not far from the delights of Hyde Park and Green Park. It was rented to them furnished for twelve months by Margot, Lady Chesham, and with the lease came a cook, maid, but-ler, and chauffeur. Such was the accepted mode of upper-middle-class life in those long-lost days.

Maud Kerr-Smiley made Wallis feel more or less at home in Lon-don, whose climate she hated. Maud gave a series of parties for her, and Wallis responded in kind. Wallis voraciously read the many London newspapers, especially following every movement of the Prince of Wales. Although she pretended to herself and others that the British obsession with royal doings was absurd and misguided, the fact is she had a hunger which drove her back again and again to read the "Court Circular," the officially authorized daily account in the *Times* of what the royal family was up to every day of the week. Her health was poor; she suffered from colds; her marriage was uninspiring. She was sad much of the time.

During the fall of 1928 the prince was continuously in the news. He was planning a visit to Egypt and to continental Africa, a trip that would include a safari in Kenya and a liaison with the aviatrix Beryl Markham; he enjoyed her favors on alternate nights with his brother, the Duke of Gloucester—a scandal that was carefully suppressed by the royal spin doctors. He appeared in public without a waistcoat, which set a new trend; he was seen helping a small boy dig worms at the sea-side; and he joined the war veterans at Ypres in France for a memorial service at that scene of bloody conflict of World War I. These seem-ingly trivial matters summed up his interests: his love of empire and his need to preserve the security of the Suez Canal, the channel whereby the trade routes to India were maintained; his informality and love of children and the poor, and his obsession with the horrors of the First World War, which he regarded as futile and stupid and the result of unnecessary conflicts between his grandfather, King Edward VII, and his cousin, Kaiser Wilhelm of Germany. That war had cost England the flower of its youth, and the Prince of Wales, who had been on the front in France, was determined, with all his heart and soul, that such a holocaust of bullet and bomb and gassing should never happen again.

All this Wallis could determine by reading his speeches, particularly the impassioned address at Ypres. She still hated war; it had caused her great anguish at Pensacola, and she had never forgotten the death of Dumaresq, Win's brother, in action in France. And then in Canton, China, she had seen firsthand the terror and danger of bloody battles between Communists and Fascists. She could not fail to sympathize with the Prince of Wales's neutralism from the beginning.

There was another matter which she soon heard about and which did not find its way into even the most garish newspapers. While still entangled with Freda Dudley Ward, Beryl Markham, and the Princess Fahmy, the prince found a new light of love: Thelma, Lady Furness, the twin sister of Gloria Vanderbilt and the younger sister of Wallis's friend Mrs. Benny (Consuelo) Thaw. Thelma had the sultry, dark good looks inherited from a partly Latin ancestry. Her American accent did the rest—the prince was always infatuated by Americans. He met her at a cattle show; he had known, he said, Benny and Consuelo when Benny was a diplomat in Buenos Aires. Thelma moved boldly into Fort Belvedere, the prince's residence on the edge of Windsor Great Park, and redecorated a guest bedroom as her own—in shocking pink, with the Prince of Wales's emblematic three white feathers at the top of each of the four wooden posts of her bed. The prince was greatly amused by this example of vulgarity. They entered into childish games: they bought teddy bears at Harrods and exchanged them as peace offerings after quarrels; they did embroidery together, an art taught them both by their mothers; and they called each other Poppa and Momma— Momma for the prince. Their sexual relationship appears to have been infantile and unsatisfactory: Thelma later complained to her friends that the prince had a very small endowment and was a very poor sexual performer. She spitefully called him, as did so many others, "the Little Man."

Wallis learned that in December 1928 the prince had to return abruptly from his trip to Dar es Salaam, Tanzania, because his father was grievously ill; Mussolini, to whom he would always be grateful, supplied transportation. Wallis, by accident or design, caught a glimpse of him one murky afternoon as he left York House, St. James's Palace, in the polished black royal Daimler to go to Buckingham Palace to attend his sick parent. She claims she was on her way to pick up her husband in the City of London when she beheld this sight; in fact, Ernest was always brought home by chauffeur, and the palace was not on the direct route from Upper Berkeley Street. It is probable, therefore, that like so many fans, she was simply waiting to catch a glimpse of the prince.

Life moved on slowly for Wallis; Ernest was a lecher who made passes at women at parties. They kept accounts together, and they played bridge games and backgammon. The only shadow on Wallis's life was the illness of her unhappy mother, who, Aunt Bessie wrote, had aged badly and was already an old woman in her fifties. In early 1929 Wallis and Ernest sailed to America on the *Mauretania* to visit with Alice. They were shocked by her appearance. They returned for a chauffeured tour of England, but the pain and sorrow remained.

The lease ran out on the Upper Berkeley Street house after a year, and Lady Chesham, who was reconciled with her husband, a captain in the Royal Hussars, from whom she had been separated, wanted the house back. Wallis and Ernest moved into a temporary flat in Hartford Street, and were house-hunting when news came from Washington that Alice was dying.

Wallis traveled alone on the *Olympic*. With her usual timing, she arrived in the midst of the Wall Street crash. The news was received aboard ship, and it was impossible to sell her shares in time. She lost almost all her $15,000 from the Warfield estate; her caveat under the name of Josephine Warfield was not heard until the following year, when it failed.*

It took only a day or two to learn that most of Ernest's American holdings had also been wiped out. It was a grievous week, and Alice's death on November 2 was the ultimate blow. Alice left nothing; she was intestate. Charles Gordon Allen, her unhappy husband, was also penniless, his meager savings wiped out by the crash. Wallis sailed back to England under a heavy cloud.

Fortunately, Simpson, Spence and Young did not depend on America; the company continued to buy and sell ships at a profit in Germany, Italy, and the Scandinavian countries. The Simpsons managed to scrape up enough money to buy some furniture, and Wallis and Ernest located a fine apartment at 5 Bryanston Court, on George Street; it was spacious and comfortable, and it came with a complete staff of servants, who were housed elsewhere on the premises. The flat had a small entrance hall, a large drawing room, a dining room that sat fourteen, three bedrooms—a master bedroom, a second bedroom, and a guest room—two bathrooms, and a large kitchen. Wallis decorated the rooms tastefully, with the exception of the guest room, which she fixed up with a huge round white bed and pink sheets and pillows. Guests entering the drawing room saw to the left an overstuffed brocade armchair and behind it a mahogany table with a Chinese vase brought from Peking; ahead a Chippendale cabinet filled with small Chinese ornaments; also straight ahead a Regency mirror over a conventional fireplace; and to the right a Queen Anne chair with a striped silk seat and a large, silk-covered sofa. Bookshelves built into the wall displayed Ernest's collection of Dickens and A. A. Milne, author of *Winnie the*

---

*But she was offered (and accepted) an alternative settlement.

Pooh, his favorite book, whose central figure he resembled in more ways than one.

Throughout much of the autumn and winter of 1929 the Prince of Wales's activities consisted of stunting in planes, remodeling his houses with Thelma, and planning another trip to Africa, which took place in January 1930. Wallis followed his movements daily: his long voyage to Cape Town through gale-swept seas; his feverish cold; his elephant hunt near Nairobi; and in March a recurrence of malaria. After a fling with Thelma Furness in Africa, he was back in England in April.

In October 1930 Benny and Consuelo Thaw moved from Paris to London, where he became first secretary of the U.S. embassy. At the same time, and to Wallis's delight, Corinne Mustin Murray also turned up in the city; her husband, George Murray, was assistant naval attaché. Wallis felt much more at home in London now. She became part of an American colony that tended to meet at least twice a week and exchange news of home.

Through Benny and Consuelo, Wallis met Thelma Furness. Bearing a son, Tony, to Lord Furness made no difference to Thelma's continuing royal liaison, and Furness, who was immensely rich from his Bermuda honeymoon ships despite the crash, was enjoying a continuous honeymoon with beautiful young women in the south of France. As if surrounding the prince on all sides, Thelma spent her weekends at Fort Belvedere while Gloria Vanderbilt, with her daughter, Little Gloria, set up house at the imposing Three Gables, directly opposite Fort Belvedere and watchable from the royal windows.

Even Mama Morgan, Laura Kilpatrick, the sisters' colorful mother, moved into Three Gables to make the siege complete. Meanwhile, inspired by Thelma's American enterprise, the prince redid Fort Belvedere from top to bottom, installing central heating—a great luxury in England—a Turkish bath, a gymnasium, and a swimming pool. The prince would arrive romantically with Thelma at this gothic hideaway by plane, his new King's Flight pilot, Flight Lieutenant Edward Fielden, expertly touching down on Smith's Lawn at Windsor Great Park.

Wallis became a friend of Thelma's; it is possible she felt that through the connection she would obtain a foothold at court. At all events, the two women met for lunch, usually at the Ritz, and enjoyed the gossip of the hour; when, in mid-January 1931, Consuelo and Benny Thaw invited Wallis to Burrough Court, the Furness house at Melton Mowbray in Leicestershire, center of the fashionable fox-hunting country, she accepted at once. The Thaws made an exciting promise: the Prince of Wales and his brother, Prince George, who annually attended the Quorn Hunt from their nearby residence of Craven Lodge, were expected to be at the house party. Lord Furness was on safari in Africa at the time.

At the last minute, Benny's mother fell ill in Paris and Consuelo flew over to take care of her. Wallis, Ernest, and Benny decided to go up to Melton Mowbray by train. It was well into January and the weather was too foggy for safe driving.

Wallis was nervous about meeting the Prince of Wales. She spent a day at the hairdresser's and beauty parlor. By Saturday she could face herself more or less calmly in mirrors—the Bryanston Court flat was full of mirrors. But she was still terrified: that she wouldn't make the right impression; that she would be out of place as she had been in Warrenton, in an environment in which horses and hunting were the main topics of conversation; and that she wouldn't be well enough to dazzle—she was coming down with a miserable winter cold.

At last she was ready. With the long-suffering Ernest, she drove to St. Pancras Station, where they met Benny Thaw for the trip. Wallis felt increasingly unwell on the journey. As the train chugged through fog and drifting snow, she was coughing and sneezing uncontrollably; she was sure she had a fever. She suddenly realized she had no idea how the prince should be addressed. Benny told her the correct form was "Sir." It dawned on her that she didn't know how to curtsey; Benny must teach her at once. In the swaying, rattling, sooty train, Benny Thaw, career diplomat and first secretary to the U.S. embassy in London, managed a very clumsy curtsey. Wallis felt too awful even to laugh. But she copied Benny, and by the end of the trip she had mastered the art to perfection.

The train steamed into Melton Mowbray in a dense yellow fog. Thelma had sent a car. The chauffeur had to struggle with painful slowness through the damp and icy murk. At last he stopped in front of a large, gabled house, with an imitation Tudor look: "Stockbrokers' Tudor," as Osbert Lancaster would later dub the architectural mode. Averill Converse, Thelma's stepdaughter by a previous marriage, was at the door instead of the butler to greet the arrivals. Averill told her guests that Thelma had gone over to Craven Lodge to return with the two princes. Wallis could only sneeze and cough miserably as she and Ernest went to their rooms to freshen up.

Averill entertained her guests to a prolonged afternoon tea. The hours ticked away on the grandfather clock; Wallis began to wonder if the princes would ever turn up, if they were marooned somewhere in the fog. Finally, after two hours, at 7 p.m., there was the sound of a car drawing up on the gravel drive, followed by a babble of voices. The butler opened the front door.

7

The Prince

Dark, vital, gorgeous, Thelma strolled in with the princes. It was the first time Wallis had seen the Prince of Wales at really close quarters: the faraway figure moving through the crowds at the Hotel del Coronado and the barely glimpsed, sad-faced presence in the royal car leaving St. James's Palace, the personage of the newsreels and the newspapers and the magazines was actually saying "Good evening" to her and shaking her hand. She curtseyed. She looked hard at him, with a burning curiosity.

She liked him at once. He was even smaller than he seemed in photographs. He looked very fit but was narrow, delicate, and slender in build. His hair was a shining gold. His eyes were a tired, haunted blue with premature pouches under them, the result, Wallis would later discover, of heavy drinking and insomnia. Almost childlike at a distance, his face was puckered and deeply lined because of too much exposure to the tropical sun on his travels to the limits of the empire. He had even, un-British white teeth, frequently displayed in an infectious quizzical smile that few could resist. He was dressed in a loudly checked tweed suit. He was informal, relaxed and laughing. His face in laughter was open, innocent, and joyous; in repose it was intensely sad, possessed of a secret pain.

Part of that pain was caused by the recurring sexual problems which Thelma Furness would later and quite ruthlessly discuss in international circles.

It was already night. Dinner would be served at nine. To make her royal guests welcome, Thelma prepared a second tea, forcing Wallis, who dieted grimly, to tackle yet another round of scones, cake, and England's favorite beverage. The conversation was desultory. At last, Wallis and Ernest went to their rooms to dress for dinner while Thelma went to the nursery to tuck her baby son, Tony, and his cousin, Little Gloria Vanderbilt, into bed; Gloria Senior was abroad in France. The conversation at the evening meal offered little inspiration to Wallis: it centered on the hunt, which she continued to dislike, hounds, and the studbook. She felt as bored and alienated as she had been at Warrenton. She was still suffering from her cold, and she was a long way down the dining table from the prince.

Feeling only slightly better after sleeping late the next morning, Wallis, still sniffling into her handkerchief, walked downstairs to find the Prince of Wales chatting with his devoted aide, Brigadier General Gerald F. "G" Trotter, a grizzled charmer who had lost his right arm in the Boer War and whose uniform sleeve was pinned to the front of his tunic. Wallis found at the luncheon table that there were no place cards now; boldly, she sat next to the prince. For something to say, he observed, "You must miss central heating, Mrs. Simpson." To which, with startling effrontery, she replied with a falsehood: "To the contrary, Sir, I like the cold houses of Great Britain." Then she added, "I am sorry, Sir, but you have disappointed me." The prince looked understandably startled by this impudence. "In what way, Mrs. Simpson?" he asked. While, no doubt, the expressions of Ernest, Thelma, "G" Trotter, and the other guests were pictures of shock and dismay, there was no stopping Wallis now. She said, "Every American woman who comes to England is asked that same question. I had hoped for something more original from the Prince of Wales!"

Wallis had grasped shrewdly from the first moment she looked into the prince's weak, sensitive, pale blue eyes that he wanted to be dominated by strong people; he liked to be confronted head-on. Her cool, expert calculation paid off. The prince was unable to shake off her sharp remark; she had caught his interest, and she knew it.

Dinner that night was an elaborate occasion. Dozens of the local gentry gathered in the dining room for hours of horsey conversation. The next day Wallis, Ernest, and Benny returned to London. Perhaps because the meeting with the prince awakened thoughts in Wallis she would rather suppress, her behavior over the next few days was nervous and drastic. She fired her chauffeur because of some slighting remark he had made to Ernest; she got rid of a maid and gave notice to the cook. She was consumed with a new ambition; she must meet the prince again. An ideal occasion would be her presentation at court. When an American acquaintance, Mrs. Reginald Anderson, suggested the presentation, she accepted immediately, even though Mrs. Anderson as a personality left her somewhat cold. Her cousin Lelia Barnett had come to London in the fall of 1929 for such a presentation, and Wallis had helped to dress her. Thelma Furness had been presented; so had Consuelo and Gloria. Wallis would not be left behind.

The conditions of presentation had a moral stringency typical of the reign of King George V, whose high standards of public conduct contrasted oddly with the decadent self-indulgence and promiscuity of fashionable London in the 1930s. For years, no divorced woman was received at court. By 1931 a divorcée could be presented, but she had to prove that the fault of adultery, cruelty, or desertion lay with the husband. Any suspicion of collusion would be frowned upon, which narrowed the field considerably.

In order to crawl through this needle-eye of official acceptance, which meant a good deal more to her than she pretended, Wallis anxiously wrote to Mrs. Sterling Larrabee, her former hostess at Warrenton, to obtain the necessary divorce documents from the Warrenton courthouse files. Why she didn't write to her lawyer, Aubrey Weaver, at Front Royal is a mystery, although she often had a poor memory for names. No sooner had she written to Mrs. Larrabee than panic seized her, and she sent a letter to Aunt Bessie expressing her interest in the prince with a cable insisting that nothing be said about the meeting at Melton Mowbray. She was afraid of a leak to the press. Then, unpredictably, after issuing this stern request, she couldn't resist bragging about her encounter. She wrote to Mary Kirk Raffray in New York about it and then impulsively gave Bessie permission to talk to Lelia Barnett, and she told Benny Thaw who told Corinne . . . It was clear she was in a spin of nervous excitement mixed with tension and scarcely knew what she was doing. And yet she claimed in her memoirs that royalty meant nothing to her.

Mrs. Larrabee proved to be a friend and sent the divorce decree to London. But since she was no expert at obtaining documents, she failed to obtain the all-important depositions of Alice and Wallis herself; Wallis most anxiously sent her back to the courthouse to obtain the depositions and mail them.

Meanwhile, the Prince of Wales and his brother George had left England, traveling via Paris to Spain and then across the Atlantic to the Caribbean and South America. The journey, taking many weeks, had the double benefit of aiding British trade problems south of Panama and spiriting the star-crossed bisexual George away from a dire situation with a boy in Paris. In the prince's absence Wallis wasted no time in capitalizing on her royal encounter. As word got around that she had met the prince, she received invitation after invitation, dragging with her the exhausted and irritable Ernest, who hated late nights after a hard day's work at the office. Her social ambition was ferocious, obsessive. Among the Simpsons' hosts that spring of 1931 were Lord and Lady Sackville, who invited them to stay at their fabled estate, Knole. At the same time, Wallis began cultivating Thelma much more intensively, clearly realizing how that friendship would bring her very close to the throne. And she also got to know Gloria Vanderbilt, who was spending more time in England, and the colorful Nadeja, known as "Nada," Milford Haven. A glamorous White Russian, Nada Milford Haven shared with Thelma and Gloria membership in a high-powered group of society lesbians who were the cause of constant hothouse gossip in the Mayfair salons.

On May 15, Thelma threw a grand welcome-home party for the two returned princes at her house in Grosvenor Square. The guests were excited as Thelma walked in, resplendent in a silver gown, with the Prince of Wales. As the prince approached Wallis, he whispered to Thelma, "Haven't I seen that lady before?" Thelma reminded him that he had met Wallis at her house. He shook hands with Wallis as she rose from her curtsey and he told her how much he had enjoyed the previous encounter. She smiled; he continued to pass down the line.

A few days later the lord chamberlain, who had accidentally overlooked the telltale American postage stamps on Win's faked letter from Canton, approved Wallis's presentation at court. Wallis was overjoyed. She could think of nothing else but the big event coming up in June. However, she had a distraction: Mary Raffray, who was separating from Jacques, announced that she would be arriving on the *Mauritania* in a few days. Wallis was far too busy to welcome this visit; the dark side of her nature was in evidence as she fretted about the arrival of her oldest and dearest friend.

Mary had a rough crossing, but she overcame seasickness to carry on elaborate flirtations with several handsome young bachelors aboard. She arrived at the railway station in London with no less than five beaux escorting her, then dropped the lot as she sped off with Wallis through the crowd. Wallis had an invitation to lunch at Consuelo and Benny Thaw's, and there was no way she was going to miss it. Suitcases and all, she whisked the exhausted Mary off to Consuelo's house to meet Thelma and Nada. On the way, she confided that the Thaws' home was used by the Prince and Thelma as a love nest.

Mary scarcely had time to powder her nose as she was whirled by high-strung Wallis from tea party to dinner party; they didn't get home to Bryanston Court until well into the early morning hours. Mary fell exhausted onto the ghastly circular guest-room bed with its pink sheets, pink plush covers, and wide satin eiderdown. Wallis spent the next few days in a constant spin with Mary. The occasional dinners at Bryanston Court had an offbeat flavor—Ernest stiffly dressed up in white tie and tails and the two girls in lounging pajamas and robes. Felipe Espil, Wallis's old flame of Washington days, was now first secretary of the Argentinean embassy and frequently entertained the Simpsons and Mary.

On Derby Day, June 3, 1931, the sleek U.S. diplomat William Galbraith and his brusque, abrupt wife Katherine took the excited Wallis and her gang to Epsom Downs to see the race from the top of a rented London double-decker bus, supping on champagne, caviar, and cold chicken from picnic hampers. At last the presentation day arrived: Wednesday, June 10. In a state of hysteria, Wallis borrowed Thelma's fan made up of three ostrich feathers, the traditional symbols of the Prince of Wales required of every presentee. She was too tall to fit into Thelma's white dress, so she wore Consuelo's instead. Thelma lent her the train. She bought an aquamarine and crystal necklace cross and a corsage brooch. The wealthy American Lester Grant lent her and Ernest his touring automobile.

The Andersons and the Simpsons left Bryanston Court early to beat the traffic jam in the Mall. Crowds had already formed and peered into the interior of the car, trying to see the occupants.

It was the first time Wallis saw Buckingham Palace. She was en-thralled. The chauffeur drove through the iron gates, parking the ve-hicle in the courtyard. Wallis and her party went to a special entrance, passing through a vestibule where liveried flunkies took the ladies' wraps. From there, the guests walked slowly up the red-carpeted grand staircase that was lined on either side by yeomen of the guard in me-dieval costumes. They made their way down a chandeliered corridor to the red-and-gold ballroom. Wallis was fascinated by the throne dais. The king and queen were seated side by side in front of the gold-embroidered canopy of crimson velvet, beneath which they had sat at the Coronation Delhi Durbar of 1911. Under the canopy's top were embroidered in gold the royal lion and unicorn, and on either side white-fluted pillars supported a display of noble classical figures.

The king was in full-dress uniform; the queen was in a beaded gown of white satin with a choker necklace of pearls and diamonds. The Prince of Wales stood behind the throne. The indispensable "G" Trotter led Wallis's party to seats near the front. Soon, the room was completely full. At a signal from the conductor of the palace orchestra, the presenters and presentees formed a line passing the thrones, the ladies curtseying one by one to the royal couple. Later, everyone re-paired to the State Apartments, and the prince joined his parents in talking briefly with the guests. Wallis heard him say to his great-uncle, the Duke of Connaught, "Something should be done about the lights. They make all the women look ghastly."

After the presentation Thelma invited Wallis, Ernest, and the Andersons to join her and the prince for a nightcap at her house. Wallis boldly challenged the prince on his remark about the lights. He ex-pressed surprise that his voice had carried so far; he had underesti-mated the intensity with which she, feigning indifference, was hanging on his every word. Once again, with great cleverness, she had piqued his royal interest.

As the Simpsons left Thelma's house at 3 a.m., their chauffeur was waiting to take them home. But the prince offered to drop them off in his own car. Wallis dismissed her driver. At Bryanston Court she in-vited the prince to come up for another drink. He declined with a smile; he was on his way to Fort Belvedere. But he indicated that he would certainly take her up on the offer another time.

In the autumn of 1931, Wallis was feeling terrible. She was ill from in-
flamed tonsils and had to have them removed. Consuelo Thaw came to
see her every day; her solicitude seemed to be beyond that called for by
normal friendship—her interest in Wallis hadn't waned. Wallis dreaded
her visits. It was a grim, foggy November; for weeks Wallis lay in bed,
exhausted by the operation, unhappy and unsettled by her penurious
condition. Word from the Prince of Wales was a long time forthcoming, but at last her patience was rewarded. In late January 1932 the
winter gloom was lightened by the longed-for invitation to go to Fort
Belvedere. The Simpsons drove down in a borrowed car, through snow-
covered countryside to Sunningdale, Berkshire, arriving in the early
evening. The road cut through forest trees until, at a moment of dramatic unexpectedness, it opened out into a gravel driveway and then to
the brightly lit turrets and battlements of the fairy-tale castle. Lamp-
light was glowing in the tall windows and a liveried footman appeared
at the sound of the car engine, to open the door and take the luggage.
With typical informality the prince, dressed in a kilt, was at the door in
person to greet his guests.

He led the again-rejuvenated and happy Wallis with Ernest through
an octagonal anteroom with black-and-white marble floors to the elaborate drawing room surrounded by Canalettos. Rich golden-yellow
satin curtains were drawn against the night; the atmosphere was cozy,
snug, and very American under Thelma's influence. There were chintz-
covered armchairs and Chippendale tables and a grand piano. Even
though a fire was roaring away cheerfully in the grate, the central heating was on full blast. Thelma was there, along with "G" Trotter and
the Thaws. The prince insisted on taking the Simpsons to their room.
When they returned after dressing for dinner, they were astonished to
see the prince, watched tenderly by Thelma, embroidering with infinite
care a backgammon table cover. He said, looking up bashfully, "This is
my secret vice. The only one, in any case, I am at pains to conceal."

Dinner took place in the handsome, paneled dining room decorated with pictures of horses by Stubbs. Wallis was very amused to see
that the prince kept his cigarette case in his sporran. After the meal the
guests joined their host in games of cards and in trying to piece together a giant jigsaw puzzle. Then they danced cheek to cheek to the
latest fox-trots and rhumbas. At last came the moment Wallis was wait-

ing for; the heir to the throne asked her to dance. "I found him a good dancer, deft, light on his feet, with a true sense of rhythm," she wrote years later.

In March 1932 Wallis's old friend from Peking, George Sebastian, issued an invitation to the Simpsons to visit him in his elegant house at Hammamet in Tunisia, North Africa. When Wallis glumly wrote her host that she was without funds, he sent her the tickets. It was a pleasant trip, and George an excellent host. Not long afterward Aunt Bessie arrived, and she treated the Simpsons to a trip around Europe. But despite these adventures, Wallis was still under severe stress; her marriage wasn't working, and the financial problems and a frustrated longing to see more of the Prince of Wales left her again in a poor state of health, suffering from ulcers. As a result, the trip with Aunt Bessie was cut short.

Wallis was also distracted with what became an open scandal that summer; Consuelo Thaw's affair with a charming foreign woman. In view of Benny's position at the U.S. embassy, this was not only a torment to that correct and decent man, but it also exposed the embarrassed Wallis to untoward gossip. The Prince of Wales found a new female distraction: the celebrated aviatrix Amelia Earhart, who had just made international headlines by being the first woman to cross the Atlantic in a solo flight. Apparently disregarding Thelma, the prince ostentatiously took Amelia dancing; she was married, and once again he seemed to have an unhealthy fascination with married women. He took Amelia to the Derby, causing a flurry of excited comment in the American press; the British newspapers primly avoided any mention of this new romance. The *New York Times* noted that he danced with Amelia at the Derby Ball—again and again and again.

He treated Thelma badly that year; he was looking for new fields to conquer. He traveled to Mussolini's Italy without her.

During the prince's long absence abroad, Wallis was increasingly unhappy, frustrated, and distracted at Bryanston Court. She still fought with her staff, firing and rehiring servants; she continued to be sickly and fretful; her ulcers caused her much pain and discomfort. However, she was consoled by the fact that the prince wasted little time after he returned before inviting her and Ernest to Fort Belvedere. In January 1933, Wallis made another visit to the fort, but it is clear from her letters that by then she was irritated by Thelma's continuing hold over the prince; she wrote an edgy note to her Aunt Bessie, clearly distracted by the sight of Edward and Thelma embroidering in unison. She didn't realize that the prince very much had his eye on her.

In March 1933, she knew. It was not customary for royal persons to send messages to passengers on ships unless those passengers were already relegated to the role of court favorite. When Wallis sailed that March aboard the *Mauritania* to visit with Aunt Bessie in Washington, a Marconigram was received for her aboard ship, wishing her bon voyage and a safe return. News of the wire rapidly spread around the ship, ensuring for her the maximum attention from officers and crew. She regarded the vacation as an opportunity to escape from her stultifying marriage. She enjoyed the attention of many men, and spent much of her time in Washington carrying on a series of giddy romantic liaisons; she added a new series of beaux on the return voyage. It is clear that it was hard on her to return to a monogamous situation even though dear, dull, devoted Ernest met her when the ship docked at Cherbourg.

After her return, Wallis's relationship with the Prince of Wales underwent a change. Evidence for this can be found in an episode involving Henry Flood Robert, the son of Grace Flood Robert, an old friend from Coronado days, who arrived in London to take part in the International Monetary Conference. Wallis, Ernest, and Grace, who was staying with them, met Henry off the train. Wallis prepared an excellent American meal for the Roberts, including fried chicken. It was an exciting occasion; Wallis was delighted to recall the good old days in southern California. Oddly, Thelma Furness was present on her own, as out of place as Ernest was in a tide of reminiscence that neither could share. Mr. Flood Robert never forgot what took place at four o'clock that afternoon:

> Suddenly the door opened and the maid came in. She announced that the royal car was at the door. And that Madam was expected to come at once to Fort Belvedere as the Prince of Wales was waiting for her! Wallis immediately, and right in front of Ernest and Thelma, picked up her coat and handbag without a word and walked out, leaving us all so stunned we couldn't speak. I looked at Ernest and saw a tear in his eye. I couldn't look at Thelma. My heart went out to Ernest, but I admit I said to Mother as we went to our hotel, "More power to Wallis!"

A certain inscription on a bracelet given by Edward to Wallis three years later, but now in the possession of the Countess of Romanones, indicates that it was not long after that incident that the relationship between Wallis and the prince became a sexual one. The countess will not reveal the exact words of the inscription, which marks a significant anniversary, but says only that it contains a highly intimate reference to "a bathtub." According to Sir Dudley Forwood, later equerry to the Duke of Windsor, the relationship between Wallis and the prince was bizarre. He said, in 1987:

> The techniques Wallis discovered in China did not entirely overcome the prince's extreme lack of virility. It is doubtful whether he and Wallis ever actually had sexual intercourse in the normal sense of the word. However, she did manage to give him relief. He had always been a repressed foot fetishist, and she discovered this and indulged the perversity completely. They also, at his request, became involved in elaborate erotic games. These included nanny-child scenes: he wore diapers, she was the master. She was dominant, he happily submissive. Thus, through satisfying his needs, needs which he probably did not even express to Mrs. Dudley Ward and Thelma Furness, she earned his everlasting gratitude and knew that he would be dependent on her for a lifetime.

Others differ with this view, among them Alberto da Zara's lieutenant, Giuseppe Pighini, who said in that same year, to my Rome correspondent Donatella Ortona:

> I was told by close friends of Wallis that indeed she in fact did introduce the prince to techniques which made it possible for him to have satisfaction during intercourse. He was so emotional that before he would climax too quickly and thus could not consummate sex.

That same year, Adolf Hitler rose to power in Germany. From the beginning he was determined to secure an alliance with Great Britain, whose foreign policy was leaning toward his chief rival among European dictators, Mussolini. He embarked upon a policy of interesting the British royal family in recementing their fractured alliances with their cousins in Germany. With great shrewdness, and in order to secure the support of the army, which maintained its traditional allegiances to the old Junker Prussian class, he did not confiscate the massive properties of Kaiser Wilhelm II, cousin of King George V. Although the kaiser remained in exile at Doorn, the Netherlands, his sons and daughters-in-law were comfortably maintained under the führer's protection in Berlin. Of these, Hitler's favorite was the Crown Princess Cecilie, the tall, buxom, and Wagnerian daughter-in-law of the former monarch. It was at her home, Cecelienhof, a looming gothic folly filled with potted plants and pictures of dead Hohenzollerns, that the young Prince of Wales had spent happy days of his childhood. Her son, Prince Louis Ferdinand, was 25 years old in 1933 and an employee of Henry Ford in Dearborn, Michigan; Ford was a keen admirer of Hitler, and Hitler had Ford's picture on his desk in the early, struggling days of the Nazi party at the Munich Brownhouse. Tall, handsome, dark-skinned, with silky black hair, Prince Louis Ferdinand was considered by the führer an ideal emissary to London. He had a romantic background, calculated to appeal to the Prince of Wales: he had just had a romance with the French movie star Lili Damita, who was soon to marry another of Hitler's idols, Errol Flynn.

Prince Louis Ferdinand was a member of the old guard of the right wing of Germany devoted to the traditions of the army. His host, the entertainingly scurrilous Sir Robert Bruce Lockhart, kept a careful diary of Louis Ferdinand's meetings with the Prince of Wales in London that season; the German visitor also met Wallis, who liked him. On July 11, 1933, the two young men met at York House, St. James's Palace. They talked partly in German and partly in Spanish. Bruce Lockhart reported in his diary entry of July 12:

> The Prince of Wales was quite pro-Hitler and said it was no business of ours to interfere in Germany's internal affairs either re Jews or re anything else, and added the dictators are very popular these days, and that we might want one in England before long.

Bruce Lockhart did not report on Prince Louis Ferdinand's response to this statement. It should be noted that at the time, due to King George V's uncertain health, Wales was taking his place at some official functions and was expected to succeed him before too long. Perhaps he himself was the dictator he had in mind. Soon afterward, Louis met Prince George, noting, as Bruce Lockhart recorded, "The prince is artistic and effeminate and uses a strong perfume. This appeals to me."

The kaiser appreciated his grandson's visit to the British capital. He wrote to Bruce Lockhart on July 22:

> My special thanks to you for your kind efforts in getting the Prince into touch with members of the Royal Family. . . . It would be particularly agreeable if, through this visit, the German-English relationship is furthered. . . . The remark of the Prince of Wales, that we have a right to deal with our affairs as we deem it right, shows sound judgement. Prince Louis Ferdinand would no doubt have agreed with him on this point.

Although Prince Louis Ferdinand was secretly anti-Nazi and later joined the German Resistance, his presence in London as a presumed symbol of Hitler's support of royal alliances ironically influenced the Prince of Wales and, through Wales, Wallis. If anything was needed to convince the Prince of Wales that the führer's intentions were to restore the old family alliances, those doubts were removed. From then on, he and Wallis seldom wavered in their naive belief in Hitler's intentions and desires for a lasting peace. On Armistice Day, November 11, Wales confided in Count Albert Mensdorff, the former Austrian ambassador, telling the count of his fondness for nazism.

Mensdorff wrote:

> It is remarkable how he expressed his sympathies for the Nazis of Germany: "Of course it is the only thing to do, we will have to come to it, as we are in great danger from the Communists here, too. . . . I hope and believe we shall never fight a war again, but if so we must be on the winning side, and that will be the German, not the French. . . ." It is . . . interesting and significant that he shows so much sympathy for Germany and the Nazis.

By a juxtaposition of significant quotations it can be seen that the prince's politics, then and later, were coincidental with those of Sir Oswald Mosley, head of the British Union of Fascists. In Mosley's memoirs, while advocating, among other things, that Goering should have come to England to secure widespread support for Nazi Germany, Sir Oswald wrote emphatically:

> I was prepared to do anything to prevent a war by maintaining good relations between English and Germans, provided it was compatible with my duty to my own country. [We should have let] the Germans go to a

possible clash with Russia, which, if it happened, would have smashed world Communism [in the 1930s], pointed Germany in the opposite direction to us, and kept its vital energies busy for at least a generation while we had time to take any precautions which might prove necessary.

In an article in the *New York Daily News* of December 13, 1966, the then Prince of Windsor wrote:

My Hanoverian and Coburg forebears were German. There was much in the German character that I admired. At their best as, alas, at their worst, they are a virile, hard-working, efficient nation. I acknowledge now that along with too many other well-meaning people, I let my admiration for the good side of the German character dim what was being done to it by the bad. I thought that the rest of us would be fence-sitters while the Nazis and the Reds slogged it out . . . the immediate task . . . was to prevent another conflict between Germany and the West that would bring down our civilization.

Wallis agreed with these attitudes of Mosley and the prince from the beginning.

In December, Thelma Furness made what for her would be a fatal decision. She returned to the United States to join her twin, Gloria, who was much vexed by conflicts with the Vanderbilt family, for an escapist trip to Hollywood to visit their old friend Constance Bennett, who was starring in a film entitled *The Affairs of Cellini*. Thelma had enjoyed an abortive if steamy career as a movie actress in the silent period and had once had an affair with Constance Bennett's father. Wallis took Thelma to a farewell lunch at the Ritz. Referring to the Prince of Wales with a rather questionable degree of concern under the circumstances, Wallis said, "Oh, Thelma, the Little Man is going to be so lonely." To which, improbably, and perhaps innocently, Thelma replied, "Well, dear, look after him while I'm away. See that he doesn't get into any mischief." Thelma wasn't being naive and absurdly trusting; she was blinded by her colossal ego and infatuated by her own unlimited power to hold the prince from any distance. She didn't realize, apparently, that he had been getting up to some mischief with Wallis already.

Thelma sailed to New York in a dream state, in a first-class suite brimming with hothouse flowers from Fort Belvedere. The prince was petulant and irritable that she should have chosen to leave him, even for a few weeks, thus disobeying his royal command. The day after she sailed, he called the Simpsons and invited them to a dinner party at the Dorchester Hotel in honor of a local representative of NBC, his old friend Fred Bate. The prince carried on all through the meal about the working-class people of the Midlands, their unemployment problems, their courage, and their misery. Wallis seized her opportunity. Although she lived in a world in which the matters of men on the dole and the breadline meant little or nothing to her, she pretended that she was touched by the prince's stories of hardship. She hung on his every word. When he went on to discuss his role in the future of the British Empire, she provided expert flattery. He wrote in his memoirs that by the time dinner was over, he was convinced that she was a woman with a social conscience.

Still fretting over Thelma's absence, apparently not satisfied by whatever brief encounters he could manage with Wallis alone, the prince became a man obsessed. He called the Simpsons at all hours of the day and night, as late as 4 a.m., just to talk; always an insomniac, tortured by his own private complexes and by the frustrations of his royal impulses, hating to be left alone even for a moment, he would turn up at Bryanston Court without warning, and Wallis would have to wake up her staff, housed in another part of the building, to satisfy his whims. He drove poor Ernest, whose days were spent trying to deal with the matters of a crumbling business, to a state now bordering on nervous breakdown.

Wallis decided to make the best of this uncomfortable situation. By now the Prince of Wales was utterly dependent on her; she held the upper hand. She knew how to make him laugh, and no matter what hour of the night he turned up, she would regale him with witty, risqué stories and observations. Sometimes he would accompany her and Ernest to such popular resorts of London nightlife as the Embassy Club. There, in the overcrowded cellar room favored by high society, with everyone in evening clothes clustered at packed tables around the tiny dance floor, the genial host Luigi in attendance, and the glittering Ambrose band playing the latest quicksteps and fox-trots, the prince and Wallis would engage each other in high-pitched, raucous conversation while Ernest sat exhausted and befuddled, in cigarette smoke thick as fog.

By December 1933, Ernest was greatly distressed. His frustration and stress emerged in a breakout of boils that had to be painfully lanced. While he was ailing, Wallis was preparing popovers for the prince in her kitchen.

Just before Christmas Wallis dragged herself from her sickbed, where she had been lying with a cold, because of an irresistible invitation: Consuelo had arranged another party for her and the prince.

In mid-March 1934 Thelma Furness was at a soirée given at the Pierre Hotel in New York by her friend, socialite Mrs. Frank Vance Storres. At dinner the hostess shrewdly placed Thelma next to the 23-year-old Prince Aly Khan, heir to the immense fortune of his father, the pro-Hitler Indian potentate Aga Khan. Aly was the ultimate lady-killer of the day. Lithe, muscular, dusky-skinned, handsome, he was an Apollo whose life was polo ponies, fast cars, and beautiful women. His reputation as a lover was second to none in society. Only Porfirio Rubirosa, the Dominican playboy, could match his boudoir reputation in later years. His father had sent him to Cairo at the age of 18 to be trained by the madams of the great bordellos in the art of Imshak, the art of withholding climax and the Egyptian equivalent of Fang Chung. A night with Aly Khan was like winning the Irish Sweepstakes. Later, a journalist commented that, like Santa Claus or Father Christmas, Aly Khan only "came" once a year.

He was instantly attracted to Thelma. He liked dark, smoldering, vaguely Latin women, and she looked her best that night. Right at the table in front of her escort, he suggested they go off together the moment they were past the coffee stage. She told him she had to pack that night because she was sailing in two days for England. He gave her a burning glance, peering into the depths of her soul, and said, "Put your trip off for a week." She was no fool; she said she would be sailing on schedule. He wasn't to be stopped. He asked her what she was doing the following night. She suggested he call her late the next morning.

She was awakened at her townhouse by a messenger bringing in an enormous bouquet of red roses with a note in a distinctive handwriting that read, "Call you at 11:30 a.m. for our dinner tonight. Prince Aly Khan." He did call, and she couldn't resist it; she had dinner with him. The next day, she sailed. When she got to her veranda-deck suite on the *Bremen*, it was filled with roses from one end to the other and Aly had scribbled on cards for each bouquet.

The next morning, when she woke up, the *Bremen* was at sea. The phone rang. It was Aly, presumably calling from New York. He suggested lunch. She laughed at this absurd idea. How about in Palm Beach? To her astonishment, he replied, "I'm on board." And he was. After that, how could she resist him?

On the crossing she had ample opportunity to learn the difference between an ardent but sexually insecure and childish Prince of Wales and a copper-skinned bedroom bombshell with an anatomical chart of the female body stored carefully in his pretty head. Thelma arrived in London looking ten years younger.

The prince had spies everywhere, and evidently some of them were on board the *Bremen* because Thelma was in trouble from the moment she landed in England. In her reckless vanity, glowing from her lover's attentions, she had apparently forgotten that royalty does not brook disobedience or infidelity. The Prince of Wales turned up at her house in London and insisted she explain herself. How could she betray him with an Indian?

It is clear that all the prince's colonial racist snobbery was aroused along with his wounded pride. The fact that he was already conducting an affair with Wallis didn't seem to strike him as in the least contradictory. Aly wisely moved on to Paris. Then Thelma, in her blindness, foolishly called Wallis and asked, on the verge of tears, for some womanly advice.

It was Wallis's moment of power, and she seized it with relish. As Thelma swept into 5 Bryanston Court, dramatically pale and tense as only she could be, Wallis told her maid to leave them alone and on no account to disturb them, no matter what the emergency. Thelma poured out her story: Aly Khan, the Prince of Wales's displeasure, her distress at his verbal punishment of her. Wallis, with expert, finely judged calculation, said, "But Thelma, the Little Man loves you so very much. The Little Man was lost without you."

At that moment, the maid walked in. Wallis glared at her furiously. "I thought I told you I was not to be disturbed," she said, with a jagged edge to her voice. The maid replied, "I know, Madam, but it's . . . His Royal Highness, the Prince of Wales!" Thelma looked as though the Tower of London had fallen on her head. Wallis went to the telephone without a word.

Thelma strained her ears to listen. All she could hear was Wallis saying, in a tight, tense voice, "Thelma is here." Then Wallis returned. Thelma could see from Wallis's face that nothing further would be said about the call. Chilled and depressed, and realizing that her reign was coming rapidly to an end, Thelma left soon afterward.

The next weekend the Prince invited the Simpsons to Fort Belvedere. It was an agonizing two days for Thelma. The prince was cold to her and scarcely listened to a word she said. By contrast, and right in front of Ernest, he was deeply and affectionately attentive to Wallis, who treated him rather the way that a nanny would treat a spoiled child. The worst happened at dinner that night. The prince picked up a lettuce leaf with his fingers to nibble it. Wallis slapped his hand and told him brusquely to use a knife and fork in the future. He smiled sheepishly and blushed like a schoolboy. Thelma looked at Wallis, who answered her gaze with an icy, triumphant stare. Wallis was reveling in her victory; that cold, haughty glance told Thelma she was finished. Lady Furness understandably took to her bed. The prince poked his nose through the door later that night. She whispered from her pillow, "Darling, is it Wallis?" "Don't be silly," he snapped. But he didn't return that night.

Meanwhile, Wallis, no doubt to the dismay of the Fort Belvedere chef, whose kitchen prerogatives were absolute, had actually invaded his sacred domain. When the prince, looking for her, at last located her there, she presented him with a plate of eggs she had scrambled herself. He sat down at the kitchen table in front of the cook and maids and ate the eggs on the spot. Thelma left at dawn.

After that, Wallis unhesitatingly left Ernest behind on many dates with her royal paramour. Syrie Maugham, wife of Somerset Maugham, who had helped Wallis redecorate Bryanston Court, gave a party to which the prince and Wallis were invited. Very late in the evening, they repaired to the library for a romantic encounter. They were startled by the sound of voices raised in the corridor outside. "Where's David?!"* a voice shrilly demanded. It was Thelma, insisting on seeing the prince. "I'll find him for you," Wallis heard Syrie Maugham reply. But at that moment Thelma flung open the library door and saw the heir to the

---

*The Prince of Wales's nickname.

throne and his American mistress locked in an embrace. Furious, she stormed out, to find consolation with Aly Khan in the south of France.

Early in 1934, Wallis's star rose rapidly. She was pleased to be the rage of London society as the prince's reigning lady, and not a soul believed the carefully arranged fiction that their relationship was platonic (although it now appears that they still were merely involved in sexual game playing and had not enjoyed conventional sexual intercourse). Suddenly, all of Wallis's financial worries disappeared; backed now by substantial sums from the royal purse, she and Ernest could afford everything they wanted, though she shrewdly cried poor in letters to Aunt Bessie. Humble, quiet Ernest was apparently quite prepared to continue with this arrangement. He seemed almost to be honored by the imperial bounty that descended upon his wife. There is not even evidence that he found consolation with a mistress of his own. Somewhere between a sheep and a saint, this foolish, fond American royalist simply got on with his daily business. It was typical of that era and place that a husband would accept the fact that he and his wife would go separate ways. Society seemed to regard marriages as a mere convenience, a conventional front covering any manner of untoward behavior. Yet Simpson's reaction seems abnormal: he was in love with Wallis, and the reaction of any man would normally have been an excess of jealousy and hatred followed by a demand that the marriage end. The situation seemed to suggest that his relationship with Wallis was essentially sadomasochistic, just as her relationship with the prince would in many ways be.

One of Wallis's newfound hostess friends and supporters was the celebrated Lady Colefax. Tiny, dark, and plump, Sibyl was a brilliant patroness of the arts, at whose dinner parties the young John Gielgud, Cecil B. DeMille, and Osbert and Edith Sitwell could easily be met. Bernard Shaw, Arnold Bennett, Somerset Maugham, and Max Beerbohm were frequently at her exquisite Georgian house in Chelsea, with its eighteenth-century furniture and green-and-yellow silk hangings. Wallis always looked forward to walking through Sibyl's tiny, walled garden with its blaze of cultivated flowers to the French-windowed living room with its air of skillfully acquired culture; the beginnings of taste.

No less prominent a hostess was Lady Cunard, yet another American arriviste who had managed to climb to the top from humble San Francisco origins. Emerald had married Sir Bache Cunard, heir to the Cunard steamship line, and had conveniently shunted her aging husband off to his country estate while she queened it in London. Small and birdlike, with dyed canary-yellow hair, enormous spots of rouge on each cheek, and Cupid's-bow painted lips, she talked in an antic, twittering voice and never sat still, darting all over the room as she provoked her guests with audacious and risqué remarks. Her lover was the conductor Sir Thomas Beecham, and she was the chief patroness of Covent Garden, with its resident ballet and opera companies. Her passions were Hitler, Shakespeare, and Balzac, not necessarily in that order. She hated her daughter Nancy, who was left-wing and had an erotic interest in blacks.

Emerald's parties at her house at 7 Grosvenor Square were the focuses of growing Nazi influences in London. Her drawing room, glowing with Marie Laurençin paintings, was alive, night after night, with excited conversation about the merits and demerits of Mussolini, British prime minister Ramsay MacDonald, and the new führer. It was Emerald who, wittingly or unwittingly, began to embroil Wallis in Nazi connections that would dog her for many years. One of Emerald's leading protégés, and her personal court favorite, was the ebullient White Russian Gabriel Wolkoff, brother of the late Czar Nicholas's admiral of the fleet. Gabriel, or "Gaby," as he was known, was the chief set designer at Covent Garden, specializing in particular in the Wagner operas which Hitler loved and which Sir Thomas Beecham also favored.

Admiral of the Fleet Wolkoff owned a humble London tea shop. He was the center of a group of rabidly anti-Semitic, intensely pro-Hitler White Russian refugees and others who were determined to crush the Soviet Union by rallying to the cause anyone and everyone in Britain who might share their point of view. Admiral Wolkoff's daughter, Anna, was a plain but determined young woman who worked as a dressmaker for Princess Marina of Greece. It was at Marina's suggestion that Wallis also engaged Anna. And it was at about that time or soon afterward that Anna became a Nazi agent; by 1940 she would be sending crucial secret intelligence to Italy for use in Berlin.

The association was sufficient to interest the Secret Intelligence Service. Nor did the SIS fail to note that among the very first individuals to whom the prince introduced Wallis were the ambassadors of Italy and Germany. Count Dino Grandi, the Italian emissary, stated through his diplomatic associate Egidio Ortona:

> I was the first ambassador who asked the prince and Mrs. Simpson together at my embassy at 4 Grosvenor Square, the purpose being the breaking of the ice which surrounded her. In fact, the dinner was not a smashing success, as a cool attitude prevailed among the guests toward the American lady. My wife, Countess Grandi, even teased me about the whole thing, saying, "You're always up to strange things!" The morning after the dinner, as early as 8:00, we received an enormous bouquet of roses from the prince with a note of thanks to us.

Soon, the coolness of the Grandi circle disappeared. Grandi confirms that he was invited on several occasions to Fort Belvedere for happy, informal gatherings, at which Wallis was present and that both Wallis and the prince were deep admirers of the Italian dictator.

Simultaneously, the prince was determined that Wallis would be part of the German Fascist circle at the highest levels in London. The Princess Ann-Mari von Bismarck, widow of Prince Otto von Bismarck, the German chargé d'affaires, has written to this author as follows:

> I remember how our association began. It was at Ascot. We separated from the crowd in the Royal enclosure. Ambassador Leopold von Hoesch told me he was in a troublesome dilemma. The prince had asked him if he would arrange a dinner party at the German Embassy for him. Naturally, the ambassador complied. The Foreign Office in Berlin was content. Then, the prince asked point-blank if Mrs. Simpson could be added to the list of guests! This was certainly a problem; it was also a royal order. Ambassador von Hoesch told me how worried he was that the German government might find it an unforgivable faux pas to include Mrs. Simpson. Not to speak of the British Foreign Office and the Royal Family of England!
>
> I remember discussing this matter for an hour and a half with the ambassador, impervious of the people around us. I tried to relax him and suggested he report to Berlin that the prince had asked him to invite Mrs. Simpson. He did not want to be disloyal to the prince. We discussed all possibilities. Finally, I said, "As the dinner is for the prince, it is important he enjoy it, and if Mrs. Simpson is not asked he will be bored, or, perhaps, not even come at all."
>
> The dinner took place. I do not know whether or not approval was given in Berlin and at Buckingham Palace, but I would assume that the

palace was not approached. I was sitting next to the prince because since
von Hoesch was unmarried I was acting as his hostess. We were at large
round tables, and my husband was sitting at the table behind me with
Mrs. Simpson. The result was that, while the prince was talking to me,
he kept turning around to look lovingly at Mrs. Simpson and to make
sure that she was enjoying herself. The evening was a great success. I
loved and admired both the prince and Wallis. She was extremely witty,
and I could see how she amused him.

Von Hoesch was the homosexual bachelor heir to a substantial
manufacturing fortune, the polished and genial German ambassador to
the Court of St. James's. This career diplomat of the von Papen school
was typical in criticizing the upstart Hitler in private but at the same
time working consistently and deviously to carry out his master's undesirable wishes. His kitchen was among the finest in London; his parties were splendidly organized; his budget from the Foreign Ministry in
Berlin was arguably the most lavish accorded to any diplomatic representative. Hitler was determined to secure the devoted interest and admiration of the British aristocracy, and he gave specific instructions that
no expense was to be spared in entertaining the cream of British society.
     Certainly, the führer was concerned that von Hoesch cement the
good feelings of the Prince of Wales. According to his diplomatic associate Paul Schwarz, von Hoesch was aware that the prince loved gypsy
music more than any other: the melancholy, thrilling strains of the
czardas. Von Hoesch hired, at great expense and on many occasions, the
gypsy band of the Hungaria Restaurant to play for Wallis and Edward
in small, exclusive soirées at his home. He invited the couple to join
him at a reception for Hitler's special adviser in foreign affairs and ambassador without portfolio, the well-tailored and fatuous Joachim von
Ribbentrop. Von Ribbentrop was fascinated by Wallis. To mark the
first anniversary of their meeting, Schwarz recorded, von Ribbentrop
sent seventeen red roses with notes of open admiration every morning,
all year round, to Wallis at Bryanston Court. She did not return them. It
was widely believed in London that she entertained him frequently at
her home, with her Jewish husband present. There was even talk of an
affair that lasted for seventeen nights. Ribbentrop represented his master in expressing great fascination for the new royal mistress. Before too
long Hitler would be obtaining films of Wallis and running them with
ecstatic pleasure at his hunting lodge at Obersalzberg.

The romance interested the Secret Intelligence Service. And another association proved to be provocative to the anti-Hitler faction in the British Secret Intelligence Service. According to Sir Dudley Forwood, that relationship was the Prince of Wales's love affair with his equerry, Edward ("Fruity") Metcalfe, one of the few servants of the Crown who was denied a knighthood in later years, perhaps because of his sexual and political affiliations. Metcalfe was tall, lean, lantern-jawed, and horsey; he had a sportive, rather grating, jocular personality that went with loud Harris tweeds and an addiction to military uniforms.

Born in Ireland, son of the head of the Irish Prisons Board in Dublin, he was described by the future Edward VIII in infatuated terms in the memoir *A King's Story*, as "gay, handsome, sympathetic and understanding." From the beginning, King George V hated him, perhaps because he suspected a romantic involvement with the heir to the throne at a time when men of that sort shot themselves; perhaps because he disliked Metcalfe's tendency to encourage the Prince of Wales's addiction to nightclubs, louche dives, and heavy drinking.

Despite an early marriage to the Fascist Lady Alexandra Curzon, known as "Ba-Ba Blackshirt," sister of Sir Oswald·Mosley, a marriage that produced children, Forwood insisted that Metcalfe was a homosexual and that he had an affair with the Prince of Wales then and later. Forwood told me in 1987:

> Of course I wasn't in the bedroom but there was every sign of intense love between him and my master. My master worshiped the ground Fruity walked on—no royal person ever felt that way about a mere servant. He was in agony whenever Fruity wasn't with him. His absences drove my master nearly mad.

On September 22, 1922, the prince wrote to Metcalfe in anguish during one of his trips away, "I miss you terribly when you are away." On September 1, 1925, he dashed off an equally pained note to his friend or lover, begging him not to leave England for a post in India to which King George had furiously sent him. Their activities as brother athletes at steeplechasing, running, swimming, golf and tennis, and mutual photograph-taking while stripped half-naked in locker rooms had all the earmarks of a "Greek" relationship and again and again the king insisted they break it off. When he refused to pay Metcalfe's salary, the prince not only restored it, but doubled it.

By 1934, the relationship was dangerous politically. Like his wife, Metcalfe was a Nazi sympathizer, an admirer of Hitler and a friend of such Fascists as William Joyce, who later in World War II would broadcast for Hitler as "Lord Haw-Haw," and would die for that crime on the gallows. If anything were needed to draw the Prince of Wales more deeply into the Nazi camp it was this superficial, silly, frivolous, and viciously anti-Semitic companion.

Although Wallis shared Metcalfe's political views, she hated him intensely. Forwood stated that she was jealous of Metcalfe, which, he said, can only have emerged from a conviction Forwood shared rightly or wrongly with her, that the two men were sexually involved.

At the same time, Metcalfe's membership in the pro-Hitler January Club, and its outright support of the Prince of Wales, was a minor danger to British security compared with another matter that surfaced at the time. Hitler and von Ribbentrop embarked upon a plan, not opposed by King George V and Queen Mary, to unite England and Nazi Germany in a permanent alliance by engineering a match for the Prince of Wales that would give Hitler a free hand in Europe, would preclude any future war with England, and, by bringing about a permanent Anglo-German alliance of the kind advocated by the January Club (and by the majority of the British Establishment), would cause the wished-for destruction of the Soviet Union.

The bride upon whom Hitler enthusiastically settled, and who was eminently acceptable at Buckingham Palace, was the beautiful Friederike, Princess of Hanover, granddaughter of Kaiser Wilhelm II, and daughter of the Duke and Duchess of Brunswick, close friends and cousins of King George and Queen Mary. Since all were directly descended from the prolific Queen Bee Victoria, Friederike was considered the perfect wife for the future English monarch. In 1911, her mother had similarly been proposed as the wife of the selfsame Prince of Wales.

In January 1934, Friederike was a pupil at North Foreland Lodge, an exclusive girls' school near Broadstairs in Kent. She was invited to London so that the king and queen could give her a looking-over at Buckingham Palace; they approved her unhesitatingly. Once back in Germany, the Brunswicks were advised by Ribbentrop that Hitler shared King George V's approval of the match, and insisted that it take place as soon as possible.

According to the Duchess of Brunswick in her memoirs, *The Kaiser's Daughter*, she and her husband were appalled by the idea, defied the führer, and canceled his plans. Nothing could be further from the truth; indeed, in the much longer (three-volume) German edition of her memoirs, the Duchess of Brunswick made no hypocritical mention of being appalled and expressed no disapproval of the potential match. Instead, she wrote:

> I left the entire matter to my daughter, whom we now know [1957] never ceased to nourish the idea of a wedding.

Certainly, that nourished ideal continued until it was clear that Wallis would always stand in the way. Princess Friederike remained on the list of approved brides until late 1937 (when she became engaged to Prince Paul of Greece) as a potential Queen of England, and not a single Buckingham Palace or Foreign Office press statement ever contradicted it.

Had the marriage taken place, with Wallis as backstreet mistress, a situation very common in British royal history, it is doubtful whether World War II would have occurred. How could England declare war on Germany with Hitler and King George V's own choice, and the granddaughter of the former ruler of Germany, installed upon the English throne? In view of this, it is ironic that King Edward VIII, in his determination to make Wallis queen, upset the very German alliance that he had wanted so desperately all his life. In the circumstances, King George's hatred of Wallis for upsetting this marital applecart can well be understood.

Among the strongest supporters of this romantic royal alliance were the wealthy and influential members of the royal house of Hesse, cousins of the Prince of Wales and of Princess Friederike, and very close to the Prince of Wales's youngest brother, Prince George, later Duke of Kent. They were great-grandsons of Queen Victoria and the sons of the Duchess of Brunswick's sister Margarethe, the youngest daughter of the kaiser. They would play a crucial role in the Prince of Wales and Wallis's Nazi-royal alliances aimed against communism and seeking an Anglo-German rapprochement then and in the future.

The two oldest boys, Philipp and Wolfgang, were twins, born on November 6, 1896. Long before Hitler came to power, they were firmly in the Nazi camp. Both were keen admirers and friends of Hitler and Hermann Goering. Hitler, with his streak of repressed—or not—homosexual hero worship, was captivated by Philipp, whose fair-haired, muscular good looks and pure Aryan royal blood left him in a state of unreasoning adoration.

From his early manhood, Philipp developed a love of Italy, and, as an architect of sorts, designed many buildings in that country. Like the Prince of Wales and Prince George of England he was bisexual, and had an unmasculine addiction to interior decoration. During the rise of Hitler he was often in Rome, where he was engaged to Princess Mafalda, daughter of King Victor Emmanuel III, to raise money from Mussolini, who presided over the civil ceremony of their spectacular marriage in Italy in September 1925.

Throughout the 1930s and until 1942, Prince Philipp was the chief personal and political link between Hitler and Mussolini. Profoundly anti-Semitic, bent upon Hitler's cause, he became, on the führer's orders, both governor and stormtrooper führer of the Hesse province; later, he would secure Mussolini's agreement to Hitler's annexation of Austria. He cleared the way also to Mussolini's reluctant acquiescence in the German conquest of Czechoslovakia. Prince Philipp never tired of seeking to secure, through the cooperation of the Prince of Wales and his brother Prince George, a permanent alliance with England ("The Jews," he said, "must be fought in all countries.") His other chief alliance was with Prince George's brother-in-law, the weak, duplicitous, and vacillating Prince Regent Paul of Yugoslavia, who was sent to Africa under arrest in 1942 by Winston Churchill for betraying his country to Germany.

And there was yet another threat to British security at the time. Sandra Rambeau was an international American adventuress and alleged Nazi agent, the mistress of the Prince of Wales, Prince George, and of Hitler's favorite, the bisexual General Franz Ritter von Epp.

Born in Springfield, Missouri, on January 26, 1909, the daughter of a naval commodore, Rambeau grew up into a spectacular beauty, with dark, wavy hair, smoldering gray-green eyes, and a perfect figure. Abandoning high school without graduating, working successively as telephone operator, waitress, and dancer in the touring Monte Carlo

Follies all over Europe, she met von Epp in Berlin while appearing with the show, and quickly lured him from a male lover who was part of the homosexual Ernst Roehm group that Hitler purged.

Von Epp was a member of the same political sect to which the Hesses subscribed; he became head of the Nazi Colonial Office, which sought the restoration of the German colonies removed after World War I as part of a permanent peace arrangement with England. He was also head of Amt VIII of the German Special Intelligence Service under Admiral Wilhelm Canaris, who as double agent for England and Germany was in pursuit of that unholy alliance.

Sandra Rambeau met the Prince of Wales and Prince George in Paris, and in 1934 they both entered into a romance with her. As late as April 4, 1938, George referred to her indirectly in a conversation in London with U.S. ambassador Joseph P. Kennedy, when he said that his brother King George VI complained that he (like their sibling Edward) was "involved with" an American woman. According to the substantial FBI files on Rambeau in Washington, Prince George gave her a number of Crown jewels, including an inherited signet ring with his royal initials on it.

Traveling restlessly from London to Paris and Berlin, Rambeau found still a fourth Nazi sympathizer, the glamorous Major General Bishnu Shumshere Jung Badahur Rana, self-styled Prince of Nepal and black-sheep son of that country's prime minister. High on the British Foreign Office list of political undesirables, later ejected from England, Bishnu wound up finally in the Bahamas, as an associate of the Duke and Duchess of Windsor when they, nazified exiles also, were governor and first lady there in the 1940s.

On June 10, 1939, when touring Canada, King George VI told Canadian premier Mackenzie King, as recorded in King's diary, "My own family relations in Germany have been used to spy and get particulars from other members of my family." Nobody could have put it more succinctly—or accurately.

Fruity Metcalfe attended, at the end of May 1934, a Fascist Blackshirt dinner at the Savoy Hotel; dressed to the teeth, he was photographed by the society magazine *The Tatler*.

The guest list included Count and Countess Paul Munster, also close to the prince and Wallis, and at whose castle they would eventually spend their honeymoon. The Fascist leader Sir Oswald Mosley and his wife Lady Cynthia (sister of Alexandra Metcalfe) were present; and last, but by no means least, William Joyce, who would one day be a traitor to England as "Lord Haw-Haw," the best-known of British Nazi broadcasters from Germany in World War II.

At that time the January Club, to which all the aforementioned individuals belonged, was under investigation both by MI5 and the Jewish Defense League. The British Union of Fascists, of which the January Club was both seedbed and participant, was financed directly by Mussolini; the funds were channeled and laundered via Minculprop, the Minister of Culture and Propaganda of the Italian government under Wallis's former lover Count Ciano, who by now was Mussolini's son-in-law and foreign minister. The same organization funded Fascist cells in several other countries.

On May 27, the same night as a January Club dinner, the prince and Wallis were at Sibyl Colefax's in the company of the Hungarian film tycoon Sir Alexander Korda; Merle Oberon; Lord Dalkeith (later the Duke of Buccleuch); and another of Wallis's new friends, the interior decorator Elsie Mendl, and her husband, Sir Charles. Two of those present, Korda and Elsie Mendl's husband, were working for the Secret Intelligence Service and noted the fact that at the party the Prince of Wales expressed his keenest admiration for Nazi Germany. Sir Robert Bruce Lockhart and the vivid diarist Henry "Chips" Channon, an American snob obsessed with the rich and titled, did not fail to note Wallis's choice of friends or her royal consort's frequent verbal indulgences in pro-Hitlerism.

One of Wallis's strongest friendships at that time was with Lady Mendl. Wallis adored this stylish, witty, irresistibly charming blue-haired doyenne of interior decoration. Elsie Mendl influenced Wallis considerably in her upward climb. When Wallis first came to London, probably because of insecurity, she was a somewhat strident, harsh, high-pitched presence on the scene, as the shrewdly perceptive Cecil Beaton noted in his diary. Lady Mendl taught her to tone down her personality to suit British requirements. She encouraged her to speak in a softer, more southern drawl instead of in harsh accents and to dress very simply, to accentuate the angular lines of her figure rather than striving to work against her physical deficiencies. Wallis's severe, classical clothes became her trademark and emblem.

Whereas dresses in the mid-1930s tended to be fussy and exaggerated, Wallis made sure hers were subdued and reserved, in pastel colors or in plain blacks and whites. Even her hats were restrained. Lady Mendl replaced Syrie Maugham's white-on-white designs at Bryanston Court with her own subtle and various color schemes. She taught Wallis how to entertain and how to present her meals, explicitly forbidding soup; her motto was, "Never build a meal on a lake." Soon Bryanston Court, aided by the royal purse, lost its slightly Early Pullman look and became a riot of spectacular effects, indicative of Lady Mendl's capacity to go to the very edge of overdecoration and then stop short. And of course the friendship provided an opportunity for Sir Charles to keep an eye on Wallis's activities and associations.

Pressing on with fierce ambition, Wallis further asserted her power in the summer of 1934. Having disposed of Thelma Furness, she now proceeded ruthlessly to make sure that nothing more was heard from Mrs. Freda Dudley Ward. The prince had not officially disconnected his relationship with Mrs. Dudley Ward. Freda's daughter, Penelope, later the wife of the movie director Carol Reed, and rumored falsely to be the child of the Prince of Wales, fell ill. Freda hoped for some word from York House or Fort Belvedere, some expression of concern or even interest. There was none. At last, Penelope rallied, and Freda called York House to inform her ex-lover that the danger was past. The switchboard operator informed her that orders had been received not to put her through. She never spoke to the Prince of Wales again.

Wallis concentrated grimly on the servants. Members of the royal staff enjoyed certain privileges that had remained unchanged from generation to generation. They tended to set the rules of the various households, instruct the lower levels of the help, and delegate duties right down the line to the lowliest levels of the kitchen and the cellars. Of these, Osborne, the majordomo of the Fort Belvedere household, was preeminent. He had been the prince's batman in World War I, and from there he had gone on to assume his position, which was considered unassailable, absolute, and final. To his horror, he, who took orders only from royalty, was informed by the Prince of Wales that henceforth he would receive his instructions from Mrs. Simpson, an American commoner. This was insupportable. However, unless he wanted to be dismissed, Osborne had no alternative but to accept this galling humiliation. Wallis instructed him to undertake all the flower arrangements at the fort himself, instead of delegating this unmasculine task to the maids. This was a complete break with tradition. She drew up the menus for each day of the week, even though she was present at the fort only on weekends. This task had always been the prerogative of the housekeeper and Osborne, working in collaboration. Not content with the decor that had been decreed by the Prince of Wales and Prince George, Wallis and Lady Mendl invaded room after room, pulling up carpets, taking down curtains, storing furniture. Then they redid the fort from top to bottom, oddly enough retaining only one room as it had been before: Thelma's pink folly of a bedroom, with its absurd bed decorated with the Prince of Wales's feathers on each post.

Wallis clashed furiously with Finch, the butler at York House. This formidable personage had played a leading role in the Prince of Wales's childhood. He had been the prince's valet from the earliest times. He saw himself as a combination nurse and surrogate father, persuading the prince repeatedly to cut down on his drinking, late nights, wild parties, and loose women. This impeccable, upright north countryman, the very epitome of gritty rectitude, found himself being bossed by a foreign woman with little regard for his finer feelings. She not only took over everything at York House, even down to ordering over a hundred gifts for Christmas, but also insisted that Finch learn to mix, serve, and put ice in drinks in the American manner; the very presence of ice in a glass was anathema to the old family retainer. When Finch refused to obey instructions, he was fired. His successor, Crisp, also failed to last. Osborne hung on, but only by a thread.

The staffs of the two households favored by the prince grew to hate Wallis for her busybody interference. They dreaded the return of their master and his mistress at three or four in the morning from the Embassy Club, the Kit Kat, or other nightclubs, laughing loudly, calling up maids and butler and cook to get out of bed and prepare a snack or otherwise attend to their imperious needs. King George V and Queen Mary were punctilious in their relationship with their staffs. They attended meals at the same time very day, and the matter of instruction to the various levels of help was always adhered to. Wallis and the Prince of Wales rode roughshod over such arrangements. Wallis was always punctual, and irritated by the prince's lax attitude toward appointments and mealtimes, but she seemed to have no understanding or consideration when it came to the employees' reaction to his unreliability.

That summer of 1934 the prince decided to flout convention to the limit and invite Wallis on a trip to Spain and France that was sure to attract attention from the press. Not in the British press; royal persons in those days could always rely upon the utmost discretion in Fleet Street. But the American reporters in particular could not fail to note his expedition with an American married woman; he seemed to care little about this, nor about the fact that Ernest Simpson would not be included in the royal party. The inclusion of Aunt Bessie Merryman in the vacation group was a sop to critics. She would supposedly be a chaperone—but few were deceived.

The prince rented a house, the Castel Meretmont, outside Biarritz, the fashionable resort in southwestern France. Piloted by Flight Lieutenant Edward Fielden, Wales arrived at Le Bourget in Paris at 5:30 p.m. on August 1, 1934; he was accompanied by his equerry, the Hon. John Aird. Wallis, as always afraid of flying, proceeded in a good humor with Aunt Bessie, "G" Trotter, and the rest of the party by boat train across the English Channel. The prince joined them for the train ride to Biarritz. The Castel Meretmont proved to be spacious and comfortable, and after the first day reporters politely withdrew to the edge of the grounds, content to watch the movements of the royal party through field glasses.

On August 5 Wallis and the prince were enjoying a drink at a swimming pool bar on the Biarritz oceanfront when a boy of 10 began screaming from the deep end that he was drowning. The prince flung off his jacket, dived in, and rescued the boy, to general applause and the mother's tearful thanks. The news spread rapidly, and the press swarmed in as the prince and Wallis left the bar. Wales was furious, shouting that the story was "lies, all lies," and pushing his way to the royal car. It was clear he was embarrassed because of Wallis's presence; he was terrified they would be photographed together. They were.

When the story appeared all over the world the next morning, the French government elected to give the prince the Lifesaving Medal. He refused it. He and Wallis went into seclusion for a week at the Castel Meretmont. Then, on August 15, they went out in wind-driven rain to dine with the celebrated Marquis and Marquise de Portago at the opulent Villa Pelican. At the party the prince told Wallis and the others he was weary of Biarritz and would fly to Cannes to join Prince George, who was now engaged to Princess Marina of Greece, and would be stopping briefly in that resort. George and Marina had been in Vienna, visiting the leaders of the Austrian government. On cabled instructions, Edward Fielden flew the royal aircraft from London, in stages, to pick up the royal party. However, it is probable that Wallis's hatred of flying influenced what the prince decided to do next.

He would now make his way to Cannes by sea. It says much for his dedication to Wallis that he would rather miss his own brother and future sister-in-law—by sailing instead of flying—than make her uncomfortable by taking the short air trip across Spain to France. He decided to obtain a vessel in Biarritz and charter it for a voyage around Gibraltar. He planned to arrive at Cannes in time to fly to Marseilles, where he would say farewell to his brother Prince Henry, later the Duke of Gloucester, who was on his way, aboard the HMS *Sussex*, to Australia and New Zealand. The only ship available was the ancient, battered, 700-ton oceangoing steamer *Rosaura*, which after thirty years of doing service as an English Channel steamer, struggling gamely through the choppy seas between Newhaven and Dieppe, had been bought by Lord Moyne, an explorer and ethnographer, as a scientific exploration vessel used mainly in the south seas. The steamer was temporarily laid up in Biarritz harbor for refueling, provisioning, and repairs.

The Mediterranean voyage around Gibraltar was rough; at last, the vessel, shipping water, was comfortably moored at Cannes. Somewhere between Portugal and France the relationship between Wallis and the prince had intensified still further.

On the third day the prince and Wallis boldly moved into the Hotel Miramar together. At 1 a.m. the prince summoned the night manager to his suite and told him to wake up the staff of the local branch of Cartier and instruct them to go to the shop. He slipped out of the hotel through a back door and made his way to the store, where he bought not only an emerald and diamond charm for Wallis's bracelet but also many other items that he held in reserve for presentation to her later on. He returned to the hotel and got Wallis and the entire party out of their beds, announcing to Lord Moyne that he wished to proceed immediately to sea.

As the vessel moved out into the moonlight ocean, the prince embraced Wallis and pressed the Cartier charm into the palm of her hand. She was flattered but not moved. The *Rosaura* continued to Nice and Genoa, in calm seas, arriving on September 17. The prince had wired ahead for reservations, and the royal party took a fleet of cars to Lake Como, situated amid the peaks of the Alps.

On September 23 the party boarded the Orient Express at Domodossola; Mussolini had provided a luxurious private car for the prince and his companions. The prince had cabled Edward Fielden to pick him up in Paris; he was anxious to get home in time to see the RMS *Queen Mary*, the newest of the Cunard ships, go down the slipways for the first time at Clydeside in Scotland. Leaving the others at the Hôtel Meurice, in the French capital, he flew to Windsor Castle, landing at Smith's Lawn, on the way to the royal residence at Balmoral. John Aird went with him; Wallis and the others followed on the USS *Manhattan* from Cherbourg. But it seemed that the prince could not tear himself away from Wallis even then. Before he left for the *Queen Mary*'s launching, he turned up at Southampton with gifts and loving words for Wallis and her aunt.

8

Moving Toward the Throne

In the fall of 1934, Prince George, the Prince of Wales's youngest brother, and Princess Marina of Greece were at the center of the world's attention. They were to be married on November 29. The royal family was greatly relieved. For years, untoward rumors had circulated about George. Some of these appeared to have a basis in truth. It was stated that he had had a romantic relationship with a black actress, the star of the sensational London revue *Blackbirds*. He was also said to have been introduced to the use of drugs by a well-known female pianist and by a society woman who would later be mentioned in connection with Lord Erroll, whose murder was commemorated in James Fox's book *White Mischief*. According to the late Laura, Duchess of Marlborough, one of her husbands, Michael Canfield, who died young, was Prince George's illegitimate son and was handed over to Cass Canfield, head of the American publisher Harper & Brothers, later Harper & Row, who raised the young man.

To this heady scenario were added some even more colorful ingredients. In his diary the incorrigible author Sir Robert Bruce Lockhart mentioned that tales were being told around London of an affair between the prince and a young boy in Paris and that blackmail was involved. According to several sources, Prince George gave the boy magnificent, personally inscribed Tiffany and Cartier cigarette boxes and lighters. The Prince of Wales had to make a disagreeable journey to France to pay money to retrieve these damaging items, but the boy sold the Prince of Wales copies, retaining the originals. There was also talk of an involvement with Noël Coward and with a dark, smoldering Argentinean youth. Everyone was greatly relieved when Prince George fell in love with the exquisitely beautiful Princess Marina of Greece. But he still saw Sandra Rambeau.

On October 24, leaving Wallis at the Hôtel Meurice in Paris, the Prince of Wales and Prince George flew together, taking turns at the controls of the royal biplane, to attend the funeral of King Alexander of Yugoslavia, who had been assassinated on the ninth of that month by a Macedonian terrorist in Marseille; the killer, who was opposed to Alexander's Nazi connections, ironically also murdered the anti-Nazi French foreign minister Léon Barthou. It was on this somber funerary occasion, with all Belgrade in mourning, that a major step was taken in the British-German royal connection that involved both Hitler and Mussolini.

Since the young King Peter succeeding to the throne was underage, his royal cousin Prince Paul was made regent; Paul's wife, Olga, was the pro-Nazi sister of the Duchess of Kent; Paul had arranged the Kent marriage. According to *Current Biography* for the year of 1941, a widely quoted comment at the time was, "The Duchess of Kent brought Balkan fashions to London—while Princess Olga brought Hitler's emissaries to the White Palace [in Belgrade]." In fact, though he has been protected by most historians, Paul was himself nervously in support of Hitler, if only for self-protective purposes, and Kent and the Prince of Wales found in him a kindred spirit along with another guest at the funeral, Prince Philipp of Hesse, führer of the storm troopers. Another guest was Field Marshal Hermann Goering, who reported to Hitler on the meetings with Windsor, Kent, and Philipp with considerable enthusiasm and a request that Paul should visit Berlin at the earliest possible opportunity. Hitler made the offer, and Paul accepted at once.

Two days before the November 29 marriage, there was a celebration ball at Buckingham Palace. King George and Queen Mary insisted that the lord chamberlain remove Wallis's name from the guest list. This was very upsetting to Wallis, and Edward was furious when he found out; as a result, he arrived with Wallis and swept through the vestibule with her, determined that she would meet his parents.

"He smuggled her into the Palace," King George later said to Count Mensdorff.

Wallis was anxious to upstage the beautiful Marina, who was dressed unpretentiously in white satin; the queen was in silver brocade. Most of the ladies were dressed in subdued colors in keeping with the dignity of the occasion. Wallis appeared in a creation of violet-colored lamé with a green sash. While many, including the monarch and his consort, stared at her in cold dismay, Prince Paul regent of Yugoslavia made a point of telling her she was the best-dressed woman in the room. Her jewels, presents from her lover, glittered at neck and wrist. She wore a tiara of diamonds, rented from Cartier.

Prince Christopher of Greece wrote in his memoirs:

> The Prince of Wales laid a hand on my arm in his impulsive way.
> "Christo, come with me. I want you to meet Mrs. Simpson."
> "Who is she?"
> "An American. She's wonderful."

With sheer effrontery, the prince introduced Wallis to his parents. She curtseyed while they stared at her. She had no warmer a reception from the Duke and Duchess of York, among the most beloved of the younger members of the royal family. The duchess took an instant dislike to Wallis. She was offended by what she felt to be Wallis's blatant and vulgar behavior and the garish colors of her dress. Wallis was equally unimpressed. She was irritated by the Duchess of York's sweet, slightly high-pitched voice, pink Scottish face, and plump figure. Later, of course, the Duchess of York would become the beloved Queen Mother.

Christmas brought new problems for the royal favorite. She had the audacity to select the 250 Christmas gifts for the Prince of Wales's staff members herself. Many of the employees were annoyed by this. There was further unfavorable gossip when the prince gave Wallis a diamond pin for Christmas with two square-cut emeralds. He also gave her a cairn puppy that was named Mr. Loo but was as often called Slipper. The prince compounded his various felonies in the eyes of his households by inviting Wallis's personal staff from Bryanston Court to join his own servants around the Christmas tree at York House. It needs no feat of the imagination to envisage the tension on that occasion.

Wearied by the prince's almost constant attentions and obsessive visits and phone calls, much as she wanted to be the prince's lady, Wallis was almost relieved when he spent the season with his family at Sandringham. Then, in January 1935, she made one of her most serious mistakes. She began imitating the Duchess of York with a harsh, mocking style that recalled her burlesques at Oldfields. One afternoon Elizabeth walked into the drawing room at Fort Belvedere and stood frozen. Wallis was performing an aggressive parody of her voice and gestures. Elizabeth stormed out. Wallis was not forgiven.

That same month, the Prince of Wales and Prince George, now the Duke of Kent, had an interesting visitor from Berlin. Kent had just returned from Munich, where he had cemented relations with his wife Princess Marina's brother-in-law, Karl Theodore, Count von Toerring-Jettenbach, husband of her pro-Nazi sister Elizabeth, who conveyed through a special agent to Berlin that Kent was reconciled to Germany's extensive rearming. He invited to London the Baron Wilhelm de Ropp, a peripatetic double agent and emissary of the Nazi theorist Alfred Rosenberg, who, during a visit to London in 1933, had placed a swastika wreath on the cenotaph to the war dead. De Ropp's purpose in being in London was to meet Kent's royal brothers in order to give them a complete picture of the qualities of Hess, Rosenberg, and the other leaders. Sir Robert Bruce Lockhart would write in his diary many years later, referring back to incidents like this, that the Duke and Duchess of Kent were "very strong in the German camp."

The Prince of Wales decided to embark upon another trip to Europe with Wallis and a group of friends. The journey was to be a combined vacation and adventure in politics. That year, the situation on the Continent was exceedingly delicate. The British Foreign Office had embarked upon a policy, emanating from Prime Minister Ramsay MacDonald, seeming to appease both Hitler and Mussolini in their territorial ambitions in order to secure for the future the British balance of power in western Europe and the defeat of communism. It was desired by the Foreign Office that at all costs Mussolini and Hitler must be kept apart, discouraged from a full-scale alliance which could imperil British hegemony. Among the British government's urgent concerns was to preserve British power in the Mediterranean and to prevent the blockade or seizure of the Suez Canal, which provided the all-important trade route to and from the British colonies in East

Africa and in India, the chief jewel in the crown of the empire. Britain was playing a dangerous game of conciliation with Mussolini, whose activities were increasingly felt to be inimical to British interests and a threat to the British fleet. At the time, Mussolini was taking a position adverse to Hitler because he feared Hitler would upstage him in the European theater. It was felt by both dictators that the possession of Austria, itself a weak, poverty-stricken, and politically flaccid nation, would swing the balance of power definitively in the direction of the country which achieved it. Britain was tending to encourage Italian influence in Vienna because Hitler must at all costs be kept within a certain circumference of power. The game was played in Whitehall for high stakes, and the Prince of Wales, both by assignment and by personal design, became part of that game.

Always an empire man, aware of the importance of India in the Commonwealth, the prince was in his own mind doing his best to execute British foreign policy in making the trip when he did. However, it was not customary or desirable for royal personages to meddle in politics in this manner, no matter how well intentioned the purpose might be. The prince's intent was to encourage the Austrians and their neighbors the Hungarians to maintain as firmly as possible their Italian connection and provide a block against Hitler's advances south. The venture was approved by a friend of his, Sir Oswald Mosley, whose British Union of Fascists was still being financed by Mussolini and Count Ciano via the Italian propaganda ministry. Wallis was a convenient "cover" for this mission to Vienna and Budapest. In view of the fact that the Prince of Wales, by his own admission in his memoirs, turned to her for advice in everything, and that we have it on his own cognizance that she was fully informed politically and read all the London newspapers from cover to cover, it is impossible to believe she was not aware of the purpose of the journey. But no proof of her knowledge exists.

The trip began as a holiday. The royal party traveled from Paris on the Simplon Express to the skiing resort of Kitzbühel in Austria. The prince and his companions were supposed to travel through the Augsburg Pass, but an avalanche swept down ahead of them, cutting the rails. Instead, they were transferred to another train, sent by the Austrian government to the town of Wörgl, which took them 100 miles off course. They had to wait several hours in freezing conditions for the train to arrive.

On February 5 they reached Kitzbühel, where a crowd of newspaper correspondents and photographers was waiting. The prince responded in fluent German to the speeches by the mayor and prefect of police. They checked into the Grand Hotel. The swirling snowflakes and leaden skies created a picture of gothic gloom. Fifteen people had been killed in avalanches, and a resort hotel and eight homes had been swept away.

While at Kitzbühel, Wallis and the prince made the acquaintance of a person whom Wallis liked; he was to play an important role in their lives. He was the young, witty, and handsome Dudley Forwood, whose neatly trimmed mustache, sturdy figure, and smart suitings instilled confidence in everyone who met him. He was the junior attaché to Sir Walford Selby, British envoy and minister to Vienna. It was customary to send an attaché or first secretary in attendance to visiting members of the royal family when they arrived within the borders of a nation. At the Grand, Forwood joined the royal entourage, which included Bruce Ogilvy, the son of Lord Airlie, who disapproved of Wallis; the Colin Buists; and the equerry, Commander Lambe.

Wallis, after an abortive skiing lesson, stayed in the hotel playing bridge, backgammon, and poker with the others in the royal party, while the prince went out in severe wind and sleet to ski from morning to night.

On February 9 the sun broke through and the sky was a sudden icy blue. That night a radiant Wallis appeared with the prince at a Tyrolean costume ball, sharing him with several pretty girls in traditional folk dances. The party lingered on for a week, leaving Kitzbühel on the midnight express for Vienna on February 16.

It was a charged time. Austria had emerged from World War I a broken and dispirited nation. Starvation, financial ruin, and spiritual despair were followed by a conviction that the only hope of the future lay in an alliance with Germany. Members of the Social Democrats and Christian Socialists, though ostensibly to the left of center, were entirely for friendly relations with the Nazis. When Hitler came to power, he made it clear that, as a born Austrian, he expected Austria to be absorbed into the Third Reich. When it was clear that Germany would not accept the country as an equal, Austria turned to Mussolini. All policy was carried out in the closest consultation and collaboration with the Italian dictator. Parliamentary government was abolished;

socialism was crushed by the Fascists. Just days before the prince and Wallis arrived in Vienna, Socialists and Communists had demonstrated and distributed leaflets in the Vienna suburbs, and ten had been arrested. There was rioting, marking the anniversary of the defeated Social Democratic revolution of the year before. More arrests followed; the day after the prince and Wallis arrived, police and Socialists clashed violently at Floridsdorf, and forty-five more were arrested during radical meetings. There were mixed demonstrations outside the Bristol; some workers felt that the Prince of Wales was on their side; others felt he was pro-Fascist. Leaving a nervous Wallis behind, he took off on the seventeenth for his first visit to the Chancellery to meet with President Miklas, Chancellor von Schuschnigg, and Vice-Chancellor von Stahremberg. George Messersmith, American minister to Austria, who had spies at the meetings, reported on the political content to the State Department later that month. The purpose was to establish the solidarity of the so-called Balkan Entente, that group of southern European nations which joined in uneasy alliance with Italy in opposing Hitler's influence. However, as Messersmith pointed out in his report, the Prince of Wales was anxious that the Labour party in England might not approve of his contact with the Austrian Fascist government, and for this reason he insisted that the high-level meetings be downplayed or ignored in the press. The prince, Messersmith's report continued, also made a special visit to the immense and elaborate worker apartments, built by the former Socialist regime.

The prince and Wallis proceeded by train to Budapest. The Hungarian capital, then at the height of its sophistication and gaiety, was ablaze with light to greet them. There, the pro-Mussolini government was even more repressive than in Austria. Conducting an uncomfortable love-hate relationship with its neighbor nation, Hungary was also firmly allied with the Balkan Entente at the time. The prince had meetings with Admiral Horthy, regent, and the ferocious General Julius Von Gombös, whose repressive regime (he would soon dissolve the existing government) had already offended many informed commentators. Once again the prince discussed the Hapsburg restoration and the necessary anti-Hitler alliances with Italy. At the same time, he and Wallis enjoyed the baroque pleasures of the Danube Palace Hotel, the casino, and shops filled with antique Hungarian jewelry. The future King of England startled the clients at the St. Gellert Thermal Bathing Palace by appearing before them stark naked.

At night, Budapest awaited: the most glamorous, corrupt, and beautiful capital city of its era, with dazzling nightclubs, restaurants, and sidewalk cafés. The prince and Wallis must have remembered Leo von Hoesch's gypsy czardas parties as they listened to the haunting strains of the local bands in various smoky cellars. Wallis loved the czardas. One night, February 23, with the sons of Regent Horthy, the prince and Wallis practiced traditional dances to a wildly applauding crowd at the Arizona Nightclub, famous for its performing animals, stripteases, trapeze acts, and multicolored strobe lighting. Wallis drew much attention, wearing a rainbow-tinted coat that appeared to be made of spun glass and an exquisite diamond clip in her hair.

The visit was a success from every point of view. Both Austria and Hungary were now more firmly bound into the Italian orbit because of the prince's influence, thereby restricting Hitler's power. When the prince and his party returned on February 28 to Paris, a huge crowd greeted them at the Gare de L'Est. Police seized cameras and smashed bulbs, but several photographs appeared. When Wallis and the prince got off the boat train in London, they fled through the crowd to York House to change hastily for dinner at Lady Cunard's. It had been an exciting, exhausting trip.

And there was a new excitement ahead: a matter of the gravest concern to the throne.

As a latter-day Victorian puritan, in marked contrast to King Edward VII, George V, whose own sexual record was far from blameless, had much to deal with in his immediate family. Though even he might have balked at condemning his sons for indulging in "normal" sexual activity on the sly, he was most emphatically opposed to their choice of certain partners. He had to face the fact that his sons the Prince of Wales and the Duke of Gloucester had shared the bed of the aviatrix Beryl Markham, who was notorious for her affairs; he had had to put up with the Prince of Wales and the Duke of Kent's romance with Sandra Rambeau, Kent's fling with a Paris ephebe, and sundry others; and with Kent's and the Prince of Wales's dalliances with Noël Coward. The fact that Kent had married Princess Marina of Greece had come as somewhat of a relief, especially since two of her sisters were married to men who might help preserve a lasting peace with Germany. But worst of all was the Prince of Wales's liaison with Wallis, a married woman of bad reputation, an obvious gold digger, and an exponent of what were called in those prelapsarian days, perverse sexual practices.

The king, with his Silver Jubilee looming, married to an even more correct and upright Queen Mary, embarked on a project that was, to say the least, against his character. This was to obtain, not to put it delicately, the dirt on Wallis Warfield Simpson.

Although once, in a fit of pique, he said that he hoped Wales would never marry, he clearly continued to hope for his son's union with Princess Friederike, a match that would prevent another world war in his lifetime. The horror of the trenches, the mud, the rats, the shells, the bloodshed, the conflict between German cousins, the loss of a world of grace and cultivation, the destruction of the flower of England's manhood—these haunted the minds of everyone of King George's generation, and he would, it is fair to say, have given almost anything to prevent it happening again.

And so, in early 1935, the king contacted Lord Trenchard, an old and devoted friend and commissioner of the London Metropolitan Police. Trenchard, the immensely distinguished creator of the Royal Air Force, was, like his royal master, a dogged puritan. In the course of revising the bureaucratic structure of Scotland Yard, he had improved the quality of the force, instituted a police training school, and cut the deadwood from the rank and file. What he emphatically did not have his officers do was pursue errant ladies of leisure in and out of bedroom sexual combat zones, obtain information on corespondents that could lead to a divorce, or undertake any other squalid duties more suitable for a private detective agency. What the king asked Trenchard to do was investigate Wallis Simpson as if she were a common prostitute.

Trenchard cannot have relished the task. In fact, from the beginning, despite his energetic reforms, it is certain he had not enjoyed his job of dealing with crime; the air force was his love.

With the high level of crime in London, his daily work was already onerous and unpleasant without a sordid extra burden; but he was a gallant old soldier and he would never fail to satisfy his king. He had in fact resigned two years earlier, wanting to enjoy a life of well-earned retirement, but the monarch had insisted he remain, first to take care of security at the marriage of the Duke and Duchess of Kent, both of whom were potential targets of pro-Communist terrorists, and later for the preparations for the jubilee.

Scotland Yard's Special Branch was used to protect, rather than expose, members of the royal family. It began its investigation into Wallis in the late spring of 1935; a certain Superintendent Albert Canning was put in charge. Canning discovered from various friends of hers that Wallis was sleeping with a man whom they would not for some reason name. It didn't take long for Canning to discover that the man was a Ford Motor Car Company sales executive named Guy Marcus Trundle.

Handsome, dashing, 35 years old at the time, Trundle was little more than a gigolo, since Wallis had given him the Prince of Wales's money for his sexual services. Reflecting their American boss Henry Ford's notorious anti-Semitism and love of Hitler, Ford employees had to be non-Jewish, politically to the extreme right, and approving of the corporation's building of trucks and armored cars for the German army, a process that did not cease with World War II. Hitler worshiped Ford, gave him honorable mention in *Mein Kampf,* and had a picture of him at all times on his desk. Thus, Trundle had to be a true-blue Aryan Fascist at heart, and a man to whom Wallis could relate.

Married at the time, described by many of Canning's informants as a "bounder" or cad, Trundle seems to have been disliked by everyone to whom Canning spoke. The question is: where could she and Trundle have conducted their affair?

Hotels, with their gossipy staffs, would not be the answer, since the Prince of Wales might hear of that. Wallis's social friends could not be trusted to supply houses or apartments. Since Trundle was married they could not meet at his home, which was a royal property near the birthplace of the Duchess of York in Bruton Street; certainly Wallis could not bring him to 5 Bryanston Court. The most likely rendezvous, as is indicated by her subsequent liaison with William Bullitt, U.S. ambassador to France, was a dressmaker's—the one place where the Prince of Wales would not follow her.

Her regular dressmaker, the Nazi agent Anna Wolkoff, had a small establishment in Mayfair; but another friend, Elsa Schiaparelli, the celebrated Italian fashion designer, whose clothes Wallis began wearing in the mid-1930s, had just opened a salon at 36 Upper Grosvenor Street, very close to Wallis's former residence at Upper Berkeley Street.

In 1990, Jean Negulesco, the Hollywood film director, told me that the building, now a block of flats, in which he had owned an apartment from 1950 on, was famous among his circle as the place where Mrs. Simpson met her lover, and where Schiaparelli (whom he knew in Paris in the late 1930s) protected them both.

Schiaparelli would be an ideal cover because she was also a Nazi sympathizer. The files on her at the FBI headquarters in Washington show that she operated continuously on behalf of Hitler and, most importantly, in view of the Wallis connection, shared Wallis's French Nazi lawyer, Armand Grégoire; he was working for Wallis as early as 1934.

One curious aspect of Canning's report is that Wallis was said, while carrying on this affair of her own, to be jealous of a certain "Austrian or Hungarian" woman in the Prince of Wales's life. The woman was not named; it was not customary to name royalty in Scotland Yard investigations. The likelihood is that the woman concerned was Princess Friederike of Hanover, who was in Vienna and London at the time. "Austro-Hungarian" would be an understandable police description of a daughter of the Duke of Brunswick, if Canning, as is likely, had little grasp of European genealogical niceties.

In the middle of the police investigation into Wallis, Lord Trenchard resigned finally and unequivocally on June 5, 1935, perhaps because he disliked this continuing sordid royal assignment, though he did linger on until December to assist his successor, Sir Philip Game. Game, after an unfortunate term as governor general of Australia, was considerably demoted by his appointment as commissioner. He now had to assist the king by conducting, in cooperation with the Secret Intelligence Service, an investigation into Wallis's life in America and with which the monarch could trump her ace when the time came.

With startling hypocrisy and effrontery, Wallis managed to keep up a pretense to the Prince of Wales. On June 15, she sat for a portrait by Cecil Beaton and gave it to the prince with a warm inscription. It appeared in *Vogue* magazine for July 10. On the twenty-seventh of July, she gave him another portrait of herself by Man Ray, inscribed, rather oddly, "SO BIG." Since Wales was scarcely known for his endowment, was this a ghastly private joke, designed to keep him guessing, and a sly and surreptitious reference to the more virile Guy Trundle?

One of George V's few abiding interests, outside field sports, was China; he had a knowledge of that country so formidable that Lord

Killearn, British ambassador to Egypt, visiting him at Buckingham Palace at the time, was astonished by it. In addition, Stanley Baldwin, who became prime minister in June, had deep interests in China, which he had visited in the 1920s. Armed with prior knowledge, both king and premier were well equipped to instruct the Secret Intelligence Service's China agent, Emmanuel Cohen, to proceed to unearth Wallis's career in that country.

Scotland Yard and the SIS supplied all of the facts that were necessary in Hong Kong, Shanghai, and Peking, while other agents in Baltimore, San Diego, Pensacola, and New York City obtained details of gambling, sexual promiscuity, and drug dealing. Baldwin delivered the resulting dossiers to the king; because of Queen Mary's sensibilities, it was left to her beloved friend and gentleman-in-waiting, the distinguished and morally impeccable Honorable John Coke, son of the Earl of Leicester, to show her the dossier himself. He recorded later that her shock and dismay were indescribable.

In January, 1951, when the much-vexed question of Wallis being allowed the title of Her Royal Highness came up, Winston Churchill summoned Coke to his holiday home in Marrakesh, where he was working on a popular history of England, to ask him point-blank why it was still being denied. Coke reminded him that in 1936, in the last month of King George V's life, he himself had heard Queen Mary say that in view of what he had shown her in the dossier, Wallis must never be queen. She, the Duchess of York, and the Duchess of Kent agreed on this matter at the time.

From that day to this, historians and biographers have denied the file's existence, one exception being Kenneth de Courcy, Duke de Grantmesnil, a friend of John Coke and the Prince of Wales, who knew that it did exist from Queen Mary and from Coke, but believed that it was a forgery. This is absurd; neither King George nor Baldwin nor John Coke would have forged it; they were not criminals by nature.

It is important to note that the royal family so deeply trusted Coke that he never left their employ. If he had been a party to a forgery arranged by Baldwin, he would have been removed and perhaps given a remote Commonwealth post, the usual treatment for erring royal servants. He remained equerry to Queen Mary to the end of her life and gentleman-equerry to King George VI (who would never have had a forger in his service) until he died. Nor did Winston Churchill reject him when he came to Marrakesh in 1951; Churchill retained great respect for Coke.

The skeptics remain vocal; in his 1991 authorized biography of King Edward VIII, Philip Ziegler asserted wrongly that everyone seemed to have known someone who saw the dossier but nobody saw it themselves, thus injuring the Hon. John Coke's memory.

During the spring of 1935 Wallis went everywhere at night triumphant, blazing with emeralds. Henry "Chips" Channon noted that at a lunch party on April 4, 1935, Wallis "already had the air of a personage who walks into a room as though she almost expected to be curtseyed to. She has complete power over the Prince of Wales." On May 31 an incident took place at the Royal Opera House, Covent Garden. The prince and Wallis were guests of Lady Cunard in her box. When the first intermission came, Wallis said sharply to the Prince of Wales, "Hurry off now, David. You'll be late for the London County Council Ball. And take that cigar out of your breast pocket. It doesn't look very pretty!"

That spring London society was agog over the upcoming Silver Jubilee of King George. Enormous sums were being spent to make the grimy city look reasonably festive; the buildings were bedecked with flags and flowers, and bonfires were lit the length and breadth of England. The king made it clear to his erring son what Wallis would not be welcome at the Jubilee Ball; as a divorced person, she would also be forbidden access to the royal enclosure at Ascot and would be denied any other privileges over which the royal family had any control.

The king confronted the prince directly in the matter of Wallis. The prince gave his father his word of honor that he had never had sexual intercourse with her. This, of course, may have been true if he and Wallis were still merely indulging in fetishistic sexual games that did not involve a total consummation of their relationship. The prince insisted Wallis was "a fine person" and had made him "supremely happy," unlike Thelma Furness, who was, he disloyally said, "a beast." He insisted once more that Wallis was not his mistress and begged that she be allowed to enter the royal enclosure and make an appearance at the Jubilee Ball. The king replied that he would, in view of the fact that the relationship with Wallis was (as he incorrectly believed it) strictly platonic, arrange for the Simpsons to be invited. Lord Wigram, the monarch's private secretary, wrote in his diary:

The Prince's staff were horrified at the audacity of the statements of [H.R.H.] the Prince of Wales. Apart from actually seeing H.R.H. and Mrs. S[impson] in bed together, they had positive proof that H.R.H. actually lived with her.

The ball took place on May 14. According to tradition, the prince opened the evening by dancing with his mother. He created a stir by walking straight to Wallis and whirling her around the floor for the second number. To make matters worse, he even danced with her straight past his parents, who gave her a look of steely distaste. She was mortified.

Throughout that month members of foreign royalty, including a number of relatives of the monarch, were pouring into London for the Silver Jubilee celebrations. Hitler correctly saw the jubilee as an ideal opportunity to cement the pro-Germanism of so many figures in British royal and aristocratic circles. Aware that the government was still leaning in the direction of Italy, seeking to restrict him in the interest of British balance of power, he strove to correct the situation by selecting a royal flush from the faded deck of cards that the deposed German royal family of Hohenzollern had become. He knew it would have been a mistake to send the ailing kaiser to London, because the British public would have risen in its wrath against the former enemy. Instead, Hitler shrewdly sent the kaiser's daughter-in-law, Crown Princess Cecilie, her daughter, Viktoria, and her son Ernst August, along with the prince's favorite, Charles, Duke of Saxe-Coburg-Gotha, who was in the SS. These figures, entirely embroiled in Hitler's cause, if only to protect their assets, could be relied upon, the führer felt, to make the necessary impression at Buckingham Palace. Wallis inevitably encountered them at the time. Among her new friends were the Prince and Princess von Bismarck, and among the other crucial connections to the royal German cousins were their devoted hosts, Sir Harold and Lady Zia Wernher. Lady Zia was the White Russian sister of Nada Milford Haven. Sir Harold was head of Electrolux in Britain, and thus an associate of the Swedish multimillionaire Electrolux tycoon Axel Wenner-Gren, royalist and friend of Field Marshal Goering, who would later play a crucial part in the lives of Wallis and the prince. At the end of May Leo von Hoesch gave an elaborate party at the embassy at Carlton House Terrace for Wallis, David, the Bismarcks, Princess Cecilie, and the Wernhers.

At the dinner, Wallis was intrigued to hear Princess Cecilie urge the Prince of Wales to make public his desire for closer alliances with Nazi Germany. She suggested that an ideal occasion might be his scheduled address at Queen's Hall to the veterans of World War I who were members of the British Legion. The Legion was already in close touch with its German counterparts, and it was anxious to repair the damage done in World War I by stretching the hand of friendship across Europe. The prince agreed that this idea was excellent. It apparently never occurred to him that by entering into such a commitment, he would expose the double game he was playing with the European powers and greatly annoy his friends in Vienna and Budapest as well as the French government, which was already hand in glove with Mussolini.

On June 19, 1935, to resounding cheers, the prince, without Wallis, walked up to the podium at Queen's Hall and delivered a speech to the Legion that included the words that made explicit his desire to have the conflicts of the Great War forgotten.

The speech caused considerable controversy. King George was furious, particularly since it was so important to continue with the appeasement policy vis-à-vis Mussolini to protect the Mediterranean and the Suez Canal. More importantly, it was essential that members of the royal family did not express themselves publicly on political issues. The prince's speech only served to illustrate his naive and confused political position. Wayward and defiant, he was being meddlesome and irritating in every possible way. Goering and General Count von der Goetz, head of the Reich League of German Officers, sent approving telegrams. A week later, at a vast assemblage of 200,000 people at Nuremberg, Goering said, after savagely denouncing the Jews, "Germans were profoundly cheered by the declaration of the British heir apparent. He can be sure the German front soldier and the German people grasp most eagerly the hand offered them."

At the same time, Britain's relationship with Italy, so warmly encouraged by the prince, became threatened by the foreign policy of Anthony Eden. After a meeting with Eden in Rome, Mussolini, Count Grandi recalls, beckoned him and with a hard and resolute tone said, "The English and the French have declared their absolute disinterest in the fate of Austria. . . . Soon the Nazi flag will wave over the Brenner frontier. This is painful but inevitable. Machiavelli wrote, 'If you can't kill your enemy, embrace him.' Some bad day we will be obliged to embrace the Germans. It will not be a pleasant embrace."

Grandi continues:

> Mussolini realized that Eden, while taking a belligerent attitude to us, also showed a certain blindness regarding our problems in Africa. Mussolini said to me, "From this moment on, there will be a shift in our foreign policy. Since we are unable to save Europe, we will move into Africa."
>
> English opposition to our actions in Africa vis-à-vis Abyssinia was indecisive. The English neither said no nor yes to our plans for the conquest for Ethiopia. In June 1935 British interests were centered on internal politics because of the imminent general election. But as the year went on, the feeling against Italy intensified.

The Prince of Wales undoubtedly brought whatever influence he had to bear in high circles to counteract the increasing opposition to Italian colonialism. In this, given her friendship with Grandi, Wallis was in complete concurrence. And yet there was still the contradiction in both cases that Wallis and the prince were paradoxically flirting with the Germans in London.

During this period of enormous publicity and conflicting currents in the world of politics, the Prince of Wales was under great stress. He depended more and more on Wallis for her support, but she still retained an ambiguous attitude toward him. On the one hand, she enjoyed flouting convention, basking in public attention, and increasing her personal power. On the other, as a chilling letter written at the time to Aunt Bessie makes clear, she was certainly not in love. She was in fact still more distressed by the prince's infantile dependence on her—despite the fact that she had engineered the situation—and his still insistent phone calls and visits. Easily bored, brittle, and restless, she impossibly wanted everything: a stolid and loyal husband and a fully enslaved prince; respectability and notoriety; the comforts of privacy and social prominence. The royal need to be satisfied in every possible way had proved catching.

In a conversation with U.S. ambassador to London Joseph P. Kennedy on June 13, 1938, as recorded in the Kennedy diaries, Sir Edward Peacock, in charge of the royal finances as receiver general of the Duchy of Cornwall, stated that at this time, the Prince of Wales began sending out royal moneys from the country, most particularly to America where, despite the Depression, good investments were more readily available than in England. Like Hitler and Goering, he put substantial sums in railroad common and preferred stocks in the northeastern American states.

In July plans were afoot for another political journey to Europe undertaken in the guise of a vacation. Using the pseudonym of Lord Chester, which fooled nobody, the prince took off with Wallis and friends to France, arriving on August 7 at Cannes by the Blue Train. Their friends Vice-Consul John Taylor and his wife met them. Apparently indifferent to the prince's support for Hitler's anti-Semitic regime, Sir Philip Sassoon had remained an intimate friend, and he arranged for them to stay at the house of his sister Lady Cholmondeley; her Villa Le Roc was next door to Maxine Elliott's famous Château de l'Horizon. The handsome white residence was situated on the ocean, with an indoor pool, like that on an ocean liner, ingeniously contained within the rocks on which the house was built. There was also a private yacht slip.

On September 11 Wallis and the prince arrived in Budapest. The headlines there were full of Hitler's speech the day before to the Nuremberg Rally, condemning Jewish Marxism and the Centerist Moderate party and promising harsher methods against both in the future. Once more, the prince had meetings with Regent Horthy, and he joined President Gombös for luncheon. He was continuing with his clumsy double game of sustaining the Italian connection to make sure that in keeping with British foreign policy there would be no interference with Mussolini's colonial expansions. The couple proceeded to Vienna, where the prince again combined visits to the Spanish Riding School, tea parties, and nightclubbing with high-level discussions at the Chancellery.

There was a quick trip to Munich to appease the Germans and then a hair-raising car ride over the Trans-Alpine Highway to France. While in Paris, the couple firmed up two more associations. The first of these was with Albert Frederic Armand Grégoire, who was described in a confidential report of the Paris Sûreté on April 9, 1934, as "one of the most dangerous of Nazi spies." Wallis's lawyer and Schiaparelli's, as we know, represented Simpson, Spence and Young's business with North German Lloyd and the Hamburg-America Line in France. He was also attorney for Joachim von Ribbentrop and for Otto Abetz, later the German ambassador to Paris, and he was Sir Oswald Mosley's chief contact in that city.

Robust, swarthy, with a dueling scar across his left cheek, Grégoire was born in Metz, Alsace-Lorraine, in 1894. He was awarded the Iron Cross, First Class, by Kaiser Wilhelm II, and he became a close friend of the Crown Prince and of the Crown Princess Cecilie. He was a founder and director of Marcel Bucard's fanatical Franciste movement, one of the leading Fascist cells in France. Under the pseudonym of Greg le Franc, he contributed pro-Hitler articles to *Le Franciste*, the inflammatory official journal of the movement.

In the issue of January 1934 (volume I, no. 2), he had written:

> Naturally, we hope with all our heart for an alliance with Nazi Germany. We fully realize that this alliance constitutes the only possible means of avoiding the universal corruption of the world. We estimate that this alliance is possible, easier in fact to realize than an alliance with the British, our hereditary former enemies, with whom we have far less in common than we have with the Germans.

Wallis's use of the notorious Grégoire as a contact and attorney (in 1937 she would have him represent her in a major libel suit) was a disaster, and the watch on her by the Secret Intelligence Service intensified. While in Paris, Wallis and the prince also became a friend of Pierre Laval, premier of France. Devious, unreliable, famous for his greasy look and his washable white tie that was never washed, Laval was married to a charming and elegant wife. He followed the policy of trying to please the Balkan nations, the Germans, and the Italians while secretly pitching one against the other. His dream was to give the Germans a free hand to smash the Soviet Union while keeping Hitler and Mussolini apart to preserve the French balance of power. He despised the British, despite their agreement with him on this issue.

While in Paris, Wallis was at last propelled into the highest levels of European power. Hitherto, the Prince of Wales had excluded her from meetings with heads of state, leaving her to go shopping while he indulged in duplicitous games of European politics. Now he made a move which was not only scandalous in the eyes of Buckingham Palace but also significant in illustrating the confidence he placed in Wallis and his need for her to become his royal consort. He arranged for her to attend a luncheon for Laval given by the British ambassador, Sir George Clerk, at the embassy on October 1.

The timing of the luncheon was extraordinary. For weeks Anthony Eden, as Britain's representative at the League of Nations, had been conferring with Laval on the delicate matter of the secret French alliance with Mussolini, which Eden opposed. That January Laval, in Rome, had entered into an agreement with the Italian dictator that would subsequently give him a free hand in Ethiopia. Now the Prince of Wales chose to confirm that he would stand behind Laval in the outright support of Mussolini's colonial ambitions, a fact to which Laval would testify in August 1945 when he stood trial on charges of treason against France.* It was a unique occasion: the heir to the throne being accompanied by his mistress to a political encounter sanctioned by a British ambassador. Laval's son-in-law, the distinguished Paris lawyer Comte René de Chambrun, a direct descendant of Lafayette, revealed in 1987 the secrets of the meeting to this author.† During the conference the prince promised to secure the approval of his father, King George, and of his government for Laval's policy vis-à-vis Mussolini. In return, the Comte de Chambrun stated, Mussolini would be made to promise that he would not enter into an alliance with the führer that would endanger Britain and France. At the same time, Laval's assurance was required and given that he would allow Britain to use French ports if at any stage in the future there should be a direct conflict with Italy in the Mediterranean.

The Comte de Chambrun in 1987 regarded this meeting as an indication of the boldness and intelligence of both his father-in-law and the Prince of Wales. But he overlooked a significant detail. One day before the embassy conference, Hitler had given assurances to Laval, widely published in the international press, though ignored by subsequent historians, that he would not take action against France no matter what arrangements Laval made with Italy. Those assurances had been made through Sir Samuel Hoare. It was clear from this announce-

---

*At his trial at Nuremberg, Ribbentrop tried unsuccessfully to summon the Duke of Windsor as a witness.
†Only part of which appears in the minutes published in Sir George Clerk's decoded report to London in the British foreign policy documents.

ment that Hitler was already planning to enter into an alliance with Mussolini in order to secure a permanent foothold in the Mediterranean and joint control of Austria and the Balkans.

During the next days Wallis, the Prince of Wales, and Laval, in the company of Madame Laval and Laval's daughter Josée, exchanged many visits. The Lavals came to dinner at the Hôtel Meurice, and Wallis and the prince went to the Lavals' house. Once again, including Wallis in such a high-level series of meetings was extraordinary; she was being treated as princess, fellow politician, and diplomat. At one meeting, at which Wallis was not present, Laval suggested that the prince should try to make an arrangement with Germany which would bring Mussolini and the führer together. Laval said that he was sure Mussolini would accept an honorable agreement and suggested to the prince that he should talk with King George. The prince replied, "My father doesn't meddle in politics, but I will certainly talk to him."

It was now clear to the Prince of Wales that it was not necessary to play a double game between the German and Italian dictators, that they could be brought together to a common purpose. That this purpose was the breaking of the Franco-Soviet pact, the prevention of the spread of bolshevism, and the crushing of the Soviet Union was made clear to the author by the Comte de Chambrun.

Meanwhile, the Duke of Kent was busy on the same political agenda. Shortly after the craven Prince Paul of Yugoslavia appointed a Fascist prime minister who doubled as foreign minister in the sinister persona of Milan Stoyadinovich, and made an infamous deal with Hitler's government for bauxite, coal, and grain, Paul met with Laval to approve the Italian invasion of Ethiopia. Also at the meeting were Prince Philipp of Hesse, whose father-in-law King Victor Emmanuel would soon illegally be made emperor of that country, and Kent, who was staying in Munich at the home of Count Toerring, his Hitlerian brother-in-law. It takes no feat of the imagination to see what alliances these devious intriguers discussed.

While all this questionable maneuvering was going on, Wallis had other things on her mind. In the spring she and the prince had attended the salon showings of the great fashion designer Mainbocher, whom she admired and loved. Main Russeau Bocher (his real name) was American born. High-strung, sensitive, and darkly handsome, he had risen from a career as illustrator to preeminence in his field under the guidance of his mother, Wallis's friend the Countess de Mun. Sponsored by the wealthy Kitty Bache, heiress and wife of the theatrical producer Gilbert Miller, Mainbocher designed for Irene Dunne, Loretta Young, Miriam Hopkins, and Constance Bennett. At the recommendation of Lady Mendl, Wallis chose him as her designer. She liked to see him selecting her fabrics, and she worked with him as closely as any colleague as he, short, stocky, relentlessly energetic, rushed from one end of the salon to the other, challenging his staff by the minute, dashing off drawings by the handful, and taking calls from Hollywood, London, Berlin, and New York. It was Mainbocher who created, in effect, the "Wallis look" that became world-famous the following year. The clothes he made for her were severe, classical, and timeless. They were the opposites of the extravagant creations favored by many of the prominent society women of the time. Even today, photographs of Wallis taken at the time show that she was stepping out of the period, dressing in styles and colors that would still look contemporary half a century later.

One day after the meeting at the British embassy, the plans of the Prince of Wales and Pierre Laval came to fruition. Mussolini was granted by the British passage of 150,000 troops through the Suez Canal. He invaded Ethiopia, wreaking devastation and destruction. His troops used mustard gas, forbidden by international law because of its horrifying effects—blindness, madness, and death.

Simpson, Spence and Young had a vested interest in pursuing the issue of the invasion of Ethiopia. The Italian commander Treves was a close associate of a partner of Ernest Simpson's. The firm was seeking to obtain a loan on the London Stock Exchange to finance the development of a cotton-growing industry in that country. Treves and the firm persistently besieged the Treasury for permission to exploit the appropriate territory. In this, documents show, they were directly backed by the Italian government through the trade attaché to the embassy in London. The argument for obtaining the loan was that if the cotton growing of Ethiopia were financed by a country other than Britain, a serious competitor to the Egyptian cotton industry would be created. The Egyptian cotton industry was under British control. The application was not favorably received, as the Treasury saw it as a combined move of Ciano and Wallis's husband. It is hardly surprising in view of this latest maneuver that the Secret Intelligence Service was even more concentrated on Wallis.

On September 7 Wallis was to add a revealing touch to this matter when she wrote to her Aunt Bessie, "If war between Italy and Abyssinia takes place, perhaps shipping will take a leap and I'll be able to come over [to America]."

Back in London, according to Laval's statement under oath at his trial, the prince took the matter of Mussolini and Hitler to King George V. The monarch then allegedly agreed that nothing must be done to stop the Italian dictator in his path of conquest. However, Anthony Eden, possibly out of guilt for having smoothed the path to the destruction of a hapless nation, began to press for sanctions against Italy at the League of Nations. In this, he was violently opposed by the Prince of Wales. Six months later the prince would be telling Ambassador Dino Grandi that he wanted Italians to know he was on their side and that he regarded the British government's attempt to support the League's sanctions policy as "grotesque and criminal." He never ceased to maintain, in later years, that Mussolini should never have been interfered with.

The late Count Grandi recalled in 1987:

> Several meetings and discussions took place between myself and leading figures of British Government upon the sanctions issue. Sir Robert Vansittart shared with Eden the view that the application of sanctions was not merely designed to give us an indication of the British attitude, but also was indirectly an indication to Nazi Germany to desist from its territorial ambitions. However, the only effect it had, unfortunately for all concerned, was to push us directly into Germany's arms.
>
> I tried to warn Eden of this, without success. I had several very difficult meetings with him. Following the meetings, I felt it necessary to confer with the Prince of Wales. I always went through Mrs. Simpson. I would telephone her at home, and ask her if she could make the necessary arrangements. She did so, and the meetings took place around ten o'clock at night. The prince was always very receptive to what I had to say and lent a very attentive ear. This was true also later, when he became king.

During the fall of 1935, the old king was ill. He was worn out by the stress of maintaining a grueling series of official appointments that taxed his waning strength unendurably. The matter of Wallis was among the greatest of his burdens. On October 31 he and Queen Mary spoke with great sadness and fierceness about the prince to the former Austrian ambassador to London, their old friend Count Mensdorff. They told Mensdorff of the prince's bringing Wallis into Buckingham Palace against their will. "That woman in my own house!" King George exclaimed. The monarch continued, "My son's former mistress, Lady Furness, was also frightful. The first, Mrs. Dudley Ward, was of a much better class and a lady of good society. [My son] has not a single friend who is a gentleman [and] does not see any decent society." Count Mensdorff said, "The Prince has so many attractive qualities, charm and giftedness." To which the king replied, "Yes, certainly. That is the pity. If he was a fool we would not mind. I hardly ever see him and don't know what he is doing."

The Prince of Wales became involved with still more questionable associations. Jewish Defense League documents show that he was in touch with Dr. Frank Buchman, an American clergyman who headed the so-called Oxford Group or Moral Rearmament Movement, which had millions of followers all over the world. Dr. Buchman was a close friend of Himmler's and had stayed with him in Germany. He would soon become notorious for his statement, "I thank heaven for a man like Adolf Hitler." Among Dr. Buchman's British admirers were Sir Samuel Hoare, Prime Minister Baldwin, the Earl of Clarendon, the Marquess of Salisbury, and the Earl of Cork and Orrery.

In the meantime, the British Union of Fascists expressed its continuing admiration of the Prince of Wales. Although Sir Oswald Mosley was careful not to be too overt in his relationships with Wallis and the prince, he was at his most drastically active in this period. Even during the jubilee celebrations, his Blackshirt brigades had given the Fascist salute to King George. Hundreds of meetings were held every week in various parts of Britain. Jews and Communists were beaten up by Mosley's gangsters. And Jews were among the leaders of the movement, including the well-known boxing champion Kid Lewis, Mosley's gauleiter. In addition, the Nazi party established its own headquarters in London and was equally interested in the Prince of Wales. Rudolf Hess, deputy to the führer, was in charge along with Ernst Wilhelm Bohle, British-born chief of the Auslands Organisation, the organization of Germans living abroad.

As 1935 grew to its close, the king weakened still further. He was greatly distressed by the death of his beloved sister Princess Victoria. Hitler sent a message of sympathy. In December the Prince of Wales, with Wallis, flew to Paris to confer once more with Pierre Laval on the matter of Ethiopia and the continuing appeasement of Mussolini. This visit was understandably kept secret, and has only now been revealed by Comte René de Chambrun. Sir Samuel Hoare joined in the discussions at Rambouillet. Laval proposed that the war would be brought to an end with the following arrangement. Ethiopia would be granted 3,000 square miles of largely useless territory in Italian Somaliland. Mussolini would be granted a huge slice of the African nation's richest cotton lands. This obnoxious arrangement was supposed to be kept hidden until the matter could be presented to the League of Nations. The accomplished "Pertinax" (André Geraud), foreign correspondent of the *Echo de Paris* and contributor to the London *Daily Telegraph*, somehow succeeded in obtaining the text of the Hoare-Laval agreement and published it in both newspapers. It was instantly denounced in the House of Commons, though none of the members knew of the Prince of Wales's role in the matter. Hoare was violently abused and gave a speech of futile explanation before the Commons. The prince rashly took the step of supporting Hoare publicly by appearing in the Distinguished Strangers' Gallery to hear the speech. He allegedly applauded it, thus attracting untoward attention amid a chorus of boos.

According to Count Grandi:

> Hoare made a fool of himself over the Hoare-Laval issue. English public opinion was not prepared by a cautious and shrewd government policy, so the pact idea fell startlingly upon the British people, like a dash of cold water against burning steel. It was a terrible mishap. Had the proposals been accepted, Italy would have been satisfied and Mussolini would never have joined Hitler. Nor would he have extended his empire.
>
> Mussolini later tried to let it be believed that he had refused the Hoare-Laval proposal, but that is not true. He called a Grand Council meeting on December 10, and the acceptance of the Hoare-Laval proposal was on the agenda. I will never forget calling from London with news of what was going on in the House of Commons. Mussolini interrupted the Grand Council meeting to talk to me, and expressed great astonishment and disillusionment.

In his frequent meetings with Grandi at the time, the Prince of Wales unquestionably was in total accord on this matter. To the end of his days he would tell anyone who would listen (and the editor and author Frank Giles went on record on this matter in his memoirs) that the biggest mistake ever made by England was in the matter of Mussolini and Ethiopia.

Wallis also remained in agreement. Nor could she forget that the foreign minister of Italy, Count Ciano, was the father of her dead child. She was happy, despite her pro-fascism, to spend Christmas with the Jewish Sir Philip Sassoon at Trent Park. Meanwhile, the prince was at Sandringham with his parents. In the wake of the China dossier and the research in Baltimore, the atmosphere was even more charged than usual. The prince made a touching effort to assuage his father by ordering the royal caterer, Frederick Corbitt, to obtain a dozen avocados as a Christmas present to the king. Corbitt had the formidable task of finding the elusive fruit in the midst of a savage English winter. According to Corbitt's memoirs (some historians have questioned the veracity of the story), when the avocados arrived, the prince had them served with vinaigrette to the king, who ungratefully snapped, "What in heaven's name is this?" His father's lack of appreciation for the gesture radically upset the prince, who telephoned and wrote Wallis that he was utterly depressed and distraught with the situation in his family.

The Prince of Wales took over for his father at several official functions. He was not at all eager when asked what would happen after he assumed the throne. He frequently said to friends, "My brother Bertie would make a much better king than I would." He even addressed the Duchess of York as "Queen Elizabeth" in private. He talked of moving to his ranch in the Canadian Rockies for the rest of his days.

January was a typically harsh month in England; the nation was swept by snow and sleet and driving winds. The old monarch developed bronchitis, a condition aggravated by his unfortunate habit of smoking heavily. On January 16 the prince, who had been shooting in Windsor Great Park, walked into the drawing room at Fort Belvedere and handed Wallis a note. It was in Queen Mary's handwriting and read: "I think you ought to know that Papa is not very well." The queen went on to suggest that the prince should come to Sandringham for the weekend, but should be careful not to reveal his concern to his ailing father.

The prince took Wallis's hands in his. They knew the king was dy-

ing. Soon the prince would be King of England. Would Wallis then divorce Ernest Simpson and become queen?

When the prince arrived at Sandringham, he found his father,
painfully thin and frail, seated in an old Tibetan robe, shivering before
a big, open log fire. The king was scarcely able to recognize his son. A
team of physicians led by the royal doctor, Lord Dawson of Penn, had
determined that, in addition to the bronchial catarrh from which the
monarch was suffering, there were signs of cardiac weakness that were
sufficient to cause alarm. Lord Wigram, the principal private secretary,
was informed that the king would not live. He discussed the arrangements that would take place for the succession with the Prince of
Wales and the Duke of York. The following day, Wales and York drove
to London to confer with Prime Minister Stanley Baldwin. The queen
was especially concerned about the upkeep of Sandringham. A joint-
stock company was discussed, in which the Prince of Wales and the
Duke of York would contribute to the upkeep. However, Wales expected to inherit a life interest in Sandringham and Balmoral when he
became monarch. The maintenance of both residences would be drawn
from Crown funds. The queen was upset; she also dreaded the thought
that her son might give the jewelry of the late Princess Victoria, whose
death had so greatly upset King George, to Mrs. Simpson. She made
sure that the will divided the jewelry between the princess royal and
the Duchesses of York, Gloucester, and Kent.

On January 17, with the king in a limbo state between life and
death, as Baldwin revealed in a conversation with Joseph P. Kennedy,
the U.S. ambassador's son, on June 13, 1938, the Prince of Wales, instead of staying by his father's bedside with all the available members
of the family who were not traveling abroad, went to Downing Street
to tell Baldwin he had hoped to get out of being king but had never had
the courage to discuss it with his father. Then, with Baldwin in a state
of shock, he upset the prime minister even further by taking off with
Wallis to a nightclub.

On January 19 the king began to sink into his final sleep. He mur-
mured to Lord Wigram, "How is the Empire?" "All is well, Sir, with the
Empire," Wigram replied. At noon the king managed to sign a document permitting the appointment of a Council of State. While Wallis
waited by the telephone at Bryanston Court, the Prince of Wales flew
back to Sandringham with the Duke of York, and after dinner he and

his brothers York and Kent drew up plans for the funeral. At 10 p.m. the king was already in a coma. It was decided that if he lived past midnight, his death announcement would miss the morning edition of the London *Times*; in view of this unfortunate potentiality, and his grievous suffering, it was decided to terminate his life immediately. At eleven o'clock Lord Dawson—improperly, according to the law, which forbade euthanasia—injected three-quarters of a grain of morphia and one grain of cocaine into the king's distended jugular vein when the nurse in attendance refused to undertake the task. Within fifteen minutes the royal life was extinct, and before the BBC broadcast of the news at ten minutes after twelve, the London *Times* was advised.

Through the night and much of the next day, the prince called the anxious but irritable Wallis countless times, telling her of each successive stage of the preparations for the next few days. There was some discussion of a possible cremation, which, according to some authorities, would have set a precedent, but this was not followed through. Everyone remembered the ghastly episode of the burial of the Duke of Teck, when the body, afflicted by a septic condition, burst open with a loud report during the funeral procession. Because of this disagreeable memory, it was decided to embalm the king.

The Prince of Wales left with the Duke of York by plane for London to discuss matters with the Accession Council, and to be officially declared king. Meanwhile, the royal coffin rested at Sandringham Church. On January 22 the official public proclamations took place in London. Wallis, at the new monarch's specific request, watched the ceremony, fascinated, from a tall window at York House. As the guns thundered, almost drowning out the words of Sir Gerald Wollaston, the garter principal king of arms, as he read the proclamation of accession, Wallis felt a firm hand gripping hers. The king stood next to her. He had again broken all tradition by coming to watch his accession with her.

They were seen driving off together in the royal car; he dropped Wallis off at Bryanston Court before continuing to Buckingham Palace. At 2:30 he was on his way to Sandringham. Upon his arrival there he joined his mother and the rest of the family to hear the reading of the will by the royal solicitor, Sir Halsey Bircham. To the king's horror, he was not included. Clause after clause was read out, and every few minutes he would interject an anguished, "Where do I come in?" Sir Halsey was obliged to say that he did not. Wigram stated that the king had not been left an inheritance because it was presumed that he had built up a substantial sum of savings from the Duchy of Cornwall. However, the king was beside himself with rage. He exclaimed, "My brothers and sister have all this money and I have nothing!" At that time he had saved from the Duchy of Cornwall an estimated million pounds sterling in investments and properties, the equivalent of $5 million. Moreover, he of course had inherited the life interest in Sandringham and Balmoral.

As it happened, the new monarch was very well-off indeed. The Duchy of Cornwall earned him at least £364,000 a year. He would receive £425,000 from the Duchy of Lancaster and £2,355,000 from the Civil List. Sandringham and Balmoral were worth at least £5 million. He also had the use of Buckingham Palace, worth £15 million, and containing £10 million in gold plate alone. The palace boasted a collection of old masters worth £5 million. The king had investments that included the ranch at Calgary, Alberta, with several hundred head of shorthorn cattle, and very substantial stocks in Jewish companies, obtained for him by the Rothschilds.

Wigram was exceedingly disaffected with the new king because of his behavior over the will. He made it clear that he would resign from his post in six months and emphatically would not act as private secretary to the new monarch. His sentiments were shared by a very high proportion of employees on the royal staff, who were appalled by the fact that the king seemed more concerned with his own financial welfare than anything else. Two days later the king stormed into the offices of the Duchy of Cornwall demanding immediate reassurance that no portion of the income, drawn in part from the rentals of the impoverished people of London, would be denied him. He was coldly informed that it would not.

In the meantime, the body of George V had been brought to London to be carried in a simple procession through the streets to Westminster Hall. Something ominous occurred on that somber journey: because of the jolting of the gun carriage that carried the dead monarch, the jeweled Maltese cross surmounting the imperial crown, which had been fixed to the coffin over the royal standard, came loose and fell into the gutter.

A much more elaborate procession, attended by a vast throng of mourning citizens, took place a few days later. The body at last reached Westminster Hall. For days and nights, close to a million people trooped past the coffin. Officers of the household brigade stood at the four corners of the platform, and funerary candles glowed in the subdued light. In the early hours of one morning, when the crowd had gone, the king, perhaps feeling a twinge of conscience because of his behavior, hit upon the touching gesture of summoning his brothers to stand with him in vigil in between the officers. On another morning he and Wallis came in through a back door and stood in silent contemplation. According to Ribbentrop's biographer, Paul Schwarz, a German agent managed to film them and send the film to Hitler, who giggled uncontrollably as he watched it. He was already in possession of motion pictures of the royal yacht cruises the previous summer and, like Eva Braun, was mesmerized by Wallis's hair, carefully made-up face, and exquisite clothes. He told Frau Ribbentrop he deeply admired Wallis.

In the midst of these sad rituals, with London black-draped in the spirit of mourning, the new monarch somehow managed to fit in meetings with representatives of Nazi Germany. Even before his father was dead, he had met Leopold von Hoesch and told him that he intended visiting Hitler's Olympic Games that summer.* He also squeezed in an audience for several groups of German servicemen and, while his father was scarcely cold in his coffin, had a fireside encounter at York House with his cousin Charles, Duke of Saxe-Coburg-Gotha. He told the Eton-educated Nazi Charles, who was a member of the SS, that he wanted to meet Hitler, that he had the highest admiration for Rudolf Hess, that Ribbentrop had done a very good job with the Anglo-German Naval Agreement. He said that von Hoesch, through a "good representative of the German Reich," was a "bad one for Hitler's Third Reich" and that he as king would require "a representative National Socialist from Germany as ambassador, who, through his personal rank in society, would belong naturally to the gentry, and who could be regarded as a representative of official policy and the confidante of Hitler." This statement suggested an urgent need for von Hoesch to be replaced by the Windsors' intimate friend the Prince von Bismarck, formerly of the Reichstag, who was to take over as chargé d'affaires in March.

One of the king's acts as monarch was to order, in person, that Lendrum and Hartman in Mayfair make an exact copy of the royal Buick,

*He was dissuaded by the Foreign Office from attending.

which had originally been manufactured in Canada. The second Buick, with identical license plates and with the royal insignia on the hood, was for Wallis's exclusive use. This was widely considered an outrage in court circles. Wallis acquired a whole series of enemies that January. Chief among these were the severely correct Major the Hon. Alexander Hardinge and Mrs. Hardinge. Helen Hardinge, a woman of old-fashioned moral character, a member of the distinguished Cecil family, detested Wallis. Several of the royal ladies-in-waiting refused to shake hands with Wallis. When Wallis came up to one of them with her hand outstretched, the woman dropped her handbag and bent to pick it up to avoid the contact.

The king proceeded to irritate almost everyone in his household. He had already annoyed many retainers by changing the clocks, which had been set half an hour fast from the time of his grandparents to save daylight hours for shooting, back to their normal time. He instructed Frederick Corbitt that lunch would no longer be served at one, as it had been for over a century, but would be eaten whenever the mood took him, usually at half past two. This put severe pressure on the kitchens. He made it clear that the staffs at all the royal houses must be ready to answer the ring of a bell at any hour of the day or night. He consulted with Wallis on the royal budget. She advised him to make a clean sweep of the staffs, cutting out deadwood and giving anyone inessential a 10 percent wage cut. To the lasting disgust of Wigram and the Hardinges, he fired many old and ailing retainers. Together, he and Wallis decided that court clothing should be modified and that frock coats should be eliminated. They appeared at York House without warning in the kitchens, maids' quarters, wine and food cellars, and basement, conducting cursory inspections and making radical changes. Years later, the king told Commander Grattidge that he was amused to find in the bowels of Buckingham Palace a group of tiny men responsible for stoking the boilers, like primitive cave dwellers who never came up for air.

Always a dieter, he cut the food purchases of each of the royal households by two-thirds; he was served salads, fruit, and small cuts of meat. His and Wallis's only indulgence was a delicious Scandinavian dessert called *rødgrød*, made of crushed raspberries, red currants, and rice. He was a little hesitant in bringing Wallis to Buckingham Palace, but one evening he gave her a tour. They decided that the entire antiquated edifice should be remodeled in a modern manner and that, outrage of outrages, it should be redecorated from top to bottom by Lady Mendl. As it turned out, this idea was never executed. By the time Lady Mendl had finished her drawings, the king was off the throne.

His rebellious informality was so extreme, and his submission to Wallis so absolute, that he did the unthinkable. When she left his royal residences, often after spending most or all of the night, on her snapped instructions he would dash past his staff all the way out of the front door and, often in rain and darkness, frantically hail cab after cab until one would draw to a halt. The driver, recognizing the monarch, would respond to the shrieked words, "Stop! I'm the king!" with a stare of astonishment that was even more wide-eyed when that elevated being actually opened the door for his notorious mistress and assisted her inside. It is fairly safe to say that no English ruler has acted in this manner, before or since.

Rear Admiral Sir Lionel Halsey of his household was let go; the king disposed of Sir Louis Greig, another loyal courtier, and tried to take his house in Richmond Park from him—but the dead king had long since made sure that Greig was given a ninety-nine-year lease and the property was no longer subject to royal confiscation. Brigadier General G. F. Trotter was another victim; the list grew longer every day.

And the king's meannesses were appalling. Even Wallis, who disliked and was jealous of Dudley Forwood, objected when the monarch made him pick up papers from the carpet on his hands and knees, papers the king had deliberately spilled there. When Forwood announced that members of the staff were drinking imported Evian water, Edward sent an announcement to the kitchen saying that Evian was only to be drunk at the royal table and anyone caught quaffing it would be dismissed on the spot without references. They were.

The King of England, according to custom, would receive official dignitaries one at a time. This practice greatly aggravated the new monarch, who instead required that groups of officials appear before him simultaneously, much to the annoyance of many of them. He disposed of the private car supplied by the railways and traveled in ordinary carriages. He did away with a stenographer and typed his own correspondence with two fingers until the sheer number of letters to be answered made him give up. He ran up colossal phone bills at the palace. When Wallis was irritated by the phone service, he told her to call the postmaster general to have the problems fixed. They were—at least for the time being.

The world was excited and impressed with the new monarch. In the United States enthralled millions watched the newsreels of his accession. One of his keenest admirers was my father, Sir Charles Higham, who, in an interview at the Waldorf-Astoria Hotel in New York, accompanied by me, his baby son, said:

> King Edward is a young people's king. And England is coming to be a young people's country, as the gap in the ranks of her youth, caused by the war, is being filled with intelligent youngsters. Edward will be their idol. He can ride, dance, fly, mix with the commoners, deal with diplomats. What can't he do? He is fully equipped for his job, if a king ever was.

The German press enthusiastically agreed. Above all, the Italians gloried in the new monarch.

Wallis was under a considerable strain during those first weeks of her lover's reign. Yet she seemed to enjoy the new game of being the king's mistress, writing to Aunt Bessie that she was "laughing a lot inside." Although her apologists have denied it, she had designs on the throne already, since on February 1 she wrote to her aunt for the Warfield and Montague family trees, determined that they would stand up against these "1066 families here." Only a week later she seemed to realize the folly of any thought of becoming queen, writing to Bessie that it would be a good idea if the king were to marry someone of appropriate background. She also made clear that she would never relinquish her power.

There was still nothing in her letters of the time to indicate the slightest degree of love or even affection for the new monarch, only a cold conflict in herself over whether or not she should seek further heights. By contrast, the king, despite his crowded schedule, seemed to hate every minute he was apart from Wallis; he sent her a stream of letters, inscribed on black-edged mourning stationery printed for his father, expressing an infantile, obsessive adoration, sprinkled with a private code in baby talk.* Sometime in the late winter he backed his written admiration with a bold financial gesture. He settled £300,000

---

*His favorite word was "einum," which, according to a reliable source, was a cross between "eenie" and "meenie" in the toe-counting nursery rhyme.

on Wallis, the equivalent of $1.5 million, or one-third of his entire life savings. According to *Time* magazine, he later panicked at the size of the gift and reduced it to £100,000. Wallis informed her Aunt Bessie Merryman that the financial arrangements, which Wallis had no doubt requested, had been taken care of. Soon the king would be spending thousands of pounds on jewels for her.

In February Ernest Simpson wished to obtain membership at the Masonic Lodge in which both the king and the Duke of Kent, who was grand master, had supreme influence and over which Sir Morris Jenks presided. Jenks turned Simpson down. The king demanded to know why. Jenks told him that it was against Masonic law to accept a cuck-olded husband as a member. Once again, the king insisted his relation-ship with Wallis was platonic. This, of course, was a mere technicality. As a result, Ernest was admitted. He was also given the unfulfilled promise of a baronetcy.

Sometime in February Ernest went to York House to visit with the king; he was accompanied by a witness, Bernard Rickatson-Hatt of Reuters. According to Rickatson-Hatt, during the course of the evening Ernest, who was by now in love with Mary Raffray, boldly told the monarch that Wallis would have to choose between them and asked the king what he meant to do about it. Did he intend to marry her? The king replied, "Do you think I would be crowned without Wallis at my side?" Ernest agreed to end the marriage provided the king promised to be faithful to Wallis and look after her.

If this conversation (the veracity of which has been questioned by certain historians) had ever leaked, it would have finished Wallis's chances of divorce the following year; a collusive arrangement would have been exposed by the king's proctor, who had to rule on the mat-ter, and the most famous marriage of the century would never have taken place.

9

Almost Glory

In March 1936, the Earl of Harewood, husband of the princess royal, the king's sister, delivered a speech to the British Legion that was a far cry from the king's speech the previous summer. He attacked Hitler's reoccupation of the Rhineland. Among other things, he was seeking to influence the Legion away from its Nazi associations. According to the present Lord Harewood's memoirs *The Tong and the Bones*, the king wrote a stinging rebuke to his brother-in-law, denouncing him for the speech and saying, "How can I make my contributions to foreign policy if my own relatives make irresponsible statements?"

That same month Wallis took off for Paris to order her spring wardrobe from Mainbocher. Wallis saw a good deal of Mrs. Beatrice Cartwright, heiress to the Standard Oil fortune; Standard Oil had substantial holdings in Germany and continued to collaborate with the Third Reich throughout World War II.*

While Wallis was in Paris, the situation in Europe darkened. On March 7 Hitler announced that German military detachments had entered the demilitarized zone of the Rhineland in defiance of the terms of the Versailles Treaty. The nineteen infantry and three artillery battalions stood on the edge of France, yet the French public seemed apathetic, still carrying memories of the misery and exhaustion of World War I, and anxious to avoid even a show of hostility to the threatening

---

*Mrs. Cartwright would soon meet and marry the Nazi collaborator Frederick G. McEvoy, the closest friend of Errol Flynn. Mrs. Cartwright was known to the State Department for her Nazi sympathies.

forces of the führer. In London the sentiment of the financial leaders was, as British Foreign Office documents make clear, overwhelmingly pro-German and anti-French. That Wallis shared their views was clear from a statement made in a letter to her Aunt Bessie in which she expressed the hope that the Germans would ill-treat the French couturiers and others who were causing her problems. Her attitude to the French was ambiguous: on the one hand, she loved French food, the Hôtel Meurice, Mainbocher's fashion salon, and the glamorous world of French society; but on the other hand she regarded the country as hopelessly corrupt, weak, and ineffectual, a natural victim of the stronger forces of Germany.

As for the King of England, in a report marked "Strictly Confidential," the London correspondent of *Berliner Tageblatt* wrote, through the German embassy, to his foreign editor on March 18: "[The monarch] has caused a number of important people in the Government to come and see him, and has said to them: 'This is a nice way to start my reign!'" He was referring directly to Hitler's reoccupation of the Rhineland. Ironically in the context, Wallis expressed concern to her aunt that, in view of the deteriorating international situation, Ernest Simpson, who was continuing to do business with Nazi-controlled shipping companies in Hamburg, might be interned.

Mary Raffray arrived in London. She had seen a good deal of Ernest in New York City the previous fall, when they became involved in a secret love affair. She was keeping a careful record of Wallis's association with Ribbentrop, which she insisted to her family was a love affair. She "hated" Wallis for it, she wrote to her sister Anne. In a curious reversal of the double standard, Wallis apparently objected to Mary's affair with Ernest; but at the same time she and the king clearly saw the liaison as a perfect way of disposing of Wallis's marriage and clearing the way to remarriage. From as early as mid-March the monarch began to plan the divorce, taking consultation with a number of trusted advisers on the best way to proceed. He was, of course, greatly discouraged by all those in his circle, and he frequently lost his temper over their objections to Wallis as the future queen. One of those whom he dismissed that spring was the honorable and devoted "G" Trotter, who also felt the headsman's ax because he was thought to be in touch with Thelma Furness. According to several sources, Trotter fell on very hard times and was even reduced to becoming a floorwalker in a department store. The king never lifted a finger to help him.

On April 9, Maundy Thursday, a sacred occasion each year at Westminster Abbey, when the reigning monarch gave alms to the poor, Edward deliberately infuriated the archbishop of Canterbury by having Wallis attend in a back-row section usually reserved for visiting royalty.

As her power grew, Wallis began to behave with even greater bold-ness. An extraordinary situation developed among herself, the king, Ernest, and Mary. They were involved in what rapidly became a fla-grant ménage à quatre: Ernest and Mary stayed with Wallis and the king at Fort Belvedere and at Lord Dudley's house, Himley Hall, and the king would spend evenings at Bryanston Court while Ernest and Mary shared the guest bedroom. On April 23 Mary wrote to her sister Anne in St. Louis:

> I meet the King often, dined at York House . . . and spent a weekend at the Fort. . . . Saturday night he took us all to Windsor Castle; at the Earl of Dudley's we met Lady Oxford [Margot Asquith], Lady Cunard, Ribbentrop, and Lady Diana Cooper. . . . Wallis is in the thick of things, received and toadied to by everyone on account of her influence with the King. (This you must absolutely not repeat.)

Ribbentrop was in London frequently that spring; while he still had the seventeen red roses delivered every day to Wallis at Bryanston Court, he was arguably the most popular party guest in London. Emerald Cunard, Laura Corrigan, and Lord and Lady Londonderry— Wallis's set—entertained him constantly; he became popularly known as the "Londonderry herr." Ribbentrop was also very close to "Chips" Channon and his wife, who paid court to him. Channon, though a gifted writer, had little power of perception when it came to dealing with leading Nazis; he was intoxicated by the idea of having a German government member at his dinner parties. In his diary entry for June 10, 1936, Channon wrote that Ribbentrop resembled "a jolly commer-cial traveler." Mrs. Ronald Greville, a friend of Queen Mary's and later of King George VI's and Queen Elizabeth's, was another of his favorite pro-Nazi hostesses. Everywhere he went, he was lavishly praised for his and the führer's defeat of unemployment and bolshevism; some even dared to praise him for the official German policy on the Jews.

It was widely believed (among the alleged witnesses was Mary Kirk Raffray) that Wallis was being paid by Ribbentrop directly from German funds in Berlin to influence—as if that were necessary—the king. Certainly, as Mary testified in a long, detailed account given to her sister Anne at the time, and subsequently written by Anne as a report to the biographer of Edward VIII, Frances Donaldson,* Ribbentrop renewed his affair with Wallis and it is hard to believe that in this case the thick smoke of gossip had no fire as its source. No such relationship could have made its way into the official files in case their contents should leak back to Ribbentrop's wealthy wife, the champagne heiress Annelise Henkell, and cause her to undermine his position by creating a public scandal. Frau Ribbentrop had young children; she had a jealous, possessive nature; and she must not be allowed to ruin Ribbentrop. As for Wallis, we know from her letters that she was not in love with the Prince of Wales, she was enjoying her power but at the same time was fearful he might want to marry her. No absolute proof exists of the relationship with Ribbentrop, but the people of Wallis's set were certain of it.

On March 27 Edward gave Wallis her finest gift of jewelry: a Van Cleef and Arpels ruby and diamond bracelet; inscribed on the clasp were the words "Hold Tight" and the date, a sly reference perhaps to the "Casanova Clip," a method of enhancing weak erections by a tight grip of the fist at the base of the penis on entry, followed by internal muscular contractions, which Wallis had, according to the late Sir Dudley Forwood, brought to a fine art.

On April 2 Wallis threw an elaborate party at Bryanston Court for the author Harold Nicolson. In a blaze of white orchids and arum lilies she received her guests, who included the king, the American wit and broadcaster Alexander Woollcott ("She has the King like *that*," he noted in his diary), and, audaciously, the archrivals Ladies Cunard and Colefax, both of whom wanted to monopolize the king. They were furious; Wallis evidently enjoyed the black joke of bringing them together under her roof.

It was typical of her mischievousness and sheer nerve that she brought off this soirée trick. That month she and the king invited the Duke of Connaught, a royal great-uncle, and his friend Lady Leslie to

---

*The contents of the report have been supplied by Kirk Hollingsworth, nephew of Mary Kirk Raffray, who inherited it. The actual document has disappeared.

Fort Belvedere for afternoon tea. According to a memoir by Lady Leslie's daughter Anita, the party strolled in the grounds; when the group returned to the house, Wallis's shoes were muddy from the damp soil. Without warning, she commanded the king, "Take off my dirty little shoes and bring me another pair!" To the stupefaction of the two guests, the monarch knelt down and smilingly complied.

On another occasion the king arrived with Wallis at a party at Lady Cunard's. He had been drinking Vichy water all through dinner, but decided to add a few drops of brandy at the coffee stage. Unable to find a bottle opener, he turned to Wallis. She instructed Ernest to take his own opener from his keychain and do the job for her lover.

Frequently, the king irritated his guests—and Wallis—by playing bagpipes after dinner at parties at the fort. One evening, in front of a fashionable crowd, Wallis made so severe a face at him during his performance that he stopped dead, blushing like a schoolboy. It was by now clear to everyone that he no longer had a will of his own. He would even yield to Wallis's entreaties to accompany her to the Royal Opera House, Covent Garden. The audience rippled when he arrived with Wallis and friends and took his place in Lady Cunard's box. He loathed opera and slipped out time and time again during the performance to chain-smoke cigarettes and fret while Wallis, who remained tone-deaf, gave the impression that she was enjoying the performance. Actually, her enjoyment was chiefly in noting that the audience was barely looking at the stage; most eyes were fixed firmly upon her.

The king had several meetings with the committee of the Civil List that spring, discussing what provisions would be made for the "future queen." He ran into resistance on the matter but persisted in pressing the subject, much to everyone's irritation. Major the Hon. Alexander Hardinge and Mrs. Hardinge were determined to block the marriage at all costs. They tried to contact the king's legal adviser, Walter Monckton, to enlist him in their cause, but he was in India. They continued to maneuver behind the scenes.

The king added Sir Robert Johnson, deputy master of the Royal Mint, to his long list of enemies. Sir Robert was in charge of the British coin designs. It was understood that in each successive reign the monarch would be photographed from the side opposite to that of his predecessor. It was a tradition that went back centuries. George V had been photographed from the left. But when the king discovered that the design for his own coins was based upon a rare photograph of his right side, he flew into a temper, convinced that his right profile was hideous, and demanded that a change be made immediately. He won.

He provoked still further criticism when, on April 20, he sent a telegram to Hitler on his birthday, wishing the führer well for his future "happiness and welfare." Five days earlier Ambassador von Hoesch had died of a heart attack. He was replaced immediately by the king's and Wallis's intimate friend, the mild and bespectacled Prince Otto von Bismarck, who was acting chargé d'affaires until Ribbentrop took over that fall. It was known that Bismarck was a frequent guest at Fort Belvedere, which suggested a very serious possible breach in security.

The reason for this fear in Whitehall was clear. Day after day, from the beginning of the reign, red dispatch boxes were sent down from London to the fort, containing secret documents from British embassies all over the world relating to the international situation. These were for the eyes of the cabinet ministers and the monarch, and were not made available to anyone else. It became a scandal that the king, bored by paperwork and troubled by eyestrain, would leave crucial documents scattered about, some of them marked by the stains of tea and coffee cups. It was suspected that certain crucial information in these documents was making its way back to Berlin. Wallis was thought to be the leak. In a biography of Prime Minister Stanley Baldwin, by Keith Middlemas and John Barnes, the following passage appears:

> About Mrs. Simpson, greater suspicions existed. She was believed to have close contact with German monarchist circles . . . she was under close scrutiny by (Sir Robert) Vansittart [Permanent Under Secretary of State for Foreign Affairs], and both she and the King would not have been pleased to realize that the Security Services were keeping a watching brief on her and some of her friends. The red boxes sent down to Fort Belvedere were carefully screened in the Foreign Office to ensure that nothing highly secret should go astray. Behind the public facade, behind the King's popularity, the Government had awakened to a danger that had nothing to do with any question of marriage.

In the files of the FBI in Washington a report, entitled "International Espionage behind Edward's Abdication," contains this statement:

Certain would-be State secrets were passed on to Edward, and when it was found that Ribbentrop actually received the same information, immediately Baldwin was forced to accept that the leakage had been located.

The same report categorically states that Wallis was responsible for this breach of security.

In his biography *This Man Ribbentrop*, Paul Schwarz, a member of Ribbentrop's Foreign Ministry staff, reported that secrets from the dispatch boxes were being widely circulated in Berlin and that materials germane to British national security and sent by British ambassador to Germany Sir Eric Phipps, were making their way back to the German capital. Again, Schwarz seemed to imply, Wallis was responsible.

Sir Robert Vansittart, the controversial éminence grise of the British Secret Intelligence Service, took charge. Tall, broad-shouldered, ruggedly athletic, exuding decency and warm common sense, Vansittart succeeded the very able Sir Ronald Lindsay as permanent under secretary in 1930. He was arguably the most daring, freethinking, brilliant, and piercingly perceptive of any political figure of his time other than his close friend and neighbor Winston Churchill. As John Connell wrote in his book on British diplomacy, *The Office*:

> He was [capable of] swiftness of analysis . . . linked indissolubly to an equivalent swiftness in his desire for action. He was impatient if the action which he believed to be obviously necessary did not immediately and resolutely follow upon the assessment of a situation which he had made or the advice which he had offered. This caused more timorous and less decisive men to regard him as imprudent and injudicious.

Poet, gambler, and bon vivant, Vansittart was a close friend and partner of Alexander Korda's; in the late 1930s, as his associate and boss in London Films, he would enlist Korda in the Secret Intelligence Service along with other German-speaking Hungarian employees of that company. Vansittart had been in the foreign service in Paris, Teheran, Cairo, and Stockholm, and he had the clearest head in London where the German menace was concerned. He was the unofficial head of the Secret Intelligence Service, MI6, which was nominally run by Admiral Sir Hugh Sinclair until 1939. "He was a leopard whose fate it was to be harnessed with a team of domesticated but sly and vindictive tabby-cats,"

Connell wrote. He was Wallis's implacable enemy from the day that he was convinced she was a Nazi collaborator.

How did Vansittart reach the conclusion that Wallis was responsible for leaking crucial documentary information to the German government? According to the late historian John Costello, the Russian secret agent Anatoly Baykalov was the source of this intelligence. The statement is confirmed in Richard Deacon's impeccably researched *The British Connection* (London, Hamish Hamilton, 1979). He wrote:

> Baykalov had [a] trump card up his sleeve, one which he played very skillfully during the later years of the Baldwin government and which paved the way towards the abdication. . . . Baykalov reported to MI5 that Mrs. Simpson was a secret agent of the Germans. He noted that she was very frequently at the German embassy. . . . The information was passed to Baldwin by his Secret Service Liaison Minister, J. C. C. Davidson.

Posing as a White Russian, Baykalov was part of the same set that included Wallis's dressmaker Anna Wolkoff, which would explain his knowledge of the matter. He appears to have acted as a double agent for the British. He took the information of the leak to the Soviets and also in February 1936 to J. C. C. Davidson, who now was chancellor of the Duchy of Lancaster. Davidson in turn took the information to Vansittart, who then conveyed it to Stanley Baldwin.

Vansittart had two reliable plants in the German embassy who could inform him when any material arrived for transmission to Germany in the diplomatic bags. Wolfgang zu Putlitz was one of these spies; later, when posted at The Hague, he would reveal the Duke of Windsor's leakage of important information on a British War Council meeting. Putlitz worked in association with another British spy, the German press attaché Iona von Ustinov, father of the actor and playwright Peter Ustinov. Nigel West wrote in his definitive book *MI6*: "For . . . years, zu Putlitz kept Ustinov . . . in touch with everything that took place within the German Embassy in London."

Wallis would have had to use the Italian embassy as a conduit for the information; Baykalov determined this. What could have been her motive? Sir Eric Phipps, British ambassador in Berlin, had greatly excited the king's displeasure because of his missives and telegrams which indicated an intense dislike and mistrust of the Hitler regime. She would not have risked acting without royal authorization; it seems likely that the king himself wished this information to flow back to Germany in order to fortify opposition to Phipps and to undermine Phipps's secret policies.

On May 4, 1936, Wallis sent a long, emotional letter to Aunt Bessie, complaining of the awful strain she had been under with the king and Ernest tearing her apart for a year and a half; she wrote of how painfully difficult it was to placate and amuse two men at the same time and to fit into their separate lives, and she said she was constantly tired, nervous, and irritable. She went on that even though she, Ernest, and the king had discussed their curious relationship on a reasonably friendly basis, and even though Ernest appeared to regard his position as a cuckold with complacency, she herself could not endure much more mental and physical stress. She knew she had outgrown Ernest; if she were to give up the king, she would regret it; and should the king become romantically involved with another woman, she would cease to have the power and possessions she now enjoyed. The letter is a harshly astonishing revelation of her ambition.

On May 27 the king invited Prime Minister Baldwin to York House to meet his "future wife." Among the guests were Charles and Anne Lindbergh. Lindbergh had just returned from Germany, where he had been given a grand tour at the specific request of his friend Field Marshal Goering. Sometime after the dinner Lucy Baldwin told her husband, "Mrs. Simpson has stolen the Fairy Prince." Walter Monckton returned to London. The Hardinges brought their influence to bear on him, but he was adamantly loyal to the king, almost certainly rejected charges of espionage against Wallis, and would only do what the king wanted. He knew that no power on earth could shake the monarch's obsessive love of Wallis. On one occasion that spring Monckton was with the monarch looking over a depressed property of the Duchy of Cornwall in London when he noticed the king staring with intense yearning out of one of the windows. He asked, "What are you looking at, Sir?" the king replied that Wallis was in that general direction. Even a brief absence from her that day was tormenting to him.

Another incident was widely discussed in London. In an effort to patch up the conflict between Wallis and his brother and sister-in-law, the Duke and Duchess of York, the king decided to take her to visit them at the Royal Lodge at Windsor. Wallis talked to them and at first they began to melt a little. She made a fuss over their children, the Princesses Elizabeth and Margaret Rose. But then Wallis destroyed all possibility of a reconciliation. The nursery governess, Marion Crawford, recalled in her memoirs that right in front of her host and hostess and their daughters, Wallis walked to the window and announced that the view would be greatly improved if certain trees were cut down or replanted and part of a hill bulldozed. The recommendation was not appreciated.

During the summer of 1936 severe censorship was applied to any mention of Wallis in England. The newspaper magnates, loyal to the king, introduced a self-imposed edict that precluded either photographs or articles which would disclose the relationship between her and the monarch. Foreign periodicals and journals were sent by their distributors to a special office where appropriate passages referring to the king and Wallis were scissored out. When the British newsweekly *Cavalcade* daringly brought out an issue covering in five columns the life of Mrs. Simpson, it sold very well but was finally dragged off the stands and confiscated. Nevertheless, black-market copies of European magazines found their way into many homes in society and were read with much surreptitious giggling over the breakfast tables.

On June 30, Superintendent Albert Canning of Scotland Yard, still pursuing Wallis on orders from Lord Trenchard and Sir Philip Game, advised Game that the Communist party of England was very much concerned with the king's relationship with Wallis and that, at a meeting led by the political firebrand Harry Pollitt at the City of Leeds Peace Conference, Pollitt had shouted, to general cheers and laughter, "If gas masks are to be given out [in a future war] we should demand the same gas masks for our wives as will be given to Mrs. Simpson." This was at a time when the Press lords of England, led by Lord Rothermere of the *Daily Mail* and Lord Beaverbrook of the *Daily Express*, followed the policy, dictated by both king and the prime minister, of behaving as if the notorious American woman did not exist.

One of the king's most characteristic acts that summer was to call a meeting of his Privy Council in late June to discuss the situation in which Mussolini had brutally subjugated and pillaged Ethiopia. In ten minutes, he suspended sanctions instituted by his father against Italian trade from July 15 on, thus greatly benefiting Ernest Simpson. He ordered Sir Samuel Hoare, first lord of the Admiralty, to withdraw war vessels from Italian waters, and he stood back while Mussolini forced Turkey, Greece, and Prince Regent Paul's Yugoslavia to withdraw their sanctions.

In an effort to forestall the king's marital plans, his opponents in the press constantly announced that he would marry this or that royal princess. Among those stated to be his choice of bride were (again) Princess Friederike, granddaughter of the kaiser, and Princess Alexandrine Louise, third daughter of Prince Harald of Denmark. It was with some difficulty that he was restrained from having Wallis assist him in receiving the guests at royal receptions; instead, he was aided by the Duchesses of York, Gloucester, and Kent.

By midsummer, all confidential documents were being withheld from the king and were not even passed from the Foreign Office as far as Major Hardinge. Foreign Secretary Anthony Eden was responsible for this restriction, along with Sir Robert Vansittart. Eden had no time for the king, and the feeling was mutual. Eden, gravely concerned over the appeasement of Mussolini, and distraught that no punishment of the Italian dictator would be permitted by the government of which he was a member, had two alternatives at this stage. Either he could accept the majority decision of the cabinet, or, if he felt sufficiently strongly about it, he could resign. Unquestionably, he should have resigned, but, as was revealed later in his career, he tended to be morally irresolute in a crisis. It was not until 1938 that he did finally resign over the official appeasement policy. The cabinet was instrumental in arranging the abrogation of Mediterranean naval pacts with Greece, Turkey, and Yugoslavia that were supposed to have ensured collective security against Mussolini. At the same time, Mussolini and Hitler had drawn together in what would turn out to be a fatally dangerous alliance. And just to be sure that Italy had unlimited power in the Mediterranean, where it was secretly involved in a submarine war with the Soviet Union,* the king planned another political vacation in Europe.

Shortly before the king left with Wallis, the deposed Sir Louis Greig discovered that the couple were staying at Blenheim Palace, ancestral home of the Dukes of Marlborough, with Ernest Simpson confined to a separate room. There, Greig determined, the three hatched

---

*The Italian submarines were disguised as Spanish.

up details for the arrangements for Wallis's upcoming divorce, for which Simpson would receive a large sum of money. Mary Raffray, who would use the pseudonym of "Buttercup," would oblige, for a financial consideration, as his sexual partner for the night and witnesses would be secured to testify to this. The king evidently still did not know that Wallis continued to sleep with Guy Trundle.

While the travel preparations were under way for the European trip, an extraordinary incident took place. On July 16 the king attended a military review in Hyde Park, surveying on horseback a fine array of guardsmen in their scarlet uniforms. He reminded them of their heroic traditions, which went back 250 years to the period in which their leader and patron was the Duke of Marlborough. He spoke of the horrors of war, encouraging his troops in their hopes that they would never suffer from fire and gunshot as their predecessors had. "With all my heart I hope, and indeed I pray, that never again will our age and generation be called upon to face such stern and terrible days. Humanity cries out for peace and assurance of peace," he said. It was a ceremony that took place only once every fifteen years.

In vivid sunshine the battalions marched past the king. The monarch rode behind the bandsmen at the head of the brigades of guards for the journey around Hyde Park Corner to Buckingham Palace. As the parade moved under Wellington Arch, a man in the second row of spectators raised a gun and pointed it directly at the king. A policeman's horse backed into the man's line of fire, and he impetuously tossed the unused revolver under the hooves of the king's horse. "Damn fool!" the king exclaimed as someone screamed, "Get the killer, don't let him go!" Three policemen apprehended the would-be assassin and hustled him off. Grim but calm, the king continued his ride to the palace.

It turned out that the assailant was one Jerome Bannigan, an Irish resident of Glasgow, who used the pseudonym George Andrew McMahon. A disgruntled alcoholic of unstable temperament, Bannigan had already been sentenced to twelve months in prison for the libeling of two police officers whom he had accused of blackmail. The conviction had been quashed by the Court of Criminal Appeal. He was allegedly distressed because a magazine he edited, entitled *The Human Gazette*, had been emasculated in an act of censorship by the authorities. He claimed in a rambling story that he had been directed to kill the king by a political group that was Nazi in origin. This absurdity was treated with appropriate contempt, and after a brief trial he was sentenced to serve twelve months in jail.*

On July 21, a storm drenched the guests at the first garden party at Buckingham Palace in six months. The king canceled the receiving line until the following day. Four days after that he sailed for France on the Admiralty yacht *Enchantress* to dedicate the Canadian war memorial at Vimy Ridge. In a solemn ceremony he unveiled the expensive white-stone monument before 50,000 veterans, and, in a speech worked on extensively by his friend Winston Churchill, he spoke eloquently of the glorious dead and once more appealed for lasting peace.

He planned to spend some time on the Riviera at the Château de l'Horizon, home of the former Broadway star Maxine Elliott, before undertaking the Mediterranean cruise. The Popular Front's left-wing Léon Blum had become premier of France after an interregnum that followed the collapse of the Laval government the previous January. It was feared that certain Communist elements attaching themselves to the Blum administration might attempt to kill the king, and he was advised by the Foreign Office to bypass the Riviera. Instead, he completed the charter of the 1,391-ton *Nahlin*, luxury yacht of the eccentric millionairess Lady Yule, who had a house full of stuffed animals and an animal graveyard in her garden. Under the command of Captain Doyle, the yacht would travel through much of the eastern Mediterranean, where the Italians and the Soviets were engaged in their secret war; the royal yacht *Victoria and Albert* at 4,700 tons was too large to voyage up the narrow inlets of Dalmatia.

It was a dangerous time to travel. The Spanish Civil War had broken out. The situation in the Balkans was potentially volatile. Yet nothing would stop the king in his determined effort to embark upon yet another misadventure in politics in the guise of a holiday trip. He was still determined to appease Italy, despite the fact that that nation's imperial policy was still flagrantly opposed to British interests in the Mediterranean. Once again, in keeping with foreign policy, his clumsy, amateurish, but on the whole well-meaning concern was to secure the permanency of the trade route to India through the Suez Canal; shortly before his departure he entertained Farouk, the teenage heir to the

---

*It is possible that Bannigan was backed by the IRA, which was at that time under Communist control.

Egyptian throne, in order to receive reassurances vis-à-vis Suez. He also was pleased to approve Baldwin's crucial appointment of his old friend Sir Samuel Hoare as first lord of the Admiralty. This was no idle choice. He needed Hoare to help him secure Italy's permanent cooperation and freedom to continue its anti-Soviet submarine war and to reinforce Gibraltar, Malta, and Cyprus. Moreover, the king considered the heavy armament installations in Yugoslavia of the British company Vickers. In Greece he could contact King George, who owed much to Britain, and General John Metaxas, newly arisen dictator and Mussolini admirer. He would also meet with Kemal Ataturk, dictator of Turkey, making sure that the Ottoman army and navy would be allied to Britain for the indefinite future.* There was fear that the Turks might be building or even floating submarines to assist their allies the Russians against Italy.

As usual, the king flew to Calais, while Wallis and the rest of the party came by Channel steamer. On this occasion the king used one of his hereditary titles: Duke of Lancaster. The royal party took the Orient Express, again in a private car supplied by Mussolini, via Salzburg in Austria, arriving at the Yugoslav frontier at Jessenice late in the afternoon. The travelers were met by Prince Regent Paul and by John Balfour, British chargé d'affaires in Belgrade. The king stepped out to chat with the regent and Balfour. Sitting in the private car, Wallis was surprised to find it was being shunted around a siding to join the royal train. There was grave concern that Edward and Wallis would be murdered either by Communists or by Croat terrorists. When Edward and Wallis broke the journey briefly to drive out into the country in the royal car to have tea with Paul and the Princess Olga, who did not approve of Wallis, the chauffeur, on instructions, drove at a frantic pace, scattering chickens and goats in every direction. The authorities were afraid that if the royal party was in a slow car, the Croats might strike.

The purpose of the meeting was not merely social. The timing had been carefully thought out, and the meeting had been preplanned, despite statements in both Wallis's and the king's memoirs that it was the result of Paul's insistence on interrupting their journey south. Two

---

*Stories that he was reluctant to visit Turkey and was forced to do so by Sir Percy Loraine, British ambassador in Ankara, cannot be substantiated by documentation.

months earlier Dr. Hjalmar Horace Greeley Schacht, Hitler's leading economist and financial wizard, had been in conference with Prince Paul on the matter of massive armaments contracts; at the same time Mussolini had been in close touch with the prince to achieve similar political and economic relations. As a result, when King Edward and Wallis arrived in Yugoslavia, half that country's exports and imports were the result of German and Italian deals. It is clear that again the King of England wanted to be reassured that the Fascist alliances established in Bucharest would not affect the British balance of power in Europe, especially in the Mediterranean basin. Prince Paul had no difficulty in giving that reassurance.

Wallis and the king then proceeded to the Dalmatian coast, joining the *Nahlin* at Sibenik. The weather was perfect, and the yacht, extensively refitted to royal instructions and freshly painted white from stem to stern, made a magnificent sight in the harbor against a background of vivid blue sea and sky. Twenty thousand people in traditional costume greeted the royal party as the group made its way by automobile to the docks. Stories about Wallis had been appearing regularly in the local press; everyone knew she was the king's mistress. Cries of "Long live the king!" rang through the warm and humid air as the white vessel slipped from her moorings and moved out into the glittering sea.

During the next three days politics was set aside as the royal party, with two destroyers as escorts, enjoyed small Adriatic ports and experienced the visual pleasures of the mountainous, magical coast. Wallis would never forget one particular evening when the *Nahlin* was moored at a pier directly under the shadow of a looming mountain peak. Several thousand peasants came to greet the yacht, carrying torches in a long procession that wound down the cliffside paths, while the sound of singing filled the night. At Dubrovnik another great crowd surrounded Wallis and the king as they went shopping, crying, "Long live love!" Despite the heat and humidity, the closeness of the cabins, and the lack of wind to aid the yacht's passage, Wallis was enjoying her role as surrogate queen, and the king was overjoyed to be giving her a taste of what it meant to be a royal person.

Among the guests on the cruise were Duff and Diana Cooper; they had joined the yachting party en route. Neither was particularly enamored of Wallis, nor was she of them. They found it sinisterly prophetic that Wallis was already wearing exact copies of the two crosses worn by the king on a gold necklet on her wrist. Diana noted in her memoirs that the couple occupied the main suite (actually, a converted library from which all the books had been removed) at the bow of the vessel, while the numerous guests were crammed into the stern.

The monarch insisted on behaving like an ordinary tourist. As the *Nahlin* nosed through the Corinth Canal, he stood stripped down to shorts on deck, causing hundreds of camera shots, as well as severe and puritanical criticism in London. King George of Greece came aboard for two hours to meet Wallis; related to the British royal family, he had known Edward on and off for many years. Then the couple went ashore with George to meet his British mistress, Mrs. Jones. The situation in Greece was very tense. Only two weeks before, General John Metaxas had seized power in Athens, appointing himself premier and minister of army, navy, air, and foreign affairs. He had cut off all telephone and telegraph communications, censored the press, and sent police to break up labor organizations. In a few days he would dissolve Parliament. Both he and King George had cemented relations with Italy and Germany; again, it was important that King Edward receive assurances that British interests would not be affected by the new regime. He did.

The royal party continued to Athens, where the king and Wallis walked their feet off exploring the Acropolis and the Parthenon. While Wallis shopped, the king and his minister of war, Alfred Duff Cooper, visited with General Metaxas for two hours of afternoon tea. According to a survey of the tour, which was made by the distinguished American magazine *Living Age*, they arranged during the course of the meeting a substantial British loan to Greece through Hambro's Bank, which in effect helped to put Britain more firmly in the Hitler-Mussolini camp.

Back on board, Lady Diana Cooper witnessed a bizarre scene. The king suddenly sank to his knees to drag the hem of Wallis's evening gown from under the foot of a chair. Instead of expressing her gratitude, Wallis stared at the monarch and snapped out: "Well, that's the *maust* extraordinary performance I've ever seen!" And then, to the astonishment of all concerned, she launched a sharp attack on the king, criticizing the way he had handled the Greek monarch and his mistress. Diana wrote in a letter, "Wallis is wearing very, very badly. Her commonness and Becky Sharpishness irritate." It was not the first time Wallis had been compared to the heroine of *Vanity Fair*. Diana noted in her diaries that Wallis kept picking on the king quite coldly, with boredom and irritation. Later, the engineer of the yacht wrote an un-published book about the cruise which indicated how bad-tempered and restless both the king and Wallis were and how they constantly badgered and bullied the crew.

"The good ship Swastika," as Malcolm Muggeridge later dubbed the *Nahlin*, now resumed its journey, hitting a bridge on the way. On September 3 Wallis watched, laughing, as the king was spilled into the water when his small rowing dinghy capsized in a heavy swell. Picnick-ing, rock climbing, collecting shells, and swimming in the warm and still sunlit sea, the royal party proceeded to Turkey, where the group received an especially tumultuous welcome. The Turkish destroyers *Adapepe* and *Kojapepe* met the royal yacht off Imbros at 8 a.m. on Sep-tember 4. General Altay of the Turkish army came aboard by launch with a welcome message from the Turkish dictator, Kemal Ataturk. Turkish destroyers joined the two British destroyer convoy ships ac-companying the royal cruise up to the landing stage at Seddul Bahr. Wallis and the king spent two hours walking through the British and Australian graveyard at Gallipoli. This caused much annoyance in Australia and New Zealand because many in those countries blamed the British, and in particular Winston Churchill, for the inefficiency that sacrificed the Anzac troops in the battle against the Turks in that region during World War I.

At noon the *Nahlin* anchored off the Dalma Bagtche Palace. The king and Wallis were greeted by Kemal Ataturk, along with the pre-mier, the foreign minister, and the Turkish ambassador to the Court of St. James's. The royal party entered open automobiles and drove at headlong speed past cheering crowds at the landing stage to the British embassy for a meeting with Ambassador Sir Percy Loraine. Again, what seemed to be merely a courtesy visit was crucial in terms of se-curing British interests in the region. After several months of negotia-tions, the League of Nations had at last agreed to permit the Turks to overcome post–World War I agreements and to refortify the Bosporus. In view of Turkey's recently cemented political and economic alliances with the Soviet Union, and Turkey's proximity to Egypt and the Suez Canal, the situation was felt to be potentially dangerous to British in-terests. During his meeting with the Turkish dictator, the king suc-ceeded in acquiring the contracts for the Dardanelles refortifications for Britain, right under the nose of Hitler's Dr. Schacht, as well as outfoxing Skoda, the Czechoslovakian company that was believed to be in Moscow's pocket.

That night Ataturk put on a Venetian regatta for the royal party, with the Turkish fleet lit from stem to stern, and a display of fireworks that illuminated the dome of Santa Sophia in a blaze of multicolored lights. It was an unforgettable night to cap an unforgettable visit.

The king and Wallis proceeded to Bulgaria, whose Czar Boris was yet another Hitler associate and admirer. The visit was absurdly mooted as an incognito affair but overnight turned predictably into a gala event. On this occasion, the couple's behavior was appalling. Not only did they boldly sleep together in the private car of the imperial train, supplied by Boris to take them from the border to the capital city of Sofia, with himself as royal engine driver, they also refused to get out of bed on arrival in the early morning, even when they were informed that hundreds of schoolchildren were outside the railroad station with flowers of greeting and a brass band.

Many in the crowd tried to peer into their bedroom, but fortunately a possible lesson in bizarre biology was avoided because the blinds were pulled firmly down. The king contemptuously ordered a British-African servant in his retinue to appear and wave and speak to the crowd. In a country noted for its racism, this was a deliberate insult, but the insult backfired; the children had never seen a "Negro" before and jumped up and down in excitement at the sight. As Czar Boris's chief of protocol, Stoyan Petrov-Tchomakov, reported in December 1965 in the *Monthly Bulgarian Review* published in Buenos Aires, "They [the kids] were quick to seize the unique opportunity [to see] a live specimen of the African race."

The king astonished his hosts by snapping pretty local girls with his Leica camera; in a sly reference to the nanny/baby relationship he had with Wallis, he responded, during a visit to the Imperial Palace, to a grumble from the king's four-year-old daughter that she had to go back to the nursery with the slyly significant words, "And so, my dear, do I." He didn't improve matters when he dubbed the queen's lady-in-waiting Helen Petrov-Tchomakov as "Petrol," the royal secretary Georghi Hanschief as "Handkerchief," and the king's close friend and aide-de-camp Alexei Bugharov as "Bugger off." The Secret Intelligence Service used all three names as codes for these officials in World War II.

Wallis and the king were met at Vienna by a royal automobile especially transported from London. As always, they checked into their favorite hostelry, the Hotel Bristol. The American hostess and columnist Elsa Maxwell was present in the lobby when they walked in with an immense number of suitcases and trunks. Miss Maxwell noticed Wallis's fixed purposeful stare and hard, determined manner.

On the morning of September 9 Wallis and the king visited the Vienna Fair, lingering at the British-Indian Pavilion. They proceeded to visit President Miklas and Chancellor von Schuschnigg. The political situation in Austria was exceedingly volatile. In June Hitler and von Schuschnigg had signed alliance agreements with guaranteed mutual political association, and Italy had concurred with the arrangement. This caused widespread discontent among the Jews and Socialists in the country, and on September 10, the second day of Wallis's and the king's visit, there was a riot in which parts of Vienna were set afire by militant rebels. Before, King Edward could always use the excuse that he was in league with von Schuschnigg in order to avoid an alliance between the Austrians, the Italians, and Hitler. But now he was lending his personal support to a government that was totally committed to Hitler. At the same time, he seemed to find nothing untoward in the fact that he and Wallis visited one of the most prominent figures in the Jewish financial community, Baron Eugene Rothschild, and the baron's American wife, Kitty, at their Schloss Enzesfeld residence. To increase the irony, he and Wallis that night attended a full-scale performance of Wagner's masterpiece, *Die Götterdammerung*, which was Hitler's favorite opera; they were accompanied by the composer's daughter, the pro-Hitler Winifred Wagner. The king also hunted chamois, visited Heinrich Neumann (a Jewish professor who had refused to attend Hitler) for the king's ear trouble, which was exacerbated by his ocean swimming, and appeared at a public Turkish bath with an embarrassed David Storrier of Scotland Yard and six leading Vienna detectives; all eight men disported themselves in the nude, with guns, before the astonished patrons.

Wallis and the king returned to the opera house to see Wagner's *The Flying Dutchman*; on this occasion the king spent most of the performance outside the royal box smoking impatiently. He was more comfortable dining at the famous restaurant The Three Hussars, revisiting the beloved Rotter Bar, and enjoying the waltzes at the Bristol.

After a weeklong stay, the couple took a train to Zurich, whence the king flew to London, and Wallis and the rest of the party continued on the express. George Weller, the *New York Times* correspondent in Athens, wrote on September 6:

In Edward's visits [in the Mediterranean] four nations envisaged a new strong British policy. They asked themselves whether a synthesis of Edward's sincerity and Hitler's zeal might not be a better protection than the League of Nations. They might not be greatly averse to being dominated by the British and Germans.

Weller had put his finger correctly on the main purpose of the voyage of the *Nahlin*.

Back in London, Wallis and Ernest finally parted company. Ernest moved to his club, and Wallis took a room at Claridges Hotel. She had a meeting with her solicitor, Theodore Goddard, who had already begun divorce proceedings. Goddard informed her that he had decided not to have the case heard in London because the calendar was so filled that it might be a year before the divorce could be granted. Instead, he settled upon the Suffolk town of Ipswich; Wallis would be represented by the celebrated barrister Norman Birkett, K.C.

The king invited Wallis and Herman and Katherine Rogers, who had been with them on one leg of the *Nahlin* cruise, to stay with him at Balmoral Castle. Among the other guests were the Duke and Duchess of Kent, Lord and Lady Mountbatten, the Duke and Duchess of Marlborough, and the Duke and Duchess of Sutherland. Canceling a scheduled opening of the infirmary of Aberdeen Hospital, the king disappeared from the castle to drive to Aberdeen Station to pick up Wallis and the Rogerses. The train was late; despite his disguise of enormous motoring goggles, everyone recognized the monarch except a policeman who reprimanded him for leaving his car in the "No Parking" zone. Wallis had never been to Balmoral before. The castle made a pretty sight, with its turrets and gables, its hundred-foot tower, and its spectacular view of mountains, forests, and the river Dee. Inside, it was an amusing royal folly, with its dark pitch-pine and tartan-covered furniture, tartan curtains, and tartan wall hangings. A life-size statue of Queen Victoria's consort, Prince Albert, stood at the foot of the grand staircase.

Wallis seemed to rejoice in the fact that she occupied rooms that had originally been used by Queen Victoria, Queen Alexandra, and Queen Mary. The incongruity evidently amused her as she issued forth in shorts each morning with the king and began shopping in the local village of Crathie. While the royal party went off deerstalking, Wallis walked through the countryside admiring the autumn-tinted leaves of the forest trees. After dinner each night, five bagpipe players paraded around the table, led by the king in Black Watch tartans, tootling away. Movies were shown, including *Strike Me Pink*, starring Wallis's favorite comedian, Eddie Cantor, and Wallis provided an additional American touch by making the guests three-decker toasted club sandwiches.

Wallis was still unpopular with the staff. It was known that she had insisted on the sackings and on pensioning off the old retainers. Her Americanization of the kitchen menus did not please the employees. She was not concerned.

She returned in a good mood to London while the king held his first Privy Council outside London at Balmoral. At the same time plans were well advanced for his coronation, which was to take place on May 12, 1937. Hotels were completely booked along the six-mile parade route. Department stores scheduled hundreds of thousands of dollars' worth of decorations. Lloyd's of London was busy with the contingency of a postponement, guaranteeing various firms against risk. It was announced that Westminster Abbey would be closed to the public, starting from January 4, to allow the Office of Works to prepare the ancient edifice for the ceremonies. The abbey organ had already been taken apart for repairs.

On her return to London at the beginning of October, Wallis sent congratulations to Sir Oswald Mosley and his new wife, Diana, sister of the Hitler-fancier Unity Mitford, upon the occasion of their wedding in Dr. Goebbels's house in Berlin, with Hitler in attendance. After a brief stay at Claridges, Wallis moved into a regency house located at 16 Cumberland Terrace, which was Crown property, subleased from the tenant, who would be going on a world cruise. Enormous, sumptuously furnished, the Nash-designed house had a huge upstairs drawing room overlooking Regent's Park that Wallis filled from end to end with her favorite flowers. She began to refurbish rooms with the help of Lady Mendl. Simultaneously, Neville Chamberlain had arranged to lease his home in Eaton Square to Ribbentrop.

As Wallis moved into Cumberland Terrace on October 7, under

the closest surveillance by the Secret Intelligence Service, she looked up at the roof, where stood figures representing Love, Justice, Wisdom, and Victory. That same day Queen Mary, who had been at Buckingham Palace for twenty-five years, symbolically left, bolt upright, staunch, and seemingly unmoved, in the back of her car for her new home at Marlborough House. The Associated Press announced that, as of that date, the king had given $1 million worth of jewels to Wallis and that $50,000 worth of silver-fox furs had been imported by a British company from Julius Greene of New York as his gift to the royal mistress. On October 11 the king officially took up residence for the first time at Buckingham Palace. He hated the endless marble corridors and enormous gloomy rooms, setting up his private headquarters in the eighteenth-century Belgian Suite. Furnished with Louis XIV and Chippendale antiques, the suite overlooked the East Terrace and the palace gardens. From Paris the king, through the good offices of the still loyal ambassador, Sir George Clerk, acquired Maxim's reigning chef. Summoned to his first audience, M. Legros was instructed to prepare the simplest menus for Wallis and the king. The monarch and Wallis would have toast and tea with lemon and a one-egg omelette for breakfast, tea and an apple for lunch, and grilled steak or sole with melon and cheese for dinner. Legros threw up his hands in despair.

The king called in the proprietors of the London newspapers and succeeded in obtaining from them the promise that Wallis's imminent divorce hearing at Ipswich would be treated with the utmost discretion in the press. However, the American press was unrestricted, and by the second week of October every hotel in the Suffolk town was crammed with reporters from the major American cities. As a result, representatives of European newspapers had to find rooms in nearby villages.

During her brief stay at Cumberland Terrace before moving to Suffolk, Wallis was under royal protection. On October 20 she went to her hairdresser, Antoine, of Dover Street. Inspector Storrier had placed her brand-new Buick, the exact copy of the monarch's that had been ordered in January, behind Cumberland Terrace; but this feeble attempt to hide her departure from the house failed, and crowds were waiting when she emerged. She was followed by car and bicycle to the hairdressing salon, and when she ran, looking flushed and uncomfortable, into the car to make the journey to her bank, the inspector had to clear the sidewalk for her. That night Wallis moved to a cottage at

Felixstowe, near Ipswich, an uninspiring residence overlooking a pebble-strewn beach and a slate-gray sea. The king disappeared from a shooting party at Sandringham to make her welcome, leaving his brother-in-law the Earl of Harewood and Sir Samuel Hoare to continue without him. Wallis's companions were her old friends George and Kitty Hunter, whom she had known from her earliest days in London and whose Mayfair flat she and the king had used for romantic evenings. Wallis was under the constant guard of David Storrier. The king visited her one more time during that difficult week of waiting.*

On October 23 the king went to London to have dinner with his mother at Marlborough House. He found her quietly distraught at the prospect of his marriage to Wallis should the divorce from Ernest Simpson go through. It proved impossible to sway her in the matter. The hearing in Ipswich was set for Saturday the twenty-fourth. Wallis had a sleepless night on Friday. She paced the floor of her room at Felixstowe, tortured by many thoughts. She was not happy about losing Ernest; nor was she happy at the prospect of being forced to become queen. She would have been content to have retained the role of royal mistress, like Mrs. Fitzherbert in the reign of King George IV or Mrs. Keppel in the reign of King Edward VII. In her reckless pursuit of power, position, and money, in her cool, dominating exercise of power, she had gotten out of her depth. Where was this plan that she had engineered going to lead her?

To prolong Wallis's agony, her case was postponed from Saturday until Tuesday, the twenty-seventh of October. The judge had too full a calendar of minor malfeasances, including rabbit poaching, to deal with her all-important matter, and, suffering from a bad cough and cold and the worst of tempers, Mr. Justice Hawke was in no mood to set her case out of the natural sequence. While Wallis went through the torments of the damned at Felixstowe, the Ipswich bars overflowed

---

*Simultaneously, an anonymous representative of Prime Minister Stanley Baldwin engaged the services of Washington, D.C., attorney Raymond Neudecker to investigate the records of Wallis's 1927 divorce from Win Spencer. Evidently, the prime minister, who was already opposed to any thought of the king's marrying Wallis, was determined to find some evidence of irregularities in the 1927 hearings. However, Aubrey Weaver, her attorney of the time at Front Royal, succeeded in having Judge Peck Alexander of Warrenton seal the files on the case. It is possible Wallis prearranged this. The files remained inaccessible until the present author obtained them in 1986.

with heavy-drinking reporters who were becoming increasingly irritable and frustrated. At last, the time arrived: 2:15 on the afternoon of October 27, 1936. Mr. Justice Hawke was ushered in by two military trumpeters playing a fanfare on their silver instruments. Ironically, the musicians were drawn from the band of the Coldstream Guards, in which Ernest Simpson had served in World War I. A uniformed marshal in black and scarlet announced the bewigged judge, who was coughing and blowing his nose into an outsize handkerchief. Wallis, looking extremely pale and exhausted in a small navy blue felt hat and double-breasted coat and skirt of matching blue, made her way from the Buick through the crowd to the witness stand. She was accompanied by Norman Birkett, in his famous shabby wig and enormous horn-rimmed glasses, and his "second," the chubby, red-faced Walter Frampton. Ernest was not present, nor was he represented by counsel; his solicitor, North Lewis, was, however, present.

Hawke, looking grim, his mouth a hard, resistant line in his red and heavily jowled face, spoke in a muffled voice for the next several minutes through his linen handkerchief and a blizzard of coughs and sneezes. This was scarcely helpful to Wallis's already frazzled nerves. She stood with her right blue kid glove already removed to take the oath. Her American accent struck an incongruous note in the drab, ultra-British courtroom. Although her hands were kept firmly from trembling by her will, she betrayed her tension in a characteristic gesture, flicking her tongue around her mouth.

Under oath, questioned by her counsel, she told of her happy marriage with Ernest until the fall of 1934, when he would leave for weekends. She described an episode that took place on Christmas day, 1934, in which she found a note on her dressing table in a woman's handwriting. She didn't say what was in it, and it was handed to the judge. It was an almost certainly manufactured two-page letter from Mary Raffray thanking Ernest for a gift of roses. Wallis said it had caused her "considerable distress."

She went on to say that at Easter of the present year, she had found a letter on identical blue stationery intended for her husband. She improbably asserted that Mary Raffray had written this love note to Ernest from the south of France and a simple letter to Wallis and had "accidentally" put them into the wrong envelopes.

Two waiters who had worked at the Hôtel de Paris in Bray stated that on July 22 and July 23, 1936, they had served breakfast in bed to Ernest and Mary Raffray, "Miss Buttercup." Norman Birkett stood and asked the judge for a decree nisi. Hawke, visibly in a bad temper, had interrupted Wallis's testimony several times for no particular reason except his obvious distaste for her. He did not respond immediately to Birkett's request. Wallis cast the barrister an anxious glance. "I assume what your Lordship has in mind," said Birkett. "What is it I have in mind?" the judge snapped. "That this is ordinary hotel evidence," Birkett said. "But the lady's name has been divulged in the petition to My Lord, and notice was served on her." The judge then said, "I suppose I must come to the conclusion that there was adultery in this case. Very well, decree nisi." It would be six months more before there was a decree absolute.

Wallis, surrounded by police who had been sent on royal instructions from Scotland Yard to shield her from the photographers, walked nervously and quickly down the stairs and into her car. The ordeal had taken less than nineteen minutes. She hadn't even had to face an audience in the public gallery. The king had had it cleared. He had not instructed the newspaper owners in vain. There was scarcely a mention of the granting of the divorce decree in the British press. The king, who was at Buckingham Palace that night, called Wallis to congratulate her.*

That night, the king presented a pleased Wallis with an engagement ring. She had heard of the fabled Mogul emerald, one of the finest stones of its kind, whose provenance went back to the ancient rulers of India. She had to have it, and the king had contacted the great jeweler, Jacques Cartier, in Paris to obtain it for her. Cartier had undertaken a worldwide search, which led him and his spies to Baghdad. There, a syndicate was prepared to sell the stone for a substantial price. It was brought to London by courier after being exquisitely set by the Cartier specialists. According to one version of the story then in circulation, the king declared that the price was too high and that he would pay only half of it. Whereupon Cartier withdrew the emerald, cut it in half, and presented the smaller stone to the monarch.

---

*In a bizarre coincidence, on exactly the same day Win Spencer was divorced by his second wife, Miriam, in San Diego, California. She charged him with cruelty, desertion, drunkenness, and breaking up the furniture in their home.

Wallis returned to Cumberland Terrace, which had been prepared for her by her cook and housemaid. The movers, Carter Patterson, had brought over much of her furniture from Bryanston Court, including many of her things from China; in addition, the king had sent over many royal possessions including sumptuous furnishings, mirrors, bed linens, china, and silverware. That night Wallis dined with the king at her home. He told her of a very unsettling incident that had taken place. A few days before the divorce, Prime Minister Baldwin had turned up at Fort Belvedere in his tiny black car and, after much meaningless talk, had gotten down to business and asked the monarch to persuade Wallis to abandon the proceedings. Wallis was appalled. Not only did she not intend to marry the king, but she was, for all her boldness, not prepared for a full-scale confrontation and conflict with the prime minister of England. Little did she foresee the storm that lay immediately ahead.

10

Abdication

E ven now, Wallis continued to sleep with Guy Trundle. It was one thing to cuckold a prince; it was quite another to cuckold a king. In a direct reference to this, on June 13, 1938, Sir Edward Peacock told U.S. ambassador Joseph P. Kennedy that Wallis was sleeping with a "young man" throughout the reign and that this "embittered the Cabinet more than ever."

Wallis was in the Distinguished Strangers' Gallery to see the king open his first Parliament. He addressed his audience directly from the throne. His speech reviewed events and legislation during the past session. He referred to the coronation, the Imperial Conference, the treaty of alliance with Egypt, the International Conference at Montreux, the tragic events in Spain, the grave concern caused by hostilities between Japan and China, the bilateral naval agreements between England and Germany, and the strengthening of the defense forces. He also mentioned the continued growth of trade, employment problems, the Physical Training and Recreation Act, progress in slum clearance, improved conditions of work in factories, defense loans, and the subsidies to shipping. He announced he would proceed immediately to India after the ceremonies and would repeat the lavish Delhi Durbar in which his parents had been proclaimed Emperor and Empress of India in 1911. This was clearly a symbolic revelation of his continuing concern with empire; it tacitly reaffirmed the views of enlightened commentators that his main concern in appeasing Mussolini and Hitler was to keep open the traditional trade routes to the East.

Count Grandi recalled in 1986:

At a ceremony connected with the opening of Parliament, I stood talking to the king and to the archbishop of Canterbury. As I walked in, I heard people applauding me. The archbishop said to me, "You do realize, Sir, the applause is for your person and not for the country you represent." To which I replied, "But I am not a person, I am my country and its flag." To which, the king then responded, "Well said! Well said!"

This publicly stated expression of support for Mussolini was discreetly left unmentioned by the ever-loyal British press. Grandi continued, "The Prince of Wales reassured me, 'There will never be a war between Italy and England.'"

An ominous rainstorm swept away all plans for the procession of the monarch from Buckingham Palace to Parliament and back again. The king celebrated the occasion by sending a four-foot-high basket of flowers to Wallis, composed of her beloved white chrysanthemums, pink and red roses, and sprays of autumn leaves. It arrived by the truck of a company granted the royal warrant displaying the lion and the unicorn and was followed an hour later by an identical truck with a supply of liquor and nonalcoholic drinks. By this stage the king was probably beyond caring whether anybody noticed or photographed these conveyances or not.

He was almost certainly equally indifferent to the fact that people might notice the house Wallis occupied was being furnished bit by bit with silver, pictures, mirrors, and even china from Buckingham Palace and Fort Belvedere. It is questionable whether the king had the right to make presents of these family heirlooms to Wallis or anyone else. Later, many of these items would be removed to his and Wallis's residences in France. Simultaneously, records show that he had paid jewelers over £100,000 of his savings from the Duchy of Cornwall to supply Wallis with her beloved gems. There were those who felt that this extravagance was in direct contradiction of his apparent concern for the sufferings of the British working class in the depths of the Depression.

On November 6 Wallis caused a ripple in the audience at Covent Garden when, in emeralds, black satin, and green-and-brocade, she sat with the Channons, Lady Diana Cooper, and Sir Victor Warrender, former vice-chamberlain and comptroller of King George V's household, in Emerald Cunard's box. She seemed unabashed by the attention. That week was saddened by the departure to Berlin of Prince Otto and

Princess Ann-Mari von Bismarck; the farewell parties went on and on. Hitler had decided to replace the prince with Ribbentrop, probably influenced by the fact that Bismarck was still under constant surveillance by the Secret Intelligence Service and Sir Robert Vansittart.

Aunt Bessie arrived in November to give Wallis moral support. On November 12 the king went to Portland harbor to inspect the home fleet from the decks of the flagship *Nelson*. Floods plunged the royal train into two feet of water, and the driver at the wheel of the royal Buick could barely plough through the drenched, badly drained streets of the seaside town. Rain poured down all afternoon as the king boarded the aircraft carrier *Courageous* and made the inspections, soaked to the skin, refusing both raincoat and umbrella. He returned to Fort Belvedere in a good mood on the night of the thirteenth. He embraced Aunt Bessie and Wallis, only to be called away by a couriered message from Buckingham Palace. He did not disclose its contents to Wallis until the following afternoon. The note was from Alexander Hardinge. Hardinge issued a dire warning. He said that there was only a matter of days before the press would break its promise of silence on the subject of Wallis. He went on to state that Prime Minister Baldwin and members of the cabinet were meeting that day to discuss the situation and that they might resign. It would be difficult for the king to form another government; the only remaining alternative would be a dissolution of Parliament and a general election, resulting in considerable damage to the Crown. It would be best, to avoid this circumstance, if Wallis were asked to go abroad.

The Hardinges had been plotting this maneuver from the very beginning. The king responded with anger. When Wallis said she would be happy to leave the country, he told her she would do no such thing and said that nothing would stop him from marrying her. She begged him to change his mind. He would not. He said to her that if the government would not approve the marriage, he would be ready to leave the throne. She began to cry. She told him it was madness to think along those lines. He was adamant. He would immediately consult with Sir Samuel Hoare and Duff Cooper, and he would summon the prime minister. Wallis agreed to stay. It was a decision she lived to regret.

———

On November 16 the king left for a tour of the South Wales coalfields, one of the grimmest areas of the British Isles, where severe unemployment and poverty had existed for many years. Welcomed wherever he went, possessed of a burning concern to improve the local conditions, he greatly upset his cabinet by making the public statement, "Something should be done." Not only were kings discouraged from doing such things as dabbling in international politics and marrying twice-divorced women, they were not supposed to express their opinions to their ministers in the matter of social reform.

Nor were they supposed to take their mistresses on the royal train. In her memoirs *Three-Cornered Heart* (New York: Viking, 1971), the wealthy American socialite Anne Fremantle recorded a conversation she had with the lord lieutenant of Monmouthshire in which he expressed his shock that Wallis was in bed with the king in the sleeping car. Later, she and her husband discussed the matter with the archbishop of Canterbury, who told them that the act of illicit sexual intercourse on the royal train would preclude forever the possibility he would preside over the couple's marriage at Westminster Abbey or anywhere else. Beside this, the king's habit of knocking on the doors of depressing miners' cottages with the words, "I am the king. May I come in?" seemed only mildly shocking.

On the third day of the tour, Wallis left the train and hastened back to London by car. She had been asked to a lunch meeting with the radical right-wing Esmond Harmsworth, son of the newspaper tycoon Lord Rothermere, owner of the *Daily Mail*, who would soon be her neighbor in the south of France, at Claridges Hotel.

Harmsworth suggested to Wallis that she should abandon any idea of being queen; she reassured him that no such thought had ever been on her mind. He recommended to her the idea of a morganatic marriage, which would keep her in England—an advantage from several points of view. There had been precedents in British history. Should such an arrangement be made, Wallis would be entitled to be a duchess or to receive another title. However, she would not be permitted to be included in the Civil List in terms of her personal income; should she have heirs, they would not be entitled to any part of the royal inheritance. Nor could the children of the marriage inherit the throne itself.

Wallis was surprised and intrigued by the suggestion. She left the matter open at the end of the luncheon, giving no opinion but at the same time by no means rejecting the idea. That was as good as saying that she accepted it.

When the monarch returned from the Welsh mines for a party at the Channons', Wallis asked him whether he would accept Harmsworth's idea. He responded adversely, but in a subsequent discussion with Harmsworth he began to show some interest. However, when he summoned Baldwin to Buckingham Palace to discuss the matter, the prime minister made it clear that the obstacles to such an arrangement would be formidable, perhaps insurmountable. A morganatic marriage would have to go through very difficult channels. The cabinet would have to approve it; special legislation would have to be passed in the form of a parliamentary bill. And Baldwin, who presumably thought it impolitic to mention the fact, no doubt bore in mind the potential danger in such an idea emanating from a highly questionable political source. This danger was known in the inner circles in Whitehall, but judiciously never mentioned in print.

According to the diaries of Chips Channon, another incident occurred that week. The king called for the Duke of Kent and the Duke of Gloucester and told them that he was going to marry Wallis. Kent was supposed to have exclaimed, "What will she call herself?" "What do you think, the Queen of England of course," the king allegedly replied. And he added, "Yes, and Empress of India, the whole bag of tricks." Kent and Gloucester were flabbergasted.

During the crisis one of the few supportive figures upon whom the king and Wallis could rely was Walter Monckton, who continued as attorney general to the Duchy of Cornwall, which associated him directly with an important source of the monarchical income. In view of the fact that the king was obsessed with money and terrified that he might lose substantial moneys were he to abdicate the throne, Monckton's support of him was crucial. Bespectacled, somewhat scholarly in appearance, Monckton had the look of a don who spent a lifetime in smoke-filled common rooms, but when his vivid, humorous, and heartfelt smile illuminated his ascetic face, he became another person entirely. He was, above all, steadfast and loyal, a rare example of a humanist lawyer; a royalist to his fingertips, he was deeply concerned with the king's welfare and clearly refused to believe Vansittart's and Hadinge's suspicions of Wallis as a Nazi contact.

Day after day in the last week of November, the king summoned

Monckton to Buckingham Palace, a procedure that involved an almost cloak-and-dagger series of movements. The king was determined that Monckton should not say anything that could be overheard by Hardinge, who was, he felt, spying constantly for Vansittart and whose offices adjoined the monarch's Belgian Suite on the ground floor. Under instruction, Monckton had to park his car at the back of the palace and then take the Privy Purse Entrance and ascend by elevator to the top floor. From there, he had to walk across the vast building to the front and then take another elevator which descended directly into the Belgian Suite. This subterfuge was useless, since members of the palace staff reported on Monckton's every movement to Hardinge, who pointedly one evening invited him to his office for a drink.

In his supposedly secret meetings with Monckton, the king made clear that nothing would shake him in his complete emotional, physical, and mental involvement with Wallis. Monckton saw at once that any argument with his old friend was totally pointless. "If they want someone exactly like my father, they can have the Duke of York," the king said, hinting that he was fully prepared to abdicate in his brother's favor.

Monckton could not help but respect the king's extraordinary devotion, which went beyond his love of empire and his desire to be in a position of power. Furthermore, Monckton had the greatest respect for Wallis. He knew that she had caused the king to stop his heavy drinking, had cut down his smoking, and had insisted he keep up his former level of physical fitness. He also knew, as Winston Churchill did, that whereas the king had been miserable, neurotic, and tortured before he met Wallis, he was now released from the bondage of his sexual and emotional problems and was a fulfilled and confident man. In the face of such a transformation, how could the monarch's gratitude be in any way limited by considerations of duty, honor, and state?

Monckton issued sage advice: he suggested to the king that he should not take any drastic action until the decree absolute of the divorce in April 1937. The coronation would soon follow, when a decision could be made more prudently and from a position of greater power. However, the king replied that this was out of the question. He could not go through a major religious ceremony as head of church and state and the Commonwealth while he had in mind that the oaths of office could soon be rendered invalid by a decision to proceed with his wedding in defiance of world opinion and the cabinet. As Lord

Birkenhead wrote in his life of Monckton, "[The king] hated and was repelled by the thought of being crowned under false pretenses." Monckton was impressed that the king was not prepared to be dishonest, however much he might be disrupting protocol and even the royal course of duty.

On this basis, Monckton felt confident in seeking to achieve a compromise between 10 Downing Street and the palace. His was no easy task. Nor was he helped by the fact that Queen Mary was tortured over the situation and appalled by the thought that her eldest son might abdicate, leaving the throne to her second son, Albert, who, shy, physically frail, and completely lacking in public charisma, would be extremely uncomfortable in high office. She was not without humor in the circumstances. As one of her meetings with Baldwin, on the fifteenth of November, she said, "This is a pretty kettle of fish!" The Duke and Duchess of York were extremely uneasy during the crisis. The duchess, still deeply dissatisfied with the very presence of Wallis on the scene, would have preferred to have her dislodged completely, but clearly that was an impossibility. She did not relish the idea of her frail husband experiencing the pressures and strains of being king. The Dukes of Kent and Gloucester were also tortured by the thought of a possible abdication.

Winston Churchill decided that Wallis had to go. ("That bitch!" he later called her.) In what he believed to be the best interests of the king and in an attempt to save the throne, he connived a plot to drive Wallis out of England. In this, he was, according to his later secretary, Sir John Colville, aided and abetted by Lord Beaverbrook, owner of the London *Daily Express*. Beaverbrook, who had been en route to a proposed vacation in Arizona, returned abruptly at the royal request but then proceeded to double-cross his monarch in the most abject manner. Sir John Colville confirmed that Beaverbrook pretended to offer the king his support, which amounted to little more than the discretion of his newspaper in dealing with the crisis, while a member of his staff cooked up a bomb plot, supposedly emanating from Amsterdam, in which a paid Australian assassin would murder Wallis. The same man arranged for threatening letters to be sent to her saying that vitriol would be thrown in her face, a substance which would scar and blind her for life.

At the same time Kenneth de Courcy, friend of the king and Wallis, stepped in. He was honorary secretary to the Imperial Policy Group, a royalist entity founded in 1934 by Sir Reginald Mitchell-Bank that included among its members such figures as Lord Mansfield, Lord Bertie of Thame, Alan Lennox Boyd, the Earl of Glasgow, Sir Charles Petrie, and Lord Phillimore. In those years, the IPG had sought at every level of government to convince the governments of France, Italy, Austria, and Spain that, despite official pronouncements, Britain's actual if secret foreign policy was to keep out of all European conflicts in order to give a free hand to Hitler and Mussolini against the Soviet Union. Needless to say, this rash disclosure ensured a more binding relationship between de Courcy, the king, and Wallis, while greatly irritating both Vansittart and Hardinge. De Courcy was close to George and Kitty Hunter, those early friends of Wallis when she had first come to London. The Hunters got wind (probably from information supplied by Sir Robert Vansittart) of the proposed assassination plot against Wallis. De Courcy remembered in 1987 that he brought word of the plot to Aunt Bessie at Cumberland Terrace. The frightened Bessie burst into tears. "She called the king, who was at Fort Belvedere; he told her not to worry. But Wallis was utterly terrified when she received the news."

One night Wallis screamed, having been awakened suddenly by the sound of breaking glass. Somebody employed by Beaverbrook had tossed a brick through the windows of the house next door. From then on, she spent most of her time in a state of terror between Claridges and Fort Belvedere, and Scotland Yard was instructed by the king to double her protection.

By November 29 Wallis was on the verge of a nervous breakdown. Even Aunt Bessie's presence could not soothe her jangled nerves. When friends, headed by Sibyl Colefax, came to see her, she was on the edge of tears. At last she realized that in her reckless ambition she might well have ruined her own cause. The king burst into hysterical rages, condemning her enemies and protesting his undying love of her. There was an ominous event on November 30: the Crystal Palace, site of many major exhibitions and a notable London landmark, burst into flames and was reduced to rubble. The sky over London was a portentous blazing red. Wallis began to think seriously about leaving England. But she was too ill at Fort Belvedere to even consider doing anything for the time being. She mentioned possibly returning to the

United States; the king said he would follow her on the next ship. On November 30 she wrote to her friend Foxy Gwynne that her heart had been acting up and she wasn't having any callers. She would remove herself and only return when "that damned crown has been firmly placed."

On December 1 the Right Reverend A. W. F. Blunt, bishop of Bradford, made a speech at the annual diocesan conference. He invoked the grace of God to inspire the king to do his duty faithfully. He expressed the hope that the king was aware of his need of God's grace; then he added, "Some of us wish he gave more positive signs of such awareness." He criticized the statement by the bishop of Birmingham that the coronation should be attended by a wide range of clergymen. He suggested that in the present situation the religious significance of the coronation ceremony would literally be endangered. The floodgates were opened to adverse comment in newspapers throughout the nation. Despite the king's supposed control of the press, a number of editorials sternly reminded him of the sacred trust of his high duty. It was clear that he had not succeeded in persuading the newspaper owners to follow his line of thought; they were too mindful of their readers' Christian sentiments and concern with moral values.

Baldwin even went to the extent of failing to send the king the minutes of the cabinet meetings at which the crisis was discussed. When the king opened the red dispatch box, all he could find was an obscure document about arms to Spain. However, he had a spy in the cabinet, who informed him that Baldwin had totally written off the morganatic marriage proposal at the last cabinet meeting without even attempting to present it to Parliament. The prime minister had forced through the decision that either the government must accept Wallis as queen or the king must abdicate. It was following this meeting that a full-scale constitutional crisis broke over England.

On the evening of December 3 the Duke and Duchess of York arrived at Fort Belvedere for a most urgent discussion on what would happen if the king were to abdicate within twenty-four hours. That same night Baldwin met the king, who drove to Buckingham Palace for a stormy encounter in which the monarch made clear that he would not budge an inch. The next day the high commissioners for Canada, Australia, and South Africa put enormous pressure on the king. Headed by the Australian commissioner, who represented the strictly Roman Catholic prime minister, Joe Lyons, the commissioners made it clear that the dominions would never accept Wallis as queen or even as morganatic wife. She herself longed to withdraw; she hated to be rejected. Even Canadian high commissioner Vincent Massey, whose brother, the actor Raymond Massey, was an old poker-playing friend of Wallis's and the king's, was obliged to convey the grimmest warnings to the palace. In each of the Commonwealth countries, the newspapers were blunt in their outright assault upon the issue. This was grievously distressing to Wallis and to the king, who had been perfectly happy to have Baldwin throw open the issue to the empire. It was clear that, hour by hour, his position was becoming increasingly untenable, and by December 3 all the costly and elaborate preparations for the coronation came to a standstill.

The Duke of York was overcome by the horror of what was to come. He detested the idea of being king as much as his older brother had, and began talking loosely about abdicating in advance and (passing over his dull brother, the Duke of Gloucester) throwing open to plebiscite the idea of the inescapable Duke of Kent as successor—still the wild card in the royal pack. Kent, endlessly flying to Munich to maintain his Nazi connections through his brother-in-law Count Toerring, was mooted for years for all kinds of thrones—Romania, Greece, Hungary, Poland—the list was long.

Like it or not, and afraid of the effect on his health and even his reason, York had to face a ghastly future of ritual and responsibility. Returning from a trip to Scotland by train on December 3, he saw at the railway station newspaper placards glaringly announcing the dreaded words, THE KING'S MARRIAGE. He drove straight to his mother Queen Mary in a state of nerves and she did her best to remind him sternly of his necessary future. He left her in near-suicidal despair. At another meeting six days later, he broke down, knelt before her, and sobbed in her lap like a child.

There was a flurry on the postage stamp market as thousands of people rushed to buy complete sets of the commemorative issue in the event that the stamps should be rendered obsolete within the week and thus increase considerably in value. Simultaneously, the king's friends in Berlin supported him once again. On Hitler's express instructions, Dr. Goebbels issued a communiqué forbidding any German newspaper or radio station to even mention the constitutional crisis. Hitler was deeply disturbed by the situation; he was counting upon the king to maintain a special relationship with Germany in the future. Similarly, Mussolini was most disappointed, and Count Grandi in London conveyed that disappointment to the monarch. When these positions of the newly formed Axis powers appeared in the American press, it was of no help to the king's cause in Whitehall.

Day and night throughout the crisis, meetings were held by the Imperial Policy Group. Kenneth de Courcy recalled the extreme tension among the members of the group as they tried to find some way through the mesh of problems involved. A preliminary meeting of interested and influential peers and members of Parliament was held in the London house of de Courcy's mother, and subsequent meetings were held at de Courcy's office in Old Queen Street. The group sent representations to the bishop of London, to Lord Salisbury, and to Walter Monckton in efforts to ameliorate the situation. The purpose was clear: the group wanted to force the king to call upon the government to resign or, at the very least, to pressure it into a position from which it would have to resign. The king would then send for Winston Churchill—who himself knew nothing of the plan—to form a new government; the IPC was convinced there were enough individuals in both the House of Commons and the House of Lords to achieve its purpose. De Courcy believed that Churchill would have swept into power with an overwhelming majority. He would immediately have achieved massive public support and would have put Britain on a much firmer footing vis-à-vis Germany and Mussolini.

However, the IPC was doomed to failure. Monckton proved obstructionist. A major problem was that Thomas Dugdale, MP, informed de Courcy and another member, Lord Mansfield, that there was a flaw in Wallis's divorce case which might make the decree absolute impossible; he also informed his visitors that the Secret Intelligence Service had a case against Wallis which, if they could see the dossier, would entirely change their attitude: a direct reference to the Chinese file, Grégoire, and Wallis's Italian and German links. Should the Secret Intelligence Service suspect Wallis was a Nazi contact, they must prepare to deliver this fatal trump card at the right moment; the group's entire case for the royal marriage and the accession of Winston Churchill to the premiership would collapse.

Faced with this revelation, de Courcy and the Imperial Policy Group felt understandably weakened in their resolve. Furthermore,

Monckton failed to convey their purpose to the king. Either he felt that they were too maverick and unreliable or he was by now sensing that the monarch was quite ready—or would even prefer—to depart from his sacred office; or he may have got wind of the plot against Wallis and feared that if Churchill did assume the premiership she would have no chance of becoming either queen or morganatic wife.

Wallis's and the king's meetings at the time were gloomy with foreboding. Geoffrey Dawson's powerful London *Times* was harshly assailing her. One evening, as the couple walked around the flagstone path at Fort Belvedere, a damp English fog crawling up from Virginia Water, the king explained to her that there was no middle way: it was either abdication or permanent separation. Wallis was beyond exhaustion, beyond being able to endure any more. She began to make arrangements to leave the country, and in London her staff was under instruction to pack up her belongings.

Wallis now wished she had left when the first inklings of disaster reached her. On Saturday, December 3, she made arrangements to move to Herman and Katherine Rogers's villa at Cannes; by long-distance telephone the Rogerses had agreed, as so often before, to provide her with safety and refuge. The king told her that he had elected to supply her with a companion and bodyguard for the journey, the slight, subdued (and very rich) Peregrine ("Perry"), Fourth Baron Brownlow. He was reliable, devoted, and a dear and trusted friend. The royal chauffeur George Ladbroke would drive them to Newhaven, where they would embark for the French port of Dieppe. In view of the leave taken by Inspector Storrier, Inspector Evans of Scotland Yard would be her official protector. Wondering whether she would be killed en route, Wallis hastily increased her jewelry insurance and drew up a will in her bedroom at Fort Belvedere, leaving most of her possessions to Aunt Bessie, her two devoted maids, and a few personal friends. Her solicitor George Allen assisted her with the document, which was written on blue Fort Belvedere stationery. In the late afternoon the king, with the assistance of Winston Churchill, Walter Monckton, and others, was at the fort finishing work on his abdication broadcast. Wallis left so hurriedly there was barely time to say good-bye to the king (who gave her a ladybug bracelet charm with the message "Fly Away Home"), Aunt Bessie, and her personal staff. To her great distress, she had to leave behind her dog, Slipper. In anguish, white with tension, she kissed the king and held him close. He told her she must wait for him no matter how long it would be. He would never give her up.

Her car moved out into the fog. Passage had been booked for her and Brownlow under the names of "Mr. and Mrs. Harris." In the wake of Wallis's departure for the Channel ferry, the king drove to Buckingham Palace to meet with Baldwin. He told him about the broadcast and placed the text in his hands. Meanwhile, Wallis refused to slow down her departure, despite the increasing fog. Wrapped in sables against the cold, she sat staring grimly into the night. The ferry left at 10 p.m. She knew there would be no sleep. During the journey she urged Lord Brownlow to find a way to have the king forget the marriage completely, end the crisis, and retain his throne. Clearly, she had in mind returning at some stage after the coronation to take up the position of royal mistress.

The fog continued during the Channel crossing and into France. Wallis and Brownlow checked into the Hôtel de la Poste in Blois on the French side at 11 a.m. on December 4. She took a room for a few hours and lay down on the bed. According to Lord Brownlow, she felt a twinge of loneliness and asked him to lie on the second bed in her room to keep her company. She cried, he recalled, with "primeval" pain. He took her hand gently but the tears would not stop.

On December 5, to avoid the reporters who had gotten wind of her movements and pursued her from the coast, Wallis was forced to abandon a plan to go to Paris to see Lady Mendl because it was clear that she would be intercepted by newspapermen. She was still terrified of assassination. Ladbroke took a circuitous route south, to make sure that there was no danger. They traveled through Evreux in Normandy. At the old coaching inn in that town, the Hôtellerie du Grand-Cerf, she asked Brownlow to put in a telephone call to Fort Belvedere. She had made a prearrangement with the king to use code names in case she was overheard. After a long wait, Brownlow succeeded in getting through. Wallis could barely hear the king's voice through a buzz of static. She said, "On no account is Mr. James to step down." In other words, the king must not abdicate. She went on, "You must get advice. You must bring in your old friends. See Duff Cooper; talk to Lord Derby; talk to the Aga Khan.* Do nothing rash. I will go to South

---

*All these names were given in code.

America or somewhere." It was so difficult for the king to hear her that she was forced to scream the words. When she left the inn, she was horrified to find she had left her notes for the conversation in the telephone booth. Brownlow warned her that if she returned to retrieve them she would be recognized. It was a miracle that she had not been recognized yet. So she decided in a state of great distress to leave the notes behind. A considerate manager locked them up in his office safe, apparently not even yielding to the temptation to read them. The following year they were retrieved for her by Harold Nicolson.

Back in England, the increasingly discredited Sir Oswald Mosley scarcely helped the king's cause by stating that he was entirely in the king's support and that the abdication issue should be submitted to the people for a referendum. This announcement only lent strength to Baldwin and to Sir Robert Vansittart and Alexander Hardinge. On December 5 Winston Churchill sent a memorandum to the king from his home, 11 Morpeth Mansions, advising him that he should not leave the country under any circumstances and that no final decision should be made until after Christmas, probably February or March. The archbishop of Canterbury that same day urged "silence and caution" in the matter of the crisis until the decision of the king be made public.

According to a diary kept by Mrs. Thomas Dugdale, wife of Baldwin's parliamentary under secretary, the king "was in a very nervous condition, threatening to do some violence to himself." Geoffrey Dawson's *Times* was thundering more loudly than ever. The prime minister, accompanied by Dugdale, had driven down that day through the fog to Fort Belvedere to confer with the king yet again. That same day Baldwin held a special cabinet meeting at 10 Downing Street. Crowds stood in the driving rain as the ministers got out of their cars and walked into the brightly lit house. Sir Samuel Hoare came first; he was followed by the chancellor of the Exchequer Neville Chamberlain, Sir Kingley Wood, Duff Cooper, and Anthony Eden, among others. As they left the building hecklers greeted them, shouting "Edward's right. Baldwin's wrong!" Hundreds more swarmed outside the gates of Buckingham Palace, yelling: "We want Edward!" A group appeared at the Piccadilly house of the Duke and Duchess of York, chanting in unison, "We want Eddie and we want his Missus!" A band of women marched from Marble Arch to the palace with huge banners upon which, in red and blue letters, was the slogan: "After South Wales you cannot let him down. Come to the Palace and cheer him. Let the king know we are with him." Later in the afternoon the crowd outside the palace began singing, "For he's a jolly good fellow!" Two hundred stood at the corner of Whitehall and Downing Street after sunset, screaming, "We want our King!" They were rapidly broken up by the police. Meanwhile, Lord Rothermere's papers had on their front pages the enormous headline in black letters, "God Save the King!" The world was breathless; the American ironist H. L. Mencken called it "the greatest news story since the Resurrection."

According to Sir Edward Peacock, in statements at meetings with U.S. ambassador Kennedy in 1938, and according also to the late Sir Dudley Forwood and the late Laura, Duchess of Marlborough, the king began to panic when Peacock pointed out to him the loss of money that would follow after the act of abdication. He might, he feared, lose much of his inheritance, of which Peacock was custodian, since he had no male heir, and any sums due to him under the provisions would have to be accorded him by his brother, who hated Wallis most bitterly.

The Labour Party was particularly anxious for him to reverse the abdication, and the king told Peacock he might consider that, and yield to the idea of morganatic marriage after all. The leading socialist John Strachey approached Claude Cockburn, well-known Irish left-wing editor of *The Week*, an aggressively liberal journal, with an intriguing if mysterious suggestion. He and Lord Louis Mountbatten, a royal cousin, would provide Cockburn with sensational facts, authorized, Strachey said, by the king, that would terminate the abdication and give Cockburn the scoop of a lifetime. The story would be delivered to him on a certain midnight—by a royal motorcyclist sent straight from Fort Belvedere.

Cockburn and his staff waited breathlessly on the king's specific instructions at the appointed hour. But no cyclist arrived, and greatly annoyed, the editor had to put his paper to bed without a lead story. The question is: what was the mysterious and absent journalistic scoop?

Cockburn in his memoirs *A Discord of Trumpets* wrote that he had no idea; his son, the political journalist Alexander Cockburn, remains equally baffled, and the Cockburn papers are inaccessible in storage in Ireland. The most likely solution is that the king knew nothing about the matter; that Mountbatten and Strachey decided to release the story of Wallis's affair with Guy Trundle to Cockburn, sending it by a man disguised as a royal messenger, thus forcing the king to give up any idea of marrying her, and thus keeping him firmly on the throne as the "people's king." Popular with the working classes, he would, they thought, serve the cause of Labour better than that of the Conservatives. But at the last minute the conspirators panicked—and backed off from the plan.

In the meantime, the other members of the royal family remained in seclusion, not leaving their separate houses. The king consistently deferred meeting with his anxious brother York, who realized that huge responsibilities lay just a step away. Sleepless, wretched, the king had no energy to see anyone except his prime minister.

Wallis continued her journey south through France. The weather was appalling, a driving wind blowing a mixture of snow and sleet against the windshield of the Buick. The party breakfasted at the Hôtel de Paris in the town of Moulins. As the group continued, against increasingly hazardous driving conditions, the car became filled with the strong smell of Scotch whiskey. Lord Brownlow, who had thrust a small glass hip flask into his overcoat pocket, had accidentally shattered the bottle and the liquor had drenched him. When he opened the window to release the stench, the snow blew in and he had to close it again.

Wallis and her companions continued to the grim old city of Lyons. The press caught up with the car there, alerted by a pedestrian of whom Brownlow had rashly asked the way. They were chased relentlessly through the city, the pursuing vehicles emitting a deafening sound of Klaxon horns. They managed to flee successfully into Vienne. It was 1:30 p.m. A single reporter, Jean Bouvard of *Paris Soir*, managed to secure an interview with Wallis as she arrived at the Restaurant de la Pyramide. She replied in schoolroom French, scarcely improved since her days at Oldfields, "You French people are very sympathetic but very bothersome. I have not been able to get any sleep for two days. In the last hotel where I stayed last night there were twenty-four newspapermen. I want rest, lots of rest. . . . I can't make any statement. The king is the only judge. I have nothing to say except that I want to be left quiet."

Wallis entered the restaurant through a back door with the aid of an old friend Madame Point, director of the Pyramide. Madame Point arranged a private room on the first floor for lunch. Wallis was able to call the Rogerses and tell them that they could expect her within hours. Madame Point was no fool. She summoned the reporters and told them she was considering changing the name of her restaurant to Mrs. Simpson's.

Wallis achieved her escape from the press in a manner that would have done justice to the Count of Monte Cristo. There was a window above the kitchen sink, which was just large enough for her to squeeze through. In order to do so, she had to climb on the kitchen table while Lord Brownlow and Madame Point held the table. Inspector Evans and Monsieur Pont stood in the alleyway to catch Wallis as she jumped down. They all dashed to the waiting Buick and took off again through driving sleet.

Meanwhile, Wallis's maid Mary Burke had arrived by train at Cannes with Wallis's sixteen trunks and thirty-six suitcases. Wallis stopped again at the town of Brignoles to buy medicine and to phone the Rogerses once again to confirm that indeed she was on the way. Lord Brownlow tried to rouse the occupants of the local post office, but at first there was no response. Then windows burst open and the occupants screamed with fury at him as he asked desperately where a telephone could be found. The group finally located one, and Brownlow, beating at the instrument in helpless rage and screaming down the mouthpiece, at last managed to get through to the Villa Lou Viei.

At 2 a.m. on the sixth, while the king was sleepless and agonized at Fort Belvedere, the Buick at long last arrived at the wrought-iron gates of the Rogerses' villa at Cannes. Hundreds of spectators were waiting, and the car could hardly edge its way through the crowd as the police strove to control the mass hysteria of the people, who had stood for many hours in the rain in expectation of Wallis's arrival. Wallis was on her knees on the car floor, a heavy rug completely concealing her.

When Wallis and Lord Brownlow walked into the hall, the Rogerses greeted them with immense relief. They had been fearful of some incident or fatal collision on the way, and their own stress was almost the equal of Wallis's. Though pale, exhausted, and fragile-looking in her brown hat and three-quarter-length sable coat, Wallis was relieved to note that Mary Burke was safely installed at the house and that the trunks and suitcases had been placed in her suite. There were ladders and pots of paint everywhere because up to that very night painters and electricians had been doing up six bedrooms and bathrooms.

Wallis walked with her host and hostess into the gloomy, damp living room, its dankness barely relieved by a log fire roaring in the grate. She collapsed into a chair.

In London, the mass demonstrations continued. The younger people of England were very much on the king's and Wallis's side. Supporters of the Labour party now found themselves in a curious alliance with the Fascists. In Berlin, the blanket of silence continued. Germans anxious to learn news of the latest developments of the crisis had to obtain newspapers from Austria. Walter Monckton tried a last-ditch stand, recommending that legislation should be passed through Parliament allowing the decree nisi of the divorce to be declared absolute immediately without the necessary six-month waiting period. This idea was rejected out of hand.

When the king drafted a proposed broadcast calling the nation to rally behind him in his love for Wallis, Baldwin refused to permit it. The prime minister again wrote off the question of a morganatic marriage, and he would not agree to change the traditional status of the king's consort to permit Wallis to assume certain privileges. He advised the Commonwealth nations of his position, and they and Dawson's *Times* went along with him in his determination to prevent Wallis from becoming the king's bride. Beaverbrook and Rothermere continued to urge a delay until the matter could be weighed in a more detached spirit, preferably after the coronation. Winston Churchill suggested to the king that he should ask for a brief respite and retreat to Windsor Castle, firmly closing the gate to the prime minister. Then Churchill would send Baldwin a letter urging him not to hurry the king to a decision and stating that it was imperative there be a delay. Even while Churchill began maneuvering in this direction, the king, alone in his bedroom, walking up and down, reached his ultimate decision. He would give up. He could not possibly consider fighting Baldwin. Any delay would only cause more agony to him and to Wallis. He couldn't fight the Commonwealth. He might even be risking civil war. He could no longer rule over a united nation. It would be torn by controversy, anger, and bitterness for the rest of his reign. Moreover, Wallis would not only be in danger if he forced the marriage, her unpopularity among the political parties and the more righteous figures of the Church of England would make her position untenable.

On December 6 Wallis wrote to the king expressing her anxiety that he should not abdicate. She was afraid that if he did so, she would be put "in the wrong light to the entire world because they will say that I could have prevented it." In the course of a long and confused letter, Wallis went on to suggest that the entire matter should somehow be postponed until the autumn of 1937. She suggested that the king should urge Baldwin to agree to the postponement. She repeated that she was "terrified of what the world will say," and she incoherently repeated her idea of the postponement again and again. Even her spelling went to pieces as she wrote of the king making an eight-month sacrifice for his people by holding off from the decision. Part of the reason that she desired the delay was to escape the situation herself; she wrote to Sibyl Colefax at a later date, clearly indicating her continuing need to flee to parts unknown. Her panic was so overpowering she was hysterical, exhausted, devastated by terror. After a sleepless night, the king at last decided on December 7 that he would abdicate. Once he made the choice, he was flooded with relief and happiness. Whereas only two days before he was on the verge of suicide, he knew now in his heart of hearts that he had made the correct decision. The two things that mattered most to him in the world were the British Empire and Wallis. By choosing Wallis, he would save the Commonwealth. He summoned Monckton and said, "I want you go go to London immediately and warn the Prime Minister that when he comes to the Fort this afternoon I shall notify him formally that I have decided to abdicate."

Monckton reminded him of what this step would mean. He told the king that within days he would be no more than a private citizen and, since he intended to go into exile, he would be pursued relentlessly by reporters. Furthermore, he must not see Wallis until her divorce became absolute, or he would risk the possibility that his enemies would bring pressure upon the king's proctor, who was in charge of the decisions in the matter of whether a divorce decree could be passed through as absolute without obstacles.

On the seventh, Winston Churchill appeared in the House of Commons protesting the king's cause, only to be greeted with screams of "Sit down!" and "Shame!" Although Baldwin had lost some of his notes, several of them in the toilet, and dropped others on the floor, banging his head on a table as he rose from picking them up, he recovered himself and gave what was probably the most accomplished speech of his career. He correctly stated the moral and political issues involved, achieving a dignity that even his many enemies were forced to admit was peerless. He was the hero of the hour in the eyes of all except the most fervent Labourites and the Communist member, Willie Gallacher.

Wallis was consumed with guilt and fear. When she got wind of the king's intention to abdicate, she wrote an impassioned letter, insisting that he reconsider her offer to back out of the situation completely. Her enemies, led by the Duke and Duchess of York, Baldwin, Vansittart, and the Hardinges, were convinced she was devising this appeal as a way of securing permanently the monarch's devotion. They refused to believe her sincerity when they learned of the gesture. She sent the letter by air mail, and on the seventh called the king at Fort Belvedere to read him a statement she was issuing to the press; she had been assisted in writing it by Lord Brownlow and Herman Rogers. Unhappily, Wallis offered "to withdraw forthwith from a situation which has been rendered both unhappy and untenable." Lord Brownlow read the statement to a mass of international newspaper reporters at a press conference at the Hôtel Majestic in Cannes. While the statement was being delivered, Associated Press noted: "In her haven of refuge of the Villa Lou Viei, a dim light glowed in Mrs. Simpson's bedroom. Faintly silhouetted against it, a slender figure paced back and forth as the American divorcée awaited the next move—Edward's acceptance, or his refusal to surrender her love even at the cost of his throne." The author of this piece did not realize that the king had already made his decision and that nothing Wallis or anyone else said would shake his inexorable resolve.

On December 5, Winston Churchill wrote to Neville Chamberlain, chancellor of the Exchequer, describing his meeting with the king at dinner at Buckingham Palace the night before. He said that the monarch began the meal in a lighthearted mood but soon succumbed to depression and had two prolonged mental blackouts during which he completely lost the thread of the conversation and was visibly on the edge of a breakdown.

Years later, Sir Edward Peacock told Ambassador Kennedy of a meeting the next day between Prime Minister Baldwin and the king at Fort Belvedere. Baldwin described the meeting to the essayist and biographer Harold Nicolson as tearful and sentimental, with both men dissolving, like Alice in Wonderland, into a pool of tears. Far more convincingly, Baldwin told Peacock that they had had a violent quarrel; when Baldwin pointed out that Wallis wasn't "the type to be queen," the monarch snapped back at him with, "So I can have her as mistress but not as wife. That's fine hypocrisy!" Baldwin had had enough. He shouted, in a direct reference to the China dossier, "If a king wants to sleep with a whore that's his private business. But the empire is concerned if he now make her queen."

The king's reaction to this exchange was to set up even more investments for Wallis in America; he told Peacock he didn't want her to "wind up like Lady Hamilton," the mistress of Lord Horatio Nelson who had died in poverty. When he tried to give Wallis a freehold in certain royal properties, including the New Gallery Cinema in Regent Street, the Criterion Restaurant, His Majesty's Theatre and the Regent Palace and Strand Palace Hotels, Peacock made clear that these were not to be bartered or given away, and that there was no possibility of her acquisition being approved in the houses of Commons and Lords. Furious, the king gave up.

By December 8 the king still had not abdicated. Nor had any public statement been made that he would do so. However, the king's decision had already filtered out through the grapevine. Mosley's Blackshirts again picketed at Buckingham Palace. At the same time, Wallis's solicitor Theodore Goddard decided to fly to Cannes in a last-ditch effort to persuade Wallis to give up the king completely. Baldwin and one of his allies in the crisis, Sir Horace Wilson, were behind Goddard's mission. The king was furious when he learned of it, and he forbade Goddard to go; but Goddard was under prime ministerial orders. Accompanied by Dr. William Kirkwood, his personal physician, who was also a gynecologist, Goddard, despite a heart condition, got into an airplane normally used for official business with a shaky engine that threatened to give out at any minute and undertook a harrowing flight through thunderstorms.

At the same time, the king at last agreed to see his brother the Duke of York, who had arrived at Fort Belvedere without being invited. It was necessary to discuss with that shy and awkward man the responsibilities that would be his within a few days. Both men were desperately weary. Their state of mind was not improved by the equally impromptu arrival of Baldwin, who walked in with Dugdale and Monckton at 5:30 p.m. To the king's horror, Baldwin arrived with a suitcase. The monarch was annoyed to think that the hated prime minister would have the nerve to want to spend the night at the fort. The king had already decided any further discussion was useless. After a meaningless dinner, Baldwin left, pale and depressed, to take his final leave of the king whose moral integrity he had so strenuously tried to preserve.

The king looked fresh and happy that evening. Now that he had made up his mind, he enjoyed his first sound sleep in longer than he could remember. Yet the newspapers continued to say that he had not made up his mind.

At Cannes on the night of the eighth, Wallis received Goddard. Lord Brownlow was furious that he had been sent. Brownlow had made it clear that the gynecologist, Dr. Kirkwood, would not be welcome in the house. The presence of such a person could only give rise to rumor that Wallis was pregnant. Goddard then said to Wallis that she should immediately withdraw the divorce action against Ernest Simpson. If she did that, the crisis would be over. As it turned out, she required little persuasion. In her state of nervous exhaustion, she would have been happy to disappear to New Zealand or Argentina and never be seen again. She replied she would do anything to keep the king on the throne. Goddard expressed his pleasure in her response. Wallis turned to Lord Brownlow for his advice. Brownlow said, "If the King does abdicate, his object will be marriage; for you to scrap your divorce will produce a hopeless climax and an all-round tragedy." However, Wallis was prepared to do what Goddard asked. She tried to reach the fort by telephone. The king could not be reached. He returned her call at noontime. Wallis said to him, "I have agreed to withdraw my divorce petition." The king responded both independently and through the solicitor George Allen that the matter had already progressed beyond the point of rescue. The abdication documents were drawn up. The king said to her, "You can go wherever you want. To China, Labrador or the South Seas. But wherever you go, I will follow you." It was clear now to Wallis that nothing would shake the royal resolve.

Wallis wondered what she should do next. She thought she might go back to Peking. For the time being, she could go to Italy, by special train, to stay with Lord and Lady Berkeley, old friends of hers with a villa in Rome and police protection. Did she think of her old lover, Count Ciano? Still determined to save the situation and bring about some form of marriage, Lord Rothermere asked Esmond Harmsworth, who was then on the Riviera, to intercede with Wallis, but Harmsworth could provide no adequate reason why she should change her mind. Goddard returned defeated to London.

On the morning of December 10 the king held a meeting with his brother York, Monckton, and other advisers on the matter of his financial future. He was entitled to a life interest in Sandringham and Balmoral. The suggestion had been made that he should return these properties to the Crown upon his abdication. However, he did not prove to be cooperative. Instead, he would compel his brother to pay him £25,000 a year in return for his releasing the two residences. He would be required to pay part of the pensions of those retainers at Sandringham and Balmoral whom he had discharged or who were retiring of their own free will or at the appropriate age. Through intermediaries, Baldwin conveyed an even sterner proviso: in return for these financial considerations, the king must never return to England unless he were granted special permission by the government. The implication was that if he refused to obey the request, he might be very restricted in terms of income under the provisions of the Civil List. The king was displeased. The news that he would not receive the income from the Duchy of Cornwall thenceforth was a matter of great distress to him. He had apparently forgotten that an abdicated monarch was not entitled to that emolument. It was stated that he very nearly withdrew the abdication at that moment. But instead he signed the Instrument of Abdication:

I, Edward VIII, of Great Britain, Ireland, and the British Dominions beyond the Seas, King, Emperor of India, do hereby declare My irrevocable determination to renounce the Throne for Myself and for My descendants, and My desire that effect should be given to this Instrument of Abdication immediately.

As the king inscribed his signature on the documents in front of his brothers York, Gloucester, and Kent, he felt marvelous, "like a swimmer surfacing from a great depth," as he wrote in his memoirs.

That same night thirty Fascists, four of whom were in Blackshirt uniforms, were seen in Regent Street. They broke up and proceeded in twos and threes to Buckingham Palace. By 9 p.m. 500 pro-Nazis had joined them. Some 200 youths and girls stood chanting, "We want Edward!" and "One two three four five, we want Baldwin, dead or alive!"

At intervals they gave the Fascist salute, cheered, and sang patriotic songs and the national anthem. Just before ten, several youths, headed by one in Fascist uniform, led 800 demonstrators to 10 Downing Street. Other Fascist demonstrators picketed the House of Commons with placards reading: "Sack Baldwin. Stand by the King!" At the same time, they gave the Fascist salute. Toward midnight the Blackshirts were screaming, "Love live the King! Long live Bessie Warfield!" The next day, according to Scotland Yard reports, 3,000 attended a mass meeting in Stepney at which Sir Oswald Mosley demanded the abdication issue be put to the people. Windows were smashed in Bancroft Road. There was a struggle between Fascists and anti-Fascists in the street.

That same day the king lunched with Winston Churchill, whose existence in the political wilderness was doomed to be extended because of his stern loyalty to his monarch. Churchill helped the king to make some last minute alterations to the abdication speech upon which Walter Monckton had already extensively worked. As Churchill, on the verge of tears, left the house he quoted two lines of a verse: "He nothing common did or mean / Upon that memorable scene . . ." The lines were by the poet Andrew Marvell and referred to the beheading of King Charles I. After lunch the king had a further meeting with the Duke of York, who was seeking to overcome his nervousness once more and his fear that his stammer would handicap him badly when he had to broadcast or make public speeches. York suggested that the king should now assume the title "the Duke of Windsor." The king was delighted with the suggestion and accepted it immediately.

In the late afternoon, Monckton arrived from London, having taken the text of the broadcast to Baldwin for a total rewrite and for his verbal approval. Baldwin asked for the insertion of a sentence saying that he had given the king "every consideration" during the crisis. The king was irritated by the audacity of this request by his archenemy, but felt that in the interest of propriety he should make the inclusion. Before leaving for Windsor Castle to make his 10 o'clock broadcast, the king called Wallis to tell her that he would be going to Switzerland and staying at a hotel near Zurich. Wallis told him she was shocked that the British government would not have provided him with a safe haven where he could be in a state of privacy. If he were in a hotel, he would face the same nightmare she was enduring, a state of being totally under siege. He would never have a minute's peace from press or public.

Instead, at Lady Mendl's suggestion, Lord Brownlow could arrange for him to stay with his old friends the Baron and Baroness Eugene Rothschild at their castle, Schloss Enzesfeld, near Vienna. Wallis said she would call him immediately to make the necessary arrangements.

She did. They at once agreed. Kitty Rothschild, a beautiful American woman, was especially overjoyed by the idea.

Accompanied by his favorite dog, Slipper, the king said good-bye to his staff at Fort Belvedere. The suitcases were carried to the royal Buick. As it swung down the driveway with Ladbroke at the wheel, the king looked back at his beloved fort, realizing he might never see it again. In a few days the furniture would be stored; most of it was to remain in storage for almost a decade. The wrench was painful. The fort had been his home for so long; he had poured so much of his thought and skill into remodeling it, creating an oasis, a haven from the cruel world. He continued to Royal Lodge, Windsor, where his mother, Queen Mary, his brothers, and his sister, the princess royal, were waiting for him. The conversation at dinner was awkward; the Duke of Kent, always highly emotional, broke down and sobbed uncontrollably at the table; the Duke of York was on the verge of tears. As the meal concluded, Monckton arrived to accompany the king to Windsor Castle. Meanwhile, Herman Rogers had managed to reach Monckton and inform him that the Rothschilds would be delighted to have the king as a houseguest.

Ironically, the monarch's old enemy Lord Wigram was now deputy constable and lieutenant governor of Windsor Castle; he impassively greeted the king and Monckton as they entered the great hallway. In the Augusta Tower the director of the British Broadcasting Corporation, Sir John Reith, surrounded by a technical team, was waiting with what was described by one eyewitness as "a basilisk stare." The tower room had been set up as a temporary studio. Then, at 10 p.m., the king spoke, warmly, confidently, released from his torment. He made clear that the decision to abdicate was his and his alone. That the woman he loved had tried to the last minute to persuade him to take a different course. That his brother the Duke of York would take his place on the throne "without interruption or injury to the life and progress of the Empire. And [Winston Churchill's addition] he has one matchless blessing, enjoyed by so many of you and not bestowed on me—a happy home with his wife and children." The king went on to mention, no doubt with a sinking feeling, how the ministers of the Crown, "and in particular Mr. Baldwin," had always treated him with full consideration. He concluded:

> I now quit altogether public affairs, and I lay down my burden. It may be some time before I return to my native land, but I shall always follow the fortunes of the British race and Empire with profound interest, and if at any time in the future I can be found of service to His Majesty in a private station I shall not fail. And now we all have a new king. I wish him, and you, his people, happiness and prosperity with all my heart. God bless you all. God save the King.

With the Rogerses, Wallis listened to the broadcast in the drawing room of the Villa Lou Viei. By her own account, she was quietly grief-stricken, but Katherine Rogers told her friend Fern Bedaux that in fact Wallis flew into a tantrum, shouting with rage and smashing things. She hated the idea of the abdication. She had wanted to be the king's mistress and to keep her husband; she had wanted to be powerful without the burdens of power and the agony of guilt. Raised like so many Americans to believe that the fulfillment of any ambition was possible and that the world was her oyster, she had learned, she wrote, "the dregs of my cup of failure and defeat." She had discovered that a prime minister and a cabinet and a Secret Intelligence Service bent upon her destruction left her no chance, no hope, of survival. Moreover, for the rest of her life she would be accused of destroying her monarch and of bringing down his rule. It was in that knowledge that she went to her room alone for a night of very great pain.

11

Exile

The Duke of Windsor, as he would now be known, though the title was not gazetted until May, had a last meeting with his mother and his three brothers; Queen Mary was, as always, superbly controlled, but the Duke of Kent was still visibly distraught and said at one stage, "This is quite mad!" He was drastically upset at the thought of not seeing Windsor again for an incalculable length of time. As Windsor left the house, he remembered his manners and bowed to the new king.

The duke had two last-minute visitors. The first was Winston Churchill, who bade him a warm farewell. The second was Count Grandi, who expressed the sympathy of the government in Italy. Neither of these visits was recorded in the press of any country; Count Grandi revealed them in 1986.

The drive, with Ladbroke at the wheel of the Buick, to Portsmouth to take the night ferry to Boulogne was dragged out because of the increasingly foul weather. The duke occupied himself by talking with Monckton, whom he had asked to travel with him to the dock, about the arrangements in Europe. He also read a letter from his sister-in-law Elizabeth, Duchess of York, who had been ill in bed but, for all her hatred of Wallis, was full of good wishes. And he told Monckton how deeply he loved his mother; there was no indication in his voice of bitterness because of her attitude to the woman he loved.

The fog, drizzle, and sudden bursts of rain delayed the vehicle's arrival at Portsmouth dock. Ladbroke drove past Nelson's famous flagship, *Victory*, which had become a tourist attraction, and realized he was lost. As he searched for the correct entrance, the Unicorn Gate, the duke pointed out various ships to Monckton, giving particulars of their histories. They drove on, looking for the HMS *Fury*, which at the last minute had been substituted for *Enchantress*; according to some versions, the latter vessel was rejected because of the unfortunate associations of the name.

The duke boarded *Fury* accompanied by Major Ulick Alexander, keeper of the privy purse, who had been delegated to take charge of his financial affairs, and by a new equerry, Sir Piers Legh. He was welcomed aboard by the fleet commodore, Admiral Sir William Fisher, and two other admirals. In his cabin the duke said farewell to his assistant private secretary, Sir Godfrey Thomas. The duke took Monckton's hands in his; never had he known a more devoted friend.

The ship sailed at 2 a.m. The Channel crossing was choppy; the duke remained secluded in his cabin. He was met at Boulogne by the Orient Express, which had been specially diverted to make the connection. The train's comptroller, Roger Tibot, greeted him as he boarded; the duke had asked that there not be a private car on this occasion, but rather a simple first-class compartment; fortunately, this ruse, plus the diversion of the train, threw the reporters off the scent. The duke told Tibot he did not want to take any meals in the restaurant car and insisted that Tibot have the sleeping-car attendant serve him in the compartment. The duke took his light and unpretentious breakfast, lunch, and dinner on trays which were set upon suitcases that filled the space between the facing seats. This was distressing to Tibot, who was used to the former king entering the dining car, after the other passengers had left it, to enjoy an exquisitely prepared repast.

Meanwhile, Wallis was far from comfortable at the Villa Lou Viei, which she had liked much better in 1928. The house was over 600 years old. The guest bedrooms were on split levels, with an ancient stone wall that ran up between the floors. The thick outer walls retained the clinging dampness of the Mediterranean winter. The living room, which seemed dark even in spring and summer, was cavernous, dank, and cheerless despite its chintz-covered chairs and bowls of green plants on the French provincial tables. There was even, Wallis learned for the first time, a ghost: Herman swore he had seen the original builder of the house flitting in a shadowy form through the corridors and rooms. The residence, which once had seemed a glowing refuge, now looked more like a expensive dungeon.

The Rogerses did everything possible to cheer Wallis up. But all she could see as she stared glumly out the windows were five gendarmes and three British policemen walking up and down, and beyond Herman's well-tended vegetable garden the misty, rain-swept slopes that led down the hill to Cannes. Even the cuisine was depressing; the old couple who acted as majordomo and cook busied themselves to little effect in the badly kept-up kitchen. Wallis began to wish she were somewhere else. In the meantime, her cook, chambermaid, and chauffeur arrived at Dieppe with a dozen suitcases and trunks, and left at once by car for Cannes. They arrived two days later; at last Wallis had some more of her things. She got in touch with George Sebastian at Hammamet in Tunisia, but finally decided not to make the move. She was very annoyed the next day when a shoal of letters arrived, many of them threatening and some of them actually stating that the assassination plan had not been abandoned. As a result, the chief of police of Cannes was called in for consultation. He stationed himself outside her rooms in person, concerned that if anything happened to her it would bring disgrace upon his community.

On December 12 Wallis wrote to the duke that she had heard there was "an organization of women" who had sworn to kill her. She urged him to arrange for full protection at all times; she was placed under armed guard.

The duke proceeded to Vienna on December 13. Upon his arrival on the Orient Express he was met by his old friend the British minister to Austria, the genial Sir Walford Selby, and by a party of journalists who behaved with uncharacteristic reserve. Among these was Douglas Reed, later the author of the book *Insanity Fair*, who observed that in spite of everything the 40-year-old duke still looked amazingly boyish, innocent, and untouched by time and stress.

Another who was present was the attaché Dudley Forwood, who had first met Wallis and the Prince of Wales at Kitzbühel.

At the duke's request, Forwood would soon become his equerry and private secretary. In the meantime, Forwood was put by Sir Walford Selby in charge of the royal arrangements. The duke wanted to proceed to the Rothschild's Schloss Enzesfeld immediately. But it wasn't possible, because protocol required that he present his respects to

President Miklas. With Forwood, the duke proceeded to pay those respects; a further requirement was that afterward the president must appear at the British Legation to present his own respects. This tiresome ritual went on and on.

Sir Dudley recalled:

When I informed the duke of the latter requirement, he said, "Oh! Miklas had better be asked to lunch!" But there was a problem. Lady Selby was a good but extremely stingy hostess. No matter who it was, if there were guests for lunch they only got one lamb chop each. I was very concerned that something better would be done for this important occasion. But the chef was under orders to supply a maximum of four lamb chops. So there could be no change. Learning of this, the duke informed me that I did not need to have lunch!

The Rothschilds sent their chauffeur to pick up the duke and his party and drive them to Enzesfeld. Dudley Forwood was in the entourage. The duke had been at the schloss briefly the year before, suffering from a bad cold. Forwood remembered:

I returned to Vienna almost immediately, but then I had to return because there were so many problems at the schloss. First, none of the duke's personal entourage spoke German, though of course he did. That made it difficult for them to communicate with the staff. The equerry, the Hon. John Aird, left, recalled to Buckingham Palace by the king. The other equerry, Sir Piers Legh, stayed on, but he wasn't at all in tune with the duke. He was an older man, very nervous and tense, horrified by the abdication, not at all sympathetic to Mrs. Simpson, and upset by the fact that he couldn't speak German. So, in this very difficult situation, I was asked to return and become equerry. I accepted at once.

Forwood soon learned the ritual of serving a royal master, a term which he still uses in reference to the duke. In the morning the valet would wake the duke, and Forwood would then enter the bedroom and announce the order of the day's business. He must bow as he did so; on the occasions when he failed to do so, the duke quietly reprimanded him. A very important matter attended to by the valet under Forwood's supervision was that of the royal clothing. When the duke played golf, he would change into a golfing outfit; he would not wear that outfit at lunch, but had to change into a suit and tie; if he wished to garden in the afternoon, he would again have to change. And then of course in the evening there would be the obligatory black tie or, for special occasions, white tie and tails.

But from the beginning, despite the onerous challenges involved, Forwood was utterly devoted to the duke. He would, in 1987, hear not a word against his master. One of his most vivid memories of Enzesfeld was that the duke called Wallis several times a day. The duke seemed reluctant to restrain himself, pouring out his agony to her, while the telephone bills in those expensive times averaged the equivalent of between $300 and $400 a week; as he walked to her, he could see in his room dozens of photographs of her that he had brought from Fort Belvedere. Although pleased to accommodate him, his host and hostess had mixed feelings about him, and he about them. Kitty Rothschild was still a very attractive woman, but the duke did not find her particularly intelligent. He had always joked that she had become a Protestant with her first husband, a Roman Catholic with her second, and a Jew with her third.*

Wallis continued to suffer the torments of the damned. She wrote to the duke, "So much scandal has been whispered about me even that I am a spy that I am shunned by people so until I have the protection of your name I must remain hidden." She expressed her desire for more and more obscurity, a pathetically futile wish in the circumstances. But she expressed hopes that the love she shared with the duke would win out against all obstacles.

In England, Emerald Cunard and Sir Philip Sassoon disowned the exiled couple outright. Following hypocritical statements of sympathy and sorrow from Stanley Baldwin in the House of Commons, the archbishop of Canterbury delivered a moralistic and protracted BBC broadcast on December 13, remarking, inter alia, of the late monarch:

> Even more strange and sad is it that he should have sought his happiness in a manner inconsistent with Christian principles of marriage and within a social circle whose standards and ways of life are alien to all the

*The political situation in Austria vis-à-vis Nazi Germany was extremely delicate where Jews were concerned. Although nothing approaching Hitler's behavior toward Jewish people existed in Austria, there was always the threat that the situation might change and the Rothschilds would have to leave.

best instincts of his people. Let those who belong in this circle know
that today they stand rebuked by the judgement of the nation which had
loved King Edward.

His comments made him singularly unpopular, and not only among
the duke's still-loyal friends. His broadcast had the disagreeable flavor
of a righteous churchman kicking an unfortunate man when he was
down. Two days later Labour member of Parliament Ellen Wilkinson,
both in the Commons and in an article in the newspaper *The Sunday
Referee*, went a step further. She said:

> There had been growing uneasiness about political tendencies around
> [Mrs. Simpson], or perhaps it would be fairer to say, in groups that had
> been using her influence over King Edward for their own purposes. . . .
> Eager to be behind Mrs. Simpson was a set that makes little secret of its
> enthusiasm for the political and social doctrines of a power not particu-
> larly friendly toward Britain. Prime Minister Baldwin recently de-
> scribed what he called a dangerous mentality in politics as being "the
> enjoyment of power without responsibility."

As a sop to the public (and perhaps to avoid a libel suit), Miss
Wilkinson added that she wasn't implying that either the duke or Wallis
knew what was being done to them politically. This scarcely soothed
the troubled brows of the two victims of the speech and the article.

At the same time, yet another blow fell. Francis Stephenson, an obscure and ancient legal clerk, intervened in what seemed to be a fairly
straightforward legal procedure toward the granting of the decree absolute of the divorce. He claimed to be able to show cause as to why
the divorce should be stopped. What information he had, if any, was
never made clear, and he subsequently was silenced. However, the likelihood is that he got wind of collusion with Ernest Simpson.

Wallis was in a state of shock when she learned of the intervention.
She wrote to the duke, "I didn't think the world could put more on two
people whose only sin is to love." She added that she looked a hundred
years old and weighed only 110 pounds, that England had made her a
"wreck." She wrote, "The world is against me and me alone." She
wondered if she could survive the ordeal.

Wallis must have worried that the truth would come out about her
earlier collusion in the matter of Spencer and that somebody might
produce evidence that she was born out of wedlock and not baptized,

which would preclude her religious marriage to the duke, even if it might reveal her marriage to Ernest to be invalid. She went out on long and meaningless drives around the curving roads of the three Corniches, the hairpin bends and sudden glimpses of the sea temporarily distracting her from her anguish. She was relieved to hear that Aunt Bessie would join her for Christmas. She wondered if the ordeal would ever end.

In that time of loneliness and sorrow, it is clear that Wallis at last began to feel a little fondness for the duke. Her letters to him at the time expressed some show of devotion and loyalty, though they still did not have the impassioned affection of his own. At that time, Newbold Noyes, who was married to Wallis's cousin Lelia of Wakefield Manor, was publishing a series of articles in the United States (and would soon do so in France) based upon what Wallis and the duke had thought were private conversations at Fort Belvedere and Cumberland Terrace in November. The articles were largely empty-headed puffery about the couple's likes and dislikes (Wallis hated cats; she loved open fires and high winds). However, Wallis felt very strongly that the pieces represented invasion of privacy; she even overreacted to them to the point that she opened a libel suit against Noyes.

She made a serious mistake. Instead of engaging a respectable French attorney, she again turned to the Nazi activist Armand Grégoire. Grégoire was still notorious—listed with the Deuxième Bureau and the Sûreté as one of the leading Nazi agents in France. Espionage files on him currently deposited at the Archives Diplomatiques in Paris and at the National Archives in Washington reveal that despite his position as a prominent lawyer, with offices in the Place Vendôme and a socially prominent wife, Crystal, who was an American by birth, he was under ceaseless watch by the authorities. France was still under the Socialist government of Léon Blum, and by a peculiar irony the head of Blum's cabinet, M. Blumel, was the brother of Maître Suzanne Blumel, later Blum, who would follow Grégoire many years later as Wallis's lawyer.

The situation was clearly monitored by Herman Rogers, whose position as an American agent was still continuing; Wallis's decision to engage Grégoire enhanced suspicions of her Nazi connections in representatives of MI6 in Paris. In short, she was in worse trouble than ever.

The phone calls and letters continued with countless bomb or other death threats, causing the Rogerses to change their telephone number again and again. An unpleasant footnote to an already disagreeable month occurred when a news announcement revealed that Wallis's old home at 212 North Biddle Street, Baltimore, had been bought by an attorney, Harry J. Green, who planned to turn it into a museum.

The duke traveled frequently to Vienna both to receive ear treatments from Professor Neumann and to renew his earlier acquaintance with Chancellor von Schuschnigg and President Miklas. Now that he was no longer on the throne, he was careful to restrict his discussions with these men to social niceties. He also renewed his friendship with the clever, sophisticated American minister to Austria, George Messersmith, who from his first day in Vienna, had kept up, through a network of intelligence contacts and a consistent interception of cables and phone calls from other embassies, what amounted to a detailed watching brief on the duke. On the evening of December 15 the duke rose from his sickbed, to which he was confined with severely aching ears and a bad headache, to join Fritz Mandl for dinner. Mandl, the husband and discoverer of the motion picture star Hedy Lamarr, was a Jewish armaments maker who was already supplying Hitler despite his ethnic origin. The duke also met with Eugene Rothschild's brother Louis, whom he would later assist to escape from Europe. Lord Brownlow had meantime arrived from Cannes with a bundle of notes and reminders from Wallis, only some of which later made their way into the pages of the selected correspondence edited by Michael Bloch.

Two problems, other than the continually tormenting matter of their separation, were paramount in the minds of Wallis and the duke. The first was the question of where they would live once they were married. There was some discussion of their going to the French estate of the Duke of Westminster, who had, of course, on a previous occasion given them the use of his yacht. But accepting this idea would have been unwise: Westminster still had very strong and notorious Nazi connections. Prince Roman Francuszko suggested they might want to move to his castle in Poland; there was talk of their buying Count Bela Zichy's 4,000-acre estate in Hungary. None of these plans seemed practicable, but another idea the couple took seriously. The Rogerses put up the idea that they might want to move, at least for a time, to the Château de Candé at Tours, not far from Paris; the château was the home of the naturalized American industrial systems tycoon Charles Bedaux and his American wife, Fern.

The second problem was the matter of the royal income from the

Civil List, which was to keep the duke in comfort for the rest of his days. Despite his brother York's verbal approval, the matter would take several weeks or months to go through the necessary committee. And there was no guarantee that, at the end of that time, the arrangement would be approved. For the moment, though he still kept it a secret, the duke of course had the very substantial sum of money he had saved from the Duchy of Cornwall. But even that bounty would not be sufficient, given the standard of living to which he was accustomed, to provide for him indefinitely. At some stage in this period Wallis agreed to give up the £300,000 he had settled on her, exchanging it for £10,000 a year for life. However, the duke was still fretful, obsessed as always with money. In London, his devoted Winston Churchill never ceased, either then or during the next few months, to press repeatedly for the cash. As a member of the Civil List Committee, Churchill did his utmost to override the objections of the others. He thought of himself still, and always would, as the duke's surrogate father or kindly uncle.

The reporters still clung relentlessly to the grounds of both Schloss Enzesfeld and the Villa Lou Viei. Wallis forced herself to make an awkward appearance one afternoon, giving a brief press conference in which she said little of interest. She was treading water, consumed with boredom and loneliness, unable to sleep; she relished prominence, publicity, and admiration and could not bear to think that she was hated as few other women had been hated in history. It was scarcely a relief to her to learn that a wax statue of her in a symbolically scarlet evening gown now stood in a chamber of Madame Tussaud's Wax Museum in London. Visitors to the exhibit noted that her startlingly realistic violet-colored glass eyes looked balefully across at the archbishop of Canterbury.

Minor troubles increased. The duke called Wallis frantically to tell her that her beloved Slipper had been mauled by Baron Rothschild's dogs and a vet had to be summoned to take care of the animal. As Christmas approached, he was not in a mood to enjoy the season. The piles of letters heaping up on his desk even surpassed Wallis's. When he advertised for a secretary, 800 women lined up for the job. He finally chose one, addressing her through sneezes and a worsening headache while sipping red wine spiced with cloves, sugar, and cinnamon.

When Wallis went shopping, press and public made her trip impossible. Her white hat and ermine coat were spotted as she took a walk along the Cannes waterfront, and she had to flee back into the car. Matters did not improve in England. His Master's Voice, which had the royal warrant for reproducing speeches, was forbidden by Sir John Reith of the BBC to issue a disk of the abdication speech. Bootleg copies sold furiously in the United States and in continental Europe.

In the meantime, Sir Horace Wilson, special adviser to the new king and diplomatic liaison between various conflicting political groups including the Labour party, the British Union of Fascists, the Anglo-German fellowship the Link and even the Communists, prepared a sixty-four-page report for the chancellor of the Exchequer, Neville Chamberlain, on the Duke and Duchess of Windsor and the circumstances of the abdication. His concluding statement was damning. It read:

> The Prime Minister not being available, I think I should refer to the point I made as to Mrs. Simpson's "plans" for the future. It is clear to me that it is her intention not only to come back here but (aided by what she expects to be a generous provision from public funds) to set up a "Court" of her own and—there can be little doubt—do her best to make things uncomfortable for the new occupant of the Throne. It must not be assumed that she has abandoned hope of becoming Queen of England. It is known that she has limitless ambition, including a desire to interfere in politics: she has been in touch with the Nazi movement and has definite ideas as to dictatorship.
>
> The essentials for her plans are (a) that she secure her divorce and (b) that she is provided with a sufficient income.
>
> As regards (a), about which she is very anxious, it is unnecessary for me to say anything. As regards (b) we have some means, at least, of saving the country from grave future trouble.

On December 19 Aunt Bessie at last arrived at Lou Viei. Wallis embraced her in tears. It was a heartfelt, eagerly longed-for reunion. The duke busied himself with preparations for Christmas. He sent Wallis a mink cape; she in turn sent him a possum coat. Recovered from his cold, he reverted to his usual custom of morning exercises and played golf and ninepins, and he even tried yodeling at a small dinner party in the newly constructed bar and dining room. And he was overjoyed when the unhappy Slipper, who had been lying in his tiny kennel, suddenly recovered from his wounds and woke the household to reveal that he had triumphantly cornered and killed a large gray mouse.

The duke was soon depressed again. On December 22 he wrote to

Wallis expressing his agony at the thought of the four months of separation to come. The ten days he had spent at the schloss had almost driven him mad with their slowness and monotony. He wrote that he lived only for their telephone conversations in the evening, that without Alexander Graham Bell's invention life would be unbearable. He complained of the cruel and inhuman newspapers; he talked of the cruelty of life itself.

On that same day the duke wrote to Aunt Bessie, describing the last two weeks as "a nightmare."

On Christmas eve, Wallis decided to ignore the press, and made her way through a large and eager crowd with the Rogerses to the Palm Beach Casino in Cannes. It was officially announced that she had stayed home. There was no Christmas tree, but she worked hard on the decorations of holly and mimosa. As an unpleasant Christmas gift to the couple, Buckingham Palace issued an announcement that sixty employees of Sandringham, who had been dismissed by the duke, had now been restored to their former positions. The duke appeared in church on Christmas day, joining George Messersmith at the services. Sir Walford Selby read the first lesson, and the duke read, in his excellent voice, still with its touches of American and cockney pronunciation, the first twenty verses of the second chapter of the Gospel according to St. Luke. He and Wallis exchanged telephone calls the same day. On the following afternoon, the duke was mobbed by hundreds of children as he gave away Christmas gifts to the children of Enzesfeld. He seemed cheerful, glowing, and in good form as he walked out into the driving snow.

During the season, the duke bombarded the king at Sandringham by (collect) telephone, according to Sir Dudley Forwood, giving him fraternal advice on how to behave as monarch. This was not particularly well received. But whatever its feelings about his advice and about Wallis, the royal family didn't hesitate to convey to the duke their love and tender thoughts. However, the cost of the duke's calls, which dragged on for hours, greatly concerned the Rothschilds. Kitty Rothschild told George Messersmith, "Edward has no sense of money. You know, we are not among the rich Rothschilds, and these telephone calls appall me." One Christmas message added fuel to the fire of the duke's enemies: the one from his friend Lloyd George, the former prime minister of England, who was vacationing in the Caribbean. Lloyd George had visited Hitler and admired the führer to distraction; so intense was the Nazi support surrounding him in England that the British Secret Intelligence Service was watching him and his friends day and night.

On Christmas night Wallis, at the invitation of her old friend Sibyl Colefax, who had remained loyal through the crisis, went with the Rogerses to dinner at the Villa Mauresque, where Somerset Maugham, then at the height of his fame as both novelist and playwright, received them with his celebrated crocodile smile. The evening was rendered somewhat embarrassing by the drunken interruptions of his "secretary," his alcoholic lover Gerald Haxton. Asked at the inquest after a rubber of bridge why she hadn't used a king of hearts, Wallis said, "My kings don't take tricks. They only abdicate." Wallis did not particularly warm to her host, nor he to her. But he had something in common with her and with Herman Rogers: all three had been involved in intelligence work—Maugham in World War I.

On January 1, 1937, Aunt Bessie wrote to Wallis's cousin Corinne Murray, who was now back at Pensacola, Florida, telling her of the life at Lou Viei: "The events of the past month are too big for my feeble mind to tackle," she said. She went on to say that Wallis was looking very well, but "too thin, of course," and that she should put on six pounds. She wished the newspapers would stop hounding Wallis; there were so many letters to answer that Bessie had to write several, like this one, herself in her place. But she did note that the tourists had stopped peeping through the gates, only the very curious were still hovering about.

Also on New Year's day the duke wrote to Wallis once again expressing his anguish and sense of strain at the separation. That night on the telephone with her, he sobbed like a child; after he had finally hung up, Wallis, clearly touched, dashed off a note to him, saying, "I couldn't bear hearing you cry."

On January 3 Wallis wrote to the duke expressing her concern at the behavior of King George VI, accusing him of being a mere puppet for government forces which had removed her beloved from the throne, using her as a "convenient tool." She expressed her annoyance that her forthcoming marriage to the duke would not be mentioned in the Court Circular; this was a disappointment because she loathed the idea of being undignified and of joining "the countless titles that roam around Europe meaning nothing." She wanted the duke to write to the king giving reasons why he should not be treated as an outcast and requesting that she be given her proper title. She disclosed her disgust with the royal family as a whole for denying her any degree of dignity.

As January wore on, Wallis's worry that the divorce would not be granted did not cease. The duke was so anxious and irritable he didn't even go to a nightclub in Vienna, nor did he even attend the Rotter Bar. On January 21 Fruity Metcalfe telephoned from the Grand Hotel at Kitzbühel to suggest that he might come by Schloss Enzesfeld and stop over for a visit. The duke unwisely agreed. Jealous as ever, Wallis urged the duke in several notes not to be alone with him. The duke ignored such advice.

He went skiing with Fruity at Semmering; Metcalfe noted in letters to his wife Lady Alexandra in London that the duke was as eager and happy as a schoolboy. He was as insomniac as ever, seldom getting to bed before 4 a.m., with Fruity, whose letters of the time to friends have a ga-ga, breathless quality of a man in love.

All through January Wallis was writing to the duke, continuing to complain about her position as an outcast and an object of international scandal. She never ceased to grumble about the ill treatment she felt the duke was getting from the king. The boredom and notoriety were eating into her more and more deeply. In her desperation, she had turned to an astrologer in Switzerland, but the written horoscope only depressed her with its prophecy of many more obstacles.

On January 27 Wallis wrote to the duke, saying she was very distressed that Baldwin would not let the Dukes of Kent and Gloucester pay a visit to the schloss. She charged Baldwin with not only ruining the family affairs but continuing to humiliate the duke.

Wallis wrote the duke expressing fears of a possible affair with Kitty Rothschild. This was absurd. Eugene went to Paris in the third week of January, transferring most of his funds to the Paris banks, but Kitty didn't finally move out until February 2, when the duke didn't even have the grace to get out of bed to bid her farewell and to thank her for her kindnesses to him.

It was not until February 3 that the duke made a public appearance at a social occasion, attending, along with Messersmith, the Selbys, and Mrs. Miklas, a concert given by the young Australian soprano Joan Hammond. The choice of program was, to say the least, unfortunate.

One *lied* by Hugo Wolf was entitled "In Retirement," and contained the words, "Leave me alone, O World / Let my heart remain alone with its pain and its bliss." Richard Strauss's "Dedication" began, "You know, dear soul, that far from you I suffer. Love makes my heart sick." In the worst taste of all was the song "The Little Foreigner" by Cyril Scott. In it, the titular figure declared that she had come from a country far away to London "to set the Thames on fire." And the final blow to an already uncomfortable duke came in the song "The Green Hills of Somerset," in which a refrain was, "No more we walk by your green hills, no more."

Two days later, the princess royal, the duke's beloved sister, and her husband, the Earl of Harewood, left London for Enzesfeld. According to the *New York Times*, the reason for the visit was to discuss the duke's financial future. Baldwin was still adamant that the duke would receive nothing from the Civil List. The princess and her husband were to bring word of this disagreeable decision and try to soothe the duke's fevered brow. When they arrived, the duke lunched with them at the Hotel Bristol and took them on a tour of several museums. Dismayed by word that his money was frozen, he reminded the princess royal that he still had possession of Balmoral and Sandringham and would not release the residences until he was paid. He said bitterly, referring to the palace of the Austrian emperors, "If the worst comes to worse, I'll always be able to pick up a living showing people around Schönbrunn." He gave his sister and brother-in-law a free tour of the moldering edifice, pointing out the pony cart belonging to the Crown Prince Rudolf, who had shot his mistress and himself in a famous double suicide. He also showed his relatives the worker apartments over which he had already embarrassed his Fascist friends in Vienna two years earlier.

In February, a series of anguished letters from Wallis to the duke indicates her extreme nervousness about the future outcome of the investigation by the king's proctor into the matter of the divorce from Ernest. One of the letters, dated the seventh, was especially confused and jumbled, filled with a sense of panic. She wanted the duke to intervene with the king on the matter, obviously an impossibility. She blamed everything that had happened upon the queen, whom she persisted in calling the Duchess of York. ("I blame it all on the wife—who hates us both.") It is quite clear from this and other letters that Wallis knew that the granting of the decree was by no means a certainty; it might be revealed that she in fact had had a form of sexual relationship with the duke. Had she (as Michael Bloch, who edited the selected letters, avers) had only the most chaste relationship with him, her letters would have assumed an entirely different character, based upon the certainty that no one would expose her in an act of adultery.

On February 12 Wallis, feeling a little better, made her 1937 social debut on the Riviera at an elaborate party given by Henry Clews, Jr., a wealthy New York socialite. The affair, at the Palm Beach Casino, was enlivened by a commotion when some tourists who had crashed the event tried to get a peek through the curtains drawn around the table at which Wallis and the Rogerses were seated with their host and hostess. In a splendid black lace gown and pearl necklace, a present from the duke, Wallis danced twice with the Greek casino owner Nicolas Zographos.

The next day the princess royal and the Earl of Harewood left Vienna by train. The princess was in tears; the duke shouted angrily at motion picture cameramen who tried to photograph the group on the railway platform, and police seized and smashed the cameras. It was widely believed that at the last minute the Harewoods had tried to convince the duke to break up his relationship with Wallis. Predictably, any such suggestion was abruptly rejected. But they did prevail upon him to postpone his wedding until after the coronation. And they were compelled to inform him, after talking with London, that there was still no arrangement for his financial prospects and provisions. He told Messersmith he had been treated "shabbily."

That the duke had ideas of returning to England and assuming the throne once more is indicated by a phrase in a letter dated February 18 to Wallis: "WE will be back in our full glory in less time than WE think."

Kent had yet again been visiting his brother-in-law, the Nazi Count Toerring, in Munich whereupon he joined his brother Windsor in Austria. The presence of two brothers as Nazi sympathizer royals with Nazi connections at the same time in a country threatened by Hitler was completely unauthorized by King George VI, and indeed all future meetings were banned by royal orders and by the Secret Intelligence Service.

In London, Joachim von Ribbentrop turned up at Buckingham Palace to present his credentials as ambassador to the king and to convey

Hitler's good wishes. He told King George about German worker apartments and social reforms; the conversation was friendly and cordial. At the end of the meeting Ribbentrop gave the monarch the Nazi salute. It is clear that Hitler's purpose was to obtain the support of the royal family in England, regardless of which particular member of it should happen to be on the throne.

In Vienna the Dukes of Kent and Windsor visited various museums and the Schönbrunn Palace; Kent stayed over for several days and nights. Lord Brownlow arrived from London the following day, February 26; he had been badly treated in London because he had backed the wrong royal horse. He was told not only that he would not be lord-in-waiting to the new king, as he had expected, but also that he was persona non grata at court; men left the bar of his club when he arrived. His name was to be banned from the Court Circular. When he asked the lord chamberlain, Lord Cromer, whether he was to be turned away like a dishonest servant without notice, he was told that that expectation was correct. The fact that he had accompanied Wallis was clearly the deathblow to his career, and even to his social life.

At the same time, rumors increased in London and in the south of France that Wallis had somehow made off with the emeralds bequeathed to the duke by his grandmother Queen Alexandra. The suggestion was either that she had wormed them out of the king or that he had retrieved them through the jewelry dealers Garrards in London as a present for her. There was no truth in either assumption; the emeralds were figments of the collective imagination. The truth was that whatever jewels were left by Queen Alexandra were divided up among the female members of the family and were never available to the duke at any time. But the story, which has persisted until recently, when it was finally quashed by the writer Leslie Field in 1987, increased the hysteria that seemed to accompany Wallis's every move.

The Duke of Kent was obliged to say that there was no prospect of Windsor's receiving any money through the Civil List. This news, on top of his sister's, threw the duke into a state of anger and depression. He and Wallis argued over it for hours on the telephone, shouting at each other night after night.

On March 2, Wallis attended her first fashion show in over a year as Captain Edward Molyneux showed his spring collection at Cannes. She bought thirteen dresses and suits, including a crepe satin evening gown of grayish blue, with a jacket fastened by three mirror buttons; the most expensive item she purchased was a silver-fox coat made of ten skins used lengthwise in straight bands. She wore it to another party at the Somerset Maugham villa that weekend.

The fear of assassination intensified in March. Wallis received another threatening letter; she was once again advised by Kenneth de Courcy of the existence of an organization determined to eliminate her—an organization that would be well paid for the killing.

There was talk that Wallis and the duke would move to the United States. The duke even began some preliminary negotiations to buy Cloisters, an immense castellated residence owned by Mr. and Mrs. Sumner A. Parker outside Baltimore. Nothing eventuated. Finally, on March 9, Wallis left with the Rogerses for Charles Bedaux's Château de Candé; she was accompanied by her maid, Mary Burke, and by twenty-seven pieces of luggage. She stored the rest of her possessions brought from England at the Villa Lou Viei. Charles Bedaux was in the United States at the time, staying at his apartment on Fifth Avenue. Fern Bedaux had broken off a trip to London and worked with tremendous concentration for over a week to prepare for her celebrated guest. An army of servants, augmented by local villagers, had scrubbed and repainted and dusted the ancient edifice virtually round the clock. The Buick, which had been garaged for most of the previous weeks while Wallis used the Rogerses' car, swept up the hill to the château's immense, arabesque doorway with its iron handles. At the ring of the hand-pulled doorbell, the door creaked open to disclose a vast hallway lined by twenty-two members of the staff, all of them uniformed. At their head was Hale, the English butler, dressed impeccably in a hand-tailored suit from Savile Row. The liveried footmen wore royal-blue and gold coats, black trousers, and gold-buckled shoes. The maids were in floor-length, black silk dresses with frilly caps and aprons, and the housekeeper was equipped with a large chatelaine of keys. Chandeliers were glowing from the ceiling on this gloomy, wet Wednesday afternoon. Ten thousand francs' worth of bought flowers sprang from crystal vases. Wallis was accommodated in Fern's own bedroom, which was decorated in orchid silk and satin and overlooked the somber woods and countryside.

Exhausted by the journey, Wallis spent her first day resting in her room. When she took a step out of doors at dusk, the rain was so heavy that she quickly returned. She called the duke several times during her first twenty-four hours there.

She gave a press conference in the library, carefully avoiding any mention of her marriage plans. Asked, rather oddly in the circumstances, for her view on the Spanish civil war, in which Fascist and Communist forces were locked in a deadly conflict, she was clever enough to say, "I'm sorry for both sides. It will be the ruin of beautiful Spain." Several reporters noted that she was wearing an enormous sapphire engagement ring on the third finger of her left hand; apparently, she had tired of the Mogul emerald engagement ring the duke had given her on the night of the granting of her decree at Ipswich and wanted a jewel that was closer to the color of her eyes.

During the next few days Wallis accustomed herself to the atmosphere of the Château de Candé. She studied everything Fern Bedaux did with the utmost care; she told Fern that the château was the best-run house she had ever stayed in. Fern, a tall, elegant, exquisitely groomed product of Grand Rapids, came from old money and ran her household with superb expertise. She was also quite a stern taskmistress: if one of the maids or manservants was heard talking or giggling outside the kitchen, the offender was immediately sent below stairs. Hale was a fussy but skillful majordomo as well as butler. Briskly, with much slapping together of his hands, he ordered about the two footmen, the ladies' maids, the upstairs maid, the downstairs maid, and the scullery maid; the only part of the house where he was not in command was the kitchen. That was the domain of Legros, who had formerly been the chef of the Duke of Alba, a chief financier of Franco; Legros was considered virtually matchless, and his three-star cuisine would have done justice to any fine restaurant in Paris. After the mediocrity of the cooking of the Rogerses' couple, Wallis was at last able to eat some decent food.

Bedaux and his architects had modernized the castle, covering the furniture with eighteenth-century patterned linens that had been found on rolls in the attic when he bought the house from its previous owners, run-down French aristocrats. He had also installed new plumbing, heating, and vast furnaces in the basement. Wallis's bathroom had heated platinum-plated towel rails and an enormous tub equipped with massive gold taps. There was even a gilded fountain to keep newly bought fish fresh; fish were always bought alive for the Château de Candé.

Dinner parties at the château were small but formal and done with great style. Two cloths were put on for evening meals. The first layer was a cloth of gold; the second was fine Brussels lace. The effect was beautiful; the gold shone through under the glistening light of the candelabra. Meals were served by Hale and the flunkies in livery. The monogrammed china and silver were of the finest quality. An individual menu was written out in copperplate for each guest and placed on a tiny silver rest in front of him or her. If Hale didn't like someone, he would turn the tray offered from the left so that the guest got the worse piece of fowl or fish; and he would never top the wine of someone he hated unless he was specifically asked to do so. The fowl were brought to the table "dressed" (with their feathers on) so everyone could see and feel them. Then they were cooked and served.

After dinner, for smaller occasions, Hale would put dance music records on the radiogramophone. For larger events Marcel Dupré, the best-known organist of his day, would perform at the enormous Skinner movie-theater organ in the living room, its bronze pipes carefully hidden under oak paneling, the music of Bach and Handel emerging through a grille. Sometimes, Fern Bedaux would take her guests to the small pavilion in the grounds, a tiny lodge rather like a shooting box. There, Wallis and her friends would join in card games or roll up the carpet and dance to the wind-up phonograph. Fern would stand on the sidelines, not joining in. Wallis could not have been more content in this sumptuous environment. Even her fastidious tastes were satisfied at last.

Meantime, on March 18 there was at last some action on the matter of the divorce. The king's proctor, Sir Thomas Barnes, announced that the case would be discussed in court the following day. Sir Boyd Merriman, president of the Divorce Court, would hear the matter at 10:30 a.m. Attorney General Sir Donald Somervell would appear to report the result of the investigations by the king's proctor. Surprisingly, neither Ernest nor Wallis was required to be present. Wallis had a sleepless night over this, but in fact she need not have worried. Somervell announced in court that he had found no ground for an intervention and that there was no basis whatsoever for any possible belief that the divorce was collusive. The judge asked if Francis Stephenson, the clerk who had entered a complaint charging that there were irregularities in the original procedures, was there. Stephenson responded that he was indeed. Small, round-shouldered, with a drooping gray mustache, he admitted he had taken legal action on December 9. He confirmed, however, that he no longer had any reason for complaint and asked that his original charges be permanently stricken from the record. Asked by newspapermen as he left the building why he had taken the action in the first place, he snapped, "You can go on wondering! Go away! I have other fish to fry!" It seemed obvious that he had been put up to his appointed task of disrupting the divorce, but had withdrawn because of his feelings as a loyal subject. The irony of course was that the divorce in fact *was* collusive; the wonder is that nobody was able to prove it.

There would still be some time before the decree absolute would be granted. Nevertheless, Wallis was greatly relieved to hear that there were no major obstacles from now on. The duke was equally pleased with the news, but he was as restless and fretful as ever; having virtually forced Kitty out of her own home, he was burdened by the problems of running Schloss Enzesfeld and began making plans to move.

Sir Walford Selby and Dudley Forwood found him a new residence: the small hotel, Appesbach House, near St. Wolfgang in the Salzhammergut lake district of Austria; it had a private bathing beach, a boat landing stage, a tennis court, and a good view of water and mountains. In the previous few weeks the duke had acquired no less than seventeen staff members, including several maids and a valet, two-thirds of whom he was compelled to dismiss. He was suffering from a bad toothache and had flown in Dr. Sumner Moore from Wimpole Street, London, to take care of the problem. His ear continued to bother him despite the numerous ministrations of Dr. Neumann. His mood was scarcely helped by the fact that Winston Churchill was still running into every possible obstacle in London on the question of the money.

By March, the duke's letters to Wallis had become almost literally hysterical. "God's curses be on the heads of those English bitches who dare to insult you!" he wrote.

On the twenty-second he wrote to Wallis saying that one day he would "get back at all those swine [in England]" and make them realize "how disgustingly and unsportingly they have behaved."

On March 28 the duke was given a farewell in the form of a torchlight procession in the village of Enzesfeld. Schoolchildren, followed by members of the local fire department and constabulary, walked through the streets and up to the castle with torches held high, chanting in unison and providing a concert of local traditional music. The next morning the duke drove to St. Wolfgang. He was accompanied by

Sir Godfrey Thomas and by Dudley Forwood. On arrival at Appesbach House, the duke walked out onto his bedroom balcony, staring
moodily at the mountains in their veil of early spring mist. He was accompanied by his new Cairn terrier, Schnuki; Slipper had already been
sent to Wallis by train. He spent the next days climbing in the mountains with Forwood and visiting local monasteries and the summer residence of the late Emperor Franz Josef. His love of the Teutonic
scenery and fascination with the relics of the Hapsburgs were characteristic. He was moving behind the scenes for the restoration of the
Archduke Otto to the Austrian throne.

On March 31 Wallis wrote to the duke once again attacking his
"wretched brother" and suggesting that if the treatment continued the
duke should announce to the world the ill-treatment he had received. She
advised the duke to make the king "ashamed of himself—if possible."

On April 8 Slipper, who had a tendency to run around looking for
rats and mice, had strayed onto the golf course near the Château de
Candé and was bitten to death by a viper. "Now the principal guest of
the wedding is no more," Wallis wrote in agony to the duke. He responded in kind, saying, "My heart is quite breaking this morning my
beloved sweetheart from sadness." They were both devastated by the
loss; Wallis couldn't bear the thought of burying the animal, so Herman
Rogers took care of it. Lady Mendl and her favorite Johnny McMullen
came down to the château to console Wallis.* Wallis had other troubles: Fern went off to Paris and London for the visit she had interrupted to receive Wallis, and Wallis was not entirely comfortable living
with only the staff for company. Moreover, she was perplexed by the
question of her birth records. For over a month she had been plaguing
Aunt Bessie to get her a certificate of some kind, as required by French
law, but of course this was not forthcoming. At last, the enterprising
Aunt Bessie found a solution. She would contact the young doctor,
Lewis M. Allen, who had been rushed to Blue Ridge Summit to take
care of the birth. He signed an affidavit stating the date and time of
Wallis's arrival.

On April 25, 212 East Biddle Street, Baltimore, was opened as a
museum. Wallis's bedroom was prominently displayed; 150 people

---

* Yet ungratefully Wallis failed to invite either of them to the wedding.

peered into it in groups of six after making their way up the narrow staircase. As it happened, none of the original furniture remained; only the kitchen, with its coal-burning Franklin stove, was more or less the same; Wallis's handwritten recipe for apple popovers was propped up on a shelf above it.

Wallis was furious when she learned that the museum offered a lifelike wax figure of herself, dressed in the wedding gown from her marriage with Ernest Simpson that Simpson had stolen and her friend Mary Raffray had sold to the owners through the agency of her friend Gloria Vanderbilt; and that, to add insult to injury, she was shown kneeling before King George and Queen Mary, her worst enemies. When a reporter asked the museum's co-owner if this was a shrine to the Duchess of Windsor, he snapped back with, "Only God and His saints are for shrines. Mrs. Simpson is neither!" When Thelma Furness told Wallis this (and admitted she got a percentage of the stolen wedding gown's sale), Wallis snapped, "Who does that man think he is? The archbishop of Canterbury?"

The duke was perturbed by the publication of a book entitled *Coronation Commentary* by Geoffrey Dennis, published by William Heinemann in London. The duke claimed that the book libeled him, even though today it seems entirely harmless. He actually sued, through the offices of George Allen, successfully seeking to enjoin the publishers against the book's appearance. At the same time, Wallis dropped her suit against Newbold Noyes, her cousin by marriage, in the matter of his articles in the American and French newspapers. Armand Grégoire remained her lawyer.

On April 14, Wallis wrote the most revealing of all her letters to the duke. She stated, referring to the king, "Well who cares let him be pushed off the throne." No doubt she expressed sentiments of this sort at dinner tables on the Riviera, ensuring the permanent disfavor in which she would be held at the palace. Read in conjunction with the duke's threats in an earlier letter to return to England and resume the throne ("WE will be back in our glory sooner than WE think") and his plans, which would soon be announced to a London journalist, to form a republic in England with himself as president and Wallis as first lady, it is clear that her statement, seditious from a naturalized British citizen, is not to be taken lightly.

At the end of April, Lord Wigram advised Winston Churchill that the king personally guaranteed he would take care of the duke's income in the future. Lloyd George was given a similar assurance. As a result, neither Churchill nor Lloyd George brought the matter up before the Civil List Committee. The duke was greatly relieved to hear the news. But there were still problems to face. British law required that the wedding of British citizens must take place at a local consulate, not at a private residence. Furthermore, it would be virtually impossible to find a British Anglican clergyman to perform the ceremony. By this stage, investigations made by Baldwin's detectives must have established the lack of legitimate birth or a baptismal certificate; in addition, under British law the marriage could not take place until six months had elapsed from the original divorce decree. Nevertheless, Wallis pressed forward with her plans. Since she couldn't face the reporters, she asked for various Paris designers to send her their latest creations for examination for her trousseau. Squadrons of couturier assistants arrived to show her an extraordinary variety of morning, afternoon, and evening clothes. Among those who submitted originals to her were Schiaparelli, Mainbocher, and Chanel. She finally decided to give Mainbocher the authorization to dress her for the wedding itself; his rivals supplied the trousseau.

Mainbocher named her wedding gown's color "Wallis blue." She had a total of sixty-six dresses, including several of a bold, not to say vulgar, design with patterns of lobsters and butterflies on white or silver backgrounds. These were in seemingly deliberate contrast to the image she had of being exquisitely tasteful at all times.

Much of the concern that the crucial figures in the Windsor matter felt was expressed in a confidential note, sent from Buckingham Palace, written by Alexander Hardinge to Sir Robert Vansittart. Dated May 1, 1937, it read as follows:

> My dear Van,
>
> As I told you during our talk yesterday, The King was asked by both Phipps and Selby for instructions as to the attitude which they should adopt in their relations with the Duke of Windsor and Mrs. Simpson, after their marriage.
>
> They wanted to know what His Majesty's wishes would be as regards their entertainment, either official or private, or their participation in official ceremonies of any kind.

The King realizes that in the future his representatives may be faced with problems of this sort at very short notice, and it would, in his Majesty's opinion, be desirable that, as far as possible, they should be given instructions in advance.

The King would therefore be obliged if you would kindly submit suggestions for dealing with the different situations which, in your opinion, are most likely to arise.

Vansittart replied on May 4, as follows:

Very many thanks for your letter of the 1st about the Duke of Windsor.

I entirely agree with the King, if I may respectfully say so, in thinking that H.R.H. should be given as much guidance as is possible in a matter which is entirely without precedent and bristling with every conceivable sort of problem.

Having said this, I need not expatiate upon the difficulty of giving suitable advice or excuse myself for the coarsity of the suggestions which I feel able to make in the circumstances.

Such as these are, they divide themselves into two categories: (1) official, (2) private. As for (1)—e.g., when the Duke and Duchess (to be) are present in a Capital where an official reception is to be given and the question arises whether steps should be taken to see that they are invited to it—I should say that the only course to follow is for H.M. representatives concerned to ask special instructions in every case, as to which we should of course consult you.

As regards (2), my feeling is that these cases might be left to the discretion of the man in charge at the moment, with the option, of course, of asking for advice if he needs it. . . . What I think we ought to avoid, if we can, is a situation in which the Duke might ask an ambassador or minister to put him and his wife up for a visit. I don't suppose this is likely to arise. Misconceptions might be created if it did, particularly if any interviews or contacts with political personages took place during the stay. . . . As a general line, Eden feels that our representatives should treat the Duke of Windsor and his wife rather as they would a member of the Royal Family on a holiday; but that if anything were contemplated which might give to the visit a more serious aspect, our representatives must necessarily refer home. . . . In any case, we shall need instructions or confirmation from the King.

Two matters emerge from the somewhat veiled wording used here by Vansittart. First, that there was real fear that the duke and Wallis would make untoward political connections through their use of the facilities of embassies in different capitals, and second, that then, as later, every one of the decisions vis-à-vis the Windsors came directly from the king. It was only possible to reach the latter conclusion in 1987, when these crucially important letters have at last become available.

On May 2 villagers at St. Wolfgang turned out en masse for a celebration in honor of the duke. They provided an elaborate pageant of local history, in traditional costumes, the mountainside glittering with a giant swastika that appeared to be on fire. When the duke inquired with false naïveté why this Nazi symbol was being used, he was told, no doubt with a touch of cynical local humor, "It is a demonstration of our sentiments." On May 3 Sir Boyd Merriman, with little ado, made the divorce absolute in London. Within minutes reporters dashed to the telephones to call the duke in Austria. He was overjoyed and immediately had his staff pack up everything; without waiting one more instant than he had to, he drove to Salzburg to join the express train for Paris. He boarded at 4:45 p.m., carrying in his arms two wrapped gifts for Wallis, one a bouquet of edelweiss and the other a dirndl. His private car was crammed with the seventeen suitcases that he refused to put in the luggage van; it was almost impossible to move. He was accompanied only by his detective bodyguard Storrier and a valet; the other members of his staff would follow by separate train. Dr. Allen's affidavit of Wallis's birth arrived via the French consul at the local British Legation the same afternoon. And also on the same day the Civil List was published in London with no mention of the duke.

On May 4, 1937, the duke arrived at Verneuil l'Etang, a small town some forty-five kilometers from Paris; Sir Eric Phipps, now ambassador to France, had arranged for the Orient Express to be stopped there and for Lloyd Thomas, who much admired the duke, to meet him on the platform. The station was cleared, and the newsreel camera team and reporters who had penetrated the thick veil of secrecy surrounding the arrival were forbidden to the station. He left the train with his equerry, Captain Greenacre, the ever-present Storrier, and several newspaper reporters who had traveled in the adjoining car. The duke, in very good spirits, chatted briefly with the officers of the Sûreté who were there to guard his safety and left almost at once for the Château de Candé, escorted by a police car and two *gardes mobiles* on motorcycles.

A crowd was waiting at the gates of the Château de Candé as the duke drove up and rapturously embraced Wallis. Charles Bedaux had arrived a week earlier from New York. Chunky, jug-eared, with the face of a prizefighter who had received several batterings in the ring, Bedaux endeared himself immediately to Wallis and the duke. With enormous charm, charisma, and energy, he had risen from penury as a tunnel sandhog in New York City, building, with intensity, a million-dollar business. His highly controversial "Bedaux B-unit system," intended to improve efficiency in factories and offices, had greatly helped management in a number of major companies while provoking considerable criticism among the more left-wing elements in the unions for its alleged exhausting effects. Although frequently accused of being pro-Nazi, Bedaux probably had no more time for Hitler or Mussolini than he did for President Roosevelt or Stanley Baldwin. He was characteristic of the internationalistic, pragmatic adventurer-businessmen of the era, crossing all frontiers, ignoring wars as temporary inconveniences, doing business with anyone who would do business with them. His Bedaux German company had been confiscated, and he was now in the process of trying to win it back. In the course of his efforts, he had become friendly with another skillful internationalist, Hitler's adjutant and World War I commanding officer, the polished and ingenious Fritz Wiedemann.

It was in those first weeks at the Château de Candé that the duke, through Wiedemann, made direct contact with Hitler, asking if it would be convenient to arrange a visit to Germany to study labor conditions there. It was typical of the duke's effrontery and defiance of Buckingham Palace that he would wish to undertake such a mission. It was understood that Ribbentrop was received, as was customary in the case of all ambassadors, by his brother the king and that Anthony Eden, who continued as foreign secretary, was pursuing a policy of not provoking the führer; however, for any member of the royal family to embark upon such a visit to Hitler could only cause the utmost distress in Whitehall. The British were still playing for time, hoping to strengthen Britain's position in terms of its military resources while seemingly not disapproving of the Nazi regime. And it was feared that, embittered as he was, the duke might do that.

Simultaneously, he rashly selected as his honeymoon residence the Castle Wasserleonburg in southern Austria, which was owned by Count Paul Munster, husband of Margaret (Peggy) Ward, who was related to the duke's former mistress Mrs. Dudley Ward. Munster, another member of the January Club with dual British and German citizenship, was on Vansittart's watch list. It seemed the duke was almost deliberately trying to provoke the interest of the Secret Intelligence Service.

The duke asked Sir Eric Phipps to request the French government to grant a special dispensation that would enable the mayor of Monts to perform the civil ceremony at the château instead of the town hall in order to minimize publicity and overcrowding. This was approved.

At Candé Wallis and the duke, their bedrooms discreetly at opposite ends of the château, spent the time playing golf and cards and chatting with their host and hostess. Now that they were reunited, they seemed to all observers to be very happy. The Bedauxes left them alone for several days, allowing them to enjoy their pleasure in each other in seclusion. They even posed for photographs on the lawn and talked in a relaxed and gracious manner with reporters.

12

Wedding of the Decade

The coronation of King George VI and Queen Elizabeth was set for May 12. It was, of course, out of the question for the Duke of Windsor and his "mistress" to attend it. On May 7 the duke and Wallis made their first motor trip out of the château. They were chased by newsreel cameramen to the village of Semblancay, where the news teams were perilously perched upon the rooftops, shouting back and refusing to budge when the local police told them to get down. The couple had lunch at an inn and then continued to the village of Vendôme, where they met with U.S. consul George Tate at the Grand Hotel. He gave Wallis the sworn statement by the doctor on the circumstances of her birth—described as "a birth certificate" in the press. As though seriously preparing for a more responsible role as a married man, the duke cut out hard liquor, replacing it with wine.

The Castle Wasserleonburg was being prepared for the couple's arrival; a new tennis court was laid and the driveway, which was badly potholed, was carefully repaired. Among those who arrived at Candé to offer their congratulations were Lady Brownlow, Mrs. Ronald Greville, Mrs. Richard Norton, and the duke's equerry, Captain W. D. C. Greenacre, just returned from leave in London. The following day Wallis completed arrangements to alter her name back to Wallis Warfield by deed poll. In her application for a marriage license, she declared herself "single."

The duke still retained a futile hope that the Dukes of Kent and Gloucester and his sister Mary would attend the wedding, with Kent as best man. On May 11 he announced his formal engagement to Wallis at last, strategically timing the press conference at Candé to occur on the eve of his brother's crowning in Westminster Abbey. Wallis displayed the Mogul emerald in her engagement ring; the sapphire had fallen out of favor. Mainbocher arrived with his staff for the third fitting of her wedding gown. The couple was now informed that the French government, on grounds of courtesy to the British government, would not permit the wedding to be broadcast on the radio. When CBS and NBC applied, they were informed that any attempt to bring microphones to the château would be stopped by police action. On the evening of the twelfth, Wallis and the duke listened to King George's hesitant postcoronation broadcast; outside, a heavy rainstorm lashed the château while the duke knitted a blue sweater for Wallis, plying the needles busily. Neither Wallis nor the duke felt inclined to toast the speech as millions were doing all over the world. A telegram arrived at the château close to midnight, announcing that Aunt Bessie had sailed on the U.S. liner *President Roosevelt*. Lelia Barnett made the mistake of giving Aunt Bessie a copy of *Coronation Commentary* for a good-bye present.

In subsequent days, the question arose of whether Wallis would be given the title "Her Royal Highness." For weeks the duke had been pestering the palace for approval of this. Walter Monckton was doing his best, and so was Winston Churchill, but their efforts were futile. It was determined that the marriage was invalid in the eyes of the church, which did not recognize divorce. The duke was seeking an announcement of the marriage in *The London Gazette*, which normally contained listings of weddings of which the king approved. There was no response from the palace on the matter.

Wallis and the duke did not fail to note a most ominous event in London. Count Grandi described it:

> Something occurred which greatly embittered our national relationship with Great Britain. As we know, the former king had refused to recognize Emperor Haile Selassie on the ground that he did not wish to provoke Mussolini. But King George VI invited the former ambassador of Ethiopia to the coronation. When Mussolini found this out, he was furious. He impulsively stopped the Prince and Princess of Piedmont, members of the Italian royal family, from attending. The British government interpreted this withdrawal as a deep offense to the Crown of England.

The Prince and Princess of Piedmont were, as we know, great friends of the Duke of Windsor. It must have been clear to the duke that everything he had feared vis-à-vis the breakdown of relations between Mussolini and the British government was coming true.

On May 16 Wallis and the duke were guests of their friends the Grafton W. Minots, wealthy socialites of Boston and New York, at a nearby château. During dinner, as the hostess toasted the happy couple, a bolt of lightning struck the electrical plant next door, ominously plunging everybody in the dining room into gloom. The next night Dudley Forwood set sail for England to escort Aunt Bessie to the château.

On May 19, in Paris, the duke visited the president of the French republic, whom he knew well from the occasion of the funeral of the assassinated M. Doumer and from a luncheon at the president's residence at Rambouillet. At the meeting, he discussed his views on maintaining peace in Europe.

That same day the final word arrived from Buckingham Palace that the king and the prime minister would not permit any member of the royal family to attend the wedding, a depressing end to almost three and a half months of negotiations. For some reason, Wallis decided that she would invite no member of her own family, apart from Aunt Bessie, to the nuptials. Perhaps she felt that to include her cousins Corinne and Lelia and their families would be offensive to Whitehall, or possibly she was still so disaffected with Newbold Noyes, married to Lelia, over his articles that she would not consider inviting him.

The wedding date was set for June 3. By what one hopes was an unfortunate coincidence, this was the date of King George V's birth. On May 16, Wallis and the duke signed their marriage contract, guaranteeing that their property would be entirely separate and that no claim would be made on either in the event of a divorce. At first, it was announced by Herman Rogers that there would be no religious ceremony, only a civil marriage performed by Charles Mercier, mayor of the nearby village of Monts. This decision, however, was quickly reversed. There was talk that the Reverend C. H. D. Grimes, rector of the Anglican church of Vienna, would officiate; the duke had read a Bible lesson for him the previous December. The archbishop of Canterbury intervened and Grimes withdrew. The wedding ring of Welsh gold, similar to that worn by several English queens, was brought from Paris. One of the first to see it was the millionaire Cornelius Vanderbilt, Jr., who, in an incongruous touch, declined to stay in the château itself, lodging himself instead in a large American trailer outside the main gate. The vulgarity of this action did not escape the attention of the French press.

On May 25 Mayor Mercier rehearsed Wallis and the duke for the civil ceremony in the music room of the château. The couple was still without a minister. When a Liverpool parson offered to preside, the archbishop of York expressly forbade him. Aunt Bessie arrived, delayed in Paris by a cold, and bustled around the château with astonishing energy, causing consternation among the staff. She even dared usurp the supreme power of the omnipotent Hale. An old friend of Wallis's, Constance Coolidge, arrived from Baltimore. She wrote to a friend of hers on May 28 under the name Constance Atherton, "I have never seen anyone as happy as the Duke—like a boy let out of school. He is gay, carefree, laughing, and terribly in love." At lunch, which he rarely attended ("His Royal Highness is doing you a great honor, Constance, as he never comes to lunch as a rule," Wallis said), he complained cheerfully about the weather, which had stopped him from playing golf, and said he hadn't enjoyed staying with the Rothschilds because he didn't like Kitty. When Constance asked him if he would want to race horses, he replied, "I can't. I'm too poor. But the one thing I would like to have if I had a lot of money is a nice yacht." After the coffee stage Hale and two liveried footmen arrived with silver trays completely covered by letters. "How many are there today?" Wallis asked. "Only four hundred and fifty," Hale replied. The letters were filled with poems, music, photographs, insults, threats, and requests for everything imaginable, including a discarded pair of shoes. The phone rang forty times in two hours. Representatives of Van Cleef and Arpels arrived from Paris with trays of jewels, followed by a case of gems, an inscribed gold box from Hitler, an onyx-and-diamond clock from Herman and Katherine Rogers, and costly gifts from Mussolini, Ciano, and Alberto da Zara of China days. Dinner that night was hot dogs and ginger beer. Randolph Churchill came to dinner. Constance Coolidge wrote:

[The duke] wore a Scottish plaid of the Black Watch—black and green kilts, and a sort of white shirt—very smart, and she had . . . such jewels: two huge leaves or feathers on the left side of her dress, one in diamonds and the other in rubies, diamond-and-ruby earrings, and diamond-and-ruby bracelets and a ruby ring. . . . After dinner we went into the living room. . . . Suddenly [the duke] noticed that Wallis's slipper was undone, and he went down on both knees and tied it up. I caught Randolph Churchill's eye at this moment, and his expression was amusing, to say the least.

When Constance went to bed at 1:30 a.m., quite exhausted from the long evening, Wallis and the duke banged on the door, announced they had come to see if she was all right, sat down on the edge of the bed, and started the conversation all over again. The duke announced that the lamp was badly situated for reading, got down on all fours on the floor, and crawled about, fixing wires and plugs until the lamp was in a better place. It was typical of his almost childlike naturalness, contrasted with his sophistication and guile.

On May 29, *The London Gazette* printed the following devastating announcement:

> The King has been pleased by letters patent under the great seal of the realm, bearing the date of the 27th of May, 1937, to declare that the Duke of Windsor shall, notwithstanding as instrument of abdication, executed on the 10th day of December, 1936, and His Majesty's Declaration of the Abdication Act of 1936, whereby effect was given to the said instrument, be entitled to hold and enjoy for himself only the title, style or attribute of Royal Highness so however that his wife and descendants, if any, shall not hold said title, style or attribute.

This decision had been reached at a meeting of the cabinet. Prime Minister Baldwin had refused to sit on the matter, and in his place the home secretary, Sir John Simon, strongly influenced the setting of the unfortunate precedent.

To the end of his life, Sir Dudley Forwood never forgot the moment when the duke was informed of the British government's—and his brother the king's—decision:

> [My master] put down his beautiful head with its golden hair in my lap and sobbed helplessly. His heart was broken, and in a sense it never healed. I never saw such agonizing grief, even from the bereaved, or from those who had been told that they had but a short time to live.

As the Joseph P. Kennedy diaries make clear, the chief influences in the matter were the women of the royal family—Queen Mary, the queen, the Duchesses of Gloucester and Kent, and the princess royal—all of whom, to use a term given to Kenneth de Courcy, Duc de Grantmesnil, regarded Wallis as "a woman of easy virtue," based upon their readings of the China dossier.

Queen Victoria is said to have issued an edict laying down the principle that the title "Royal Highness" was to be enjoyed only by relatives of the reigning monarch. But, in fact, this edict had been overridden in at least two famous cases. Her Majesty Queen Elizabeth was a commoner as Lady Elizabeth Bowes-Lyon, but she had been granted the title "Her Royal Highness" when she became Duchess of York. Lady Alice Montagu Douglas-Scott had also assumed that title when she married the Duke of Gloucester. To this day, no satisfactory documentation has been produced to support a legal basis for the denial of the title to Wallis; in fact, she and the duke spent the rest of their lives ignoring the gazetted notice. The duke insisted—with what to many was an irritating degree of persistence—upon Wallis's being called "Your Royal Highness" by everyone, and he demanded that she be curtseyed to both in private and on public occasions. In many cases, ladies obeyed his command only to please him, fully aware of the fact that their action might bring displeasure at the palace. Wallis was never curtseyed to by members of the queen's household. Members of foreign royal families were forbidden to do so. Wallis used the royal insignia, either a coronet surmounted by a lion rampant or a monogram of two entwined Ws under a royal coronet, on her stationery. She and the duke took the view that she was entitled as his wife to use whatever royal imprints she chose. There were many who disagreed. It was not until 1972 that the College of Arms would officially authorize her use of the royal coronet, and then only after the duke's death.

"The wedding will be very small," Aunt Bessie wrote to Corinne in Washington, D.C., on May 31. "Wallis is very well. Thin, but she looks splendidly and she is in fine spirits." On May 30 Helena Normanton of the *New York Times* boldly asked Wallis about her Nazi connections. Wallis replied, quite contradicting Mary Kirk Raffray, "I cannot recall ever being in Herr von Ribbentrop's company more than twice, once at a party at Lady Cunard's before he became Ambassador, and once at another big reception. I was never alone in his company, and I never had more than a few words of conversation with him—simply the usual small talk, that is all. I took no interest at all in politics." Miss Normanton did not have the temerity to question this statement.

More wedding guests began to arrive on June 1. They included Hugh Lloyd Thomas, first secretary of the British embassy in Paris; Lady (Walford) Selby; Walter Monckton; Fruity and Alexandra Metcalfe; the Eugene Rothschilds; George Allen; and Dudley Forwood. At the last minute, a clergyman had been found to officiate: the Reverend R. Anderson Jardine, vicar of St. Paul's Church of Darlington, in the county of Durham. Although it was claimed that Charles Bedaux had bribed Jardine to defy his church and conduct the ceremony, in fact Jardine had volunteered by letter. Despite dire threats from his bishop and from the archbishop of York, he made his way to the château and began working on the arrangements immediately. Jardine had become infuriated by the press announcement that there would be no religious ceremony; abandoning his breakfast, he paced agitatedly around the room, went to his garden, and entered an old army tent, where he sank to his knees in prayer. When he rose to his feet, his mind was made up: he would write to Herman Rogers congratulating the duke and stating that he would be prepared to officiate. That Sunday morning, while he was conducting the children's services, he received a telegram from George Allen asking him to call. The following day he met in London with Allen, who arranged his passport with amazing speed and in the utmost secrecy. The next morning he boarded the boat train. After a brief stay in Paris he was picked up at the local station and driven to the château by the duke's chauffeur.

Cecil Beaton was already there, taking photographs of Wallis and the duke. The Rogerses had entertained Beaton with after-dinner films of Peking, the *Nahlin* cruise, and Wallis's stay at Balmoral. The château was in a turmoil as Constance Spry, the famous florist from London, arrived with her assistant to decorate the residence with flower displays. Wallis watched everything carefully; she was visibly exhausted by the strain of the occasion. But the duke looked fit and sunburned and very happy. The Reverend Jardine drove up. The Rogerses met him at the front steps. Rogers said to him as he shook his hand, "Thank God you have arrived. Now I shall have something to say to the Press."

A few minutes later Rogers read to the crowd of reporters in French and English the astonishing statement that the civil ceremony would be followed by a religious one. This turned the tables on a newspaper hoax that had been proposed, in which the columnist Logan Glendenning would suddenly turn up, wearing a clerical outfit, and perform a fake wedding which would be instantly declared a practical joke. Photographs had even been planned for this vicious leg-pull. The would-be hoaxers were dumbfounded by Rogers's announcement.

Jardine was introduced to the duke and Wallis by George Allen. The duke, dressed in open-neck shirt and shorts, said to Jardine, "Why wouldn't they give us a religious ceremony? We are both Christians. . . . You are the only one who had the guts to do this for me." Jardine gave a prayer book to Wallis; then everybody began searching for an appropriate "holy table" in the absence of an altar. In the frantic hunt somebody broke an Italian lamp. Finally, Jardine discovered a hall chest. The problem was that it was faced with plump nude nymphs holding up a fake Renaissance carving. Protesting against the chest's vulgarity, Wallis managed to find a cream-colored, embroidered silk tea cloth from one of her linen trunks, and she and Katherine began draping the chest to cover the offending nudes. George Allen came in with two silver candlesticks, but Wallis rejected them as they were to be used for dinner. Jardine asked if there was a cross available. Charles Bedaux replied that he had several, but all of them showed the Christ figure. Jardine refused to have a crucifix. The duke suggested contacting the British embassy or even London for a suitable cross. Another crucifix arrived and was rejected. Finally, Charles Bedaux obtained a plain cross from a local church.

There was a hunt for cushions for the couple to kneel on. Beaton took shots of the duke in Wallis's room, followed by photographs of the couple. The session continued after lunch and well into the afternoon. As the duke and Wallis were standing before a turret window for the wedding shots, a communication from Walter Monckton arrived stating that the duke's last-minute appeal to his brother on the matter of "Her Royal Highness" had failed. However, the duke pulled himself together and continued to cooperate with Beaton. When he left that night, Beaton was appalled to discover that a conventional photographer for the London *Evening Standard* had published a photograph ahead of him. Forwood was under great pressure from reporters. He remembered one saying to him, "Do you think the duke has fucked Mrs. Simpson yet?" To which Forwood replied, "I haven't been in the bed." The reporter laughed. Forwood continued, "Right up to the last

minute the duke hoped that his brothers the Dukes of Kent and
Gloucester would come, that somehow the Royal Family would relent.
But they did not. He was deeply, deeply hurt."

There was a prewedding dinner. Everyone at the table was in the
best of spirits. Charles Bedaux sat at the head, the duke at the lower
end. After separating, the men for brandy and cigars and the women
for light conversation, the guests gathered in the library for a recital by
Marcel Dupré. Bored as usual by music, the duke left the recital, drew
Jardine aside, and questioned him, with surprisingly detailed knowledge, on the problems of poverty and unemployment in Durham.

Thursday, June 3, at last arrived. The weather was perfect. "King's
weather," many of the press called it, not quite appropriately. By 7 a.m.
a complete ring of police surrounded the château. There were many
detectives of the Sûreté. The government had forbidden planes to fly
overhead. The entire village of Monts was lined up along the avenue of
pines that led to the gates. Jardine went to see the duke at 7:15. He
was, Jardine wrote, "as happy as a schoolboy." "I suppose I should have
a prayer book," the duke said, and ran out and fetched one given to him
by his mother when he was a child. With tears in his eyes, he showed
Jardine the loving message inscribed in it. By contrast, Lady Alexandra
Metcalfe later recalled that Wallis looked hard, cold, and quietly triumphant now that her hour had arrived.

The civil service took place at 11:42 a.m. Only four newspapermen
were permitted to witness the ceremony. The duke's wedding gift to
Wallis was a diamond tiara. The duke wore a black morning coat and
striped trousers, with a white carnation in his buttonhole. Wallis looked
almost too stiff and formal in Mainbocher's box-shouldered blue outfit.
She wore matching jewelry: diamond-and-sapphire brooch, bracelet,
and earrings. The nearsighted Mayor Mercier was extremely nervous.
The duke kept clasping and unclasping his fingers behind his back.
The religious service followed. Above the holy table stood two golden
candelabra with sixty-two candles apiece. Two more candles flanked
the gilt ormolu mirror at the back of the improvised altar. Marcel
Dupré struck up the strains of Handel's "Wedding March" from *Judas
Maccabeus*. During the benediction Dupré played "O Perfect Love."
Only the duke's excessively loud and high-pitched "I will" disrupted

the composed atmosphere of the ceremony. The wedding ring, of gold mined from the Welsh hills,* made Wallis the Duchess of Windsor. There was no incense, no choir, no pomp. Yet no one who witnessed this occasion would ever forget it.

As Herman Rogers walked out to the porch to announce that the wedding was over, and the couple joined their guests in a buffet lunch of lobster, salad, chicken à la king, and strawberries, the elderly French housekeeper took a bottle of champagne and ritually broke it against the gate, a local tradition; with characteristic neatness, she then removed the broken glass with a broom. Rogers managed to extract a promise from the reporters that they would not pursue the newlyweds to the train station.

Back in England, *The Church Times*, the clerics of St. Paul's Anglican Church at Darlington, and several religious bodies condemned Jardine's action outright. He returned to England to a blizzard of criticism and, unswervingly loyal to the duke and duchess, he decided in the face of widespread criticism to leave his parsonage and make his way to the United States, where he and his wife opened a modest house of religion which they called the Windsor Cathedral of Los Angeles. They were deported back to England in 1942 for overstaying their visas.

Forwood did not forget the events that followed the wedding. The duke and duchess and their large entourage made their way in a convoy of cars to join the Simplon–Orient Express at Laroche-Migennes. They were accompanied by two armed motorcyclists in uniform and a car filled with French gendarmes. Another car was filled with English detectives, including Storrier. Dressers, footmen, the household comptroller M. James, the duchess's maids, and numerous others followed. Because Forwood had not realized that the police escort would drive at a slow speed according to tradition, he had misjudged the length of time it would take to meet the train. He was already worried about the delay and the fact that the train might be missed when, to his horror, the duke announced, "We're going to have a lovely picnic!" Forwood dared not break rank to announce that this might mean missing the express. Following the royal command, every car stopped and a procession led by Wallis and the duke made its way into the fields. The duke

---

*A platinum copy was auctioned in 1987 at Sotheby's.

told Forwood he wanted the dogs to be let off their leashes so that they could relieve themselves. Forwood said that if that were the case, they might be lost. The duchess agreed with Forwood.

The duke then ordered Forwood to take the dogs on their leashes into a cornfield and, in front of everyone, raise his leg repeatedly so that they would follow suit. By the time he had achieved his purpose, tables had been set up for what presumably would be a royal banquet. But when M. James opened the large picnic hampers, it was discovered that all they contained was peaches. Due to some error in the kitchens of the Château de Candé, the rest of the food had all been sent to the train in advance and only the fruit was passed through in the royal caravan. Everyone had to eat the peaches until several felt ill. It could have been a scene from Saint-Simon's journals of the court of Louis XIV.

By the time this disagreeable feast was over, it became obvious even to the duke that the Orient Express might leave without the party. Everyone piled back into the cars, and the chauffeurs drove at reckless speed to the station. Fortunately, though much to the annoyance of the passengers, the express had been held. Then there was the laborious business of putting 266 pieces of royal luggage aboard; the duke insisted that 50 pieces be placed in his private car, leaving scarcely any room even to move. The car was ablaze from one end to the other with red and yellow roses.

The train's departure was still further delayed because one of the Cairn terriers escaped and had to be retrieved. The duchess in her hurry had left her hat in her car, and another automobile with numerous suitcases turned up late.

The Orient Express stopped in Venice on the way to Austria. After so many restrictions on their visits to Italy because of the Foreign Office's sensitivity, the Windsors were delighted to begin their honeymoon in Italy. The Foreign Office under Anthony Eden had, as we know, not allowed the duke to visit Italy before, since such a visit not only would expose the duke's Italian connections but would appear to give a too overt picture of support for Mussolini to the rest of the world. No doubt this, along with the romantic appeal of the Venetian canals, influenced the royal decision to stop off there. A tremendous mass of people greeted them at the station with the Fascist salute, to which the duke responded in kind. Forwood recalls that Mussolini had arranged an elaborate escort of gondolas to accompany the royal party to the Lido, where the group was housed at the Hotel Excelsior. The Windsors had a crowded three and a half hours in the city. It was clear that they were hugely popular in Italy. Gondoliers took them in a brilliantly painted craft down the Grand Canal; they walked through St. Mark's Square, where they fed the pigeons; they saw St. Mark's Cathedral and the Ducal Palace. They took tea at the Excelsior. They boarded the train in the early evening, and as they waved farewell, a hundred carnations arrived from Mussolini in Rome. As they stood at the window of their private car, the duke once again gave the Fascist salute.

The train arrived at Arnoldstein in Austria at 11:45 on the night of the fourth. Dozens of young people dressed in traditional costumes arrived to bid the royal party welcome, but they were rudely turned away by the police. Instead, the Windsors were greeted by six journalists. They stepped off the train in a buoyant mood, accompanied by Dudley Forwood, Chief Inspector Storrier, and Inspector Attfield of Scotland Yard. Paul and Peggy Munster were absent, but the Countess Munster's Mercedes was there to meet them. The chauffeur drove them up a steep, dangerous road to the Castle Wasserleonburg, which dated back to the fifteenth century. The imposing forty-room gothic pile stood framed against the southern escarpments of a mountain. As the couple reached the huge gray-stone doorway, the duke laughed, picked up Wallis, and carried her over the threshold to the hall, where thirty servants were waiting. The ancient housekeeper sagely remarked that the fact that the duke didn't stumble meant the couple would be very happy.

Like Villa Lou Viei, Wasserleonburg had a ghost. Anna Neumann had murdered, according to legend, six husbands; on each honeymoon, she had had a portrait painted of the new husband, and in days he had perished of poison. Achieving her last murder at the age of 82, the blushing bride was caught and executed, leaving a full confession. She was allegedly seen by many, including the Munsters, drifting, a semitransparent gray figure, through the castle's ancient halls.

Wallis immediately made changes in the castle. She stored the horns, tusks, and heads of various hippopotamuses, elephants, and deer in the attic, rearranged the heavy, ugly gothic furniture, and sent an army of newly hired maids to sweep and dust. However, she retained Anna Neumann's enormous sinister oil portrait which glared down from the north wall of the sitting rooms.

The couple seemed happy. The weather was perfect. There was a tremendous view across an Austrian river valley to the snow-capped Julian Alps on the Italian-Yugoslav border, and there was a multiterraced garden with clumps of chrysanthemums and rhododendrons. The village of Noetsch nearby was blissfully free of photographers; it was almost empty because the menfolk were spread through the Alps searching for a savage wolf that had killed five children. World news seemed distant and insignificant in this beautiful spot. There were small ripples of information from the outside world during the days that followed: Ernest Simpson, in London, was pursuing a libel suit against a woman who had charged that he had been paid a substantial sum to yield to Wallis's divorce action. The case was subsequently settled out of court with an apology. The British and American newspapers reported Jardine's drawn-out struggle with the church in England. Otherwise, the couple had little to think about, and they slowly but surely grew bored. Wallis started to scold the duke for having abdicated and denied her the role of royal mistress. On June 8 the couple sent a telegram to Hitler, belatedly thanking him for his good wishes and gift on the occasion of their marriage. The following day they thanked Winston and Mrs. Churchill for a "lovely piece of plate" sent as a wedding present. They also expressed their admiration for Randolph Churchill's article about the wedding in the London *Daily Express*. They posed happily for photographs; then they sent a note to George Allen asking him about Fort Belvedere. He reported that it would be left unoccupied for the indefinite future. Scene of the alleged leakage of the official documents, tainted by the presence of a woman who was utterly evil in the eyes of both court and church, it fell into a sad state of disrepair.

On June 20 the Windsors arrived in Vienna for a stay at the Hotel Bristol. Shortly afterward, Sam Gracie, honorary Brazilian minister in Vienna, and his British wife gave a dinner party for the Windsors at the Brazilian Legation. Among the guests was a young secretary of the Italian embassy and George Messersmith. At dinner, Messersmith reported to Washington, Wallis was very bitter about the American press. The duke hung on her every word. It was then that an extraordinary episode took place. At coffee, the secretary of Chancellor von Schuschnigg arrived unexpectedly. He called Messersmith aside and gave him a sealed message stating that a train from Germany to Italy had been wrecked and that naval shells had been found in it, sent by the Berlin admiralty for use by Mussolini's navy. This was top-secret information, of gravest concern to neutralist Austria and the United States, because it proved that Germany was directly supplying the Italian war machine. When Messersmith returned from his meeting with the chancellor's secretary to the party, the duke asked Messersmith why von Schuschnigg had sent somebody to see him. Foolishly, Messersmith breached the confidence and gave the duke the secret intelligence that had been conveyed to him. Soon afterward, Messersmith noticed that the duke was talking to the secretary of the Italian embassy, who left immediately. The next day the military attaché of the U.S. Legation brought to Messersmith an intercepted and decoded telegram that the Italian ambassador, Prezziozi, had sent the night before to the Foreign Office in Rome; it said that, at the dinner, the duke had revealed the secret information of the train crash and that "the cat was out of the bag so far as the Naval shells were concerned." The duke had given away to the Italians the fact that the American government had obtained secret information about Nazi-Italian connections.

In the FBI files on the Windsors in Washington, a lengthy report shows that an American secret agent named Helga Stultz, planted in the archives at Hitler's country eyrie of Berchtesgaden, listened to a conversation between Hitler and Robert Ley, labor leader, discussing the upcoming royal visit to Germany. Ley said he had been in touch with the pro-Nazi former British prime minister David Lloyd George, who had recently visited the führer for consultations, to discuss what capital could be made from the Windsors' tour.

Hitler told Ley he must convey to the Windsors, and to Lloyd George, that the only hope for the future of the world was if the Duke of Windsor returned to the English throne with Lloyd George as prime minister. He added:

This cannot happen unless there is a war. Though the British don't want to fight and have no stomach for it, I believe they may blunder into war. If that happens, they will collapse within a year. We will have new rulers to deal with and I am certain [from our talks] that Lloyd George will give us back our colonies without a fuss. He promised me he would agree to this.

The Windsors continued in Vienna until the beginning of July. Both celebrated their birthdays in the city. Gifts poured in from all over the world. On June 25 word came from distant San Diego that Commander Earl Winfield Spencer had announced his engagement to a Miss Norma Reese Johnson.* On June 30 a story appeared in the London *Evening Standard* in which Sir Gerald Wollaston, garter king of arms, stated that the duke "had hurried arrangements for his father's funeral." The duke was upset when he read the piece. Back at Wasserleonburg on July 1, he denied the charges to local reporters and told the newspaper's editor by telephone that Wollaston was the only person involved who wanted the funeral delayed. In New York the Reverend Jardine ran into trouble when he threatened to "blow the lid off" the abdication story by revealing that the duke was driven from England by "a political consortium." He claimed to have "inside information." Since he did not, and his remarks were irresponsible, many of his lecture engagements were canceled by their sponsors out of consideration for the British government.

Aunt Bessie arrived at the castle on July 22. The Windsors were accompanying her to Salzburg for the annual music festival when their chauffeur collided with a trolley car in the packed central city square; no one was injured. The following night all three attended Beethoven's opera *Fidelio*, under the direction of Arturo Toscanini. There was a dazzling society audience for the opera. Toscanini's conducting of the overture brought an ovation of an intensity which even that great maestro had seldom experienced. Lotte Lehmann was the star, overcoming the notorious flaws in her voice by the sheer force of her dramatic temperament. When the Windsors and Aunt Bessie fought their way through the crowd to the buffet at intermission, they were greeted by a burst of applause. The 83-year-old Mrs. Sara Delano Roosevelt, mother of the president, was upstaged in the bar as more than 200 Americans gazed, transfixed, at Wallis, who looked magnificent in a white taffeta Schiaparelli gown illuminated with a thousand sequins.

On July 28 the Windsors returned to Venice by train. Once more,

---

*He had been involved in a horrible incident at the St. Francis Hotel in San Francisco in which a newlywed bride had left her husband for him and after a quarrel with him had flung herself from a window to her death.

the Italians greeted them ecstatically; they could hardly make their way down the Grand Canal as hundreds of gondolas swarmed about them. Hundreds more gathered at the Lido to catch a glimpse of them as they entered the Excelsior. Scores of photographs were taken when they sunbathed and swam the next day.

That same evening, Barbara Hutton and her fierce husband Count Haugwitz-Reventlow gave a party for the Windsors on the terrace of the Grand Hotel; among the guests were Wallis's old friends the theatrical producer Gilbert Miller and his wife Kitty Bache, the Maharaja and Maharani of Jaipur, and, interestingly enough, Count Ciano and his wife Edda Mussolini. Wallis was not told of the guest list in advance, and it is easy to imagine her feelings when she walked onto the terrace and saw her former lover, the father of her aborted child, rising to greet her. How she carried the evening off is not recorded; however, Barbara Hutton, who kept a diary entry on the occasion, noted that Wallis and the duke emphasized the virtues of fascism to their companions and that Wallis snapped at the duke constantly, instructing him on what to say and what to eat. Next day, Wallis and Barbara spent an estimated $25,000 between them shopping at the exclusive linen store Olga Asta's.

On the night of the thirtieth, they appeared at a performance of the Monte Carlo Ballet in *Romeo and Juliet*, and they danced for three hours after that at the Pergola nightclub. Their best friend in Venice was the Duke of Genoa, a cousin of King Victor Emmanuel. Once again, the duke frequently gave the Fascist salute to the delight of the Venetians and the consternation of Whitehall. He was, after all, still a member of the royal family, and whatever British foreign policy was regarding appeasement of Mussolini, this public indication of support for the Italian dictator was highly inadvisable.

By August 7 the Windsors were back at Wasserleonburg. Plans were advancing further for the trip to Nazi Germany. The key figure in the arrangements was still Fritz Wiedemann. A seeming Anglophile, Wiedemann held firm to the idea of peace with Great Britain for the indefinite future. He represented the group in Germany that was in support of a restoration of the powers of the German royal family. He believed, as much as the Duke of Windsor did, in recementing the royal family alliances that had been broken in World War I. As a political moderate, he was not in tune with the extremist elements of the

Nazis, but nonetheless, despite statements to the contrary, he was a devout servant of the führer. He had several strong connections in London. Among these was his mistress, the egregious, half-Jewish Nazi agent Princess Stephanie Hohenlohe. Hitler had a surprising sexual interest in her despite her part-Jewish origin; he was prepared to overlook ethnic prejudice when employing certain loyal servants of the Third Reich. Later, he would give her the producer Max Reinhardt's castle as a present.

It was Wiedemann, under direct instructions of the führer, rather than Charles Bedaux, who was responsible for the Windsors' arrangements for their German trip in the fall. Dr. Robert Ley, Reich labor leader, was helping to sort out the details. It was agreed with the duke while he was in Austria that all payments for the trip would be made available from the special funds of the Hitler-controlled Reichsbank. Needless to say, the duke preferred it to be thought that he subsidized the trip himself.

On August 19, 1937, Charles Bedaux, who was in Budapest, called to see Howard K. Travers, chargé d'affaires at the U.S. Legation. Bedaux announced that he was acting for the Duke of Windsor and said that the duke wished to study the lot of the lower classes and desired "to make a complete study of working conditions in various countries." This seemed harmless enough until Bedaux, somewhat indiscreetly, added the dangerous words, "with a view to returning to England at a later date as the champion of the working classes." This was a deadly, dynamite-laden statement. What it implied was that the duke wished to upstage King George VI and reenter Great Britain, probably to seek political office. With the enthusiastic support of the peoples of Europe and the United States, he hoped to reassemble his vast following in Britain.

The statement that Bedaux made on his behalf had leaked back to London when Howard Travers reported it in a "strictly confidential" memorandum to the State Department on August 19. By that time, George Messersmith had returned to Washington as assistant secretary of state in charge of the Balkans, and when he received the document on September 10, there can be no question that he referred it to the appropriate British authorities. The result would seriously affect the Windsors' entire future.

There was another reason for the duke's desire to visit Germany, which has been confirmed by Sir Dudley Forwood. He told me:

Why did they go to Germany? I have very strong views on this. It was not to give a public statement of his approval for the Nazis. We went because he wanted his beloved wife to experience a state visit. And the only way such a state visit was possible was to make the arrangements with Hitler.

Sir Dudley did not explain why a visit to Mussolini would not have been equally possible, and perhaps slightly less dangerous.

Sir Dudley continued:

It must be admitted that, whereas the duke, duchess and I had no idea that the Germans were or would be committing mass murder of Jews, we were none of us averse to Hitler politically. We all felt that the Nazi regime was a more appropriate government that the Weimar Republic which had been extremely Socialist and under which, we felt, Germany might have turned Socialist. Instead of *National* Socialist, which we felt was the lesser of two evils.

On September 2, Hardinge wrote to Vansittart clarifying the Windsors' status:

His Royal Highness the Duke of Windsor and the Duchess should not be treated by His Majesty's representatives as having any official status in the countries which they visit. For this reason it seems to the King that, except under special instructions, His Majesty's representatives should not have any hand in arranging official interviews for them, or countenance their participation in any official ceremonies.

He continued by stating that it was the king's wish that the duke and duchess not be invited to stay as guests in any embassy or legation. Ambassadors or ministers should not meet the couple at a station, and entertainment at the embassy would be strictly private and informal. The Duchess of Windsor must be placed on the right of His Majesty's representative on each occasion. "Anything of an official nature should be avoided."

The same day, Vansittart wrote to Sir Geoffrey Knox, British ambassador to Hungary, stating:

H.R.H. the Duke of Windsor and the Duchess should be treated on the same lines as a member of the Royal Family on a holiday. If anything were contemplated which might give to the visit a more serious aspect,

you should refer home at once. It is not considered that you should
yourself meet them at the station, but that you should send a senior
member of your staff. If they seem to wish to lunch or dine at the legation, there would be no harm in your inviting them, but you should
avoid asking any politically prominent Hungarians to meet them.

The Windsors arrived in Hungary to stay with Bedaux at his Borsodivanka Castle on September 9. By now, both Washington and the Secret
Intelligence Service were again keeping a very sharp eye on them.
Messersmith hadn't forgotten the incident in Vienna when the duke had
leaked the fact that Messersmith was informed about the arms shipment from Germany to Italy.

On September 14 Bedaux was back at the U.S. Legation in Budapest,
saying that Travers should inform the State Department that the duke
would make a public announcement on October 3. In the statement he
would disclose the fact that he and the duchess would visit Germany at
Hitler's invitation for twelve days, beginning October 11, and that "the
German government [had] placed two airplanes and eight automobiles
at [their] disposal." The British ambassador at Berlin, Sir Eric Phipps,
would be informed on the same day. The Windsors would leave for
New York on the German steamer *Bremen* on November 11, and the
duke "would appreciate being received by the President in order to discuss social welfare." In his memorandum to Assistant Secretary of State
Wilson, Travers wrote, "[The duke] desires that his forthcoming visit
[plans] be kept entirely secret, but will telegraph the British Ambassador
in Washington at the same time he informs [the] British Ambassador in
Berlin, October 3. The British government is not yet informed of the
proposed visits, and he desires to keep them confidential until his October 3 announcement."

Meantime, despite Bedaux's great air of secrecy, the duke informed
Sir Ronald Lindsay, British ambassador in Washington, who was on
leave in England, that he would be going to America; Lindsay, in a memorandum of that date to the Foreign Office in London, warned that there
might be a subsequent attempt by the duke "to stage a semi-Fascist
comeback in England by playing up to labor in America."

Sir Robert Vansittart summoned Lindsay to the Foreign Office to
show him the secret file on the duchess's espionage activities. What he
saw there appalled him. Vansittart told him that instructions had been

sent to every British minister and ambassador in the world forbidding them to accommodate the Windsors, give them dinners, or present them officially to anyone; at any railroad station, they were to be met by no one more important than a third secretary. The Windsors were to be given only "a bite of luncheon," a contemptuous final touch. That was how severe and damaging the contents of Vansittart's files had become.

The degree of Nazi (and more emphatically Italian) collaboration determined by Vansittart was extreme, going far beyond mere sympathy or approval. The Windsors traveled to Bucharest, Romania, on September 13. They were in Vienna on the fourteenth and then continued to Czechoslovakia where they contacted members of the Sports and Shooting Club of Austria, who were visiting there. On November 1 of the following year, Ribbentrop's Dienststelle, or Special Intelligence Service, reported that Windsor was president of the club. This cadre of wealthy socialites and members of minor royalty, some of whom were bisexuals, was considered dangerous and illegal, and it was under watch order by the gestapo and the Austrian police.

The report reads in full:

> On German territory, in the neighborhood of Salzburg, is situated the Scholss Mittersill, which belongs to the company known as SIMAG, owned by the Princes of Lichtenstein. The aforementioned SIMAG has lent the castle to the Sports and Shooting Club, including its golf course and tennis courts.
>
> The Duke of Windsor is honorary President of the club. From the membership roster, it is clear that a number of noted representatives of the royal families of Europe as well as foreign politicians are members. The club's exclusiveness may be judged by the fact that the membership fees are enormously high.
>
> The club is now looking for German and other supporters. The local Police Chief and Salzburg Civil Authorities for State and Foreign Policy as well as [the gestapo] for ideological reasons are interested in investigating the activities of the club. According to a report by a Professor Lehofrich of Vienna, a clean-up of the club's activities will be impossible without full German control. As an example, [one royal member] has recently fled Vienna because he was under threat of arrest on charges of homosexuality. In connection with this the [police] report also charges the Duke of Windsor with allegations of bisexuality.

That week of mid-September, Wallis and the duke were at Charles Bedaux's Borsodivanka Castle. On September 18 Cordell Hull, U.S.

secretary of state, sent a memorandum to Budapest via consul Hugh
Wilson saying that the president would be happy to receive the duke,
but General Watson, the presidential secretary, added in handwriting
the note "subject of course to consultation with the British Embassy at
the appropriate time." He scratched out the words "who do not want
this matter made public." Hull's memorandum continued, "It is difficult and even somewhat embarrassing to take a definite position until
this government knows the relationship of the British Embassy toward
the proposed visit." By now, all cables in the matter were being sent in
confidential code and marked "No Distribution." The matter was explosive: in view of the duke's popularity, the U.S. government did not
want to seem to be insulting him, but at the same time the security files
on the Windsors were so damaging that Washington was nervous of
causing offense in Whitehall by arranging for him to be received.
Matters were scarcely helped by the fact that the duke wanted to be
accompanied on the whole tour by an executive of Eastman Kodak,
which was in direct partnership with its equivalent German company.
On September 14, 1937, Victor Mallet, British chargé d'affaires in
Washington, referred to the Bedaux approach in Budapest in a memorandum to Eden:

> The Duke has now ceased being front-page news over here, but if he
> were to come out this autumn we shall have all the old ballyhoo revived
> again. What is more, the tale of his sympathy for the South Wales min-
> ers and the consequent wrath of Mr. Baldwin, which is still widely be-
> lieved in the middle west, will be revived by his proposed investigation
> of the life of the American working man. I can only hope that nothing
> will come of this suggested trip, but I should be very grateful for any
> news which you may have about it.

On September 30, Oliver Harvey of the Foreign Office in London
sent a lengthy memorandum to Vansittart about the Windsors' proposed tour of Germany. The memorandum revealed that the prime
minister took the view that it would be impossible to stop the duke
from making the visit, but that care should be taken to prevent representatives of the British government from taking any action which could
be construed as countenancing the visit. In the same report Harvey revealed that it was known to the king that the German government had
arranged the visit and that it was considered at the palace "most im-

proper that the German Government should take upon itself to arrange such a visit without informing us." It was felt at the palace that no member of the British embassy staff in Berlin should meet the royal train, "lest it might appear as giving a British official nature to the tour in Germany." Vansittart scribbled in the margin, "I quite agree. This is really a monstrous innovation—for propaganda purposes. . . . I agree with Sir Alexander Hardinge. We have not been consulted and should therefore stand aloof."

On October 1, Vansittart wrote a memorandum to Hardinge confirming that "nothing can be done to prevent [the visit] but that His Majesty's representatives should not take any action which could be regarded as countenancing it." He added: "Personally I think these tours, prearranged without a word to us, are a bit too much. And I hope our missions abroad will be instructed to have as little as possible to do with them. If we are to be expected to assist, we are entitled to be consulted, and to have a chance at dissuasion. The direct approach to our missions, without our knowledge, is hardly fair." In a response of the following day, Hardinge wrote in a postscript, "I entirely agree with what you say about these tours, and I feel strongly that nothing should be done to make them appear other than what they are. I.e., private stunts for political purposes—they can obviously bring no benefit to the workers themselves." The same day Sir George Ogilvie-Forbes, British chargé d'affaires in Berlin, cabled in a mood of anxiety, saying:

> If this visit comes off, I earnestly hope that your instructions will be to accord to the Duke of Windsor courtesies not less than is the authorized practice at Vienna Legation. German Government are certain to make the maximum capital and publicity out of this visit, and it will be extremely embarrassing and painful for me if I am instructed to ignore His Royal Highness's presence, for this will not be understood here. . . . While I will of course scrupulously comply with the King's wishes, I trust that above will be taken into consideration.

On October 3 Ronald Lindsay wrote, from his house in Dorset, to Vansittart, saying among other things that "the intended visit of the Duke and Duchess of Windsor to Washington fills me with unmitigated horror. . . . Of course the general lines of my conduct will be dictated to me by the Palace and the Prime Minister, and I shall do nothing till I receive from you the necessary indications of what is wished; but it will not have escaped your notice that there is a purely American side to this affair."

He added:

> The visit will be a tremendous sensation—I think it certain that from the first moment [the Windsors] will be in the fullest glare of publicity and will be fairly mobbed wherever they go. The attitude of the Embassy will be a matter of the greatest public interest.
>
> In my opinion it will be important to allow nothing to transpire indicating that *the visit to America in itself* is in any way disapproved, and I think therefore that I ought certainly to put the Duke and Duchess up at the Embassy while they are in Washington; and I think they should be presented at the White House and that I should at least give them a large Belshazzar [feast].
>
> But I imagine that I should dissociate myself, tacitly, from the undeclared objects of the visit—that is from most of the Duke's activities in America outside Washington.

From the tenor of the memorandum, it is clear that the duke's extracurricular activities were again thought to be dangerously political.

With the Windsors now in Vienna after a brief trip to Paris, the discomfort of the U.S. government increased. Hugh Wilson, now in charge of the matter at the State Department, wrote a memorandum to Cordell Hull saying that there was clearly "a distinct political purpose" in the Windsor trip to Germany. The government was still "not taking sides" in what was, "after all, a strictly British internal question."

On October 4 Vansittart wrote to Hardinge stating it would be preferable that the royal couple not be entertained at the British embassy. Moreover, the ambassadorial staff should be instructed to refuse any invitations of a ceremonial character issued during the tour.

In a memorandum dated October 6 Hardinge made clear to Oliver Harvey of the Foreign Office that is was now known for certain that the German government was sponsoring the tour.

Hardinge cabled Sir George Ogilvie-Forbes in Berlin on October 6, categorically stating that the king forbade Forbes to attend the Windsors' arrival at the station in Berlin, that no member of the staff should accept any invitations connected with the tour, that Ogilvie-Forbes should have no hand in arranging any official engagements or interviews, that the Windsors were not to be entertained by any member of the embassy, nor should the staff accept invitations from the duke, and the consular officials should not meet the royal party on arrival anywhere. Above all, "The Embassy must scrupulously avoid in any way giving the appearance that His Majesty the King and His Majesty's government countenance the proposed tour."

Forbes replied on October 7 in the following terms:

> The instructions will be carefully carried out. Nevertheless I feel I should tell you they will leave an unfavorable impression of the attitude of the Embassy and of [His Majesty's government] which the Germans in all probability will view as another snub to a friendly gesture. They will closely watch the measure of recognition the Duke receives from H.M. missions in other foreign countries.

At last, the arrangements for the visit to Germany were concluded. It was announced in the *New York Times* on October 9 that a conversation would take place between Adolf Hitler and "the English guest" which would be "an open discussion of those questions interesting the Duke." These questions would involve "the new Germany in its varied aspects, its hopes and aspirations and Hitler's hopes for the future." The Windsors would visit nine cities. The main purpose of their trip would be to study working conditions.

On October 9 Sir Ronald Lindsay was summoned by the king to Balmoral for an extraordinary meeting on the matter of the Windsors. The queen was there, and among those present were two of the duke's worst enemies, Alan Lascelles and the recently knighted Sir Alexander Hardinge. Lindsay pointed out that if the Windsors were not accommodated at the British embassy, it would be regarded by millions of Americans as a snub and an act of disapproval of the duke's interest in labor. The king, Hardinge, and Lascelles variously stated that the duke was behaving abominably: it was his duty not to embarrass the king; he was dropping bombshell after bombshell; and what would come next? Lindsay wrote to his wife two days later:

> [In their view] he was trying to stage a comeback, and his friends and advisors were semi-Nazis. He was not straight—he hadn't let the King have an inkling of his plans, and the first news of them was a letter from him to the King's own agent. . . . What if he were to go to a Dominion? Or to cross over from the United States into Canada? There was a lot of talk about a scheme by which I should invite him to stay at the Embassy, and then a swift emissary should speed over and persuade him to decline.

This absolutely horrified me and it was, thank God, discarded because [they realized] "that woman" would never allow him to decline, and because there exists no emissary who would command confidence and at the same time stand the smallest chance of influencing the Duke.

The queen joined in the conversation. She expressed grief rather than indignation as she mentioned the duke. "He's so changed now," she said, "and he used to be so kind to us." She had no good words to say about Wallis. It was clear that the royal family was uniform in its resolve that the Windsors would receive absolutely no privileges on their American visit. The king and queen would not even allow them to be accompanied by Lindsay when they went to the White House. Lindsay wrote to his wife on October 17, "[The duke] is being turned into a purely Nazi show, and of course he is known here to have decided Nazi tendencies." Later, Lindsay managed to arrange through the Secret Intelligence Service to have two letters that were written by Bedaux intercepted and smuggled to the embassy. The letters were to private contacts in the United States and indicated that the duke planned to be the leader of an international peace movement, which was considerably more sinister than it sounded.

The Windsors left Paris by train for Berlin, a crowd of 300 waving them good-bye. When the Nord Express chugged into the Friedrichstrasse Station in Berlin, hundreds more were waiting to greet them. The crowd screamed, "Heil Windsor!" interspersed with "Heil Edward!" as they stepped down from the platform to meet with Dr. Robert Ley, Fritz Wiedemann, the deputy political leader Artur Goerlitzer, and, amid a swarm of uniformed officials and a gestapo guard, a rather embarrassed third secretary of the British embassy.

The Windsors checked into the Kaiserhof Hotel. Again, an immense crowd was waiting for them, chanting a specially composed song provided by the Propaganda Ministry. In defiance of the British Foreign Office, Sir George Ogilvie-Forbes, continuing chargé d'affaires in the absence of Sir Neville Henderson, the British ambassador who had sagely taken leave of absence, arrived at the Kaiserhof to pay his respects. He noted that the Windsors' suite directly overlooked Hitler's Chancellery.

Sir George Ogilvie-Forbes explained to the duke that the king regarded the visit as purely private and unofficial and laid down the rules vis-à-vis no entertaining, etc. Forbes cabled Harvey in London, "I shall . . . be very glad when the visit is over, as the absence of the Embassy from participation is marked and the subject of comment. The Ambassador is fortunate to be away."

Wallis stayed at the hotel resting while, shortly after noon, the duke visited the Stock Machine Works at Grünewald. Swastikas flew from the roof as the duke examined the ultramodern buildings in which 3,000 workers enjoyed an elaborate restaurant, an assembly and concert hall, a swimming pool, and handsomely planted lawns and flower beds. The duke asked several questions in German and obtained details of factory life from workers whom Dr. Ley brought forward one by one. With loud laughs and hearty slaps on the back, Ley encouraged each man to tell the duke of the conditions of work, how disputes were resolved, and how labor and management conferred openly, unhampered by the spirit of class. Several men told the duke of their high wages, physical fitness classes each morning, and the nourishing food served in the restaurant. That afternoon the duke, along with 1,000 workers, attended a concert of Wagner and Liszt given by the Berlin Labor Front Orchestra; it featured the "Grail Aria" from *Lohengrin*, sung by Hitler's favorite American operatic tenor, F. Eyvind Laholm. At the end of the concert, "Deutschland Uber Alles" and the "Horst Wessel" were played, followed by "God Save the King." The duke returned at 4:30 p.m. and went shopping with Wallis.

That night Robert Ley gave an elaborate party at his thirty-seven-room house in the Grünewald. Among the guests were Dr. Joseph Goebbels, Ribbentrop, Goerlitzer, Himmler, and Hess. Goering could not be there because his brother-in-law had just been killed in the Bavarian Alps. The next day, while Wallis again stayed at the hotel, breaking her solitude only for a brief drive to Potsdam and back, the duke undertook a grueling inspection tour. An elaborate observation coach, described by Frederick T. Birchall of the *New York Times* as resembling somewhat "a streamlined duck," was used for the journey. It included nine seats, a bar, a small dining area, a wireless telephone, and a parlor car. Ley slowed its normal speed of eighty miles per hour to forty along the autobahns so that the duke could get a good view of the countryside. At the Pomeranian border the coach halted to take aboard the local governor, who joined the party headed by Ley on the journey to Crossensee, headquarters of the training school of the Death's Head Division of the Elite Squad of the SS. The Death's Head band greeted the party, playing the British national anthem, to which the duke responded with a detailed inspection as the men presented arms and he gave them a full Hitler salute. The sprawling barracks buildings, with their thatched roofs, were dominated by a vast tower with ancient gateway. Here, the cream of Hitler youth studied and trained for four years, undergoing rigorous physical training for five hours a day. The duke's hosts explained to him that the main subjects of teaching were racial biology, German archaeology, history, and politics. After lunch he went on to the Stargard military airport. In Dr. Ley's twelve-passenger plane, he flew over the Baltic coast to see a four-mile beach and luxury hotel which was being built to accommodate members of the Nazi youth movement. He returned to Berlin at 6 p.m.

That evening the Aga Khan, having just presided over the League of Nations Assembly, dropped by the hotel after dinner. His sympathies were in accord with the Windsors'. Three years later, on July 25, 1940, German Foreign Ministry documents would reveal that he planned to join Hitler at Windsor Castle and that he recommended renewed bombing of England a few days before more bombing took place. The next day, October 14, heavy rain prevented the duke from flying to Brunswick; instead, he and Wallis visited the Berlin War Museum and the Pergamon Museum; later, the duke went to a Turkish bath. That afternoon the couple visited with the Goerings for tea at the air minister's famous hunting lodge, Karinhall. They saw the plump field marshal's electric train and chatted away happily; Frau Goering never forgot the encounter, writing of it warmly in her memoirs many years later.

Forwood remembered:

We had a meal at Karinhall, at which Goering and the Duke and Duchess sat at a high table on a raised dais while the rest of us sat below. Behind Goering's desk there was a large map in marquetry. Except for England, the map was completely covered in colors indicating that it was in the possession of Germany. My master looked at Goering and said, "Isn't this a little impertinent? A little premature?" Goering replied, "It is fated. It must be." I remember the field marshal saying, "My wife is pregnant. If it's a son, a thousand planes will fly overhead. If it's a daughter, only five hundred." There was one vulgar touch I remember. There were paintings of nude women over his bed.

Another evening was set aside on Hitler's orders for a banquet in the private dining room of Horchers, the leading restaurant of Berlin, with Dr. Goebbels as host. Next day, Goebbels invited them to his country estate without telling his wife, who was appalled to find she had no cakes or scones ready for the teatime hour and had a servant go out and buy them. The only detail of the meeting to have survived appears in the memoirs of the propaganda minister's press secretary, Wilfred Von Oven (*Mit Goebbels bis zum Ende* [*With Goebbels to the End*], privately published in Buenos Aires in 1948). The discussion was predictably occupied with the theme that Germany and England must join against Russia, the common enemy. Goebbels told Van Oven after the tea, "Meeting [the duke] was one of the greatest impressions of my life." Later he was to call him "that tender seedling of reason."

That evening, the Windsors had a very interesting visitor: Ernst Wilhelm Bohle.* Yet another visitor in the next twenty-four hours was again Dr. Goebbels. He had, of course, been host for the Oswald Mosleys when they were married the previous year in his house. Goebbels always regretted that Windsor had left the throne. During World War II Goebbels wrote in his diary that he regarded as a tragedy the failure of Germany to make an arrangement with the duke toward permanent alliance. He regarded his meeting with the duke as one of "the great impressions of my life." The Duke of Windsor struck him as "a far-sighted, clever and yet modern man." He recognized the supreme importance of the social problem in Germany. Goebbels continued, "He was too clever, too progressive, too appreciative of the problem of the underprivileged, and too pro-German" (to have remained on the throne). Goebbels concluded, "This tragic figure could have saved Europe from her doom. But instead, as Governor of the

_____

*Born in Bradford, England, Bohle was raised in South Africa and had renounced his British citizenship just before the Windsors arrived. Intelligent, forceful, and domineering, he had joined the Nazi party in 1932. In 1933 he became head of the Auslands Organisation, known familiarly as the AO. It was the organization of Germans abroad. In November 1933 he was elected to the Reichstag. He was bent upon securing a permanent alliance of all international peoples of German descent against the Soviet Union. Later, he would be secretly instrumental in the flight of Rudolf Hess to Scotland, and he undertook the translations of Hess's letters to the Duke of Hamilton concerning a negotiated peace. Most historians have thought that Hess undertook the mission without help from the government.

Bahamas, he had to witness the disintegration of the British Empire and perhaps of Europe and the West altogether."

On the fifteenth, the Windsors went to Essen by train to visit a large coal mine. The duke went down 1,500 feet into the bowels of the earth, with Dudley Forwood, negotiating a series of awkward steel ladders, with water splashing on his head, to the base of the shaft, and then went on to Krupp's armaments factory, the leading German armament manufacturers. A reception was given by the president of the Rhine province that night in honor of the distinguished guests.

On the sixteenth, the Windsors were in Düsseldorf, where they attended a so-called creative folk exposition. Surrounded by yelling, laughing, and frantically gesturing people, the duke, flanked by a flying squad of SS men, responded in kind to a chorus of "Heils." The duke was impressed and deeply fascinated, but the duchess was bored, as the guide, Dr. Maiwald, whom the duke had met during the Paris Exposition, explained the exhibits of every aspect of German industry. They saw examples of artificial textiles being made, buna rubber, and displays of the uses of coal, sand, stone, and wood. Dr. Maiwald said for years afterward that no other person he had ever entertained knew as much about the technical details of industry as the duke, who yet again gave the Nazi salute as he journeyed through the crowded streets.* There was an incident in which an Englishwoman had to be arrested because she was screaming out threats. The Windsors went on to see a miners' hospital, where they talked with injured men; then the duke went alone to see the Krupp colony for workers, unexpectedly dropping in on some old-age pensioners. The Windsors returned to their hotel, going over the details of their American trip. They were still completely ignored by the local British consular representatives.

They visited a concentration camp which appeared to be quite deserted. Forwood said, "We saw this enormous concrete building which of course I now know contained inmates. The duke asked, 'What is that?' Our host replied, 'It is where they store the cold meat.' In a horrible sense, that was true."

On October 17, the Windsors were in Leipzig. Once more, a crowd of several thousand greeted them at the station with the Hitler salute, and this time there were forty swastika banners waved overhead. Iron-

---

*The newsreels were tampered with in England to remove his "heiling" arm.

ically, the best hotel in Leipzig was closed because it had a Jewish owner, and they had to take second best in an unsatisfactory hotel. As thousands more stood in the street below their windows, the duke thanked them in German for their kindness, saluted them, and then said good-night. That same evening he made it clear to Ley that he would not be prepared to meet Herr Julius Streicher, the Nuremberg party chief; the reason can be deduced from an article that appeared several months earlier in Streicher's newspaper *Stürmer*, accusing the duchess of being Jewish.

That same day, Sir George Ogilvie-Forbes wrote to Eden, who handed the letter to Hardinge and Sir Roland Lindsay, discussing a meeting Forbes had just had on the fifteenth with Prentiss Gilbert, new counselor and chargé d'affaires at the U.S. embassy. He reported that Gilbert had discussed with him the matter of the Windsor visit to the United States and had mentioned that Bedaux had approached him to get U.S. government approval of the visit and treatment in America of the duchess as royalty. Gilbert told Ogilvie-Forbes that he did not encourage these proposals. Bedaux had made it plain to Gilbert that he would be paying the Windsors' expenses for the American tour; Bedaux also revealed the illuminating fact that following the official visit to the United States the duke would make a similar one to Italy and Sweden. In Sweden he would be put in touch, by Bedaux, with Axel Wenner-Gren, the multimillionaire Swedish Nazi collaborator and inventor of the vacuum cleaner. The report added:

> [The Swedish millionaire] . . . was interested in world peace through labor reconciliation. Bedaux said it was also intended that H.R.H. should take up this line and even went so far as to express the opinion that H.R.H. might in due course be the "savior" of the monarchy! Bedaux also tried behind Gilbert's back to get Miss Frances Perkins, the American Secretary of Labor, to send an invitation direct to H.R.H., an attempt which has been foiled. . . . Much of the above will, I fear, be painful reading, but I feel you ought to know what has been going on here and that it would be as well to keep an eye on Mr. Bedaux's activities.

On the twentieth, the Windsors' old friend and cousin Charles, Duke of Saxe-Coburg-Gotha, gave an elaborate dinner party for the Windsors and a hundred guests at the Grand Hotel in Nuremberg. The guests included many of the aristocrats with whom the duke had hobnobbed during his father's jubilee and funeral. Coburg told the Windsors at the dinner that he totally accepted Wallis's right to be "Her Royal Highness." His wife and all the other women guests curt-seyed to her deeply. Even her place card carried the German equiva-lent of H.R.H.

The Windsors visited what the *New York Times* called "the altars and temples of the National Socialist Cult." The couple continued to Stuttgart. An awkward incident took place there. While returning from a factory visit, the duke, who had left Wallis at the hotel, on an impulse decided he wanted to see the palace of the kings of Württem-berg. Dr. Ley looked embarrassed, but the duke insisted. When he en-tered, he was interested to see a huge illuminated map of the world in lights, showing those portions which represented the German colonies "improperly" seized from the Reich after World War I. He grimaced with displeasure when he noted that certain of these were now British possessions. He also saw a display of photographs of Nazi storm troops marching through Chicago and New Jersey. He was shown more maps, marked in red to indicate how many Germans lived in certain countries. That night the duke and duchess went to the great municipal audito-rium to attend a "Strength through Joy" festival. They saw a pageant and play illustrating the glories of German youth; their arrival and de-parture were marked by frantic shouting, applause, and Nazi salutes.

And now at last came the climax of the trip: the meeting with Adolf Hitler on October 22, which took place just twenty-five days after Hitler had entered Berlin with Mussolini, joining him in an exchange of toasts at an official banquet. That encounter had sealed the doom of all the early dreams of the Duke of Windsor that by his appeasing the Italian dictator, Mussolini and the führer would be kept firmly apart. Three days before the ducal visit, Lord Halifax had visited Hitler, hop-ing to sustain the British balance of power in western Europe by at least seeming to encourage Hitler's now unbridled ambitions. In the course of the conversation, Halifax had stated that the new prime min-ister, Neville Chamberlain, wanted to make a permanent settlement with Germany and encourage talks on the cabinet level between Lon-don and Berlin; Britain would concede to Hitler certain colonies in Africa and would give him a free hand in eastern Europe. Nothing much came of this conversation. As it happened, Hitler had already de-cided in secrecy on a policy of obtaining "living space" by going to war.

He would strike west as well as east; but it was part of his policy to pretend to representatives of the British Empire that he wanted only peace with England. From the führer's point of view, the timing of the duke's visit was extremely appropriate. He knew that the duke, obsessed with bolshevism as he was, would be very happy to encourage the führer in his desire to strike at Russia. Hitler was prepared to encourage any folly, even from an abdicated monarch, that would allow him to carry off his supreme bluff in the matter of foreign policy.

Hitler's mistress, Eva Braun, eagerly awaited the arrival of the duke and duchess. Her biographer, Nerin E. Gun, wrote:

> Eva begged Hitler to let her be introduced to the Duchess of Windsor. [She] had subjected her lover to endless eulogies of the ex-monarch who "had renounced an Empire for love of a woman. . . ." . . . According to some, she hinted that Mrs. Simpson [*sic*] had something in common with Eva Braun, and that a sincere lover could accept a small sacrifice— not the loss of a crown like Edward, but the risk of a slight blow to his prestige, by marrying the woman that he declared he loved. Hitler pretended not to understand and in order not to aggravate the situation, claimed that the demands of protocol prohibited meeting.

Hitler looked forward to that meeting. There is no question that in the führer's grand design for the future, Lloyd George, who had visited with him the previous year and who was his favorite British politician, would become head of the puppet English government under his control, with the royal family exiled to Canada and the duke restored to the throne with Wallis as queen. Paul Schwarz recalled he still constantly ran the films of various yacht voyages and of the duke conferring with Wallis at the time of his father's funeral. He never ceased raving to Ribbentrop about Wallis's lack of makeup, "not bad figure and impeccable grooming and couture."

At 1:10 p.m. the train arrived at the foot of the mountain at Obersalzberg, where, in the company of Robert Ley and Dr. Paul Schmidt, special interpreter for the Foreign Office, they took a trip to Lake Königssee. At 2:30 p.m. the couple was driven up the mountainside in the company of Dudley Forwood; they were followed to the hunting lodge by three carloads of detectives and SS men. The roads had been completely cleared of tourists; under normal conditions thousands would be seen on the steep incline, making their way up the mountainside to see Hitler's lair. Now, only twenty, who had special influence, stood waiting on special permit at the gates as the procession of cars swept through.

Surrounded by officials, Hitler stood waiting for the Windsors at the bottom of a flight of steps, wearing the brown jacket of a Nazi party official, black trousers, and patent-leather shoes. He conducted the Windsors into the entrance hall. It was dominated by a painting of Bismarck, grandfather of the Windsors' close friend Prince Otto. As the duke and duchess walked along the passageway behind their famous host, a series of tall, fair-haired, muscular guards, dressed in brass-buttoned uniforms, stood at attention. The Windsors were taken to an anteroom where servants removed their coats. They walked down three marble steps into an enormous reception hall. One wall of the room was filled entirely with a bay window which overlooked the Unsterberg mountain. Hitler pointed to the view, a sweeping display of peaks and sloping green meadows where workers toiled with hoes.

As the führer ordered afternoon tea, the couple had the opportunity to observe the details of the room. The walls were white, relieved by paneling of fumed oak. There was an enormous marble fireplace with great heaps of cordwood on either side. There were tapestries of figures of the period of Frederick the Great mounted on immense, powerful white horses. The carpet was cherry red, the marble in the room a matching red. The furniture covers were stitched in a series of swastika motifs and Nazi mottoes. There was a grand piano with a bust on it of Richard Wagner, and a large globe of the world. Everywhere there were white and yellow flowers: hydrangeas, zinnias, pansies, roses, carnations. Hitler's special adviser Walter Hewell, his official interpreter Paul Schmidt, and his photographer Heinrich Hoffman were present.

For all except twenty minutes of the two-hour visit, Hitler was with both the Windsors. While tea was being prepared, he showed his guests the entire house and gardens. He pointed out Salzburg from one of the balconies. Albion Ross of the *New York Times* was one of the few reporters permitted to enter the building and receive information as to what was going on. He described the intense interest that the führer had in both of his guests.

Successive biographers and historians have claimed that aside from some generalized remarks recorded by Paul Schmidt, no word of the conversation between Hitler and his visitors survives. This is incorrect.

There was in 1987 a still-living eyewitness. Sir Dudley Forwood was present at the encounter. He told me:

> I vividly recall how the conversation began. My master said to Hitler, "The Germans and the British races are one. They should *always* be one. They are of Hun origin." I fear that His Royal Highness had over-looked the Norman Conquest!
>
> The Duke was very annoyed because Schmidt had been hired. The duke spoke, as we know, flawless high German. He said to Hitler, in German, "I do not require this man." Hitler did not respond correctly, but said to the translator in German that the conversation would be contin-ued as scheduled, and that he expected the duke to speak English. The un-fortunate Schmidt had to convey this statement in English to my master. And so it went on. Every few minutes, the duke would say, irritably, to Schmidt, "That is not what I said to the führer." Or he would say, "That is not what the führer said to me." They also discussed comparative con-ditions of the Welsh and German miners. Hitler was most attentive.

On November 4 William Bullitt, U.S. ambassador to France, would write to President Roosevelt giving an account of the duchess's description of her discussion with Hitler. Hitler told her that the Nazi buildings would one day "make more magnificent ruins than [those of] the Greeks." It seems clear that most of the füher's conversation with the Windsors was deliberately generalized, socially welcoming, and in-consequential. However, he drew the duke into another room for a twenty-minute talk that was of much greater moment. The duke him-self in an article published in the *New York Daily News* on December 13, 1966, described what was said:

> My ostensible [*sic*] reason for going to Germany was to see for myself what national Socialism was doing in housing and welfare for the work-ers, and I tried to keep my conversation with the Führer to these sub-jects, not wishing to be drawn into a discussion of politics. Hitler, for his part, talked a lot, but I realized that he was only showing the tip of the German iceberg. In a roundabout way, he encouraged me to infer that Red Russia was the only enemy, and that it was in Britain's interest and in Europe's too, that Germany be encouraged to strike east and smash Communism forever. Hitler was then at the zenith of his power. His eyes were piercing and magnetic. I confess frankly that he took me in. I believed him when he implied that he sought no war with England . . . I thought that the rest of us could be fence-sitters while the Nazis and the Reds slogged it out.

It is thus clear that the duke encouraged Hitler in his ambition to strike against Russia. The duke had other suggestions to make. In his table talk on May 13, 1942, according to records obtained by the historian David Irving, Hitler said, "The King [sic] offered to meet Germany's colonial needs by allowing Germans to settle northern Australia, thereby creating a powerful shield for British interests against Japan." That is a very curious statement. One can see from other documentation that Britain was afraid of a Soviet-Japanese alliance, and in 1939 a group of British businessmen acting as secret agents would be arrested in Tokyo, tried and imprisoned for spying on Japanese officials in regard to this matter. According to Irving, the duke went on to tell Hitler that his brother George VI was "weak and vacillating and wholly in the grip of his evil and anti-German advisors." This was of course a reference to Sir Alexander Hardinge and Sir Robert Vansittart. The duke also discussed his conversation with Hitler with J. Paul Getty, a close friend of his who also had Nazi connections. In his memoirs, Getty remembered asking the duke, "Did Hitler listen to you when you spoke with him?" The duke replied, "Yes, I think so. The way was opened— ever so slightly—for further progress. Had there been any proper follow-through action in London or Paris, millions of lives might have been saved." He meant that he proposed permanent peace with Germany and (Getty said) mass emigration of Jews from Germany, also advocated by Charles Bedaux and Sir Oswald Mosley, rather than slaughter.

Getty added the following revealing paragraph:

Although [the duke] never said as much to me, I had reason to suspect that he was not acting on his own when he went on Germany and spoke to Hitler and other Nazi leaders. It would not surprise me if one day a musty EYES ONLY file is fished out of some top security vault and new light is thrown on the episode.

In part because of his friendships and personal contacts, the duke, and Wallis with him, apparently did not approve of Hitler's genocidal methods or mass imprisonment of Jews, despite the somewhat generalized anti-Semitism, typical of the time, which the Windsors had a tendency to express. The highly charged meeting with the führer, due to be dismissed as insignificant by enemies of the duke and partisans alike, ended with a warm parting. The *New York Times* noted:

Members of the entourage of the Duke and Duchess of Windsor reported after their visit . . . that the Duchess was visibly impressed with the Führer's personality, and he apparently indicated that they had become fast friends by giving her an affectionate farewell. He took both her hands in his saying a long goodbye, after which he stiffened to a rigid Nazi salute that the Duke returned.

After that, Hitler turned to Schmidt and said, "She would have made a good queen."

That night, the Windsors dined with Rudolf Hess and his wife in Munich; Frau Hess wrote to friends in Alexandria, Egypt, saying how warmly impressed she was, especially with the duchess. She recalled later that she was nervous about meeting Wallis because she felt dowdy; but once they met she relaxed and enjoyed Wallis's company. Ernst Wilhelm Bohle turned up to act as the interpreter, cementing his friendship with the Windsors. Hess shared the Windsors' preference for mass Jewish emigration rather than wholesale slaughter. After leaving Munich, Dr. Ley returned to Berlin, and two Labor Front officials drove the Windsors to the Austrian border. It is said that as they arrived, the duchess gave a bag of money to an SS official with the words, "This is for the Strength through Joy Fund."

After giving a dinner party for Dr. Ley's assistant, Stabsleiter Simon, and four other officials who had escorted the party around, the couple returned to Paris on the twenty-third.

That same day Vansittart wrote to Hardinge, referring to the letter from Ogilvie-Forbes sent on the seventeenth. In a postscript Vansittart said:

> I see . . . in this disturbing letter a reference to visits to Italy and Sweden. You will remember that I prophesied the former, and that was why in my conversations with [Sir Ronald] Lindsay I was very anxious to set no precedents in the United States which would be embarrassing when the inevitable visit to Italy was brought forward.

On October 24 Bedaux wrote from the Château de Candé, sending Sir Ronald Lindsay, at the Traveler's Club in Pall Mall, London, the first draft of the Duke of Windsor's schedule of visits. It was to start in Washington on Armistice Day and finish in Los Angeles and San Francisco in mid-December.

Exhausted, the Windsors rested for several days at the Hôtel

Meurice, the duke at last mustering enough strength for indifferent games of golf while Wallis, with a battery of secretaries, continued plans for the American trip.

In a conversation with Ambassador Kennedy on June 13, 1938, Sir Edward Peacock described a telephone call he made from London to the Windsors that week at the Meurice. The matter was pressing; much as he disliked doing it, King George VI, evidently afraid of public criticism if Windsor charged him with stinginess, had been paying the income from the hereditary Duchy of Lancaster (about £20,000—$100,000) while at the same time not charging him income tax on that sum; he paid it himself.

Impatient and irritable with this arrangement, the king asked Peacock to call Windsor to ask him to pay the tax; certainly that was a reasonable request. The duke picked up the phone; Wallis listened intently on the extension line. Peacock conveyed the royal request; the duke said he wasn't sure if he would oblige. Peacock pointed out that if he refused, the matter could leak to the newspapers (he implied he would make sure it did) and the Windsors would be plunged into the worst of public scandals. Nervous, the duke asked Peacock to hold the line. He went to Wallis and asked her what she thought. She shouted in anger, "There will be no concessions!" Peacock could hear her clearly. The duke came back to the phone and told Peacock he could not agree; his brother must pay the tax. Peacock advised the king, who was exasperated; so were the queen, Queen Mary, and the Duchesses of Gloucester and Kent. If there were any question of their relenting in the matter of Wallis's Royal Highness title, this incident ended it.

On October 27, the duke appeared at the weekly luncheon of the Anglo-American Press Association in Paris, denying that his visit to Germany had any political significance, a statement which, of course, was totally false. Asked why he had chosen to sail to New York aboard the German ship *Bremen*, he pointed out that the only reason for the choice was that he had promised not to enter British waters, and the *Bremen* was the only ship that did not enter Portsmouth or Southampton after leaving Cherbourg. On the same day Charles Bedaux and his wife Fern sailed aboard the *Europa* for Manhattan; also on board was, by coincidence, Ernest Simpson, who was en route to marry Mary Kirk Raffray. His company was selling the SS *Leviathan* for scrap. On the twenty-eighth, Winston Churchill wrote to the duke:

I have followed with great interest your German tour. I am told that when scenes of it were produced in the newsreels in the cinemas here, Your Royal Highness's pictures were always very loudly cheered. I was rather afraid beforehand that your tour in Germany would offend the great numbers of anti-Nazis in this country, many of whom are your friends and admirers; but I must admit that it does not seem to have had that effect, and I am glad it all passed off with so much distinction and success.

The Windsors continued to prepare for America. The Department of State in Washington sent out a blizzard of memorandums concerning the visit. Everybody in the government, especially the anti-Nazi secretary of the interior, Harold L. Ickes, was extremely uneasy about the matter. According to Charles Bedaux, Jr., Mrs. Roosevelt even contacted the labor leaders in Wallis's hometown of Baltimore, urging them to boycott the visit on the ground that the Charles Bedaux system of time-and-motion study in industry was unacceptable and that anyone Bedaux sponsored would be unwelcome. On November 2 Sir Ronald Lindsay visited with Sumner Welles, under secretary of state, in Washington, to convey the details of the royal attitude toward the Windsors. He said, inter alia:

[The king and queen] felt that at this time when the new King [is] in a difficult situation and [is] trying to win the affection and confidence of his countrypeople, without possessing the popular appeal which the Duke of Windsor [possesses], it is singularly unfortunate that the Duke ... [is] placing himself in a position where he would seem constantly to be courting the limelight. ... [I have found] on the part of all the governing class in England a very vehement feeling of indignation against the course of the Duke of Windsor based in part on the resentment created by his relinquishment of his responsibilities, and in ever greater part due to the apparent unfairness of his present attitude with regard to his brother, the King. ... In court circles and in the Foreign Office and on the part of the heads of the political parties, this feeling [borders] upon [a] state of hysteria. ... There has been a widening of this sentiment of indignation because of the fact that the active supporters of the Duke of Windsor within England are those elements known to have inclinations towards Fascist dictatorships, and that the recent tour of Germany by the Duke of Windsor and his ostentatious reception by Hitler and his regime [can] only be construed as a willingness on the part of the Duke of Windsor to lend himself to these tendencies.

Lindsay, expressing his own opinion, said he didn't think the duke was aware of being exploited in this manner, an indication, like the rest of his statement, that he didn't fully understand the duke's actual purpose: to be a statesman without portfolio. However, he went on to say that the British government was anxious to avoid taking any action that would make Windsor a martyr; at the same time, he would not be permitted to present the duke to the president, clearly upon royal orders. In response, Welles said that no representative of the U.S. government would accompany the Windsors on the tour; the duke would be received by officials in each city and shown what he wanted to see, and that would be the end of the matter. Welles made it painfully clear that although the duke would be received informally at the White House, this would not be regarded as a state visit or anything approaching it and no special privileges would be accorded via George T. Summerlin, chief of the Protocol Division of the State Department, who would act as Washington host. The question of whether the duchess would be called "Her Royal Highness" arose. The duke made it clear he required that the title be used. Sir Ronald Lindsay particularly requested that it not be. The matter remained unresolved.

The tour would resemble the German excursion in terms of the emphasis on industry and working and housing conditions. It would begin in Newark, New Jersey, on November 11, and would then be followed by the visit to the White House and an NBC radio speech urging peace upon the world. There would follow a visit to several major corporations that had powerful German connections, including General Electric at Schenectady, Eastman Kodak at Rochester, Standard Oil in Bayonne, and du Pont in Wilmington. The Windsors would then journey to Virginia to visit with Wallis's Montague cousins, to Washington again to see Aunt Bessie, and on to North Carolina, Georgia, Ohio, Detroit (General Motors), Dearborn (Ford), Washington, Oregon, California, and then (secretly) to Hawaii and Pearl Harbor.

On November 3, while the duke was working on his broadcast, recovering from a strenuous walk around a model housing project in the Paris slums as Wallis shopped extravagantly and had fittings with Mainbocher, and while Charles Bedaux gave a press conference in New York, the Baltimore Federation of Labor unanimously adopted a resolution to condemn the Windsors' visit, attacking Charles Bedaux as "the arch-enemy of organized labor." At a stormy meeting the Baltimore AFL leader, Joseph P. McCurdy, said, unnecessarily, "The Duchess, when she lived here, had no interest whatsoever in labor or the laboring classes of her fellow citizens." Even while he was delivering the speech, the British Broadcasting Corporation announced that it would not be relaying the NBC broadcast, even though the Canadian Broadcasting Corporation would be participating.

On November 4 Dr. William E. Dodd, Jr., son of the passionately anti-Nazi U.S. ambassador to Germany, said at a meeting of a citizens' committee in Philadelphia, and later on a local broadcast, that Windsor might "try to convince Americans of the achievements of National Socialism in Germany." More labor organizations attacked the visit, taking their cue from Baltimore, as the Windsors attended an elaborate banquet at the U.S. embassy in Paris, ironically with the anti-Nazi ex-premier, Léon Blum, and his wife among the guests. The Windsors were disturbed by the fact that Charles Bedaux suddenly crumbled in the face of opposition, offering to withdraw from his role as organizer of the tour. The duke declined this suggestion, but he and Wallis were given pause by a further statement of Bedaux: "Out of one hundred chances that [the Windsors] will come, about ninety are gone." He had just received word that the State Department, in answer to a request by Sir Ronald Lindsay, would not accord the duchess the title "Her Royal Highness."

Bedaux's statement, not conveyed to the Windsors in person, reached them most inconveniently and disagreeably by radio. They were very upset indeed. It is clear that if Bedaux had stood firm, they would probably still have continued with the trip, and indeed on November 5 their trunks were still packed.

In the afternoon Sir Ronald Lindsay telephoned the duke in Paris. Lindsay told the duke he had noticed with deepest distress the trend of present opinion against the visit. The duke said he was considering dropping Bedaux and touring without him; Lindsay replied that he did not know how dependent the duke was on Bedaux's arrangements in regard to the tour. The duke revealed that U.S. ambassador to France William Bullitt was urging him to go ahead, while Bedaux was urging him to desist. He thought he might perhaps curtail the tour, recasting it on the spot in Washington. Lindsay told him that would cause dreadful difficulties. Then, ever restless, the duke said perhaps he should just postpone the trip; if he did so, he asked, would he be able to make the tour later? Lindsay replied, "If you do, you will not be able to do it ever."

"Are you alarmed?" the duke said.

"Sir," Lindsay replied, "I feel the tour will cast a certain discredit on the American view of British monarchy."

An hour later, the duke telephoned a number which he thought was that of William Bullitt and instead accidentally dialed the private number of Sir Eric Phipps. He began by saying that he was grateful for Bullitt's advice to go to the United States in spite of the campaign against him. Phipps urged the duke to ignore Bullitt's recommendations, and the duke listened.

The following night the Windsors issued a press communiqué to the effect that they had decided to postpone their trip. In a desperate effort to overcome Nazi charges against them, they unwisely stated that they would be going to the Soviet Union. According to an Associated Press release, authorized by the duke, the purpose of the Russian visit would be "to balance the German tour" and "prove to the world that the Duke played no politics."

Later, Mrs. Roosevelt told Lady Lindsay a curious story. The ship that would have carried the Windsors was supposed to dock on November 11, Armistice Day. The Windsors would have arrived in Washington in time to allow them to go to Arlington and lay a wreath on the Unknown Soldier's tomb. Mrs. Roosevelt, determined to prevent this, had arranged it so that the train would be delayed deliberately to prevent the wreath being laid.

American socialite Wallis Spencer, wife of U.S. Navy officer Lieutenant Earl Spencer, in 1919

Wallis in the gown she wore when presented at court, c. 1925

British demonstrators protesting against the
proposed marriage

Mrs. Simpson's offer to withdraw made the English headlines

INSTRUMENT OF ABDICATION

         I, Edward the Eighth, of Great Britain, Ireland, and the British Dominions beyond the Seas, King, Emperor of India, do hereby declare My irrevocable determination to renounce the Throne for Myself and for My descendants, and My desire that effect should be given to this Instrument of Abdication immediately.

         In token whereof I have hereunto set My hand this tenth day of December, nineteen hundred and thirty six, in the presence of the witnesses whose signatures are subscribed.

SIGNED AT
FORT BELVEDERE
IN THE PRESENCE
OF

The Instrument of Abdication in which Edward VIII renounced his throne on December 10, 1936

The duke and duchess on their wedding day, June 3, 1937, at the Château de Condé in France

The Duke and Duchess of Windsor in Paris in 1937

The duke and duchess on honeymoon in Venice

The duke and duchess in Nazi Germany in October 1937 with Dr. Robert Ley, leader of the German Labor Front

The duke and duchess greeting their host, Adolf Hitler, in October 1937

At right, William Bullitt, Ambassador to France, with Senator Allen Bankly at the U.S. Embassy

The duke and duchess with Major Edward Dudley Metcalfe at his country house in Sussex in September 1939

The duke becoming Governor General of the Bahamas in 1940 as Wallis watches

The duke and duchess in the Government House in the Bahamas

The duke and duchess receiving a warm welcome on arrival in Miami in
May 1941

The duke and duchess at the Washington Stage Door Canteen in 1943

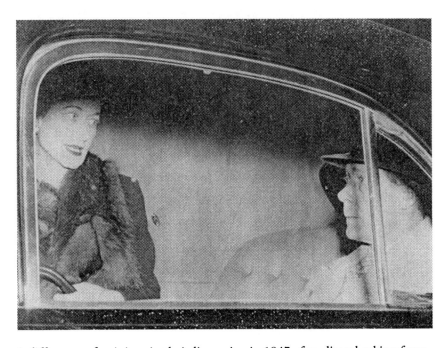

A difference of opinion: in their limousine in 1947 after disembarking from the Queen Mary; the duke and duchess were returning from England, which was eagerly anticipating Princess Elizabeth's upcoming marriage, to which the duke and duchess were not invited.

In Portofino, Italy, during a cruise of the Mediterranean in 1951

The duchess with her luggage in Florida in 1956

The duke and duchess at the International Canine Exhibition in Paris in 1956; the duchess's dog, Davy Crockett, won a first prize.

The duchess adjusting the duke's hair in January 1958

A Time Life portrait of the Duchess and Duke of Windsor in 1960

The duke and duchess with Maurice Chevalier enjoying the 1963
International Dance Festival in Paris

Stylishly arriving in Southampton, England, on board the liner United
States on New Year's Day, 1965

The duke and duchess with Rose Kennedy (at center) at the Everglades Club in Palm Beach

The duchess and duke with ballerina Ludmilla Tcherina in November 1966 at a Paris gala celebrating the twentieth anniversary of UNICEF

Members of the House of Windsor at a June 1967 at an unveiling ceremony for a memorial plaque of the duke's mother, Queen Mary. From left to right: The Duke of Edinburgh, Queen Elizabeth II, the Queen Mother, the Duke and the Duchess of Gloucester, and the Duke and Duchess of Windsor

The duchess being escorted by President Nixon at the White House in April 1970 as the duke stands nearby

Emperor Hirohito and Empress Nagako visiting the duke and duchess at their home in the Bois de Boulogne near Paris in October 1971. The last time the emperor and duke had met was in Tokyo in 1922.

In June 1972, the duchess with Earl Mountbatten en route to Buckingham Palace, where she stayed while attending the duke's funeral

Two days before the duke's funeral, the duchess watching Queen Elizabeth and the Trooping of the Color ceremony from a window in Buckingham Palace

A grudging reconciliation on June 5, 1972: Queen Elizabeth accompanying the heavily veiled duchess outside St. George's Chapel after the funeral

A frail duchess dining at Maxim's in Paris in September 1975

Princess Anne and the Queen
Mother talk to a clergyman at
the funeral of Wallis, Duchess
of Windsor, on April 29, 1986

Prince Charles and Princess
Diana leaving St. George's
Chapel after the funeral

13

Outer Darkness

It was at this time that Wallis embarked upon the most dangerous emotional and sexual adventure of her life. Abandoning Guy Trundle, she became the lover of U.S. ambassador to France William Christian Bullitt.

Bullitt's first interest in Wallis was indicated on February 22, 1935, when he wrote to Roosevelt saying that, while in London that week, he had received an invitation from "a very charming Maryland lady" to go to Fort Belvedere but had to decline as he was due in Moscow that week. Little did he know that the "charming Marylander" whom he would visit several times as her husband's guest at Bryanston Court would ensnare him in a liaison that could have wrecked his diplomatic career.

Philadelphia blueblood, son of a wealthy coal merchant, with George Washington, Pocahantas, and Fletcher Christian of *Mutiny on the Bounty* fame numbered among those he claimed as his ancestors, Bullitt was raised in luxury by his doting parents. He grew up sleek, superficial and devious—in other words, he had the makings of a perfect diplomat.

Bald from an early age, he was nevertheless attractive, with regular features, lively blue eyes, and a slim figure dressed in tailor-made clothing from Savile Row. His wealth and enormous charm added to his appeal as both social figure and career politician. His passion for Germany began in 1916 when he and his first wife, Ernesta Drinker, were guests in Berlin of the kaiser and his high command. Later, he endeared himself to the up-and-coming Adolf Hitler when he publicly attacked, in terms scarcely less incendiary than Hitler's own, the Versailles Treaty, which stripped Germany of its power and its colonies at the end of World War I.

In the early 1930s, his unauthorized efforts to have Germany's war debts waived or reduced by 80 percent were so dangerous that he came close to being arrested under the terms of the Logan Act, which precluded private American citizens from making arrangements with foreign powers without presidential authorization.

Seeking to obtain inside intelligence on the Soviet Union, which, as a secret anti-Communist, Bullitt could well supply, President Roosevelt, with his customary cunning, appointed him ambassador to Moscow, where the Russians sensibly mistrusted him. On December 23, 1923, he had married his second wife, Louise Bryant, widow of the American Communist John Reed; the Reeds became the subjects of Warren Beatty's film *Reds*. Bryant was a lesbian, the lover of the great Broadway star Eva Le Gallienne; in a novel he wrote based on their relationship, entitled *It's Not Done*, Bullitt portrayed a hero rendered impotent by his wife's frigidity. Rudely, he dedicated it to Bryant.

The truth is that his impotence with his wife was caused by his discovery that he was bisexual; he fell in love, in 1934, with his young and appealing male private secretary, Carmel Offie, a Philadelphian with Nazi connections like himself, whom he first met in Washington and had transferred from a post in Honduras to his embassy in Moscow. In Russia, where sex between males could result in beheading, he daringly conducted his affair with Offie under the protection of the embassy, and installed him in his house, on the excuse that he needed to consult with Offie at all hours of the day or night.

He was tortured by his dual nature, and for psychosexual treatments he turned to no less than his friend Dr. Sigmund Freud in Vienna. Freud shared his detestation of Woodrow Wilson, architect of the Versailles Treaty, and as early as 1925 they jointly produced a sensational book which was not published until 1966, condemning Wilson outright.

Bullitt's connections to the German royal conspirators led by the Hesse family began with the Wilson project and continued for many years as he worked with Freud's cooperation; forming a friendship with Wolfgang, Prince of Hesse, Wolfgang's wife, Marie Alexandra, and his twin brother Prince Philipp, he spent much time at their Castle

Friedrichshof at Krönberg reading the papers of World War I German chancellor Maximilian Von Baden, Alexandra von Hesse's father, to show, through Wilson's correspondence with him, the American president's designing of Germany's complete destruction in 1918–1919.

In 1934 Bullitt divorced Louise and left Russia; appointed ambassador to France in 1935, he supported the breaking of the Franco-Soviet pact that Liberals believed could have prevented World War II. He worked against the anti-Nazi French Popular Front, conspired with the Paris Fifth Column, prompted the French to send 350,000 men to Iraq, Syria, and Turkey, thus dangerously undermining the national defense, and gave full support to such flagrantly pro-Nazi figures as the journalist Stéphane Lauzanne, editor of *Le Matin*, a frequent visitor to Hitler, Lauzanne's boss, Maurice Bunau-Varilla, brother of a chief backer of the Panama Canal, and Wallis's lawyer Armand Grégoire, who represented Bullitt as well as Elsa Schiaparelli and Wallis's ex-lover Ribbentrop.

Bullitt had yet another high-level Fascist connection that directly involved the Hesses. At a time when Prince Philipp of Hesse was acting as emissary of Hitler to Mussolini, and Philipp was husband of Princess Mafalda, daughter of King Victor Emmanuel, Bullitt's Aunt Louise married one of the highest-ranking figures of the pro-Mussolini Italian hierarchy, the Duke of Assergio, and set up a Fascist salon in Rome that Bullitt often visited.

Exactly when Wallis's affair with Bullitt began is uncertain, but his absence from her wedding, an astonishment in view of his presence as ambassador in Paris at the time, may indicate that at least there were the beginnings of romantic feelings between them even then. The late Charles Bedaux, Jr., son of Wallis's friend and host, believed their liaison started in November 1937. The question is, why did Bullitt, who had money, looks, charm, and peerless diplomatic status, and could have the pick of Paris females, risk his career by having an affair with the most notorious woman in Europe? Cuckolding the Duke of Windsor could have made a ruinous news story, followed by an even more sensational divorce.

The answer lies clearly in the fact that he—still involved with Carmel Offie, with whom ironically Wallis often played gin rummy at the American embassy in Paris—needed a woman again, but was threatened, as he had been with his wife Louise Bryant, by the problem of impotence for which Freud was treating him. Wallis, with her Chinese sexual techniques, could arouse and satisfy him, restoring his confidence as a man at a time when gays of his class were often guilty and dysfunctional; after all, had she not done the same for her husband?

The question, as with Guy Trundle, was where Wallis could conduct the affair without the jealous and possessive duke finding out about it. With most society marriages at the time, adultery on the side was considered acceptable, perhaps even desirable. But the Duke of Windsor was neither sophisticated nor amenable. At all costs, the truth must be kept from him.

The answer, again, was Elsa Schiaparelli. Her sumptuous salon at the Place Vendôme had numerous private rooms used for fittings, any one of which could be converted into a bedroom. The designer Mainbocher, with whom Wallis also shopped, was a giddy gossip who could not be trusted to keep his mouth shut. Others who assisted Bullitt in the cover-up were the Nazi emissary Otto Abetz, a friend of Hitler, and his wife, the French patroness of the arts Suzanne de Bruyker. Still another cover was provided by the young attorney Suzanne Blum, a close friend of Bullitt's who would one day be Wallis's lawyer.

Because of Bullitt's Fascist connections, Sir Robert Vansittart and Sir Alexander Cadogan of the Foreign Office in London sought, through the Paris Secret Intelligence Service agent Wilfred Alfred Dunderdale, a suitable spy who could observe Wallis's relationship at first hand and avoid a royal scandal by making sure the Duke of Windsor didn't find out about it. From his headquarters apartment at 1 Avenue Charles-Floquet, Dunderdale began searching for the appropriate agent. He settled on one of his favorite society operatives, the remarkable Lady Jane Williams-Taylor, whom Wallis knew very well.

The daughter of a Canadian lumber tycoon, Lady Williams-Taylor was the reigning queen of Montreal and Bahamian society, as well as one of the most prominent figures of New York, London, Paris, and Palm Beach. Tall and imposing, with a beautifully modulated voice and a strong, single-minded will, she was 72 years old when Dunderdale and his team engaged her for her important task.

She was born at Hyacinth, in the province of Quebec, in 1865. Her family was quite distinguished; one of her uncles had been tutor to the children of Queen Victoria. She combined a formidably authoritative manner with a contradictory streak of vulgarity; she would at parties point to the crotches of men's trousers and remark on their contents, causing thrills of horror or amusement to pass through the guests. She was noted for the strings of lovers she commanded—handsome one and all, they satisfied her quickly or were discarded as hastily as lame horses from her stable of thoroughbreds.

She settled on a husband, not among the rich, but rather among the poor, whom she could control for life. Frederick Williams-Taylor was handsome, finely proportioned and muscular—just her physical type. Starting out as a humble clerk at the Bank of Montreal, he rose rapidly through her influence, and his command of finance took him to the very top. An excellent horseman, polished and personable, proficient at tennis, swimming, badminton, and bridge, he joined his wife in dazzling society, and nobody was surprised when he was knighted in 1913 for his services to the British Crown.

In 1934, Lady Jane met an admiring Adolf Hitler in Munich and when she joined Admiral Sinclair's Secret Intelligence Service in London soon afterward; her calling card was that she would pretend to be the führer's ardent supporter. For years she maintained an oil painting of Hitler at her various homes—Claridges Hotel and Hans Court in London; the Ritz in Paris; and Star Acres, her legendary estate in the Bahamas.

Her chief claim to international fame was her granddaughter, Brenda Frazier, one of the most talked-about women of her day. The society debutante and legendary beauty whose photographs and interviews were in almost every women's magazine in America, Brenda, in league with her husband, John "Shipwreck" Kelly, worked with Lady Jane in the Secret Intelligence Service.

On Wilfred Dunderdale's instructions and with the cooperation of Millard E. Tydings, senator from Maryland, and Marjorie Merriweather Post, heiress to the Post Toasties cereals fortune, Lady Williams-Taylor made arrangements to shop at Schiaparelli's, and various parties that Wallis and her husband attended, and report on the political and sexual connection to Bullitt on a regular basis. At the same time she acted as a decoy, inviting the Duke of Windsor to various afternoon teas and other events so that he would not insist on accompanying Wallis to her fittings at Schiaparelli's. With Constance Coolidge, that friend of

Wallis's, she could ensure that Wallis entered the salon by a secret back door, protected by police, so that the inevitable crowd of celebrity hunters would not mob her.

Throughout the liaison, interrupted frequently when Bullitt made visits to Washington or Berlin, the duplicitous ambassador continued to entertain the duke and duchess at dinners at the townhouse he shared with Carmel Offie—2 Avenue Iéna, and at his country home, Saint-Firmin, at Chantilly on the river Oise, where Offie also lived. He carried off this breathtaking hypocrisy with his usual polished skill. In one letter, he wrote to Roosevelt saying approvingly that the duke was "still very much in love with his wife."

Bullitt, up to his eyes in appeasing the Nazis and opposing the Russians, matters in which he found Wallis a continuing ally, in Berlin that month met with Goering and his Aunt Louise's old friend, Mussolini's ambassador Bernardo Attolico, also a contact of Philipp of Hesse. The result of the meeting was a recommendation to Roosevelt in a letter from Paris on November 23 in which he said, after a lengthy and sly account of the Nazi hatred of the liberal ambassador in Berlin, William E. Dodd, a hatred he shared:

> The only way that I can see that the growth of German strength can be used for constructive instead of destructive purposes is by a general effort to the giving of . . . concessions to Germany as part of a general plan of unification of Europe.

The concessions referred to were the imminent acquisition of Austria and Czechoslovakia. He added, "The Germans have the most profound desire to improve relations with us and we can influence them." The next night he found a condign audience in the Windsors when he had them to dinner and Wallis told him of Hitler's remark to her that future civilizations would compare the ruins of the Germany of the time as equivalent to those of the Greeks—an absurd comparison at best, but received with pleasure by the ambassador.

The failure of Bullitt's plan to have them tour the United States was a disaster for the Windsors. They had made two mistakes: first, in not undertaking the venture before the German tour, and second, in crumbling so easily under the objections of very few labor unions. John L. Lewis, the American labor leader, was, according to Charles Bedaux,

Jr., a keen admirer of Bedaux, and certainly there could have been no general strike in the towns they visited. Their enemies, however, were deeply grateful that the tour was called off.

On November 10, the Reverend J. L. C. Dart, vicar of the Church of England at St. George's in Paris, announced that he would not welcome the Windsors if they attended the Armistice Day services the following day. He would not fail to provide good seats, but he would certainly not speak to the Windsors. So far as he was concerned, "Marriage only ends before God when it is ended by death," and Wallis was still married to her first husband. The duke and duchess did not appear. Meanwhile, the *New York Times* reported that Buckingham Palace was relieved by the Windsors' decision not to go to the United States, and at the same time the Loyalist government in Spain acclaimed it. The *Voz*, the Loyalist newspaper, said in an editorial:

> The Windsors abandoned their proposed visit to America. . . . First it was Mussolini's son, and now the Duke and Duchess. At this rate no Fascist traveller will be able to leave Berlin and Rome.

Arriving in New York aboard the French ship *Normandie*, Lord Beaverbrook, not content with having driven Wallis out of England a year earlier, said the duke should "quit public life."

For some weeks he and the duchess did. They stayed on at the Meurice for several weeks, their suite overlooking the long stretch of the tree-studded Tuileries Gardens and the distant Seine. Chief Inspector Storrier still remained in constant attendance. So did Dudley Forwood.

Several events took place that month. On November 9 Mary Kirk divorced Jacques Raffray, and just nine days later she married Ernest Simpson in a ceremony at her family home in Fairfield, Connecticut. They were to spend their honeymoon in London. He was 40; she was 41. Both had tragic futures. Their son, Henry, was born on September 28, 1939; he was evacuated to the United States, and his mother accompanied him there. She was returning aboard ship through U-boat-infested waters when she discovered an early cancer symptom. The ship was diverted to Lisbon because of U-boat action, and she insisted on proceeding to London to work with the Red Cross first-aid stations as a volunteer nurse during the blitz. Becoming seriously ill, she returned to the United States, but then went back to England to die, at the age of 43, on October 2, 1941. Ernest died at 62 of cancer of the throat, on November 30, 1958. It was the same cause of death that would take the Duke of Windsor.

That same month the Grand Duchess of Hesse, the duke's cousin, was killed when the plane she was traveling in for the wedding of Prince Ludwig, her husband's brother, and the daughter of Sir Auckland Geddes, collided with a brickworks chimney in Ostend, Belgium. The wedding, which the duke and duchess were unable to attend, was held entirely in black, with the bride in a black wedding gown.

In the third week of November, the libel suit filed by the duke against Geoffrey Dennis, author of *Coronation Commentary*, was settled in London. The duke's counsel, Sir William Jowitt, K.C., called for dismissal; he stated that the duke had withdrawn the suit in return for unspecified damages and an apology. The chief passage complained of included the statement, "The lady who is now the plaintiff's wife occupied, before his marriage to her, the position of his mistress."

On November 25 the Windsors attended Thanksgiving services at the American Church. They sat with William C. Bullitt, who read President Roosevelt's Thanksgiving Proclamation.

On November 30 it was mentioned in the press that the Windsors (who had not thought of it) would be going to visit Argentina. With dry humor Hardinge wrote to Vansittart, "There would, of course, be no possible objection to the Duke and Duchess of Windsor paying a prolonged visit to the Argentine." He clearly hoped they would never come back.

At Christmas the Rogerses, who had sailed to New York, made arrangements to lend the Windsors Lou Viei. Dudley Forwood and the staff went ahead by auto to the villa to prepare everything while the Windsors followed by train. In the duke's luggage was a complete set of photographs of his visit to Hitler. Two years later the Rogerses' niece by marriage, Mrs. Edmund Pendleton Rogers, was visiting France when the duke proudly showed her the same pictures. The duchess seemed quite indifferent.

After Christmas eve dinner with several Canadian friends, the duke visited a florist's and bought just under $300 worth of orchids, white violets, and lilacs for the delighted duchess. However, Christmas day itself was miserable because the duke had an ulcerated jawbone from neglected teeth and had to undergo orthodontic surgery.

On December 28 Sir Eric Phipps wrote to Anthony Eden from Paris, referring to a statement made by his predecessor as ambassador, Tyrrell:

> Tyrrell, who has been staying here for a week, told a member of my staff the following astonishing story:
>
> Some time ago, a special correspondent of the *Daily Herald* came over here to interview the Duke of Windsor. Tyrrell was shown the account of this interview, in which it was stated that His Royal Highness said that if the Labour Party wished, and were in a position to offer it, he would be prepared to be president of the English Republic. Tyrrell urged Greenwood to have this left out of any published account of his interview, as he was so shocked and horrified. This Greenwood promised to do, and I understand that, so far, the interview has not seen the light of day. In reply to a question put by a member of my staff as to whether the government knew of the declaration, Tyrrell said, "I think not the government, but possibly the Prime Minister." I am not informing anyone of the above except yourself.

The Windsors lingered on in the south of France. On New Year's eve they were with their friend the Hon. Mrs. Reginald Fellowes when the duke won a substantial sum at baccarat at the Monte Carlo Sporting Club. Three days later Lloyd George arrived from London for a visit; he reported that it was in the Paris newspapers that the bishop of Bermuda had ordered the Windsors' portraits taken down from the window of a local shop; when the shopkeeper refused, the bishop tore down and destroyed the photographs himself. Winston Churchill also arrived; the conversation circled around all the problems raised by the royal visit to Germany. On the seventh, the Windsors attended a dinner party given by Maxine Elliott at the Château de l'Horizon. Lloyd George and Churchill were there.

When the Windsors arrived, across a small bridge, they were greeted at the door by Maxine's nephew by marriage, the political journalist Vincent Sheean. Maxine, once a legendary American beauty, still looked attractive with her piled-high white hair and white Chanel gown. The duchess, who had been forewarned that Maxine would be in white, succeeded in upstaging her hostess by wearing black. Maxine managed a curtsey, while Vincent Sheean, equally briefed, bowed. At dinner the duke sat at the head of the table, and the conversation was brisk. Sheean noted in his memoirs, *Between the Thunder and the Sun*, that the talk revolved around the conditions of the Welsh coal miners and the necessity of improving their plight through legislation. Either unaware or mischievously aware of the fact that Sheean was decidedly left-wing, and a keen supporter of the Loyalists in Spain, the duke praised the social legislation of the Nazis:

> He and the Duchess had been assured by Dr. Ley that every mine in Germany had the most ample, and indeed luxurious, arrangements for bathing at the pithead. They had indeed visited these baths on their tour of the Reich some months before. Mr. Churchill did not particularly enjoy praise of the Nazi regime, and although he had been remarkably silent throughout the meal (deferring like a schoolboy to the authority of Mr. Lloyd George and the Duke) he now spoke up to say that he had proposed compulsory shower-baths at the pithead long ago.

Sheean observed that the seriousness of the interest of everyone present could not be doubted, yet it was "confounded with an incurable frivolity owing to their astronomical remoteness from the conditions of life of which they spoke." Clearly, the duke wanted to see the miners "clean, healthy and contented, as you might wish your horses or dogs to be; to him they were not men and brothers." Sheean added, with equal shrewdness:

> The Duchess, so slim and elegant, so suggestive of innumerable fashionable shops, dressmakers, manicurists and hairdressers, seemed at the uttermost removed from the pithead of a mine, and I tried to imagine what she must have been like when Dr. Ley, all puffed out with . . . the snobbery of a German official, showed her the men's baths in the Ruhr.

The evening became increasingly surrealistic as the hard-bitten journalist watched in a daze of disbelief Churchill, Lloyd George, the duke and duchess, and the one or two other guests discussing matters of poverty and struggle while surrounded with expensive furniture, glassware, silver:

> It was like lunch, I thought, in a traffic policeman's tower; if you turned your back and chewed hard on the ham you were unaware of the street.

On January 9, 1938, the Windsors returned to the Meurice; three nights later police arrested a man who was trying to penetrate their suite. A Swedish anti-Nazi, he was suspected of attempting an assassination. On January 18 the duke interceded with the Spanish government to arrange, through Ambassador Sir Henry Chilton, for the release from prison of the Franco diplomat Don Javier Bermejillo, whom he and Wallis had known in London, when Bermejillo was on the embassy staff. This fact only came to light because Chilton's wallet was stolen in London, and he had to give a list of contents to the police. It contained the duke's written request. This act of assistance to a Fascist scarcely improved his image.

On January 26, after a prolonged search, the Windsors at last found a Paris residence that they both liked: the Château La Maye, located at Versailles, a property of the American widow of a French politician, Paul Dupuy. Magnificently furnished, it had a tennis court, a golf course, and a swimming pool. They took a six-month lease and moved in on February 7. However, they tired of the house within two months, after bringing over much of the stored furniture from Fort Belvedere, York House, and Wallis's home at Cumberland Terrace.

In this period the duke and duchess engaged a young and skillful secretary, Dana Wells Hood, whom the duke had met in South America and who was presently working for the Brazilian embassy in London. While in the British capital, she consulted with Thomas Carter, of the Department of the Privy Purse, to master the necessary details of the duke and duchess's bookkeeping. She was to be in charge of the same complex cash-entry system formerly used at York House and Fort Belvedere. She noted that the bookkeeping methods dated back to Queen Anne's time.

She joined Gertrude Bedford, the duchess's secretary, and the two women formed a reliable team. They shared a double bedroom at the Meurice; the adjoining rooms were occupied by the valet, the duchess's lady's maid, and Storrier or whichever detective was standing in for him. Dana Hood was pleased by the open affection the duke showed for the duchess and the fact that he was constantly trying to find ways to make her happy. He always called her "darling" or "sweetheart." She called him "David" or "Dave." She had only to call him for him to run to her, even from the middle of a haircut.

The discipline of the household was severe. Dana was never allowed to sit in the duke's presence, even when she was taking dictation. She would even deal with as many as fifty letters at a stretch while remaining standing. She noted that the carpet was usually covered with heaps of letters and documents and that the duchess disliked the mess. The duchess imposed on the duke a complex filing system which apparently he reluctantly used.

In March, William Bullitt was summoned to Washington by President Roosevelt, who was far from satisfied with his ambassador's Nazi-Italian connections. He offered Bullitt, with barely disguised humor and contempt, the suggestion that he might run for governor of Pennsylvania. It took all of Bullitt's skills of persuasion to retain his post in Paris.

It was a stormy month in France. The treacherous and slippery premier, Camille Chautemps, presiding over a cabinet feebly composed of right- and left-wing elements, resigned in the face of public fury for his antilabor policies, and the nation was crippled by strikes in industry and transportation. The so-called friend of labor, Léon Blum, was forced to assemble a new government in haste to avoid a national collapse, and for several days the country had no official administration.

Wallis had her rich woman's distractions. Chief among them was the racetrack at Auteuil where she and the duke were guests of the Steeplechase Club president Comte Delaire de Cambacérès, Duke of Parma, and his popular associate, the Marquis du Crozet. There, Wallis often saw her trusted friend, Constance Coolidge, who had recently become the mistress of British novelist H. G. Wells.

Constance was a fascinating if dizzy companion, a Boston blueblood who had been immortalized by John Singer Sargent. Beautiful, dark, as promiscuous as Wallis herself, she often entertained the Windsors at her luxurious apartment near the racetrack at 11 Rue Maspéro.

Her innumerable love affairs with attractive men were interspersed with brief and ill-fated marriages; first to the American diplomat Ray Atherton, who took her to China just ahead of Wallis's stay there, second to the flamboyant Comte Chapelle du Jumilhac, of the Château du Dreux-Bresée, at Chèze Sur Argos (who later married another American, Ethel Barbey), and third, a step down in the world, to the humdrum California newspaperman Eliot Rogers, whom she shed when he failed to meet her exacting standards in the bedroom.

In March 1938, Constance was sleeping with the prominent and strikingly attractive political journalist and long-term Berlin correspondent of the pro-Hitler *Le Matin*, Philippe Barrès. His father was the world-famous nationalist and author Maurice Barrès, for whom a street in Paris is named to this day.

Constance herself was profoundly anti-Nazi, recording that month in her diary her horror of Hitler moving through Europe like a fatal disease, a view she kept hidden from the Windsors, perhaps in order to determine what they were up to. Barrès had been a strong supporter of the Nazis; his *Sous la Vague Hitlerienne* (Plon, 1933) was a somewhat critical but mostly ecstatic account of the führer's rise to power. But by 1938, when he met and fell in love with Constance, he had already begun to feel disillusionment, seeing a threat to French power and autonomy to which his life, like his father's, was dedicated.

He had left the post of Berlin correspondent when even his mildest critiques of Hitler were relegated to the middle or back pages. Now he was preparing to resign as Paris feature writer in conflict with Stéphane Lauzanne, the inflammatory Hitler-supporting editor in chief, and Maurice Bunau-Varilla, the dictatorial Hitler-loving owner. Like Constance, he put up with the Windsors' fascism, presumably in order to determine how dangerous they were.

One evening at dinner at Constance's apartment at 11 Rue Maspéro, the duke annoyed her by saying, all too characteristically, in reference to stories that Czechoslovakia was next on Hitler's list of conquests after Austria, "It's a ridiculous country. It isn't a nation at all but an invention of Woodrow Wilson's. How could anyone go to war for a place like that?" He was referring to Wilson's September 3, 1918, agreement to grant Czechoslovakia her ill-fated independence from the Austro-Hungarian Empire in dissolution; a noble action excoriated by Bullitt in his book written with Sigmund Freud.

On March 22, Wallis and the duke left by car for the south of France to visit with the American millionaire Ogden Codman, to discuss renting his Antibes Château Leopolda, named for its former owner, the pro-Nazi King Leopold of the Belgians. Next day, Constance Coolidge had lunch in Paris with the Comte de Cambacérès, who informed her that she must attend to certain important matters concerning the Windsors.

He said that he had been contacted by a certain Madame Maroni, who wished to see her at once. Madame Maroni lived just a few minutes' walk from Constance's apartment—at 36 Boulevard Emile Augier, also in the 16th Arrondissement and very close to the Auteuil racetrack.

Despite the comte's distinction, Constance felt uneasy. When Madame Maroni called her twice, she told her butler, Victor, to say she was out. But the woman persisted; her manservant made further calls; and at last Constance gave in. Asked to tea on March 23, she went that evening instead. Unwisely, she didn't check the social registers (*Tout Paris* and *Bottin Mondain*), which would have shown her that the only Maroni listed in Paris, Fernand Maroni, editor in chief of the legendary conservative newspaper *Journal des Débats*, was unmarried and living at 10 Avenue Bugeaud, also quite close to her, in the same 16th Arrondissement near Auteuil.

Once arrived at the apartment building, she wasn't impressed by the ancient and disheveled concierge in the vestibule. She took the elevator to the third floor, to an apartment which, had she consulted the social registers, she would have seen was occupied not by Maroni, but by a certain Gustave Badollet of Le Touquet. The white-coated butler who opened the door left her equally unimpressed and she felt even more uneasy when she met her Italian hostess, who was badly painted and dyed and had the atmosphere of an adventuress on the make. The background of vulgar white satin couches and curtains proved no more reassuring to the visitor.

The woman talked in hints, suggestions, and half-whispers. Essentially, she was saying that she was acting on behalf of a friend who was very highly placed; after a while, she announced that the friend was a duchess. Foolishly, Constance didn't ask for the duchess's name, but listened uneasily while Madame Maroni said the peeress concerned had in her possession letters, documents, and photographs of a sensational character that would be of great potential damage to the Windsors and to the royal family of England as a whole. The smell of blackmail lay heavily on the air.

"The papers are not to be believed," the woman said, as Constance grew more and more uncomfortable. Madame Maroni pressed on; Constance didn't have the sense to ask why if the friend were a duchess she couldn't have met the Windsors herself. Maroni said that a "certain group" was prepared to force her hand to buy the materials and publish them in America unless they were preempted; Constance must act at once to protect her royal friends.

She added that all she needed was to see the duke alone. To make him happy she would burn the photographs and documents in his presence— a potential scene of blackmail and high drama that could have come from an overdose of Dostoyevsky or of low-grade romantic fiction.

At that moment, the doorbell rang repeatedly; the butler had disappeared and there was no one to answer it; nor did Constance's mysterious hostess bother to excuse herself and go to the door.

Knock after noisy knock followed; at last the door burst open and Constance's butler Victor ran, badly upset, into the drawing room. He was, he said, worried that something bad had happened to his mistress.

Constance rose from the sofa and told Madame Maroni she would have nothing to do with the matter, thus making it clear that blackmail did not appeal to her. Then she and Victor walked out.

Back at her apartment, badly upset, Constance wrote Wallis a letter to the Hôtel du Cap at Antibes, describing the unsavory encounter, but thought better of it and didn't mail it. She needed to look further into the matter.

Next day, she had a visit from her friend Dr. Edmond Gros, the distinguished physician and director of the American Hospital at Neuilly. She told him the story and he was shocked; he at once contacted his brother-in-law, Stéphane Lauzanne of *Le Matin*. This was a smart decision; if Madame Maroni had incriminating documents connecting the Windsors to a Fascist scandal, then she could be silenced by the Fascists instead of paid.

Later that morning, Constance's lover, Philippe Barrès, who had just handed in his resignation to Maurice Bunau-Varilla, arrived at her flat and told her that Lauzanne had brought the matter to the *Le Matin* staff's attention but that the story had been quashed immediately—he didn't say by whom. But clearly, the decision was Bunau-Varilla's.

Constance called the Comte de Cambacérès and arranged to have lunch with him and the Marquis du Crozet at the racetrack at Maison-Laffitte. She chided the comte severely for getting her involved in so unsavory a matter. She made no record of his response.

Still upset, Constance returned to her apartment that afternoon only to find that a "police inspector," as she called him in her diary, was waiting to see her; she did not record his name, but it is clear that he was assistant to Superintendent Gilbert Rochès, commissioner of police at the Quai des Orfèvres, the city headquarters of the Sûreté, an indication of the importance of the case. Bunau-Varilla and Stéphane Lauzanne had clearly asked him to take charge.

Constance told him the story. The superintendent told her that the only Maroni in Paris was indeed the distinguished Fernand Maroni of the *Journal des Débats*. Maroni's corruption extended to his being a paid servant of the Lazard Frères banking empire, which connected him directly, and Bunau-Varilla and Stéphane Lauzanne with him, to the internationally conspiratorial Synarchiste movement, which also had strong Mussolini connections.

The superintendent informed her that the Comte de Cambacérès had unwittingly led her into a trap; the woman was not Madame Maroni, wife of the financial journalist, but an obscure niece; Constance said she was relieved, as she could not believe so important a man would involve his wife in a flagrant blackmail plot.

On a visit next day, the "inspector" said that the woman had been a maid in the Duke of Windsor's household; that she herself was the mysterious highly placed figure, the so-called duchess who owned the letters and photographs, and that she had a bad reputation in the arrondissement.

He added that she had followed the duke from Vienna to Le Touquet, a town some two and a half hours out of Paris, which he had visited on more than one occasion, and that she had sent him two letters, which he had handed over to the police. It is obvious they were of a similar blackmailing character.

The mention of Le Touquet provides a significant clue. Gustave Badollet, the retired industrialist who rented the apartment in which the Maroni woman spoke to Constance, owned the Villa Savaral in that town, and may well have entertained the Windsors there.

The assistant superintendent went on to say that he had called Maroni in for questioning at police headquarters at the Quai des Orfèvres; that Maroni had denied any knowledge of the matter and would not allow his divorced wife, the writer Mathilde Maroni, whom he had married in Switzerland, to be asked questions. He had enough power in Paris to stop that interrogation.

When Constance conveyed this to Philippe Barrès, he wasn't satisfied. Almost his last act as contributor to *Le Matin* was to go with a reporter to 36 Boulevard Emile Augier to talk to the Maroni woman.

Asking her, as Constance should have done, what exactly she had on the Windsors, she provided the astonishing revelation that the documents and photographs concerned the duke's and the royal family of England's links to Prince Philipp of Hesse.

When Barrès told Constance what he had found out, she would, if she had any political inside knowledge, which she did not, have been in a state of shock. If it were made public that Windsor and Kent had been in intimate contact with Philipp, to the point that they exchanged letters of a dangerous character in favor of Hitler and Mussolini and appeasement of fascism and that they were photographed together, when not one trace of such a direct association was ever made public (or has been since), it could have blown the lid off the British monarchy, especially since Kent was a hero in the world's eyes as a patriotic Englishman. Worse than anything, the woman clearly had evidence that King George VI had personally authorized the Kent-Hesse connection, as would surface in the papers of Neville Chamberlain the following year. This meant that, contrary to popular opinion then and now, the English king was in improbable accord with Windsor and Kent—determined to achieve peace at any cost.

What is certain is that the woman had royal-Nazi connections. As publisher and editor of *Le Matin*, Maurice Bunau-Varilla and Stéphane Lauzanne would be familiar with the Philipp of Hesse association and would want to protect the Windsors to the limit. There could never be any question of "Madame Maroni's" charges leaking in their newspaper, nor of course in the pages of Fernand Maroni's distinguished *Journal des Débats*. And given the political censorship and the libel laws of the time, even such liberal publications as *Paris Soir* or *Paris-Match*, of which Philippe Barrès soon became joint editor, would never have published the facts.

Constance, at Commissioner of Police Gilbert Rochès's request, finally mailed the letter describing everything to Wallis, whose urgent telegram of receipt from Antibes can today be seen in the Coolidge files at the Massachusetts Historical Society. She and the duke must have been in a state of shock, because, despite a national strike, they drove helter-skelter to Paris on roads crowded with trainless people in cars and buses to a Paris that was virtually paralyzed; dodging both their home at Versailles and the Hôtel Meurice, they checked in secrecy into the Hôtel Crillon on April 4, where they had never stayed before.

The duke immediately contacted Sir Philip Game, commissioner of Scotland Yard, to come to the hotel at once. Game came over, dropping everything.

Wallis must have been petrified. Game was still in charge of the Guy Trundle affair, of which the duke remained oblivious. The Duke also summoned Game's friend and French counterpart Roger Langeron, prefect of the Paris police. After lunch next day with Wallis, the duchess called her at home and said she must come to the Crillon to meet the police chiefs.

They asked her to tell all she knew; when she was told to describe any woman other than Maroni who was romantically interested in the duke she mentioned an Austrian. She probably meant Friederike of Prussia, now Princess of Greece. Next day, Gilbert Rochès came to Constance's apartment and took her statement yet again. And that was the last she heard of the matter.

A major problem for the historian examining Constance Coolidge's journal is the identity of the mysterious niece of Fernand and Madame Maroni.

A slip in Constance's diary entries gives us a clue. When Gilbert Rochès told her who Maroni was, she noted down him saying that, as well as being involved with the *Journal des Débats*, he was also an architect. But he wasn't.

It seems that in his haste to deal with the matter, Rochès had confused Fernand Maroni with his cousin and namesake, the Italian Fascist architect Gian Carlo Maroni, who was at the time attending a series of valedictory celebrations in Rome and Florence that followed the death of his friend, Italian Fascist poet Gabriele d'Annunzio, for whom he had designed Il Vittoriale, the most famous private house in Italy. Gian Carlo Maroni had a direct link to Prince Philipp of Hesse; Philipp was a fellow architect and they both designed for Philipp's wife, Princess Mafalda, and for her father, King Victor Emmanuel III.

Gian Carlo Maroni had several nieces, all of them poor. It is likely that one of them worked as a maid in Philipp's household and stole the photographs and documents from him, at his Castle Friedrichshof, and then stole more, from the Windsors, whom she could have joined as a maid in their Austrian-German entourage.

The final question is: what became of the photographs and documents? Normally, the proposed victim of a blackmail plot would prosecute, and the appropriate proof would be filed with the advocates of court of Paris, pending preliminary hearings and a criminal trial. But in this case, the Windsors predictably didn't press charges; a trial would have exposed far too much.

Instead, the woman was let go, presumably to return to Italy, and more work as a housemaid with her uncle Gian Carlo Maroni's assistance. The documents would be held for at least ten years, with copies supplied to the potential plaintiffs, in case they should change their minds and pursue the case before the statute of limitations expired.

The British government probably believed that the dossier was sent, on orders of the Germans who occupied Paris in June 1940, to Prince Philipp of Hesse at the time of that occupation; hence the fact that in 1945 the Secret Intelligence Service sent the double agent Anthony Blunt to retrieve them from Philipp's castle in 1975. Prince Wolfgang, twin brother of Prince Philipp, would, as we shall see, confirm there were strong links between the Dukes of Kent and Duke of Windsor and Philipp that the Blunt intelligence team was looking for. But more of this later.

On April 20 the Windsors were back on the Riviera; they decided to take a lease on a house which had originally been recommended as the site of their marriage. This was the Château La Croë, at Cap d'Antibes, the home of the British newspaper magnate and Hearst associate Sir Pomeroy Burton. Modernized in 1928 at a cost of $2 million, the château had a 20-karat gilded bathtub, twelve bedrooms, a swimming pool, two bathing pavilions, and a tennis court; it also had a large dining room that seated twenty-four at the table and a magnificent drawing room lined with tapestries and painted panels. Once again, their furniture from England was shifted in an elaborate convoy by road. Thomas Carter arrived with everything expertly packed and inventoried. When he turned up with the truck and van convoy, the entire drive and lawn were completely covered with an immense (as the duchess put it in her memoirs) "avalanche of crates, linen baskets, furniture, trunks of clothing, bales of draperies, chests of silver." Lady Mendl sent from Paris her indispensable assistant, Johnny McMullen, and his associate, Tony Montgomery, to help redecorate. Lady Mendl herself turned up to assist. Soon the house carried the authentic Mendl touch: a riot of mirrors, extravagantly elaborate gold-and-white moldings, yellow-and-white-and-blue draperies, and whirlwinds of satin, silk, lace, lacquer, and tapestries. The royal bedroom was a flourish of black, scarlet, and gold, the furniture painted in trompe l'oeil. The dressing table displayed many silver objects from brushes to mirrors, but none was real; they were merely painted. On the chest the artist had with audacious vulgarity achieved a kind of microcosm of the Windsors' early relationship: it included an invitation to Fort Belvedere with Wallis's name on it, a piece of love letter, a bunch of flowers with the Prince of Wales's card on it decorated by feathers, two satin gloves, and a pair of socks.

The footmen at La Croë wore the red and gold livery of the British royal household. As in a hotel, the guest room bedside tables had a list of the house's many services, including a hairdresser, three secretaries, a footman, and a "manicure specialist." The duke's study suite was decorated like the cabin of a ship's captain, an imitation of a similar room at the home of Lord Louis Mountbatten in London. Deprived of any political influence, stripped of her true power, the duchess poured all her frustration into La Croë, which she and the duke finally moved into on June 1. They celebrated their first wedding anniversary there on the third, posing for pictures on the lawn.

Dana Hood gave a vivid account of life at La Croë in her memoirs. The duke named his quarters on the top floor "Belvedere." He had a telescope that enhanced the already nautical decor and through it he would gaze out to sea, like a captain on a bridge. Dana was struck by the prodigiousness of the duke's memory. He could remember people he had only run into casually years before. He dictated official letters jerkily, throwing out phrases or sentences and then replacing them with alarming speed. Sometimes, he would leap from his chair, drag a key out of his pocket, rush across the room, and open a dispatch case; he would then pull out a document and use it as a point of reference.

His personal correspondence he handled with extreme secretiveness, and even Dana was not permitted to know what he was writing. He tapped with two fingers on a portable typewriter. He did his own accounts and typed out his own checks. He would respond to gifts personally, provided they came from intimate friends. At Christmas, he insisted on reading every one of the vast flood of Christmas cards and messages. He and the duchess received a stream of baby socks, rattles, and other indications that stories she was pregnant were making their way into the gossip mill.

Ill or well, the duchess ran her household with great expertise. Each morning, after dictating her letters, she interviewed the chef. Dana Hood remembered that he would submit the day's menus, and the duchess would go over them very carefully, sometimes approving of them, sometimes altering or adding to his suggestions. She never forgot if a guest disliked a particular dish, and if the chef accidentally included it when that guest was invited to dinner, she would change it.

A constant stream of hairdressers, masseuses, manicurists, and chiropodists turned up at the house. Every night the duchess's hair was shampooed and set. Beauty specialists were brought in from Nice or Cannes. She changed her jewelry several times a day. The same was true in Paris. She completely revised the old-fashioned royal cashbook and ledger system used by her husband. There was not a penny or a franc exchanged that she did not know about. The butler had to prove that he had not spent beyond the limit on groceries, cleaning materials, and soaps. The chauffeur was under constant instruction not to fiddle the gasoline accounts. The huge telephone bills were relentlessly monitored.

The duchess constantly went all over the house, as her grandmother had in Baltimore, checking lights in broom closets, switches that didn't work properly, or even the cords on the draw blinds to see that they were not knotted. She used a thermometer to test the temperature of the wine; during a meal she would jot down on the copperplate-written menu tiny remarks such as "Too hot," "Too cold," or "Cigars handed at the wrong time." Her gold-covered notebook of complaints became known as the "Grumble Book." The staff put up with everything.

Her mania for tidiness rivaled that of Craig's wife in the play of that name. The slightest movement of a clock, vase, or figurine she would notice. She was very annoyed when she found letters placed in front of a clock, a typical servant's habit. She would move a chair a fraction of an inch if its position had been changed by a cleaning woman.

The duchess, Dana Hood reported, spent hours inexhaustibly standing doing the flower arrangements. She was incapable of lounging in a chair. She would sit bolt upright at all times. Any member of the staff who did not have perfect posture would earn her reproof. Round shoulders infuriated her. The unfortunate victim of her tongue would learn to straighten up immediately. She and the duke bargained incessantly. They would wrangle over plumbers, electricians, and carpenters, who were notoriously inefficient in Paris and had a tendency to overcharge. They read every newspaper and magazine they could get their hands on from cover to cover. Few newspapers escaped their attention. They read countless biographies. The duchess was obsessed with mascots. She tired of her collection of elephants with their trunks up, considered lucky and begun in China, and she suddenly gave them away. But she did believe in frogs and had them everywhere. Later, she would collect pug figures.

The bed linen had to be ironed every night and replaced every other night. Every sheet and pillowcase, towel, tablecloth, and table napkin was, Dana Hood reported, "finely embroidered with initials and coronet." Both in Paris and in the south of France there was a special lingerie room presided over by various expert women.

Despite the couple's pleasure in their houses, they cannot be said to have been happy or comfortable. In particular, the duke continued to fret over his situation vis-à-vis the royal family. He harassed Sir Walter Monckton and the palace ceaselessly for an increase in money and for the opportunity to return to England with Wallis, where she would be recognized at last as "Her Royal Highness." So complete was this obsession, and so absolute the duke's removal from the realities of his own situation, that those who dealt with him could do little more than humor him in what appeared to be a form of madness. Monckton visited with the Windsors twice that year, doing his utmost to soothe their fevered brows, returning to the king and queen with not much more than faint reassurances and subdued requests for more consideration for his friends, which were rejected out of hand.

It is easy to see why. The situation in Europe had deteriorated rapidly in Hitler's favor during the past few months. While the Windsors were wrangling over details of their move to La Croë in March, Austria had collapsed completely, failing even to respond when Hitler, having forced the resignation of the Windsors' old friend Chancellor von Schuschnigg, had marched into Vienna. Many opponents of the Nazis who could be identified either committed suicide or were committed to concentration camps. Von Schuschnigg was arrested without trial.

The fact that the duke made no protest at this assault on his favorite European country, and in fact continued to hobnob with certain figures of the Nazi regime in Paris, could only sit badly with the royal couple in London. But Monckton and the ever-loyal Winston Churchill seemed to forgive everything. Neville Chamberlain's government was impotent in the face of Nazi power.

One unfortunate aspect of Hitler's seizure of Austria was that Baron Louis Rothschild, brother of the Windsors' close friend Eugene, who now commuted between Zurich and Paris, had been arrested by the gestapo and installed under house arrest with von Schuschnigg on the top floor of the Metropole Hotel in Vienna. Louis had been the president of the Creditanstalt Bank when it went bankrupt in 1931, carrying with it substantial amounts of German investors' money. The Nazi government insisted it would not release him until it had received full settlement; the storm troopers had already seized his estates in lower Austria and his house in a fashionable district of Vienna. His imprisonment greatly concerned the Windsors. The duke and duchess immediately began to take steps to arrange for go-betweens to have an appropriate ransom paid. This would include handing over to Himmler the complete ownership of a Czechoslovakian factory complex, along with sums of money which were being held in Switzerland and France. Since the German government obviously could not deal with any other member of the Rothschild family, it was clear that the Windsors, with their impeccable reputation in Berlin, were ideally placed to undertake the refined task of freeing the distinguished captive. Others involved in the negotiations were said to have been Fritz Wiedemann and Princess Stefanie von Hohenlohe. In May 1939 Louis Rothschild, his hair completely white, his health adversely affected, flew to Paris for a reunion with his benefactors.

In the meantime, the Windsors continued to travel restlessly. On July 12 they sailed with the Herman Rogerses from Cannes to Genoa, Italy, aboard the chartered yacht, *Gulzar*, continuing to Rapallo, and terminating the first leg of the journey by meeting with Princess Maria, daughter of King Victor Emmanuel, sister of Princess Mafalda of Hesse. There was a certain black humor in the fact that they would choose to make further appearances in a country which was now second only to Hitler's among dictatorships. The gesture seemed almost willfully tasteless and aggressively affirmative of the Windsors' political position. There were unconfirmed rumors that they had met with Count Ciano; the Foreign Office was very concerned about the visit, and managed to persuade, possibly on threats of discontinuing the Windsors' income, the couple from traveling to Vienna or Italy-dominated Tunisia to visit George Sebastian. They were also talked out of accepting a Panamanian decoration because of the authoritarian regime in Panama.

While the tour continued, the Duke of Kent was acting as an instrument of British pacification of Hitler and Mussolini. Foreign Office minutes of July 15, 1938, make clear that his frequent visits to Munich were approved, and that it was desirable he should shortly make a return visit to Germany, where "a personal gesture of that sort would be appreciated by Herr Hitler." In return, Field Marshal Goering, whose importance was rather oddly considered to be equivalent to Kent's, would be invited to London; but the Foreign Office stopped short of a suggestion, source not stated, that German paintings of recent origin should be displayed at the British National Gallery. It was felt, not without reason, that their artistic quality would scarcely improve public opinion of the country from which they emanated.

Meanwhile, temporarily eclipsing even the Windsors, King George VI and Queen Elizabeth had made a triumphal visit to Paris. They did not contact the Windsors, who were advised by the Foreign Office to stay firmly in the south of France. As it turned out, the royal tour of the city almost ended in tragedy: a Catalan group, allied with the Spanish falangists, or extreme right-wing Fascists, planned to kill the monarch and his wife, pinning the blame on the Communist-backed government in Spain.

The plot was hatched in the back room of a popular nightclub, the celebrated Boeuf sur le Toit, and at the Restaurante Le Cour and Café George V, as well as at an apartment rendezvous on the Rue Chateaubriand. A spy, the Marqués Rabalso, head of the Spanish government's intelligence service stationed at St. Jean de Luz, uncovered the plot just in time and, despite bureaucratic indifference when he reported it to the British embassy in Paris, managed to get the Sûreté, headed by the overworked Gilbert Rochès of the Maroni blackmail affair, to raid the appropriate clubs and arrest the various conspirators.

Within days, a perfect reason was found for Kent's trip, designed to please the führer. Queen Marie of Romania died conveniently and he and his wife, the duchess, flew at once to attend her funeral in Bucharest, where Goering, Mussolini, Ribbentrop, Prince Philipp of Hesse, and Crown Prince Paul of Yugoslavia and their wives were in attendance. After a no-doubt useful discussion on the need for peace, Kent left for Munich and his sister-in-law Countess Toerring. And all this just four months after the destruction of Austria. Could pacification of Hitler's policies at the British royal level go any further?

The delights of Fascist Italy apparently overcame some of the disgruntlement the Windsors felt over the glory of the British royal reception in the city they had adopted. Besieged by irritable memorandums from the Foreign Office, they impatiently canceled the remainder of their yacht cruise on August 14 at Genoa, dismissed the captain and crew, and boarded the liner *Conte di Savoia*, arriving at Cannes the following day. They returned to La Croë for two weeks, where Wallis did some new remodeling. During that period the duke had disturbing news. Schloss Mittersill had burned down, and no doubt the duke was worried that details of his so-called Sports and Shooting Club would be revealed in the press. It was on November 1 that Himmler supplied Ribbentrop with the sensational report on the duke's membership in the club. But nothing ever appeared in print, and it was not until the West German government declassified the files in 1986 that the truth could be determined by this author.

On September 22 the Windsors left for Paris. The situation in Europe was darkening still further. Czechoslovakia was falling apart, and it would obviously only be a question of time before it was added to Hitler's list of conquests. On August 3 the British mediator Walter Runciman had arrived in Prague, preparing the groundwork for Hitler's imminent invasion. He was encouraging the leaders of the Sudetenland in their determination to assist in the dismemberment of the country. On September 12, after a speech by Hitler at Nuremberg, an international crisis erupted, followed by the surrender of Britain and France to Hitler's demands. On October 2 the London *Sunday Dispatch* published a statement from the duke's publicity staff saying, in response to Neville Chamberlain's notorious crumbling before Hitler:

His Royal Highness has never lost hope [for the solution of the crisis] as he had unqualified confidence in the Prime Minister, although there seemed to be slender hope of success. His Royal Highness was convinced that Mr. Chamberlain's personality would prevail and his policy of peace would succeed.

In this conviction the duke was, it goes without saying, reflecting the majority of conservative political opinion in Great Britain. And that opinion, unhappily, is believed to have been shared by a majority of the public and even of the Labour party.

Once again, that left no one in any doubt of where the duke stood. Nor was anyone surprised when he was seen hobnobbing with the Pierre Lavals at parties, or with Otto Abetz, the German diplomat and Hitler fanatic who would soon become ambassador to Paris (a specially created title) and play a crucial role in the collapse of the Third Republic.

On September 29, the duke, without Wallis, held an extraordinary meeting at the Hôtel Meurice, a meeting that was monitored through discs in the walls by the British Secret Intelligence Service. Those in attendance at the meeting were Hitler's deputy, Rudolf Hess, Hitler's private secretary Martin Bormann, and the Nazi agent and motion picture star Errol Flynn, who had recently been in Spain with the Nazi spy Dr. Hermann Erben, going behind the Loyalist lines to inform Hitler and Franco, as exposed in such important books as Peter Wyden's history of the Spanish Civil War and George Seldes's *Witness to the Century*. After the meeting Hess wrote to Hitler:

> The Duke is proud of his German blood. Says he is more German than he is British. There is no need to lose a single German life in invading Britain. The Duke and his wife will deliver the goods.

Records of the meeting remain classified in 2004. However, it would be reasonable to deduce that Flynn promised support for the ducal tour of the United States, where he had strong connections with Nazi groups in New York (he was a frequent attendant at German-American Bund underground meetings) and in California, where a Japanese-German network existed, as well as with the Irish pro-Nazi supporters of the IRA, mostly located in the San Francisco Bay area and Marin County. And that Hess and Bormann promised a warm reception from Hitler and from the Nazi leaders as a whole.

Money was a continuing problem for the Windsors. Their £21,000 a year,* though the equivalent of over $100,000, was barely enough to sustain their extraordinary standard of living. The duchess's addiction to jewelry required constant satisfaction. Her clothes still had to be originals by Mainbocher, Schiaparelli, Chanel, or Molyneux. The duke auctioned off his entire herd of shorthorn cattle, grazed at his High River, Alberta, ranch, for a total of $10,000. That helped a little, and the investing skills of Eugene Rothschild helped more. Ironically, much of the Windsors' money was invested in the Jewish-owned Lyons' Corner Houses, a popular chain of what would today be called fast-food restaurants in England. These were enormously profitable and popular, and the income from them substantially improved as time went on.

On November 11 the Duke and Duchess of Gloucester, returning from a vacation in East Africa, flew to Paris and joined the Windsors for lunch at the Hôtel Meurice. They went for a drive and stopped by the Eugene Rothschilds' for tea. During the evening they dropped by a new house which the Windsors had just rented and were fixing up: an imitation Louis XVI residence owned by the Italian Countess Sabini, situated at 24 Boulevard Suchet, facing the wind-stripped autumn trees of the Bois de Boulogne. They would retain this elegant and charming house for many years.

The visit of the Gloucesters ended with a farewell at Le Bourget Airport. There was no question that the duke used the visit to press for Wallis's recognition and a return to London, but every effort made by the Gloucesters to sway the king and queen in the matter of Wallis's title failed.

On November 24 Prime Minister Neville Chamberlain and Foreign Secretary Viscount Halifax, who were locked in meetings with French statesmen that would lead to the moral disintegration of the Quai d'Orsay, found time for an evening with the Windsors. The *New York Times* reported that at the meeting the duke and duchess clearly expressed their support of the government's foreign policy. On December 11, at a party in Paris given by Lady Mendl, Lady Diana Cooper, and Wallis's friend Mrs. Euan Wallace, wife of the parliamentary secretary of the British Board of Trade, both curtseyed to the duchess.

---

*£25,000 less the pensions for the dismissed staff.

The Countess of Pembroke objected to this, clearly reflecting the views of Buckingham Palace. She said to the two ladies, "Nothing would induce me to curtsey to the Duchess, as it is not customary to curtsey to any but royal personages." Lady Diana later said, "I only did it to please the Duke."

On December 10, Prime Minister Baldwin was in Paris to answer yet another futile plea from the Duke of Windsor to have Wallis given the title of "Her Royal Highness" and to be received by his family in London. In the circumstances, as Sir Dudley Forwood told me, the duke can only be described as virtually insane in the degree of this obsession. That same day, the king wrote Baldwin from the Buckingham Palace what was perhaps the fiercest letter of that quiet man's life, stating that he had canvassed people "of all classes" and that the consensus was clear: the duke must not come to England with Wallis as his companion for even the shortest of visits; that neither his wife nor his mother Queen Mary had any desire to meet the Duchess of Windsor; and that any visit made for the purpose of such meetings was out of the question. He closed the letter by stating that the matter was so intimate that he thought Baldwin would best convey this statement rather than himself—that Windsor might take the refusal in a more friendly manner if it came from the prime minister. This was humorous, to say the least; the king knew that Windsor hated Baldwin even more than he hated him.

On December 17 the Windsors left for La Croë for the Christmas holidays. Their next-door neighbors for the season were none other than Thelma Furness and Gloria Vanderbilt; it goes without saying that visits were not exchanged. Their houseguests were Lord and Lady Brownlow and children, Aunt Bessie, Sir Charles and Lady Mendl, Johnny McMullen, and the Herman Rogerses. Another storm in a teacup blew up when, at an elaborate party given by Somerset Maugham, a couple of the female guests refused to curtsey and were reprimanded to their faces by the duke. On the other hand, the opera star Grace Moore did curtsey deeply to the duchess at the Cannes Casino following a recital, and this brought a storm of criticism, to which Miss Moore responded with great vigor. Mischievously, the duke sent a cable through the wire services stating, "Her Royal Highness is displeased at the public criticism of Miss Grace Moore." This episode, absurd and trivial though it seemed, increased the determination against the Windsors at Buckingham Palace.

In January, while Ambassador Joseph P. Kennedy was in Washington, the Windsors invited his wife, Rose, who was visiting Paris, to dinner. She called her husband by transatlantic telephone and asked him if she should accept. He thought it better that she did not, because of the couple's continuing Nazi connections. Accordingly, she declined. Shortly afterward, Bullitt called her and invited her to his house to meet the couple, saying it was important that Rose attend. She did.

Later, referring to Rose's refusal, Kennedy told an American newspaper reporter, "I know of no position that I could hold that would involve my wife in any obligation to dine with a tart." When Kennedy told the queen the story at dinner at Windsor Castle on April 14, she laughed joyously and said, "It serves [Mrs. Simpson] right." She added, "I understand, Mr. Kennedy, that the Windsors are talking about my husband and I. Our conscience is clear. They are deplorable!" And Kennedy noted that the decorative motif of the Buckingham Palace ballroom when Windsor was king was a motif of swastikas. The queen changed it at once.

Early in February, Victor Cazalet, an old pro-Fascist friend, visited the Windsors in Paris. They told him that the duke would have gone to see Hitler himself if Chamberlain had not. He noted that the duke still adored Wallis and that she had him under her complete domination. Charming as always, the duke received Cazalet in a kilt. He criticized Baldwin to Cazalet because Baldwin had not mentioned Wallis in his famous speech to the House of Commons.

In those early months of 1939 the duke asked Walter Monckton to make inquiries at 10 Downing Street as to how Chamberlain would react to his returning with the duchess for a short visit. On February 22 a letter from Neville Chamberlain arrived at Boulevard Suchet. The prime minister stated that it was his desire that the visit of the duke and duchess should be completely successful, and not provoke heated controversy of any kind. However, he was forced to conclude that a controversy would arise if the duke and duchess were to come to England at that time. Of course, this did not mean a permanent postponement, and the prime minister promised to keep a weather eye on the development of public opinion and to give a signal as soon as matters had improved to the point that such a visit would be officially acceptable.

On February 22 French premier Edouard Daladier spoke at a Washington's Birthday dinner at the American Club in Paris at which the Windsors were present. Introduced by a beaming William C. Bullitt, who stressed that the United States would not "start a war with any nation," Daladier spoke of permanent peace in Europe despite the fact that Italy was mustering on the border of Libya and French Tunisia. Only sixteen days later, Hitler annihilated the Czechoslovak state. And on May 8, in the wake of that annihilation, the duke, with Wallis at his side, broadcast on NBC from a country inn in Verdun, famous as a battlefield of World War I; his message was a plea for peace. Although he claimed that his brother the king, who was now on his way to Canada and the United States for a goodwill tour, approved this ill-timed address, nothing could be further from the truth. In fact, the British Broadcasting Corporation flatly refused to relay it. During the king's tour Nazi-controlled Sean Russell, head of the Irish Republican Army and an admirer of the Windsors, planned and almost brought off an assassination of the royal couple as they took the train from Windsor, Ontario, to Detroit. Simultaneously, serious consideration was given to the possibility of sending the Duke of Gloucester to Australia in the Duke of Kent's place.

On June 11, with great boldness, the Windsors went to a dinner party at the home of Count Johannes von Welczek, the German ambassador to France, with whom they had been friendly for many years. It was a season of elaborate parties, a summer of golden indulgence on the very edge of war. The most elaborate of all the soirées was given by Lady Mendl, apparently under the patronage of Paul-Louis Weiller, at her Villa Trianon. It was the last tremendous evening before night fell over Europe. The hostess invited 700 guests The distinguished French decorator Stephane Boudin of the House of Jansen created a magically beautiful dance pavilion that was open to the rolling lawns on three of its four sides. The exterior of the pavilion was painted green and white. Inside, there were blackamoor lacquered statues bearing parasols, white leather banquettes, and marble pillars. There was a champagne bar that framed an ancient oak tree. The dance floor was built on springs and was made specially in London. Constance Spry supplied thousands of white, red, and yellow roses. The entire garden including the fountains and statues was lit with great cunning to create a fairyland effect. Lady Mendl also hired a circus, including clowns, dwarf jugglers, acrobats, high-wire walkers, and an elephant. There were three orchestras, including the Windsors' favorite—an all-woman band that had played at the Bristol in Vienna—another Austrian group that had played at the Rotter, and Jimmy's Orchestra, famous at Jimmy's Bar in Paris.

Dressed in a diamond-and-aquamarine tiara and a Mainbocher white gown, the hostess received a striking array of guests. Aside from the Windsors, there were, among dozens of well-known names, Coco Chanel, Schiaparelli, Mainbocher, Eve Curie, Syrie Maugham, Sir George Clerk, and Foreign Minister Bonnet. The Fascist author Paul Morand, the Duc de Gramont, and members of the royal house of Monaco were also there. Ambassador Bullitt and the famous society beauty Mrs. Harrison Williams completed the list. The social crowd was present in force. The prominent political journalist Pertinax observed that many pro-Nazis and admirers of Mussolini's regime used the party, as they used many similar events, to improve their connections on behalf of fascism. Anything went in the glamorous and corrupt atmosphere of Paris in those days.

By now, the Windsors were fully settled in their home at 24 Boulevard Suchet, a four-storied residence with a small front garden, redecorated with inspired skill by Wallis, with the help of Boudin. The staff was large and headed by two secretaries, the butler, Hale, who had been wooed away from the Bedauxes, and Dudley Forwood. There were twelve servants' bedrooms, which were always fully occupied. The new chauffeur, Webster, had his own room. In the south of France a separate staff was maintained, including the reliable Anna, Antoine, and Valat. The chef Dyot, who had originally been with the Duke of Alba, chief supporter with Juan March of Franco in Spain and presently ambassador to the Court of St. James's, was in residence at both houses. His canapés were famous; his specialty was white grapes, peeled, pitted, and filled with a delicate white French cheese.

In early June, the Duke and Duchess of Kent had received an invitation to attend, in Florence, Italy, the most spectacular wedding in years—of Mussolini's admiral, Prince Aimone Roberto, son of the Duke of Aosta, a crucial figure in Fascist-royal politics, and Princess Irene, sister-in-law of Princess Friederike, the former proposed Queen of England, now married to Prince Paul of Greece.

Documents show that the Foreign Office in London urged Kent to undertake the trip in order to confirm the existing and anomalous allegiance between Great Britain and Italy—between Neville Chamberlain and Mussolini, King George VI and King Victor Emmanuel III—

when Italy was to all intents and purposes a part of the Axis. If statements made in 1975 by Prince Wolfgang of Hesse, twin brother of Prince Philipp, are to be believed, the Duke of Windsor had another purpose in mind. Like King George VI, he wanted Kent to meet with Prince Philipp toward the purpose of a permanent peace, through an intervention with Hitler.

The Foreign Office's only proviso was that Kent should not show British approval of Mussolini's recent invasion and conquest of the hapless nation of Albania by proposing a toast to King Victor Emmanuel at the wedding banquet as King of Albania and Emperor of Ethiopia, which nation he and Mussolini had, of course, wantonly conquered. Nevertheless, he would join in the toast; so the restriction was pointless.

On their way to Florence, according to the Paris socialite Ginette Spanier, the Kents surreptitiously met the Duke of Windsor (they were not talking to the duchess, whom they hated) at the Ritz Hotel on June 30. There, a Croatian terrorist threatened their lives; the anti-Nazi group of Croatian origin was certain that they were bent upon Hitler's business. The Sûreté defused the plot, coming to the Windsors' rescue as they had done in the year before in the Maroni affair; Gilbert Rochès was in charge of the Place Vendôme, location of the Ritz.

At the last minute, a bizarre invitation had to be brushed off. Mrs. George Keppel, the former mistress of King Edward VII, grandfather of Windsor and Kent, offered her summer home in Florence as accommodation during the wedding. The Kents declined, stating politely that they had already secured a suite at the Hotel Excelsior.

No sooner had the Kents arrived in Florence than the British ambassador Sir Percy Loraine warned of another assassination plot. This time a pro-Nazi group was behind it: Croatians were furious that the Duchess of Kent was talking to her sister Olga, Princess Regent of Yugoslavia, to prevent Paul, Olga's husband, from forming an alliance with Mussolini. This plot also was defused; such were the dangers of royal meddlers on both sides of the political spectrum.

After the glowing nuptials were over, the Duke of Kent had his scheduled meeting with Prince Philipp of Hesse, the only one of many encounters referred to by Prince Wolfgang of his brother in 1975 of which written documentation survives. This meeting was specifically authorized by King George VI.

At the meeting, Kent had the king's urgent message, not authorized, indeed forbidden by Neville Chamberlain, and undertaken without authorization of the Foreign Office, to convey to Hitler in Berlin. He was to warn the führer, in King George's words, that "we mean business," and that Britain would declare war on Germany if Hitler were to invade Poland, a sign of panic on King George's part.

Kent was entirely out of order in saying so. Although Britain had entered into guarantees with Poland, there was still, in Whitehall's eyes, room for negotiation. But hidden inside Kent's warning was a fear far deeper than that of German aims; both he and the king knew that it was only a matter of weeks before Ribbentrop signed a pact with the Soviet Union that would carve up Poland; it was Russia they were still afraid of, haunted by the slaughter of their royal cousins Czar Nicholas and his family at Ekaterinburg.

Hence, Kent's second statement, which was to urge Philipp to have Hitler dismiss Ribbentrop as a "perpetual insult to England." To call for Hitler to dismiss his foreign minister was something that Kent had no right or authorization to do.

Hesse left Florence for Berlin but had to wait for an audience with Hitler until August; this was an early sign that this handsome object of Hitler's adoration had not only started to lose his hair and his looks but also his influence.

Back in London, the Duke of Kent formed an alliance as dangerous as that with Philipp of Hesse. He had for some time been an intimate friend and perhaps the lover of his cousin, the handsome, blond, and athletic Prince Friedrich of Prussia, cousin of Princess Friederike, Queen of Greece, and a favorite grandson of the kaiser.

Beloved of Hitler, the glamorous youth, the toast of pro-Nazi elements in London society, member of the Anglo-German Fellowship and the pro-Nazi The Link, worked as a junior executive at the Schröder Bank, a chief backer of Hitler in London, as well as taking classes in history at Corpus Christi College, Cambridge. In a tight-fitting white army uniform, he had been the scene-stealer at the funeral of King George V and the coronation of George VI.

Friedrich was, following the death of his father, and in view of his grandfather's abdication and exile in Holland, the favored successor to the throne of Germany. The direct heir, his oldest brother Wilhelm, had renounced his rights; his second oldest, Louis Ferdinand, was rejected out of hand by the Reichswehr, the German army faction,

chiefly because of his louche succession of love affairs, including a prolonged liaison with Lili Damita, the Hollywood star and wife of Errol
Flynn, and because of suspicions of disloyalty to the führer. Friedrich
was, as recently declassified Foreign Office documents show, also the
choice of the British government for the German monarchy, as part of
the endless plans for negotiated peace—a knitting together of the broken strands of royal British and German cousins.

The Duke of Kent urged Friedrich to return to Germany as soon
as possible—undoubtedly for the purpose stated, but technically an act
of betrayal. Even after war broke out on September 3, Kent was writing to Prince Regent Paul of Yugoslavia through the diplomatic bags,
stating his disappointment that Friedrich (Fritzi) had decided to stay.
He wrote on December 5, 1939:

> I saw Fritzi who said he couldn't fight for the Nazis, etc. I think he is
> wrong as he is in the army. He should have gone back and they would
> have given him work. Now I doubt if he would ever go back again.

Such thoughts were treasonable in wartime.

On June 23 the Windsors celebrated the duke's forty-fifth birthday
party at the restaurant on the first platform of the Eiffel Tower. It was
also the fiftieth anniversary of the celebrated monument. The Windsors'
guest was a 6-foot 3-inch girl, Jacqueline Vialle, who had been elected
Mademoiselle Eiffel Tower in a tallest woman contest. In the middle of
dinner, Bedrich Benes, military attaché of the Czechoslovak government in exile, who may or may not have been attempting an assassination, was poised 186 feet up the tower outside a window gazing at the
Windsors from a perilous metal strut. The Windsors were startled by
a horrifying scream. The man had lost his balance, and was clinging to
a girder. A minute later he plunged to his death on the sidewalk below.
Wallis screamed with terror.

As the world drifted closer to war, the Windsors returned via
Switzerland to La Croë. That they realized the future was grim can be
illustrated by the fact that they bought a macadamia nut plantation in
Hawaii for $135,000; the plantation, composed of rich tropical soil,
was 2,000 feet up Diamond Head. On August 22 the announcement
that the Nazi government had signed a pact with the Soviet Union ap-

palled the duke; he cannot have been oblivious, however, after some reflection, of the sheer cynicism of this move toward an artificial relationship, engineered by Ribbentrop, which would simply allow Hitler to move as freely as he wished in western Europe and to ship oil and other supplies from Mexico through Siberia. Whether the Windsors knew it or not, the alliance with Russia was encouraged by Ribbentrop because of his own desire to confront his rival, Rudolf Hess, who agreed with the policy the duke advocated, that of a joint onslaught by Britain, the United States, Germany, and Italy on Russia. Stalin seized the opportunity to make the alliance so that he could move into some of the satellite countries such as Bessarabia without being interfered with and could strengthen his army in anticipation of an all-out confrontation. The most serious aspect of this artificial truce between ideological enemies was, from the duke's point of view, that it would no longer be possible for Britain to allow Hitler to move into Poland. Before the pact the English would have been happy to allow the attack if it were to follow that Hitler would then proceed against the Soviets. By August 24 the Windsors' social set had fled La Croë. Fruity Metcalfe was still there, offering any help that might be required. A squad of Senegalese black troops camped in the grounds along with an anti-aircraft battery. On August 29 the duke sent a telegram to Hitler, followed by one to King Victor Emmanuel of Italy, urging both to intercede in the interest of securing peace. Even as Hitler marched into Poland, the führer sent a telegram in response, saying that England was responsible for the situation and that "if war came" it would be England's fault. However, Victor Emmanuel, presumably with the authorization of Mussolini, cabled that he would do his best to see that Italy remained neutral.

War broke out on September 3. The Windsors' position was extremely delicate. If they remained in France, they ran the risk that the Germans would kidnap them as accomplices in a plan for the duke to resume the British throne. On the other hand, if they fled to the United States, it would reflect appallingly upon them and would suggest that they were cowards. The only alternative was to go to England. They could scarcely do so without at least offering to assist the war effort, since not offering to help would only add strength to their enemies, led by the Hardinges and Sir Robert Vansittart. From the point of view of the king and queen, there were numerous problems connected with the Windsors' return. Vansittart and the Secret Intelligence Service would have to keep a close eye on them as there was always the danger that they might sell official secrets to the enemy, or at least that Wallis might. Moreover, there was already afoot in England a disorganized series of movements allegedly bent upon overthrowing the throne in the interests of fascism should Britain be invaded and sue for peace. These included The Link, which was headed by Sir Barry Domvile, former chief of naval intelligence; it was made up of a group of right-wing and reactionary politicians and their hangers-on. Two other such groups were the Right Club and the Nordic League, the latter headed by Archibald Maule Ramsay, an anti-Semitic member of Parliament for Peebles and Southern in Scotland. These were largely eccentric frondes, with no common leadership and rather scattered resources, but it was well known that if Britain were attacked they would do everything to encourage a general laying down of arms and the setting up of a puppet state. Churchill would be put under house arrest and the royal family exiled to the Bahamas (Churchill, with great dark humor, would instead sent the Windsors there). At the beginning of September Domvile recorded in his diaries his excitement at enlisting "D of W" in The Link as one of his members. Opinion differed as to whether this was the Duke of Windsor or the Duke of Westminster: it was the latter.

Sir Walter Monckton moved rapidly to assist the Windsors to return to London. After an uncomfortable flight to the south of France, he told the duke and duchess what the situation would be when they returned. No royal accommodation would be offered. Fort Belvedere was in disrepair and uninhabitable; not a soul had touched it from the day the duke left. They must make their own arrangements for a house. The duke would be offered by the king, his brother, one of two meaningless posts, deputy regional commissioner of Wales or liaison officer with the number-one British military mission to French general headquarters under Major General Sir Richard Howard-Vyse. The first of these suggestions was a very serious mistake, the second scarcely less so.

The Windsors would not fly to London; the duchess remained terrified of airplanes. In the aforementioned article in the *New York Daily News* on December 14, 1966, the duke would meaningfully write, "The Duchess . . . at Pensacola . . . was witness to many crashes that left her with little confidence in airplanes." Sir Ronald Campbell was now ambassador to France. He advised the Windsors to drive to the Channel coast, where they would be informed of the arrangements for their being picked up. However, when they reached Vichy and tried to get some more information as to which port they should stay at, Campbell told them to do nothing for the time being. It is clear that arrangements were being made for them to be watched.

They continued to Paris. Finally, they were told to go to Cherbourg, after closing up their house at the Boulevard Suchet for the indefinite future. They reached Cherbourg on the twelfth. Ironically, Lord Louis Mountbatten, whose politics were the exact opposite of theirs, had been sent by Winston Churchill to pick them up in the HMS *Kelly*. Randolph Churchill was also there.

Dodging possible U-boats, the *Kelly* arrived at Portsmouth in blackout conditions; Churchill, as admiral of the fleet, had arranged for the Royal Marines' Band to greet them with the national anthem. Lady Alexandra Metcalfe and Walter Monckton were there to make them welcome; Fruity Metcalfe had been with them throughout the journey. Lady Alexandra had been told by officials at Buckingham Palace that no automobile would be placed at the couple's disposal. Churchill arranged for them to stay at Admiralty House for the night. Clearly, their host and hostess, Commander in Chief Admiral Sir William James and his wife, had been told of the suspicions of espionage surrounding Wallis, who mistook their excessive interest and probing glances to mean simply that she was still considered a notorious abductor of the king.

The queen, at dinner with Ambassador Kennedy on the eleventh, told him that the only bad moment on her recent royal tour of the United States was when, in Wallis's hometown of Baltimore, a woman stepped up to her with a large bouquet of flowers and for one horrible moment she thought it was Wallis.

She told Kennedy, referring to the Windsors' presence in England, that it was "terribly embarrassing" to have them in the vicinity; she certainly would not in any circumstances receive "Mrs. Simpson"—as she persisted in calling her.

The Windsors continued to the Metcalfes' house in Sussex, where they posed and smiled for reporters in the garden.

On September 14, without the duchess, the duke went to see the king. It was a superficially friendly meeting that meant nothing. The duke said he would "prefer the Welsh appointment." The king, already briefed on the problems in Wales, nodded. Queen Mary refused to see the duke, and by royal instruction he was not permitted to visit the Duke of Kent.

The next day the king visited Winston Churchill. Churchill made it clear he disapproved of the duke's visit to Hitler and his speech at Verdun. He had apparently changed his mind following his previous letter praising that very visit, possibly in view of the changing European situation. However, he was sure the duke would now, as "one of us," be loyal to the British cause. Where the duke was concerned, Churchill's incurable romanticism again seemed to overrule his famous common sense.

Within twenty-four hours, the Welsh appointment was withdrawn for obvious reasons on the advice of Vansittart. The very fact that the duke wanted it was sufficient cause for it not to be given. On September 14 the Earl of Crawford noted in his diary:

[The Duke of Windsor] was too irresponsible as a chatterbox to be entrusted with confidential information which will all be passed on to Wally at the dinner table. That is where the danger lies—namely that after nearly three years of complete obscurity, the temptation to show that he knows, that he is again at the centers of information will prove irresistible, and that he will blab and babble out State secrets without realizing the danger. I dined with Howe [Francis Curzon, Fifth Earl Howe] at the Club. He is working at the Admiralty, and to his consternation saw the door of the Secret Room open—the basement apartment where the position of our fleet and the enemy is marked out by hour—and lo! out come Churchill and the Duke of Windsor. Howe . . . was horrified.

It was decided that the duke would proceed to France as major general. Actually, the duke never officially accepted the position, but two advantages can be seen in the decision to make the French appointment. First, it would get the duke out of the British Isles. Second, it would be possible for agents of the Secret Intelligence Service to keep an eye on him while he performed various assignments, including the formulation of reports on French military weaknesses.

The duke went to see Prime Minister Neville Chamberlain at 10 Downing Street. Chamberlain felt extremely awkward, since he had on his desk much material (and not just hate letters) suggesting it would be unwise to have the duke around in wartime. Chamberlain also undoubtedly knew that the duke was dangerously talkative. The ebullient Leslie Hore-Belisha was minister of war. He was Jewish and certainly cannot have liked the duke's politics. (Hore-Belisha would soon be pushed out of office for allegedly trading improperly in the City and for having criticized the inadequacy of British military strength in France.) When the duke asked if the duchess could go with him to visit the troops in Scotland, a very dangerous request, Hore-Belisha naturally declined. It was inconceivable that, in view of emergency conditions, he would not have been briefed on the security problems involved. It was obvious that the sooner the duke went to France the better. At all events, he must not be permitted to visit British troops there either, because he could so easily give away their secret transit arrangements in loose talk in Paris.

Several of the days before the departure of the duke and duchess were spent in London. One afternoon, they went to see Fort Belvedere, only to find it falling into disuse, not a sign of life in it anywhere.

In severe weather on September 29, with Fruity Metcalfe and Captain Purvis of the British army, the Windsors took the destroyer *Express* to Cherbourg. They continued to Paris, deciding not to move back into their Boulevard Suchet house, which was still closed and shuttered. Instead, they checked into the Trianon Palace Hotel in Versailles, partly in order to be close to Lady Mendl. The duke reported for duty on September 30 at the military headquarters under Major General Sir Richard Howard-Vyse. His duties were explained to him with fake seriousness and an air of heavy import. He was to be in charge of an "investigative mission" surveying the strengths and weaknesses of the French defense forces, including the Maginot line, and he was to report his considered impressions of French leaders. Although described as an intelligence assignment, this was in fact a survey which had already been undertaken by other officers; Winston Churchill had made a tour of the line in mid-August, reporting on its problems, and in January would make another journey of inspection. General Gamelin made no secret of the line's deficiencies in meetings with Lord Gort. As General Lelong, of the French forces, had written to Gamelin on September 19:

The assignment of the Duke of Windsor is a matter of pure expediency. They do not quite know what to do with this encumbering personage, especially in England; but they do not wish it to be said that he is sitting on his hands. They have therefore found a way out through Howard-Vyse, who is not too proud of the fact.

Thus, a waste of the taxpayers' money was undertaken. That Gamelin had no time for it was indicated by the fact that, according to the famous French journalist Pertinax in his book *The Betrayal of France*, Gamelin dismissed General Alexandre Montagne for having told the duke the secrets of how the enemy could break through the Maginot line. It was the only dismissal from that French general's staff at the time; Pertinax made clear that the information was leaked to the Germans—it is believed that Wallis was the conduit.

Lord Ironside, son of the late commander in chief, said in 1987:

My father determined that the duke was a serious security leak. He was giving the duchess a great deal of information that was classified in the matter of the defenses of France and Belgium. She in turn was passing this information on to extremely dangerous enemy-connected people over dinner tables in Paris. As a result, the information made its way into German hands.

Wallis stayed in Paris, helping in a public relations stunt to prepare mess kits including clothing and toilet articles and to knit socks for the French troops. While the Windsors made sure these contributions to the war effort were publicized, it was typical of their impudence and almost humorous perversity that the first person they saw, entertained, and visited in Paris was Charles Bedaux. One would have thought even the minimum of common sense would have urged them to avoid any such encounter, in view of the fact that Bedaux, whether guilty of Nazi collaboration or not, was under constant surveillance by the Secret Intelligence Service. The fact that Fruity Metcalfe organized the meeting makes one wonder about his motives.

On October 2, the queen wrote a very long letter to Prince Paul of Yugoslavia on Buckingham Palace stationery, relating directly to the duke and Wallis's visit to England. Still referring contemptuously to Wallis not as the Duchess of Windsor but as "Mrs. S," she revealed that she had written to her stating that in all honesty and to make things clear she would emphatically not be prepared to receive her; she hoped that the duke would stay in France and not return to England; there was no place for him in England and "the mass of people do not forgive quickly the sort of thing he did to this country and they HATE her!" She added, "What a curse black sheep are to a family!" The rest of the letter illustrated her horror of the war. The missive was fired less by a burning patriotism than by a need to bring the conflict to a hasty end; for her, the two world wars seemed to run together. She wrote that she even had the horrifying experience of thinking she saw her brother, dead in World War I, in a palace parade of the Black Watch regiment.

The same day, the Duke of Windsor wrote to Sir Walter Monckton in London, stating that he didn't like the tone of Churchill's broadcast of the day before. That statement gave him away: Churchill had said on the BBC that a defeated Poland would "rise again like a rock" emerging from the tidal wave of defeat, and he had praised the action of British submarines, "hunting the U-boats with zeal." Churchill had added that though the war might last for three years, Britain would fight to the end; as proponents of a negotiated peace, these were the last words the Windsors (or Kent) wanted to hear. Five days later, Hitler issued a peace proposal to England which was summarily rejected, on Churchill's specific advice.

On October 6 the duke met with the British commander in chief, Lord Gort; the Duke of Gloucester was attached to Gort's staff as liaison officer. In a revealing sentence in his diary, the British chief of staff, Major General Pownall, wrote on October 7: "There is, for the moment at any rate, an 'inhibition' against his going around troops, indeed I believe he was not supposed to come to G.H.Q., but we can't help saying 'yes' when we are told he is coming." On October 10, after a tour of inspection, the duke provided a report on the problems of the French defenses on the Belgian frontier. The report merely confirmed the findings of Churchill in August. When it arrived in London, it was, needless to say, shelved as redundant. On October 14 Gamelin gave an elaborate luncheon for the duke at the military headquarters at the Château de Vincennes. The duchess was not present; no wives were there. Meanwhile, the duchess decided to reopen her house after all. Astonishingly, she entertained Charles and Fern Bedaux at that address, which took a great deal of nerve.

On October 17 the duke arrived uninvited at the Gort headquarters in Arras; in defiance of his brother the king's orders, he joined his brother Gloucester in inspecting the troops. Unfortunately, according to a United Press release on January 8 of the following year, he wore suede shoes with his uniform. He also infuriated Gloucester by returning a salute to which it was his brother's privilege to respond. As a result of this, plus the fact that he had behaved improperly in arriving as he did, the duke was forbidden any further visits to the British front line. On October 26 he made a further tour of the French troops. But as the war began to look more serious and German attacks were expected, he was increasingly deactivated and sent to places where there was even less information to be obtained which could be of use to the enemy. He spent most of his time in Paris, where Gray Phillips, an experienced staff officer, had arrived to take up the role of the duke's aide and comptroller. Providing Phillips's services was a gesture by the palace, but the fact that the duke was in the outer darkness was further indicated when neither War Minister Hore-Belisha nor King George contacted him when they came to France in November and December. A third inspection tour by the duke of the French forces was equally futile and redundant. Nobody in Whitehall was impressed when the duchess turned up distributing gift parcels to the French troops. The duchess, they knew, had no business being there.

On October 11, Sir Stewart Menzies of the SIS and his colleagues in Whitehall, in cooperation with the BBC, brought off an ingenious ruse, designed to test the Windsors' popularity in Nazi Germany, as well as the response of the German public should England lose the war and the Windsors, as Hitler hoped, be returned to the throne. The Secret Intelligence Service team arranged for a fake BBC broadcast to be relayed throughout the Nazi empire announcing that there had been a coup d'etat in England; that the public had risen up and forced King George's abdication; and that Neville Chamberlain and the cabinet had resigned, to be replaced by the supporters of the Duke of Windsor, who would now be returning to Britain to reassume the throne.

The Nazi propaganda minister, Dr. Joseph Goebbels, in charge of radio as he was in charge of films and newspapers, dictated the facts to his secretary for his diary in progress. He stated, based on telephone reports received from all over the country, that the German public was swept up into a "veritable storm of joy"; that people were embracing each other in the street; and that factories were "exploding," even government departments were "on fire with excitement" at the news.

In her memoirs, Cristabel Bielenberg, British wife of a German official, gave an eyewitness account of the matter. She was shopping for vegetables in a Berlin market when she heard a hubbub; people were crying out that England had changed hands and the beloved "Duke of Vindzor" would at once be restored to the throne; German women shook this Englishwoman's hand. Suddenly a police sergeant appeared and announced a broadcast bulletin; a plane with a British peace delegation would be arriving within a few hours at Tempelhof Airport in Berlin.

Goebbels saw through Menzies' Secret Intelligence Service plot; that it was designed to show the danger of the Duke of Windsor and his threat to the British throne—the degree, in short, of Hitler's and the German people's passion for him. Goebbels himself broadcast that the story was a fabrication; every newspaper in Germany was ordered to run the headline: FURTHER INSOLENCE FROM THE BRITISH MINISTRY OF LIES.

It isn't surprising to note that within hours of the broadcasts, King George issued an order restricting Windsor from entering areas occupied by British troops in France. On October 14, infuriated by the edict and convinced incorrectly that it had been in force from before his assignment, the duke fired off an angry letter to Sir Walter Monckton from Paris, saying that he had heard of the order "by accident," and that this was "a back door intrigue." He also addressed a furious note to whoever steamed open the letter. Given the juxtaposition of dates, it can scarcely be doubted that the royal order came as a direct result of the SIS broadcast. He wasted no time in disobeying it: a court-martial offense.

When Kim Philby, later to become famous as a Communist spy, was on special duty for the Secret Intelligence Service disguised as a journalist, he found the Duke of Windsor at Bruges, suspiciously close to the German lines, and reported it; seeing him, the frightened duke fled at once to Paris.

On November 4, the duke wrote to Hitler, under the name of EP (Edward Prince), saying that he had information regarding his trip to the north (to survey the British troops) in disobedience of his brother's command, and that the Nazi Charles Bedaux, as his emissary, had the information with him. ("I am hardly able to stress the importance of the information, which is why I have gone into so much detail in explaining it to our friend.") Bedaux handed the letter, and the treasonable intelligence report, to Hitler in Berlin on the ninth.

According to the writer Peter Miller, in an article in the *Sunday Times* of London, dated January 26, 2003, the Duke of Kent was still involved in questionable peace negotiations at the time. Although his constant stream of letters to Prince Regent Paul of Yugoslavia emanated from his home at Coppins, Iver, Buckinghamshire, Miller states that he bought a house near Rosyth in Scotland, where he had at least ten secret meetings with the Polish prime minister in exile, General Wladyslav Sikorski, who was prepared to offer Kent the Polish throne in the event of a negotiated peace.

Kent's response to previous offers of thrones had resulted, his papers show, in a consignment of the proposals to the nearest wastepaper basket, and there is no reason to believe that he responded to Sikorski's offer any differently. With Russia as England's ally (disgracefully, since it sliced up Poland with Hitler) no monarch would have been allowed by Stalin to be part of any peace arrangement with his own ally, Germany. As with Italy, Britain was playing the dangerous game of maintaining full diplomatic arrangements with a member of Hitler's Axis.

Nevertheless, the appeasement group in London led by Sir Robert Vansittart, and Sir Stewart Menzies of the Secret Intelligence Service took a dim view of the Kent-Sikorski meetings just as they took a dim view of the Kent–Paul of Yugoslavia letters.

On December 12 the duke visited the sector of the French Second Army between Thionville and Sedan. He delivered himself of the futile observation, "I gained the general impression that the Maginot Line is an effective barrier, but cannot be looked upon as impregnable." According to the duke's biographer Michael Bloch, this and subsequent reports amounted to important intelligence, yet the problems with the Maginot line were well known to both the French and British forces; it might well be asked also how a visit to the line could be considered a useful intelligence mission when the French arranged it in the full knowledge that little or nothing of significance could or would be reported.

Christmas was depressing, a time for the embattled couple to weigh in the balance how much had been lost and how little had been gained.

The Windsors were under constant surveillance by British agents and undoubtedly knew it.

In January the duke was again at the front line, commenting rather futilely upon the problems of the defenses. Although historians have not found any records of the visit, such records do exist; they are on a level with the duke's previous reports. The chief advantage any of these reports had was, arguably, to the Germans, who apparently received them via the duchess during this period.

On January 12, still continuing his affair with Wallis in Paris, William Bullitt was busy cementing his connections with Mussolini. He advised Roosevelt by telegram that he was leaving for Rome to visit with his aunt, the Fascist Duchess of Assergio. He was also cementing relations between his pro-Fascist friend F. Pinckney Tuck and the Italian government. In fact, Tuck became, under Bullitt's advisement, emissary to Rome and later U.S. ambassador to collaborationist Vichy; Bullitt's other close friend, Gaston Henry-Haye, mayor of Versailles, who, at his request, had provided the Windsors' house there, almost free of rent, would become Vichy ambassador to the United States, where Wallis became both contact and friend.

On January 26, the peace for which Kent and Windsor so profoundly wished was the subject of a letter sent from Prince Paul of Yugoslavia via his aunt, Queen Marie, to King George VI at Buckingham Palace. Paul said that a member of his appeasement delegation in Düsseldorf, Germany, had word from a German general that there was to be a coup d'etat before winter was over and that Hitler and Goering would be assassinated. Paul thought this might result in an armistice, but then he added with typically disgraceful emphasis that of course, after peace was arranged, the Allies should not ask for the restoration of Austria, Czechoslovakia, and Poland. Even for the outrageously duplicitous Prince Paul, this was too much.

In mid-January the Duke of Windsor flew to London for what was described as "business." The date of his arrival was altered in the newspapers in order to allow him some extra days of secret meetings. One of these meetings was with Major General John Fuller, who recorded the event in his date book. Fuller, described as the inventor of modern warfare, was a leading member of fascistic organizations in Britain and had written books and articles praising Hitler. He was under suspicion of being prominent among those individuals in England who supported the idea of a negotiated peace with Germany and would assist the Germans if they were to invade Great Britain. The duke also met with Ironside at the War Office, grumbling about his unhappiness and frustration in his present role. A memorandum was sent by Julius Count von Zech-Burckesroda, German minister to the Netherlands, to the Nazi secretary of state in Berlin for Hitler's personal attention on January 27, 1940:

> Through personal relationships I might have the opportunity to establish certain lines leading to the Duke of Windsor. . . . He does not . . . feel entirely satisfied with his position and seeks a field of activity in which he would not have merely a representative character, and which would permit him a more active role. In order to attain this objective, he was recently in London. . . . There seems to be something like the beginning of a Fronde [secret organization] forming around W. . . . When he was recently in London, I had explained to him through an intermediary why it is completely utopian for England to attempt to effect a change of regime in Germany, and the statements of my intermediary are believed to have made a certain impression on him. . . . Heil Hitler!

On February 19 the same diplomat was back in touch with the secretary of state. He wrote:

> The Duke of W, about whom I wrote to you in my letter of the 27th of last month, has said that the Allied War Council devoted an exhaustive discussion at its last meeting to the situation that would arise if Germany invaded Belgium. On the military side, it was held that the best plan would be to make the main resistance effort in the line behind the Belgian-French border, even at the risk that Belgium should be occupied by us. The political authorities are said to have at first opposed this plan: after the humiliation suffered in Poland, it would be impossible to surrender Belgium and the Netherlands also to the Germans. In the end, however, the political authorities became more yielding.

This is a very interesting document. In fact, the Allied War Council did not discuss the matter concerned at its meeting. It was a topic of detailed conversation at a War Cabinet meeting in London presided over by Winston Churchill. Some member of the War Cabinet (possibly the ever-trusting Winston Churchill himself) relied upon the Duke of Windsor sufficiently to tell him what was discussed, and in turn the duke unwisely conveyed the information to the duchess, who in turn relayed it to Nazi-associated people in Paris. For the duke (and more importantly the duchess) to have leaked the secrets of such a meeting to the enemy can only be described as treasonous, assuming that the ambassador to the Netherlands had not invented the story. A career diplomat of the old school, not particularly enamored of the Hitler regime, Zech would scarcely have had a motive for concocting such a thing. That the Secret Intelligence Service and Sir Robert Vansittart* were alerted to this leakage of privileged information can be seen from the fact that Wolfgang zu Putlitz, the British spy who had been at the British embassy when Wallis was suspected of obtaining classified materials at Fort Belvedere, was at Zech-Burckesroda's embassy in the Hague at the time the telegram was sent to Berlin. No doubt this latest disclosure only served to confirm the fears of Wallis's archenemy Vansittart. Just three days earlier, there had been another serious leak. In *War Propaganda 1939–1944: Secret Ministry Conferences in the Reich's Ministry for Propaganda*, edited by Willi A. Boelcke, the following entry appears:

> February 16, 1940, Friday: The message of the Duke of Windsor to the King of England [sic] about the miserable condition of the English troops at the Front shall be used for the language service.

The duke had only just returned from inspecting the land and sea defenses at Dunkerque on February 10, and he had noted in his report that the British pilots, among others, were nervous wrecks. Again, Ironside was convinced that the duke and duchess were leaking crucial information to the enemy through contacts in Paris.

On December 23, 1941, President Roosevelt, in a private conversation at the White House with Fulton Oursler, author and editor of *Liberty* magazine, made the following statement:

> The Duke [of Windsor] was present at the most intimate councils of the commanders in chief of the two armies. He knew everything that was going on. Sometimes he would suddenly decide that there was nothing more for him to do and he would go back to Paris, not just overnight but for three or four days. . . . I know that there were nine shortwave wireless sets in Paris constantly sending information to the German troops, and

---

*Though officially kicked upstairs, Vansittart was permitted to continue operating, largely behind the cover of London Films, his own special spy system.

no one has ever been able to decide how such accurate information could be sent over those wireless stations.

The duke's inspection tours continued. They were completed at the end of February. His reports on the French generals continued to be futile. Instead of analyzing their technical approach to the war, he restricted himself to meaningless generalities. Commenting on General Condé, he wrote, "He is shy by nature, and it takes a little time to appreciate his real qualities as a soldier, but an afternoon spent in his company revealed these to be remarkable." Dealing with General Freydenberg, he said, "He has a very comfortable appearance and his features are those of a good-looking man. While in no way interfering with his military work, he seems to enjoy his creature comforts." And so forth in a similar vein. In mid-March the Windsors returned to La Croë. They had offered the château as a convalescent home for British army officers, but clearly that idea could not be entertained in Whitehall. It was a fairly commonplace device for enemy agents to milk wounded soldiers for information, and the duchess's membership in the Red Cross was scarcely encouraging to the more sophisticated members of the Secret Intelligence Service. The Red Cross was unwittingly a sieve in terms of security, used by Germany in various skillful ways to allow traffic in individuals and information across every border. This is not to say that the duchess used the Red Cross for this purpose, only that she would quickly fall under suspicion of doing so.

On May 10 the American journalist and playwright Mrs. Henry (Clare Boothe) Luce was in Paris; she was invited to dinner at the Boulevard Suchet. There was a BBC broadcast that Germans had bombed London and coastal villages. Mrs. Luce said, "I've driven through many of those villages. I hate to see the British so wantonly attacked." The duchess replied, "After what they did to me, I can't say I feel sorry for them—a whole nation against a lone woman!"

On May 20 Wallis's cause was not helped by the fact that her dressmaker, Anna Wolkoff, was arrested in London on Vansittart's advice and charged with having leaked to the Germans the secrets of the British attack on Norway. These secrets had been discussed at the Supreme War Council meeting which Ironside attended and to which the German ambassador to the Netherlands had incorrectly referred. Is it possible that Miss Wolkoff, who certainly had continuing high-level connections, had obtained some of this information from the duchess? She had delivered the crucial intelligence to the Italian Duco del Monte at 6 Cadogan Square, for transmission to Count Ciano in Rome via the Italian embassy.

That month Chamberlain resigned, and on May 10 Winston Churchill became prime minister of England and formed a coalition government. Pressed by Labour leader Clement Attlee, he instantly moved to deactivate the entire group that was planning a negotiated peace with Hitler. A close friend of the Windsors, the Duke of Buccleuch, the brother-in-law of the Duke of Gloucester, resigned from his position as lord steward of the royal household. The *New York Times* reported the matter, implying that Buccleuch was part of the appeasement faction in England. No word of the removal appeared in the British press. The Duke of Westminster was warned not to take part in any serious appeasement efforts. At the same time, Sir Oswald Mosley, Lady Mosley, Archibald Maule Ramsay, and several others were imprisoned under the recently introduced regulations. Vernon Kell, head of MI5, was dismissed on May 25, according to some sources because of the leak of official secrets to Germany, but according to others because of personality conflicts with Churchill. Major General Fuller was warned to be inactive on pain of instant arrest. Sir Samuel Hoare was under grave suspicion of wanting a negotiated peace, and arrangements were made to send him out of the country as ambassador to neutral Spain. Among those who had the gravest misgivings about him was Sir Alexander Cadogan, who had replaced Vansittart as permanent under secretary of the Foreign Office on January 1, 1938. In a diary entry for May 20, 1940, he wrote:

> The quicker we get [the Hoares] out of the country the better. But I'd sooner send them to a penal settlement. He'll be the Quisling of England when Germany conquers us and I am dead.

There was a War Cabinet meeting in London on May 26. During it Lord Halifax, as foreign secretary, suggested the idea that there might be a negotiated peace. Entirely echoing the views of the Windsors, he said that the issue now was "not so much . . . a question of imposing a complete defeat upon Germany, but of safe-guarding the independence of our own Empire and if possible that of France." Halifax said that the evening before he had had an interview with the Italian ambassador,

Signor Bastianini (who had replaced Grandi), and that Bastianini had suggested a peace conference at which Mussolini would appear in order to obtain peace in Europe. Halifax had responded that he looked upon the suggestion favorably. Churchill dismissed the idea at once. The lord president of the council said that Italy might send an ultimatum to France threatening that unless such a conference were held, Italy would join Germany. This was exactly the position taken by the Windsors and by their friend Laval. The matter was discussed at length. It was taken up again the following day. Churchill revealed the surprising fact that, whereas he was opposed to a direct approach to Mussolini, he had maneuvered to have Roosevelt make such an approach "ostensibly on his own initiative." This put a new complexion on the matter. Churchill wanted to avoid any direct negotiation, but was not as adverse to an indirect one as he had appeared the day before. Halifax then revealed that in fact Roosevelt had made the appropriate approach to Rome. The lord president of the council announced that Sir Percy Loraine, who was now British ambassador to Italy, had sent a telegram advising that Hitler had informed the Italian government he did not want the Italians to enter the war and was sure he could reach a satisfactory arrangement with the French. The secretary of state for air was opposed to any such approach to Italy, and so was the lord president of the council. The lord privy seal was also opposed. The prime minister talked of the "futility" of the suggested approach to Mussolini. He added, "At the moment our prestige in Europe [is] very low. The only way we can get it back is by showing the world that Germany has not beaten us. . . . Let us therefore avoid being dragged down the slippery slope with France." After much further discussion, the meeting was adjourned. The final outcome was made clear by the prime minister at the end of a meeting held on the twenty-eighth:

> If we make a bold stand against Germany, that would command their admiration and respect; but a grovelling appeal, if made now, would have the worst possible effect. I do not favour making any approach on the subject at the present time.

Word of the decision was brought to the Duke of Windsor. He was infuriated; he was still pressing for a negotiated peace via Mussolini, and he was almost certainly in touch with Count Ciano and others in Italy on the matter in the hope that his friendship with Churchill might prove influential. It of course did not. Halifax remained unregenerately in support of the peace plan and wrote in his diary that Churchill had talked "a lot of rot."

Churchill had another secret meeting at 10 Downing Street on the twenty-eighth at which it was agreed (minutes of this were not taken) that the Windsors should be brought to Britain immediately, at the very least for interrogation by Cadogan and Vansittart on their peculiar role in Nazi collaboration. However, Churchill's sentimental attachment to the duke overcame his normal sensibility.

Quite suddenly, and on the orders of Sir Stewart Menzies, the Windsors were told to leave Paris as security risks, abandoning Fruity Metcalfe, and make their way to the Villa La Croë at Antibes. This has been put down incorrectly as a desertion of duty that could have been a court-martial offense. Removal in the certainty of treason was worse. Bullitt was left in charge of their Paris house, which he protected when the Germans marched in; actually Ribbentrop, who was at the Ritz Hotel, had arranged for that protection already—and so had Winston Churchill.

In a detailed report by Edward A. Tamm, leading FBI executive operative, to J. Edgar Hoover in Washington written on September 13, 1940, he made clear that the Secret Intelligence Service, headed by Menzies in London, was very much in pursuit of the Windsors throughout their trip south:

> The contacts of the Duchess of Windsor with von Ribbentrop from the Villa [La Croë] . . . became so serious that it was necessary for the British government to compel them to move. The Duchess was obtaining a variety of information concerning the British and French Government official activities, which she was passing on to the Germans. . . . [I]mmediately upon their checking into a hotel in Biarritz, a British Secret Service man turned on a radio on a German commercial station and heard a news commentator in Berlin state that the Duke and Duchess had moved into [the Palace] hotel where they were occupying Suite 104–E. This was in fact the suite occupied by the Windsors and they had been there hardly a matter of minutes when this announcement was heard.

The report went on:

> The British Secret Service [sic] ascertained that the Duchess had informed von Ribbentrop of her itinerary, schedule, etc., prior to her departure from the villa.

It may be asked, how could Wallis communicate so easily with Ribbentrop at the time? The fact is that it would not require more than the slightest of efforts. The German foreign minister was still in France, located at the Ritz or at the Château d'Ardenne near Dinant, which could be reached either by telegram or telephone; until communications became difficult, when a messenger could be sent by car or motorcycle. Ribbentrop was present for the signing of the French armistice at Compiègne on June 22 and of course was in touch with all foreign ambassadors, including Bullitt, who had moved into Charles Bedaux's Château de Candé, a perfect vespiary of Nazi spies and collaborators.

The Tamm report went on to state that in view of the leakage of information to Ribbentrop, the Windsors were told by the SIS to leave for Spain at once. Even at this early stage it was decided they must go to the Bahamas; an appointment in Africa or New Zealand would have been more appropriate, but there was a clear-cut reason, stated directly in the Tamm report: as the most prominent figure of the Bahamian island colony, Jane Williams-Taylor would once again be able to spy on them.

Back at La Croë, the Windsors left the incriminating documents from Fort Belvedere with Herman and Katherine Rogers for safekeeping; still acting for the Secret Intelligence Service, the couple locked them in a safe instead of handing them to the Italian or German authorities as the Windsors would have wished; along with the records of collusion went the contents of the official red dispatch boxes sent to Windsor when king, an act of theft for which he cannot be excused. The abdication documents went to Switzerland.

The duke cabled Sir Samuel Hoare in Madrid for a ship, but Hoare could do nothing without authorization from the Foreign Office. Finally, according to Sir John Colville, Winston Churchill's secretary, the Windsors persuaded Hugh Dodds, consul general at Nice, to leave his post and take them across the border. When Churchill found out that a number of wounded war veterans who needed assistance in Nice had been denied it, he went, Colville says, "through the roof." Colville mentioned that Dodds was his uncle by marriage. "I couldn't care less!" Churchill exploded.

But, while Churchill was furious at the duke and duchess's behavior, it was clearly essential that they leave Europe as soon as possible.

14

A Dark Plot

On June 19, Wallis's birthday, the duke and duchess, driven by Ladbroke, began the long and difficult journey to Spain. Accompanying them in a fleet of cars were the equerry Captain George Wood and his wife, Gray Phillips, Major Hugh Dodds, and Martin Dean, vice-counsul at Menton. Italian bombers were attacking the seafront; the travelers had an uncomfortable night in Arles, and were not pleased to be removed from the hotel in Perpignan by the sudden arrival of the chief of French intelligence, who had no time for them, probably because of their Nazi connections, and unceremoniously commandeered their suite.* Unable to find any other accommodation, they proceeded irritably through the night and almost got stopped twice. The British embassy in Paris had failed to obtain authorization from London or Madrid to secure the necessary safe-conduct passes, and the party was barely allowed to scrape through. At midnight on the twentieth, the group arrived at Barcelona.

Simultaneously, Sir Stewart Menzies was concerned about the arrival of the Duke of Kent on an official visit to Lisbon. It was feared that he would contact the Windsors for purposes that would be inimical to British interests in the region. Such concern was conveyed through William Strang, a special agent of the Foreign Office in London reporting to Sir Alexander Cadogan of the Foreign Office; Strang made it clear through Arjando Monteiro, Portuguese ambassador to the Court

---

*In order not to reveal his presence, the chief had the mayhor of Perpignan tell the Windsors that "the entire French government" was arriving.

of St. James's, to President Salazar of Portugal in a letter dated June 21, that the exact location of Kent's whereabouts must be kept secret during his visit.

There was a double reason for this; Prince Philipp of Hesse was in Lisbon to see Kent. It is clear from a letter sent by Kent to Prince Paul of Yugoslavia shortly after his return to London on July 17 that he wouldn't have wanted to meet the Windsors; he considered his brother's behavior disgraceful—a case of the royal pot calling the kettle black—and said he was greatly relieved that the duke and duchess (whom he called, like Churchill, "the Bitch") hadn't come back to England. With false naïveté he told Paul he was surprised that his brother would accept so lowly a position as governor of the Bahamas. "W[inston] C[hurchill] doesn't want him back," he wrote. He added that he had fought against his brother's possible return.

On the twenty-second, Churchill cabled Windsor care of Sir Samuel Hoare: "We should like Your Royal Highness to come home as soon as possible. Arrangements will be made through His Majesty's Ambassador at Madrid with whom you should communicate." On the same day, Eberhard von Stohrer, German ambassador to Spain, cabled Ribbentrop in Berlin seeking advice on how the Windsors were to be treated. The question arose of whether "we might perhaps be interested in detaining the Duke . . . here, and eventually in establishing contact with him." The next day Ribbentrop replied, "Is it possible . . . to detain the Duke and Duchess of Windsor before they are granted an exit visa? It would be necessary at all events to be sure that it did not appear in any way that the suggestion came from Germany."

On June 24 Sir Alexander Hardinge wrote from Buckingham Palace to W. I. Mallet of the Foreign Office that it had been observed by the king that in certain correspondences the duke and duchess were referred to as "Their Royal Highnesses." Hardinge added: "For obvious reasons it is very undesirable that this incorrect description of the Duke and Duchess should be included in any official communication, and the King trusts that steps will be taken to prevent this mistake being repeated." It was not repeated.

In the meantime the Windsors arrived on the twenty-third at an impoverished, beggar-haunted, shabby Madrid. Sir Samuel Hoare had arranged accommodation for them at the Ritz Hotel. The slippery British ambassador conveniently suspended all activities of the Secret

Intelligence Service in the Spanish capital for the duration of the Windsors' visit. They were thus free of surveillance, which must have greatly aggravated the appropriate authorities in London.

Meantime, their old friend Don Javier Bermejillo was proving to be a Good Samaritan. The Spanish Fascist government under Franco was prepared to offer its hospitality for an indefinite period. Characteristically, the duke arranged with Bermejillo to deal directly with the enemy. Bermejillo went to the German and Italian embassies and asked them to be sure that the Windsors' properties in the south of France and Paris were protected and carefully maintained. Actually, neither house was in danger; La Croë was in unoccupied France and Boulevard Suchet was of course being maintained by Bullitt, who had just moved into Charles Bedaux's Château de Candé, which he used as the embassy. After Pearl Harbor and after the German occupation of the whole of France, and Italian guardianship of La Croë, the Windsors' requirements were still met. This breach of the Trading with the Enemy Act was absurdly described by Michael Bloch in his book *Operation Willi* as "indiscreet." The Windsors' account at the Banque de France was never confiscated by the German alien property custodian, Carl Schaefer.

The duke was determined that he would not go to England unless the duchess was accorded her proper rank. In what looks very much like a device to avoid going to London, he insisted upon her being given full status with other members of the family. He knew by now that any such request must meet with a direct refusal. Churchill was furious at the Windsors' intransigence, and he cabled the duke on June 28:

> Your Royal Highness has taken active military rank, and refusal to obey direct orders of competent military authority will create a serious situation. I hope it will not be necessary for such orders to be sent.

Sentimentally, Churchill struck out the following suggestive sentence: "Already there is a great deal of doubt as to the circumstances in which Your Royal Highness left Paris. I most strongly urge immediate compliance with wishes of the government." The duke now shifted his ground to ask only that he and the duchess should be received for a short meeting by the king and queen. Again, he knew that such a request was totally out of order, and it was of course rejected outright. On June 28 the Italian chargé d'affaires in Spain, Count Zoppi, cabled

Wallis's former lover Count Ciano with the request that La Croë should be committed to the protection of the Italian government in the event that Italy should invade France. The request was promptly granted. On June 30 Ribbentrop instructed Otto Abetz to "unofficially and confidentially" provide "an unobtrusive observation of the [Paris] residence of the Duke." The ambassador to Spain was instructed to inform the duke that Ribbentrop was looking out for the house's protection.

Late that week, U.S. ambassador to Spain A. W. Weddall sent a secret memorandum to the State Department. It read:

> In conversation last night, the Duke of Windsor declared that the most important thing now was to end the war before thousands more were killed or maimed to save the faces of a few politicians.
>
> With regard to the defeat of France . . . the Duke stated that stories that the French troops would not fight were not true. They had fought magnificently, but the organization behind them was totally inadequate. In the past ten years Germany has totally reorganized the order of its society in preparation for this war. Countries which were unwilling to accept such a reorganization of society and concomitant sacrifices should direct their policies accordingly and thereby avoid dangerous adventures. He stated this applied not merely to Europe, but to the United States also.
>
> The Duchess put the same thing more directly by declaring that France had lost because it was internally diseased and that a country which was not in a condition to fight a war should never have declared war.
>
> These observations have their value, if any, as doubtless reflecting the views of an element in England, possibly a growing one, who [sic] would find in Windsor and his circle of friends a group who are realists in world politics and who hope to come into their own in the event of world peace.

Sumner Welles, under secretary of state, forwarded this document to Whitehall, with the inevitable result of increased disfavor for the Windsors. Hoare was anxious for the Windsors to leave Madrid. They were an embarrassment and a burden to the embassy, particularly since there were widespread and probably well-founded comments in the European press that he and the Windsors were meeting with Germans to arrange a negotiated peace. Nevertheless, Hoare did his best to make them comfortable. He arranged introductions for them to such figures as Prince Alfonso, who had flown in the Franco air force, bombing defenseless villages, and he seemed not to object to their association with the fascistic Marqués de Estella, Don Miguel Primo de Rivera, civil governor of Madrid.

On June 29, Bullitt, still using Berlin Foreign Ministry facilities, left Paris and traveled to unoccupied France, where he set up the collaborationist government at Vichy, conferred with Marshal Pétain and Pierre Laval, the betrayers of France, and assured them of Washington's cooperation. Staying at the home of the American millionaire Frank Jay Gould in Vichy, he advised Washington by radio via Berlin that all the necessary arrangements for full-scale collusion were in place. Ribbentrop could not have asked for more.

Pieter G. Hansen, of the Abwehr, German military intelligence, in 1940, writes from Germany, basing his information on a clear memory of the subject of discussion in his office at the time:

> [The British secret agent Claude] Dansey had been handling private jobs for Churchill and Churchill's henchman Professor Frederick W. Lindemann; he had been caught misappropriating government funds for his personal advantage and charging expenses to the government. He would have been fired if he hadn't continued to do jobs for Churchill.

According to Hansen, the ferocious Dansey, acting on orders that were emphatically not from Churchill but from Sir Stewart Menzies, made a terrifying threat at a meeting with the duke and Wallis. He told them they would be murdered in cold blood if they did not leave Europe for the Bahamas as soon as it could be arranged.

Hansen goes on to state that it was known in the Abwehr that the duke and duchess were making financial and other demands of Ribbentrop toward their assuming the English throne which had to be approved by Hitler himself. Hitler was hesitant to pay them, as he "wanted a German in charge [in London] and not some figurehead." This caused the Windsors considerable concern; if they weren't going to be paid to resume the throne in the event of a negotiated peace they certainly weren't going to cooperate. Soon, Hitler changed his mind.

On July 2, as the Windsors began the next stage of their journey of exile, the German ambassador cabled Ribbentrop that the duke was about to leave. The duke planned eventually to return to Spain, where he had been offered as a residence the palace of the caliph at Ronda. The Windsors arrived in a still glittery and raffish, refugee-filled Lisbon on July 3.

In his book *Total Espionage* (New York: G. P. Putnam's Sons, 1940) the political journalist Curt Riess gave a vivid picture of Lisbon, and the fashionable district of Estoril, at the time. No less than two hundred German agents were housed at the Nazi legation; The Link, the dangerous pro-Nazi organization in London that had supported the duke and duchess for years, was active in the area, particularly its leader, Sir Ivone Kirkpatrick, who flooded his contacts at the Park and Palace hotels with appeasement literature.

Others present included Camille Chautemps, whose craven abandonment of his premiership of France had occurred in the week of blackmail and intrigue involving the Windsors in March 1938, and who had now betrayed his country's cause; the Windsors' close friend and fellow intriguer, the French airplane tycoon Paul Louis Weiller; Friedrich Sieberg, right-hand man of Otto Abetz, Hitler's ambassador to Paris . . . and soon to arrive, William Bullitt himself, up to no good as usual.

The situation in Portugal was explosive. Members of the Himmler-trained secret police were on guard everywhere. There was a German plan afoot to bring about a coup d'état which would overthrow the ineffectual neutralist Salazar. Sir Walford Selby was bombarding the Foreign Office with anxious cables on the matter. The Portuguese government, fearful that any close association with Britain might result in such a coup, was refusing to allow the Secret Intelligence Service to have access to encoded telegrams; by June Selby was trying to organize a British landing force to forestall German plans. The Germans were contemplating an attack on Portuguese East Africa; the Japanese, already contemplating war, were pushing for oil concessions in Portuguese Timor.

A villa had been arranged for the Windsors at the appropriately named Boca di Inferno, or "Mouth of Hell," at Cascais. The couple's host was Ricardo Espírito Santo e Silva, owner of a private bank and a friend of the Rothschilds; he was also of Jewish origin. The Duke of Kent had stayed with him until his departure a few days earlier. Silva was under constant watch by the Secret Intelligence Service, and it turned out that he had considerable Nazi connections. It seems incredible in the circumstances that such a residence was authorized by the British ambassador, Sir Walford Selby, the Windsors' old friend from Vienna. Asked to explain his father's curious action, Ralph Selby replied in the following manner:

> The Windsors were originally booked in Lisbon's main hotel, the Aviz. As the flood of refugees from occupied Europe grew larger, the hotel manager contacted my father and told him he would find it difficult to provide the duke and duchess with adequate accommodations and he wondered whether it would not be preferable to house him in a suitable villa. He thought he would be able to find him one. My father agreed, and the house at Cascais was found. As my father drove to the airport with his air attaché to greet the duke, the air attaché said that he had heard that the villa's owner had the reputation of being a Nazi sympathizer. My father said that he had heard the same thing but did not see what they could do about it now.
>
> It was thought at the time that the duke would only be in Lisbon for 48 hours or so, and that he would be taking one of the York aircraft sent out to bring him back to England. Little harm could be done in so short a time. My father's papers reveal how surprised and pained he was to see the owner of the villa on its doorstep to greet the duke on his arrival there. Neither before nor afterwards did my father have any reason to suppose that the manager of the hotel who had made the arrangement was in any way a Nazi sympathizer.

On July 4, the duke telegraphed Churchill, "I will accept appointment as Governor of Bahamas, as I am sure you have done your best for me in a difficult situation. I am sending Major Phillips to England tomorrow, and will appreciate your receiving him personally to explain some details." Churchill replied, "I am very glad Your Royal Highness has accepted the appointment, for I am sure useful service can be rendered to the Empire at the present time. I will arrange all details with Major Phillips if you will send him home. Sincere good wishes." The appointment was published in London on the tenth. However, Sir Alexander Hardinge was worried about the duchess's activities in Lisbon. He sent a memorandum on July 9 to Eric Seal of the prime minister's staff at 10 Downing Street: "As I told you once before, this is not the first time that this lady has come under suspicion for her anti-British activities, and as long as we never forget the power she has exerted over [the duke] in her efforts to avenge herself on this country, we shall be all right."

It is clear from this extraordinary message that Hardinge remained unshakable in his conviction that the duchess was a Nazi collaborator or agent. Evidently, the Secret Intelligence Service in Lisbon had reported unfavorably on her activities. These cannot have been merely associating with Nazis, who certainly would be welcome in the home in which the Windsors were housed. The activities would have to have been more serious than that.

Among the numerous acquaintances of the Windsors at the time was the German ambassador, Oswald Baron von Hoyningen-Huene, a career diplomat of the von Papen school. Polished and ingenious, he was bent upon cultural exchanges between Portugal and Germany. An OSS report on him dated October 11, 1945, reads: "His self-appointed task of cultivating the Portuguese [for political objectives] was facilitated by the lax British practice of regarding Portugal as traditionally within the British orbit." He found that Portuguese distrust of Germany sprang largely from a fear that Germany might wish to compensate itself for the loss of its colonies at Portugal's expense. It was his main objective to allay this distress.

Huene was, the OSS reports confirm, an instrument of the Nazis. He reported to Berlin on July 10 that the duke was convinced that "had he remained on the throne, war could have been avoided and [he] describes himself as a firm supporter of a compromise peace with Germany. The Duke believes with certainty that continued heavy bombing will make England ready for peace." This disagreeable sentiment was, as we know, precisely matched in an identical observation by the Aga Khan to the Nazi agent Prince Max von Hohenlohe later that year. And it is worth noting that not too long after the cable was received in Germany, the heaviest bombing of England began.

On July 7, a secret Foreign Office report signed "L." (Reginald Leeper) to Sir Alexander Cadogan at the Foreign Office read:

> Germans expect assistance from Duke and Duchess, latter desiring at any price to become Queen. Germans have been negotiating with her since June 27th. Status quo in England to expect undertaking to form anti-Russian alliance. Germans propose to form opposition government under Duke of Windsor having first changed public opinion by propaganda. Germans think King George will abdicate during attack on London.

Ribbentrop decided at this stage that it was important to have the duke and Wallis return to Spain on some pretext no matter what money they demanded from Hitler. The result would be "the assump-

THE DUCHESS OF WINDSOR

tion of the English throne by the Duke and Duchess." Ribbentrop's message added: "Should the Duke have other plans, but still be prepared to cooperate in the restoration of good relations between England and Germany, we would likewise be prepared to assure him and his wife an existence which would enable him, either as a private citizen or in some other position, to lead a life suitable for a King." Ribbentrop added further that he had received information from a London source that the duke would be killed on official instructions as soon as he reached the Bahamas. Ribbentrop sent for Walter Schellenberg, head of the SD, German secret intelligence, and instructed him to make an offer to the duke based on the Windsors' proposals. Schellenberg was to deposit 50 million Swiss francs in an account in the duke's name. The Windsors were to be invited across the Spanish border, from where they would be conducted to an appropriate location at which the necessary arrangements with Germany could be made. Ribbentrop said that if the British Secret Intelligence Service gave any trouble, it should be dealt with by force, but that the duke should be treated similarly only if he were seized by "a fear psychosis." If 50 million francs wasn't enough, the figure could be increased. At that moment in the conversation the phone rang; Hitler was on the line. Schellenberg was given the extension phone so that he could listen in. He heard Hitler say, "Schellenberg should particularly bear in mind the importance of the Duchess's attitude and try as hard as possible to get her support. She has great influence over the Duke."

There was concern in London that the Windsors might wish to go to the United States on their way to the Bahamas. Such a visit would be highly undesirable. With their immense following in America, they might easily influence public feeling toward the isolationists who wished to keep the United States out of the world conflict. It was Winston Churchill's unequivocal policy to involve America in the war. The 1940 elections were looming, and even within the Democratic party, such extreme right-wing Democrats as Senator Burton K. Wheeler of Montana were determined that the Rooseveltian policies of collaboration with Britain would see no chance of fruition. The Windsors had a double reason for wanting to go to the United States. Not only did they wish to make contact with isolationists and appeasers, but the duchess had the mundane motive of wanting some surgery done on her nose. By now, Major Gray Phillips was in London at the Bath

Club, and the duke was cabling him via Sir Walford Selby that it was essential that the duchess see the "specialist" in New York.

At the same time, the Windsors were worried about getting their property out of Paris and Antibes. Joseph Kennedy, as ambassador in London, cabled Cordell Hull in Washington about the matter on July 10, stating that the British Foreign Office was requesting the U.S. consul at Nice to make arrangements for the shipping of personal effects, clothing, and linen from La Croë. This would be taken care of on Kennedy's authorization. However, Paris was a slightly more complicated problem. The duchess, seemingly confident of her reception from Otto Abetz and the other Nazi figures in the French capital, actually planned to go back to the Boulevard Suchet and supervise the packing of her belongings. Fortunately, this plan was prevented by Selby, who clearly saw the outrageous nature of the request. Wallis contacted one of her former chefs in Vichy, France, to pick up as much as he could from La Croë; at the same time she contacted the Germans to allow her lingère and maid, Jeanne-Marguerite Moulichon, to proceed to Paris to collect silver, china, and linen for shipment to the Bahamas. This, of course, was in breach of the British Trading with the Enemy Act, and, under the provisions of the recently amended British Defense Regulations, would normally result in imprisonment without trial. Don Javier Bermejillo undertook to act as a go-between in this peculiar act of outright treason. In Madrid he spoke to the German ambassador, Eberhard von Stohrer, who in turn contacted Ribbentrop. He sent Ribbentrop two telegrams, the first of which dealt with the duke's appointment in Nassau and revealed that Churchill had threatened the duke with court-martial if he did not obey orders. The second (July 11) read as follows:

> The Duke of Windsor, through the confidential emissary of the Foreign Minister, has again expressed thanks for cooperation in the matter of his house in Paris, and has requested that a maid of the Duchess be allowed to travel to Paris in order to pick up various objects there and transport them by van to Lisbon, as they are required by him and the Duchess for the Bahamas.

The German ambassador continued by stating that these wishes should be satisfied because the maid could always be held as hostage against the Windsors' decision to cooperate or not to cooperate with the German government in the event that they should hesitate.

At the same time, the duke met with an emissary of Ribbentrop in Lisbon and confirmed that Churchill had threatened a court-martial by telephone if he did not proceed to the Bahamas. On the 15th, William Bullitt met with the Windsors and, in a conversation which President Roosevelt repeated to the writer Fulton Oursler, referred to their imminent departure. "We sail for our Saint Helena," Wallis said. St. Helena was, of course, the island location of Napoleon Bonaparte's final exile and death. On the seventeenth, arrangements were made to bump some passengers from the *Excalibur* to make room for the Windsor party.

Also on July 17 Wallis planned Mme. Moulichon's trip to Paris with the expertise of a general. Armed with a German passport and clearance documents stamped by the gestapo, the adventurous maid flew into Madrid to obtain further documents from the German consulate. She was held up by red tape; authorities in Paris and Berlin were questioning this matter of collaborating with their enemy. In the meantime, Wallis was worried about acquiring a new secretary. She cabled Johnny McMullen at the St. Regis Hotel in New York, asking him whether the girl he had recommended knew shorthand, typing and accountancy; "Would she be free to meet us in New York on 7 August?" the duchess wanted to know. She also asked McMullen to find her a butler as London "impossible." Apparently, even Wallis quailed at the thought of having to hire a butler in London when Great Britain was fighting for its life.

Meanwhile, Sir John Colville recalled that at 10 Downing Street, Churchill was furious at being bothered by such trivial matters as the Windsors' requests at this time of crisis. The duke was bombarding Churchill with requests for the proper transportation, complaining that the neutrality laws made it difficult for him to find passage on an American ship. There was always the danger of attack or boarding parties when British subjects were aboard American vessels. The duke advised Phillips that he should send all British luggage to New York direct and that he wanted a member of the Scots Guards as a solider servant. He ruled out a recommended maid, but asked Phillips to continue the search. He wanted a second cook hired in Nassau. He was

sending his other equerry, George Wood, to London with further instructions that his cigarettes and tobacco were to be sent to Lisbon on
the next flying boat.

It is possible that at this stage the Windsors may have had a narrow
escape from death. Squadron Leader Frederick W. Winterbotham, head
of Air Intelligence of the Secret Intelligence Service, co-creator of the
famous Ultra system that broke the German Enigma code, specialized
in sabotaging airplanes by the simple device of dropping sulfuric acid
through a drip bottle on the insulation wires, a device he would, by his
own assertion (to the author Peter Allen), apply in disposing of the
Duke of Kent and of General Wladyslav Sikorski, exiled premier of
Poland, and his Nazi associate Victor Cazalet.

On the advice of David Eccles, who worked with Winterbotham
and with Sir Stewart Menzies in the Secret Intelligence Service, the
Windsors were, the SIS decided, to return from Lisbon to London by
Sunderland flying boat, the same make of plane in which Kent was to
die in 1942, and which could easily be tampered with. Churchill may
have gotten wind of this and canceled the plan. On no account now
must the Windsors return to England; they planned to stay there with
the pro-Nazi Duke of Westminster, the most powerful property owner
in London, setting up his country estate Eaton Hall as a second Buckingham Palace.

By July 17, when Wallis's maid was waiting in Madrid for clearance,
it was settled in London that the Windsors would sail to Bermuda and
be conveyed from there by warship to Nassau. Lord Lothian, the British
ambassador to the United States, would be taking care of the necessary
arrangements. However, there must be no question of the ship's touching American ports or even entering U.S. territorial waters. Cordell
Hull was adamant about this. Reservations were made on the Export
Lines' vessel *Excalibur*, sailing from Lisbon on August 1. At the same
time, with considerable difficulty, Wallis arranged for furniture and
paintings to be moved from La Croë to storage in Italy, yet another
breach of the Trading with the Enemy Act.

On July 18 Gray Phillips telegrammed from London that the duke
could not be granted the services of various noncommissioned officers
he wanted to accompany him, because they were required for immediate wartime service, and under no circumstances would he be permitted to go to the United States. Lord Lloyd cabled the duke, "War

Office represent that to take fit and efficient soldiers out of Army at this junction would set an unfortunate precedent." The Foreign Office cabled Lord Lothian that it would be necessary for the *Excalibur* to make a 350-mile diversion from its normal route to Bermuda. The British government would, of course, be ready to meet any extra expense involved. That same day, Windsor, impatient with a number of frustrations vis-à-vis his voyage, sent an irritable telegram to Churchill which included the words, "Have been messed about quite long enough and detect in Colonial Office attitude very same hands at work as in my last job. Strongly urge you to support arrangements I have made, as otherwise will have to reconsider my position."

On July 20 Herbert Claiborne Pell, U.S. minister to Portugal, had dinner with the Windsors at the house of Espírito Santo e Silva at Cascais. Another of the guests was David Eccles. After dinner the duke and duchess said several extremely dangerous things. Pell cabled a top-secret telegram to Cordell Hull on July 20. It read as follows:

Duke and Duchess of Windsor are indiscreet and outspoken against British government. Consider their presence in United States might be disturbing and confusing. They say that they intend remaining in the United States whether Churchill likes it or not and desire apparently to make propaganda for peace. If Department cancels their visas, they can take clipper to Bermuda, thence to Bahamas. Visas were given by Consulate General.

This devastating telegram made its way through the normal channels to London. Written by an impeccable personage, it set the seal of doom on the Windsors forever. The fact that they would be prepared to press for peace with Hitler in the United States against the expressed policy of Churchill and Roosevelt made both of them about as welcome in the U.S. and British corridors of power as a resurrected Bonnie and Clyde.

On July 22 there was a secret communication to Ribbentrop from his agents in London, stating that the duke had addressed a memorandum to King George VI urging upon him the appointment of a new cabinet which in pro-Hitler appeasement would replace the existing coalition cabinet headed by Churchill. The report said the new cabinet was also being pressed upon the king by Lloyd George. The German ambassador to Ireland cabled Ribbentrop the same day, saying that such a revised cabinet would be prepared to make immediate peace with Germany. Among those who would be willing to make such a peace would be Lord Halifax, Sir John Simon, and Sir Samuel Hoare ("whose delegation to Spain was viewed in the appropriate perspective").

Also on the same day, neutral Italy's newspapers headlined the story. The *Gazetta del Popolo* of Turin provided a detailed account in which it was stated rightly or wrongly that the duke wanted Lloyd George as prime minister of a Fascist England. The actual telegram remains classified to this day.

On July 23 it was determined in London that the cost of the diversion of the *Excalibur* would be £7,500, or about $37,200, plus £10,000 ($50,000)* of insurance when England needed every penny. By now, the telegrams to and from Major Phillips were assuming a fantastic absurdity in time of war. On the twenty-third, Phillips cabled the duchess:

> Have choice of two maids, one hundred pounds. One nine years Lady Duncan, seven Countess Vitetti. Recommendations excellent. Other five years Clare Beck. Since then dressmaking four years, appearance distinctly plain. Either could leave Sunday with me.

On the twenty-third, German ambassador Stohrer reported to Ribbentrop that his emissary had learned the following from the Windsors:

> In Portugal [the duke] felt almost like a prisoner. He was surrounded by agents, etc. Politically he was more and more distant from the King and the present English government. The Duke and Duchess have less fear of the King, who was quite foolish, than of the shrewd Queen, who was intriguing skillfully against the Duke, and particularly against the Duchess. The Duke was considering making a public statement and thereby disavowing present English policy and breaking with his brother.

It was also reported to Ribbentrop that the duke and duchess would be willing to come to Spain instead of going to the United States, but it is probable the Windsors were only talking about this possibility and had no intention of actually returning.

On July 24 arrangements were made for another vessel, the Cana-

---

*Multiply by 30 for the modern equivalent.

dian *Lady Somers*, to meet the Windsors in Bermuda and take them to
Nassau. They would have to be accommodated for several days in
Hamilton, the Bermudian capital. In the meantime, after several postponements due to the pressure of other work, Walter Schellenberg at
last made preparations to depart for Lisbon. On July 26, apparently
still uncertain of what he would do, the duke began playing desperately
for time. He stated that the American Export Lines agent wanted him
to sail with Wallis on August 8 instead of August 1, because they would
"create bad feeling" by displacing other passengers. This was a blatant
lie, easily exposed. But a later departure would provide the chance of
perhaps getting some possessions from La Croë. He urged Phillips to
find an August 8 sailing. He remained greatly irritated by the refusal to
let him stop in New York. He cabled Churchill on the twenty-sixth:

> Regarding not landing in the United States at this juncture, I take it to
> mean that this only applies until after the events of November [the pres-
> idential election]. May I, therefore, have confirmation that it is not to be
> the policy of His Majesty's government that I should not set foot on
> American soil during my term of office in the Bahamas? Otherwise I
> could not feel justified in representing the King in a British colony so
> geographically close to the United States if I was to be prevented from
> ever going to that country. I appreciate your successful efforts regarding
> my soldier servant.

In other words, he would not assume his position if he were to be
forbidden visits to America indefinitely. This threat greatly irritated
Churchill, particularly since by now bombs were raining on London.
Churchill's days and nights were filled with countless crushing problems involving millions of human lives. Much as he was devoted to the
Duke of Windsor, he simply could not spend any great amount of time
dealing with the stream of trivial difficulties that were relayed in telegram
after neurotic telegram from the irritable personage in Portugal. He
exploded several times to his staff about the duke's lack of consideration during Britain's desperate crisis.

Walter Schellenberg arrived in Lisbon on July 26, carrying with him
Hitler's authority to do everything in his power to dissuade the Windsors from leaving Lisbon and to convince them to return to Spain and
thence to Germany prior to the duke's reassuming the English throne

following a negotiated peace. Schellenberg had some reason to be optimistic. The following telegram was sent from Ambassador Stohrer to Ribbentrop on the twenty-sixth:

> Strictly secret. A wire message from the Spanish Embassy in Lisbon is now in the Spanish Ministry of Foreign Affairs. According to it, the Duke and Duchess of Windsor have had their visas [for Spain] organized for them after considerable pressure on the British Embassy in Lisbon. Confirming messages to be awaited. . . . The plan, as developed in previous telegram, will under all circumstances be followed through, since even after issue of visas, counteraction Intelligence service is possible.

In a separate telegram of the same date, Stohrer made clear that if the Secret Intelligence Service should intervene, the Windsors could be taken to Spain. Intermediaries for Schellenberg pointed out to the Windsors the danger that when they went to the Bahamas they would be killed by British intelligence agents. It now became imperative in London that the Windsors leave at once. Churchill cabled the duke on the twenty-seventh:

> I have seen your telegram to Major Phillips suggesting postponement for one week. I believe Lord Lloyd is telegraphing to you in reply suggesting that you should sail on August 1 as arranged, and I do very much hope that you will be able to fall in with this proposal. As regards your visiting the United States, we should naturally wish to fall in with Your Royal Highness's wishes. It is difficult to see far ahead these days, but in accordance with the standing royal instructions to colonial governors which you already have, you would no doubt consult the Secretary of State of the colonies before leaving the colony, and we should naturally do our best to suit Your Royal Highness's convenience.

At the same time, the Windsors talked of moving to the Hotel Aviz in Lisbon, probably under pressure from Sir Walford Selby, who must have gotten wind through the Secret Intelligence Service of Schellenberg's arrival. The SIS had complete control over the Aviz. Needless to say, the house at Cascais with its pro-Nazi owner was a more convenient location from the German point of view. An associate of Schellenberg's warned the Windsors that the Aviz was dangerous and that they might be murdered there on British orders. The duchess was particularly frightened by this suggestion. That same day a Spanish agent delivered to the Windsors a letter signed by Miguel Primo de Rivera, civil governor of Madrid, directly proposing the Schellenberg plan for them to go to Spain in the guise of a hunting expedition, where they would be met by the appropriate contacts. The duke read this document in a state of bemusement; of course, it would be impossible for him to take such a risk, since were he to do so, he could easily be arrested by the British authorities in Lisbon and shipped to London for court-martial. On the twenty-eighth Gray Phillips and the duke's newly appointed valet, Piper Alistair Fletcher, were flown into Lisbon by Edward Fielden. Sir Walter Monckton had accompanied them on Churchill's instructions to make sure that the Windsors left on the scheduled sailing.* Monckton was greeted warmly by the Windsors; they had never forgotten his help to them during the abdication crisis. They were also pleased by his moderating influence in London. They did not know he was under orders to deactivate and remove them.

Monckton carried with him to the house at Cascais several documents, including a letter from the king stating that he was pleased the duke had agreed to accept the post in the Bahamas, and a letter from Churchill dated the twenty-seventh warning the duke in the friendliest spirit to be extremely careful:

> Many sharp and unfriendly ears will be pricked up to catch any suggestion that Your Royal Highness takes a view about the war, or about the Germans, or about Hitlerism, which is different from that adopted by the British nation and Parliament.

Churchill went on to refer to various reports that might have been used to the duke's disadvantage. Churchill's cleverness in the matter is undeniable. He had followed his original threats of possible action with an indirect command that the duke would not make his Nazi sympathies public. At the same time, he had expressed respect along with his concern, which was sure to appeal to the duke's inflated ego. The duke told Monckton that he was pleased with the communications but still was concerned that certain figures of the British government might wish to remove him. In this, he was entirely accurate. Monckton warned the Windsors that Churchill had gotten wind of a plot to put them on

---

*Monckton was on the Appeals Committee in the matter of the Fascists aiming for a negotiated peace in England.

the throne in the event of an invasion of England and a negotiated peace. Monckton felt Churchill was right.

Monckton also felt it desirable to have a Criminal Investigation Department detective from Scotland Yard accompany the Windsors on the *Excalibur*, both to keep them under watch and to protect them in case there should be an attempt to abduct the duke and duchess at sea. Meanwhile, the duke was determined to go to America despite instructions to the contrary; as early as July 29 he booked a whole floor of New York's Wickersham Hospital and the services of Dr. Daniel Shorell to give the duchess her nose job. Apparently, the Secret Intelligence Service got wind of this, because further communications between London and Lisbon indicated that there was no relinquishing of the worry over the Windsors' making a trip to New York.

Amazingly, Sir Walter Monckton, a true-blue British to the core, actually stayed in the Nazi household at Cascais, where he and the Windsors were watched day and night by an odd variety of amateur and professional secret agents. Presumably unknown to Monckton, the duchess's maid, Jeanne-Marguerite Moulichon, had obtained the necessary documents in Madrid from the German embassy and was on her way to Paris. When she arrived at the house on Boulevard Suchet, she and the butler and his wife carefully packed the silver, china, and linen in numerous cabin trunks and boxes. Nobody was able to figure out the combination to the safe, so it remained closed for the duration of the war. The German high command in Paris and the German embassy were, of course, privy to Jeanne-Marguerite's arrival, turning a blind eye to this breach of the German Trading with the Enemy regulations.

Meanwhile, in Lisbon, Schellenberg was growing desperate. He was even thinking of kidnapping the Windsors, but this, of course, was an absurdity. His next idea was to advise the Windsors that a communication line would be opened up to the German government. But the warnings from Churchill via Monckton again rendered any such action impossible. Schellenberg cabled Berlin for instructions. It was later claimed by Schellenberg that Ribbentrop ordered a kidnap after all, but this was almost certainly sheer invention. However, it was leaked by someone that something similar to this idea was being discussed. The Americans shared the alarm. A week later, on August 6, a confidential report to Ribbentrop by a member of his staff stated:

The American fears are at present along the following lines: That [there could be] intermediate negotiations with Germany through the Duke of Windsor, and thus via Spain, with the goal of removing the Churchill government and achieving a cease fire pact with strong colonial concessions.

On July 30, from his special train at Füschl, Germany, Ribbentrop fired off a long telegram to Schellenberg that amounted to a last-ditch effort. The duke's pro-Nazi host was to talk to him in an effort to persuade him that Germany would now, following the British rejection of the führer's last peace speech, force England to a position of surrender. Germany would be willing to cooperate with the Windsors in any future alliance between Germany and England, and in response, Hitler would ensure their future. They should be warned that Churchill would keep the Windsors permanently in the Bahamas in order to be in complete control of them. The duke's response to this message was that though he was in favor of the führer's policy, the present moment was "inopportune . . . to manifest [myself] on the political scene." On the other hand, his departure for the Bahamas need not imply a rupture, since he could easily return to Europe in twenty-four hours via Florida. The next day, July 31, Detective Sergeant Harold Holder of Scotland Yard and a maid named Evelyn Fyrth arrived in Lisbon by flying boat. According to a German report of that date, Miss Fyrth was a British Secret Intelligence Service agent; if this is true, she almost certainly did not make it known to the duchess, but was used to survey the couple during the voyage. At the eleventh hour the duke sent a letter to Churchill sourly stating that he didn't consider his appointment first class, but since it was clear that his brother the king and Queen Elizabeth would not bring the family feud to an end, he would agree that the Bahamas post was "a temporary solution." Shortly after sending this letter, he went to the Spanish embassy to discuss the entire matter with the ambassador, Nicolás Franco y Bahamonde. The ambassador urged him to stay, to assist the British people in favor of a negotiated peace to find a new leader. The duke listened carefully, but realized he could still do nothing.

That night, Selby gave a farewell party for the Windsors at the Hotel Aviz. The next day Primo de Rivera delivered a warning to the Windsors that they mustn't leave or they would risk their lives. Other warnings were delivered. The duke told Santo e Silva that he was impressed by the führer's desire for peace, which was in complete agreement with his own point of view; he was convinced that if he had been king, it would never have come to war; it was too early for him to come forward with such a plan at the present time; and he would make himself available to Germany immediately once he received a particular code word. He concluded with an expression of admiration and sympathy for the führer.

Meanwhile, Schellenberg acted with incredible stupidity. Highly strung, overwrought, and afraid of repercussions over his abject failure in Berlin, he arranged for Gray Phillips to receive a passenger list of the *Excalibur* on which the Jews aboard were marked, suggesting that danger might come from them. The wife of a Portuguese official called on the duchess and told her that if the Windsors sailed, her husband would be dismissed. A bouquet of flowers arrived at the Cascais house with a warning on the enclosed card. An anonymous letter advised the duchess she was in grave danger. An English driver told the Windsors he was afraid to go to the Bahamas because of a murder plot. A scene was staged on board the *Excalibur* in which there was a fake arrest of a German agent disguised as a regular passenger who informed the Portuguese police that there was a bomb intended for the Windsors on board. A plan to fire shots in the night, breaking the Windsors' bedroom window, was abandoned.

Dr. Salazar, prime minister of Portugal, who had been advised to neither encourage nor discourage the duke's travel plan, received the duke on the day of the sailing while the duchess completed the packing. The Spanish ambassador had warned Salazar that the duke was a probable peace mediator "in spite of his temper" and that he could have an important role to play: "As peace mediators are not many, the ones that are left should not be disregarded nor should we allow them to be destroyed." At the meeting, which quite improperly was not reported to Sir Walford Selby, it appears that such proposals were put forward by the duke and that Salazar most skillfully avoided any kind of commitment. Up to the very last minute, the Windsors were still trying to play for more time, and even requested that the *Excalibur* should be held for a week for their convenience. This, of course, was impossible. All ideas of going to Spain at last abandoned, the duke and duchess finally made their way on board on August 1, as scheduled.

The British authorities had clamped down a rigid censorship on the Windsors' every movement. Sir Samuel Hoare turned up at the eleventh hour to see them off; recently declassified U.S. State Department documents suggest that he too was still discussing with them the potential of peaceful arrangements between Britain and Germany. There was some talk of a convoy's being supplied for the *Excalibur*. But the American under secretary of state, Sumner Welles, absolutely rejected any such idea as a breach of neutrality arrangements. The Windsors, who had done a thorough inspection of their ten cabins and Veranda Suite the previous week, were driven to the ship in the early afternoon. The vessel was crowded with British and American citizens making their way out of Lisbon to safety in the United States. Among the passengers were Anthony J. Drexel Biddle, U.S. ambassador to Poland and a friend of the Windsors, George Gordon, U.S. minister at The Hague, and William Phillips, U.S. ambassador to Italy. The Windsors' party included Major Gray Phillips, the mysterious Evelyn Fyrth, Captain and Mrs. George Wood, and Harold Holder. All were accommodated in the Veranda Suite of cabins.

The *Excalibur* sailed slowly in a northwesterly direction. The Windsors were advised by radiogram that their baggage had arrived in New York from Liverpool aboard the Cunard White Star liner *Britannic*. They had an early night, followed by a leisurely day on the second. In the afternoon they strolled the deck, chatting informally with their fellow passengers. They visited the bridge to see the captain and looked out at a flat, brilliantly blue sea.

The next day, the Windsors were on the bridge when the Pan American Yankee Clipper, en route with wealthy refugees to New York, flew overhead at a low altitude. Baron Eugene de Rothschild and Kitty were on board the flying boat. Captain Sullivan of the Clipper descended to within 200 feet of the *Excalibur* and greeted the Windsors by wireless. They waved and sent a message back. "Thank you. . . . We reciprocate and bon voyage."

The Windsors entertained the Drexel Biddles and William Phillips and his daughter at dinner; the next day they answered their correspondence, the duchess by hand and the duke on a portable typewriter. The sea remained calm. The duke and duchess sunbathed and attended movies in the ships' theater. They might as well have been on vacation; there was no inkling of their awkward and disagreeable exile.

15

Elba

T he *Excalibur* steamed into pale green Bermudian waters on August 7, as Sir Charles Dundas, retiring governor of the Bahamas, and Lady Dundas left Nassau en route to Rio de Janeiro, whence they would fly to Africa to a new appointment in Uganda. Sir Charles had not wanted to leave. His wife was ill, and the journey would be exceedingly uncomfortable for her. But Winston Churchill had given him no alternative.*

The Windsors came ashore by tender to the Royal Bermuda Yacht Club at 2:45 p.m.; hundreds of spectators burst into applause as the duke stood to attention on a small palm tree–flanked grass oval while the national anthem was played. Wallis remained beside the wharf, talking with Mrs. Francis Hastings-Brooke, sister of Governor Lieutenant-General Sir Denis Bernard. Among the welcoming party was Frank Giles, aide-de-camp to the governor. Detective Inspector Holder, the royal bodyguard, advised Giles that the Windsors were in danger every moment of the day and night and should never be allowed out of sight.

The duke carried out an inspection of the guard of honor, pausing briefly to talk to a youth in the Bermuda Volunteer Rifle Corps. He then departed for Government House in a state carriage with Sir Denis Bernard and with Lieutenant Giles, while Wallis and Mrs. Hastings-Brooke followed with the rest of the entourage in another carriage. Although the duke seemed to be cheerful, composed, and in the best of

---

*Dundas was known to be anti-American, another reason for Churchill's desire for a change.

tempers, in fact he was not. The reason was that Mrs. Hastings-Brooke and the ladies accompanying her had so far failed to curtsey to Wallis and that nobody had addressed her as "Your Royal Highness." At dinner that night they again failed to do what he wanted. Instructions had come from London that on no account was Wallis to be treated as royalty and that, in extremis, the most that could be accorded to the duke would be a half-curtsey. The duchess was to be addressed as "Your Grace."

Red-faced and flustered at the lack of respect for his wife, the duke sulked all through the banquet. After dinner, when the ladies repaired to the drawing room and the gentlemen made their way to the library for brandy and cigars, the duke burst out with, "If I had been King, there would have been no war." This characteristic statement at a time when Britain had her back against the wall so infuriated Sir Denis Bernard that he almost lost his temper. The duke's former equerry, Charles Lambe, who was now commander of a British cruiser, stepped in and changed the conversation, but the governor remained furious.

The pleasant and relaxed Frank Giles accompanied the Windsors day and night during the following days. He wrote in his memoirs *Sundry Times*:

> I had ample opportunity for observing them and every night made some copious notes about my impressions. They included the curious fact, imparted by seeing the Duke take a shower after a game of golf, that he had absolutely no hair on his body, even in the places where one would most expect it to be.

Giles noted:

> It was fascinating to watch this famous couple together and assess the impact of each personality upon the other. He [was] more in love with her than she with him, I noted, though her feelings assumed a watchful, almost maternal devotion. Each night, before the Government House party went to bed, she would ask me about arrangements for the next day, in particular the time of the Duke's first engagement—for I am the alarm clock in this family. As well as timekeeper, she was also watch dog.

Giles recalled that a bridge game was in progress one evening. The duke was supposed to be preparing a speech that he would make upon assuming his new position at Government House in Nassau, but instead he was chatting away while the duchess played cards. She left the table and walked into the drawing room saying, "Now, David, what about that work?" He replied sheepishly, "All right, darling, I'm going up now." As it turned out, he didn't go up to his bedroom to work until close to midnight. When he told Wallis he was at last going to attend to his work, she looked at him like a nanny "whose charge had forgotten the precepts she had taught him, thereby grieving more than annoying her."

Although day after day the duke insisted that Wallis be curtseyed to and addressed as "Your Royal Highness," his wishes went unsatisfied. The governor did his best to suppress his finer feelings and made the couple as welcome as possible in the circumstances. After a lengthy press conference on the night of August 9, Mrs. Hastings-Brooke gave a dinner party for the famous guests; it was attended by Admiral and Lady Kennedy Purvis, Colonial Secretary Eric Button and Mrs. Button, Charles Lambe, and the George Woods.

The next day, while the duke reviewed the Canadian troops stationed on the island and continued with a game of golf, Wallis visited the local aquarium. At a cocktail party that night an American woman, Mrs. Beck, caused considerable adverse comment when she, followed by three other Americans, curtseyed to the duchess. The Englishwomen present glared at them. A notable absentee from the cocktail party was the bishop of Bermuda, the Right Reverend Arthur H. Browne, the same dignitary who had personally ripped the couple's photographs from the shop window in Hamilton when the abdication took place. However, the Windsors boldly attended the bishop's service at the cathedral on Sunday, the eleventh. The bishop made a very curious reference during the sermon. At some stage during the previous two days, the duke had sent an unwise telegram to Lisbon indicating to his Nazi contacts that he would be willing to return as agreed to discuss the negotiated peace arrangements. Censorship was very strict in Bermuda; even if the duke had sent a message via a neutral consulate or in a diplomatic bag for transmission from a neutral island, it is doubtful whether he could have evaded interception. Looking directly at the Windsor's, the bishop said, as he analyzed St. Paul's Epistle to Philemon, "St. Paul's letters reveal much. As censors these days come to know, correspondences can afford the most intimate revelation of the writer's personality." On the night of the eleventh, the duke visited St. George's

Island and spoke with the officers and crew of an interned French vessel; on the twelve he inspected many troops on the island. He planted a poinciana tree next to the mango that his father had planted in 1880. Meantime, Wallis took several cruises around the bays and inlets, and she had tea with Aunt Bessie's good friend Jeffrey Dodge, of the Dodge auto family.

On August 15 the couple sailed for the Bahamas. Nassau had been scrubbed, repainted, and extensively brushed up for the royal arrival. The Windsors were taken aboard the Canadian vessel *Lady Somers*, in normal circumstances a risky procedure for royalty in time of war. However, a British destroyer did keep the *Lady Somers* in sight the whole way. Among the passengers was, by chance, Eugene Rothschild's cousin the Baron Maurice, who proved to be a genial companion of the voyage.

Thousands were lined up behind the police cordons along the wharf at Nassau as the official welcoming party led by the colonial secretary and John W. Dye, the American consul, all dressed in white suits, stood along the pier with their wives beside them. American and British flags flapped feebly in the slight breeze. The heat was enveloping and stifling.

The duke was in a general's uniform; Wallis was in a navy blue silk coat, a simple print dress, and a white cap stitched with mother-of-pearl. The Windsors gave no inkling of the discomfort they were feeling in the humidity as they shook hands with the officials. Without further ado, the duke and duchess made their way directly to the Council Chamber, where, watched by 150 fascinated citizens, they sat under a red canopy bearing the insignia of the golden crown. Wallis sat one step below the duke, but one above the normal place reserved for the wife of a governor. It was a discreet touch that the local authorities had taken hours to work out.

The duke removed his army cap and wiped his perspiring brow with a large white linen handkerchief withdrawn from his left sleeve, while Lieutenant Colonel R. A. Erskine-Lindop, commissioner of police of the Bahamas, read the commission of office. Then Chief Justice Sir Oscar Daly stepped forward to administer the sacred oath. Reflected in a huge mirror that filled much of the wall opposite him, the duke swore his allegiance to his brother the king and signed a written form of the same declaration with a tortoiseshell pen. Wallis stood to watch him, thereby breaking protocol. As he completed his second signature, he looked directly at her. Neither smiled. The duke delivered the official speech he had worked on in Bermuda, which contained an extremely veiled reference to his desire for peace in a remark about "the changed conditions which hostilities have imposed." The couple then shook hands with 285 people, all of whom were visibly wilting in the airless, suffocating chamber. The couple proceeded to the balcony as the band played the national anthem and the crowd cheered.

That afternoon the Windsors arrived with their hosts at Government House. Wallis was appalled by its condition. Unlike the Nassau building, which was spruce, well constructed, and attractively furnished, their new residence was crumbling into decay. The swimming pool was disused and filled with brown palm leaves blown there during a recent storm. The Windsors could barely make out the "H.M. King Edward VII" accompanied by the royal seal that a previous governor had painted on the bottom.

At the reception at the house that night, Lady Jane Williams-Taylor's husband, Sir Frederick, gave a stiff and awkward welcome speech. Apparently the shock and distress Sir Frederick felt over Wallis's treasonable activities conveyed through his wife were such that he forgot the importance of pretending to be favorable to her in order to assist his wife in milking her of secret information; he even, to the duke's fury, could not bring himself to mention Wallis.

He continued to snub Wallis for weeks until Jane convinced him that his attitude was unhelpful; she began to be friendly with Wallis and even to make her feel better, invited her to her magnificent estate of Star Acres in the Bahamas, reminding her of other times together in Paris, and showing her in her drawing room, as a false picture of her true sympathies, the encouraging oil painting of Hitler the führer had given her on her visit to Munich in 1934. That even outdid Wallis's photograph of Ribbentrop on her own bedroom dressing table, the first thing the duke and she saw when they got up in the morning.

By August 19 the Windsors had already given three press conferences. They began talking with the American consul general about wanting to go to Canada to visit the Alberta ranch, and an anxious John W. Dye cabled Washington warning of this possibility. There was great fear that the Windsors might move from Alberta to Washington, and the State Department advised Whitehall that any such idea must not be entertained. When the duke cabled the Colonial Office asking to be allowed to go to Canada, Lord Lloyd got in touch with Ambassador Lothian, who instantly stated that there must be no question of the Windsors' making the journey. A telegram dated August 24 to the Colonial Office read in part:

> If the Duke and Duchess visit the United States en route to Canada, they will certainly attract a great deal of publicity and much commercial interest of a rather undesirable character. But reaction of the press might be even more unfortunate if it were thought the Duke was being prevented from visiting this country. . . . In view of great pressure on the President and for other reasons, it is obviously undesirable that any such visit should be [paid] until after the elections, and I think, therefore, that the idea of His Royal Highness coming to this country should be postponed until after that date. In any case, public opinion here might well be surprised if His Royal Highness were to leave his post now, so soon after his arrival there. It is most desirable that the general public here should not get an impression that he is not taking his public duties seriously.

The Windsors hated the colonial atmosphere of niggling provincialism and inbred gossip. Moreover, Secret Intelligence Service agents were watching them, and they knew it. They were somewhat cheered by the arrival from New York of a newly appointed equerry, Captain Vyvyan Drury, and his wife, Nina. The Drurys proved to be congenial companions as well as loyal servants.

Wallis began to look around the island, trying to make the best of a bad job. Nassau was extraordinarily cramped, claustrophobic, and provincial. Its faded colonial charm and pleasant quasi-American shops, its palm trees and coral beaches, scarcely compensated for the sense of remoteness and futility it engendered. The duke and duchess unwittingly grew closer to Lady Jane Williams-Taylor and to other dominating figures of the islands. Sir Harry Oakes, the wealthy uncrowned king of the Bahamas, offered them the use of his house, Westbourne; they stayed there for weeks, and Wallis gratefully gave him her favorite Chinese screen from Peking. He had been a penniless gold prospector in Canada when, after years of futile searching, he had at last discovered the world's second-largest gold mine. His coarse, loudmouthed, vulgar personality had not changed from the days when he had explored the wilderness armed with a pick and shovel. A big man, with massive shoulders and a once-powerful physique that had run to fat, he had a harsh, grating voice and a strident, challenging manner that were excused only because of his money. His Australian wife, Eunice, was by contrast a gentle charmer, and he had a pretty daughter, Nancy, who would soon marry the playboy and Bahamian businessman Alfred de Marigny. Oakes also had two handsome sons.

Oake's partner in Nassau and in the Nazi Banco Continental in Mexico was a very sinister character. Swarthy, green-eyed, muscular, Harold Christie was a former rumrunner who had bootlegged alcohol during Prohibition. Christie had become the leading real estate dealer in the islands. He lived extravagantly, running an expensive household and traveling to and from the United States ceaselessly trying to rustle up interest in his properties. But it was wartime, and in spite of the allure of living in a tax-free zone, many potential investors were concerned that because the Bahamas were British colonial property, they might be seized in a German attempt to obtain airfields from which the American mainland could be attacked. Thus Christie was running into considerable financial difficulties at the time. He tried to take up the slack by wheeling and dealing in large numbers of low-priced properties, making loans to blacks. He was a prominent and aggressive figure in the Bahamian Assembly, using his considerable influence in Bay Street, the business and shopping district, to push through his various shady or legitimate projects.

Axel Wenner-Gren, the notorious multimillionaire Swede, was a very powerful figure in the Bahamas; at the time, he was sailing around the United States after the U.S. authorities denied him permission to land in Alaska. He was Christie and Oakes's partner in the Bank of the Bahamas and the Nazi Banco Continental. A tall, fleshy, pink-faced man with white hair, Wenner-Gren had made his vast fortune through inventing the vacuum cleaner and the refrigerator, which he had patented early in the century. His Electrolux industries had spread all over the world. An internationalist with a foot in every camp, Wenner-Gren dealt openly with Nazi Germany, Britain, and the United States, preaching a convenient doctrine of peace and maneuvering behind the scenes to preserve his massive interests. On May 25, 1939, he had met with Goering in Berlin and listened sagely as Goering called for a permanent peace with England that would entail the restoration of African colonies and no interference in the Polish corridor. He had carried Goering's message directly to Neville Chamberlain to secure a negotiated armistice; as Chamberlain remarked in a memorandum without date, all of Wenner-Gren's ideas favored Germany and offered only futile promises in return. He also was in ceaseless conference with Krupp, whose interests he protected in Sweden. He manufactured munitions for the Germans through his Swedish company, Bofors, which was protected by Sweden's neutrality. He also had a share in S.K.F. ball bearings; the company supplied commodities to the belligerents on both sides of the war.

Wenner-Gren owned the *Southern Cross*, which he had bought from Howard Hughes for $2 million. The largest yacht afloat, the vessel was magnificently furnished and had a private radio station on board. He had settled in Nassau at the end of 1939 and had founded the Bank of the Bahamas, which was connected to the Stein Bank of Cologne, which financed the gestapo, and he bought Hog Island, renaming it Paradise Island and creating a luxury resort there. He constantly changed the registry of the *Southern Cross* to avoid seizure on the high seas, and he tried to sell arms from aboard the vessel to the American republics at a time when the Panama Canal was under threat of seizure by Nazi-controlled elements in the Panamanian republic.

Wenner-Gren's agents in Nassau advised him of the Windsors' arrival, and he left messages for them to be welcomed, albeit belatedly, on his behalf. He had in fact been in touch with them before, corresponding via Charles Bedaux in the matter of negotiated peace. Soon he would return and form a fast friendship with them.

In mid-September Wallis was fretting over the whereabouts of her maid, Jeanne-Marguerite Moulichon. The State Department's Division of European Affairs cabled the American embassy at Vichy on the sixteenth to approach Maynard Barnes of the American embassy in Paris. Mme. Moulichon had had a dramatic series of experiences. In August a German official met her in Paris and helped her carry the precious trunks containing linen, silver, and china to the Spanish frontier. Although he left her before the frontier was actually reached, she succeeded in having movers complete the rest of the journey to Spain; then she was held up for a month by the British consul in San Sebastian. Meanwhile, Gray Phillips in Lisbon, working with Bermejillo and the U.S. consulate in Madrid, had organized the shipment of the trunks from La Croë to the Bahamas. After further vicissitudes, Jeanne-Marguerite at last managed to make her way to Nassau with the aid of Gray Phillips in November. Simultaneously, the duchess, who was determined to find some way of getting into the United States, had succeeded in securing an American passport via the head of the Visa Division of the State Department, Breckinridge Long.*

On September 19 the following urgent message was sent by Lord Lothian to the Foreign and Colonial offices in London:

> *Possible visit of Duke of Windsor to U.S.A.* President Roosevelt's opinion [is] that in no circumstances should H.R.H. come to America *before* the election. He himself hopes soon to visit Eleuthera Island and meet him there. Possibility of the Windsors visiting Washington later.

The reference in this secret message was to the fact that Roosevelt was interested in establishing a base at Eleuthera, where American warships could be berthed in expectation of U.S. involvement in the war. In a written memorandum John Balfour of the Foreign Office provided a footnote to this cable, saying:

> It seems to me that the President is going ahead rather fast. In the first place, we have not yet agreed that the Americans shall have a base on Eleuthera Island, though we know that they have cast tentative eyes on it. Secondly, the President can surely not visit a British dependency without finding out first from us whether such a visit is agreeable. Nothing is said as to the date of the visit.

Copies of Balfour's memo and the telegram were sent to, among others, Sir Alexander Hardinge at Buckingham Palace. Later that month, the duke had somehow influenced Lord Lothian to the point that Lothian himself was pressing the Colonial Office to allow the duke to visit America. On September 28 Lord Lloyd sent a memorandum to Foreign Secretary Lord Halifax, secretary of state, which read as follows:

> I think Lothian is being a nuisance in sounding the President about a possible visit of the Duke of Windsor to the U.S.A. I have just got the

---

*The same day that he authorized the passport, September 9, 1940, Long refused permission for a Jewish refugee ship to land its passengers at Norfolk, Virginia, with the result that the vessel was turned back and many died in the concentration camps.

Duke, as I thought, clamped down securely in the Bahamas for awhile, and now Lord Lothian is stirring up the waters again.

An appropriate memorandum was sent to Lothian suggesting that it would be advisable to discourage any further ideas along these lines. On October 8 a German newscast in English, relayed to England, stated that the duke might play a part in possible peace negotiations in Europe by President Roosevelt. The report added:

> The government sent him to the Bahamas to get him out of the way, but he accepted the appointment so that he could be within easy access of the U.S.A. He will shortly leave the Bahamas for the U.S. in order to talk with the President.

John De La Vautry of the Censorship Division of the Intelligence Unit of the Ministry of Information wrote in a memorandum of the same date, forwarded to Sir Walter Monckton:

> The Germans have . . . started a peace rumor campaign. Now they are again linking it up with the Duke of Windsor, and bringing in his announced trip to U.S.A.—which, for that if no other reason, might usefully be put off.

Monckton sent a secret memorandum to Sir Alexander Cadogan on October 9 which read:

> I have seen the telegrams passing between the office and Lothian about the suggestion that the Duke and the President might meet in the apparently not too distant future. The . . . German broadcast in English . . . sent to me by the Censorship Intelligence Unit, may suggest some confirmation of the Office view that even discussion of such a meeting is not without risk. You may have heard from the Secretary of State of the efforts made by some circles in Spain to prevent the Duke from leaving Lisbon. I had and have no doubt this was because the Germans could make use of his presence, particularly after an expressed intention to go away—in much the same way as they are now using the possibility of his meeting with the President.

Cadogan added a handwritten footnote: "We might perhaps inform Lord Lothian of the broadcast to illustrate the danger of this." Lothian telegrammed London on October 10 that he had no intention of implying that he wished to encourage an early visit of the duke to America, and he reassured the Colonial Office that the president's visit to the Bahamas would be of a purely private character and would not take place until after the election. Winston Churchill personally confirmed the necessity for caution in the matter, and he approved the Colonial Office's and Monckton's attitudes in a secret memorandum dated October 15. Four days later, the duchess sent two shipments of personal effects to Miami, including clothing for cleaning and repairing. The following memorandum was sent on the nineteenth by an FBI staff operative to J. Edgar Hoover's second-in-command, Clyde Tolson. It read:

> In the course of my duties as classifier, I noticed that the Duchess of Windsor was reported as being violently pro-German; on subsequent date I noticed that her clothes were sent to New York City for dry-cleaning. The possibility arises the transferring of messages through the clothes may be taking place.

She was prevented from sending any more.

In October, an incident occurred at the Château de Candé, still being used as the American embassy, with supposedly secret current files and archives still available to the German government as William Bullitt had wished. On the twenty-third of that month, Hitler met with General Franco of Spain at Hendaye on the French border for a meeting intended to involve Franco in the war; the meeting failed.

Next day, he met with Marshal Pétain at Montoire, with the result that Pétain offered him full support in the war against England in return for the promise of certain British African dependencies. From there, Hitler, accompanied by Goering and Ribbentrop, made a pilgrimage to the Château de Candé, where, seeing the duke and duchess's portraits in oils hanging in the library, they stood solemnly side by side and gave those loyal friends and exiles the Nazi salute.

The matter was reported by Whitney Shepherdson, American agent in France, to William Donovan, the OSS leader in Washington, on October 25.

On October 29 the duke opened Parliament in Nassau. He delivered a carefully worded speech calling for certain reforms in legislation and discussing electricity and communications, sponge fisheries, and unemployment problems. It was all conventional material, of little or no significance.

On November 11, after several postponements because of bad weather, the Windsors sailed on a six-day visit to the Out Islands of the Bahamian group to make real estate deals with Harold Christie. Meantime, Whitehall was still concerned about the Windsors having any contact with Roosevelt, who was still determined that they wouldn't come to Washington. Secret message after secret message crossed the Atlantic, all inevitably forwarded to Alexander Hardinge at the palace. Lothian even went to see the president's secretary, General Watson, to confirm that no immediate meeting would take place. In November Jeanne-Marguerite Moulichon arrived, and John W. Dye sent a message to C. W. Gray, assistant to Cordell Hull in Washington, on the fifteenth, reading:

> The maid arrived in Nassau some days ago and according to her, the British authorities were not very helpful. In fact she declares that she was unnecessarily delayed nearly a month in Spain because of their inaction, and during this time no effort was made to recover her lost luggage. The Duke expressed his sincere thanks for the real help rendered by all the American officials concerned.

That same week Axel Wenner-Gren arrived in Nassau aboard the *Southern Cross*. He was accompanied by his wife, the alcoholic American singer Marguerite Liggett. A Department of State official, G. A. Gordon, wrote to Fletcher Warren of that same department on November 20:

> Axel Wenner-Gren has since November 1, 1939, been constantly steaming in and out of Nassau Harbor on his yacht, equipped with high-powered radio atennae. This yacht is manned by ex–Swedish Navy officers, all of whom, according to my informant, are definitely and professedly pro-Nazi.

In meetings with Wenner-Gren the Windsors agreed with him on his policies of supporting a separate peace with Nazi Germany. They also arranged for him to meet with pro-Nazi general Maximino Camacho of Mexico, an improper act since Anglo-Mexican diplomatic relations had been broken off. The purpose was to shift money to Mexico.

Early in December Wallis suffered from a severe dental problem which needed to be treated immediately. She would (she said) have to be operated on by a periodontist, Dr. Horace Cartee, in Miami. The Windsors were stubbornly bent upon going to the mainland. Of course, Cartee could have flown to Nassau. In the meantime, President Roosevelt had been triumphantly reelected, and it was now agreed in Washington that he should go to the Bahamas for the long-deferred meeting to forestall the duke's coming to see him. The Colonial Office was still opposed. Lord Lloyd pressed the couple to avoid the encounter, and he skillfully engineered that the duke's requested leave dates coincide with the very period in which the president was due. Then, by a quirk of fate, the *Munargo*, the passenger ferry to Miami, had to be dry-docked because of engine trouble. Ironically, in order to get rid of the Windsors during the week of December 9, the Colonial Office had to authorize them to sail on Axel Wenner-Gren's *Southern Cross*. They were thus pitched directly into a situation that under normal conditions would be considered highly inadvisable.

The party sailed on schedule. It included Harold Holder, who was under investigation for anti-British sentiments, Piper Alistair Fletcher, and Evelyn Fyrth. The *Southern Cross* docked in Miami, causing a great deal of critical comment in the left-wing press. Twelve thousand people were gathered at the docks to greet the couple, and 8,000 more were lined up along the eight-mile route to the St. Francis Hospital. Wallis was in great pain, but showed no sign of it; when she arrived in the outpatients' room, Dr. Cartee told her it would be a tough operation as her jawbone condition was quite serious. She was operated on immediately, and her lower right molar was extracted. There was considerable infection and the postoperative recovery was miserable. That same week Lord Lothian died of a sudden illness; a Christian Scientist, he had refused the treatment that might have saved him. Stubbornly seizing the advantage of the death, the duke flew in a U.S. naval patrol bomber to the Bahamas. He met with Roosevelt after all, in a three-hour visit on board the presidential cruiser *Tuscaloosa*, anchored off Eleuthera. The duke, with characteristic determination and along with many defeatist statements, asked the president on the spot whether he could visit the CCC camps set up for young people during the Depression. This was a way of ensuring that he and Wallis would at last make their way farther onto the American mainland. The question of base sites for the U.S. Navy was discussed, but the results were inconclusive.

The duke flew back to Miami to join Wallis for the return voyage on the *Southern Cross*. They sailed on December 17. The duke announced to reporters that he would be happy to accept the post of British ambassador to the United States if he was appointed, a remark that caused the usual disapproval in Whitehall.

After a brief cruise of the western Bahamas, Wenner-Gren took the couple back to Nassau. The trip to Florida had been undertaken in defiance of Churchill's orders and as an act of defiance also against Jane Williams-Taylor's efforts to stop it, seconded by her husband, Sir Frederick, and by her friends Marjorie Merriweather Post, and the Maryland senator Millard E. Tydings. Soon, the Secret Intelligence Service would engage the unlikely agents Greta Garbo and her friend the diet authority Gayelord Houser to keep an eye on Wenner-Gren and his royal associates.

When the Windsors returned to Nassau, they were told that a prominent American isolationist editor and author whose magazine *Liberty* was owned by that other leading diet guru, Bernarr McFadden, was waiting to see the duke for an interview.

Oursler was unaware of the Windsors' Nazi associations, or at least so it seems. In turn, the Windsors subscribed to *Liberty*, which had engaged Errol Flynn in 1937 as a cover for his Nazi adventure in the Spanish Civil War. What the duke overlooked was that, isolationist or not, Oursler was a loyal, anti-Nazi American.

Oursler had been seeking the interview for weeks. The White House had discouraged it, probably because Roosevelt didn't want Windsor to spout his defeatist views in print at a time of Lend-Lease to Great Britain. The British government had similarly vetoed the idea. But Oursler was determined to press ahead. He obtained the support of one of the Windsors' social acquaintances, the wealthy Thompson Rich, who promised to do what he could.

On the plane to Nassau, Oursler had as traveling companion Charles A. Taussig, head of Roosevelt's presidential mission to investigate labor conditions in the Caribbean. Taussig snubbed him and did everything possible to stop the Windsor interview from taking place.

But then Thomson Rich turned up suddenly and showed Oursler a letter which Captain Vyvyan Drury, the duke's aide-de-camp, had written to Roosevelt, saying that the duke would be pleased to receive Oursler at any time. Just how Rich had gotten his hands on the letter he chose not to explain.

Oursler secured a meeting with Drury on the eighteenth; he was astonished to see the ballroom at Government House lined with much of the Windsors' luggage, still unpacked after more than four months. Drury was cordial and said that the duke would be pleased to receive him—at six o'clock that night.

The duke strolled into the drawing room at the appointed hour, shook Oursler's hand, and offered him a seat. Oursler plunged right in. He asked Windsor what he thought of the collaborationist Marshal Pétain's act in removing his second-in-command Pierre Laval; in fact, Laval had been reinstated in a matter of days. But the question brought a hoped-for expression of approval of Pétain that proved Windsor's support of Vichy. Oursler also spoke of Italy's "defeat"—actually a minor frontier setback—and put forth the deliberately absurd statement designed to provoke his interviewee, that Italy's collapse before the Allies would cause an antiwar revolution in Germany that would result in Hitler's removal by the masses. The duke fell into the trap. He said, irritably:

That is wishful thinking, Mr. Oursler. There will be no revolution in Germany and it would be a tragic thing for the world if Hitler were to be overthrown. Hitler is the right and logical leader of the German people. It is a pity you never met Hitler, just as it is a pity I never met Mussolini. Hitler is a very great man.

He added:

Do you suppose your President would consider acting as a mediator when, and if the proper time should arrive?

Oursler replied that the president would do so if he thought it in humanity's best interests. But he hadn't seen him in three months and that was only a guess.

Windsor plunged in deeper:

Few people are aware what a serious situation Britain is in. England is blockading Germany but Germany is blockading England. The submarine losses are enormous and getting worse, and creating havoc. The time is coming when something has to be done. Someone will have to make a move.

His pulse racing, Oursler flew to Washington, where the president granted him an audience at the White House. He repeated everything Windsor had said and Roosevelt shook in anger, mentioning the high-level appeasement group in England that Windsor represented. The president seemed appalled by the duke's mentioning of Hitler's great-ness and the certainty of a revolution in England; he knew that such a revolution would ensure Windsor's placement on the English throne.

It was then that Roosevelt delivered the bombshell about the nine shortwave Paris radio broadcasts to Berlin that, he was told, relayed in-formation supplied by Windsor to the German government. The pres-ident discreetly made no mention of Bullitt, whom he despised and had now dismissed. He said: "After [the broadcasts] it was suggested to the Duke he go to Cannes with his wife and stay there."

Oursler never published the whole story; his son, Fulton Junior, says he feared for his life if he did so. Instead, he published a much milder version, which in itself annoyed Churchill and King George VI; had the full account appeared it would, in Oursler Senior's words in his diary, have "blown the lid off the English throne."

As is clear today from recently declassified documents of the British Foreign Office, Roosevelt deceived Oursler in the matter. Far from being genuinely appalled by the appeasement policies of Hitler, he had been involved until May—when the new prime minister, Winston Churchill, swayed him—in continuing attempts to appease Nazi Ger-many and bring the war to an end. The only difference was that, in-stead of initiating such a plan, as Windsor suggested, he would support Britain under the table, and once it had put out the feelers to Berlin he would bring the matter to Hitler.

The inspiration for this ignoble idea came from Sumner Welles of the Department of State, an old friend of Roosevelt's who had been at school with him at Groton. Welles, as special emissary to Italy, had been unduly impressed by Mussolini, King Victor Emmanuel, and Count Ciano, and believed that they might act as intermediaries with Hitler, as none wanted war, despite the fact that they had entered it that summer—the führer's incompetent allies.

Lord Lothian had met secretly with Roosevelt on April 5 to discuss the president's plan for a negotiated peace. Roosevelt ironically matched and echoed the Duke of Windsor's fundamental hope that in any peace arrangement Germany would retain its "living space" and would never be cut up into sections then or in the future. All that Roosevelt would require was that Hitler would agree to a European peace force arranged jointly with the United States; the president even went to the unique and improper length of drafting a memorandum for Chamberlain to convey to Hitler in the matter.

The Foreign Office in London was appalled. On April 8, 1940, Sir Robert Vansittart wrote in disgust to Chamberlain, "We should on no account go into this. It would be a real trap." He added, "Let us go on fighting the war. Let us not be drawn into this embarrassing rigmarole by these distant and inexperienced amateurs [Welles and Roosevelt]." He went on:

> These loose ideas [in Washington] are very dangerous. No sane man will consider disarmament unless (a) Prussia is broken up and (b) The German military caste is destroyed. Both these conditions are absolutely indispensable to anything resembling peace and Roosevelt and Welles never mention them. On no account must His Majesty's government be influenced by tyros.

That winter, Frazier Jelke of New York, a well-known stockbroker, paid several visits to the Windsors. He was astonished to hear them stating quite categorically to their guests that they were totally opposed to America's entering the war. On one occasion the duke said to Jelke, "It was too late for America to save democracy in Europe. She had better save it in America for herself." In view of the expression of such sentiments, which were conveyed by Jelke to Churchill, it is hardly surprising that Churchill felt very strongly along with the king and Roosevelt that in no circumstances was the duke to go back to the United States, where he might give strength to the arms of the isolationists. It is worth noting that at the time many of those isolationists were not merely well-meaning but misguided pacifists, bent upon protecting the lives of young Americans, but were in the direct pay of the Nazi government, a fact that was generally known in Whitehall and to the intelligence services in Washington.

Christmas of 1940 was spent informally, with parties at Government House for the poor children of the islands. The winter season began; in more comfortable weather, society flocked from the mainland to Nassau for a series of major events. Axel Wenner-Gren entertained aboard the *Southern Cross*, anchored off Paradise Island; among the guests with whom the Windsors became very close was the extroverted James D. Mooney, European chief of General Motors.* After failing to obtain a visa for London because of the intercession of Sir Robert Vansittart, Mooney was traveling in the Americas with a charter from Goering to negotiate peace on Hitler's behalf. Mooney was visiting Cat Cay, an island to the north of Nassau, along with another Nazi sympathizer, Alfred P. Sloan, the chairman of General Motors, aboard Sloan's yacht the *René*. According to American intelligence reports, the duke had several meetings with Mooney to discuss plans for a separate peace with Hitler. To protect himself, Mooney, according to several sources, had been a double agent for Vansittart for several years; he may possibly have reported on the Windsor-Nazi connections in the Bahamas.

An actual eyewitness of the Windsors' malfeasances in the matter of evading currency restrictions was the British secret agent H. Montgomery Hyde, on the staff of Sir William Stephenson, of British Security Coordination. Montgomery Hyde visited Nassau at the time, observing much to his annoyance that Harold Christie and Maximino Camacho were blatantly meeting with the duke to discuss arrangements with the Banco Continental that would illegally benefit the

---

*Protective of his company's substantial holdings in Nazi Germany, Mooney was directly in charge of Hitler's enormous Adam-Opel factories, manufacturing armored cars and tanks that had led the invasions of Czechoslovakia and France. On December 22, 1936, in Vienna, Mooney had told the Windsors' acquaintance George Messersmith, "We ought to make some arrangement with Germany for the future. There is no reason why we should let our moral indignation over what happens in that country stand in the way." In an interview with the *New York Times* on October 8, 1937, U.S. ambassador to Germany William E. Dodd reported that Mooney was part of a "clique of U.S. industrialists hell-bent to bring a fascist state to supplant our democratic government." In 1938 Mooney received the Order of the Golden Eagle from Hitler. In April 1939 he conferred with U.S. ambassador Joseph Kennedy in London, arranging for a visit to that city by Emil Puhl of the Hitler-controlled Reichsbank and Helmuth Wohlthat, Goering's American-educated economic adviser. In a series of conferences, these men organized a plan in which Germany would be given a secret loan of $500 million to $1 billion in British gold, and in a future reorganization of Europe, Germany would control all currencies through a restoration of the gold standard. Mooney proposed a scheme whereby, in a negotiated peace with Hitler, Germany would receive back her lost African colonies.

Windsors in time of war. Montgomery Hyde declines to state whether
he reported this matter to the British and U.S. treasuries; however, it
was already known both in Washington and Whitehall, as numerous
documents of the time reveal.

On January 25, 1941, Summer Welles sent a confidential memorandum to Fletcher Warren of the State Department that read as follows:

> The most recent information I have regarding Mr. Wenner-Gren indi-
> cates that he is in constant and close touch with the Duke of Windsor
> and that both of them are seeing a great deal of prominent and influen-
> tial businessmen, particularly from the Middle Western states, where a
> strictly commercial point of view would appear to prevail in business
> circles with regard to relations between the United States and Germany.
>
> There would appear to be certain indications that Mr. Wenner-
> Gren, as well as the Duke of Windsor, is stressing the need for a nego-
> tiated peace at this time on account of the advantages which this would
> present to American business interests. This angle, I think, should be
> closely observed.
>
> The other information I have is that the brother of the new Presi-
> dent of Mexico, General Maximino Avila Camacho, is due to arrive in
> Nassau early in February, apparently to confer with Mr. Wenner-Gren.
> Reports have reached me that Mr. Wenner-Gren is anxious to partici-
> pate in an American consortium planning the investment of a consider-
> able amount of new capital in Mexico. For all of these reasons I think it
> is highly important that we have more than the customary routine re-
> ports of Mr. Wenner-Gren's activities.

Camacho would in fact soon be back in the Bahamas as the Windsors' guest, for discussions about setting up the complex of German,
American, and British interests in Mexico in which the Windsors
would be involved.

On February 5 James B. Stewart, American consul general in
Zurich, Switzerland, sent a strictly confidential memorandum to Fletcher
Warren. The document, headed "Alleged Nazi Subversive Activities in
the U.S. of James D. Mooney," read in part as follows:

> Mr. Eduard Winter, formerly General Motors distributor in Berlin, and
> at present this company's representative in Paris, acts as courier in de-
> livering communications from Mr. James D. Mooney, president of the
> General Motors Overseas Corporation, to high German officials in
> Paris. Mr. Winter has a special passport which enables him to travel
> freely between occupied and unoccupied France. Mr. Mooney is known

to be in sympathy with the German government, and the persons who supplied this information believe that the General Motors official is transmitting information of a confidential nature through Mr. Winter.

In other words, Mooney was involved in espionage on behalf of Germany. Messersmith, who was now U.S. minister in Cuba, wrote in a long report dated March 4, 1941:

> Something has fundamentally gone wrong with Mooney's [brain], and I consider him a dangerous individual. He is one of those Irishmen who is so against England that he would be prepared to see the whole world go down in order to satisfy his feelings with respect to England. In my opinion, his is as mad as any Nazi and is one of those who nourishes the hope that when the United States may turn fascist he will be our Quisling or our Laval.

Messersmith, unbriefed on Mooney's role as a double agent, also added that the General Motors executive had recently had an affair with the daughter of a well-known German official, "the girl being somewhat unbalanced in character and a pronounced Nazi." Mooney was an "even more dangerous person than Wenner-Gren for the Duke and Duchess of Windsor to be associated with." The American government intensified its watch on the Windsors. The FBI was not empowered to operate in the Bahama Islands, and the OSS was newly formed and somewhat restricted in its operation in British territories. Nevertheless, various U.S. secret agents flew to and from Cuba, Florida, Bermuda, and Haiti in an effort to try to unravel the truth of what was going on. Meanwhile, German propaganda never ceased to emphasize the Windsors. It was asserted on radio that in the new order of things the duke would be viceroy of America (!) and (again) that the British royal family would be banished to the Bahamas in his place. Yet another visitor to Cat Cay was Errol Flynn, ostensibly for deep-sea fishing, but in fact to become a guest of Alfred P. Sloan and James Mooney. The egregious movie star, with extensive Nazi connections, had reason to support the discussions of future negotiated peace.

Harold Christie deepened his associations with the Windsors. On February 6 he gave them the first big party of the season and the first ever by a Bahamian for a governor and his wife. Among the guests were Aunt Bessie, Sir Harry and Lady Oakes, Captain and Mrs. Vyvyan Drury, and the Wenner-Grens.

On February 20, Wallis watched excitedly as the duke won the local golf tourney, renamed the "Duke of Windsor Cup," with a score of 74. On February 22 the couple attended the George Washington Birthday dinner given by U.S. consul John Dye. On March 4 Dye sent a memorandum marked "Confidential" to the Department of State, indicating that the duchess had been making secret visits to San Juan, Puerto Rico; the source of the information was Mrs. William Leahy, wife of the former Puerto Rican governor, Admiral Leahy, who was currently U.S. ambassador to Vichy. Oddly, Aunt Bessie conveyed this information to the authorities. Dye dismissed the report as being baseless, but was it? The Foreign Office had grave suspicions in the matter, and it was anxious to prevent either the duke or duchess from visiting Santo Domingo, where other undesirable contacts might be made; President Trujillo was known to be pro-Nazi. The British embassy in Washington expressly forbade the Windsors to travel there.

With the aid of an increased increment up to some £5,000 and the use of an interior decorator from New York City, Wallis gradually converted Government House into a comfortable residence. Over the fireplace in the sitting room hung the famous portrait of her by Gerald Brockhurst. Chintz-covered sofas faced each other along with imitation Queen Anne chairs, and a large coffee table in front of the fireplace sported displays of flowers. The atmosphere was American rather than British, undistinguished but at least adequate. But her modest pleasure in improving her living conditions and her typically energetic work in the Red Cross (which sustained its unfortunate German connections) and in the hospitals and orphanages of the islands were at all times undermined by her deep bitterness and misery in exile. She and the duke ceased to rail against everyone who had put them into their present predicament, although the duke, to his credit, would not tolerate direct criticism of his brother, sister-in-law, or mother, even from Wallis. Wallis had no such sense of restraint. She breathed fire at the merest mention of the British royal family in her presence. Many of her insults made their way back to the palace—with the inevitable results.

Wallis's letters to Aunt Bessie then and in the years to come contain a constant rumble of discontent. The heat, the isolation, the humidity, the sense of rejection—these emotional and physical problems weighed more heavily with her in her self-centeredness and self-pity than the torments Europe was undergoing in the middle of a world conflict. Pouring herself into work, running her staff with the determined efficiency of a general, toiling round the clock on the Bahamas Assistance Fund, which sent thousands of milk cans to remote islands to feed children, she was at once trying to assuage her depression and sense of futility and improve her battered image in the eyes of the world. When magazines and newspapers notably failed to give her credit for what she was doing, she became testier than ever. Somehow, the world refused to regard her as a saint; she was still, in the eyes of most, the fascinating, hypnotic, and intriguing wicked witch of the West, as elusive and sinister as the dead villainess of Daphne du Maurier's *Rebecca*.

On March 4 the duchess wrote to a friend, P. G. ("Nick") Sedley of the Carter Carburetor Corporation in St. Louis, Missouri. Sedley had been assisting her in communicating with Sir Pomeroy and Lady Burton, owners of La Croë, who were living under house arrest in France; in the letter she revealed that she had been paying the rent for La Croë to the Burtons' account at Coutts Bank in London. She also revealed that she had been sending money to Herman Rogers to pay the wages of Antoine and Anna, her staff at the villa. She was concerned about rumors that the house had been sold. She was determined, she said, to keep La Croë going, no matter what happened in the future. Sedley was acting as a go-between in the matter. He was married to Lady Burton's sister, and his mother, Mrs. Sedley, was living at her house at Dinard. In a letter dated March 5 to a contact of his, Hugh R. Wilson of the Department of State, Sedley wrote the following message, which made its way into the Special Intelligence Division:

> I know nothing of these things, but conceivably there might be some German in authority at Berlin who would permit this copy [of the duchess's letter] to be delivered *as a courtesy to you or to the Duke of Windsor, or to both*. [Italics added.] It is said that an occasional 25-word message may be sent through and I am trying that, asking whether my people need ready money, but obviously the Duchess of Windsor's message could not be compressed to 25 words, because if I tried to do that, with mention of names and places, the German censor would no doubt hold it up because of lack of understanding, whereas the complete message, as written by the duchess, is quite clear and harmless from any point of view.

U.S. assistant secretary of state Breckinridge Long, in a note dated April 4 to Mr. Sedley, stated that he would be glad to transmit the text of the letter to France but only with the authority of the British. He would have to be in touch with the British embassy in Washington before he could proceed, since clearly this was on the edge of breaching the security regulations and could be interpreted as going beyond the limitations of the Trading with the Enemy Act. The duchess's letter was forwarded to the Foreign Office in London, where it proved to be of particular interest to Wallis's old enemy Sir Robert Vansittart. As far as it can be determined, the letter was stopped. The fact that Wallis would countenance obtaining the support of Berlin authorities in order to get a letter through in the matter of her house was naturally frowned upon in Whitehall.

On March 18 Churchill cabled Windsor that the proposed visit to the United States was neither in the public interest nor in the duke's own. Churchill did not object to Windsor's cruising the West Indian islands, as long as it was not done in Wenner-Gren's yacht. Churchill continued:

This gentleman is, according to reports I have received, regarded as a pro-German international financier, with strong leanings towards appeasement, and suspected of being in communication with the enemy. Your Royal Highness may not perhaps realize the tensity of feeling in the United States about people of this kind and the offense which is given the administration when any countenance is given to them.

Referring to the watered-down article in *Liberty*, he added:

The language, whatever was meant, will certainly be interpreted as defeatist and pro-Nazi, and by implication approving of the isolationist aim to keep America out of the war. . . . I could wish, indeed, that your Royal Highness would seek advice before making public statements of this kind.

He hadn't forgotten his investiture of the Prince of Wales at Caenarvon Castle; he was still a sentimental godfather and guardian in the last sentence: "I should always be ready to help as I used to be in the past."

There could be no relinquishing of the secret watch on the duchess as long as such activities continued. It was not until July that H. Freeman Matthews, first secretary of the U.S. embassy in Vichy, informed the State Department that the telltale letter had actually slipped through the mesh despite the stoppage in London. Breckinridge Long, who had frequently breached the Trading with the Enemy regulations (while precluding foreign payments for Jewish refugees because such payments would be in breach of the Trading with the Enemy Act), had passed Wallis's letter under the table via diplomatic pouch. Ironically, however, as Matthews reported on March 16:

> Due to the interruption of the pouch and ordinary postal services by the German authorities between the Embassy at Vichy and the American Consular offices in occupied France, the Embassy has unfortunately been unable to communicate copies of the letter from the Duchess of Windsor to our Consular offices in the occupied zone for transmission to the persons concerned.

On March 17 Winston Churchill sent a secret message to Windsor urging him not to continue his association with the "pro-Nazi" Wenner-Gren. At the same time, as Churchill was issuing his warnings and admonitions to the duke—and, by extension, to Wallis—he was also taking care of the duke's property in France. The following memorandum (X2153/188/503) was sent by the Foreign Office on April 7, 1941, to the American embassy in Paris:

> Mr. Winston Churchill presents his compliments to the United States Ambassador, and has the honor to request that His Excellency may be so good as to ask the United States Consul at Cannes, to pay, from British funds at his disposal, the sum of 44,156.25 Francs (being the equivalent of 250 pounds at 176.625 Francs to the pound) to Mr. Herman Rogers, Villa Lou Viei, Cannes, against his receipt for the upkeep of the property of His Royal Highness the Duke of Windsor, for whom Mr. Herman Rogers is acting as agent.

On March 27 the duke had sent an angry official note to Churchill, in care of Lord Moyne at the Colonial Office. He began, "Any repudiation of Oursler article in American press would only serve to attract attention and publicity. Besides, were I to hold views at complete variance with your policies, I would use more direct means of expressing them." He had, of course.

He went on:

> I wonder if [the new ambassador] Lord Halifax has been long enough in America to be able to predict that a visit of ours would become a

slow. . . . In Miami last December . . . our visit was most dignified and no harm was done to British interest that I am aware. . . . The importance you attach to American magazine articles prompts me to tell you that I strongly resent and take great exception to the article in the magazine *Life* of the 17th March entitled "The Queen" in which the latter is quoted as referring to the Duchess as "that woman." I understand that articles about the Royal Family are censored in Britain before release, and this remark is a direct insult to my wife and is, I can assure you, no encouragement in our efforts to uphold the monarchical system in a British Colony. Added to this is the chronic anomaly of my wife not having the same official status as myself, which is not without its unpleasant and undignified [aspects]. It is not necessary for you to remind me of the sacrifices and sufferings that are being endured by Great Britain. . . . Had my simple request conveyed to you by [ambassador to Spain] Sam Hoare been granted by my brother, I would have been proud to share these sad and critical times with my countrymen. I have both valued and enjoyed your friendship in the past, but after your telegram FO No. 458 of the 1st July and the tone of your recent messages to me here, I find it difficult to believe that you are still the friend you used to be.

Sir John Colville told the present author of Churchill's fury at this missive; no reply was sent.

At a Bundles-for-Britain party in Nassau, the socialite William Rhinelander Stewart reported (April 21, 1941) to Percy Foxworth of the FBI that the duke had been vigorously singing the words, "There'll always be an England," when he suddenly stopped and said, freezing the room, "There'll always be a Scotland Yard," almost as if he knew that his hostess, Lady Williams-Taylor, was a British spy. At another dinner party, at Government House, a bagpipe player working for the Secret Intelligence Service accompanied the guests' arrivals. Making an inflammatory anti-British remark to someone at the table, the duke turned to the bagpipe player and said, sharply, "You can report what I've said to 10 Downing Street"—namely to Winston Churchill.

On June 23 a meeting took place in Washington between Hoyer Millar, first secretary of the British embassy, and J. W. Hickerson of the U.S. State Department on an extremely urgent matter. With the collusion of the Windsors, and of Harold Christie, Wenner-Gren was planning to buy large tracts of land in the Bahamas. Word of this had been transmitted by Hickerson to the War and Navy departments. Both departments had informed Hickerson of their hope that the

British government would not permit Wenner-Gren to gain control of lands in the vicinity of proposed American naval and military bases. Millar was pleased to hear of these responses from the departments concerned, and he gave the concurrence of the British government that Wenner-Gren must not be permitted to continue with his plans. On June 24 the duke rashly interceded on behalf of Wenner-Gren, thus giving his whole game away. He actually wrote to Lord Halifax, who was now British ambassador in Washington, asking him to find out what it might be that the United States government had against Wenner-Gren. The duke claimed that Wenner-Gren was disposed to make large investments in the Bahamas which would be very helpful to the native population and said that as governor of the islands he desired to know officially what reason there might be for "not approving and encouraging such activities on the part of Wenner-Gren."

Halifax took this note to Summer Welles, and they had a discussion in the State Department the same day. Welles explained to Halifax that Wenner-Gren's associations with high members of the German government were intimate, and he made it clear to Halifax that Wenner-Gren's activities could only be regarded as suspicious in view of the world situation. As a result of this meeting, Halifax replied to the duke on the twenty-third: "I will look into the matter, but since it is a delicate subject I doubt if I can obtain any information." The duke's furious reaction can easily be imagined. At the same time, Wenner-Gren had joined, along with Sir Harry Oakes, Harold Christie, former senator John D. Hastings, Wall Street plunger Ben Smith, and Ed Flynn, Democratic boss of the Bronx, the Banco Continental in Mexico City. According to U.S. Treasury reports, Camacho yet again met the duke and duchess in the spring of 1941 to discuss ways and means of evading British currency regulations at a time when diplomatic and political relations between Great Britain and Mexico had been discontinued following a dispute over oil concessions in 1938. It was widely believed that the Windsors had succeeded in siphoning over a million pounds of illegal currency to the Banco Continental through the medium of its various shareholders.

Simultaneously, Winston Churchill, in a breach of the Trading with the Enemy Act which his government had ratified in 1940, made arrangements of so disturbing a character that only a complete quotation of the appropriate document can fully illustrate it. Restricted by the Foreign Office, the document, dated April 7, 1941, made its way into the State Department and was declassified, for the present author, for the first time on October 28, 1986, under the enumeration NND 70032L:

No. X1937/188/503

Mr. Winston Churchill presents his compliments to His Excellency the United States Ambassador and, with reference to Mr. Achilles' letter of 1st March to Sir George Warner of the Foreign Office concerning the property in Paris of His Royal Highness the Duke of Windsor, has the honour to request that the United States Embassy in Paris may be asked to be so good as to make the following payments on behalf of the Duke of Windsor, from British funds as their disposal, the payments to be shown as separate items in their account with the Foreign Office:

1 Rent of 55,000 Francs for the current year, but not to continue the purchase option.

Renew the insurance, costing 10,000 Francs.

Pay back wages to Fernand Lelorrain at the rate of 2000 Francs monthly to 31st December, 1940 and at the rate of 1000 Francs monthly for January, February and March, 1941, plus 30 Francs daily for food for the whole period. It should be explained to Lelorrain that this latter rate is the rate paid to the servants at La Croë, His Royal Highness's house at Antibes.

Continue to pay Lelorrain monthly, upon presenting himself, his 1000 Francs, plus 30 Francs a day for food.

2 The Duke of Windsor would also be grateful if the United States Embassy could enquire the situation regarding his possessions in the Banque de France and pay 15,000 Francs for the current year's rent of his strong room there, which expired last November.

3 Mr. Churchill would be obliged if an expression of His Royal Highness's appreciation could be conveyed to the United States Embassy in Paris for the able assistance they are giving to his affairs.

Paris was fully occupied by the Nazis, of course; the rent would be paid to the German authorities; the Banque de France was totally under Nazi control.

On April 11, 1941, at dinner at Government House, Windsor told his guests that it would be very unwise for America to enter the war against Germany as Europe was finished anyway, and what little help she could give would be too late. Several nights later at another party the duchess said that if the United States did come in the war it would go down to history as "the greatest sucker of all time." And they both spoke of their admiration of Hitler.

The Windsors succeeded in obtaining permission to land once more on United States soil. On April 18 they sailed to Miami aboard the SS *Berkshire*; they were met by a welcoming crowd estimated at 2,000. The purpose of the trip was to meet with Sir Edward Peacock, now head of the British Purchasing Commission and a director of the Bank of England, to discuss financial matters. The British Purchasing Commission was under surveillance by both British and American intelligence. Montagu Norman, Sir Otto Niemeyer, and F. W. Tiarks* of the Bank of England were all partners in the Bank for International Settlements in Basel, Switzerland; also on the Swiss bank's board of directors was Dr. Walther Funk, president of the Hitler-controlled Reichsbank. The Bank of England had also played a crucial role in stealing the Czechoslovakian gold reserve, sent from Prague in 1938 for safekeeping in London. Montagu Norman had sent the gold of that defeated country directly to Berlin.

The meeting with Peacock, so far as can be determined, was of little consequence and only generalities were discussed. The duke issued a press announcement through Gray Phillips on April 19, saying, "The talk [with Sir Edward Peacock] will be private, and no announcement of its contents will be made." In Palm Beach the Windsors met with the mysterious Walter Foskett, attorney for Sir Harry Oakes and Harold Christie, and partner with both men in a consortium that was suspected of shady dealings in both the United States and the Caribbean. It was called the Tesden Corporation. Foskett also had another connection to the Windsors. He was a member of the board of directors of Alleghany, the massive railroad empire of which the presiding genius was the Windsor's friend, the multimillionaire Robert R. Young. Young warmly welcomed the couple.

While the Windsors were in Palm Beach in May, they saw a good deal of the handsome socialite Captain Alastair "Ali" MacKintosh, one of Wallis's first friends of London days; he was a self-appointed informant for the FBI and was about to enlist in the British army. He issued a secret report to J. Edgar Hoover on May 2. As a result, on May 3 Hoover wrote to Roosevelt via the presidential secretary, Major General "Pa" Watson:

---

*Friend and adviser of Prince Otto von Bismarck.

Information has been received at this Bureau from a source that is so-cially prominent and known to be in touch with some of the people in-volved, but for whom we cannot vouch, to the effect that Joseph B. [*sic*] Kennedy, the former Ambassador to England, and Ben Smith, the Wall Street operator, had a meeting with Goering in Vichy, France, and that thereafter Kennedy and Smith had donated a considerable amount of money to the German cause. They are both described as being very anti-British and pro-German.

This same source of information advised that it was reported that the Duke of Windsor entered into an agreement which in substance was to the effect that if Germany was victorious in the war, Hermann Goering through his control of the Army would overthrow Hitler and would thereafter install the Duke of Windsor as the King of England.

After that memorandum, the Windsors were, in the words of a presidential aide of the time, "about as welcome at the White House as two pickpockets." Yet they were allowed to tour the nearby Army air base, which was nearing completion at Morrison Field. It was during that visit that the duchess made her first ever flight by air. She was aboard Harold S. Vanderbilt's air transport piloted by Benjamin Thaw's brother Russell. She seemed to enjoy the tour of naval and military in-stallations.

Another event that May was the flight of Rudolf Hess to England. The Windsors' old friend Ernst Wilhelm Bohle was of course partly re-sponsible for this, though it was generally believed that Hess made the decision on his own. The flight had originally been planned for Spain, where Hess would undoubtedly have conferred with Sir Samuel Hoare.

Wallis wrote to Aunt Bessie on May 16, referring to the flight. In a significant sentence, she said, "If only [Hess's journey] meant the end of this war." In the wake of the flight the Windsors became seized by an alarming thought. They wondered if the Germans would try to kid-nap them and hold them as hostage against the release of Hess; over the next two years, the jittery duke, for all his Nazi sympathies, kept announcing the real or imaginary sighting of U-boats off the Out Is-lands of the Bahamian group.

The Windsors celebrated their birthdays in devastating heat. The day before the duke's birthday Hitler invaded Russia.

On June 30 the duke sent an immensely long letter to Winston Churchill pouring out his feelings. While admitting that "banishment to these islands was as good a war-time expedient for a hopeless and insoluble situation as could be found," he complained that his services were not rated "very high by any [*sic*] British government" and that "I have the same old court clique to thank for keeping me out of my country. I hope the latter is the correct conclusion, but whatever the true facts of the case, I have learned a very good lesson, and that is never to become involved with official England again, from which I intend to extricate myself the day the 'cease fire' is sounded."

He promised to continue in the Bahamas, "so long as I can conscientiously feel that I am pulling as much of my weight as this restricted appointment allows." He mentioned the duchess's work for the Red Cross and other local charities, and he complained because Churchill had not advised the king to grant the duchess royal rank. He said his demand was not based on snobbery, since he would readily drop his own title if the occasion arose, "but it is to protect her from the world being able to say, and indeed they do, that she has not really got my name. Some newspapers have even gone so far as to infer that ours is a morganatic marriage." The letter continued to press for the American trip, urging the establishment of a steamship line to the islands and saying it was important that he visit the president. He assured Churchill he would not speak against British policy, and he said, "I have no desire whatsoever to make any speeches outside the Bahamas or to discuss politics, for in these days it is far too dangerous a topic with people's emotions keyed to such a high pitch." He asked, "I only wish you would do something to dispel this atmosphere of suspicion that has been created around me, for actually there is a good deal more I could do to help on this side of the Atlantic."

The Windsors bought a cabin cruiser, the *Gemini*, and toured around in her against orders, meeting their various questionable friends. Wenner-Gren departed for Peru, using the excuse of an archaeological expedition to the Inca ruins, to help set up (or so the FBI believed) a network of pro-Nazi connections in that region. Vincent Astor turned up on his yacht the *Nourmahal*, on an unofficial investigative mission for Roosevelt; Astor was an unpaid special agent for the president, and the reports the millionaire sent back to the White House were of great assistance in determining the Windsors' activities.

Meantime, the Windsors stubbornly began planning yet a third trip to America, this time an extended tour that would take them all the way to Canada and the ranch in Alberta. It was virtually a reworking of the canceled trip of 1937, with a few cities left out. The British Foreign Office was understandably alarmed by such a proposal, and in fact Vansittart once again influenced policy against the Windsors. At Buckingham Palace, Sir Alexander Hardinge felt equally disturbed by the idea. The anxiety in London was exacerbated by the fact that the Duke of Kent was due to make an official visit to America in August and on no account must Kent and Windsor be present on the American mainland at the same time. There was still fear of a double conspiracy. It was felt once again that, given their great popularity among an unsuspecting public, the two dukes might easily try to swing their weight behind the various senators and congressman who wanted to keep America out of the war. But it was virtually impossible to refuse the Windsors' request for the appropriate visas and travel documents. All that could be done was to deny them, once more, full-scale diplomatic assistance or the hospitality of the embassy and the various consulates. They must on no account be given the impression that their visits had even the most tacit approval in Whitehall.

Lunch at the White House was inevitable, since to decline the Windsors' suggestion that they should be entertained there would create unfavorable publicity against the president at a time when it was necessary for him to have complete public support. He was already fighting an undeclared war with Hitler in the Atlantic and was under a storm of criticism in Congress over it. He had begun Lend-Lease, and in everything except name was England's ally against the Nazis.

At the last minute, Churchill sent the duke a long and deeply felt memorandum, urging him to do everything in his power to influence the Roosevelts—not that they needed influencing—in Britain's cause. He included these words:

[Remind the president that] the whole British Empire is one in its inflexible, unwearying resolve to fight against Hitlerism until the Nazi tyranny has been forever destroyed. . . . This time of struggle and of sorrow might be long, but it cannot last forever. It will only last until victory of the righteous cause has been won.

There was, of course, no chance that sentiments of this noble sort would be conveyed, and in any event, the meeting with the president was called off because of a bereavement of Mrs. Roosevelt's that week.

By an odd and rather disagreeable coincidence, the week the couple arrived in the United States, so did Wallis's Paris lawyer, the Nazi agent Armand Grégoire. A huge FBI file, accompanied by State Department documents and OSS records, appeared on the desk of Adolf A. Berle, assistant secretary of state, an able and patriotic man who reported directly to the president on secret intelligence matters at regular weekly meetings. Often bypassing the FBI, Berle used his own information gleaned from a network of vice-consuls acting as spies and trained in cyphers in neutral countries overseas. He was in many ways the equivalent of Sir Robert Vansittart, who had retired. Berle shared Vansittart's unfavorable view of the Windsors; he was certain they were Nazi collaborators. He found an ally in George Messersmith, who was now minister to Mexico and no longer adhered to his moderate view of the duke and duchess. Their connections to Wenner-Gren, whose Nazi links were known to Messersmith in Berlin and Vienna, had been sufficient to make that accomplished diplomat their enemy.

The Grégoire file proved to be of interest to Berle. It spelled out the French lawyer's representation of the duchess in 1937, and it revealed his handling of Ribbentrop and Sir Oswald Mosley as well as Ernest Simpson's French and German shipping contracts.

Berle kept a watch on Grégoire for the next twelve months, tracing him to Berkeley, California; he authorized Grégoire's seizure and imprisonment by the Department of Justice in March. In jail for the rest of the war, defined as a Nazi agent, Grégoire was tried and found guilty of collaboration with Germany by the French government in 1946 and sentenced to hard labor for life.

Berle now relentlessly focused on the Windsors, and the FBI opened a substantial file. Letters poured in, some of them obviously crank missives, others written or typed in a more rational mode. Preserved in the Windsors' main file at the FBI in Washington, D.C., the letters are filled with charges, almost all of them against the duchess rather than the duke. Several name her point-blank as a Nazi spy; all warn American against the Windsors' presence and demand that they be refused courtesies or access to strategic areas.

The Windsors' position was not aided by the fact that they were taken from Miami to Washington on a special train supplied by the millionaire president of Alleghany, their old friend Robert R. Young. John Balfour, basing his statement upon evidence, wrote in his memoirs

that Young was a Nazi sympathizer. Young was yet another in a long
line of wealthy people who wished to create a negotiated peace with
Hitler. He was introduced to the Windsors by a member of the Alleghany board of directors, Walter Foskett, the prominent and questionable Palm Beach lawyer who was both a partner and friend of
Harold Christie and Sir Harry Oakes in the much-investigated, allegedly shady Tesden Corporation.

In view of the nature of the Windsors' host, whose bulging file was
already on Berle's desk, it is not surprising that the Windsors received
a chilly welcome when their train chugged into Union Station, Washington, on September 25. The chargé d'affaires was notable by his absence. The British and American officials were cold and unwelcoming.
The unsuspecting public, always the last to know about anything,
cheered the duke and duchess as they made their way to the embassy. On
this occasion, Ambassador Sir Ronald Campbell* proved to be at least
polite. In the wake of President Roosevelt's reelection the previous year,
the Foreign Office, presumably under Churchill's guidance, this time
did not refuse to permit the ambassador to give at least the appearance
of hospitality to his erring visitors. Despite the canceled lunch at the
White House, the Windsors actually made their way there and the
president, unaccompanied by his disapproving wife, and no doubt ap-
prised of their activities to the full, gave them a token welcome. His
motive was still the securing of those troubled bases in the Bahamas.

At the National Press Club, the duke, with the duchess smiling on,
delivered a much watered-down version of Churchill's suggested patriotic address, unwisely but predictably removing the more aggressive
elements and replacing them with an outrageous addendum calling for
peace in direct contradiction of Churchill's insistence on unconditional surrender and a total destruction of Germany. That evening, a
number of high-ranking officials of Roosevelt's cabinet came to a party
for the duke and duchess at the British embassy. Among the guests
were Berle, seeing first-hand what he was up against, and the strongly
anti-Nazi secretary of the treasury, Henry Morgenthau, who also had
highly damaging files on the Windsors on his desk and pretended

---

*Campbell by now was privy to the Windsors' secret file in London, and the whole
mass of telegraphic correspondence between the Windsors in Nassau and the Foreign
and Colonial offices in London was automatically sent to him.

friendliness in order to lay the ground for determining more information in the future.

The duke and duchess gave a party to meet old friends and relatives, including Lelia Barnett and several Warfields. Then they left for Canada to see the royal ranch in Alberta. It was a thrilling journey for Wallis. They were rapturously received, the duchess noted excitedly, as they traveled through the Midwest, the center of isolationism. The crowds were filled with large numbers of German-Americans who had elected pro-Nazi politicians as senators and congressmen, including the dangerous Montana senator, Burton K. Wheeler, best friend of Robert Young. The isolationist *Chicago Tribune* announced the Windsors' arrival in huge headlines, embarrassingly endorsing their appeasement stance. They crossed into Canada. The prime minister, Churchill's friend Mackenzie King, was in an embarrassing position, since he had not wanted the Windsors to come. He knew their record only too well. The Royal Canadian Mounted Police not only guarded the Windsors but kept an eye on them throughout their visit. They arrived at the ranch. It was handsomely situated in magnificent countryside, and Wallis much enjoyed the rest. The duke dreamed of striking oil on the ranch; there was much discussion with the duchess of selling the property in return for his retaining 50 percent of the petroleum rights. He was to call this off at a later stage on her advice and to start to drill himself.

In the couple's absence the Bahamas were swept by a disastrous hurricane. It would have been advisable for the Windsors to have returned to take care of the situation, but they did not, causing much criticism among the blacks whose properties had been wiped out.

The Windsors went to Baltimore, where they visited Lelia Barnett. Wallis was delighted to see her uncle, General Henry M. Warfield, at Salona Farms in the Harford hunting country. Uncle Henry was waiting for the couple at the station, along with a large crowd of cheering people. The duke and duchess very much enjoyed their stay at the farm, which was only a few miles away from Oldfields School and Grandmother Warfield's house, Manor Glen. Wallis was pleased to show the duke paintings of the clan. She did not go to Oldfields; the reason may have been that Mary Kirk Raffray had so recently died. The Windsors returned to Baltimore for a full-scale motorcade attended by 200,000 cheering people. During the procession Wallis caught a glimpse of 212 Biddle Street, in which she had spent so much of her youth. She was delighted at a country club reception when an elderly lady came up to her and announced she was Ada O'Donnell, her kindergarten mistress.

While the Windsors were enjoying the delights of Baltimore, a naval intelligence report on them, dated October 14, appeared on the desk of Adolf Berle and J. Edgar Hoover. Supplied by Major Hayne G. Boyden, naval and air attaché of the U.S. Marine Corps, it read as follows:

DURING CONFERENCE IN GERMAN LEGATION [IN WASHINGTON, D.C.] DUKE OF WINDSOR WAS LABELED AS NO ENEMY OF GERMANY. [HE WAS] CONSIDERED TO BE THE ONLY ENGLISHMAN WITH WHOM HITLER WOULD NEGOTIATE ANY PEACE TERMS, THE LOGICAL DIRECTOR OF ENGLAND'S DESTINY AFTER THE WAR.

HITLER WELL KNOWS THAT EDWARD AT PRESENT CANNOT WORK IN A MATTER THAT WOULD APPEAR TO BE AGAINST HIS COUNTRY AND HE DOES NOT URGE IT (A RELIABLE INFORMANT ON CLOSE TERMS WITH A NAZI AGENT REPORTED). BUT WHEN THE PROPER MOMENT ARRIVES HE WILL BE THE ONLY PERSON CAPABLE OF DIRECTING THE DESTINY OF ENGLAND.

That weekend the couple stayed with Wallis's old friend, Mrs. Sterling Larrabee, at Oakwood, Warrenton, Wallis's home during the first weeks of sitting out her divorce from Winfield Spencer. The Windsors continued to New York City for a five-day visit that at first turned out to be something of a frost. Less than twenty people, all of them reporters and railroad workers, were on the platform when the duke and duchess stepped off the train. They made their journey through the almost deserted streets to the Waldorf Towers in a custom-built limousine supplied to them by GM's Alfred P. Sloan. Vyvyan Drury met them at the Towers; they were delighted with their twenty-eighth-floor suite, a magnificently preserved art deco masterpiece overlooking the sweep of Park Avenue. The duchess was suffering from recurrent stomach ulcer pain, and she saw three specialists during the stay. Either separately or together, the duke and duchess visited various housing developments, baby crèches, and clubs. When they went to City Hall, they received a welcome from a large crowd as they were greeted by the mayor, the ever-popular Fiorello La Guardia, whom Wallis loved.

She was delighted that the Herman Rogerses were in town. Rogers had finally left France after setting up the basis for the Voice of America broadcasts that were proving to be of great value in stimulating anti-Nazi feeling in the Americas. A curious incident occurred on October 21. A German-born 18-year-old farmhand, Fritz Otto Gebhardt, made his way up to the Windsors' suite, only to be arrested as he stepped out of the elevator. Asked what his purpose was, he said that he wanted to interview the Windsors for a newspaper in Vienna, and he admitted that he was a supporter of the America First isolationist group. He was charged with being a member of the German-American Bund and was held for questioning. By now, thousands of people had poured in from out of town in response to widespread publicity of the royal visit, and they swept down on the Windsors en masse everywhere they went. The duke and duchess continued to Detroit. There they happily joined Henry Ford for tea; they had much in common with Ford, who had been a favorite of Hitler's and had published in his *Dearborn Independent* a reprint of the notorious forgery "The Protocols of the Learned Elders of Zion," and outrageous anti-Semitic tract. Hitler had Ford's photograph on display in his Brown House in Munich. At the time of the duke's visit, and even after the United States entered the war a few weeks later, Ford was building trucks and armored cars for the Nazis in occupied France, a procedure he would follow until the end of the conflict.

The duke also visited General Motors, which likewise retained German connections after Pearl Harbor; James D. Mooney received them.

On November 18, 1941, Sir Ronald Campbell, now the ambassador in Washington, sent a personal and secret memorandum to Anthony Eden in London, saying that Henry Morgenthau, Jr., secretary of the Treasury, was inquiring about the dollars which the Windsors used during their visit to the United States. The report continued, "The Secretary of the Treasury made it plain that he was not asking the question for frivolous reasons but because there were stories going about in connection with which information was required. . . . The United States Treasury are checking on any dollar accounts which the Duchess may have in the United States." The report to London continued, "If you wish to avoid supplying any information, can you give me a formula for reply?" The surrounding documents are missing from Lord Avon's files at the Public Record Office in London, but it is clear from this report that the gravest suspicions had yet again been aroused of the Windsors' improper use of currency against all restrictions of the time. Documents located in the Washington, D.C., National Archives indicate that the couple had obtained even more black-market currency through Wenner-Gren. The Windsors returned to Miami, and for the second time the duchess got into an airplane as they returned to Nassau.

On December 7 the Japanese attacked Pearl Harbor. Immediately, President Roosevelt declared that a state of war existed with Japan. However, despite the fact that Japan was part of the Axis, the United States did not declare war on Germany. Hitler took consultation with Ribbentrop, asking him whether it would now be necessary for Germany to declare war on America. Ribbentrop advised the führer that the terms of the present Tripartite Pact between Germany, Italy, and Japan called for aggressive action by each partner if another partner was subjected to attack or invasion. Since Japan was the aggressor in this instance, the terms of the pact did not apply. However, Hitler decided to declare war because of information the *Chicago Tribune* had published on its front page. Based on a leak from the U.S. War Department, the article stated that Roosevelt planned, in an operation entitled "Rainbow Five," to invade Europe and defeat Germany in 1943. The leak was caused by Robert R. Young's close friend Senator Wheeler.

After Pearl Harbor Charles Lindbergh held a meeting of pro-Nazi America Firsters at which he stated that although he had no quarrel with Germany, he was disgusted by the yellow hordes of Japan threatening the United States; the duke expressed an equal horror of the "Nipponese hordes." While he was appalled by news of the attack because clearly it would end forever the chance of a negotiated peace with Germany, he would, like Lindbergh, fight Japan. It is generally acknowledged that the duchess was, according to the apologist biographer Michael Bloch, "thrilled by the news" of Pearl Harbor. What does this mean? Was she delighted that America was entering the war, thus ensuring a swift end to the conflict, or was she pleased it had been attacked?

Seven days after Pearl Harbor, under the most severe pressure from Whitehall and Washington, Axel Wenner-Gren was blacklisted for the duration of the war. In view of the fact that the Swede was a resident of the Bahamas, the duke was placed in the awkward position of having to sign the blacklisting document himself. Among the companies included on the document to which the duke's signature was appended was the Bank of the Bahamas, in which the duke and duchess had a substantial interest. Other companies were enumerated, all quite clearly having German connections. Wenner-Gren was on his way to

Mexico at the time aboard the *Southern Cross*, and he was compelled to stay at his home in Cuernavaca for the duration of the war. All his operations in the Bahamas were closed down. President Roosevelt, Under Secretary of State Sumner Welles, and Adolf Berle jointly were responsible for the action that was taken. As stated by Berle in a memorandum to the president dated February 9, 1942, the purpose was "to put Wenner-Gren out of the general promoting business and to make it perfectly plain that he was politically unacceptable in the United States. I should not think it necessary to go further at this time."

There were other reasons. A British intelligence report dated January 29, 1941, stated: "Wenner-Gren is . . . attempting to form in America a cartel to control the wood trade, and this has been discussed with various persons who have got the impression that his real object is to cut off Britain's supply of wood."

Most seriously, Wenner-Gren was a partner in the H. A. Brassert Company, which had multinational connections and was located in both New York and Berlin; it was handling Goering's affairs in the steel industry. The Treasury was interested in the possibility that through Brassert and the Bank of the Bahamas, Wenner-Gren had assisted the Windsors in investments and had transferred laundered money owned by them through the Banco Continental.

There was much discussion in 1942 of U-boat sightings in the outer islands of the Bahamas. The duke advised that he was still fearful that he and the duchess would be kidnapped and exchanged for Rudolf Hess. Thus, the guard, both British and American, was greatly increased in the islands. Windsor bombarded London with telegrams expressing the gravest concern over the situation.

Wallis was afraid to go out of doors; there was considerable labor unrest in Nassau and throughout the island of New Providence. Conditions, already very bad, were not helped by the departure of Wenner-Gren, whose tenants in many cases were left homeless. The Windsors once again ran into trouble with the British Secret Intelligence Service and the FBI. William Stephenson, head of British Security Coordination in New York, determined through his Censorship Office in Bermuda that a letter addressed to Prince Redolfo del Drago in Rome from Wallis's close friend Mrs. Harrison (Mona) Williams, later the Countess von Bismarck, contained a card from Government House used only by the Windsors. The card contained a message, the contents of which are still classified in 2004, from Major Gray Phillips, who used the code name Grigio. For Phillips to communicate with a resident of an enemy country was in breach of the Trading with the Enemy Act. By now, British and American authorities on both sides of the Atlantic, all the way up to the White House and Buckingham Palace, were finding their worst suspicions of Wallis and her contacts confirmed. However, the matter was allowed to drop. In a memorandum to the British agent Charles Howard Ellis on Stephenson's staff and occupying the role of British consul general in New York, the duke wrote, with unconscious humor:

> I am entirely satisfied with [Major Phillips's] explanation of this incident, and that his endeavor to communicate with an Italian was in no way prompted by any sinister motive. . . . I can vouch for his integrity. I hope, therefore, that under the circumstances British Security Coordination will overlook the serious breach of security regulations which he has unfortunately committed.

In April 1942 Harold Christie was negotiating with Sir Harry Oakes to sell him a substantial stretch of land, which in turn would be sold to the British government for use as a RAF base. The land would adjoin the existing Oakes Field, which was used as a civil airport. Oakes was quibbling over the money, and Christie went behind his back, making arrangements to sell the property at a high price to a questionable American syndicate. The syndicate, in turn, would make a substantial profit by reselling land that in the first place should have been given to Britain in support of the war effort. It was not until several months later that Oakes realized he had been double-crossed.

In May 1942 the Windsors were thinking of visiting South America, but Anthony Eden sent Churchill a memorandum dated the fourteenth strongly discouraging such a move. Latin America was torn apart by Nazi influences and, Eden added, "[Such a visit] would certainly arouse suspicions in Washington."

On May 28 the Windsors returned to Miami aboard the *Gemini;* they went on to Washington and joined the Rogerses at a small luncheon at the White House. In their absence, the long-smoldering fires of antiwhite hatred and resentment burst into flames in Nassau.

On June 1 there was a full-scale riot. Wallis was appalled when the duke told her that 1,000 black workers had looted and pillaged Bay

Street. The U.S. Marines arrived, in the guise of military policemen, on direct instructions from the president; all businesses closed down, and there was a general strike. Soon, the rioters had swelled to 2,000 in number, demanding that the government act immediately to improve their conditions. Finding no response, they used anything they could carry, from broken bottles to antique swords snatched from the local museum, to smash the shop windows, hurl the contents into the street, and invade the bars to consume large quantities of liquor. When troops, led by the Cameron Highlanders, confronted them, they beat one of the Scot soldiers violently. The Highlanders shot at random into the crowd, killing seven and injuring forty others. In a lull in the fighting, there was a hysterical meeting of leading businessmen, who demanded that the acting governor, Colonial Secretary Leslie Heape, act immediately. Lieutenant Colonel R. A. Erskine-Lindop, commissioner of police, was under special fire from Christie, Oakes, and the other business leaders for not having acted promptly.

A curfew was instituted in Nassau. That night two blacks were shot and killed. Reports reached Government House that the mob had torched the local Grant's Town public buildings, including the police and fire stations.

Leaving the duchess behind to shop and visit friends in Washington with Aunt Bessie, the duke returned to Nassau immediately. Despite the fact that he was opposed to blacks joining local clubs or having any place in government, his personal charisma in a British colony, his charm and presence, ensured a sudden cessation of the local insurgence. To give him credit, the duke did his best to achieve a semblance of order. He no doubt enjoyed his first serious challenge as governor, and it must not be forgotten that the blood of empire ran in his veins. Although he would undoubtedly rather have been viceroy of India, he still took pleasure in making high decisions even in this unlikely place. He calmed down the jangled nerves of the Bay Street boys and, on advice well taken from Eric Hallinan, attorney general of the Bahamas, set up a commission of inquiry. On June 8 he broadcast to the people of the islands in a tone of imperial authority and not a little condescension, urging general cooperation and somehow contriving to give his listeners the impression that while he was intensely problack, he would not tolerate any further displays of rebellious lack of discipline.

The duke telephoned Winston Churchill in London and told him of these events. Churchill's response, on June 10, was to offer him slyly the governorship of Bermuda, describing it, in a letter of that date, with a certain amount of tongue in cheek as "a key point in the relationship between Great Britain and the United States with a better climate than Nassau." Since this was an even more meaningless post than his present one—Bermuda was not more than a flat and featureless holiday resort with a naval base—he rejected the idea on the tenth. As it happened, Roosevelt had a motive the duke no doubt saw through: Bermuda was the headquarters of the British censorship and espionage operation in the North Atlantic, and whereas Lady Williams-Taylor had failed in her authorized mission to keep Windsor away from Wenner-Gren, Sir William Stephenson, head of the Secret Intelligence Service in North America, with frequent stays in the Bermudian capital of Hamilton, perhaps would not fail.

The duke seized the opportunity to return to the United States on June 12 to obtain advice from Roosevelt. As in their previous encounters, the president gave the impression of sympathy and interest, acting with his customary skill a role meticulously rehearsed and typical in its fully realized falsity. In fact, he said nothing of interest; with great geniality, he left the duke to fend for himself in the situation.

Meanwhile, Nassau looked as though it had been struck by a hurricane, storm shutters hastily nailed to the great gashes and holes in the public buildings. The duke joined Wallis in New York on the seventeenth, celebrating her birthday there two days later, followed by his own on the twenty-third. On June 27 they joined Herman and Katherine Rogers aboard the *Gemini*, sailing through a storm.

No sooner had they returned to Nassau than a new and dramatic incident occurred. The duke and duchess were sitting with Mr. and Mrs. Rogers, celebrating Katherine's birthday on the twenty-eighth, when they were astonished to see a gust of fire bursting out of Bay Street and flaring against the sky. Accompanied by Sergeant Harold Holder and a butler from Government House, the duke, as excited as a schoolboy, ran along the street and began helping the volunteer groups and the fire brigade. In a fit of heroics he began running in and out of buildings to see if anyone was trapped. He and the duchess formed chains with numerous citizens to try to salvage furniture and equipment. The culprit turned out to be a local businessman seeking to collect on the fire insurance.

The Bay Street Boys were furious with the duke for failing to take extreme measures against the looters and arsonists of the riots. His policy, to avoid a full-scale revolution, which would place him and the duchess in mortal danger, was sensible enough: pragmatic rather than liberal, as some people considered it. While he faced many angry complaints, the summer heat once more intensified unbearably. Then came shattering news. At 1:15 p.m. on August 25, 1942, the Duke of Kent took off with eleven other people in a Sunderland flying boat from Invergordon, Scotland, en route for Iceland and Newfoundland. Shortly afterward it crashed, killing all except one man aboard. Rudolf Likus, Ribbentrop's chief of intelligence in the German Foreign Ministry, made a statement, issued widely through the various media, that:

> the so-called accident has been engineered by the nefarious British Secret Intelligence Service to get [Kent] out of the way before he would embarrass the royal family any further with his outspoken sympathies for the German cause.

Ladislas Farago, formerly of the U.S. Office of Naval Intelligence, recorded this fact in his book *The Game of the Foxes* (New York: David McKay, 1971).

The biographer Martin Allen wrote to the present author on July 4, 2003:

> The Duke had descended into the murky world inhabited by British Intelligence, and so it is not impossible that he was becoming a problem, had outlived his usefulness. My father knew Freddy Winterbotham [of the SIS], and in a discussion they had in the late 1970s, asked him about the matter. My father said that all Winterbotham would say was that "We got rid of Kent as we got rid of the Sikorski problem."

The reference was to an almost identical air crash of July 1943 that killed Wladyslav Sikorski, premier of Poland in exile. In both cases, according to Winterbotham (Allen says), the method used was putting sulfuric acid on the insulation wires.

How was this done? With no knowledge of the actual murder, Georg von Zirk, a former Luftwaffe pilot, explains:

If you wanted to destroy a flying boat in those days, a member of the ground crew would be engaged to carry out the job. He would fit a bottle, rather like those used in hospitals for intravenous feeding, to a section of the internal insulation wiring, and, using a timer, allow it to drip, drop by drop, until the connections were burned through. Then, when the plane took off, it would only be a matter of minutes before it lost altitude; the pilot would try to make a forced landing but it would already be too late.

What reason can there have been for Sir Stewart Menzies of the SIS to take so desperate a step as eliminating the king's brother and a possible heir to the throne?

According to Martin Allen, there was a primary reason in Kent's increasing drunkenness and outspokenness on his missions. Bitter and disappointed in tasks in navy and air force, and jealous of his royal cousin Lord Louis Mountbatten, he was unhappy in his life. The war he had so desperately wanted to avoid, hence his many missions to Germany, filled him with horror; his numerous letters to Prince Paul of Yugoslavia, exiled under arrest to Africa by Winston Churchill, show hatred of Germany for betraying his trust, but at the same time no love of his country either. Instead of the burning patriotism expressed by his brother King George and sister-in-law Queen Elizabeth, his letters are full of misery. And misery and drunkenness can cause so high a personage to be a dangerous potential security leak, especially since he was privy to both British and American air force activities and spies laced his frequent destinations of Canada and Iceland.

Kent had an intriguing connection to William Bullitt, overlooked by historians. In a dissertation for a master's degree in economics at Cornell University in the United States, the scholar Jonathan Victor Marshall showed the two men involved in a highly questionable matter concerning the purchase of bomber planes in Canada, which led to personal profit and to security leaks to Germany that caused considerable concern in Whitehall. By their working with French contacts, over a million dollars was extracted from the Banque de France in one swooping measure; in view of Kent's comparative lack of grasp of money maters, Bullitt must bear the brunt of the blame for this. But Kent's close contact with General Spaatz of the U.S. Army Air Force in terms of securing vital information as liaison was thought to be highly dangerous by the British Secret Intelligence Service, especially in view of his drinking and looseness of mouth.

It is only fair to add, as a final comment on this distressing matter, that British Establishment critics of the events categorically deny that Kent was assassinated. Nigel West (Rupert Allason) believes the crash was caused by general drunkenness among captain and crew. The historian and biographer Hugo Vickers opts for mistakes in piloting caused by weather conditions. Yet the official inquiry showed no evidence of drinking, and indeed it is unthinkable that the trained pilot and officers would have risked the life of the possible future heir to the throne by leaving in that condition. As for faulty piloting, the team was the best-trained in England, with a complete knowledge of that Scottish terrain; they had flown in all weathers over it for years without a mishap. On balance, the sabotage/explosion theory will works best.

Yet another motive for murder is asserted by Martin Allen. Kent had been involved in a complex scheme to lure to England the same British-born Nazi agent Ernst Wilhelm Bohle who had met with the Windsors in Germany; the purpose was to pretend to set up a negotiated peace, while capturing Bohle on a flight to Scotland. Bohle could be a fountain of information on Hitler's high-level tactics. Allen says that Kent had been chosen for the task because of his links to Nazis in the 1930s, particularly in Munich; he was allowed to work with the Duke of Buccleuch, recently dismissed from the royal household for his Nazi sympathies, because Buccleuch also had made connections in Germany.

As it turned out, Rudolf Hess flew famously to Scotland in Bohle's place; his flight and landing were put down, by both German and British government sources, as the random trip of a madman. The truth of his coming as a result of an invitation by Kent toward peace discussions had, Allen says, at all costs to be hidden from the world—and the Germans also wanted it hidden. Thus, if Kent was getting drunk and talking loosely, was it not possible that particularly in Iceland, where the American press had many representatives, and in Newfoundland, his next port of call, the biggest secret of World War II might leak and bring disgrace on the English government?

Whatever the truth, once Kent was dead, his chief German contact toward a negotiated peace in Hitler's favor was no longer of value to the führer, Prince Philipp of Hesse. His brother Wolfgang, his cousin Princess Viktoria Luise, her daughter now Queen Friederike of Greece, and all other royals who had been involved with Hitler were summarily dropped and in some cases punished. Behind Hitler's dissatisfaction with his former favorites, which rapidly turned to hatred, was the implacably antiroyal and petit bourgeois propaganda minister Dr. Joseph Goebbels, whose diaries of the time show the relentless process whereby he destroyed Philipp of Hesse and Hesse's wife, Princess Mafalda.

Philipp was certain, and not without reason, after the German defeat by the Russians at Stalingrad, that Hitler was a definite liability toward a knitting together of the royal families in the interest of anticommunism and the destruction of Russia. Only by a hasty replacement of Hitler by Himmler and Goering could Germany ally with England and create a new state, in which the German royals could flourish and Russia be defeated. With Kent dead, he was finished, as no doubt Sir Stewart Menzies and Winterbotham knew when they killed Kent. Hitler sent both Philipp and Mafalda (whom Goebbels accused of poisoning to death the collaborationist Czar Boris of Bulgaria) to concentration camps.

Ironically, Mafalda died in an Allied bombing raid; Philipp's imprisonment was significantly with the double agent and intelligence chief Admiral Canaris, who was hanged in a nearby cell and for years had been Menzies' and Winterbotham's contact in Berlin.

The news of his brother's death was a devastating shock to the duke. Scarcely able to believe his ears, he sobbed like a child when he heard it on the radio. He was in tears again at the memorial service on the twenty-ninth. He was so distraught that he even forgot to send a letter of sympathy to the Duchess of Kent, an oversight for which he was unfairly criticized. Wallis also failed to write.

Meanwhile, an extraordinary report in the Axel Wenner-Gren file of the State Department (RG 59/Box 2682K/1940–1944) had been made. The following statement (July 21, 1942) appeared:

Axel Wenner-Gren is supposed to have according to my information the following sums of money on deposit and now all frozen:

London	$50 millions.
Bahamas	$2,500,000.
United States	$32 millions.
Mexico	Two millions.
Norway	$32 millions.

It is understood that the deposits of $2,500,000 in the Bahamas were made at the express request and *in part for the benefit of* the Duke of Windsor . . . he is a very close friend of the Duke.

Subpoenaed accounts later confirmed the statement, proving the duke's aforementioned evasion of currency restrictions and his partnership in questionable business organizations.

Meantime, Churchill continued through the Foreign Office to be concerned with the upkeep of the Windsors' property in France. On August 11 a memorandum was sent from the American consulate in Nice to John G. Winant, American ambassador in London. Marked confidential, it reads, in part:

It will be recalled that the Foreign Office authorized payments sufficient for the upkeep of the property [La Croë] up to June 30, 1942. I am now informed by Mr. Antoine Carletti, the personal servant of the Duke, that the funds deposited to Mr. Herman Rogers' account with the Société Générale at Antibes for the upkeep of the Duke's property are now exhausted. He states that he will be able to manage until about September 15, and accordingly hopes that the money will arrive by that time.

Sometime back, Antoine called to report that he was becoming anxious to know what to do to protect the movable property belonging to His Royal Highness. He referred to eight cases of silver which he had packed up and hidden in his own villa situated nearby, which he recently rented. He had also packed up the china and glassware and is attempting to find a suitable place for the storage of the twenty cases involved. I informed Antoine that there was little this office could do to assist him. However, I expressed approval of the precautions he had taken, to allay his fears. Nevertheless, as he is very conscientious, he is very much concerned at the possible seizure of the silver in the event of occupation by enemy forces.

Antoine asked that His Royal Highness be informed that everything is in good order and that there have been no changes in the personnel.

In the midst of all this high-level finagling, the duchess was running the local Red Cross in temporary quarters, making charity arrangements for orphans.

The duke opened the Bahama Assembly on September 1. At a stormy meeting, members of the House demanded that Colonial Secretary Leslie Heape, Sir Eric Hallinan, Senior Commissioner for the Out Islands John Hughes, and Lieutenant Colonel Erskine-Lindop be summoned for immediate action for their disgraceful role in failing to quell the June riots. It was at this moment that, as so often before, the Windsors' guardian angel Sir Walter Monckton turned up from England. He stayed for several days, advising the Windsors to refuse to allow the House to gobble up the aforementioned officials in any form of kangaroo court. Instead, he said he had made arrangements for a British judge to appear to conduct the authorized Commission of Investigation. Sir Alison Russell, retired Tanganyika chief justice, turned up on October 1, and the commission convened on the fifth. The report was completed by the end of the month. Erskine-Lindop stood condemned on evidence for inadequate treatment of the rioters. However, Mr. Justice Russell also condemned the wholesale corruption of Bay Street for having brought about the riots in the first place. This still further pitched the Bay Street figures against the duke; in order to avoid a direct confrontation, he sent the report to London with very little comment.

At that time, Sir Stewart Menzies of the Secret Intelligence Service, tirelessly vigilant in his efforts to obtain still more damaging evidence on Wallis Windsor, sent Eddie Chapman, one of his most peripatetic agents, on a special mission from the Channel Islands to Germany to retrieve the duchess's files from the Abwehr, showing her continuing contacts with Ribbentrop until at least August 1940. Operating out of Jersey, which was under German occupation, Chapman, posing as a Nazi spy, had undertaken several similar missions for Menzies during the war; he succeeded in bringing not only the duchess's but the duke's Abwehr files back to London, along with Errol Flynn's—no doubt because of the Windsor-Hess-Flynn meeting at the Hôtel Meurice in Paris in March 1938.

On May 8, 1943, the Windsors undertook their third tour of the United States. The day they arrived at Robert R. Young's Palm Beach house, word reached them that the U.S. government had in 1942 deported the Reverend Jardine and his wife for outstaying their visas. Since there was some suspicion attached to them, the duke said he could do nothing; he let them be sent home. The Windsors traveled again to New York and saw the Ringling Brothers Circus.

They continued to Washington, where the duke took a drastic and revealing step. On the morning of May 18 he visited with Secretary of State Cordell Hull, not the most sympathetic person in the circumstances, and he asked Hull if he would be good enough to discontinue any future censorship of Wallis's letters. The request was made under great pressure from Wallis. The duke's own letters were uncensored because he had royal and diplomatic status. Unfortunately for him, the matter wound up on Adolf A. Berle's desk. In a memorandum dated June 18, 1943, addressed to all appropriate departments of the government, Berle wrote:

> I believe that the Duchess of Windsor should emphatically be denied exemption from censorship. Quite aside from the shadowy reports about the activities of this family, it is to be recalled that both the Duke and Duchess of Windsor were in contact with Mr. James Mooney of General Motors, who attempted to act as mediator of a negotiated peace in the early winter of 1940; that they have maintained correspondence with [Charles] Bedaux, now in prison under charges of trading with the enemy, and possibly of treasonous correspondence with the enemy; that they have been in constant contact with Axel Wenner-Gren, presently on our blacklist for suspicious activity, etc. The Duke of Windsor had been finding many excuses to attend to private business in the United States, which he is doing at present.

Permission for exemption from censorship was denied. Bedaux, whose desire to maintain his international businesses despite the interruption of war had put him in a position in which he was charged with treason, was in a jail in North Africa; he would be brought to Miami in 1944. His son, Charles Eugene Bedaux, insisted in 1986 that his father was innocent, saying he was deliberately fooling the Germans about supplying them with plans of pipelines in Africa in order to protect his Jewish friends in France. In support of his case, Bedaux Jr. stated that his father was, along with his companies, posthumously awarded the Légion d'Honneur and had a street named after him. Berle, J. Edgar Hoover, and General Sherman Miles of U.S. military intelligence took a less favorable view.

It is worth noting, too, that after the first wave of condemnation and revenge, the postwar de Gaulle government began reinstating certain figures of Vichy; de Gaulle attended the funeral of Marshal Pétain; and the Académie Française did not eject those of its members who had been of Fascist sympathy. By the 1960s, more had been forgiven, and former supporters of the Vichy regime were given certain awards and raised to high office after convenient periods of exile.

Winston Churchill was visiting Washington, and on May 19 he

delivered a characteristically resounding address to Congress. The duke had two meetings with Churchill, who had never relinquished his belief in his beloved prince. The duke begged Churchill for a new appointment. The prime minister contacted the Foreign Office, the Colonial Office, and the palace, and the result had more than a slight bit of black humor in it.

On June 12, 1943, the duke cabled Eden:

> Mr. [George] Allen has informed me that my fourteen boxes of documents have been removed from South of France to Switzerland. Will you please convey to the Swiss Government my gratitude and sincere appreciation of their action in removing my documents to their archives, and their continued interest in the security of my belongings at Cap d'Antibes.

On July 4, in an echo of the death of the Duke of Kent, the exiled and deposed premier of Poland Wladyslav Sikorski took off from Gibraltar on a secret mission in a Liberator flying boat with the Windsors' and Kent's close friend and Nazi associate, Victor Cazalet of the Anglo-German Fellowship and The Link, and, in identical circumstances, all aboard were killed in a crash arranged (he claimed) by Frederick Winterbotham through the use of sulfuric acid on the insulation lines.

Cazalet, who had acted as Churchill's special emissary in visits to the United States, and Sikorski himself had become security problems because they were playing a dangerous game against the Allies' Russian partners. As in the case of Kent, within an hour the German radio stations announced that Sikorski had been killed by the British Secret Intelligence Service; it is clear that someone very high-level in the SIS was a German-British-Soviet triple agent. Denials were issued very swiftly from Whitehall.

Shortly after the Windsors returned to Nassau, the newspapers announced that Win Spencer had been found bleeding on the porch of his house in San Diego, a knife protruding from his chest. He announced feebly that he had been "peeling fruit." Nobody believed him; it was probably a clumsy attempt at suicide. He survived.

16

Murder in Nassau

Despite the many conflicts arising with Bay Street, the Windsors remained friendly throughout the spring and summer of 1943 with Sir Harry Oakes and with his partners, Harold Christie and Walter Foskett and (in Mexico) Axel Wenner-Gren. They were also fond of Lady Oakes and gave a small farewell party for her when she left in June with her sons and daughter for Bar Harbor, Maine, to escape the Nassau summer heat.

However, the duke emphatically did not like (though the duchess had a soft spot for him) Alfred de Marigny, the husband of Nancy Oakes, a prosperous up-and-coming young businessman in the Nassau community. The brisk and fun-loving de Marigny, facing much criticism in a racist and anti-Semitic community, was involved in building apartments to which he admitted Jews. He even managed to persuade restricted local clubs to accept Jews as members, and he pushed, with a determination that many people found maddening, for an improvement of water supplies to the impoverished blacks during the many rain-free months outside the hurricane season.

Born in Mauritius, de Marigny was a tall, lanky, attractive man with a wide mouth that often curled into a mischievous, challenging, and crinkly smile. A charming but opinionated gadfly, possessed of immense vitality, he made the mistake in a tiny, tight community of talking far too loudly and far too often against the people he disliked. Most notably, the objects of his detestation were Oakes and Christie, but above all, he hated the Duke of Windsor.

That summer of 1943 de Marigny had become infuriated because water rights had been granted to the well-known travel writer Rosita Forbes, who had bought a large property on New Providence. As a result of this diversion of the supply, many poor blacks were threatened with thirst and perhaps disease from polluted springs. De Marigny stormed into Government House and demanded to speak to the duke, who listened with barely concealed impatience as he puffed away at a briar pipe. Vyvyan Drury stepped in and said coldly, "The audience is at an end." De Marigny shouted, "You may be impressed by His Royal Highness! He doesn't impress me! Here he is ruling this pimple on the ass of the British Empire! If he amounted to anything, he would be in high office in England or the United States!"

From that moment, de Marigny was a marked man.

At the same time, Sir Harry Oakes had found out that Christie had sold the land for a new RAF base behind his back to an American syndicate, thus cutting him out of the deal. In revenge, Oakes began to make preparations to call in Christie's IOU notes and repossess Christie's only fully owned asset, his beloved island of Lyford Cay. Christie realized that his world was falling apart. With the blacklisting of Wenner-Gren, Christie's partnership in the Banco Continental and in the Tesden Corporation and Bahamas General Trust was useless. Oakes was talking about going to the mainland to join his family, planning not to return until the fall, by which time Christie would be ruined.

What follows is based upon a fresh reexamination of the evidence of what would turn out to be one of the most famous unsolved murder cases of the century. Dr. Joseph Choi, chief of forensic medicine of the Los Angeles County Coroner's Office, the late John Ball, well-known author and special adviser to the LAPD Homicide Division, and Sergeant Louis Danoff of the LAPD, assisted the present author in reaching the conclusions presented here. This analysis of the case is based upon an inspection of the original autopsy reports obtained from the Bahamas, the evidence given under oath by the Nassau forensic specialists, the recently declassified FBI files, the photographs hitherto unavailable, and the judge's notes and subsequent murder trial transcript in his own handwriting obtained by the author in person from the

Bahamian archive in Nassau. No detail herein departs from the fully documented (and only now available) facts; the late Alfred de Marigny also contributed much valuable information and confirmed the guilt of the murderer, which he knew of from the beginning. But he differed from the present author in the matter of the murder weapon.

On the evening of July 7 Sir Harry Oakes entertained a small party of visitors at Westbourne, including Harold Christie; Mrs. Dulcibel ("Babs") Heneage; and Charles Hubbard, a retired Woolworth's executive. Dinner was prepared by the cook, Mrs. Fernandez, and served by the maid, Mabel Ellis, at 8:45 p.m. The guests finished eating shortly before ten. They played Chinese checkers until 11 p.m. Christie announced unexpectedly that he had decided to stay the night; a tropical storm was blowing up, and he did not feel like driving home. He had also stayed at Westbourne the previous night. At about 11:15 Hubbard drove Mrs. Heneage to her house, which was close by, on Eastern Road; Hubbard then drove back to his own house, just a few doors away from Westbourne.

Meanwhile, Christie had dismissed the two night watchmen, one of whom doubled at the country club next door, saying that he would take care of the house and grounds. The only people within both view and earshot of the house now were Mrs. Newell Kelly, wife of the property manager, who was on a fishing trip to a remote Out Island of the Bahamian group, and her mother, an elderly lady. They were housed in a small guest cottage in the grounds.

It was Oakes's custom to have no doors or windows fastened, bolted, or locked at any time, despite the fact that he was so nervous of possible intruders that he constantly changed his bedroom and he kept a gun, at all times, in the drawer of the bedside table, with his pound notes fixed in a Canadian gold money clip underneath the weapon. Like many of pioneer stock, Oakes seemed to invite the prospect of confronting a potential burglar or would-be murderer with a firearm; a very light sleeper, he would often rise several times in the night to prowl around, keeping his weapon ready. He liked having Christie for company, despite the fact that Christie was already plotting against him and that he had never forgiven Christie for going behind his back in the airfield deal. Lady Oakes and their children were still in the United States.

After Mabel Ellis left at 11:30 p.m., having washed up the dishes and laid the table for breakfast, the wind increased from the sea, sending black waves pounding against the beach below the house. Lightning began to flash in a murky sky. Thunder burst in enormous peals. Rain beat down with the intensity typical of the region. As the storm broke, Christie went up to visit with Oakes in the master bedroom where the Windsors had slept almost three years before. They talked for a while; at some stage during the conversation Christie almost certainly laced Oakes's nightcap with a drug that would be sufficiently powerful to give Oakes—a very light, nervous sleeper—a deep, not easily disturbed sleep. Christie watched. After a while Oakes began to show signs of drowsiness. Satisfied, Christie left the room. Sir Harry fell into a profound slumber with a feather pillow pressed for comfort against his body, an oddly childlike habit for a man of 69. Another pillow was tucked at an angle under his head, with a third tossed aside on the floor. The doomed millionaire tucked the *Miami Herald* for July 7, which he had been reading, under his right thigh as he turned over on his right side, his face buried in the pillow.

Christie had no time to waste. Leaving all the lights on to give Mrs. Kelly and her mother the impression, if they should waken and look out the guesthouse windows (they did), that he was still inside Westbourne, he went out through a back door and along a newly constructed connecting passage that led to the country club. He walked to the front of the club, looking to right and left to make sure he was not observed. His car was parked there, allegedly to save gasoline because of wartime rationing, but actually to enable him to drive off without the sound of his motor alerting Mrs. Kelly and her mother. He made his way through the storm into Nassau.

It is not certain where he contacted the hit man whom he had engaged to dispose of Oakes. However, it is most likely, in view of his subsequent movements, that he met him at his Bay Street office, where any such encounter would be safe from detection. It is possible to reconstruct the nature of the hired killer from accumulated indirect evidence. He was a very short but powerfully built spear fisherman, expert—as Christie was—in the art. He was a member of the Brujeria sect of south Florida, a practitioner of witchcraft and malevolent sorcery. The Brujeria sect emanated from the Congo region of Africa and practiced the diabolical cult of Palo Mayombe. The cult figured prominently in the Bahamas. An initiate who wished to be involved in murder was required to wear the dead man's clothes. Christie was wearing Sir Harry's pajamas before, during, and after the murder. In Palo Mayombe murder, the head must never be injured except for the precise purposes of the killing itself. It must not be burned, decapitated, or in any other way molested. Feathers, spears, and gunpowder were invariably used; the gunpowder was placed traditionally in small piles on the floor near the victim and set afire, causing tiny explosions that would make burns in the carpet and smoke smudges on the walls. Stab wounds to the head were intensely characteristic, because the figure of the diabolical Palo Mayombe god, Eleggua, was portrayed in drawings and paintings with swords or arrows embedded in its cranium. The use of a lanza or a fishing spear in such killings was common; it was a symbol of the interwoven Abaqua cult, also of south Florida and the islands, a symbol of that particular subsect which was committed to ritual assassination and which denied membership to homosexuals.

Palo Mayombe murderers were available for hire in the region. Christie, who had numerous connections in the underworld and who probably, if only for convenience, was an adherent of the cult (few who did not belong could obtain hit men for any price), must have imported the nameless killer from south Florida. It would have been too risky to engage the services of a local resident. In so crammed and closeted a society as Nassau, and with so much drinking common in the bars and shanties of Grants Town (the native district), word would have gotten around very quickly of such a person in the neighborhood.

In a station wagon borrowed for the purpose, the hit man, or an associate with the hit man as passenger, drove Christie through the driving rain and wind along Bay Street, preparing to head toward the beach. As the station wagon swung out around a corner, it was stopped by a traffic light. At that exact instant Edward Sears, chief of police of Nassau, passed it going in the opposite direction at a distance of six to eight feet and at 15 miles per hour. He saw Christie clearly through the side window of the passenger seat, but the visibility was not good enough to enable him to make out the driver's face or color.

The driver took Christie to a girlfriend's house, where he stayed for several hours. His stopovers at Oakes's two or three nights a week were mere disguises, in a community noted for gossip, for his nocturnal sojourns at that house. His girlfriend was married to a man in the forces.

Meantime, the black magician drove the station wagon around the back of Westbourne, near the country club, in order not to disturb

Mrs. Kelly and her mother in the guesthouse. He climbed the long wooden staircase that led up from the beach to the three levels of the house, his footsteps on the creaky wooden slats concealed by the sound of the storm. He was carrying with him a fishing spear, gunpowder, matches, and an insecticide spray can.

Sir Harry had not moved; overcome by the drug, he still had his face in the pillow with his body pressed against the second pillow. The hit man walked soundlessly across the thick brown carpet to the bed. He now stood almost exactly level with Oakes's head in its prone position. At extremely close range he hauled back and struck with the fishing spear exactly four times, with ritualistic precision; the apex of the triangular spearhead each time faced in the same direction toward the nose, and the wounds formed were almost exactly equidistant from one another. They made, according to Palo Mayombe tradition, a crescent pattern around and above the ear.

The cuts were at different depths, none deeper than an inch, and were insufficient to kill. The arteries and veins spurted in fountains, drenching the killer in blood. The murderer tried to wipe away the blood from his eyes. He took out his insecticide can and aimed the nozzle at Oakes's chest. Oakes stirred a fraction; at that moment the killer flung a match so that the petroleum-based flammable liquid caught fire. Then the hit man stabbed the second pillow against the body with his spear. He pulled handfuls of feathers from it and scattered them over the burning body in the time-worn practice of Palo Mayombe killers.

According to the autopsy report, Oakes died of shock combined with a fractured skull and the fierce heat of the flames. He probably never knew what had happened. At the moment of death, he evacuated so completely that the mattress was soaked through. The burning flesh and the heat made the feathers adhere to him, as the killer had wished. But the effort of committing the murder, and perhaps the effect of drink or drugs, temporarily affected the assailant. He staggered to the opposite wall of the room, leaving bloody, smoky marks of his fingers at his full height of just over four feet. He tried to wipe the blood from his face and body, using a towel Sir Harry had left on the second of the two twin beds. Then he flung the towel impatiently on Sir Harry's bed and began looking for the bathroom, groping through the smoke and still unsteady on his legs.

In doing so, he took a wrong turn and left more bloody marks on the walls of the corridor and even, ironically, on the glass handle of the door to Christie's room and on a panel of the door itself. He turned back, realizing he had made a mistake; at last he found a bathroom and began washing off the blood, leaving some specks on the basin. Meanwhile, Sir Harry's bed had burned only in small patches; though the corpse had collapsed under the blazing feathers and the force of the flames, the window burst open in the force of the storm and the mattress smoldered in its rain-dampened condition. In a reflex action, the dying man had swallowed some smoke, which, mixed with mucus, had formed a viscous black substance in the digestive tract that for some reason (they claimed) puzzled investigating physicians and police later on. He hadn't breathed the smoke in; his lungs were unblackened. His nose was too buried in the pillow to allow him to inhale.

The killer had more work to do. Remembering his ritualistic task, he began dropping small mounds of gunpowder on the floor of the murder room and the corridor outside, igniting them with his store of matches so that they burned and exploded but did not spread fire through the house. Had arson been his purpose, or an attempt to conceal the crime rather than give it an unmistakable signature, the killer would have brought a flame gun and used it on draperies, flammable chairs, woodwork, paintings, and hanging tapestries; none of these was touched. Sometimes, he sprayed small amounts of insecticide on the walls or floors, lighting them one by one; again, the fire did not spread. In one place he tried to set a small gunpowder charge on an inside windowsill and, significantly, another giveaway of his height, had to climb up on a chair to do so.

He left at last, again using the back door to escape any possible sighting by Mrs. Kelly or her mother. He drove the station wagon to pick up Christie and take him back into Nassau to collect Christie's car. Before dawn he was on his way back to the mainland; the storm had blown out, and the sea was navigable by motor launch.

Christie returned to Westbourne. As he walked through the hall, he found the numerous small burnt patches where the powder or flammable liquid had made holes in the carpet or smoke smudges on the walls. He went upstairs. Oakes was still in the position in which the murderer had left him; theoretically, all Christie now had to do was call the police. But he couldn't reveal he had been absent from the house.

He had planted the idea that he would be staying there when he spoke to the other guests at the party the night before; moreover, he had to protect his girlfriend, who could be ruined by gossip and might turn against him. He must turn the body over and go through a pretense of trying to revive Sir Harry, deliberately leaving his fingerprints on the thermos flask and the glass by the bed. He would say that he had tried to make Sir Harry drink the water and that in order to do so he had raised his head. He overlooked the fact that rigor mortis had long since set in, given Oakes's weight and the temperature of just over 75 degrees, and that in order to raise the head he would have had to break the neck. The jaws would have been clenched, even without the teeth, which still lay in a second glass on the bedside table. No one on earth could have managed to force a glass of water between the dead man's lips.

Christie dared not wait until the maid, Mrs. Ellis, appeared at her usual time between 7:00 and 7:30 a.m. He shouted from the veranda to waken Mrs. Kelly and her mother; sleeping, they did not respond, so he called them on the telephone in Sir Harry's room. Mrs. Kelly came to Westbourne immediately. Next, Christie telephoned Government House; he reached Gray Phillips, who wakened the Windsors with the news. The duke cannot have doubted for a moment that given Christie's description this was a black crime, with sinister overtones. The riots were fresh in his memory, and the fire, the feathers, the wound or wounds to the head clearly spelled ritual murder. If this indeed were the case, then any arrest or punishment would lead to further bloodshed and desperate danger for him and for Wallis and for every other white person in the Bahamas. It cannot be doubted that the duke was in an agony of indecision. Unquestionably, Wallis shared that agony. In desperation, to give himself time to think, the duke absurdly told Gray Phillips to put an embargo, a total censorship, on all news of the case. Phillips was to call Sir Etienne Dupuch, publisher of the *Nassau Tribune*, at home to tell him to suppress the story; he was to contact the local radio station and say that on no account was it to beam the news out on the morning broadcast.

But Phillips was too late. Christie, playing to the full his role of frantic and bereaved friend, had already called Dupuch, who, scenting the story of the century, rushed an immediate announcement onto the wire services. Dupuch also advised the local radio station. Meantime, Christie called Erskine-Lindop, who arrived twenty minutes later, summoned by his wife from the police headquarters, where he had gone on an early morning call. At 7:30 Mrs. Kelly telephoned Dr. H. A. Quackenbush, a rather curious choice since Quackenbush was an autopsy surgeon normally called in only by the police. Oakes's own physician was never summoned, nor was his mainland doctor flown in. Two minutes after 7:30 Christie called Charles Hubbard, who in turn called Mrs. Heneage. Christie dared not risk a direct call to her because the wires of Westbourne were tapped by the U.S. State Department. At 7:40 Erskine-Lindop, now at Westbourne, summoned his associate Charles Pemberton. Five minutes after that, Mrs. Ellis reported for work an unusual thirty minutes late. Meanwhile, urgent messages were sent to the Out Islands to find Mrs. Kelly's husband on his fishing trip.

By 8 a.m. the murder room was filled with people milling about the corpse and discussing the mysterious crime. This was totally against all possible regulations. Erskine-Lindop and Pemberton should immediately have sealed the room and ordered everyone out. By having all and sundry move around the room touching everything, there would be so complete a puzzle of fingerprints that nobody would ever be able to make out the nature of the intruder. Dr. Quackenbush did not examine the head fully, despite his twenty years of experience as an autopsy physician. He announced to all concerned, including Sir Eric Hallinan, the attorney general, who arrived at 10 a.m., that there was only one wound, and he put his finger into it. He concluded that the death must be "suicide disguised as murder." The other three wounds were obscured by blood. It was not until his abler associate Dr. FitzMaurice arrived at Hallinan's behest at 11:30 that it was determined through swabbing that there were in fact four wounds.

Neither Quackenbush nor FitzMaurice was able, it seemed, to determine that the wounds were caused by a sharp, triangular instrument, either an arrow or a fishing spear. Yet both talked from that moment on about "blunt instruments" and bludgeons. No blunt instrument or bludgeon existed with that shape head. Christie, then and later, repeated his story that he had tried to waken Sir Harry, had lifted his head and forced water between his lips. Nobody questioned his statement, despite the accepted effects of rigor mortis.

At 10:30 a.m. after much tortuous indecision and many conferences with Wallis, Erskine-Lindop, Pemberton, Christie, and everybody else available, the duke called the Miami Police Department. It is clear that he dared not call Scotland Yard or the FBI because too much would have been disclosed by the expert investigative methods of either one. Neither would have hesitated to reveal that this was a black crime, a disaster for island unity. The duke had already established an association with Captain Edward W. Melchen, chief of the Miami Homicide Department, who had accompanied him on some of his more questionable journeys in Florida, in particular to meet Walter Foskett at Palm Beach. He could trust Melchen; moreover, Melchen had a long record of criminal associations, and for that reason J. Edgar Hoover had him on his suspect list for years. The duke's phone call was intercepted by the Foreign Activities Correlation branch of the State Department under Adolf A. Berle; the intercept file, declassified for the present author in 1986, still exists. The duke did not, as every historian has said he did, speak to Melchen of "suicide disguised as murder"; rather, he spoke of a crime of "a most extraordinary character," without specifying either victim or method of murder. Melchen must come at once, and he was "not in any circumstances to obtain a passport." The Pan American Airways noon flight from Miami would be held for Melchen and one or two of his men; the duke would arrange it.* Melchen applied to the State Department for immediate passport-free clearance despite the duke's instruction; he was aware that not to do so could cost him his badge. He brought with him Captain James O. Barker, supervisor of the Miami Police Laboratory and his number one fingerprint expert. According to the declassified FBI file on the Oakes case, J. Edgar Hoover was convinced that Barker also had strong contacts with criminals and confidence men in south Florida.

The two detectives clearly knew that a cover-up would be involved, since they deliberately left behind the fingerprint identification camera that was mandatory in every examination of the circumstances of a violent crime. They later used the lying excuse that the duke had told them on the telephone that this was a suicide case. Even when they arrived, met at the airport by Erskine-Lindop and Pemberton, they failed to pick up the perfectly usable fingerprint camera maintained by the Nassau police, and apparently neither Erskine-Lindop nor Pemberton offered it to them, nor did they fly in their own cam-

---

*He knew Juan Trippe, chairman of Pan Am.

era from Miami on the next plane. The danger of using such a camera was that, by mandate, they would have to photograph every object in the murder room; therefore, it would be impossible for them to plant any fingerprints there once the photographic coverage was completed.

Contrary to every published report, Erskine-Lindop and Pemberton were not instructed by the duke or anyone else to place Melchen and Barker in exclusive charge of the case. First, in a British colony, such a situation would be out of the question. Second, it was necessary for everyone concerned to hold together in this difficult predicament. However, there is no evidence that either Erskine-Lindop or Pemberton was privy to the conspiracy that followed.

It was decided by all concerned that the killer, whoever he was, must have signs of singes or burns. This was an entirely arbitrary decision since the killer could easily have used a fire helmet, a mask, and asbestos-lined gloves. Indeed, anyone not committing a ritual murder would have obtained such protections. Naturally, Christie came through the examination of his body hairs with his reputation unscathed. None of the rest of the staff, including the black stableman, was asked to submit to the examination. By now, everyone had decided on who it was that would be declared a suspect. Inevitably, it was Alfred de Marigny. He was the perfect fall guy: he had irritated almost every major figure of Bay Street; he was known to have had violent quarrels with Oakes; he hated Oakes as much as Oakes hated him; and he had an irritating gadfly presence most people would be happy to see rubbed out. Most important, he would take the heat off the black issue that was threatening to plunge Nassau into bloody violence. A white man as the accused would be perfect in every way.

Yet there wasn't a shred of evidence on which to arrest him. He stood to inherit nothing if Oakes died; Nancy, his wife, had herself been cut out of the will. He had no record of crime; he wasn't the type to stab and burn an old man in his bed, no matter what people thought of him; and he had a perfect alibi. He himself had given a party on the night of the murder. And his closest friend, Georges de Visdelou, had been with him at the time the murder was committed.

Yet de Marigny was arrested, on the pretext that some hairs on his forearms were lightly singed; he had been putting a match to a hurricane lamp at the house during the party, and the lamp had flared up. He was charged and placed in the Nassau prison. Bail was not granted.

In the meantime, the duke visited the murder room. Barker announced that he had found a fingerprint of de Marigny on the Chinese screen. He had chosen to overlook the fact that the screen had been removed from the room when de Marigny was brought to it and was encouraged to pick up a glass, leaving the print that was later and most improperly transferred.

At the preliminary magistrate's hearing in the first week of August, the ritual of folly was repeated: Christie's lying statements, Quackenbush's inadequate summation of the forensic evidence, and the ineptitude of the successive police reports. Not a soul tried to look through hardware or sporting goods stores to match the size and shape of the weapon head; nobody came forward to contradict the blunt-instrument story; there wasn't an inkling in the press either in Nassau or overseas (the story made headline news even in the middle of the war) to draw attention to the sinister and magical elements of the murder. At the preliminary hearing Melchen, rapidly embroidering his fake story, insisted without producing a shred of evidence that Oakes, after being struck the first blows, had staggered into the hall (*sic*), his clothes aflame, before being dragged back to his bed and finished off. No one exposed this lie for what it was; even the most amateurish student of medicine would have seen that Oakes died without moving.

The Windsors took off to the mainland for a tour that included a visit to Aunt Bessie, who had broken her hip and was lying in a hospital in Boston. They left de Marigny to his fate; Erskine-Lindop, who was clearly disturbed by the nature of what he was involved in, was transferred to Trinidad as he had wanted to be since the riots. The fingerprints were taken to New York for analysis in a laboratory; by a curious irony, just as the trial began on October 17, 1943, the Windsors turned up at the FBI headquarters in Washington and were given a conducted tour by a grimly humorous J. Edgar Hoover of the very fingerprint laboratories whose expertise they had so skillfully avoided using. The duchess was feeling ill, perhaps because of strain over the case, and the duke proceeded alone to the Quantico base where marines were being trained. While de Marigny fought for his life, the duke inspected the honor guard, the shower facilities, the dormitories, the gun vaults, and the rifle ranges.

The trial, which the Windsors followed closely, was a sinister farce from beginning to end. De Marigny's able counsel, Godfrey Higgs,

K.C., exposed Christie as an outright liar on the stand. Again and again Higgs pressed him on the matter of his pretending that he thought Sir Harry was alive; thrusting a picture of the dead man in front of Christie, the figure burned away and covered in feathers, the face streaked with blood, Higgs asked him if anyone could think that such a devastated corpse could possibly have any life in it. He attacked Christie on the issue of his sleeping through fire, blood, and storm; Christie screamed at him in anger, yet never cracked, holding firmly to the exact letter of his evidence at the preliminary hearing. Disgracefully, Christie's girlfriend was never called on the matter of his whereabouts. Higgs made one major mistake: he did not summon to the witness stand an independent pathologist to testify to the effects of rigor mortis, testimony which have shattered Christie's credibility at a blow. Higgs did effectively destroy Barker; he showed him up to be a liar and revealed to everyone in court that Barker had planted de Marigny's fingerprint. He as good as stated that the duke was an accessory to the planting. The following exchange took place:

HIGGS: Did not His Royal Highness visit you at Westbourne and come to Sir Harry's room at the time you were processing for fingerprints?

BARKER: Yes, he came up to see the crime scene.

HIGGS: I do not think it would be proper for me to inquire as to why he came or to what was said.

De Marigny was saved by the fingerprint evidence. However, three jurymen held out against nine. In Great Britain the result would have been a hung jury; in the United States, a mistrial. But in the Bahamas a nine-to-three verdict was sufficient. De Marigny was acquitted. In the tremendous hubbub that filled the courtroom, few people heard the jury foreman's addendum: the absence of Erskine-Lindop from the trial was deplored, and it was recommended that de Marigny and his friend Georges de Visdelou Guimbeau should be deported at once. Such a recommendation was unprecedented in law and was totally unsupported by any existing statute. However, the duke acted upon it immediately. Having returned to Nassau, he besieged the Colonial Office in London and the authorities in Washington to make sure that the deportation suggestion was implemented. Meanwhile, Harold Christie returned to his normal role on the Executive Council.

After several attempts to find de Marigny a new domicile, the duke packed him off to Cuba. The duke's drastic impatience is conveyed in a telegram dated November 25, 1943. Addressed to the secretary of state for the colonies, it reads as follows:

Immediate confidential.

De Marigny and Guimbeau. I will telegraph the Governor of Mauritius. . . . De Marigny has made inquiries as to the chances of his getting [to Haiti], but must point out that, unless the government has the means to transport him compulsorily, de Marigny may remain in this Colony, as the only inducement for him to leave of his own volition is the threat that he may be sent to Mauritius. I, therefore, very greatly regret your decision that transport by Royal Air Force cannot be justified, and I very strongly urge that Air Marshal Bowhill be given an opportunity to consider my request, and that copies of all telegrams which have passed between us be sent to him for consideration. I am sure that you will meet me thus far. Although I would be loath to worry the Prime Minister at this time, I feel so strongly on this question that I would not hesitate, as a last resort, to approach him direct, because I am convinced that unless the Bahamas Government is armed with the power to move both deportees, the British Colonial Administration will be subject to derision in the United States, and the relations of the Government with the local people strained to a breaking point.

De Marigny recalls that within a few weeks more than one attempt was made on his life; on one occasion a series of shots was fired into his bed. He charges that the duke was accessory to this attempted murder. It is impossible to corroborate this charge.

De Visdelou Guimbeau went to Haiti, securing a permit to enter Great Britain. De Marigny led a vagabond life for years, threatened, pursued, repeatedly refused documents because of ducal influence, repeatedly denied the right to emigrate anywhere. He was convinced that the duke was responsible for his appalling plight. He went to Canada, and thence to South America, on a seemingly endless journey until, at last, with the duke's death, he seemed to find relief in exile. He and Nancy divorced and he married the daughter of one of Roosevelt's trusted aides and found much happiness with her and in raising a family.

Over the years Christie was repeatedly asked why he was absent from Westbourne on the night of the crime; nobody believed he could have slept there and not heard the murder. He always held to the story that he was trying to protect his girlfriend's reputation, an odd way of protecting her since, as a result of his false alibi, she spent the rest of her life under a cloud of gossip.

There was a theory, propounded in three books on the case, that Oakes was killed by the Mafia, that Meyer Lansky ordered the crime from his headquarters in Key West. The motive was supposed to have been that Oakes was refusing to allow the mob to run a gambling concession in Nassau. But, in fact, Oakes had no power to make that decision, and no Mafia crime has ever been committed in the manner in which Oakes was disposed of. The same authors suggested that Oakes was killed somewhere else, probably with a winch lever on his boat or at the dock, and carried back to the house, placed on the bed, and then set afire. Yet these theorists overlook some important details. No man leaves his home without his false teeth; trial testimony showed they never left the glass by his bed. Moreover, if he had been struck with a winch lever, the nails would have gone in at the same depth; the nails of a winch lever do not match either the size or shape of the implement used on Oakes. Furthermore, if he had been hit while standing or sitting, as was suggested, the blood would have flowed down vertically on his cheeks, instead of horizontally from left to right as in fact was the case.

The great unsolved murder case refused to die. On June 26, 1944, Raymond Schindler, a famous private eye of the era whom Nancy Oakes had brought in on the case, asked the duke to reopen it. The request was refused. Schindler responded by exposing some new evidence unearthed in Nassau establishing black magic elements in the case.* His reputable associate Leonard Keeler, inventor of the lie detector, and Homer S. Cummings, distinguished former U.S. attorney general, also appealed to the duke, but both were refused. They were told in a memorandum that "the matter is closed."

On April 18, 1946, de Marigny called for a new investigation, claiming that Oakes died by a bullet wound. By then the duke had left the Bahamas; there was no response to de Marigny's request. Then something startling happened. On September 16, 1950, Edward Majava, a

---

*Though he believed the black magician killed Oakes because Oakes was having an affair with the magician's wife.

New York City stevedore on vacation in California, got drunk in a bar in Berkeley and said that he knew the killer's name. It had been given to him by Mrs. Hildegarde Hamilton, society portrait painter of Fort Lauderdale, who had heard the story on the local grapevine and perhaps had been told it by friends of Walter Foskett.

It seemed a highly dubious lead, but the Berkeley police decided to take action. They contacted Augustus Robinson, Nassau police chief, who was rushed to Berkeley to interrogate Majava. Majava told him (declassified FBI files revealed) that the killer was Harold Christie. Robinson confirmed that Majava was correct. However, Robinson did not explain how he had obtained this information, or why he had failed to act on it by charging Christie with murder. The press never printed Christie's name; it revealed only that Robinson had confirmed the guilt of the person Majava had named. According to FBI rules, if the bureau was not involved in a case, it would not deal with the case in the future, so the FBI chose to do nothing. Scotland Yard remained silent; royalty was involved.

Five days later, a young woman in Toronto reported to the FBI (which has not declassified her name) that Christie had hired a killer; that Christie was a secret mulatto, son of a white father and a black mother; and that he had acted in concert with a still more powerful figure. In a declassified FBI report that figure was named as Walter Foskett.

In the late 1950s Cyril St. John Stevenson, a prominent figure of the Bahamian government, directly charged Harold Christie in the Assembly with the murder. Christie did not reply. The press still refused to name Christie; Stevenson applied to Scotland Yard to begin a full-scale inquiry, which the upper and lower houses of the Bahamian Assembly uniformly voted for. Christie himself, to avoid risk of exposure, had to vote along with the rest. Scotland Yard refused to act, and the file was closed. Christie became immensely rich after the war; he was knighted by Queen Elizabeth II for his services to the islands. He died of a heart attack in 1973, in Munich, peacefully in his bed.

The Oakes case remains closed. At a party in a house in the south of France in the 1960s, Lord Beaverbrook asked Christie, "Harold, now that you're free and clear, why not tell us all how you did it?" Christie only smiled.

He spent the rest of his life seeking to convince anyone who would listen that the crime was committed by a voodoo priest out of jealousy—as Schindler had opined. Many still believe him in 2004.

A final question remains. Were the duke and duchess accessories after the fact? There is no proof that they were. But there is circumstantial evidence that the duke knew this was a black crime and that therefore his treatment of de Marigny remains a mark against him forever. And it is impossible to believe that he did not share this guilt with Wallis, Duchess of Windsor.

17

Return to Europe

In the wake of this horrific event, Christmas came; while de Marigny, his marriage shattered, languished in Cuba, Wallis worked very hard to cast off the shadow of the murder and supervise special dinners for 1,000 enlisted men. Despite the fact that she was unregenerately convinced there should never have been a war, Wallis tried to make the best of a bad job and flung herself with all her customary energy into the Red Cross work, the infant welfare clinics, and the Nassau canteen. From Pearl Harbor on, she had been tireless in her efforts to improve conditions in the islands, and so had the duke, except for his mysterious blind spot over the water supply issue. It was one of the many paradoxes of their personalities that the Windsors still retained the fascination with the question of social reform that had helped propel them so disastrously into Hitler's camp.

However, in one of his local concerns, the duke was not entirely liberal and altruistic. He still had a consuming interest in developing the Out Islands, and in this he was more than ever secretly hand in glove with his friend's murderer Harold Christie. Christie, still overextended, was concerned that his landholdings in the Out Islands would simply remain just that—meaningless holdings. Because of the war scare, and now the lack of money available to make something of the distant Cays, he feared his land would have no future. By pressing constantly in the upper and lower houses in Nassau for the Out Islands development scheme, the duke clearly hoped to profit from rake-offs from Christie. In consistently blocking the duke in the matter, at least until the middle of 1943, the Assembly was bearing in mind the nefarious involvement of its own member, Christie, in get-rich-quick real estate schemes. To the duke, stubborn as ever, the colonial government was being stupid, obstructive, and pigheaded.

There were symbolic changes in the administration at the outset of 1944. Sir Eric Hallinan, worn out by the stress of the riot and the murder trial, followed Erskine-Lindop to Trinidad, where no doubt those embattled gentlemen had a great deal to discuss. Colonial Secretary Leslie Heape applied for a transfer and was granted the depressing post of acting governor of British Guyana. He accepted it immediately.

In the early months of the new year, Wallis received a series of shocks. At Verona, Italy, on January 11, 1944, Count Galeazzo Ciano, her long-lost lover of China days, went to the firing squad on the instructions of his father-in-law, Mussolini, who accused him of treason. Ciano died bravely, refusing a blindfold and asking that he be permitted to look directly at his executioners as they fired. The first round of shots failed to kill him. The chair in which he was bound toppled over and he lay on the floor, groaning. Even when the commander of the firing squad shot him in the temple with a revolver, the stubborn young man did not die. It was only with a second shot that life was terminated. How Wallis responded to the news is unknown. It takes no great feat of the imagination to envisage the torment she must have felt and the flood of memories that must have poured into her brain. Soon, the Windsors' dear friend Pierre Laval would be dragged, half-sensible from terror, after an abortive suicide attempt, before another firing squad for betraying France.

There was another echo of the past when the newspapers announced that Alberto da Zara, Wallis's other China flame, who was now admiral of the Italian fleet, had handed his ships over to the Allies at Malta.

Charles Bedaux, who had been arrested and imprisoned in North Africa on suspicion of treason against the United States and had been brought to Miami for incarceration in a detention home, died by his own hand. He had managed to hoard a supply of sleeping pills, probably in his rectum, a practice later adopted by Field Marshal Goering.

On February 10 he retired to bed and swallowed all the pills. Max Lerner and I. F. Stone disclosed in the newspaper *P.M.* and in *The Nation* that they were convinced Bedaux was encouraged to take the easy way out. Had he stood trial, he might have exposed a whole network of internationalist American businessmen (and a royal duke) who traded on both sides of the war.* Again, no record exists of Wallis's reaction to this second and shattering piece of news. She could not communicate with Fern Bedaux, her beloved hostess of the days of Château de Candé, Madame Laval, Edda Mussolini Ciano, or the Lavals' daughter Renee, because all the mail was still censored and even the telephone, as we know, was monitored by the State Department Foreign Activities Correlation staff.

On March 10 a flash fire mysteriously swept through the top floor of a luxury hotel in Richmond, Virginia; among those who were burned to death was Wallis's friend and lawyer from Warrenton days, Aubrey "Kingfish" Weaver. This news must have been a shock to Wallis; she always felt that Weaver had waved a magic wand over the judge who had granted her divorce from Spencer.

She was driven almost beyond endurance by stress during the spring of 1944. In her exasperation, her increasing irritation with everyone and everything in Nassau, she even let her racism slip into a letter to Aunt Bessie ("Government House with only a colored staff would put me in my grave!"). She increased the white staff. Later, she wrote, not for the first time, that she and the duke had been "dumped here solely by family jealousy!"—a refrain Aunt Bessie was scarcely unaccustomed to. In another missive she wailed about "being a prisoner of war or worse"—and there she was closer to the mark. She told Rosita Forbes, "They [*sic*] only murdered Sir Harry Oakes once. They will *never* stop murdering the Duke of Windsor."

The duke tried one last desperate ploy to improve his embarrassingly pathetic position. He urged Whitehall to approve his becoming viceroy of a new Caribbean federation over which he would preside. The Germans had again announced in their propaganda broadcasts that he was to be viceroy of an America that lay conquered by Ger-

---

*According to Charles Bedaux, Jr., his father suicided to protect his wife and family in France; if he used as a defense that he had aided Jews in his companies, his kindred would have been punished.

many and Japan. He applied for this position through friends in London. His lawyer, George Allen, and his long-term economic adviser, Professor Henry Richardson, ran into a brick wall. Even the reliable Sir Walter Monckton proved unhelpful. The duke had the nerve to take the matter to Buckingham Palace. Sir Alexander Hardinge had resigned his post the previous year because of ill health, and perhaps Windsor hoped that Hardinge's successor, the now knighted Sir Alan Lascelles, would take a more favorable view of him. This seems incredible. Hardinge had thoroughly briefed Sir Alan in the matter of the Secret Intelligence Service files on the Windsors. Like Hardinge, Lascelles was trained in cyphers and had been privy, like Sir John Balfour, to all the intricate maneuverings of the Windsors on the international Fascist scene. Moreover, Lascelles had never liked the duke from the time he had known him in World War I, and surely the duke, self-centered though he was, must have known this. Sir Alan was devoted to King George VI and Queen Elizabeth and shared their horror of Wallis. Nothing came of the application, and the federation concept was never acted upon.

That summer the Allied forces reoccupied Paris. There was word of both Windsor properties in France: the Foreign Office files were abrim with intercepted telegrams and secret reports. Although all of these have conveniently disappeared, due to an oversight the Foreign Office printed a synopsis of what was going on in its published indexes that were unwisely issued in 1972. The furniture still remained stored at Maples in Nazi-occupied Paris, protected by special arrangements with the Berlin authorities. More was at Antibes and Grenoble; still more remained at the Hotel Majestic and the Maison Camerlo at Cannes. Other effects were hidden in the fastnesses of the Alpes Maritimes. Some objects were stored at the town of Tarn, others—with audacious disregard for the rules of war—in Italy. The strong room at the Banque de France was still being paid for on Churchill's orders, at this time through Switzerland. The Germans had of course hardly touched Boulevard Suchet. Otto Abetz had planted soldiers at the gate to make sure nothing was disturbed. Even if the Windsors were not on Hitler's special list of favorites, the house would have been preserved because it had an Italian owner, the Countess Sabini, at least until Italy made a negotiated peace with Britain and the United States in 1943.

As for La Croë, it was also scarcely disturbed. Even when the

Germans occupied all of France, the château remained carefully kept up, its lawns leading to the sea laced with land mines to protect it still further. According to Foreign Office indexes, the Germans had paid rent on the property throughout the latter part of the war, when it was no longer possible for America to filter through funds to Sir Pomeroy Burton. The Swiss had paid out of British funds for the Suchet rental.

Sailings to Europe were prohibited at the time, so the Windsors had to remain in a state of frustration, unable even to take a vacation to inspect their property. And perhaps it was just as well that they couldn't go, because two of Wallis's intimate friends and sometime designers, Gabrielle "Coco" Chanel and Elsa Schiaparelli, came under suspicion of espionage. Schiaparelli was able to scrape through because her many powerful friends in high places used their influence on her behalf. But Chanel had actually spied for the enemy, and Walter Schellenberg had been her employer. In a British intelligence secret report, declassified in 1985, she stands revealed as an organizer of a negotiated peace plan in April 1944. The report reads, in part:

> [I was] told of the existence of a certain Frau Chanel, a French subject and proprietress of the noted perfumery factory. This woman was referred to me as a person who knew Churchill sufficiently to undertake political negotiations with him as an enemy of Russia and as desirous of helping France and Germany, whose destinies she believed to be closely linked together.

The report continued in the following vein. Chanel had been brought to Berlin, where Schellenberg briefed her as a direct agent of foreign intelligence, the SD; a friend of hers, a Signora Lombardi, was released from internment in Italy to go to Madrid to lay the groundwork for Chanel with Sir Samuel Hoare. She would bring with her a letter from Chanel urging Hoare to contact Churchill. But no sooner was Signora Lombardi in Madrid than she reported that Chanel was a Nazi agent. Chanel was charged with treason against the French state and arrested as soon as she arrived in Paris. She was held by the American authorities for twenty-four hours. Then, with amazing swiftness, she was released. It seems that she had several aces up her sleeve. Had she been forced to stand trial with threat of execution as an employee of an enemy government, she could easily have exposed as Nazi collaborators the Windsors, and dozens of others highly placed in society.

Despite the hatred of the Windsors at Buckingham Palace, the royal family would not willingly tolerate an exposé of a family member.

In August 1944, Wallis and the duke stayed once more with their great friend Robert Young, both at Palm Beach and at Newport. Wallis was stricken with stomach pains; on this occasion they were not symptoms of perforated ulcers but of cancer. She checked into a ten-room suite with six full-time nurses at Roosevelt Hospital in New York City, where she was attended by Dr. Henry W. Cave and by Dr. Lay Martin of Baltimore.

She went through a successful operation with her usual resolution and strength and left the hospital on September 11; as she walked shakily down the steps to her car, she was met by a carefully organized group of cheering children from a nearby high school. The Windsors stayed at their favorite Waldorf Towers for several weeks. The duke was still bombarding London with requests for another job. Finally, and with negligible chance of success, he asked to be engaged in intelligence work, presumably against the Russians; the application only suggested to his enemies at court that he couldn't have applied for such work unless he knew something about it.

The duke and duchess returned to the Bahamas in a depressed mood that fall. They were disappointed when, after many attempts at drilling, it was proved that there was no oil at the ranch in Alberta. There was a small consolation prize in January 1945 when, at long last, the Bahamian government approved the sum of £77,000 for developing the Out Islands, an investment which finally paid off and incidentally paved the way for Harold Christie's financial future and his ultimate knighthood. After many threats the duke finally resigned his post on March 15, 1945, and handed over his seals of office to the mild-mannered William L. Murphy, colonial secretary and frequent acting governor of Bermuda. The duke's brother King George personally signed the papers authorizing the resignation some months before the actual appointment term would normally expire.

The duke stayed on for a few weeks to tie up any loose ends. On April 5 he met with both houses of the legislature to sign bills passed during the previous session.

President Roosevelt died that month. The Windsors sent conventional condolences, but in letters given to this author by Kenneth de Courcy, the duke deplored Roosevelt and blamed him for what the duke called his intervention in World War II. He spoke with contempt of the great man whose statue would later stand in Grosvenor Square. As Frank Giles, his former aide in 1940, reported in his memoirs, the duke complained that World War II could have been avoided had it not been for "Roosevelt and the Jews."

On August 4, 1945, John Balfour, who was now acting chargé d'affaires in Washington, made arrangements for the duke (Wallis was ailing) to meet President Truman at the White House. Balfour, like Sir Alan Lascelles, was still in the anti-Windsor camp in London and had been privy to all the many encoded documents relating to the couple. He liaised with Adolf A. Berle (before the latter's resignation that year) in keeping a constant watch on the couple.

It was a dramatic moment for the duke's encounter with the president. Truman had issued an ultimatum to the Japanese calling for unconditional surrender. That morning the Japanese government replied through Switzerland that it would not accede to the request. When the duke and Balfour walked into the Oval Office, Truman told them the news. He said, in a voice dark with foreboding, "I now have no alternative but to drop the atomic bomb on Japan."

In the next few days, at the Balfours' house, the news came through that Hiroshima and Nagasaki had been destroyed and that Japan had given in. The duke tried to call Wallis at the Waldorf Towers in New York, but the circuits were busy and he couldn't make the connection. He took a hot bath, trying to relax and gather his thoughts together. As he lay in the water, the Balfours' Irish maid burst into the bathroom and, without turning a hair, shouted at the top of her voice, "Get out of the water at once! Yer wife wants to speak to yer on the telephone!"

Two nights later Robert and Anita Young came to dinner with Wallis and the duke. Balfour's purpose in having the duke stay with him was to keep an eye on him. The Youngs showed their true colors that evening. Balfour wrote in his memoirs, "They all seem to be oblivious of Nazi misdeeds and seem to feel that if Hitler had been differently handled war might have been avoided."

It was in that period that Young, always weaving in and out of the Windsors' lives, assumed a temporary predominance. Let us pause for a moment in the narrative to consider this remarkable individual. From 1937 he had been in virtual control of Alleghany. This had been Wallis's first investment favorite; her Warfield uncles had managed to secure her some of the preferred stock issued in a storm of controversy by the banker J. P. Morgan, who was chief investor for King George VI and Queen Elizabeth at the time they were Duke and Duchess of York. Aleghany stock was among the few to survive the Wall Street crash. Young had risen higher and higher, keeping Wall Street in a constant state of turmoil as he fought the investment banks and Capitol Hill to plunge forward with his wild and reckless schemes for a multibillion-dollar railroad empire that would link the nation coast to coast without a need for changing trains. His particular obsession was Chicago, where travelers had to stop, often for a whole night, before proceeding to the West of East Coast. But despite every effort he was unable to cut through red tape and vigorous opposition by rival railroad tycoons; the change of trains continues in 2004.

The Windsors were intoxicated by Young. In particular, the duke, who clung to the past of his youth, longed to see the railroads combat what would undoubtedly be the postwar rise of commercial domestic airlines; because of her only partly conquered fear of flying, as well as her love of trains, Wallis also found Young a crusader and a hero. The Windsors decided to invest substantial sums in Young.

That same August the embattled couple ran into further trouble. At his trial for treason in France, Pierre Laval testified of his dangerous political association with the duke. He mentioned their secret meeting in Paris to discuss the handing over of Ethiopia to Mussolini and to secure the permanence of Fascist alliances. The duke responded to this sworn statement with fury. When an alert *New York Times* called him for comment, he lied, saying that although he had met Laval at "a social function at the British Embassy in Paris in 1935," it was "untrue that any conversation on political matters took place between us." Quite apart from the fact that British government documents, published after the war, contained an apparently doctored but revealing paragraph, disclosing the very text of the political conversation at that luncheon presided over by Ambassador Sir George Clerk, Laval's son-in-law, the indispensable Comte René de Chambrun, emphatically stated that the Mussolini plan was laid down at the subsequent secret meeting.

That month, a very curious and since much-discussed mission was instigated at Buckingham Palace. Owen Morshead, archivist of Windsor Castle, that formidable catchall for every document likely to be even marginally threatening to the British royal family, was dispatched to

Friedrichshof, the traditional home of the Hesse family in Germany. His seemingly innocuous purpose was to retrieve letters by Queen Victoria to her eldest daughter, Princess Viktoria, wife of Emperor Frederick I of Prussia, and grandmother of Prince Philipp and his twin brother Wolfgang of Hesse, as well as their Nazi brothers. The ostensible purpose was to extract the letters from the U.S. Army, which might misuse or destroy them.

No indication of such vandalism had reached Buckingham Palace, and if the letters were required, Margarethe, mother of Philipp and Wolfgang, could have sent them. They were of no great value, nor was King George VI a student of his ancestor Victoria's progeny. Therefore, why was Morshead sent on so expensive and difficult a mission? Further questions could be—and have been—asked as to why Anthony Blunt, of the Secret Intelligence Service, was also sent.

At the time, Philipp was a prisoner of the Allies. The existing interrogatory reports, most of which concern Hitler's imprisonment of him on suspicion of treason and his wife's similar imprisonment, naturally and completely avoid, no doubt on high-level orders, any discussion of his prewar (and during the war) role in appeasement arrangements with the Duke of Kent and Prince Paul of Yugoslavia—the royal mafia. No mention was made then or later of the blackmail plot in Paris in March 1938, or who was behind it, namely the supposed Madame Maroni, or the role in it of her architect uncle Gian Carlo Maroni and his cousin, the editor of the *Journal des Débats*. Certainly, records of the matter, the documents and photographs for sale, would have been known to the Secret Intelligence Service, which also failed to act upon the denazification interrogatories in which Philipp disclosed his meeting with a Hitler-pacifying Duke of Kent on the very brink of war.

Only royal orders could have so completely squelched any proper talks with Philipp, and it was not until November 25, 1979, more than fifteen years later, that his twin, Prince Wolfgang, revealed to the London *Sunday Times* "Insight" team that Blunt and Morshead were looking for the Philipp-Windsor-Hesse documents that showed collusion among all three.

The likelihood is that the documents, thought by the royal family to have been returned to the Hesses by the Germans when they seized the files of the Paris Sûreté at the Quai d'Orsay in June 1940 and shipped them to Berlin, were in fact not at Castle Friedrichshof at all. The evidence suggests that, busy fighting a war, the Germans didn't have time to sift through the vast mass of materials of the Paris police, and simply stored them away for the duration.

In 1945, the Russians seized them and took them to Moscow; some records have been returned to Paris over the years, but these have yet to be fully sorted and filed. If the records of the Rochès investigation into the Maroni affair survive, they are undoubtedly still in the French capital, either at the archives of the Sûreté at Fontainbleu, or in the Deuxième Bureau files at Versailles. It will be many years before they are catalogued and released for public inspection, but it is doubtful if more details than are available from the indispensable Coolidge diaries will surface even then.

This still doesn't answer the question of what became of the records of the Windsor-Kent-Philipp connections *after* April 1938. The answer very probably is that the Duke of Windsor, in collusion with the Duke of Kent, made sure that no records of meetings were preserved, and most certainly no photographs. And there the matter rests.

In October there were more embarrassments. British and American forces seized the archives of the German Foreign Ministry, including a high proportion of the documents relating to the Portuguese episode. The telegrams, now decoded and clearly readable, lay on the desk of every appropriate official in London and Washington. Also disclosed was the most serious matter of the duke's leaking the contents of the War Cabinet meeting of January 1940 at which the defense plan for Belgium and France was discussed. John Balfour was put in charge of the matter in Washington. Dean Acheson, in the wake of Adolf A. Berle (who was thereby cheated of his prey), was in constant touch with Balfour in the matter. Top-secret memorandums flew to and fro. London requested that all documents be forwarded to the appropriate authorities. The documents were considered highly embarrassing to the royal family, and Winston Churchill stepped in, making a keen effort to suppress them entirely. He did not want the public to get wind of what had been going on. However, the Windsor enemies in Whitehall were moving rapidly, and the advent of a Labour government under Clement Attlee ensured that the documents would see the light. It has to be emphasized that the disclosures were totally without the approval of King George VI or Queen Elizabeth. Once again, much as they disliked Wallis and were uneasy about the duke, they did not want to have the royal family's dirty linen washed before the world.

The Windsors sailed to France for the first time in nearly six years. They traveled aboard the troopship *Argentina*, one of the first vessels permitted to make the journey at the end of the world conflict. The ship did not anchor at Plymouth, but stayed out at sea, where she was boarded by a team of thirty British and American reporters who came by launch to interview the duke. They noted that by now he had a more pronounced American accent. The duchess was not with him in the purser's cabin, where the press conference took place.

Asked if he planned to visit England, the duke said, "I'm certainly not going to hide, and people will have a chance to see me." After the press conference Wallis joined the duke on deck and smilingly posed for photographers and newsreel cameramen. "It will be lovely to be back in England," the duchess said.

The ship docked at Le Havre. The Windsors were met by a British embassy chauffeur, who drove them to the Boulevard Suchet. They discovered that the house would be sold, by the Countess Sabini, but they were allowed to stay on to organize their furniture and bring it out of storage. They were given at least six months' grace, a remarkable consideration in the circumstances.

As it turned out, Wallis did not accompany the duke to Britain. She was, it would be reasonable to suppose, uncertain of how she would be received, and of course it would be embarrassing to receive a direct snub from the palace. Certainly, the Attlee government would not make her feel welcome or comfortable.

The duke arrived at Hendon Airfield in a Royal Air Force transport command Dakota airplane. He was driven to Marlborough House to see his mother. A crowd was waiting for him; as the car approached the royal residence, hundreds burst through the police cordon and shouted at him joyously, "Good old Edward!" and "You must come back, Teddy, we want you back!" So violent was the crush that a number of very young children were almost trampled underfoot. At last, the car entered the courtyard of Marlborough House.

That evening there was a partial family reunion. The Duke of Gloucester was in Australia and was unable to attend. However, the king did appear, unaccompanied by his wife. The Duchess of Kent was also notable by her absence. It has been claimed that she had never forgiven the Windsors, who had disliked her from the 1930s, for not writing a letter of condolence to her and her children upon her husband's untimely death. The princess royal, who still adored the duke, had been in residence at Marlborough House for several days.

It was on the whole a pleasant evening. Old enmities and strains were temporarily forgotten, and the conversation was brisk. On October 7 the duke and his mother visited the East End, exploring the bombed areas. They visited the home of James Kirby, a 47-year-old gas company clerk, to see his newly prefabricated house, a sample of cheap but adequate dwellings that were a special venture of the Labour government. On October 11 the duke flew back to Paris, announcing ominously, "I shall certainly be back, and next time the duchess will be coming with me."

Both in London and in Paris, the duke saw a good deal of Winston Churchill, who showed little or no interest in meeting the duchess. The Windsors stayed on in Paris through the winter. They began house-hunting, aware of the fact that they had long outstayed their welcome at Boulevard Suchet, and they also discovered, on a visit to La Croë, that although they would spend a good deal of time there, it was unlikely to be their permanent home. The costs of upkeep in more expensive times would prove to be crippling.

In January 1946 Wallis, to her delight, topped the New York Dress Institute's list of the ten best-dressed women in the world. She had been on the list for years, tying on one occasion with Courtney Espil, who had replaced her in the affections of the Argentinean diplomat she had loved. On January 7 the duke was again unaccompanied as he revisited London to see his mother. Once more, he was greeted by excited crowds; he proceeded on January 8 to visit with his brother at Buckingham Palace. He had what must have been very uncomfortable meetings with his enemies Attlee, Ernest Bevin, and other Labour government figures regarding his desire to be made ambassador at large in the United States, or perhaps viceroy of India. But he was offered nothing; eventually, governor general of Australia was suggested. He refused the post.

Unfortunately, while the duke was in London, another disagreeable echo of his past was heard. The New York Times reporter Tania Long, stationed in Nuremberg to cover the International Military Tribunal's trial of the major Nazi war criminals, got hold of a secret document from the files of Alfred Rosenberg. The document referred to Sir Samuel Hoare's interest in nazism; to Rosenberg's 1931 visit to London, in which he found many pro-Nazi figures in the general staff; and to the visit of the special agent de Ropp to London in January 1935 to discuss National Socialist philosophy with the Duke of Kent, who had conveyed the details directly to his brother. This was most embarrassing, and the article appeared in the *New York Times* on January 10, while the duke was still in residence at Marlborough House. On this occasion he declined to make any comment.

The Windsors spent the next several months in Paris and at La Croë, the arrangement whereby they were permitted to stay on at Boulevard Suchet extended until 1948. The duke was ceaseless in his requests to return to Great Britain in some official capacity. In this, he was most keenly supported by Wallis and by public feeling; his popularity still proved to be of grave concern at Buckingham Palace.

The Windsors' chief concern during 1946 was, as always, the Russian threat. At the outbreak of World War II, when he heard the news at La Croë that Russia had helped conquer Poland, the duke had said to Wallis that it would mean the influx of bolshevism and the destruction of Europe as he knew it. He was not entirely mistaken, of course, no matter how misguided were the political principles which had provoked the remark. The notorious decision at the Yalta Conference to give almost all of eastern Europe to Stalin was surely of gravest concern to every thinking person not of the far left. The hysterical fear that Russia would move rapidly westward and absorb all of European civilization did not have an equal foundation in logic. But the duke cannot be blamed for such fear at the time, nor for his continuing belief that the only possibility now was to launch an immediate attack upon the Soviet Union. The fact that such an attack would be totally illegal, unprovoked, and unsupported by international regulations and restrictions did not have the slightest interest for him; he believed to the end of his life (and many agree) that the Russian people should have been freed by the defeat of Stalin.

Soon, the world would be plunged into a cold war, and that year Churchill's famous Fulton, Missouri, Iron Curtain speech on Russia found the Windsors in total concurrence.

Finally resigned to the fact that the duchess would never be accepted at the palace, the Windsors arrived in London for a private visit on October 11, 1946. It was the duchess's first appearance on British soil in more that eight years. The Earl and Countess of Dudley, whom the Windsors had entertained at La Croë on the eve of World War II, had offered them Ednam Lodge, their country house at Sunningdale, Berkshire, only a stone's throw from Fort Belvedere. The Dudleys were staying at Claridges in London.

Gray Philips and the reliable Thomas Carter, who continued to represent the Windsors' interest vis-à-vis the royal allowance in London, met the duke and duchess at Dover and drove them to Ednam Lodge, where they were very comfortable. They made a brief and nostalgic drive to Fort Belvedere, which they found in a sad state of disrepair; later, it would be restored and occupied by Mr. and Mrs. Gerald Lascelles. Lascelles was the duke's nephew, the son of his sister, the princess royal. The duke had been quietly disposing of the furniture at the fort piece by piece through private channels, anxious that no word of the matter would leak out. George Allen arrived from London to pay his respects and reassure the duke on that score. On October 16 the Windsors made a visit to London and stayed, like the Dudleys, at Claridges.

The duchess kept a large number of her jewels in a box, almost the size of an overnight suitcase, which was normally placed under her maid's bed. The night before she and the duke left for London, she moved the box, placing it in front of the fireplace in her bedroom, where it could not have been any more conspicuous. The excuse she later gave was that her maid was going on vacation to Scotland and that the following day the box would be placed under the bed of Lady Dudley's maid. She had completely ignored Lord Dudley's urgent request that she put the jewels in the well-protected and burglar-alarmed strong room where the family silver was stored. Celebrity burglaries were headlined every week that season.

At 6 p.m. on the night of the sixteenth, the detective on watch outside Wallis's bedroom apparently joined the rest of the staff for an early dinner in the kitchen. It was still twilight when thieves climbed up a white rope attached to a window in the room of Lady Dudley's daughter. Ignoring all other rooms and the strong room, the thieves walked down a corridor directly to the duchess's bedroom. Without touching any of the items on the dressing table or in the drawers, searching closets, or even taking Lady Dudley's gems, which were on her dressing table in the neighboring room for all to see, they picked up the jewel box and carried it back down the same corridor. Despite the fact that the Windsors' Cairn and pug dogs were upstairs, neither barked. Is it possible that they recognized the thieves?

The duchess's maid went to her mistress's room to fetch something. She noted the absence of the box. She immediately called the police. Soon, the house was in an uproar. It seemed incredible that burglars could have made their way into the house in clear daylight, walked across an entire floor, picked up a heavy box, and made their way down the rope with it without disturbing anyone. The maid advised the Windsors, who instantly drove down to Ednam Lodge, where the police were already interrogating everybody. The Dudleys followed immediately. R. M. Howe, assistant commissioner of Scotland Yard's Criminal Investigation Department, and Chief Inspector Capstick were in charge of the investigation.

A golf course caddie reported that he found a number of earrings, none of them matching, scattered through the bunkers. Staff members reported finding expensive Fabergé boxes lying about on and near a windowsill. There was no trace of the jewel box. There was talk of people seeing a large Canadian armored car parked in the vicinity, and it was mentioned that a somewhat demented individual seen prowling around the local golf club might have been responsible. The duke reacted very much as he had done in the Oakes case. He decided on the spot that the madman was responsible and had him arrested on the most flimsy evidence and held in prison; after a short time the unfortunate man was released on the ground that it was clear the crime had been carried out by highly skilled professionals.

Lady Dudley, later the Duchess of Marlborough, recalled that the duchess behaved with artificial fury. Much to the Dudleys' annoyance, she insisted that all their valued retainers and maids, as well as their cook, be thoroughly searched and subjected to a police grilling. Only one scullery maid was new to the household. The police questioned her mercilessly, but they could prove nothing against her.

One of the duchess's brooches, supposedly not in the box, proved to be missing that night. The duchess compelled the duke to search high and low for it, turning out cushions, getting on all fours to peek under chairs, ransacking closets, and generally turning a beautifully ordered and elegantly maintained house upside down. This inelegant and humiliating performance ended with the duke at last recalling that he had hidden the brooch for some inexplicable reason under a mantel shelf vase. He produced it, pale, exhausted, and on the verge of tears, to Wallis's cold, shrugging approval.

The Duchess of Marlborough remembered how extremely annoyed she was by Wallis's misbehavior in the matter. A few days after the theft she had been walking in Mayfair when, to her astonishment, she was stopped by a plainclothes policeman who asked to inspect her diamond clip. It was in the form of the Prince of Wales's feathers and was a family heirloom. He had evidently mistaken it for the sapphire and diamond 1936 Cartier clip which the duchess had worn at her wedding.

Summers, Henderson, the insurance assessors, issued under pressure a list of the items in the jewel box. It was extremely brief and was followed by the tantalizing word, "etcetera." In view of the fact that the Duchess of Marlborough examined the contents of the box and saw a vast number of items in it that were not included on the assessor's list, it is possible that Summers, Henderson chose not to reveal the vast majority of the items. The reason for this is mysterious. Among the very significant pieces that went unlisted, but which the duchess mentioned to reporters, was the magnificent diamond tiara that the duke had given her as a wedding gift; made by Cartier in 1936, it included four large center diamonds and three curved upright fingers of smaller diamonds mounted on platinum. The tiara had been intended for wear at the wedding, but this idea was decided against at the last moment because of the implied insult to Buckingham Palace. It was worn only for photographs.

Later in 1946 Frances Goldwyn, wife of the movie tycoon Samuel Goldwyn, was in a jewelry store in Bond Street, asking for a book of samples of important items that were offered for sale. She was astonished to see in the book certain gems that were supposed to have been stolen. The book was hurriedly removed with the words, "We regret, madam, this sample was offered to you in error." For years, people claimed they saw the gems, worn by the duchess in different settings, which were supposed to have been in the stolen box.

A rumor flew around London, not discouraged by the Windsors, that Buckingham Palace was responsible for the robbery. The reason adduced was that the mysterious and fictional Alexandra emeralds were in the box and that the palace wanted them back at all costs. This absurdity has persisted to the present day.

A number of theories have been put forward on this matter. Among them is that of the official historian of the queen's jewels, Leslie Field. She charged in 1987:

> I believe the Duchess of Windsor defrauded the insurers by overstating the numbers and identifications of the jewels which had been disposed of. At least thirty items she named as being stolen turned up in the Sotheby's catalog at Geneva in April 1987 and were sold for high prices. She clearly could never wear those jewels again after she and her husband had collected the insurance. They had from the beginning been in a strongbox in Paris and remained there.

According to the author and fashion editor Suzy Menkes, a thief confessed in 1960 to the crime. However, he appears not to have revealed to which fence he disposed of the gems.

With the theft officially unsolved and Scotland Yard in a great state of embarrassment, the Windsors wisely sailed for the United States on the *Queen Elizabeth* on November 6. The sailing was rendered uncomfortable by the presence on board of Sir Alexander Korda, the close friend and colleague of Sir Robert Vansittart. Korda had been in the Secret Intelligence Service throughout World War II, and he was well aware of Vansittart's investigations of the Windsors. Korda was coolly polite, but the Windsors generally gave him a wide berth. By contrast, they found a keen supporter and friend in Captain Henry Grattidge, and they enjoyed his company at the captain's table. The duke had sailed with him before on Cunard ships in the 1920s; the captain was a genial soul, uncomplicated and extroverted, and he made the Windsors feel entirely welcome aboard the *Queen*. They occupied Suite 58A on the main deck. They traveled with 155 pieces of luggage: 80 suitcases in their suite and 75 cabin trunks in the hold. According to Grattidge, at 7 a.m. each morning during the crossing, the duke went unfailingly to the restaurant to watch the bellboys attend morning roll call under the second steward. He and the duchess made a tour of the dog kennels, where their own animals were housed. "Everything here except lampposts," the duke said as he left the "dog hotel" before lunch one day.

When the ship docked, the Windsors were met by Robert and Anita Young. Young was still locked in his continuing battle to obtain ultimate control of the New York Central Railroad; questioned by reporters, both Young and the duke denied that royal money was invested in the struggle. It was a futile denial.

On November 21 the Windsors attended with the Youngs the world premiere of William Wyler's classic movie *The Best Years of Our Lives*; they were given an elaborate late-night supper by Edith Baker, heiress to the $500 million banking fortune of her husband, George. On December 10 the duke presented a check (not his own money, but the Bakers') to the Salvation Army national commandant, Ernest I. Pugmire, at the army's 120 West 14th Street headquarters. Just before Christmas, the Windsors paid a visit to President and Mrs. Truman at the White House.

They spent Christmas happily at the Waldorf Towers. In January 1947 a new and remarkable personality entered their lives. Tiny, sharp-eyed, twinkling, Guido Orlando was one of the ace publicists of his era. Among his clients had been Mussolini, Greta Garbo, and Aimée Semple McPherson. Dapper and fast-talking, he could buy or sell any gimmick.

The duchess met Orlando at the Waldorf Towers and told him that the duke was worried because the German diplomatic records relating to their pro-Hitler activities might see publication despite Winston Churchill's determined efforts to suppress them. Orlando recalled that, without thinking twice, he immediately cooked up an enterprising "patriotic" scheme. He would arrange a party at Delmonico's Hotel which would be attended by 100 Purple Heart veterans, and the duke and duchess would attend. Photographs would be taken and distributed to the press in foreign nations; the domestic press would be there in full force. At the end of the party the veterans would send bouquets to Wallis with notes of thanks; she would, of course, pay for these.*

The party went off according to plan. The official hostess was the wealthy Mrs. Sailing Baruch, sister-in-law of Bernard Baruch. At a certain stage during the evening the New York playboy Jimmy Donahue turned up and said to Mrs. Baruch, "I understand the Duke likes you very much. He always did have a weakness for sailors!"

The Windsors had not met Donahue before. Orlando introduced

---

*In the end, she did not.

them. Slim, oval-faced, with slicked-down hair, Donahue was a remarkable personality. His mother, Jessie, with whom he lived at 834 Fifth Avenue, was the daughter of the billionaire Frank Woolworth; Barbara Hutton was her cousin. His father had committed suicide in April 1931, taking an overdose of mercury tablets. The elder James Donahue had been noted for his homosexual activities, and he had allegedly taken his own life because he had been jilted by a young serviceman.

By 1947, when he met the Windsors, Donahue was as notorious in society as his father had been. Despite the fact that press agents organized numerous women for him as well-publicized dates, he remained exclusively interested in men. With unlimited cash, he could afford the most expensive call-boys; he staged elaborate orgies during his mother's absences in Palm Beach. A close friend was Cardinal Spellman, the leading Catholic dignitary in the United States, whose indulgences with male prostitutes and handsome young priests were an open scandal in Manhattan. On one memorable occasion Donahue gave a dinner party for the cardinal and appeared at the table in a ball gown. The stories about him were legion. An informant who wished to be anonymous said that Donahue and a friend had cornered a waiter at the Waldorf Towers and tried to rape him; when the man resisted their advances, they allegedly castrated him.

An extraordinary incident took place on March 18, 1946, according to the late Truman Capote, who is quoted at length in C. David Heymann's *Poor Little Rich Girl: The Life and Legend of Barbara Hutton* (New York: Lyle Stuart, Inc., 1985). Donahue walked into the elegant Cerutti's, a gay bar on Madison Avenue. It was full of men in uniform. Accompanied by the jewelry designer Fulco di Verdura, Donahue took a number of sailors, soldiers, and marines to a party at Mrs. Donahue's Fifth Avenue apartment. They stripped a GI and began shaving off his body hair. They were using an old-fashioned open razor. Then Jimmy castrated the soldier. Everyone became hysterical, and the man was thrown into Jimmy's car, driven to the 59th Street Bridge, and tossed onto the sidewalk. Donahue was arrested but released when Mrs. Donahue paid the unhappy victim close to a quarter of a million dollars to drop charges.

According to the author Stephen Birmingham, when a male prostitute failed to satisfy Donahue's requirements, he forced him to eat an excrement sandwich. Guido Orlando claimed in 1987 that, after he introduced Donahue to the Windsors, the duke fell in love with

Donahue and that within a year they were involved in an affair. It is impossible to corroborate this story. Certainly, the three were notoriously inseparable for the next several years. Orlando says that he encouraged Donahue to flirt continuously with the duchess in public places in order to give the impression that it was they, not Donahue and the duke, who were romantically interested in each other. At the same time, Orlando claims, he urged the duke to put on a full-scale display of detesting all homosexuals.

The Windsors' surviving friends deny Orlando's story. Certainly, gossips suggested that Wallis was seeking to convert Donahue to heterosexuality by having a surreptitious affair with him. There is no proof whatsoever of that eventuality. But there is no question that their association with Donahue was the most sordid of the Windsors' lives, more sordid even than the episode involving Sir Harry Oakes, and if Orlando is correct, Wallis must have hated the situation. Not even Orlando's most determined efforts could make the Windsors acceptable socially at the highest levels; true, they never ceased to go to parties, but many people would not receive them in view of Donahue's presence. As for England, it would clearly be insupportable that Donahue should accompany the duke and duchess to the homes of those few members of the aristocracy who would be generous enough to receive them.

By 1947 the duke, perhaps because of stress over his relationship with Wallis and Jimmy, was drinking heavily for the first time since the mid 1930s. In February 1947 the Windsors found a temporary escape from this ghastly liaison and traveled to Florida, where the Youngs joined them at the Horse Shoe Plantation, Tallahassee, owned by the millionaire banking heir George Baker and his mother, Edith, for a turkey, quail, and dove shoot. Surprisingly, they returned to the hated Bahamas to stay with friends of the Baker family, the explorer Arthur Vernay and his wife, at Los Cayos. They returned to attend the Hialeah Park Handicap at Miami, and throughout March they were at the Youngs'. Back in New York, they were reunited with Donahue and, at Orlando's behest, formally opened the New York Book Week, designed to refurbish the Merchant Marine Coast Guard Station libraries. They visited the east side settlement and toured the New York police headquarters, where unflattering files on the Oakes case were inconveniently maintained.

On April 15 an episode not organized by Guido Orlando put the duke in a heroic light. A fire broke out in one of the suites of the Waldorf

Towers at 11:55 p.m. and the hotel alarm went off. The duke, always at-tracted by fires, made his way, followed by the duchess, from the twenty-ninth to the thirty-fifth floor, where flames were emerging from the apartments of the Baron and Baroness Egmont van Zuylen of Holland. The duke helped an emergency crew of hotel employees break open a firebox and carry the long hose down the corridor, aiming the water into the suite. By the time firemen arrived, the worst of the problem had been solved.

Six days later, Mr. and Mrs. Harry Truman arrived at the Towers, and the Windsors saw a good deal of them. On April 26 they watched the Maryland Hunt Cup at Glyndon, the first time Wallis had seen the race since childhood. On May 10 Aunt Bessie saw the Windsors off for England on the *Queen Elizabeth*, this time with only eighty-five pieces of luggage, a secretary, a valet, and a maid. They renewed their happy relationship with Captain Grattidge. In England the duke again made efforts to secure some form of employment, but without success. He was greatly hurt by the fact that he was forbidden to attend his mother's birthday celebrations on May 27; he was allowed to go to Marlborough House alone to present his greetings. That same week the engagement of Princess Elizabeth to Lieutenant Philip Mountbatten was being widely discussed. It was made clear that there would be no question of the Windsors' being asked to the wedding. Asked for his comments, the duke said only that he wished the couple the very best. The duchess found herself unable to make any comment.

In Paris that summer, still at Boulevard Suchet, the Windsors saw a good deal of Noël Coward. They had much to talk about concerning the tragic past. Coward had never approved of the Windsors up till that time, but now, his diaries indicate, he warmed to them. He also saw them, then and later, in the south of France, where he invited them to dinner and they often invited him to La Croë.

In August the Windsors were in the south of France. Among their many visitors was a close friend from Baltimore, Mrs. Eleanor Miles, who left a detailed record of her visit in the form of a letter to her cousin Edith in Maine. The letter is dated August 5, 1947. She observed that the duke drank only gin; he was almost on the wagon again. Wallis took only a Dubonnet or "one of those nasty weak Vermouth tasting things." The duke was fondly handling a letter from his mother, looking at the seal in black wax with the letter "M" surmounted by a crown. "It is pretty," he said to Eleanor. "Don't you think for an old lady of eighty my mother writes with a steady hand?" Eleanor couldn't resist a peek at the letter itself. It mentioned Princess Elizabeth's engagement; clearly, it implied that Queen Mary would be deeply pleased if the duke would appear at the wedding, but there was no mention of Wallis. The duke talked with deep affection of his mother. It was a sad and touching moment.

He told Eleanor that he wished he would be given the governor generalship of Canada. He mentioned he had declined the Australian post. Eleanor joined the Windsors in laughing loudly at magazine photographs of the dreadful clothes worn by everyone at Ascot. The next day they all took off to an elaborate party at the Hôtel du Cap at Eden Roc. Eleanor was fascinated by the furniture at La Croë. She described the trompe l'oeil desk with painted panels of roses and thistles in a Louis Quinze design. A chest of drawers was painted as though lace underwear were falling out of it, and one drawer was painted with a letter addressed to Wallis at Cumberland Terrace in 1936. The handwriting was the duke's.

That fall, London was en fête for the royal wedding. Through the pages of his own *Evening Standard*, Lord Beaverbrook urged Britain to demand that Buckingham Palace invite the Windsors. "What has the Duchess done that she should be held up to ridicule in this way?" the *Standard* Londoner's Diary columnist asked. "As the wife of the bride's uncle, if for no other reason, the Duchess should be accorded the dignity of an invitation to her niece's marriage." There was no response to the plea. Drew Middleton of the *New York Times* went into various London public houses asking the people at the bar what they thought about this royal snub. Without exception, the comments were unfavorable. Churchill did his best to sway the palace, but without success. As the guest list of the wedding swelled to 2,200 more newspapers clamored for the duchess's acceptance. By mid-October the matter had blown up into a full-scale sensation. Fuming in Paris, the duchess had a small compensation: her uncle, General Henry Warfield, had died and left her $15,000 from his $850,000 estate. On November 11 the Windsors arrived at Southampton aboard the *Queen Mary* from Cherbourg. They were met by more than fifty representatives of the radio, film newsreels, and press. Again, they were pressed on the matter of the marriage. And again, they effectively dodged questions. They had sagely decided to proceed to the United States immediately.

18

Wandering Years

B y the late 1940s the Windsors were adrift. Their lives had begun to assume a circular monotony as they moved between Paris, the south of France, London, and New York City. Their galère of friends remained limited: the Youngs, George and Edith Baker, and, in Paris, the Mendls, the Rochefoucaulds. The duke tried to alleviate Wallis's frequent periods of depression by bestowing on her a whole new series of gifts of jewelry. In 1947 he presented her with a magnificent gold, turquoise, amethyst, and diamond bib necklace, set in a lattice design on a chain of Prince of Wales linking, signed by Cartier. In 1948 he presented Wallis with the first of a series of panther clips, which were to become legendary. The 1948 gift was made of gold, enamel, and emeralds; the whole was crouched upon a single cabochon emerald of 90 karats. It was Cartier's first use of the motif. In 1949 it was followed by the present of a sapphire and diamond panther clip, the cobochon sapphire of 152.35 karats, the whole including 106 sapphires. For many years after that, the duchess would accumulate a marvelous menagerie of similar gems.

In 1948 a presence entered the restricted inner circle of the Windsors. By a curious coincidence, the arrival of this new personage on the scene coincided with the punishment of her predecessor. On October 8, 1947, Armand Grégoire was found guilty in absentia of the crime of intelligence with the enemy in 1940 and 1941, in a judgment of the Court of Justice, First Subsection, Department of the Seine. He was sentenced to hard labor for life, and his property was confiscated; the court declared that he was in a state of national indignity, of which the penalty was national degradation. There were several other similar cases of collaborators protected by the U.S. government, as the Barbie case and others have illustrated.

The Windsors' new lawyer was the remarkable Maître Suzanne Blum. Then Madame Paul Weill, she was, as we know, the sister of André Blumel, a lifelong friend, law partner, and associate of France's former premier, Léon Blum. Blumel had been administrative assistant or chef de cabinet in the Socialist and Russian-allied Blum administration during Edward VIII's reign. A convinced left-winger, he was, like Blum, Jewish. During World War II, when Léon Blum was imprisoned following the preposterous Riom trial in which the collaborative government of France sought hypocritically to blacken his name as an aide in the downfall of the Third Republic, Suzanne Weill and her husband managed to reach New York, where she altered her name to Blum. Tirelessly, during her exile, she sought to obtain public support to alleviate ex-premier Blum's conditions of imprisonment. Before America entered the war, on April 9, 1941, she secured over a hundred signatures, among them that of Eleanor Roosevelt, to a telegram of goodwill that was forwarded to the distinguished prisoner in his cell. The following year she organized another telegram celebrative of his seventieth birthday.

It seems peculiarly ironic that Blum, as a Socialist, a relative of Blumel whom the Windsors politely deplored, and an apparent disliker of Nazis, could attach herself to them, or that they would want her to handle their affairs. How did she manage, in short, to obtain a stranglehold on the Duchess of Windsor that she never relinquished until the duchess's death?

The answer can be given in two words: William Bullitt. As his intimate friend, from the first day she and her late husband met him in Paris, perhaps misunderstanding his political role which on the face of it seemed publicly opposed to Hitler, a naive, driven, self-deceiving control freak who believed only what she wanted to believe, she worshiped Bullitt, and he had the cunning, since he was being connected dangerously to Armand Grégoire, Laval, and other traitors, to take her up in wartime America and co-edit, write the introduction to, and help publish her book of Léon Blum's writings in French in Montreal in 1943.

Thus she was privy to Wallis's greatest secret, the secret her besotted

Duke of Windsor must (and would) never find out: the Bullitt affair, which, according to Eleanor Davies Tydings Ditzen, went on in Washington during the Bahamian exile period and even later. Had the truth come out, the greatest love story of the century would have seemed a brutal sham—the story of a ruthless woman and a hapless cuckold.

When I wrote the original edition of this book in 1987, I stated that Maître Blum was clearly oblivious of the duke and duchess's politics. I no longer retain this view; Maître Blum wanted these rich and famous clients and cared nothing about their associations, of which she was well aware.

During 1946 and 1947, though still in his fifties, the duke felt that impulse which usually seizes upon somewhat older men: the desire to write his official memoirs. He engaged for the purpose an accomplished journalist, Charles J. V. Murphy, a frequent contributor to *Life* magazine. Despite the fact that Clare Boothe Luce, wife of Henry Luce, chairman of Time/Life Incorporated, remained convinced that the Windsors were Nazi collaborators, her husband was less fussy and encouraged Murphy to go ahead with the assignment. It proved, like many arrangements of the sort, to be somewhat of a crucifixion for both partners. The duke proved to be maddeningly skittish and unreliable in terms of schedules; he would say a great deal that appeared to be revealing and would then withdraw it. He fussed over every detail. Sometimes he would appear to be involved in the work, but at other times he would be totally abstracted and indifferent. Murphy pressed on doggedly, clearly realizing that the book could be a best-seller. In the midst of the writing, Robert Young, George Baker, and Kenneth de Courcy all indicated to the Windsors that war with Russia might break out at any minute. They began to make arrangements to sell La Croë, and shifted a lot of their personal belongings to the United States. All of this absorbed a great deal of their time, and the matter of the memoirs kept being delayed. Moreover, according to Murphy, the duchess proved to be infuriatingly interruptive, constantly irritable, and resentful of the irregular absorption of her husband in the task in hand. She would burst into the various dens of the homes they occupied, dragging the duke off to this or that luncheon; she would scream out, "Stop talking about the past!" and she would insist that the duke go, with or without Jimmy Donahue, to nightclubs and restaurants very late at night so that he would be too exhausted to tackle the writing in the morning. It was only by sheer force that the determined Murphy squeezed a series of articles out of the duke; they appeared in *Life* magazine beginning on December 8, 1947. It gives some indication of the laboriousness of the task in hand that it was 1950 before the second part of the series appeared.

In April 1948, following a winter with the Youngs at Palm Beach and a long cruise with Joseph E. Davies, the former ambassador to Russia, and his wife aboard the yacht *Sea Cloud* in Caribbean waters, the Windsors unexpectedly took a lease on Severn, the elaborate estate of Mrs. Brooks Howe at Cedar Creek, Locust Valley, Long Island. The house had been built for George Baker's sister, then Mrs. Stanley Martineau, about fifteen years earlier. It was French provincial in style, a comparatively small, twenty-five room château overlooking a golf course. The building was turreted, with a circular staircase that went from the ground floor to the top in what appeared to be an imitation-medieval effect. Wallis worked hard with carpenters, decorators, and plumbers, assisted by Mrs. Howe's majordomo, Patrick Cunningham.

In June the Windsors, with 120 pieces of luggage, sailed for England aboard the *Queen Mary*; among the other passengers was Lord Beaverbrook, who no doubt had much to discuss with them at the captain's table about the abdication years. They made a second visit later in the year, and on each occasion the duke paid a loving visit to his mother, to whom he had grown closer and closer over the years. Whenever Wallis made a sharp remark about any member of his family, he would gently but firmly reprove her, and it is clear that despite all the differences among the members of his family, they began to draw closer together in the late 1940s. Only Queen Elizabeth stood firm in her resolution never to forgive the duchess for her activities on behalf of the enemy or for provoking the abdication.

Much of Queen Elizabeth's concern and sense of unforgiveness still centered upon her husband's health. Although still not far advanced into middle age, King George VI was suffering from declining strength by the late 1940s. Always lacking his older brother's athleticism, energy, drive, and sheer charm, he had, with courage, decency, and resolution, sustained his royal duties without flinching, and his role in World War II was nothing short of heroic. But the stress of working against his shy nature as the most conspicuously exposed of public figures had at last worn down his health. By November 1948 he was suffering from a failure of arterial circulation in his legs, which had become a mass of swollen varicose veins. A lifelong smoker, like the Duke of Windsor, he was also showing symptoms which Lord Horder, the royal physician, would two years later indicate to his family might suggest a possible carcinoma. Further bronchoscopic examinations in 1950 suggested that this supposition was not without a basis. The king was not informed of this discovery.

The Duke of Windsor was disturbed and moved by the news of his brother's ill health. The duchess's indifference made him fretful, even though there was a perfectly understandable basis for it. While in England he stayed either with his mother at Marlborough House or, when Wallis accompanied him that year, again with the long-suffering Earl and Countess of Dudley at Ednam Lodge. He showed no forgiveness of his enemies. Writing to Kenneth de Courcy on August 28, 1948, he referred to the Franklin D. Roosevelt statue in Mayfair, London: "I would not be surprised if you by-passed Grosvenor Square nowadays to spare yourself the disgust of having to look at the statue of the man most responsible for the jam in which the Western Powers now find themselves." Elsewhere in the letter he said that "if we had given a free hand to Hitler, we would have destroyed the Soviet Union, instead of America forming a wartime alliance with the Soviets."

At the end of 1949 the Windsors stayed with Margaret, Mrs. Anthony Drexel Biddle, their old friend from Paris days, at her Mayfair home. They had by now given up their Paris residence and had moved to a rather unsatisfactory house at 85 Rue de la Faisanderie, near the Bois de Boulogne, which by mid-1949 was ready for occupancy. It was in essence a gift of that old friend, Paul-Louis Weiller, French millionaire and controller of the airline that was nationalized and became Air France. This leader of French commerce had continued to be the mentor and patron of Sir Charles and Lady Mendl, and he made it possible for this perennially charming pair to sustain their exquisite house, the Villa Trianon, near Paris.

These friendships and associations with people of very different political histories proved to be highly supportive at the time. Yet it cannot be said that the Windsors were ever entirely comfortable during those years. The palace's continuing refusal to accept the duchess still nagged and irritated. There were people who avoided them at parties or aboard the Cunard ships they favored. The Donahue situation continued to be maddening to everyone. The column items on the trio were increasingly unflattering. The ferocious Walter Winchell in particular rejoiced in exposing the ghastliness of the ménage à trois while discreetly failing to reveal its true nature. Laura, Duchess of Marlborough told me that she found Donahue's very presence insupportable. She recalled a dreadful episode at the popular nightclub Scheherazade in Paris, sometime in 1950. There was a Windsor party of twelve, all of them watched most closely by the other diners, who barely attended to their food. Jimmy and the duke had drunk far too much wine. Donahue had placed large numbers of red roses in front of all the plates, including his own. Suddenly, in an extravagant gesture, Wallis flung her Prince of Wales feather fan into Jimmy's roses. The duke turned to Lady Dudley in horror, his eyes full of tears. Although Lady Dudley naturally assumed his jealousy was provoked by the alleged affair between Jimmy and the duchess, she did not understand the true reason for his discomfiture.

Charles Murphy recalled that one evening "at the Monseigneur . . . the duke left early, after buying the duchess a gardenia from the flower girl's tray. Jimmy had bought her one, too. As soon as the duke had gone, the duchess snatched his flower from her corsage, flung it into the champagne bucket, and tamped it down in the ice with a bottle. Jimmy's flower she then tucked into its place. . . .[Jimmy] took her hand and they wept."

According to Murphy, Donahue was determined to have Wallis become a Roman Catholic. He enlisted the aid of the popular Monsignor Fulton J. Sheen, who had already won Clare Boothe Luce, the journalist Heywood Broun, and the Communist Louis Bendunz to the faith. Wallis somewhat frivolously discussed the matter, but of course to have entered into any such arrangement would have caused extreme offense to her husband; it was clear at all events that she was by now entirely agnostic.

She also carried with her some odd echoes of the past. Nancy Mitford, gifted authoress and sister of Lady Mosley, wrote to Evelyn Waugh on January 11, 1950, saying that during a dinner party at the Windsors' she had gone into the bedroom and had seen there an erotic painting by Boucher of two lesbians making love. Surprised, she had asked Wallis what the painting signified. Wallis replied, "Well it seems there was some god called Neptune, who could change himself into anything he liked—once he was a swan you know—and this woman liked other women so he turned himself into one."

The seemingly endless work on the duke's memoirs was finally completed, and the rights were sold to G. P. Putnam's Sons in December 1949. Kennett L. Rawson, vice president and editor in chief at Putnam's, made the necessary arrangements. He flew to Paris to obtain the duke's signature on January 21, 1950. Later that month the Windsors took off on an elaborate trip to New York, Florida, Louisiana, Texas, and Mexico. As usual, they used the private railroad car of Robert Young. En route they stayed with the Bakers at their Tallahassee Horse Shoe Plantation in Florida. In Mexico City they were the guests of President Miguel Alemán, who discreetly made no reference to their association with his rebellious and pro-Nazi former associate, General Maximino Camacho. In association with Axel Wenner-Gren, who had survived blacklisting to continue acting as a cloak for Krupp in Europe, Alemán and his close friend Bruno Pagliai had acquired many of Wenner-Gren's interests; the Windsors thus moved back rapidly into the orbit of the very group they had allegedly broken with nine years earlier. They spent three days in Mexico City. They then proceeded via Texas and other points (many of which Wallis described in letters to her old friend Corinne Murray) to Alberta, to the ranch they had not seen for nine years. All efforts to strike oil there had of course long since failed. They returned to Europe on May 24, the duke still laboring at the third draft of the autobiography. News of King George VI's health was very bad.

In July 1950 Herman Rogers wrote to Wallis to invite her to his wedding. Katherine had died in May 1949, and he was marrying Lucy Wann, widow of a retired Royal Air Force officer. The date was set for August 6, but Wallis was unable to attend that day and asked Herman to put back the date by several days. According to friends of Wallis's, she was not at all happy about this new union. In various telephone conversations, she criticized Herman for becoming involved with another woman so soon after Katherine had died. When Wallis did arrive at Villa Lou Viei to attend the wedding, she presented the couple with a sterling silver salver, having omitted any mention of Lucy in the inscription. As the Rogerses set off on their honeymoon after the nuptials, Wallis deliberately pulled at Lucy's wedding gown, twisting the cloth until the whole collar was totally ruined. The Windsors turned up late for the wedding breakfast at a restaurant near Antibes, and during lunch Wallis's behavior was even more irritating, as she ignored Lucy and talked across her to Herman.

The Windsors left with Herman and Lucy on the yacht cruise honeymoon. Wallis became a little more polite during the voyage, and at last began talking to Lucy. After dinner at the Hôtel de Paris in Monte Carlo, the two women found themselves in the powder room together. Wallis stared at a ring of gold and diamonds on Lucy's finger. Lucy said she felt she had enough jewelry and going to insist that Herman return it for a refund. Wallis revealed herself all too clearly when she exclaimed, "Don't send it back! Don't be a fool! It's money!"

At the beginning of 1951, Wallis, without perhaps knowing it, faced a new threat: the emergence from secret files of the 1935 China dossier. The Honorable John Coke, son of the Earl of Leicester, who had originally taken the dossier to Queen Mary, and had himself examined its contents, felt that sufficient time had passed and the old queen had little time left to live, to discuss the dossier, of which he had kept a copy, with Winston Churchill, who was writing and painting in Marrakesh, Morocco, on a monthlong stay throughout January of that year.

Churchill made no comment; he told Coke he had heard about the dossier in 1936, when it was much discussed in the circles that wanted to see the removal of Edward VIII from the English throne; he certainly knew that Baldwin on instruction from George V had obtained it; and that when Queen Mary saw it, in shock and outrage she decided Wallis would never be queen. It will be recalled that is was she, as well as the Duchesses of Gloucester and Kent, who decided after the abdication that Wallis would never receive the title of "Her Royal Highness."

From Marrakesh, Coke came to stay with the Windsors' old friend and confidant, Kenneth de Courcy, Duc de Grantmesnil, who was renting the Windsors' old home, the Villa La Croë, in the south of France. The Duke and Duchess of Westminster joined Coke as de Courcy's guests for lunch on March 9 and Coke described the contents of the dossier to the group. He added that Queen Mary, whom he still served as attendant gentleman-in-waiting, had never forgotten the dossier and thus would not relent in the matter of agreeing to Wallis having the title of H.R.H. He added that there was no question at any time of her receiving a former prostitute who indulged in "perverse sexual practices." Cole asked de Courcy if whether, after hearing such facts, he could expect Queen Mary to relent? De Courcy replied that in the circumstances he could not.

Later, after forming a friendship with the Windsors' lawyer Maître Suzanne Blum, de Courcy wrote to her frequently, appeasing her by saying that the dossier did exist but was "a forgery." In fact, it was conceivable, indeed it fitted with his investigation into Guy Trundle via Scotland Yard, that King George had the dossier obtained; what is inconceivable is that he and the Secret Intelligence Service would have provided false witnesses and faked Hong Kong, Shanghai, and Peking police reports in Chinese—a criminal act indeed. When the National Archives of Great Britain opened the Scotland Yard files on Trundle in 2003, they issued an official statement that the China dossier never existed. No further comment seems necessary.

The house at the Rue de la Faisanderie was proving less and less satisfactory. Wallis was not at all happy with it. Although its salon was large and its bedrooms quite spacious, the house suffered from a smallish dining room, a particular irritation in view of her desire to give large dinner parties. It was a somewhat cold, unwelcoming residence, and she decided they must move. The Windsors did finally leave the house in 1953. They had already given up their residence on Long Island. It was unfortunate that the publication of the excellent royal autobiography *A King's Story* in the spring of 1951 coincided with King George VI's total collapse and disintegration. The book, however, was very successful, earning the duke a much-needed $1 million. He apparently invested part of this in Robert Young's continuing adventure in railroad acquisition. In September King George was found to have a malignant growth in his throat. His left lung was removed on the twenty-third. The Windsors were in London that October, staying with Margaret Biddle. Perhaps unfortunately, the duke chose the occasion to press Winston Churchill once more for a position in government. When the stricken monarch sharply refused any such suggestion, the duke was obliged to inform the duchess. She stood at the window of the house gazing out into the foggy day and said, with intense bitterness, "I hate this country. I shall hate it to my grave." Soon after that, when the Windsors' nemesis John Balfour happened to visit them at

Biarritz and the duchess dropped something on the floor, Balfour, unfailingly British and polite, got on his knees to pick it up. "I always did
like to see the British grovel," the duchess said.

On November 12 C. L. Sulzberger of the *New York Times* attended
a dinner party at the Windsors' house in Paris. Among the guests were
Prime Minister René Pleven and Senator Warren Austin of the UN
delegation. According to Sulzberger, the other guests consisted of "a
weird collection of social derelicts." The dinner comprised ten courses
and was "heavily spiced with sherry, white wine, red wine, pink champagne, and huge slugs of brandy." At the seventh course, a string orchestra appeared and played nostalgically in the mode of the bands the
Windsors had admired in 1930s Vienna. Everyone sang a birthday song
to Senator Austin. After dinner all the guests disappeared except the
Sulzbergers. The Windsors insisted on buttonholing them and launching into a diatribe against the British royal family, the duchess saying
she would never return to England because of the shabby treatment of
her husband. The duke complained that when he had recorded a speech
for a publisher's dinner announcing his book of memoirs, he was told to
cancel it because of the king's illness. Yet on the same afternoon that
the speech was to be delivered, Princesses Elizabeth and Margaret had
gone to the races. Both the Windsors repeatedly said it was disgraceful
that the princesses had gone to see the horses despite their father's
condition while the duke was forbidden to promote his book.

The Sulzbergers were now invited to listen to the forbidden
recording. At the end of it, the duchess exclaimed, "What hypocrisy!
What jealousy!" And she repeated her critique of the princesses going
to the racetrack. The Sulzbergers left in a state of numb boredom.

In December 1951, the king gallantly made a Christmas broadcast. He
rallied a little in January, but on February 6, 1952, his valet found him
dead. The Windsors received the news in New York. The duke sailed
at once aboard the *Queen Mary* for England. He held a press conference in the Veranda Grill on the sun deck of the ship before sailing on
February 7. He said:

> This voyage, upon which I am embarking on the *Queen Mary* tonight, is
> indeed sad—and is indeed all the sadder for me because I am undertak-
> ing it alone. The Duchess is remaining here to await my return. I am

sailing for Great Britain, for the funeral of a dear brother, and to comfort Her Majesty, my mother, in the overwhelming sorrow which has overtaken my family and the commonwealth of British nations.

Referring to the fact that he had participated in the funerals of three previous British monarchs, his great-grandmother, his grandfather, and his father, the duke added, hypocritically:

The late King and I were very close, and the outstanding qualities of kingship he possessed made easier for me the passing on of the interrupted succession to the throne of the United Kingdom. That was over fifteen years ago—a turbulent decade and a half during which my brother's reign ran its noble course. Harassed by the dangers and tribulations of a second world war, and beset by more than his share of political strife, King George VI steadily maintained the highest standards of constitutional monarchy. . . .

But Queen Elizabeth is only 25—how young to assume the responsibilities of a great throne in these precarious times! But she has the good wishes and support of us all.

Throughout the voyage, Commander Grattidge reported, the duke's misery was enhanced by Wallis's absence, and he paced the decks day and night like a lost soul, yearning for her. Others reported that he tied up the radiotelephone and cable rooms of the liner talking with Wallis through the crackling interference or besieging her with messages of affection. He was still as much in love with her as ever.

As the *Queen Mary* sailed past the Isle of Wight, the duke stood on the bridge, pointing to the outlines of Osborne House, where Queen Victoria had died. He spoke to Grattidge with tear-filled eyes about his many bereavements. Then he went down to the Veranda Grill to meet the press representatives, who had come out by launch and climbed a Jacob's ladder to talk to him. "God save the Queen," he said to the reporters, who spontaneously applauded.

He drove straight from the docks of Southampton to Marlborough House, where he found Queen Mary in mourning, stricken with grief. He gave her what comfort he could. She was too infirm, too advanced in years at 84, to go to the funeral. Instead, she accompanied the duke to Westminster Hall, where, with the princess royal, they stood and looked at the royal catafalque, covered in a purple and gold pall, while the crowd of visitors was held back. It was the same dais upon which King

George V's remains had lain in 1936. Later in the day, after dropping off his mother and sister at Marlborough House, the duke proceeded to Buckingham Palace for his first meeting in many years with the 25-year-old queen. They were joined for tea by the Queen Mother and the royal consort, the Duke of Edinburgh. As at the time of King George V's state funeral, London was filled with royalty: Prince Paul of Yugoslavia, King Paul of Greece, the Spanish pretender Don Juan, King Gustav and Queen Louise of Sweden, and many others poured into London to pay their last respects. Queen Juliana flew in by plane, piloted by her husband Prince Bernhard. The King and Queen of Denmark arrived by ship. Prince Albert of the Belgians represented his brother King Baudouin, who for controversial reasons had refused to attend. The King of Norway and the Crown Prince of Ethiopia also were in attendance.

The duke arrived at 10 Downing Street on the night of February 14 for a closed conference with Winston Churchill. At the funeral procession the duke was accompanied by the Duke of Edinburgh, his brother the Duke of Gloucester, and his young nephew the Duke of Kent in the long walk behind the royal coffin. Thousands of people dressed in black lined the streets, and many were weeping. The Duke of Windsor caused unfavorable comment by walking out of step, pushing forward, possibly in an attempt to draw attention to himself.

Wallis remained at the Waldorf Towers, listening to the broadcast of the funeral and perhaps remembering with sadness that other occasion long ago at which she had urged the then king to wear his father's greatcoat to block out the intense and bitter winter cold.

In the wake of this tragic hour, a controversy blew up. The duke was back in New York with Wallis in May; they returned to Paris later that month. It was then that Lord Beaverbrook rashly embarked upon a BBC broadcast on the subject of the abdication. He charged Geoffrey Dawson, editor of the London *Times*, with having terrified King Edward VIII and swayed public opinion against him. He charged Dawson with having used methods "which many would condemn," and said that Dawson "pursued his quest with a vigor that seemed more like venom." The broadcast immediately provoked an outburst of fury from every direction. Wickham Steed, colleague of the late Mr. Dawson, denounced the broadcast in the pages of the *Times* itself. He claimed that the charges were "wholly fantastic." The *Daily Telegraph* and almost all other papers rallied to the support of the deceased editor.

The truth was, of course, that Dawson had played a role in the abdication, but in the long run he most certainly could not be blamed for it.

Following what turned out to be something of a storm in a thimble, the Windsors took off on their first yacht cruise of the Mediterranean in many years. They chartered the yacht *Amazon* and sailed to Genoa, Portofino, and other Italian coastal towns, proceeding to Rome, where they were received in audience by a person of like political views, Pope Pius XII. They were accompanied by Sir Walter Roberts, British minister to the Vatican. They avoided, for obvious reasons, U.S. ambassador Clare Boothe Luce and Edda Mussolini Ciano. On the next leg of the cruise the duke was stricken with a severe case of gastroenteritis due to poisoned food and had to be taken by train from Montecatini to Paris for immediate treatment. Still feeling ill, he was a victim of a severe attack of lumbago, and even a trip to Biarritz did not prove to be particularly reviving. At close to 60, he was feeling the first symptoms of approaching old age. His temper cannot have been helped by the publication that year of a book entitled *Lèse Majesty: The Private Lives of the Duke and Duchess of Windsor*, by Norman Lockridge. Chapter 1 was entitled "The Worst of the Charges: Homosexualism." The book, with a degree of readable scurrilousness, contained alleged interviews by the author with the author Sir Edmund Gosse and with a psychiatrist; the former denied the charge that the duke was homosexual, while the latter confirmed it. There was no suit for libel.

In late 1952, the Windsors finally wearied of the Rue de la Faisanderie. They began house-hunting, deciding that at last they must obtain a residence which would satisfy their every requirement and from which they would never have to move. They settled at first upon 29 Rue Barbey-de-Jouet, but discovered that this was French government property and was not available. There was some discussion of their obtaining the historic home that had once belonged to Madame du Barry, but the notoriety of its previous occupant finally made them decide against it. They had continued their friendship with Paul-Louis Weiller, and it was this personage who recommended to the Paris municipal authorities that the Windsors should be allowed to live, at a peppercorn rent, in a magnificent house, 4 Route du Champ d'Entrainement. The rent was only $50 a year; a magnificent establishment, the house stood in a two-acre park, on the edge of the leafy Bois de Boulogne.

It was in these years that the duchess again set the tone of the style of life that defied postwar austerity and would forever be associated with her name. She embarked upon close to thirty years of a fine degree of extravagance in households in which she saw herself as surrogate queen. Sydney Johnson, a black who had been with the couple since the Bahamas, would greet arrivals with great circumstance, dressed attractively in scarlet and gold. He was accompanied by a Spanish butler, Georges Sanègre, who customarily wore white tie and tails. As always, Wallis ran the household with fanatical expertise. As a hostess, she was more dazzling than ever. She supervised minutely every detail of her perfect dinner parties, even making sure that the lettuce leaves were trimmed to the same size and shape. At the cocktail hour the staff in livery carried fine silver trays with such Legros delicacies from prewar years as grapes individually hollowed out and filled with tiny dollops of cream cheese, bacon bits fried in brown sugar, cabbage leaf pieces with shrimps or prawns attached to them by picks, fried mussels, and chipolata sausages. Dinner was customarily served in the blue chinoiserie dining room at two round tables set for eight. Wallis did not copy her prewar habit of having flowers on the tables. She always made sure that, in a tradition she had learned in Britain, there would be delicate savories for the guests following the dessert. There were, of course, silver and gold monogrammed cigarette boxes and exquisite cut-glass fingerbowls; the dinner service and silver were souvenirs of York House and Fort Belvedere. According to Suzy Menkes, Wallis especially favored as main courses roast partridge, chicken Maryland—a nostalgic touch— grouse, and faux filets, and then, for dessert, the luscious dark chocolate cake known to the world as Sacher torte.

The Windsors decided that they also needed a country home, a gentle and subdued place of escape; despite the fact that the Paris house had its tiny park and its greenhouses, the duke yearned for a garden. From the beginning, one of his greatest pleasures in life had been pottering about among flowers, crossbreeding, applying a vigorous watering can, and dibbling the soil for new plantings. Under his green thumb even the most reluctant earth would flourish and multiply. Give him a packet of seeds and a set of instructions and he was in seventh heaven.

The duke and duchess managed with great good fortune to locate the house which of all houses in their lives they were to love the most. It was known familiarly as "The Mill." Only the fort approached it in terms of the magic it held for the duke. Its real name was the Moulin de la Tuilerie, and it was just fifteen miles southwest of the fashionable Paris suburb of Neuilly, outside the charming but rather gloomy village of Gif-sur-Yvette. It was a seventeenth-century structure, brown, with white shutters, redolent of a more leisurely and comfortable era when kings were kings and a leisurely aristocracy ruled France. It was owned by the distinguished painter, designer, and creator of theatrical spectacles Etienne Drian; it was rented initially, and then bought, for no more than $80,000.

If Wallis poured all her energy into the Paris house, assisted the while by the irreplaceable Stephane Boudin, the duke flung his creative passion headlong into The Mill. To begin with, he completely redesigned the garden. It became a haven, a bower of flowers and grass and delicate trees adored and frolicked in by the pugs Imp, Trooper, Davy Crockett, and Disraeli. The house itself was reconstructed from top to bottom. With skill, the duke managed to preserve the original, powerful, two-foot-thick walls, the massive oak beams, and even the slate tiles on the roof. Like so many French buildings of the period, The Mill was surrounded by three other buildings that flanked a cobbled courtyard. It was a private enclave, ancient in mood even after the extensive changes. The duchess added many touches of her own to the duke's workmanship. She created a white bedroom and bought an immense antique bed, canopied and covered in plump silk pillows. The duke's room was spartan, not much more than a soldier would enjoy in a country billet. And, once again, every inch of the room was crowded with pictures of the duchess.

Fastidious visitors like Cecil Beaton and Kitty Bache (Mrs. Gilbert) Miller made some criticisms of the house to Charles Murphy as they walked through it. Beaton thought the whole thing excessive, and he disapproved of the use of war medallions, bamboo chairs, and gimmicky poufs. Kitty Miller hated the clutter; like many Americans, she objected to the British habit, now mimicked by Wallis, of wanting to fill every bit of space in the Victorian tradition. There was one fantastic import from York House: the immense war map that had illuminated the duke's rooms there, representing the earth from sea to sea, from pole to pole, and marked with all the illuminated journeys he had undertaken in his lifetime. From as early as 1933 such visitors as Gloria Vanderbilt and her mother had been captivated by the map, and now

another generation of friends and acquaintances would stand transfixed before it. Two grenadier bass drums formed the coffee table in
the living room. The stables and cattle stalls became a guest wing.
There, the atmosphere was exceptionally military and nautical, with
Highland banners and tartans, contest trophies, World War I buttons,
and other souvenirs everywhere. The abdication table formed part of
this private museum. It was said that years later, when the duchess died,
the table was offered to the British royal family. "The Queen needs the
abdication table like a hole in the head," a palace representative is, with
unaccustomed informality, supposed to have said.

Much of 1952 and 1953 was absorbed in work on the two houses. During this period the duke resumed and the duchess acquired a warm
friendship. They became very close to Sir Oswald and Lady Mosley.
The Mosleys lived at the Temple de la Gloire, only a few miles from
The Mill. Since the duke had known them in the 1930s, they had had
a checkered career. It will be recalled that in May 1940 Winston
Churchill, acting on the recommendation of Sir Robert Vansittart and
Clement Attlee, had imprisoned them in London for activities that
were considered inimical to the public safety under the provisions of
the specially introduced Regulation 18B. They had suffered considerable privations in jail. For a long time Lady Mosley did not see her
children, because she was anxious that they should be kept away from
the scandal. The effects of an icy winter of 1940, the bad food, and the
insanitary conditions seriously affected Sir Oswald's normally robust
health; by 1943 he was a victim of phlebitis, and it was felt that he
might not survive another year. A much-embattled home secretary,
Herbert Morrison, and Winston Churchill apparently decided that
Mosely must not be a martyr, and they arranged for both his and Lady
Mosley's release. At the end of the war it was the Mosleys' misfortune
that Clement Attlee was elected prime minister; as head of the Labour
government, he made sure that life continued to be uncomfortable for
the pair. According to Lady Mosley, she and her husband were forbidden
the use of passports and had to flee the country aboard a chartered yacht
for Ireland. They later proceeded to France, where they at last settled in
the temple. It had once been the property of General Moreau, chief of
the armies of the Rhine, who was considered to have been a rival of
Napoleon until his death in 1810. For years the building had belonged

to the family of the Comtes de Noailles. When the Mosleys purchased it in 1951, it was in a state of extreme disrepair, a dank and pathetic structure that had lost most of its character. They proceeded to remodel it with great taste and style, and the Windsors very much enjoyed going there.

It was unwise for the Windsors to associate with the Mosleys at this particular juncture. The Mosleys not only were personae non grata in London but were not to be received by British diplomatic representatives in Europe. One would have thought that, in the wake of all they had been through, the Windsors would have wished to associate only with those who were apolitical or who, by no stretch of the imagination, could recall the disastrous commitment to a now vanquished and deceased Adolf Hitler and Mussolini. Instead, they chose to enjoy a public friendship with the British knight most clearly associated in the minds of thinking people with nazism. In fact, Lady Mosley's sister Unity Mitford had been notorious among the more celebrated British supporters of Hitler, had flung herself at the führer himself, and had attempted suicide following public condemnation.

In 1986, the late Lady Mosley made no bones to me about her continuing feeling that Hitler was a genius and a potential savior of the twentieth century. Still resident at the Temple de la Gloire, retaining the delicate beauty of a moonbeam in her old age, she recalled her friendship with the Windsors. She made it entirely clear that, starting in the 1930s and right up until their deaths, the Windsors shared her views on Nazi Germany. They felt, as she and her husband did, that if a separate peace had been made with the führer in 1939 and Hitler had been given a free hand against the Soviet Union, the world would have been saved from communism and the British Empire would never have fallen into decay. She said:

> The Windsors agreed with me, and the Duchess was certainly politically sophisticated and knew exactly what she was doing and saying, that World War I had been a total failure, that it was a disaster the Austro-Hungarian Empire had been broken up, that the Versailles Treaty was grossly unfair, and that Germany should never have been encircled in the 1930s. If Hitler had been given a free hand to destroy communism, and if he had been allowed to deport the Jews, if Britain and America had accepted them, there would have been no need for a holocaust. There was of course no room in Palestine for them. Hitler felt the Jews

behaved abominably in Germany after World War I, and all he wanted
to do was be rid of them. And one mustn't forget that anti-Semitism was
endemic everywhere in central Europe: the Poles hated them, the Czechs
hated them, everyone did. Of course, my husband, the Windsors and I
felt that we could not exonerate Hitler for being impatient and provoking World War II. With two egos like Churchill and Hitler, there was
little chance for peace in the world. But still, if the right people had been
in power in England, particularly Lloyd George, there could have been
a negotiated peace.

The Mosleys dined at The Mill twice a week, and the Windsors almost that frequently at the Temple de la Gloire. One of their perennial
topics of conversation was the idea that after World War II ended the
Allied forces should have occupied satellite countries of the Soviets before the Russians got to them and should have proceeded to conquer
the Soviet Union itself. In none of these retrospective views were the
Windsors in any way exceptional in aristocratic or royal society. Such
opinions were bruited about clubland and right-wing dinner tables
from shore to shining shore, and still are in 2004.

In April 1950 Wallis learned of the death of Win Spencer at 62.
During the early 1950s she continued to suffer from poor health. In
February 1951 she was at the Harkness Pavilion at the Columbia Pres-
byterian Medical Center in New York for tests, followed by elective
surgery to remove her apparently cancerous ovaries. Dr. Benjamin P.
Watson, fellow of the Scottish Royal College of Surgeons and an emi-
nent gynecologist, assisted the American doctor, Henry Wisdom
Cave. Wallis was depressed and miserable. After she had gained sufficient strength, she began desultory work on her own memoirs, using a
variety of collaborators, including Cleveland Amory, who later became
the author of the witty and perceptive volume *Who Killed Society?*, and
the hardworking Charles Murphy. Like so many authors of memoirs,
she naturally selected from the past those facts which would flatter her,
while omitting those which would not. She was particularly evasive in
the matter of China. That entire chapter of the book was so completely
fabricated that she even altered the name of the hotel she stayed at in
Shanghai from the Astor House to the Palace; she scarcely mentioned
the Chinese civil war, and apart from her arrivals on the *Chaumont* and
the *Empress of Canada*, she scrambled her dates so completely that she
confused and tripped up subsequent biographers, who followed her

blindly. One might legitimately conclude that, concerned over her oath of secrecy, she was anxious to disguise the fact that she had been working for U.S. naval intelligence, and of course she would also have been concerned about hiding her affair with Count Ciano. Throughout the book, however, facts were remorselessly rearranged in what amounted to a self-performed face-lift. The Oakes case was dismissed in brief paragraphs; only in the passages dealing with her childhood and her flight to France at the time of the abdication did she rise to the drama of the occasion. Yet in spite of everything the book, finally issued in 1956 under the excellent title *The Heart Has Its Reasons*, had enormous charm, reflecting its author's politically misguided but winning and desirable personality in abundance. Though it did not equal the critical success of the duke's own volume, the book sold well and attracted a new generation of readers to this charismatic, electric, and compulsively ambitious personality.

Old friends turned up in the 1950s, and new friendships were formed. One of the most embattled of these was with the dumpy, smart, sophisticated hostess and society mascot Elsa Maxwell. She had, of course, encountered the Windsors before, most notably when they arrived in Vienna on one of their visits in 1935, when she was riveted by the duchess's strong, forceful stride across the lobby of the Hotel Bristol on her way to the elevator. Miss Maxwell had known the duke when he was Prince of Wales, and like everyone else she was captivated by him. By the late 1930s Miss Maxwell was the party organizer par excellence of her era. Despite her phenomenal lack of personal attractiveness and a figure that resembled an advertisement doughnut, she was called upon by everyone who mattered to organize spectacular occasions that people talked about for decades. Miss Maxwell had a knack for engaging the most skilled caterers, the finest decorators, the very best chefs, waiters, and attendants, the most glittering dance bands, and the most exotic and beautiful young men and woman. She created, for the bored and exhausted members of high society, a range of stimuli in the form of soirées that featured a mixture of movie stars, playwrights, authors, politicians, composers, and artists. She brought them all together and moved among her guests, with a somewhat toadlike but persistent waddle, fixing everyone in sight with her charming, always fascinated stare, snapping out deliciously squalid gossip, and making sure that all the guests were happy with their company and that their champagne or cocktail glasses were never empty.

Elsa Maxwell was infuriated by the Windsors' interest in Hitler and strongly felt that the duke should never have abdicated, but should have retained Wallis as his mistress. She would even confront them at parties and tell them point-blank what she thought of them, her effrontery causing them only to smile. She ran into them in both New York and Europe during this period, enjoying a mutual friendship with Mrs. George Baker.

In December 1952, she helped Mrs. Lytle Hull, sister-in-law of the former secretary of state, Cordell Hull, gave a tremendous benefit party in New York and invited the Windsors. Wallis asked that her name not be mentioned as a sponsor; she was always crying poor and trying to find ways out of paying income tax. Elsa was annoyed about this, as she had expected to display the duchess as her trump card, showing not only the end of a long hostility but also her capacity to attract the very greatest to her occasions. She was even more annoyed the following year when Mrs. Hull queened it over a similar Maxwellized benefit. On this occasion Miss Maxwell chose the beautiful Duchess of Argyll, the Duchesse de Brissac, the Duchess of Alba, and the Duchess Disera as her sponsors. Cholly Knickerbocker, the popular columnist, asked Wallis her opinion of the choices. Wallis snapped back, "It would take four ordinary duchesses to make one duchess of Windsor." Elsa was phenomenally upset about that. And she was also annoyed because, despite many pleadings, she could never get the Windsors to speak publicly in her favor. However, she was mollified when the duchess hired her to present the Windsor Ball at the Waldorf Astoria in 1953, with the decor done by Cecil Beaton. It was a tremendous occasion: the duchess caused a flurry when she entered the ball, not on the arm of the duke, but on that of the socialite Prince Serge Obolensky.

The Windsors and Elsa quarreled again soon afterward, chiefly over the omnipresent Jimmy Donahue, whom Elsa could not abide and whose behavior, particularly in front of his adored mother Jessie, the somewhat prim and proper Miss Maxwell found insupportably offensive, despite the fact that she herself was a lesbian. She begged the duchess not to drag Jimmy along on a cruise of the Mediterranean in 1954, and she was continually worried that his ménage of male prostitutes and other lowlife might threaten the Windsors' safety or make off with their possessions. As it turned out, these fears were ground-less, but that did not prevent Miss Maxwell from retaining them.

By the mid-1950s the Windsors were growing tired of Donahue. He was losing his looks all too rapidly under the onslaughts of drink-ing, smoking, and endless late nights. A ghastly incident brought the whole miserable matter to an end. Charles Murphy was privy to it. The embattled trio were at Baden Baden in Germany, staying at a ho-tel and apparently taking the waters. During a quarrel in the hotel restaurant one evening, Jimmy kicked the duchess so hard that she bled. She screamed in combined shock and fury, and the duke, scowl-ing and red-faced, assisted her to a sofa. He shrieked at Jimmy to get out. Soon after Jimmy left the dining room, the unfazable playboy phoned the duke and said, "I can't find my valet to pack. He's off with yours." The duke slammed down the receiver; the most atrocious rela-tionship of the Windsors' lives was almost at an end. According to the author Hugo Vickers, basing his findings upon the diaries of Cecil Beaton, the final rift was caused by a petty detail. Donahue was eating too much garlic, and his breath offended the duke and duchess.

19

Late Afternoon

In the early months of 1953 Queen Mary, then in her mid-eighties, began to fail. On March 6 the duke, accompanied by the princess royal, who had been visiting New York, sailed aboard the *Queen Elizabeth* for England to see his stricken mother. The duchess again stayed behind at the Waldorf Towers.

No sooner had he arrived than the old queen passed away. The duchess heard the news on the radio at the Towers; her secretary, Anne Seagrin, recalled later that, to her surprise, the duchess wept when she heard the news. It was a remarkable feature of the duchess's character that despite all the calumny heaped upon her from the palace, and her own hatred of England, knowing how much Queen Mary meant to her husband she shared his grief almost as though she had known Queen Mary herself. For years afterward she kept a picture of the deceased former monarch on a table in her bedroom Paris.

The coronation of Queen Elizabeth II was to take place on June 2. This presented a unique problem because the normal period of court respect was six months of full mourning followed by six months more of half mourning. The Duke of Windsor as monarch had set a precedent by shortening the time to six months. Elizabeth had reduced the period to four months for her father. In order not to upset the order of the coronation, the new period was reduced to one month. Queen Mary had left explicit instructions that nothing must affect the coronation; this was typical of her.

For the second time in a little over two years, London was draped with black banners. Flags again flew at half-mast. A long stream of visitors appeared at Marlborough House to leave notes of condolence along with visiting cards. Members of both houses of Parliament convened in black suits. Prime Minister Churchill again moved the duke to tears as he delivered a BBC broadcast, stating incorrectly that Queen Mary was the last living link with Queen Victoria. It was yet another excruciating reminder to the duke of the world of his childhood, a world now irrevocably lost in an increasingly pragmatic and democratic age, with the Soviets looming; dangerous. He must have realized the poignant irony contained within Churchill's statement:

> She [Queen Mary] died in the knowledge that the crown of these realms, worn so gloriously by her husband and by her son, and soon to be set with all solemnity on the head of her granddaughter, is far more broadly and securely based on the people's love and the nation's will than in the sedate days of her youth, when rank and privilege ruled society.

The duke can scarcely have failed to note that only one son of his late father was mentioned by the prime minister.

Lord Beaverbrook seized the occasion to express through his newspapers an urgent request to the world at large that the long exile of the Duke and Duchess of Windsor should be terminated. The *Daily Express* stated in an editorial: "It is the deep and earnest desire of the nation that [the former king] should make his home in this, the land that gave him birth." Other newspapers pointed out that while Queen Mary was alive, the duke had announced repeatedly to her that he would take up residence in Great Britain only if the duchess were to be received by his family. Queen Mary, the newspapers pointed out, had remained unalterably opposed to the duchess's reception. These were painful things for the duchess to read.

Once again, thousands of saddened Londoners filed past the royal coffin lying in state in Westminster Hall. The drums sounded; the salute of guns rang through the air; the gun carriage, drawn by six black horses, lumbered through the streets. Behind the carriage the Duke of Windsor walked in company with the Duke of Edinburgh, the Duke of Gloucester, and the Duke of Kent. At Westminster Hall the new queen, Princess Margaret, the princess royal, the Queen Mother, and the Duchesses of Kent and Gloucester were waiting. The burial at St. George's Chapel, Windsor, was a further ordeal for the duke. As at the time of his brother's interment, he could not hold back the tears. At the end he stood quietly beside the tomb and then made a deep bow toward it, whispering words of farewell to the mother he loved. He sailed on the *Queen Elizabeth* the following day for the United States, and remained confined to his cabin for most of the voyage. He would not attend his niece's coronation since, despite all his pleas, it was decided not to invite the duchess. According to some sources, the duke himself was not invited.

The Windsors remained in New York during the June celebrations, listening with mixed feelings to the skillful running commentaries by Richard Dimbleby and others in the broadcasts from London.

Soon afterward the couple faced the unpleasant ordeal of the publication of the German Foreign Ministry documents which disclosed the duke's leakage of the discussion that took place at the War Cabinet meeting of February 1940 on the matter of the Belgian invasion plan. Confronted with the matter by reporters during a visit to London on November 9, the duke denied the entire affair and said that he was not responsible and the documents were false. No one had the temerity to cross-question him or to seek further investigation, and his denial was allowed to stand. Churchill, as always, defended him. When a question was asked in Parliament, Churchill stated that the charges against the duke were, "of course, quite untrue." He added: "I naturally thought it proper to show [the documents] to the Duke of Windsor and, on May 25, told him they were to be published in the United States and in this country later in the year. His Royal Highness did not raise any objection. He thought, and I agree with him, that they can be treated with contempt."

In January 1955 the Windsors visited President Eisenhower at the While House. They had first encountered him as a colonel on their first wartime visit to Washington in 1941. In March they were present at White Plains, New York, where they exhibited their favorite three-year-old pug, Goldengleam Trooper, in the fifteenth event of the Saw Mill River Kennel Club. The dog won out against 950 competitors in the contest. However, it lost the gold rosette to Mr. and Mrs. Arnold J. Canton's Golden Note.

In October Mrs. George Baker gave a party for the Windsors at her elaborate home at Locust Valley, Long Island. Fifty-eight guests attended for a banquet and dancing. Among the guests were two recent acquaintances of the duchess, the wealthy and handsome 35-year-old sportsman and racehorse owner William Woodward, Jr., and his wife Ann. Wallis very much liked Woodward's mother, the still glamorous and fascinating former Elsie Ogden Cryder. The Woodwards left the party at 1 a.m., returning to their house at Oyster Bay. Mrs. Woodward was nervous that night because there had been talk of prowlers in the neighborhood.

At 2:08 a.m. an emergency operator answered a call from the Woodward house. Ann was shrieking hysterically. Lieutenant Haff arrived at the house and found Mrs. Woodward in a state of desperation. Woodward was lying naked on his face on his bedroom floor, shot through the right temple.

It was discovered that Ann Woodward had taken a duck-hunting rifle and loaded it with shells, placing it next to her bed. She said through floods of tears that she had heard her watchdog barking and was convinced there was an intruder. She turned on the lamp next to her bed, picked up the rifle, and made her way to the door. Seeing a man standing there, she fired twice, right into his face.

The Windsors, who were staying with Mrs. Baker, were advised of the shooting that night. The news was of course a considerable shock to them. Wallis had even danced with Bill Woodward at the party. The duke shared Woodward's interest in horses, and they had enjoyed their meetings socially over the previous months. They followed the subsequent events with deep interest; Wallis was questioned twice by the police. Mrs. Woodward was held for questioning while society flew into an uproar. The Windsors were asked about the killing wherever they went. They decided wisely not to get involved; they made no attempt to contact Ann during her long ordeal, though they did remain in close touch with Mrs. Baker and with Elsie Woodward on the matter.

On November 25 a Nassau County grand jury heard Mrs. Woodward tell her story. On the advice of her lawyers, she appeared voluntarily and signed a waiver of immunity against the possible consequences of what she might say. In a state of great distress, sobbing helplessly, she told her version of the facts simply, poignantly, and with apparent honesty, her face devoid of makeup, her cheeks drained of color. The jury accepted her account and reached the conclusion that she was not guilty of the crime. However, many refused to believe her. The most persistent skeptic was Truman Capote, who in the late 1960s and 1970s would pursue the matter. He made clear that his book in progress, *Answered Prayers*, would disclose the fact that Ann Woodward was guilty of murder.

Capote's destructive campaign had a result. Ann Woodward, met by suspicious glances from those who believed Capote's story, and still haunted by the horror of what she had done, committed suicide. As a result, Capote himself was adversely affected. His whole life hinged upon society; many members of that society closed their doors to him. The Windsors were as angry with Capote as everyone else.

The late 1950s brought two serious bereavements. Herman Rogers, whose wife Katherine had passed away in 1948, died of cancer in the south of France. He had remarried and left a son. Ernest Simpson died, also of cancer, in 1958. Wallis did not visit him in the hospital in London where he lay dying. She sent a large bouquet of his favorite chrysanthemums, a nostalgic reminiscence of their early times together, with a note that said, simply: "From the Duchess of Windsor."

In April 1956 the Windsors embarked on the first of a series of charitable projects that did much to restore their tarnished image in the eyes of thinking people. They set up a clinic for the rehabilitation of civilian handicapped people in New York. In this, they were assisted by Dr. Howard A. Rusk, director of the Institute of Physical Medicine and Rehabilitation at the New York University–Bellevue Medical Center. They also set up a similar clinic in Paris with the aid of Dr. Jacques Hindermayer, director of the rehabilitation program at the Paris Children's Hospital.

But while their public relations image was being burnished by these adventures in charity, the Windsors with apparent perversity seemed to encourage relationships which could only reconfirm the more unfair suspicions of those who wished to cast aspersions on them. They resumed their prewar friendship with Prince Otto and Princess Ann-Mari von Bismarck. The Princess von Bismarck recalled in 1987 that she lent the Windsors her home in Marbella, Spain, and stayed with them at their house in Paris. Her husband had been cleared of Nazi associations at the end of World War II, but nevertheless the fact that the prince had been a representative of Germany in London as chargé d'affaires at the embassy throughout much of 1936, the year of Edward VIII's reign, showed the duke's persistent political interests, memories, and concerns.

In 1960, the duchess made another of her rather serious mistakes. She decided to embark upon a critique of the British royal family and government for its "twenty-four years of persecution" against the duke. In an article in *McCall's* magazine, published in January 1961, she wrote, "My husband has been punished like a small boy who gets a spanking every day of his life for a single transgression." She continued, "I think the monarchy's lack of dignity toward him [at the time of the abdication crisis] and occasionally now, has been resented." She also wrote, "It suddenly occurred to me how ridiculous it is to go on behind a family-designed, government-manufactured curtain of asbestos that protects the British Commonwealth from dangerous us. . . . This man, with his unparalleled knowledge, trained in the affairs of State . . . was first given an insignificant military post. Eventually, he was 'put out of harm's way' with an appointment of little consequence—the Governorship of the Bahamas."

This outburst was singularly ill-advised and, had it not been for the consideration of the queen, might have closed the door to the Windsors at Buckingham Palace forever. It seemed almost deliberately designed to infuriate the Queen Mother, who continued to tell people that it was the influence of Wallis that had forced her husband to assume the throne, thereby destroying his health. For the duchess to portray the royal family as mean, vindictive, and destructive on some absurdly hypocritical moral basis was a falsification of the truth. Unhappily, her point of view has been perpetuated by her authorized biographer, Michael Bloch.

In the early 1960s the Windsors finally decided to dispose of the Alberta ranch. Visits there were so infrequent, and the couple's disappointment in the failure to discover oil on the property so intense, there seemed to be no purpose in retaining it. Colonel Douglas Kennedy, who had managed the ranch since 1956, put it on the market at the beginning of November 1961. A substantial number of Hereford and Galloway cattle, 800 hogs, and a team of Welsh ponies were offered with the 4,000 acres. In addition, there was a large stable of Clydesdale and thoroughbred horses, as well as imported collie dogs and German shepherds. The estimated value was $300,000.

The sale was completed on February 28, 1962. The purchaser was Jim Cartwright, owner of a neighboring ranch, who wished to extend his own territory. That same year the duke and duchess celebrated their silver wedding anniversary aboard the ship that they now favored over British vessels, the SS *United States*. The Windsors gave an elaborate party in a private room, attended by the captain and several of the senior officers. They seemed radiantly happy and gave interviews by radiotelephone to the *New York Times* and other newspapers.

In Paris in the 1960s the Windsors surpassed even their own previous record as party givers. Sir John Colville recalled that everything at the Bois de Boulogne house was "perfection itself." The food, the service, the exquisite elegance of the hostess, the collection of French aristocracy and representatives of the diplomatic corps, all in a setting of matchless elegance created by Boudin, made an unforgettable impression. Lady Mosley in her turn did not forget those evenings, the candlelight shining on polished mahogany, the period mirrors glowing from the walls, the paintings and tapestries and fine silver.

The guests were served by footmen dressed in royal scarlet livery. The table was decorated with six immense Venetian sterling silver candelabra. Each guest had beside his or her plate a small, perfectly fashioned snuffbox, containing either cigarettes or small gifts. If there were Spanish or German guests present, the duke would talk to them expertly in their own language. Oddly, in view of their place of residence, neither of the Windsors could manage more than fourth-form French.

The duke remained more outspoken than the duchess on political themes. He continued to say, at these dinner parties often preaching to the converted, that a negotiated peace should have been made with Hitler in 1940 and that England should have retained a neutral position, as Sweden did, while the Germans and Italians were free to destroy communism. He would point out that all his predictions had come true and that now, because there had been no World War III in 1945 and Russia had not been crushed, one had to face the menace of the Soviets. If the Rothschilds or other figures of the Jewish community were not present, he would drag out his old theme of blaming Roosevelt and the Jews for the confrontation and total surrender policy of World War II.

As the 1960s wore on, the duke acted with an increasing eccentricity, watched with disapproving frowns by his more composed and restrained wife. Charles Murphy has recorded that the duke would rather awkwardly attempt to conduct the dance band hired for the evening or would suddenly stand up and perform as though on an invisible cello or violin. He would join the band, clumsily tapping away at the drums.

He would even sing, most raucously, in reprises of the hit numbers of *Annie Get Your Gun* or *South Pacific*. At times he would break out in Spanish or German. During one party he danced a clumsy Charleston with Noël Coward.

While Wallis shopped or went to fashion salons, was massaged or spent hours in beauty parlors, the duke continued to display his passion for golf. He remained rather a poor hand at the sport. He had been through the hands of numerous golfing pros but still, according to Murphy, could only manage to score in the 90s. He was as stingy as ever, failing to tip even the caddies, who in France depended upon largesse to exist. At the same time, he never ceased going over his accounting books, watching everything meticulously, jiggling his knee in a state of nervous tension. Chain-smoking, he would scatter ash over the ledger pages, brushing it irritably aside as he found some real or imaginary mistake in his accountant's work. He remained shrewd in his investments, taking the money he had pulled out of the Central Railroad and investing it in reliable blue-chip stocks. The money from his memoirs was expertly placed in a varied portfolio. His lawyers and London advisers on his royal interests were on their toes day and night to satisfy him. But, above all, the garden of The Mill absorbed him and satisfied him. He still loved working there, puttering about in old shoes, blissfully cross-pollinating in a large, floppy hat.

Much of the mid-1960s was taken up with elaborate social events: parties at the New York World's Fair of 1964; major functions in honor of President Lyndon B. Johnson; benefits at the Waldorf, including the big Heart of America Ball, held in the Sert Room, where a columned gazebo, covered with elder vines, was ablaze with multicolored lights. In June 1964 the duke and duchess celebrated their birthdays.

But at the same time, life was not without its many problems and anguishes. The duchess had two face-lifts; she did not respond well to surgery, and the postoperative recoveries caused her considerable distress. The duke was suffering from severe eye problems; ever since he had read the difficult and complex official documents during his reign in 1936, he had had almost consistent strain in his eyes, and now the ravages of advancing age had drastically affected his vision. The retina of his left eye had become detached in late 1964, and an operation was recommended in London. It was feared that he might go blind in that eye and that the other eye might be affected in what was known as sympathetic blindness.

In August 1964 Aunt Bessie turned 100, and Lelia Noyes gave a big party for her at Wakefield Manor. The house was as beautifully preserved as it had been during Wallis's childhood. Twenty-five relatives and friends attended the dinner, at which Mrs. Noyes proposed the toast, saying, "This is for Aunt Bessie to all the world, a great lady, once called by the King of England a 'wise and gentle woman.'" The Windsors' health problems prevented them from attending the dinner. According to Mrs. Dale St. Dennis, Aunt Bessie was very disappointed. The family was chagrined when Wallis failed to attend Aunt Bessie's funeral; Mrs. Merryman died on November 29. But at the time Wallis, recovering from surgery on her right foot, was in a hospital in New York City. She was upset that the doctors would not let her go. However, the duke did put in an appearance.

To Wallis's distress, he was ailing seriously by this stage. He was suffering from an aneurysm in the aorta artery of the abdomen below the arterial branches that led to the kidneys. The decision was made to have an immediate operation because the weakening of the artery wall through which blood was circulated from the heart could present serious potential danger. It could rupture suddenly, with at least a 7 percent chance of immediate death. Only in recent years has the corrective surgery become available, in which a Dacron graft or section can be used. The preeminent expert in the field was Dr. Michael de Bakey, professor of surgery at Baylor University College of Medicine in Houston. On December 11 the Windsors arrived by train in that city and were met by British consul general Peter Hope. They decided to take up residence in the Methodist Hospital together, arriving with a police motorcycle escort in a $35,000 Rolls Royce gray Phantom limousine. Despite their personal distress the Windsors gave a buoyant interview to reporters, carrying off the situation with their customary style and grace. They were touched and surprised when, upon entering the suite of rooms, they found bouquets of flowers from the queen and the princess royal. This was yet another subtle and welcome indication of the present queen's moderate attitude toward the Windsors, or at least toward the duke.

Michael de Bakey is one of the most remarkable figures of medicine.

Even though he was 56 at the time, he was immaculately trim, fit, and muscular, and he exuded an atmosphere of striking physical and mental health. Often up at dawn, he was known to be at the operating table for as many as twelve to fourteen hours in the course of a day, and he was capable of doing as many as forty-five operations a week. He would run many of the young and athletic members of his staff completely off their feet. He was a delightfully comic figure, racing along the hospital corridors, bent forward, his long legs loping away, in his shapeless surgeon's scrub suit that flapped around his ankles, looking, according to a *New York Times* reporter, "like Groucho Marx without a mustache." He talked sharply and rapidly, earning his nickname of "The Texas Tornado." Nobody really believed that he slept at all. He seemed like a man possessed, and the human cardiovascular system was as familiar to him as an African jungle to an explorer. His antic genius enthralled the Windsors, and he became a lifelong friend.

The surgery took place on December 16; it began at 7:35 a.m. and lasted exactly sixty-seven minutes. Though the duke was thin and generally devoid of body fat, the operation was still strenuous and delicate for a man of his age. Had he been overweight, it would have been much more drastic. De Bakey found that the aneurysm was the size of a large grapefruit and there was severe erosion of the aorta wall. In fact, the duke was in more danger than had hitherto been expected. The duchess was not present during the operation itself—she was stoic and calm as she waited—but she was with the duke every other minute. As he came round from the anesthetic, he was remarkably perky and talked to the duchess and de Bakey with an eager smile. Letters and telegrams poured in from all over the world. Two days afterward the duke managed to struggle to his feet and take a few steps, feeling chipper but undeniably and understandably weak. He sat down hard on the bed, breaking into a charming laugh at his own expense.

Everyone in the hospital adored him. He was the best possible patient, considerate of the nurses and always ready with a joke. He never complained about the liquid diet or the subsequent use of soft foods. His eye was still giving him much trouble, and when he waved to the cameras during his first Christmas photography session, his left eye, sadly, was closed. He pulled himself together for the traditional turkey dinner on Christmas day.

————

On New Year's day the Windsors checked out of the Methodist Hospital and moved into a ninth-floor suite at the Warwick Hotel. Six days later they flew to New York, accompanied by the duke's personal physician, Dr. Arthur Antenucci. This was the first time the duchess had set foot on a jet plane: a Delta Airlines Convaire 880. The couple sailed for Europe on January 29 aboard the USS *United States*. They were greatly saddened by the death of Winston Churchill; because of the medical problems of the moment, they were unable to attend the funeral, and the duke was represented by Sir John Aird. His persistent eye trouble would be taken care of at the London Clinic under the supervision of the distinguished Sir Stewart Duke-Elder, surgeon oculist to the queen herself. Again, the queen sent a magnificent bouquet to the clinic. The operation, which took place on the night of February 26, was successful. Sir Stewart Duke-Elder used recently improved high-intensity laser beams, now a standard in eye surgery, to weld the troublesome retina to the back of the eyeball. A second operation was involved, treating the membrane that delivered the images to the eye's optic nerve. On March 15, after the duke had a third corrective treatment, the queen arrived at London Clinic with her principal private secretary, Sir Michael Adeane, and her bodyguard, Detective Inspector Albert Perkins. Sir Stewart Duke-Elder and two of his associates greeted her as she proceeded to the suite. It was made clear that she would accept the duchess's presence, and in a historic act she greeted Wallis, who curtseyed deeply. They had not seen each other since that awkward moment when Wallis appeared at the Royal Lodge in 1936 and suggested that the garden be rearranged according to her specifications.

The duke presented a smiling but sad figure as he sat in an armchair, wearing a robe over his pajamas, his left eye concealed behind bandages. The meeting was somewhat strained, but both the queen and the duke behaved with an appropriate royal composure and refused to allow past differences to affect them. The duke seized the occasion to ask the queen if she would permit him to be buried, when death came, in the private burial ground of the royal family at Frogmore. And he had a further request—a request of the highest moment that would call upon the monarch's consideration. The duke understandably wanted Wallis buried next to him, and he wanted both of them to be accorded the privilege of funeral services at St. George's Chapel.

The queen promised to attend to the matter. She did not respond immediately. The queen felt somewhat composed about the thought of the duke's being buried at Frogmore, but she was said to have been opposed to the idea of the duchess's being buried there. The Queen Mother is said to have felt even more strongly on the matter. Of course, in the eyes of the queen and those of her mother Wallis still was not "Her Royal Highness," nor by any stretch of the imagination could she be called a royal person, nor was she acknowledged even at that late hour as a member of the family. But the queen, who was fond of her uncle, could not bear to hurt him. She was faced with a considerable quandary, which she did not immediately resolve.

The Duchess of Kent turned up, quite disguising her ill feelings about the failure of the Windsors to send her a note of condolence following the death of her husband. The Duke and Duchess of Gloucester were in Australia; the Queen Mother, who did send flowers, was not present in the hospital. Nor, so far as is known, did she speak to the duke on the telephone.

On March 19 the Windsors left the London Clinic. Caught by a cruel camera, the duke was wearing dark glasses and looked pathetically frail. The queen visited the duke and duchess at Claridges, and she brought with her pleasing news. She would grant the duke permission to be buried at Frogmore, and the duchess would be accorded an identical privilege. Moreover, both would be given the special funeral service requested at St. George's Chapel. This indication of understanding from the palace was of the utmost importance to the Windsors.

But in the wake of this display of forgiveness, bad news came. On March 28 the princess royal died of a coronary thrombosis during a walk through the grounds of her home in Yorkshire. Doctors advised the Windsors not to attempt the journey to Leeds to attend the funeral. The couple sent a white carnation wreath; the duke was deeply distressed by his beloved sister's death. However, they did attend the memorial service at Westminster Abbey, their first "royal" outing in Britain. The stricken Lady Churchill, still overcome by her husband's death, was also present. These were grievous, stressful times. Death and the prospect of death seemed to haunt the Windsors every hour— the inevitable burden of growing old.

The Queen Mother remained adamant in her attitude toward the duchess. Wallis's disdain for the Queen Mother was equally intense. The duchess did nothing to overcome the problem when, following the Queen Mother's stomach operation in 1966, she said, "It must be all those chocolates she's eating."

Like Errol Flynn before her—forgiven his wartime treason, he had been used as a CIA agent against Castro in Cuba—Wallis joined the same agency in the winter of 1966. She used her position as a famous hostess to determine whether one of her regular dinner guests was acting as a mole in the Paris headquarters of NATO, leaking secrets of American conventional and atomic weapons to Moscow.

Her control was John Derby, code name Jupiter, head of the CIA operation in France; she was to report to her old friend Aline, Countess of Romanones, who had been an American secret agent since the war years. Ironically, Wallis was accorded the code name Willy, almost exactly the German code name for the Duke of Windsor in 1940. Smartly, she made no mention of this.

Wallis settled on the innocent American NATO officer Paul Ferguson as the possible mole, but efforts to have him make a slip in conversation at her dinner parties failed. His wife, Maureen, proved to be a mistress of the leg-pull: realizing Wallis was investigating her husband, she talked of mysterious visits out of town, attendance at classical concerts—thought at the time to be used for conveying information through music scores—and that he was actually his twin brother Peter, exchanged for him in her marital bed without a demur.

Following this, Wallis targeted a certain official of NATO; according to the Countess of Romanones, as soon as she did so a CIA agent was found murdered, his death staged as a suicide by gas oven. A letter from him arrived at John Derby's office the next day saying that "Willy" should find out if the official concerned would be in Paris on February 1, and for her to "beware." Unafraid, Wallis invited Chandler and his wife to dinner on the second; they didn't turn up, and after that (she charged), they fled—to Austria, Hungary, and then Russia, without the secrets they had promised the Soviet KGB. At lunch at Maxim's soon after, Gilbert congratulated Wallis on her feat. It was her last adventure in spying.

In the summer of 1967 the Windsors were invited to attend the unveiling of a plaque in honor of Queen Mary's memory. When the Windsors announced that they could not get to England from New York in time for the originally scheduled date of May 26, the centenary of Queen Mary's birth, the monarch postponed the unveiling until

June 5. Lord Mountbatten, who had apparently softened in his attitude toward the Windsors, greeted them at Southampton as they disembarked from the *United States*. He had them stay with him at his house, Broadlands, at Romsey. The next day the Windsors appeared at York House for the first time in thirty years, where they lunched with the Duke and Duchess of Gloucester. Gloucester was also suffering from the ravages of time: he was partly deaf, his circulation was sluggish, and his memory poor. It was a tormenting meeting for all concerned.

The following day the streets were crowded with well-wishers as the Windsors drove from Claridges to St. James's Palace for the unveiling. There was a tremendous cheer from the hundreds of people thronging the street as the duchess, in an exquisite Givenchy costume, blue coat, and pillbox hat, and the duke, haggard, with an expression of deep sadness, left the royal limousine and made their way to the wall where the plaque had been inserted. The Queen Mother was present; the duchess stared at her intently, no doubt to the recipient's annoyance. According to the countess of Ramanones, the duchess appeared to be counting the berries in the Queen Mother's hat. The countess described the scene as told to her by Wallis. The Queen Mother graciously, if coolly, extended her hand to Wallis, who with great audacity and singular lack of taste failed to drop a curtsey. When asked about this later, the duchess snapped, "She stopped people from curtseying to me. Why should I curtsey to her?"

With great composure the elder Queen Elizabeth gave no inkling of the irritation she must have felt at this outrageous breach of etiquette. She talked to her old bête noire with all the seeming warmth and dignity which she, above all others save the queen herself, could summon up when necessary. Her private thoughts, it goes without saying, must have been another matter. It is most unfortunate that the duchess, when curtseying to the queen, could not resist a direct glance at the queen's already offended parent.

After the service of dedication, the Queen Mother said a temporary farewell to the Windsors. Once again, Wallis failed to curtsey. "I do hope we meet again," the Queen Mother said, probably not meaning it. Wallis quite rudely replied, "Oh? When?"

The Windsors attended a small luncheon given by Princess Marina at Kensington Palace. Then they returned on the Queen's Flight to Paris. Prince Michael of Kent came to see the Windsors, followed by

Prince William of Gloucester; they now addressed the duchess as "Aunt Wallis." Her apparent rehabilitation continued. Burke's Peerage urged that she be granted the title of "Royal Highness" as the previous refusal to accord her this title was "the most flagrant act of discrimination in the whole history of our dynasty." But flagrant or not, the act of discrimination was not revoked. The duchess was never accorded the title of H.R.H.

20

Evening and Night

In a determined effort to stave off the advance of old age, the duke yielded to suggestions from several of his friends and, emulating Somerset Maugham, traveled to Switzerland on more than one occasion in the late 1960s to attend the Paul Niehans Clinic at Vevey, near Lausanne. The duchess apparently did not undertake Niehans rejuvenating treatment until later, though by now she had had at least three face-lifts.

The duke and duchess indulged themselves with an extraordinary degree of extravagance. By the late 1960s they had a staff of thirty servants; they had separate chauffeurs to drive them to shopping, and the kitchen staff alone consisted of seven, including the chef, assistant chef, washers-up, and scullery maids. When guests arrived, they were greeted by seven liveried footmen. Needless to say, when they addressed the duchess, her household members invariably used the title "Your Royal Highness."

By 1969 the Windsors were forced to offer their beloved Mill for sale. The reason was not only that they needed to obtain some extra capital. The journey from Paris to the country was proving excessively tiring for the now shockingly fragile Windsor. He was improved in spirits by the investiture of Prince Charles as Prince of Wales on July 1, 1969.

In October 1971, the Windsors received Emperor Hirohito of Japan with the empress at the Bois de Boulogne house. The duke had not seen the emperor since 1922, when he was on a tour of Japan. He showed the emperor the screen Hirohito had given him. The emperor recalled that on the previous occasion he had been too young and too shy to utter a single word to the Prince of Wales. Albin Krebs of the *New York Times* affectionately recorded this pleasant and relaxing reunion.

But by now the duke was in a more grievous state of health. Even when the emperor and empress visited him, he was suffering from almost complete loss of voice. His French physicians took a biopsy and found that he had a cancerous tumor in his larynx. A further biopsy on November 17 confirmed that the cancer was deep-seated and beyond direct surgery. He was to be given a series of cobalt treatments which would last a total of forty-one days. Despite this horrifying news, which left him and the duchess in a severe state of shock, the duke was as stubborn and childish as ever, insisting upon smoking an expensive cigar after dinner every night. His doctors were in despair.

Lord Mountbatten came to visit the duke in February of 1972 when the duchess had gone to Switzerland for what was described as an operation but may well have been a Niehans treatment. (Some sources place the meeting four years earlier, in 1968.) According to Charles Murphy, the duke complained about the fact that Mountbatten hadn't attended his wedding. Mountbatten replied that he had not been invited. The truth was, of course, that he had been invited but that the royal family was adamant that he must not go. Murphy said that at midnight the duke croaked to Mountbatten, "There's something I bet you don't realize. If I hadn't abdicated, I'd have completed thirty-six years of my reign by now." Mountbatten left with the conviction that the duke had finally buried the last traces of bitterness toward him and the rest of the family in London.

In March the duke was operated on for a double hernia at the American Hospital in Neuilly. He had lost a good deal of weight and was now a mere 100 pounds. Wallis, in anguish, almost never left his side. Her constant concern for him was touching to everyone who observed it. Word was conveyed to the queen in London that she should visit her uncle while there was still time. Lady Monckton (Walter had died) visited the Windsors; she urged Her Majesty's principal private secretary, Sir Martin Charteris, to advise the queen of the urgency of the situation. Elizabeth was due to visit Paris anyway for a state visit in connection with Britain's joining the Common Market.

At first, the queen was adamant she would not revise her schedule to see her uncle. When one of Wallis's doctors, Jean Thin, called Buckingham Palace to say that he might not live more than a few days, he received a telephone message from Christopher Soames, Churchill's son-in-law and ambassador to France; Soames told Dr. Thin that the duke must die "before or after the royal visit—but not during." It was another indication that royalty would even seek to influence the Grim Reaper—just as King George V, the queen's grandfather, had been disposed of before his death overtook him in order to make the morning edition of the London *Times*. When Thin became irritable, the palace issued a statement to him saying that "*You* know he's dying. *We* know he's dying. But WE [meaning the queen] don't know he's dying." Then the queen did the unthinkable and changed her schedule to see him.

By now the duke was being intravenously fed glucose. He hated the idea that Lilibet, as he affectionately called the queen, would see him in this condition, with tubes descending from his nose and a bristle of radium needles. He demanded that Dr. Thin have the nurses remove the "damn rigging." Thin agreed.

According to Murphy, it took close to four hours for Thin to prepare the duke for the royal visit. Wallis was impressed by his marvelous control, and the duke gave the performance of his lifetime. Wallis, curtseying as the queen entered the room, took her to the chair where the duke sat. He had carefully dressed in his favorite navy blue blazer with its brass buttons, and he struggled to make a small, wan smile. The queen was determined to show no inkling of her shock at his appearance. She also played out her part with expertise. She spoke warmly and consolingly, while the duchess sat nearby. Then the duchess withdrew to join Prince Phillip and Prince Charles for tea, while the queen and her uncle remained à deux.

The visit gave the duke great pleasure and eased his suffering somewhat.

On May 27, according to Murphy, the duke asked his nurse, "Am I dying?" She replied, with alarming briskness, "You're quite intelligent enough to decide that for yourself." He still fretted over his hair color, augmented with iodine.

Dr. Arthur Antenucci, the duke's favorite doctor from Roosevelt Hospital in New York, flew to Paris. The duke was able to take feeble hold of his hands. On Saturday, May 28, Sydney Johnson told the British writer Ingrid Seward that the duke had asked Johnson to take him to his desk so he could write some letters. Johnson added:

I got him up and sat him at his desk, but he couldn't hold his pen as he was shaking too much. I suggested that he have something to eat—perhaps his favorite finnan haddies and scrambled eggs, but he insisted that it wasn't food he needed. [He said] "They're feeding me through my veins, Sydney. All that is behind me now, and I don't want anything. I don't feel like anything . . . except maybe some peaches and cream."

I ran downstairs to the kitchen and got some fresh peaches and cream and put [them] in front of him. He started putting the spoon to his mouth, but he was trembling so much he couldn't eat. So I fed him and he drank all the cream. Then he felt tired and wanted to go back to bed, so I sponged him down as I always did and put him to bed with the curtains drawn. It was the last time I ever saw him alive.

At two or three in the afternoon, the Duke was still sleeping. I went to see Her Royal Highness and told her it was getting late and he was still sleeping. "Don't worry, Sydney," she said. "Let him sleep." But I knew she was worried as I heard her mumbling, "This is a bad sign."

That evening the duke woke and again feebly requested stewed peaches—a favorite dish from his nursery days. Then he began to sink into his final coma. The duchess was determined to remain in control of her emotions, refusing to break into tears in front of the staff.

There is more than one version of the duke's death. The late John Utter told his friend Hugo Vickers that Wallis was asleep in the early morning hours of May 29 when the duke quietly passed away. It fell upon Utter to waken her with the sad news. She took it with stoic resignation.

According to the Countess of Romanones, soon after 2 a.m. on the twenty-ninth, the doctors called the duchess from her rooms to the bedside. As life drained away from the man with whom she had shared most of her days, the duchess took him tenderly in her arms. He let out a deep breath; his blue eyes gazed tenderly into hers; he uttered the one word "Darling," and then he was gone. According to Sydney Johnson, the duke also said, "Mama, Mama, Mama, Mama." Johnson apparently felt that he was referring to Wallis, but of course he could also have been addressing his long-dead unforgiving parent. The duchess was frozen, paralyzed, speechless. She was gently taken to her room, where she sat silent, staring into space. She still refused to display hysterics. And from then on, she never for an instant lost her dignity.

The news was relayed on the late-night radio and television services. Millions of people, remembering the golden image of the Prince of Wales and the man who gave up his throne for the woman he loved, felt a wave of grief. Young people, who were scarcely aware of the abdication crisis and all that followed, had not forgotten their history. The queen ordered a period of mourning.

According to Sydney Johnson, when the embalmers arrived from London, the duchess was crying and told him to take care of everything. Johnson advised the embalmers that he proposed dressing the duke in nightshirt and robe. The embalmers said this was impossible because of rigor mortis and he would be covered, naked, with a satin sheet. The clothes should be given away to the needy. The appalled Johnson asked the duchess about this. She allegedly said briskly, "Don't interfere. Just brush his hair the way he does it and leave him. They know what they are doing."

Through the media the public was requested by the grief-stricken but outwardly composed Wallis not to besiege the house; people answered that request with appropriate consideration. Those who wished to express their sympathies were asked to come to the British embassy in Paris, where they would be able to sign a book bound in black leather. On May 29 hundreds turned up, close to an hour before the embassy opened, to make the tender and deeply felt endorsements. Not a few of the signatures were accompanied by special notes of remembrance.

A flock of private visitors did come to the house, led by the duchess's favorite hairdresser, Alexandre; King Umberto of Italy; and Maurice Schumann, French foreign minister and former journalist, who had been present at the wedding at the Château de Candé in 1937. Hubert de Givenchy arrived to fit her mourning dress and coat. The next day the body was taken by motorcycle escort to Le Bourget Airport, where it was accompanied by a special French guard of honor before being taken to England on the Queen's Flight to the base known as RAF Benson, Oxfordshire. The duchess was not in a condition to accompany the coffin. She was seized by uncontrollable fits of crying, despite all her efforts to maintain her dignity.

At Benson the Duke and Duchess of Kent led the party that greeted the dead former monarch. The national anthem was played. The next morning the body was carried in a somber procession to Windsor Castle, for the special lying in state at St. George's Chapel. Some indication of the affection in which the duke was held by the people of England can be given by the fact that the crowd of mourners stood for many hours outside the chapel to pay their last respects. The catafalque, draped in royal blue, stood at the center of the sixteenth-century nave. Wallis had sent a cross formed of Easter lilies picked from the gardens of The Mill; the coffin was flanked by tall black candles. Thousands of people filed past the catafalque each hour. Alvin Shuster of the *New York Times* reported that many in the long line, which stretched from the Henry VIII gate down Castle Hill past the railroad station and beyond, remembered the abdication speech as though it were yesterday. Joan Hutchinson, who had stood for twelve hours in line, told Schuster that she was 15 years old and working in a knitwear factory when she heard the speech. "I cried and cried," she said. "He should have stayed on. The wife he wanted would have just slipped into the background. We wouldn't have cared at all. She's a lovely woman."

With great determination, the stoic and courageous but miserable duchess managed to summon up the strength to go to London. The Queen's Flight pilot took her to Heathrow; with her were her friend Grace, Countess of Dudley; Mary Churchill, wife of British ambassador to France Sir Christopher Soames; Dr. Antenucci; and John Utter, her secretary. Upright, her face a mask, the duchess stepped down the ramp to be greeted by Lord Mountbatten. She was reported to have asked Utter, "Why couldn't Prince Charles have been here?" She said querulously to Mountbatten, "I am afraid of the Queen Mother. She never approved of me." Mountbatten did his best to reassure her.

Even in her extremity the duchess was appalled (as she had been in 1936) by what she felt to be the lifeless and gloomy interior of Buckingham Palace. She was accommodated in the State Suite at the front of the palace. The royal family did everything possible to make her comfortable, making sure that the bathroom was well equipped. The suite itself was exceptionally comfortable and her later complaints about it were quite unjustified. Princess Anne was reintroduced to her, and she was touched and happy to see her. A revealing newspaper photograph showed the duchess at a window of the palace, her face stamped with grief. But in her Givenchy mourning dress, exquisitely fashioned of black silk, she succeeded in being among the most elegant and fashionable members of the royal family—even though that membership was still denied to her.

The queen had an unfortunate and difficult decision to make. June 3 had been long since declared her official birthday. This was always a major public event. She would ride out and take the salute at the Trooping the Color. She had thought of canceling this, but was prevailed upon not to do so. Instead, she introduced the touch of having the bagpipe bands play a sad dirge, an appropriate reminiscence in view of the duke's love of the bagpipes; inappropriate as the duchess still hated them.

Still barely able to move or talk, the duchess watched the ceremonies on television in the State Suite. It was her wedding anniversary. She was under sedation, but even so the playing of the bagpipes her husband loved provoked uncontrollable tears. She was so badly shaken she could hardly remember what was said to her from one moment to the next. Finally, pressed hard by Lady Monckton, she agreed to go with Lady Dudley to the official lying in state after the public had gone. At 8:52 p.m. on June 3 the duchess left Buckingham Palace in a royal automobile to go to St. George's Chapel at Windsor. Accompanied by the Prince of Wales and Lord Mountbatten, she walked slowly around the catafalque on which her husband's coffin lay at the center of the nave of the chapel. Then she stood staring at the flower-heaped coffin, proceeding to an examination of the many wreathes in the cloisters. She said, over and over again, to Mountbatten and Prince Charles, "Thirty-five years! Thirty-five years!" And added, "He was my entire life. I can't begin to think what I will do without him, he gave up so much for me, and now he has gone. I always hoped I would die before him." Before her, 57,903 people had by now stood in line to pay their last respects. The queen, Prince Philip, and Princess Anne had also paid visits to the chapel earlier that day.

The service lasted half an hour. It began at 11:15 a.m. on the fifth of June. The public was not admitted. The duchess sat next to the queen, with the Duke of Edinburgh to her right. The Queen Mother did appear. The prime minister, Edward Heath, was there. So was the Earl of Avon, Anthony Eden, who had so radically disagreed with the duke during the time he was king. Lord Mountbatten, Prince Charles, the Duke of Kent, Prince William and Richard of Gloucester, and King Olav of Norway were also present. The Duke of Gloucester was too ill to be present.

The dean of Windsor, the Very Reverend Launcelot Fleming, presided. The blessing was given by Dr. Michael Ramsey, archbishop of Canterbury. The coffin stayed in the chapel while the royal family members accompanied the duchess to a luncheon. After lunch the Queen Mother made a sudden decision to attend the interment at Frogmore. The mourners continued to the place of burial. The duke was lowered gently into the rich English earth, alongside his beloved George, Duke of Kent, and Princess Marina, his adored great-uncle, the Duke of Connaught, and his father's favorite sister, Princess Victoria. The duchess was reassured that when the time came she would be laid beside her husband, but she did note with an old, characteristic touch of cynicism that the space available to her was exceptionally tiny and cramped. She told the archbishop of Canterbury, "I realize that I'm a very thin, small woman, but I do not think that even I could fit into that miserable little narrow piece of ground." The duchess told her friend the Countess of Romanones (who is the source of this story) that the archbishop then replied, "I don't see that there's much that can be done about it. You'll fit, all right." To which the duchess responded that she didn't think she would. She wanted the hedge removed to give her more room. "After all, I am not a hedgehog, you know." This Alice-in-Wonderland conversation concluded with the archbishop's promise to move the hedge. He did; there was, at last, more than ample space for both graves.

There followed an unfortunate lapse. The lord chamberlain, who was in charge of the arrangements, neglected to arrange for any member of the royal family to go to Heathrow Airport to see the duchess off on her flight to France. Instead, and touchingly, all the members of the family who were present bade her farewell at Windsor Castle. Fighting back tears, Wallis was accompanied by the Hon. Mary Morrison, lady-in-waiting to Her Majesty, and by the lord chamberlain. A third member of the party was Lieutenant Colonel John Johnston, who happened to be Sir Alexander Hardinge's son-in-law. The Hon. Mary Morrison was not permitted to curtsey to the duchess even at this stage. Summoning a remarkable amount of energy, the duchess walked unaided up the ramp to the plane, filmed as she did so by the television crews. She then proceeded, with her beloved Lady Dudley doing her best to console her, on the Queen's Flight to Paris. In the House of Commons, Prime Minister Edward Heath spoke movingly of the death of the former monarch, concluding with words of praise for the duchess, "who had repaid his devotion with an equal loyalty, companionship and love. His death is, above all, her loss, and to her the House will wish to extend its profound sympathy." Harold Wilson, leader of the Opposition, added words of admiration, saying, "We hope that she will feel free at any time to come among and freely communicate with the people whom her husband, Prince of Wales, King, and Duke, lived to serve." The ill-fated Liberal leader Jeremy Thorpe confirmed these sentiments. However, despite the feelings of the entire House, and the considerable softening toward the duchess of several members of the royal family, she was emphatically not permitted the title of "Her Royal Highness" even now. She would still be addressed as "Her Grace, the Duchess of Windsor."

Exhausted, the duchess returned to her house in Paris. Disturbingly, she dismissed Sydney Johnson, allegedly because he had asked to go home early one evening to be with his family. These sudden twists of behavior were uncharacteristic and suggested either the adverse effects of certain medications or the imminent onset of senility, or both.

The duke left her his entire fortune of £3 million, and of course there was her brilliant collection of jewelry. She was informed by Maurice Schumann, representing the French government, that she would not be charged death duties and that she would continue to live free of income tax for the rest of her life. Moreover, the house would be hers in perpetuity. The Mill was still for sale, but in June 1973 a buyer was finally found: Edmond Antar, a Swiss businessman, paid close to $1 million for it. Still burdened by the duchess's expenses, Maître Blum deemed it necessary to sell many Windsor possessions during the next decade.

For some weeks the duchess remained in almost complete seclusion, tended to by a dedicated small staff led by her elegant French butler Georges Sanègre and his wife Ofelia. John Utter, a former American diplomat, who had once, ironically, been emissary to Haile Selassie,* continued his duties as secretary. Johanna Schutz assisted him. Maître Blum was constantly at the house attending to all the complex details of the estate. She also assumed a protective role, discouraging members of the press from prying into the duchess's solitude, seeking to prevent them from invading the duchess's territory and taking shots of her through the windows. She gradually became the guardian that the late Walter Monckton had once been.

---

*The Ethiopian monarch had fallen victim to the king's special relationship with Mussolini; the king had refused to receive him at Buckingham Palace.

The duchess had hoped to go to a wedding in Salzburg, but her old problem of ulcers flared up again and prevented the trip. Instead, she invited two newlyweds, the son and daughter-in-law of the Countess of Romanones, to stay with her when they concluded their honeymoon. In one of her rare public appearances she took them to Maxim's for dinner. They were astonished when she ordered a hamburger. Now that her life seemed to all intents and purposes to have come to an end, she saw no reason to put on any pretense and her old, intense American feelings and appetites were resurfacing.

She continued to fret about the size of her grave at Frogmore. She was at last reassured by a letter from her solicitors in London, stating, somewhat bizarrely, "There is plenty of room between the Duke's grave and the border, approximately nine yards." The letter added that there were six yards on the other side to the base of the plane tree which overshadowed that part of the garden. A sketch was enclosed showing the exact position. The duchess sent a note to the Countess of Romanones asking her to be sure "when my rock-a-bye time comes" that the tree would not fall on the two adjoining graves.

Wallis's attorney, Maître Suzanne Blum, still had the supreme advantage of knowing of Wallis's affairs with Guy Trundle and William Bullitt from 1937 to 1940; of her use of Armand Grégoire as Nazi lawyer; of her true connection to Ribbentrop; of her espionage activities, and surely of the China dossier. The duchess would never dare let her go, and her stranglehold increased by the day, the week, the month. The lawyer ruled her royal captive from a grim and gloomy nineteenth-century apartment on the Rue de Varenne on the Left Bank of the Seine. The few visitors intrepid enough to visit her and risk her flaring wrath had to make their way up to her quarters in an arthritic creaky elevator that seemed in imminent danger of crashing to the basement. When visitors arrived, a maid, hobbling and bent with age, opened the door to a dusty chamber with six imposing doors, furnished in the familiar browns and dull ochres of Parisian sitting rooms dating from the 1930s. Many of the decorations were oriental—relics no doubt of Wallis's stay in China in the 1920s.

Despite the smudges of age, the liver spots and wrinkled hands, the tiny monster had benefited from facial surgery and looked younger than her 84 years. She hated meeting journalists or would-be biographers; she would hiss at them threateningly like a cobra. She dismissed every book or article written about the duchess as "ordure" or "stew" made out of discards from a second-rate kitchen. She insisted absurdly that the duke had never had sex with the duchess; that the duchess was a virgin the day she died and was actually a man. When the Irish novelist Caroline Blackwood had the temerity to mention the fact that the duke, after a team of porters carried as many as eighty-six pieces of luggage to various suites, tipped none of them, she snapped, "Tip! Him tip! Tipping would have been demeaning!" She went on to call Miss Blackwood a "jackal." Then she suddenly weakened and trembled, looking old and shaken when the question of the duchess's medical bills came up. "They are fearful," she groaned.

Slowly but surely, the duchess began to experience a minimal social life once again. Patrick O'Higgins, the intimate friend and biographer of the cosmetics queen Helena Rubinstein, took her out to small dinner parties in Paris. She occasionally saw Sir Oswald and Lady Mosley and the Rochefoucaulds. She gave very intimate, limited soirées, with never more than eight guests. When she went out to dinner, she always made sure that there was a guard on duty outside the restaurant. She was terrified of murder or kidnap; there was no doubt that she remained extremely unpopular in Communist circles, although it is doubtful whether at this stage she would be considered seriously as a target. She talked about having a Duchess of Windsor Museum set up at Oldfields School, where she had spent so much of her childhood. But the scheme lay fallow, and finally disintegrated. Sometimes, her memory would fail, and she would forget names or even faces. She became obsessed with a fear of burglars. She had a toy revolver placed next to her bed (she thought it was real) and increased the complexity of her electronic warning system, threaded through every inch of the doors and windows. She would sometimes rise in the night and peer out of the window with her increasingly myopic eyes, trying to see whether the former French soldier she had hired was standing on duty. She stumbled and broke her hip. Admitted to the American Hospital in Neuilly, she was petulant, muddled, and difficult, searching in vain for her light switch, besieging the staff with questions over and over again, and ignoring the answers. Sometimes, her old, flashing humor would reemerge in an eccentric form. An old friend came to see her. He was limping heavily on a stick and told her that he had also broken his hip. She hooted, gleefully, "Hip, hip, hooray!"

The duchess kept everything in the house exactly the way it was when her husband died. She even retained the cigarettes she hated, the pipes were still in their racks, and the cigars lay neatly in their expensive boxes. The desk was exactly preserved, even down to the full inkwells. The duke's room remained crowded with pictures of Wallis from one end to the other. Visitors noted that all the pictures were of her alone; only a few displayed the duke with her. Even the wardrobe was unchanged. In the closets hung all the duke's suits, immaculately preserved in mothballs.

The duchess worried constantly about her pug dogs, adoring them as passionately as ever and drastically concerned that they were not getting the right food. She began cutting down her staff, applying the same principles of somewhat ruthless economy that she had applied to the staffs at Fort Belvedere and York House in London. While visiting Biarritz, still one of her favorite resorts, she fell once more, breaking some ribs. It proved to be difficult to place an anesthetic tube down her throat because of the extensive plastic surgery that had been done on her neck.

Even when back in the hospital, she still had considerable style. She rejected the American food, introducing her own three-star menu supplied by her personal chef. Appalled by the inexpensive linen used in the normal hospital bed, she brought in her own pillows and sheets. She freshened up her rooms with magnificent displays of flowers and, at one stage, her favorite motto cushion, which carried the legend, "You can't be too thin or too rich."

The absurd story appeared in 1972 in the French newspaper *France-Dimanche* that she would marry John Utter. This gave her a much-needed laugh. Utter always could be relied upon, despite some misgivings about the duchess, to cheer her up and give her satisfactory company. He was a warm and lovable man. He did not live at the house, but had his own home in the country at Osmoi, where he had established a foundation for up-and-coming musicians who could not afford to pay the high rents of the French capital. Utter was not impressed with Lord Mountbatten, who had a tendency to turn up at the duchess's house and, acting as though he owned the place and was Utter's employer, would say to him, "Get your notebook out, John," and then proceed to dictate letters to him. This infuriated the retired diplomat.

Mountbatten also annoyed John Utter in those years by walking around the rooms of the house in Paris, pointing out this or that expensive objet d'art, particularly some Fabergé gold boxes that had been left behind by the burglars at Ednam Lodge, saying that the duke had intended those for him and that he proposed removing them. Utter and Johanna Schutz advised Maître Blum of this, and she accordingly made sure she was present during Mountbatten's visits to preclude any possible theft. Another who was asked to be present was Aline, Countess of Romanones. The duchess told Aline, "[Mountbatten's] always asking for things. And after my kind husband bestowed all those honors on him! Even Georges [Sanègre] I suspect dreads his visits. . . . But what can one expect from a man who threw his wife into the sea?" This was a reference to the widely believed story that Lady Mountbatten, after dying in Borneo, had been committed to the waves.

According to the duchess, Mountbatten insisted upon her making out a will during one of his visits, in 1973, leaving everything to the royal family. Naturally, she alleged, Mountbatten wanted to be included in the legacy. He had even drawn up a working version of the document himself, stating where everything should go. The duchess apparently intended that certain legacies would be left, in particular to Prince Charles, but she told the Countess of Romanones, "They [all] did David out of properties which were his own." This, of course, was a false charge. In fact, as the duchess well knew, she had enjoyed the benefits of a life income from the act of blackmail her husband had performed against the royal family members in forcing them to pay him an income as a reward for his ceding his life interest in Sandringham and Balmoral.

According to Maître Blum, Mountbatten now tried to make the duchess sign a document in which she placed all her property in a foundation which Mountbatten would administrate, with the Prince of Wales as its chairman. He urged her to reinstate her dismissed English firm of solicitors, Allen and Overy. The duchess authorized certain innocuous papers and military and other insignia of her husband to be taken back to London for the benefit of the queen; these were housed, as far as can be determined, at Windsor Castle. But later Maître Blum made extremely serious charges in a series of letters dated March 24, April 5, and April 7, 1979, to the Windsors' old friend, Kenneth de Courcy, Duke de Grantmesnil. She stated that whereas the duchess was perfectly willing to have letters from King George VI and Queen

Elizabeth to the duke, historical souvenirs, and other documents given to the palace, that was the limit of the duchess's agreement.

Maître Blum stated to Grantmesnil that two individuals, authorized either by Lord Mountbatten or "some other person," acting upon what she alleged to be royal authority, somehow obtained the keys to the duke's boxes and confidential filing cabinets and burgled the contents, placing everything in packing cases which were carried under secret conditions to the concierge's lodge, where as night fell a truck appeared to remove them. The contents included the duke's private correspondence, the documents of divorce from Win Spencer and Ernest Simpson, bills from tradesmen and department stores, and a certain amount of the duchess's personal correspondence. Maître Blum confirmed her charges with supporting statements in writing from Utter, Sydney Johnson, and Johanna Schutz. Each supported Maître Blum's claim that when the duchess requested that her filing cabinets and boxes be opened, the duchess was appalled to find them empty.

Grantmesnil decided to take the matter of the alleged royal burglary up with Sir Robin Mackworth-Young, librarian of Windsor Castle. On April 11, 1979, Sir Robin replied, stating that the allegations were without foundation. He said that the first consignment of documents was given to him by John Utter on June 15, 1972, in the presence of Maître Blum. The duchess had personally received Sir Robin. She gave permission herself for the movement of the papers. The second consignment was delivered, again in person and again by Utter, on December 13. The third was handed over on July 22, 1977. On this occasion the duchess was not present and John Utter had left her employ. In 1987 in answer to a question a similar letter was sent to the present author by the Windsor Castle librarian who had succeeded Mackworth-Young.

In 1974, Wallis was able to muster the strength to take a ship to New York City. Accompanied by Johanna Schutz and two of her pugs, she sailed aboard the Italian *Rafaello*, arriving on April 9. A *New York Times* reporter managed to obtain a brief quote from her. She said, "I don't go out as much and I'm much lonelier. [The royal family] made a fuss at the time of the abdication, but I don't think they would make a fuss now. I get on well with the royal family." Her old wit flashed again. The reporter ignorantly asked her, quite forgetting the publication of *The Heart Has Its Reasons*, whether she would one day write an autobiography.

"That would be the most dreadful thing to do!" she snapped back, and the reporter still didn't understand. She was fascinated, while at the Waldorf Towers (in Suite 40F, twelve floors above her old beloved 28A, a suite which belonged to the millionaire art collector and food tycoon Nathan "Nate" Cummings), to learn that Prince Charles had recently been in San Diego, scene of that memorable night when she had glimpsed the Prince of Wales across the room.

She seemed to rally under the vibrant stimulation of Manhattan. Princess Margaret and Lord Snowdon called on her and were photographed with her. Nate Cummings freshened up the Waldorf suite with a Sisley painting and a Renoir. The duchess bought a few decorative pieces to improve the rather somber furnishings, and she again brimmed the rooms from end to end with her favorite flowers. Walking on a cane, ravishingly dressed by Givency, she always caused a flurry in the elevator and the lobby during her arrivals and departures. Stooped now, visibly frail, staring straight ahead, her voice somewhat tremulous, she carried with her an atmosphere of extraordinary dignity, resolution, and intrinsic power. Even in her precipitate decline, she was undoubtedly *someone*.

The duchess returned to England to make a private visit to her husband's grave at Frogmore. She sent a simply but beautifully worded letter of thanks to the queen for her consideration, and she was touched to receive a thoughtful and sensitive telegram from Prince Charles. She adored Charles and again talked of leaving him some small but significant legacies. But on December 9, 1974, she wrote to Mountbatten, stating categorically that his efforts to retrieve objets d'art of the duke were permanently rejected. John Utter was helpful to the duchess when she fell seriously ill on November 13, 1975, and went back into the American Hospital at Neuilly. She almost died from her old problem of bleeding ulcers. In May 1976 she wanted to take some sunshine, and her two nurses carried her out onto the terrace of her house. Two cameramen took cruel and devastating photographs of her, looking thin, weak, and sunken-cheeked. The photographs were published in *France-Soir.* Maître Blum sued the paper for invasion of privacy on her behalf and was awarded a verdict of 80,000 francs.

That summer Wallis began to suffer from the characteristic hallucinations of senility. She cried out, "I'm frightened! They've been here again! They've moved my things! This is the second time they've hijacked me!" This did not seem to be a reference to the missing documents; the duchess appeared to be convinced that certain of her decorative objects had been stolen by Mountbatten.

There was again talk that June, when she had her birthday, that a left-wing political group was planning to kidnap her, and she increased the guard on the house. When John Utter retired, disturbed and uncomfortable with the duchess's sudden alarming shifts of mood, he continued to see her from time to time, taking her to dinner about once every eight weeks and calling her every day to see how she was. Then, quite suddenly, and without the slightest explanation, the duchess rang the curtain down on him. When he telephoned from his country house, the receptionist informed him that Johanna Schutz had given out instructions that his call must not be put through. It was the same fate that had befallen Freda Dudley Ward when she had tried to reach the Prince of Wales at York House some forty years earlier.

The duchess grew weaker and weaker. The American Hospital doctors succeeded in having her cut down her consumption of alcohol to a minimum; she had been drinking more and more heavily during the previous years. She would scarcely eat anything, and she lost so much weight that she was positively emaciated by 1976. Her mind continued to wander. Unable to reach the telephone, she would pick up an imaginary instrument and ask quietly, "Miss Schutz, please come up here immediately!" Everyone in her circle felt that it would be very important for her if the Queen Mother would finally relent and pay her a personal visit. It says much for the Queen Mother's character that, despite all that had taken place, and her continuing hatred of Wallis, she was prepared to oblige.

The Queen Mother was due to come to Paris in October 1976, and it was decided that she would undertake her mission of compassion at that time. On the twenty-fifth, she was at the British embassy for an official luncheon in her honor. The next day she opened the British Cultural Center in Paris. It was agreed that at 4 p.m. she would drive to the duchess's house in the embassy car. But at the last minute the duchess was too ill to receive her. Johanna Schutz called the embassy and stated that the duchess would not, as a result of her poor state of health, be able to see Her Majesty. It was later explained to the Queen Mother that the duchess was suffering from severe hallucinations, and that Dr. Jean Thin and Maître Blum both felt that the moment was not opportune for the meeting. The Queen Mother then displayed the splendor of her character in full force. She sent to the duchess a bouquet of two dozen roses, red and white, with a note that read, "In friendship, Elizabeth."

Late in 1976 Miss Schutz on behalf of the duchess agreed to lend a number of the duke's personal possessions for a special exhibition at Windsor to commemorate the fiftieth birthday of the queen. Hugo Vickers flew to Paris on September 14 to pick up the twelve items on loan. According to Vickers, "The Queen Mother examined the abdication items with interest, while she expressed disapproval at seeing Mussolini and Hitler on display."

In May 1978 Verity Lambert, director of drama at Thames Television, went to see Maître Blum to inform her that Simon Raven would be writing the script for the seven-part series *Edward and Mrs. Simpson*, based on the biography of Edward VIII by Frances Donaldson. Maître Blum was not at all happy with Lady Donaldson's book, but apparently under the existing laws was unable to intervene. She certainly would like to have done so. She demanded that she see the scripts, but she was told that was out of the question. The duchess also hated the idea of being portrayed on the screen, and perhaps fortunately her mental and physical condition precluded her from knowing about the series.

She was by now very seriously ill. Maître Blum took over everything. The house was like a morgue. There remained only the butler, Georges Sanègre, and his wife; a maid, Germaine; the receptionist; and the day and night nurses. The duchess had lost the use of her hands and feet and had to be carried from her bed to a clinical couch. Visitors were for a time forbidden, because when they arrived, she seemed to become excited and her blood pressure reached a dangerous height. She had to be spoon-fed. John Utter told a friend, "For everyone's sake, the sooner she dies the better." She was for periods in a world of her own. Eventually, she had to be fed intravenously because in her semiparalyzed condition she was unable to swallow. Tragically, she was not in a coma, which at least would have rendered her oblivious to her fate. She had moments of vivid awareness, which to anyone of her essential vitality and love of life must have been very nearly unendurable.

According to the Countess of Romanones, the duchess called her, saying, "Aline, you must come to see me right away. I need you desperately." The countess was up to her eyes organizing the first free elections in Spain since General Franco had taken over the government. He had died; King Juan Carlos had assumed the throne. The countess asked Wallis if she could possibly come the following week. The duchess said that was fine. The next day the countess called to give the exact hour of her arrival so that the chauffeur could pick her up at the airport. She asked to be put through to Wallis. A secretary replied that was out of the question; if there were any messages for the duchess, she would be glad to convey them. The countess was shocked and upset. She said she intended to come anyway.

Any further effort to contact the duchess proved fruitless. The Countess of Romanones wrote several times and called, but there was no response.

The duchess was not even able to read; she was almost completely blind. Sometimes, she would ask feebly to be taken to the window, where she could hear the birds singing. Hugo Vickers, observing the house from the road, wrote in his diary:

> Over the wall through the gray, misty atmosphere one could see a kind of living tomb. All the windows on the ground floor were shuttered from the outside world, but I thought the drawing room window was open. Upstairs where what remains of the Duchess [sat,] surrounded by nurses, there were two lights—one on the side, which is her bedroom, and one in the far window of what I think is the upstairs sitting room.

The duchess was unaware of her birthday in June 1980. A new person entered the scene: Michael Bloch, the scion of a well-to-do family resident in Ireland. He was born in 1953 and was a graduate of St. John's College, Cambridge. He had written to Maître Blum for assistance on a book he was writing on the historian and biographer Philip Guedalla, an old friend of the Duke of Windsor's. He wanted to interview Maître Blum and obtain access to certain papers. The Paris lawyer became very fond of him and appointed him her assistant; he had been admitted to the London Bar. He took over as official custodian of the Windsor papers and also authorized biographer. He was appointed editor and annotator of the duchess's letters, most of which had escaped the alleged removal of the papers to Windsor Castle by unauthorized persons. By the time he assumed his position, the duchess was quite unable to talk to him or assist him in his researches. However, she signed full power of attorney to Maître Blum, allowing the lawyer to publish whatever she chose. In answer to certain queries Maître Blum stated that the duchess wanted her correspondence to be made public. Many of the letters, which appeared after the duchess's death (with great success, particularly in England), were of a painfully personal character. But they are of indispensable value to the biographer. They give an extraordinarily vivid picture of her multifaceted personality.

After two years of trying to see the duchess, the Countess of Romanones at last succeeded in obtaining permission from Maître Blum to pay a visit. This was an extremely rare privilege. The duchess had had several hemorrhages. When the countess arrived at the house, she noted an eerie, disturbing silence. She knew at once what was missing: the loud, excited barking of the pug dogs. The duchess had no longer been able to tolerate the sound that she had once adored, and the pugs had been given away. When the countess entered the boudoir, the exquisitely furnished room that stood between the two main bedrooms, she found the duchess, seated with immense and majestic poise in her wheeled chair, wearing a handsome brocade dressing gown the color of her blue eyes. Her hair was elegantly drawn back behind her ears, showing the still impressive cheekbones and the firm line of the jaw. She was wearing her favorite sapphires. Surprisingly, and for the first time in weeks, she was coherent, and when the countess said she looked like a Chinese empress, Wallis sparked up with an old, significant memory. "People told me that when I was living in Peking in 1924," she said.

Even when the countess returned several months later, the duchess was still able to talk to her. Her hearing was so amazingly sharp that she even caught the countess's footfall as the countess entered the room. The countess was saddened to see that Wallis had not been manicured or made up and that her hair was white and lifeless now. But she still had an appreciation of beauty. Staring out the window, she said, "Look at the way the sun is lighting the trees. You can see so many different colors." But then she uttered a sentence that for the countess was like a knife to the heart. She said, "Tell David to come in. He wouldn't want to miss this!" On her third and fourth visits the countess heard not a single word from the duchess's lips.

The duchess did not leave her house after 1981. Dr. Thomas

Hewes, senior physician at the American Hospital in Neuilly, answered a question about her condition with the following words: "The Duchess is a vegetable. She is in a pitiable state. I don't believe she suffers anything at all anymore." A pianist was engaged to play, hour after hour, a medley of popular songs, once beloved of the duke, including "Bye Bye Birdie" and "I Get a Kick Out of You," in an effort to stir her moribund mind. The effort was useless.

Interested people would walk by the house and stare across the wall at the bedroom window, beyond which her silent figure lay immobile. Occasionally, they would see nurses in white moving to and fro, but otherwise there was no sign of life. Bizarre rumors began to circulate, that she was already dead and had been refrigerated, or that she was on a sophisticated computer that could tell Maître Blum what sustenance she needed and whether the nurses had fulfilled their duties.

At last, all the unwelcome publicity surrounding her illness ceased. For months nothing appeared in the press. Then, on April 24, 1986, her heart finally and mercifully gave out. She was 90 years old.

The lord chamberlain flew to Paris to escort the body home in its plain oak coffin. The Duke of Gloucester, her nephew by marriage, whose father had died some years before, greeted the remains at RAF Benson and accompanied them to Windsor Castle. The castle was closed and a guard of honor was waiting to salute the duchess on her last journey.

There was a twenty-eight-minute private service in St. George's Chapel, attended by 175 people. Queen Elizabeth II entered the chapel with Prince Philip and the Queen Mother. American ambassador Charles Price was among those present. Sixteen members of the royal family sat in the quire, directly opposite the coffin, which was flanked by the Military Knights of Windsor in red uniforms with gold braid. The duchess was accorded the honor of lying in the same position and place as King George V, King George VI, Queen Mary, and the Duke of Windsor. The queen's wreath of yellow and white lilies lay at the center of the coffin. The words "Her Royal Highness" did not appear upon the plaque; the duchess's name was omitted from the service. The St. George's Chapel Choir sang the anthem "Thy will keep him in perfect peace." Among those who mourned that day were Lady Mosley, whose husband had died in 1980, the Countess of Romanones, the Princess Ann-Mari von Bismarck, Grace, Lady Dudley, Lady Alexandra Metcalfe, the Duke and Duchess of Marlborough, and Laura, Duchess of Marlborough. Very few others of the duchess's friends were still alive. Maître Blum was notable by her absence.

At the end of the service the coffin was taken in procession from the quire, led by the constable of Windsor Castle, Marshal of the RAF Sir John Grandy, and the Military Knights of Windsor, and preceded by the dean of the American Pro-Cathedral in Paris, the archbishop of Canterbury, the dean and canons of Windsor, and the lord chamberlain. The queen, the Queen Mother, Prince Philip, Princess Anne, and the Prince and Princess of Wales followed the coffin through the nave and down the Great West Steps. And then the duchess was at last lowered into her grave next to that of the duke.

The obituaries for the duchess both in Great Britain and the United States were on the whole respectful. Indeed, more than one newspaper incorrectly stated that any suggestion that she had any Nazi connections was without foundation. The Countess of Romanones published an article in the June 1986 issue of *Vanity Fair* in which, among a great deal of colorful—and contested—reminiscence, she included some shockingly unflattering remarks the duchess had allegedly made about the Queen Mother. The duchess apparently had mocked the Queen Mother in conversations with the countess, calling her "Cookie" and saying that she resembled "a pudding." With considerable ingratitude in view of the Queen Mother's consideration toward her at the time of the duke's death, she insultingly described that great lady's black hat as having a "white plastic arrow sticking up through it." She said that she almost laughed in the Queen Mother's face even though she was stricken with grief. Elsewhere in the piece, the countess, who as a former OSS agent in Spain should have been better informed, said that the duchess was falsely charged with Nazi associations. Although seeming to be in the duchess's favor, the article turned out in the end to be somewhat unflattering.

The love letters appeared in newspaper serialization during the very week of the duchess's death, which some have regarded as an error of taste. Soon after, they were published in a book form. An important letter by Alistair Cooke appeared in the *New York Times* of May 9. Mr. Cooke pointed out that the real reason for the abdication was that, according to the terms of the Statute of Westminster passed in 1931, any alteration in the law touching the succession of the throne required the assent of the parliaments of the dominions as well as of the Parliament of the United Kingdom. Thus, the secretary of state for the dominions was required to put the matter before the Commonwealth parliaments. Whereas New Zealand was prepared to follow the majority decision of the British Parliament, and India was divided between Hindus and Moslems, Canada, Australia, and South Africa were adamant that they would neither sanction Wallis as queen nor permit her to enter into a morganatic marriage. The Labour party in London was, of course, equally opposed.

Although it is questionable, to say the least, whether the duke would have wished his childlike romantic correspondence to have been examined by a large and interested public, it is probable that the duchess (though not the duke) would have been happy to have had her magnificent collection of jewelry displayed to the world. The decision was made by Maître Blum to auction the entire lot at Sotheby's. At least twelve major items of jewelry had been sold before the duchess's death, along with the duke's royal silver, the china pug dogs, and the wines. The auction took place in Geneva on April 2 and 3, 1987.

The spectacular and dazzling array consisted of 230 lots valued at more than $7 million and including 87 Cartier pieces and 23 emanating from Van Cleef and Arpels. According to Sotheby's Nicholas Rayner, the duchess's favorite piece was a Burmese ruby-and-diamond necklace given to Wallis by Kind Edward VIII on the occasion of her forty-first birthday on June 19, 1936, and inscribed, "My Wallis from her David." The Mogul emerald engagement ring given by the king to Wallis on the evening after her divorce decree nisi was granted at Ipswich was another major item.

From the 1930s came a platinum-and-diamond necklace; a diamond dress suite of great beauty; a pearl, emerald, and diamond bracelet; the diamond-and-sapphire Prince of Wales feather clips; and the diamond bracelet which included the many Latin crosses inscribed with mementos of various occasions, including a visit to St. Wolfgang in 1935 and Wallis's appendectomy in 1944. An 18-karat gold-and-gem-set cigarette case by Cartier had a map of the couple's travels from London via Calais, Paris, Biarritz, Spain, and Cannes to Italy, Germany, Austria, Yugoslavia, Turkey, Bulgaria, and Hungary and then back to London, a grand prize for anyone who acquired it. An exquisite gold-and-gem-set powder compact was studded with sapphires, rubies, emeralds, citrines, and amethysts; on the back was another journey map, identical to the one on the cigarette case.

From the 1940s came a sapphire bracelet; a gold, sapphire, ruby, and diamond-hinged bangle; golden ruby ear clips; sapphire-and-diamond ear clips; a sapphire, emerald, citrine, and diamond clip in the form of a flamingo; and the gorgeous panther clips designed by Jeanne Toussaint, the beloved friend of Jacques Cartier, who had nicknamed Mlle. Toussaint his "Panther."

From the 1950s there were an onyx-and-diamond panther bracelet, an onyx-and-diamond tiger clip, and pearl-and-diamond ear clips; from the 1960s, a superb gold, cultured-pearl-and-diamond choker necklace, an emerald-and-diamond pendant designed by Harry Winston, a Cartier emerald-and-diamond necklace, and ruby-and-diamond ear clips.

Included in the auction were many historic items of the Duke of Windsor, including legacies of extreme value. There were gold snuff-boxes, silver cigarette cases, an 1820 silver-gilt seal box, a 1910 silver-gilt inkstand, an 1823 desk seal, and a motley collection of clocks, watches, and even gold replica train tickets supplied by the Canadian Pacific Railway Company in 1919 and 1927. One of the most splendid items was a cigar box presented to the Prince of Wales in 1915 by the members of the king and queen's households while the prince was on active service in the First Battalion Grenadier Guards in northern France.

The Mogul emerald went for $2.1 million, and the 1936 birthday present, the ruby-and-diamond necklace, went for $2.6 million. A tiny cigar piercer raised a staggering $3,700. Mohammed Al Fayed, Egyptian owner of Harrods department store in London, who had just been granted by the French government a continuing lease on the Windsors' house in Paris, obtained the memento charm bracelet. Los Angeles divorce attorney Marvin Mitchelson paid over half a million dollars for the amethyst necklace. He bought sapphires for $300,000 apiece. Elizabeth Taylor snapped up the Prince of Wales feather brooch for $575,000. According to some sources, she also obtained the panther brooches, outbidding Prince Charles, who was determined to obtain them for Diana, the Princess of Wales, who had set her heart on them.

At the end of the second day the total of the sale was $50,281,887. This was seven times what Sotheby's had estimated. The highest price of all was paid by an anonymous buyer. It was $1,466,653 for a Royal Navy sword presented by King George V to the Prince of Wales. This was, of course, vastly beyond its true value. All the money from the auction went to the Louis Pasteur Institute in Paris, where it would be applied to research into AIDS. In view of the fact that two of her husbands were bisexual and that many of her friends and admirers were gay, this seemed appropriate.

Thus, in death, the duchess was more famous than ever, and the jewels that were her main love in life became her monument.

Unhappily, Mohammed Al Fayed did not keep the Windsor house's contents for long. He decided to close the residence after its brief spell as a museum and to sell the furniture, paintings, and china to support his son Dodi's charities. After announcing an auction at Sotheby's in New York City, he had to suspend it because of the death of Dodi and Princess Diana of Wales, his son's lover. When the auction did finally take place, it fetched considerably more than its anticipated value; but it entirely lacked the glamour and excitement of the jewelry auction and, attended by almost no celebrities, came as a sad anticlimax to the duchess's life.

On June 6, 1995, Prince Edward, the nephew of the Duke of Windsor and who had been working for Andrew Lloyd Webber, embarked on a whitewash documentary on his uncle for ITV, London. Housed in Mohamed Al Fayed's Ritz Hotel in Paris, appropriately in the Duke of Windsor Suite (at $5,120 a night), Edward, on the first day of shooting, found himself, perhaps for the first time in his life, compelled to make himself a sandwich—on the set.

Although the documentary, as shallow and misguided as its royal subject, was a typical example of Buckingham Palace spin-doctoring, it gave rise to at least one entertaining story, told by Wendy Leigh, author of *Edward Windsor: Royal Enigma* (New York: Pocket Books, 1999). According to Leigh, the prince told Desmond Wilcox, his producer, that contrary to the "facts" presented in the finished film, his uncle was a thief, and took into exile oil paintings and furniture that belonged to the royal family. In this, he had inherited his great-grandmother's

Queen Mary's tendencies: the rooms of her various residences were notoriously magpies' nests of stolen items and to "lock up the silver" was the watchword when she came to visit.

A series of protective books appeared in the 1990s. Philip Ziegler's *King Edward VIII* was a direct result of authorization by the queen, who allowed him access to the collection of papers at Windsor Castle, with predictable results. He failed to deal satisfactorily with any of the controversial aspects of the Windsors' life, using the time-worn device of their somewhat dim authorized chroniclers in replacing any suggestion of treasonable activities with the lesser charges of foolishness and naïveté (the duke) and greed and selfishness (the duchess). This had the effect of diminishing the couple; at least their espionage and treason had shown a degree of intelligent enterprise, if only in the wrong direction.

The worst biography to date was Michael Bloch's hagiography *The Duchess of Windsor* (1996), which suggested, like Maître Blum, his mentor, that Wallis was a man, or at least that she had male sexual characteristics. How then could she have become pregnant to Count Ciano or had cancer of the ovaries? *Hidden Agenda* by Martin Allen (2000) is much contested and fascinating; but only one book, *Hostage to Fortune: The Letters of Joseph P. Kennedy*, edited by his granddaughter, Amanda Smith (2001), can be said to provide astonishments even for the seasoned Windsor biographer, revealing as it does at first hand the true nature of the figures of the abdication crisis as nobody else has done.

The last words must go to an anonymous poet. Among the items found in the inventory of the duchess's house in Paris, and not included in the Sotheby's auction, was a small gold-framed illuminated manuscript; the verse text was surmounted by a coronet. The words were:

> *My friend to live with thee alone*
> *I think t'were better than to own*
> *A crown, a scepter or a throne.*

Notes on Sources

Chapter 1: A Baltimore Childhood

The details of Bessie Wallis Warfield's childhood are based upon research conducted by the genealogist Robert Barnes of Perry Hall, Maryland. Mr. Barnes obtained census reports for Baltimore for 1900 and 1910 listing birth dates for the Warfield and Montague families; an autobiographical document by Solomon Davies Warfield incorporated into his last will and testament dated August 22, 1927; an administration account book of Anna E. Warfield, giving details of house and land transactions, deeds, and certifications; the will of Anna Emory Warfield incorporated into a document dated March 26, 1929, and found in the papers of Solomon Davies Warfield; and birth, marriage, and death certificates for the principal figures, along with *Baltimore Sun* newspaper reports of these events. At the time of the Orphans' Court hearing in which Josephine Metcalf Warfield filed against the estate of Solomon Warfield on August 9, 1929, numerous other documents were subpoenaed and have been examined, giving a clear picture of the family history. Dr. Beale Thomas, with the assistance of numerous officials of the Episcopalian Church of Baltimore, searched all church records and conclusively determined that Bessie Wallis Warfield was not baptized. This was subsequently confirmed by the local archdiocese; Dr. Winthrop Brainerd, Mrs. Jewel Vroonland, John Zeren, and Dr. Beale Thomas supplied more information. Dr. Thomas also obtained the confirmation record and was able to establish that, in entering it, the Warfield family falsified the truth concerning the lack of a baptism. Todd Dorsett did research at Blue Ridge Summit, Pennsylvania, searching valuable records. The *American Dictionary of Biography* contains exhaustive biographies of the principal figures of the Warfield clan. City directories disclosed addresses. Baltimore guidebooks gave particulars of the schools that Bessie Wallis attended. The Baltimore

Historical Society supplied documents of the Oldfields School published at the time of the fiftieth anniversary in 1917. These included memorabilia of members of Bessie Wallis's class. A Warfield genealogy in handwriting, accompanied by a Montague genealogy, was also obtained from the Baltimore Historical Society. Society visiting lists for the period proved to be of value. *The Heart Has Its Reasons* provided some pictorial detail. Articles in *Harper's* magazine, *World's Work*, *Good Housekeeping*, *The Delineator*, and *The North American* were illuminating. Cleveland Amory's book *Who Killed Society?*, F. F. Beirne's *Baltimore: A Picture History* and his indispensable *The Amiable Baltimoreans*, and S. E. Greene's *Baltimore, an Illustrated History* were all good sources. Mrs. Edward D. Whitman gave a vivid interview. Archdeacon Moseley of the Los Angeles Episcopalian Archdiocese provided me with details of the religious issues involved in the failure to baptize Wallis and confirmed that, according to the orthodoxy of the 1890s, condemnation to hell was the consequence of not being baptized.

Chapter 2: A Stubborn Young Lady

The very substantial number of letters written by Mary Kirk to her mother at a rate of three or four a week describing her school days with Bessie Wallis proved to be a treasure trove. The correspondence has been preserved at Radcliffe. Records of the du Pont family maintained at the Eleutherian Mills Library in Delaware have been drawn from. The syndicated columnist who called himself Cholly Knickerbocker ran a series of articles at the time of the abdication crisis in which he interviewed many of the then-living contemporaries of Bessie Wallis, including Lloyd Tabb, Tom Shyrock, and the principals of Wallis's schools. Robert Barnes obtained records on John Freeman Rasin. Mrs. Dale St. Dennis, granddaughter of Corinne De Forest Montague Mustin Murray, was very kind in handing me the substantial and extraordinary correspondence between her grandmother and Bessie Wallis.

Chapter 3: Running Up the Ladder

The Amiable Baltimoreans is the best source on the Bachelors Cotillon. Here again *The Heart Has Its Reasons* and the Anna Warfield and Solomon Warfield accounts and probate records proved to be of value. In the matter of Pensacola, I had the invaluable help of a Navy wife, Anna Irwin, who spent weeks checking up on descriptive details of the naval base in the teens of the century, talking with various survivors of that era, and searching the microfilms of the *Pensacola Journal*, which supplied many of the particulars. Professor George F. Pearce was most helpful. The U.S. Navy Air Force records in Washington were obtained, along with the correspondence files kept in boxes at the Library of Congress of Henry Mustin and Mark L. Bristol, among others. Annual reports of the U.S. Navy were searched, along with the files of the naval academy at Annapolis. Several railroad historians were contacted for descriptions of the journey to that region in 1916, and an examination of maps and street directories showed the journey a visitor would take to reach specific destinations at that time. Brochures of the San Carlos Hotel came to light in the Pensacola Public Library. The history of Earl Winfield Spencer's father was found in Chicago records searched by Eleanor Campbell, qualified genealogist, in that city; she also visited Highland Park, Illinois, to obtain more information on the spot. Obituaries of the family members revealed much. These appeared in the *Chicago Tribune*. Annapolis supplied the class, demerit, and graduation records of Spencer.

Chapter 4: A Stylish Marriage

The best description of the nuptials appeared in the *Baltimore Sun* and was supplemented by the wedding certificate obtained by Robert Barnes. The resident historian of the Greenbriar Hotel at White Sulphur Springs, West Virginia, Dr. Robert Conte, was kind enough to send me prospectuses of that period, the room number, location and view of the Spencers' honeymoon room, and other particulars. Rear Admiral George Van Deurs, U.S. Navy (retired), supplied more information in his little-known book *Wings for the Fleet*. Records of the U.S. Navy aeronautic station at Pensacola were searched. Paolo E. Coletta, working on the editing of the unpublished manuscript *The Goonie Bird*, sent me notes. Katherine Carlin King, daughter of Gustav and Katherine Eitzen, left memorabilia, now to be discovered in San Diego. The Boston Historical Society was helpful. The San Diego *Tribune, Union*, and *Transcript* files were searched for details of that city in the teens of the century. I had a very pleasant visit to San Diego, assisted in both driving and research by John Baron, of the University of California. I enjoyed visiting the houses rented by the Spencers at the time. Eileen Jackson, veteran journalist of the *San Diego Union,* supplied me with the addresses. I then contacted the owners of the houses, T. Hyrum Callister of 1143 Alameda Street, Mr. and Mrs. Leo Hansen of Pinewood Cottage, and Mr. and Mrs. Jennings Brown of 1023 Encino Row, and they were good enough to allow me to visit them. I stayed at the Hotel del Coronado, where the publicity staff generously supplied me with period information. The manager of the Palomar apartment building was equally helpful. Members of the Fullam and Spreckels families cooperated with me, as did Neil Morgan, editor of the *Tribune,* and the aforementioned Mrs. Dale St. Dennis, who was hospitable to a degree. Captain Arthur Sinclair Hill showed me a moving photographic gallery of his tragically star-crossed Montague family, with bereavement after bereavement in every generation and so many magnificent-looking young people struck down. Mary Carlin King and her family were extraordinarily hospitable. Vastly changed though it is, San Diego still has the sense of warmth and welcome it had when the young Mrs. Spencer lived there. The San Diego newspapers all described the Armistice Day celebrations of November 11, 1918, and the Prince of Wales's visit on April 7, 1920. I obtained the complete guest list of the party at which he was received by the local citizens, thus determining that Wallis was not on the special short list. Joan Alban of the Coronado Chamber of Commerce and the staffs of the San Diego and Coronado Historical Societies provided much material. Back east, the Chevy Chase Country Club was cooperative; so was the Army and Navy Club. The divorce files of *Spencer v. Spencer,* unsealed for me at Warrenton, Virginia, contain the important depositions of Wallis and her mother which provide transcripts of conversations between them and Earl Spencer. Mrs. Milton E. Miles, widow of Rear Admiral Miles, gave me her recollections as a young Navy wife. I interviewed Professor Immanuel C. Y. Hsue, author of the excellent *The Rise of Modern China,* at his home in Santa Barbara, California, on the general background. Navy annual reports were drawn from. Record Groups 24 and 38, containing general correspondence of the Navy Department and records of the chief of naval operations, were searched. So were files of Record Group 45, the naval records collection of the Office of Naval Records and Library.

Chapter 5: China

The Operational Archives Branch of the Naval Historical Center of the Washington Navy Yard supplied declassified data. So did Evelyn M. Cherpak, head of the Naval Historical Collection, Department of the Navy, Naval War College, Newport, Rhode Island. Oral histories of wives of that time in China were used. An obituary of Mrs. F. H. Sadler in the *New York Times,* June 20, 1951, and O.A.B. materials on Rear Admiral Sadler were used. The Biographies Branch of the U.S. Department of the Navy supplied details of Admiral Luke McNamee. U.S. Navy intelligence files and the U.S. State Department passport files on Mrs. Earl Winfield Spencer were declassified under the Freedom of Information Act and were available on supply of her death certificate. These established circumstantial evidence that she was on government business. Record Group 59 of the State Department, records relating to internal affairs in China, M.F. 329 rolls 38, 39, 40, 43, 103, 128, and 163 were consulted. So were boxes 6432, 6254, and 930. More specific frame references can be obtained in the author's collection of documents at the University of Southern California. The complete log of the USS *Chaumont* was obtained. Professor Hsue was again helpful on the political background. Files of the *Hong Kong Telegraph, North China Herald, China Press, Celestial Empire,* and *North China Daily News* were read on microfilm. Details of the China dossier were determined through interviews and correspondence with the Duc de Grantmesnil and Leslie Field. The passenger lists of the *Empress of Russia,* the *Empress of Canada,* the *President Garfield,* and the *Shuntien* were fortunately published in the local newspapers. U.S. military intelligence reports at U.S.C. were examined. The guest lists of the Astor House Hotel in Shanghai and the Grand Hôtel de Pékin were also published, a curious lapse of security for U.S. citizens in time of civil war that was amended by 1925. U.S. State Department consular records were searched to obtain details of Mrs. Spencer's movements. U.S. military intelligence reports were consulted on train details. Several members of Herman Rogers's family, most notably his nephew, Richard D. Schley, and his niece, the former Mrs. Edmund Pendleton Rogers (Mrs. Beatrice Tremain), were interviewed at length on Rogers's background in intelligence work. The U.S. State Department maintained quarterly lists of U.S. citizens resident in Peking, which enabled the author to discover the address at which Herman Rogers was resident. This was quite at variance with that given in *The Heart Has Its Reasons*. FBI files were examined, along with published railroad schedules preserved at the Library of Congress. Naval and Marine files were looked at on the matter of Commander Little. The Ciano relationship was confirmed by Mrs. Miles; an oblique reference to it, with Wallis's name omitted, is in Giordano Bruno Guerri's *Galeazzo Ciano: A Life, 1903-1944*. (Milan: Bompini, 1979). The most difficult task was determining the date of Wallis's return to the United States, which she described quite incorrectly in her memoirs. James P. Maloney spent a week searching U.S. Department of Justice immigration and naturalization records for vessels arriving in Seattle before, late one night, he at last lit upon her name as a passenger aboard the *President McKinley*.

Log books of the USS *Wright* were examined. U.S. Navy records of Spencer (R.G. 1959: 1930–1939, box 79) established his Mussolini connections.

Chapter 6: Ernest

The New York Genealogical Society confirmed Ernest Simpson's Jewish origins. Barbara Goldsmith, in *Little Gloria, Happy at Last*, disclosed details of the Vanderbilt and Morgan families. The Pittsburgh Historical Society and Pennsylvania Historical Society supplied information about Mary Thaw. The divorce records of *Spencer v. Spencer*, preserved at Warrenton, Virginia, were unsealed for the author on request. The London *Times* and *New York Times* helped me to clarify the social background in London in 1927. Luc Nemeth in Paris, a specialist in Italian political history, and John Hope in London unraveled the pro-Italian background. Kenneth Rose and Lady Donaldson in interviews in London helped illuminate the character of the Prince of Wales. The *New York Times* files revealed the engagement to Lady Bowes-Lyon and the Max Beerbohm caricature which created such a fuss. Samuel Marx revealed the prince's affair with Marguerite Laurent in his entertaining book *Queen of the Ritz*. The author visited the various addresses in London where Wallis and her husband lived. They are scarcely changed in 2004. Barbara Goldsmith was the best source on the relationship of the prince with Thelma Furness. Contemporary photographs in *The Tatler*, *The Sketch*, and *The Bystander* revealed the contents of 5 Bryanston

Court. The dual memoir of Gloria Vanderbilt and Thelma Furness entitled *Double Exposure* was an excellent source. *The Heart Has Its Reasons* was also drawn from here.

Chapter 7: The Prince

Barbara Goldsmith was excellent on Thelma Furness and the prince. Mary Kirk, later Mary Kirk Raffray, wrote vivid letters home on her visit to London. Again, these were obtained from Radcliffe. The Windsor letters edited by Michael Bloch supplied more information. The *New York Times*, a great source neglected by all Windsor biographers, gave particulars of the prince's movements in those years. The London *Times* gave a more censored calendar of events, notably avoiding the Italian connections. The *New York Times* had no such compunctions. Henry Flood Robert of San Diego supplied the anecdote about the ill-fated afternoon party. Sir Robert Bruce Lockhart revealed in his diaries the particulars of Prince Louis Ferdinand's visit to London. Kenneth Rose kindly supplied me with diary excerpts of Graf Albert Mensdorff, former Austrian ambassador to the Court of St. James. The Duke of Windsor's *New York Daily News* article was indispensable. The biography of Aly Khan by Leonard Slater was a witty source on the Furness-Khan affair. Stanley Jackson's *The Sassoons* filled me in on the background of that remarkable family. *The Long Party* by Stella Margetson was very useful. John Costello supplied me with details of Admiral Wolkoff and his daughter Anna, supplemented by information obtained from transcripts of the trial of Tyler Kent, available at Yale University. Donatella Ortona interviewed her father, who in turn interviewed the 94-year-old Count Dino Gradi in Bologna, Italy, for an irreplaceable firsthand account of the Italian connection in London. I spoke with the Princess Ann-Mari von Bismarck at her home in Marbella, Spain, on the matter of the German connection, and she followed up our conversation with a letter which, of great historical value, has been somewhat adapted in the actual wording to conform with current English usage. Paul Schwarz's excellent book *This Man Ribbentrop* supplied much information. *The Tatler* had a memorable full-page photograph of the guests at the May 27 January Club dinner (only William Joyce was without a black tie). The biography of Elsie de Wolfe by Jane S. Smith was a good source on her and was supplemented in my research by the late Tony Duquette, her protégé and a leading California decorator and artist, and his associate Hutton Wilkinson. Frederick Corbitt, in charge of catering for the royal household, left an entertaining memoir, entitled *Fit for a King*. This book has been much neglected by historians. The *New York Times* and London *Times* followed the prince's movements throughout Europe. Several members of Lord Moyne's family, including his son and the Duchess of Normanby, have filled me in on matters relating to the *Rosaura*.

Chapter 8: Moving Toward the Throne

The late Laura, Duchess of Marlborough was the authority on the matter of the illegitimate child of Prince George. She married Michael Canfield, who died tragically young. The affair with Noël Coward was discussed in Michael Thornton's *Royal Feud*. The memoirs of Prince Christopher of Greece have been consulted. Thornton is the best source on Wallis's burlesque imitation of Princess Elizabeth. Frederick Winterbotham, through correspondence and telephone calls, and the late Ladislas Farago, both on the telephone with me and in his *The Day of the Foxes*, discussed the de Ropp episode.

The account of the journey to Europe is drawn in part from the *New York Times*; the untapped papers of George Messersmith, American minister to Austria, housed at the University of Delaware, contains more useful information. The British journalist G. E. R. Gedye's book *Betrayal in Central Europe* gives a vivid picture of the Prince of Wales in Vienna. Austrian newspapers of the period supply further details. These include the *Arbeiter Zeitung* and the *Neue Freie Presse*. Prince Otto von Hapsburg confirmed the Prince of Wales's interest in him. Research in the Budapest newspapers *Kis Ujsag*, *Neps Java*, and *Budap* brought to light useful information. The diaries of Henry Channon were consulted. A most helpful article by Francis Watson in *History Today* (December 1986) supplied excerpts from the Wigram diaries, which were not then open to public inspection. The *New York Times* expertly covered the Silver Jubilee and pointed to the involvement of Princess Cecilie in the prince's German connections. Further information on the matter of the British Legion was drawn from the legion's official history by Graham Wooten. Hansard was referred to for questions asked by Aneurin Bevan. The Londonderry connection is dealt with in many sources, including *England's Money Lords* by Simon Haxey, a most useful work. The Windsor letters have again been consulted.

Once again, the *New York Times* exhaustively covered the royal tour. George Messersmith was on the case as always. The matter of Armand Grégoire is dealt with in the FBI and Army intelligence files on Grégoire and in the Sûreté files in Paris, now lodged at the Diplomatic Archives along with numerous other reports on him drawn from a variety of intelligence sources. The magazine *La Franciste* has been read, and so has the book *Bucard et le Francisme* by Alain Deniel. *Deadline* by Pierre Lazareff, former editor of *Paris Soir*, and *Campaign of Treachery* by the distinguished Paris lawyer Henry Torres confirm FBI and State Department reports that Wallis engaged Grégoire as her lawyer. The Laval connection was established by the evidence given by Laval at his trial for treason in France after World War II, and both transcripts and *New York Times'* accounts have been drawn from. Comte René de Chambrun confirmed the relationship, which he discussed in his book *Pierre Laval: Traitor or Patriot?* British Foreign Office documents were looked at. *Current Biography* for 1942 gives particulars of Mainbocher. Again, Kenneth Rose supplied the Mensdorff diaries.

Kenneth de Courcy, the Duke de Grantmesnil, was the main source on the China dossier. George Seldes discussed in *In Fact* the matter of Dr. Frank Buchman and his Nazi connections. The biography of Sir Oswald Mosley by Robert Skidelsky supplies much information, supplemented by additional details in Colin Cross's book *The Fascists in Britain* and in the memoirs of Nicholas Mosley, Lord Ravensdale. The matter of Simpson's cotton concessions, referred to in the indexes to the documents of the Foreign Office published in 1972, is recorded in the existing Foreign Office files at the National Archives, London. Frederick Corbitt's aforementioned memoirs supplied the avocado story. Kenneth Rose's *King George V* is excellent on the old king's decline. The *History Today* article was most valuable here; in confirmed from both Lord Dawson's and Lord Wigram's documents the fact of the euthanasia matter. *Business Week*, March 21, 1936, supplied the details of the royal income based on careful research in British archives. Helen Lombard's *Washington Waltz*, a most reliable work, gives further details of the royal investments in Lyons. Henry Grattidge's book *Captain of the Queens* includes the story of the disturbing event that took place during the funeral procession. Paul Schwarz's

This Man Ribbentrop contains the account of the secret films taken of the king and Wallis and sent to Hitler. Schwarz was among the few people in a position to know about this.

The German Foreign Ministry documents contain descriptions of the meetings between the king and his German visitors at the time. *Loyal to Three Kings* was consulted. The idea of Lady Mendl's redecorating the palace came from a *New York Times* article. So did the interview with my father Sir Charles Higham. The love letters were once more a good source. *Time* magazine expertly covered these events. The papers of J. C. C. Davidson, former chairman of the Conservative party and later chancellor of the duchy of Lancaster, were consulted on the Masonic issue.

Chapter 9: Almost Glory

The intelligence files on Mrs. Cartwright are in the Diplomatic Records Branch of the National Archives in Washington. Mary Kirk Raffray's letters were again a good source. Paul Schwarz dealt with the matter of the seventeen red roses, and Channon gave a detailed account of Ribbentrop in England. Harold Nicolson's diaries were consulted. Again, Sir Robert Bruce Lockhart's diaries provided much colorful information. Keith Middlemas and John Barnes's *Stanley Baldwin* is a most reliable source. The FBI files were looked at in connection with the documentary leakage. Schwarz confirms it. John Connell gave the best account of Vansittart in his book *The Office*. John Costello provided more information from intelligence sources in Britain. Nigel West filled me in on zu Putlitz. The Phipps leak is confirmed in British Foreign Office document indexes. The Baldwin papers were consulted. Marion Crawford's controversial book *The Little Princess* supplied the anecdote about Wallis's visit to the little princesses. The matter of the secret submarine war between Italy and Russia was confirmed by Donatella Ortona in discussions with her father, and by Henry Gris, journalist, who interviewed Count Ciano at the time. The attempted assassination was well covered by the London *Times* and *New York Times* and by *Time* magazine. Yet again, the *New York Times* was the best source on the royal tour. J. Charlet in *The Living Age* described the political significance of the trip, basing his information on interviews on the spot. George Weller, the indispensable Athens correspondent of the *New York Times*, dealt with the political purposes of the journey in the issue of September 20, 1936, and so, again, did the equally indispensable George Messersmith. The British press and subsequent historians swept aside much of this information, dealt with further in the Windsor State Department files. John Balfour's memoirs *Not Too Correct an Aureole* are of great value to the historian in this connection. The biography of Sir Percy Loraine by Gordon Waterfield was consulted. Lady Hardinge continued to be a good source on the couple's activities. The *New York Times* kept a constant watch on Wallis at Cumberland Terrace, and at Felixstowe and Ipswich. *Time* magazine also expertly covered the divorce matter. Mrs. Belloc Lowndes revealed the provenance of the Mogul emerald.

Chapter 10: Abdication

Here, the *New York Times* was especially indispensable, and ignored by all biographers. Copies of the *Daily Mail* for the period were read. Rudolf Stoiber, the leading authority on Princess Stephanie Hohenlohe, supplied background on the Rothermere family. Lord Birkenhead provided judicious comments and much information in his excellent life of Walter Monckton. Birkenhead was the source of the anecdote about Monckton's "secret" visits to Buckingham Palace. The Duke de Grantmesnil was the source on the attempted assassination of Wallis. He also described meetings of the Imperial Policy Group. The diaries of Blanche Dugdale were drawn from. The account of Wallis's flight from England was obtained from a great variety of sources, including her own memoirs, the *New York Times*, the London *Times*, the memoirs of Diana Vreeland, a close friend of Lord Brownlow, Lady Donaldson's *Edward VIII*, etc. Martin Gilbert's monumental biography of Winston Churchill was a great source. Copies of all London newspapers for the period were examined. So were the Scotland Yard reports. (The cabinet minutes on the abdication crisis will remain classified for many years.) The journey to the south of France was exhaustively discussed by the *New York Times*. The London *Times* was notably inadequate on the subject. Birkenhead was again an excellent source. French newspapers, especially *Paris Soir*, *Le Figaro*, *Le Matin*, and *Le Temps*, were indispensable. Michael Bloch's annotations on the love letters filled in many useful details. Kenneth Rose was the chief source on the matter of Sandringham and Balmoral, as well as on the Civil List issue concerning the royal income. Charles

Bedaux, Jr., Betty Hanley, and the former Mrs. Edmund Livingstone Rogers were marvelously helpful in the matter of Wallis's stay in France.

Chapter 11: Exile

Donatella Ferrario Ortona, in consultation with her father, obtained the quote from Count Grandi. Birkenhead on Monckton was the best source on the king's journey to Europe. The history of the *Orient Express* by E. H. Cookridge gave a good account of the duke's travels aboard that legendary train. The former Mrs. Edmund Livingston Rogers gave me an exhaustive description of Lou Viei at the time. Douglas Reed in his memorable book *Insanity Fair* covered the duke's activities in Vienna. Frederick Morton's book on the Rothschilds was a useful source. *The Sunday Referee* contained the article by Ellen Wilkinson. Newbold Noyes's pieces in the *Washington Star* and *Paris Soir* were read. The *New York Times* covered every inch of both the duke's and Wallis's movements at the time. So did *Time* magazine. Aunt Bessie's letter included in the Windsor love letters book were valuable; Corinne Murray's granddaughter Mrs. Dale St. Dennis supplied me with several of her notes from the south of France. Lady Donaldson obtained exclusive access to the Metcalfe letters and quoted them in her *Edward VIII*. The *New York Times* covered the concert in Vienna and the visit of the princess royal and the Earl of Harewood. Leslie Field has effectively disposed of the Alexandra emeralds theory. For her book on the royal jewels, Mrs. Field spent years of research at Buckingham Palace. Betty Hanley was indispensable on the life at the Château de Candé. She is one of the very few surviving eyewitnesses, and Charles Bedaux, Jr., read these passages and confirmed their authenticity. The *New York Times* and London *Times* covered the hearing on the divorce. Reporters from the *New York Times* were present every day at Enzesfeld. The large State Department file 033.4111 on the Duke of Windsor contains information on his relationship with Bedaux and on the problems that relationship provoked.

Chapter 12: Wedding of the Decade

A good source on the wedding was the hitherto neglected memoir *At Long Last* by the Reverend Jardine. Constance Coolidge's account is to be found in her correspondence in the Maryland Historical Society. *The London Gazette* was consulted. So were Aunt Bessie's letters to Corinne, supplied by Mrs. St. Dennis. As always, the *New York Times* was in the forefront in covering the nuptials. Betty Hanley obtained many details from her Aunt Fern, even though she herself was not present. The *New York Times* covered the visit to Italy, largely ignored by the London *Times*. The stay at Wasserleonburg was drawn from aforementioned Austrian papers as well as British and American newspapers. The *Daily Express* was an especially good source. Messersmith's report on the duke's leakage of information regarding the armaments shipment was to be found in his collection at the University of Delaware. The further travels were covered by the *New York Times*, as usual. The Duke of Windsor State Department files exhaustively document in letters and telegrams the preparations for the American tour. None of these files had been consulted by historians. The Earl of Crawford's diaries are an excellent source for the grave concern of the king and queen in the matter of the Windsors' Nazi connections. The *New York Times* and Austrian and Italian newspapers covered the German tour in detail. The Duchess of Windsor's account in her memoirs was grossly distorted and self-serving. Nerine Gun in his entertaining biography of Eva Braun was a good descriptive source; William Bullitt's *Personal and Secret*, his correspondence with President Roosevelt, was also a much ignored source of information. So was J. Paul Getty's *As I See It*. The late Adrian Liddell Hart interviewed Frau Hess, who told him of her meeting with the duchess. Army intelligence, OSS, and State Department files were consulted on the matter of Bohle. Martin Gilbert is the source of the Churchill letter on Germany; it is reproduced in the accompanying volume of Gilbert's work that includes correspondence. Files of the Protocol Division of the State Department were drawn from. So were the documents of Sir Eric Phipps; the Hardinge-Vansittart correspondence cited is from the Lord Avon files at the Public Record Office, London.

Chapter 13: Outer Darkness

The Loyalist newspaper *Voz* was examined. Vincent Sheean's admirable book *Between the Thunder and the Sun* provided the best account of the events at Maxine Elliott's house in the south of France. The *New York*

Times continued to follow the Windsor's every move. Tony Duquette kindly supplied much information, as well as telegrams and correspondence, relating to Lady Mendl and the Windsors. George Seldes exposed William Bullitt definitively in *In Fact*. The *New York Times* dealt with the Louis Rothschild matter in some detail; the duke's involvement in the ransom arrangements was supplied by a confidential source. The Ribbentrop document on the Duke Windsor's involvement with the Sports and Shooting Club at the Schloss Mittersill is included in the German Foreign Ministry Dienststelle Ribbentrop documents entitled "Personliche Inlander" file, volume 11, period: 17 December 1936–31 August 1940, serial number 314, negative frame numbers 190707–190708 T120/roll 250. The document may be found in the Charles Higham collection at the University of Southern California or at the National Archives in Washington. The *Sunday Dispatch* report was examined. Nigel West was most helpful on the matter of the Duke of Kent. The attempted murder of the King and Queen of England by Sean Russell can be traced through Russell documents in the author's collection at USC or in the files of the FBI, Diplomatic Records Branch of the National Archives, Scotland Yard, and State Department files. Mrs. Smith's life of Lady Mendl and the French newspapers were combined for my account of the party which signaled the end of an era in Europe. The death of Bedrich Benes was described by the *New York Times*. John Hope in England pulled together details of the many fascistic groups functioning at the time. Malcolm Muggeridge's memoirs *Chronicles of Wasted Time* describe the suspicions that attached to General Ironside. Donald McCormick in his biography of Lloyd George described the dangers that existed in Wales and at Hindhead. The Earl of Crawford's diaries were again consulted. The French Military Archives at Vincennes, the State Department files, *The Gravediggers of France* by Petinax, Lady Donaldson's *Edward VIII*, Major General Pownall's diaries, my interviews with the present Lord Ironside in London, the memoirs of Hore-Belisha, the German Foreign Ministry documents, War Cabinet meeting transcriptions, and massive numbers of documents from the Public Record Office were consulted vis-à-vis the duke's service in France. Boelcke's book on war propaganda was read. The Red Cross security problems are exhaustively dealt with in State Department files in the Diplomatic Branch record room at the National Archives in Washington.

Chapter 14: A Dark Plot

Michael Bloch's *Operation Willi* contains much original research in this controversial area. The former British Public Record Office's files were consulted, including the all-important Portuguese file, to which Mr. Bloch first drew attention. State Department files on the Windsors proved to be another source. The Portuguese government archives supplied materials relating to the Duke of Kent's visit. Martin Gilbert, completing in many volumes Randolph Churchill's unfinished biography of his late father Winston Churchill, has given the historian a fine record to draw from. The memoirs of David Eccles were useful OSS reports on Serrano Suñer and Baron von Hoyningen-Huene were declassified for the author. With the assistance of John Taylor of the National Archives in Washington, German Foreign Ministry documents were reexamined. I also drew from previously unavailable and specially declassified reports on and by Walter Schellenberg, obtained under the Freedom of Information Act from U.S. intelligence sources. The late Sir John Colville granted me an all-important interview. Hutton Wilkinson, on behalf of Tony Duquette, gave me the duchess's cables to Johnny McMullen. The Herbert Claiborne Pell telegram is in the Windsors' State Department documents. These apparently were not consulted by Michael Bloch. The Schellenberg memoirs were used. Birkenhead's biography of Monckton was again a good source. Portuguese files of Dr. Salazar had not hitherto been available. The *New York Times* had a report on board the *Excalibur* and on the *Yankee Clipper*. Thus it was possible to reconstruct the events of the voyage and the air-sea encounter with the Rothschilds.

Chapter 15: Elba

The Windsors' declassified State Department files indicate that on a day-to-day basis the local authorities were keeping a constant surveillance on the couple. Frank Giles wrote amusingly about the duke and duchess in his memoir *Sundry Times*. The *Nassau Tribune* covered the duke and duchess's activities, and so, from a defending counsel's point of view, did Michael Bloch in his *The Duke of Windsor's War*. The U.K. National Archives had substantial files on the Windsors in the Bahamas. Not all of these were consulted by Bloch. The FBI files on Sir Harry

Oakes, Harold Christie, Walter Foskett, Axel Wenner-Gren, Mrs. Wenner-Gren, and the Bahamas as a whole were declassified in 1986. J. Edgar Hoover, frustrated by the restrictions of his activities in the Caribbean, characteristically embarked upon a full-scale separate investigation. The Wenner-Gren FBI files alone amount to almost 3,000 pages. Bloch's account of the journeys of the duchess's maid were supplemented by reference to the State Department files. The Windsors' FBI file contains the report on the duchess's alleged shipping of messages to New York City. John W. Dye, while seeming to be a friend to the Windsors, reported on them somewhat unfavorably. The *New York Times* filled in the details of their travels to the mainland, supplemented by the *Miami Herald* files. The James D. Mooney documents were drawn from his collection at Georgetown University. The State Department and FBI files on Mooney were also of value. Previously undiscovered letters from the Duke of Windsor to Churchill were found by Daniel Re'em in the Avon files at the Public Record Office, London. Messersmith's documents at the University of Delaware were again used. Errol Flynn's movements were determined from the Warner Bros. files at the University of Southern California Doheny Library, Department of Special Collections. The duchess's letters to P. G. Sedley are in her State Department files. The *Liberty* magazine article was read and annotated. Churchill's telegram concerning it is in both the State Department files and Martin Gilbert's. The material concerning the Banco Continental is to be found in the Diplomatic Records Branch of the National Archives in Washington. The substantial Mexico files in that same room were drawn from. Churchill's memorandum concerning the Windsors' property in France is in the Windsors' State Department files. FBI files on the British Purchasing Commission are included with the massive documentation on Princess Stephanie Hohenlohe, declassified on appeal. Details of the Tesden Corporation were also obtained from the FBI. The Mackintosh report is to be found in the Franklin D. Roosevelt Memorial Library at Hyde Park, New York, in the J. Edgar Hoover collection. Hoover reported each Wednesday afternoon to the president. The Hess documents were obtained from Madelyn Sorel, who in turn obtained them from Hess's jailer at Nuremberg. Adrian Liddell Hart supplied more information. The Windsor letters were used. Vincent Astor's investigative mission is recorded in files in the Diplomatic Records Branch. The *Washington*

Post and *New York Times* were consulted. Once again, the Armand Grégoire FBI files and his OSS file were useful. The Adolf Berle documents are at the Diplomatic Records Branch. John Balfour's *Not Too Correct an Aureole* was a source. The *Chicago Tribune*, *Toronto Star*, and Montreal and Ottawa papers were consulted. For a more detailed account of the Windsors' tours, read Bloch. But he missed some details supplied by the *New York Times* and incorporated here. The Ribbentrop-declaration of war matter was found only in the Ribbentrop documents declassified by the Department of Army Security and Intelligence Command at Fort Meade, Maryland. The British intelligence report on Wenner-Gren is quoted in U.S. intelligence reports; the British report is still unavailable in England. The Brassert Company files are with the U.S. Treasury. The information on the Williams–del Drago correspondence comes from Bloch. It is supplemented by material in the Windsors' State Department files. The information about Christie's conflicts with Oakes came from interviews with the only surviving eyewitness, the late Alfred de Marigny, in 1987. The account of the riot was drawn from the *Nassau Tribune*. So was the account of the subsequent fire. The description of the death of the Duke of Kent comes from a declassified report available from the Public Record Office. The Axel Wenner-Gren State Department files yielded particulars of the Windsors' improper investments. The Berle memorandum re censorship is available from the Diplomatic Records Branch. The FBI and Army intelligence files on Charles Bedaux were examined, and his son was in fairness allowed his say in the matter. The judicious historian will examine the intelligence records before reaching a conclusion. The account of Spencer's near death came from the *San Diego Union* and *Tribune*.

Chapter 16: Murder in Nassau

De Marigny gave excellent interviews discussing the entire scene in Nassau in 1943 and his collisions with the Duke of Windsor. He also explained in full Christie's motive for murder. It was necessary to represent all the forensic and circumstantial evidence, along with the details for the judge's previously unavailable handwritten trial transcript obtained by the author on a visit to Nassau. In Los Angeles I was assisted by Dr. Joseph Choi, former assistant to the famous Dr. Thomas

Noguchi, and John Ball, an expert on murder and author of the admirable *roman policier In the Heat of the Night*. The moment I mentioned the size and shape of the wounds to Mr. Ball, he identified them as being caused by a fishing spear, and he also knew from other cases with which he had dealt that this method of killing was exclusive to the Santeria–Palo Mayombe cult. On approaching Dr. Choi, I had exactly the same response. In Los Angeles in recent years there have been a number of murders that can be described in precisely identical terms. I also showed both gentlemen the photographs of the deceased, and they confirmed instantly that nobody seeing that body could have believed the victim was alive. Thus, Harold Christie is proved to be perjurious. Alfred de Marigny, as indicated in the text, believed Oakes was killed by a bullet. He averred that the two autopsy surgeons lied in court in the matter. But there is nothing to indicate that they did, and in fact the wiser policy would have been to lie, saying that the crime was committed by gunshot, so as to remove any suggestion of a black ritual murder, which could only cause another riot in the islands. Dr. Fitz Maurice's testimony was especially valuable since he precisely stated the details of the wounds and declined to give an opinion on the cause of them. The author visited many boating stores in Los Angeles and Newport Beach, examining winch levers and other possible instruments of murder, ruling them all out and returning confidently to the decision of Choi and Ball. The precise details of everyone's movements on the night of the crime were obtained both from the judge's notes and from the *Nassau Tribune*'s files. None of the participants appears to have survived. Sergeant Louis Danoff of the LAPD Homicide Division kindly sent me detailed printed brochures, normally only for use by the police force itself, with diagrams and descriptions of Palo Mayombe killings. I consulted with experts on arson in the matter of gunpowder, an inevitable feature of Palo Mayombe. The matter of rigor mortis was explained to me by Dr. Choi. The Foreign Activities Correlation Department of the State Department kept records of the duke's conversations, carefully monitored through RCA and Western Union sources in Miami. The Windsors' mainland visit was extremely well covered by the FBI and is contained in the FBI files. The visit to the FBI headquarters in Washington was discreetly ignored by all newspapers. Alfred de Marigny directly charged the Duke of Windsor with being an accessory after the fact of the crime and claimed that the duke pursued him through intermediaries who made attempts on his life and also that the duke blocked him from migration. *Inside Detective*, November 1944, has been read. The fine detective Raymond Schindler got part of the story right. The Majava report is in the J. Edgar Hoover special file on the case. Whereas the newspapers neglected to mention whom Robinson identified as the killer, the FBI files specifically name him. Surprisingly, the FBI declassified this information for this author in 1981 without requesting Christie's death certificate, an indication to the historian that they had conclusive proof of his guilt. The Toronto report is in the Windsor FBI files. Stevenson's charges were recorded by *Time* magazine and the *Saturday Evening Post*.

Chapter 17: Return to Europe

Ciano's death was recorded in newspapers all over the world. The demise of Charles Bedaux was also extensively reported. The Richmond newspapers gave an account of Aubrey Weaver's death in a fire. *The Duke of Windsor's War* by Bloch shows Wallis's increasing distress in Nassau and the duke's efforts to reinstate himself in Britain. (As usual, Bloch blames the British royal family for their pettifogging attitude, an incorrect approach in my opinion.) The Foreign Office Indexes published in 1972 list the whereabouts of the Windsors' properties. The Chanel file comes from the Schellenberg report. Balfour's memoirs again were excellent on the Young matter. Joseph R. Borkin's biography *Robert R. Young: The Populist of Wall Street* is a carefully documented source. The State Department Windsor files give uncomfortably revealing details of the attempts to suppress the German Foreign Ministry files. The trip to England was covered by the *New York Times* and most other newspapers. Tania Long covered the Nuremberg-Rosenberg matter thoroughly. The Duke de Grantmesnil supplied me with all correspondence of the period housed at the Hoover Institution on War, Revolution and Peace at Stanford University, California. The Duchess of Marlborough was a main source on the jewel robbery, her account supplemented by the London *Times* and *New York Times*, the London *Daily Mail* and *Daily Express*, Scotland Yard reports, and an interview with Leslie Field. Captain Harry Grattidge's *Captain of the Queens* supplies much little-known information. An interview with Guido Orlando proved invaluable. Stephen Birmingham in his *Duchess* gave an amusing picture of Jimmy Donahue. The New York newspapers covered the Windsors' movements thoroughly in the late 1940s, including the fire episode at the Waldorf Towers. Mrs. Eleanor Miles's letter about the Windsors in the south of France is to be found at the Maryland Historical Society. The Henry M. Warfield will is obtainable from the Maryland Archives.

Chapter 18: Wandering Years

Sotheby's catalog of the famous jewelry auction at Geneva in April 1987 was examined. The details of the history of Suzanne Blum are contained in several existing biographies of Léon Blum. *The Windsor Story* by Charles J. V. Murphy and Birmingham's book reveal Murphy's problems with the duke and duchess in the matter of working on the memoirs. The late Laura, Duchess of Marlborough and the late Duchess of Argyll supplied much new information. Details of the tour of the southern states and Mexico are to be found in the Corinne Murray correspondence; it has only been possible to include some highlights in this account. Balfour provided the Biarritz anecdote. C. L. Sulzberger in his memoir *A Long Row of Candles* gave the strong description of the Windsors incorporated here. Most newspapers recorded the duke's speech about Queen Elizabeth's accession, as well as the subsequent controversy. Hugo Vickers admirably described the Windsors' successive homes in Paris. Cecil Beaton wrote characteristically of the couple in his diaries, drawn from by Vickers in his definitive biography of that artist. Lady Mosley granted the author one of the most memorable interviews of his life at her home near Paris. I drew from this rather than from her biography of the duchess, which was based almost entirely on published sources. Elsa Maxwell wrote with a surprising sharpness and intelligence about the Windsors in her neglected memoir *RSVP*, one of the best books of its kind and an indispensable guide to the social life of an era. Cholly Knickerbocker's syndicated columns were read. The story of the collapse of the Donahue relationship is drawn from Birmingham and Murphy, and supplemented with an interview conducted in 1980 with Jerome Zerbe.

Chapter 19: Late Afternoon

The *New York Times* expertly dealt with the matter of Queen Mary's death. Biographies by Anne Edwards and James Pope-Hennessy were consulted. The *Daily Express* was read. The *New York Times* was the most reliable source on the Woodward killing, the Capote account the least reliable. *McCall's* magazine, January 1961, was read. The late Sir John Colville and Lady Mosley were the best sources on the Windsors' social life and brilliant capacity to entertain in those years. Murphy's account was also valuable. Members of the Murray and Mustin families described Aunt Bessie's hundredth birthday party and her funeral. The New York and Texas newspapers covered the duke's surgery at Houston. Michael Thornton's *Royal Feud* brought together most reliable sources on the visit to the London Clinic and on immediately subsequent events. Hugo Vickers filled in more information.

Chapter 20: Evening and Night

The Niehans Clinic information was researched in Switzerland. Murphy was the best source on the Mountbatten matter. Thornton supplied more details. Hugo Vickers confirmed or corrected published information. The best account of the death of the duke and the subsequent service is to be found in the London *Times*, with additional details supplied by Thornhill. Vickers gave me long and invaluable interviews on the final years. The Countess of Romanones, in an article in *Vanity Fair*, June 1986, gave an intimate, if controversial, memoir of that difficult time. Most importantly, the Duc de Grantmesnil Collection at the Hoover Institute at Stanford, contains the extraordinary correspondence between himself and Maître Blum on the matter of the removed documents. The Duchess of Marlborough, Princess von Bismarck, and Hugo Vickers discussed the duchess's funeral with me. Alistair Cooke in the *New York Times* provided the last word on the reasons for Wallis's being denied the throne. Once again, the Sotheby's jewel catalog was used as a source on the auction, and various newspaper and television reports were drawn from.

Notes on the New Material

The late Sir Dudley Forwood was the source on Edward "Fruity" Metcalfe, in an interview at his house in the New Forest at Ringwood, Hampshire, on October 9, 1987, which was to be kept confidential until his death. *The Kaiser's Daughter*, the memoirs of Princess Viktoria Luise, Duchess of Brunswick (Englewood Cliffs, NJ: Prentice Hall, 1977) provided the details of the proposed marriage of Princess Friederike of Prussia and the Prince of Wales. The matter of Prince Philipp of Hesse was drawn from the denazification files on the prince (1945–46) supplied by Professor Jonathan Petropoulos of Claremont College, California, the world authority on the subject; from the *New York Times* from 1924 to 1945; from seized German records on microfilm at the National Archives and Records Service in Washington, D.C., Modern Military Branch; from the Foreign Office files at the National Archive of Great Britain; and from State Department files, obtained by Jill Cairns-Gallimore, courtesy John Taylor. The Sandra Rambeau matter comes from the State Department espionage files on her and on her fellow agents Frederick G. McEvoy and Errol Leslie Flynn; from the files of the *Los Angeles Herald-Examiner* at the University of California; and from her master FBI file.

The connections of the Duke of Kent, Prince Paul of Yugoslavia, Prince Philipp of Hesse, Goering, and Hitler are clearly stated in the State Department files on each and in Philipp's denazification files as well as from private information. The affair with Guy Trundle, recorded in the Albert Canning reports at Scotland Yard to Lord Trenchard and then to Sir Philip Game, were originally classified until 2037 but were released in January, 2003. The matter of the China dossier can be found discussed in the correspondences and diaries of Kenneth de Courcy, Duc de Grantmesnil, housed at the Hoover Institution on War, Revolution and Peace at Stanford University, California. The actual dossier may or may not exist in the closed (until 2017) de Courcy files or at the vespiary of Windsor Castle, where its presence even at the time of the abdication has been consistently denied by Buckingham Palace sources and official biographers. Sir John Coke can be regarded as reliable and the record stands. The conversations of Sir Edward (Robert) Peacock and Joseph P. Kennedy are contained in the aforementioned *Hostages to Fortune: The Letters of Joseph P. Kennedy*, edited by his granddaughter Amanda Smith and published by Viking Penguin in 2001. They represent the only leak to date of the most careful cover-up in the royal chronicle—the matter of the finances and of the queen's (later Queen Mother's) attitude to the Windsors, which has also been carefully hidden to date, with one entire box of files (24) removed from the Bodleian Library at Oxford, it is believed on royal orders. Happily, her letter on the matter to Prince Paul of Yugoslavia (October 2, 1940) survives at Columbia University, along with her acid comments in the Kennedy diaries. The involvement of Prince Paul with the Nazis, hidden by generations of whitewashers, is exhaustively dealt with in his former minister Ilija Jukie's *The Fall of Yugoslavia* (New York, Harcourt Brace Jovanovich, 1971), the only insider's account available. The Prince of Wales's behavior at the time of his father's death can be found in the Kennedy diaries. His behavior when he became king—hailing taxis and so forth—is to be found in an anonymous but reliable report to be found at Churchill College, Cambridge, and confirmed as authentic by the son and grandson of Sir Louis Greig.

The Maundy Thursday occasion was mentioned in the *New York Times*. The May 4, 1936, letter of complaint from Wallis to her aunt Bessie Merryman is at the Baltimore Historical Society. The report on Communist activity regarding the king is in the Scotland Yard reports by Superintendent Albert Canning. The Privy Council meeting regarding Ethiopia is in the Royal Archives at Windsor Castle. The Blenheim Palace divorce conspiracy is discussed in the anonymous report at Cambridge. The Bulgarian visit was published in the *Bulgarian Monthly Review* as cited in the narrative, and in *Crown of Thorns, the Reign of King Boris III of Bulgaria* by Stéphane Grovet (New York, Madison Books, 1987). Wallis's continuing affair with Trundle when her husband was king is recorded in the Kennedy diaries; the source, as given, was Sir Edward Peacock; the visit to Wales is in the Anne Fremantle book cited in the narrative. The account of the Duke of York's horror at being king is shown in a long and anguished confession preserved in the Royal Archives at Windsor Castle. The desire to reverse the abdication is in the Peacock-Kennedy discussions. The Cockburn matter is to be found without a solution in his memoirs *A Discord of Trumpets* (New York, Simon and Schuster, 1956); the account of the king's blackouts at dinner and the meeting with Peacock comes from the Churchill papers at Cambridge.

Sir Horace Wilson's 64-page report on the abdication is indispensable, and damning in its conclusions. Dismissed as "inaccurate" and "ill-advised" by the royal spin doctors when declassified in 2003, it is based upon exhaustive research by a devoted, reliable, and royalist civil servant. The report also contains documentation on cabinet discussions as to whether Wallis should be bribed, confirming my findings on the matter in the 1987 edition. The visits to Count Toerring by the Duke of Kent are recorded in the Foreign Office files of the British National Archives. The exhibition of Wallis in the Baltimore museum was recorded in that city's newspapers.

Sir Dudley Forwood supplied me with details of the duke's grief on the H.R.H. issue at his home at Ringwood, Hampshire, England, on October 8, 1987. The Helga Stultz matter is in the FBI files of the Windsors in Washington, D.C. The meeting with Errol Flynn, Hesse, and Bormann at the Hotel Meurice is in the Flynn SIS files, described in detail to the writer Gerald Brown at the Ministry of Defense in February 1980. The historians Martin and Peter Allen have since enlarged the picture from reliable eyewitness sources in the intelligence services. The Horchers banquet and the visit to Goebbels were recorded in the van Oven work cited in the narrative. The Peacock-Windsor discussion over money by telephone from London to Paris is in the Peacock-Kennedy conversations in the Kennedy diaries.

Wallis's love affair with William Bullitt was described to the author in telephone interviews with Eleanor Davies Tydings Ditzen, a close friend of Lady Jane Williams-Taylor, at her home in Washington, D.C., on March 4, 8, 12, and 19, 2003, and referred to her memoirs, overlooked by all historians, *My Golden Spoon* (New York: Lanham Books, 1997). Bullitt's background can be found discussed in various issues in George Seldes's weekly *In Fact* (1940–1945) and is closely documented in the damning Bullitt State Department files at the National Archives in Washington, including the illicit use of the German Foreign Ministry for transmitting top secret messages to Washington. The details of his sexual life are to be found in *Friend and Lover: A Life of Louise Bryant* by Virginia Gardner (New York: Horizon Press, 1982); the Freud connection is documented in Peter Gay's biography of the doctor (New York: W.W. Norton, 1988). The Bullitt-Offie affair comes from Rosemary Murphy, actress daughter of Bullitt's close friend and diplomatic associate Robert Murphy, who was in Paris at the time. The secret rendezvous at Schiaparelli's is from Mrs. Ditzen; details of Lady Williams-Taylor come from Gioia Diliberto's *Debutante: The Life of Brenda Frazier* (New York: Simon and Schuster, 1987) and from the records of the Bank of Montreal and the Montreal Historical Society. The Maroni blackmail story, as stated in the narrative, comes from the Constance Coolidge diaries, courtesy Andrea Lynn of the University of Illinois; it is supplemented by Coolidge's letters to her father of the time, maintained at the Massachusetts Historical Society in Boston; and from research in the social registers *Bottin Mondain* and *Tout Paris*, sundry books in French, and Pierre Lazareff's *Deadline*, as well as the files of *Le Matin* in Paris, records of the Sûreté at Fontainbleu, and interviews in Paris in October 2003, as well as an exploration of that city for all the appropriate addresses. The meeting at the funeral of Queen Marie of Rumania is in the Romanian newspapers and in the *New York Times*; the letter from King George V to Baldwin regarding the Windsors is in the Royal Archives at Windsor Castle; the insult following Rose's refusal of the dinner invitation is in the Kennedy diaries. The resuming of the Kent-Rambeau relationship is in the files of the *Los Angeles Herald-Examiner* for 1939; the meeting of Prince Philipp of Hesse and the Duke of Kent in July of that year is in the files on Philipp maintained by Professor Jonathan Petropoulos; the letters of the Duke of Kent to Prince Paul on the subject of Prince Friedrich of Prussia are at Columbia University. The conversation between the queen and Kennedy on the American tour is in the Kennedy diaries. The letter dated October 2, 1939, from the Queen of England is the only record of her contempt of Wallis to have been rescued from generations of royal weeders and is at Columbia University in the Prince Paul papers. It is a unique and invaluable picture of her personality (it also displays a humorous homophobia in its mocking picture of the society photographer and designer Cecil Beaton.) The fake broadcast on October 11, 1939, is recorded in the Goebbels diaries housed at the National Archives, Washington, and in the book by Cristabel Bielenberg, *The Past Is Myself* (London: Corgi 1968). The treasonable note sent to Hitler by the Duke of Windsor via Bedaux is in the possession of Martin Allen. It was given to his father Peter Allen by Albert Speer, who said he obtained it from Hitler in the last days of the führer's life in the Berlin bunker. The Bullitt-Assergio-Mussolini connection is in the U.S. State Department file of Bullitt's letters. The report of Fulton Oursler's conversations with Roosevelt is recorded in his diaries and private papers at Georgetown University, Washington, supplied courtesy Fulton Oursler, Jr. The Bullitt mention of British assets in Paris is in the State Department files. The Edward A. Tamm report on the Windsors, classified when I wrote the original book, was declassified by the FBI in March 2003. However, the name "British Secret Intelligence Service" was blacked out. My assistant Jill Cairns-Gallimore found the same document with the SIS name not excised as the source in a long-lost file on Axel Wenner-Gren at the National Archives, thus supplying the indispensable fact that the report came from Sir Stuart Menzies and not from some unreliable society source.

The information on Claude Dansey and the Windsors came by letter from the former Abwehr agent Peter Hansen, who is at work on a memoir, courtesy of Harry C. Cooper of the Sharkhunters. The Bullitt-Vichy story is in the Bullitt files at the State Department. The Strang report is in the files of the British National Archives. The July memorandum is also at the National Archives. Frederick W. Winterbotham spoke of his killing of the Duke of Kent on SIS orders to historian Peter Allen—facts courtesy of Martin Allen, July 4, 2003. German comments on the crash were in the *New York Times*.

The Williams-Taylor matter is from an interview I conducted with Eleanor Davis Tydings Ditzen on July 3, 2003. The William Rhinelander Stewart story is in the Windsor FBI files declassified in March 2003. The Bullitt-Welles matter is in the files of Secretary of the Interior Harold L. Ickes at the Franklin D. Roosevelt Memorial Library at Hyde Park, New York. The Monnet mission is in the cited Marshall thesis; for this I am in debt to Cornell University. The Eddie Chapman mission is from Chapman himself, in an interview with Gerald Brown of the Murdoch newspapers at an Arab health farm near London on February 3, 1980. The Sikorski death was recorded in the *New York Times* on July 5, 1943; the cause was given by Frederick W. Winterbotham to Martin Allen. Windsor's comment on Roosevelt is from the de Courcy papers at Stanford. So, too, is the revival of the China dossier issue in Marrakesh and in the south of France in 1951.

The Susan Mary Alsop story is from her *To Marietta from Paris* (New York: Doubleday, 1975). The story of Wallis as a CIA agent comes from Aline, Countess of Romanones's *The Spy Went Dancing* (New York: G.P. Putnam's Sons, 1990). The matter of the duke being required to die on schedule is from my interview with Dr. Jean Thin in Paris on October 4, 1991. The matter of the auction of furniture and effects by Mohammed Al-Fayed is supplied courtesy of Sotheby's New York.

Index

Page numbers in italic type refer to photographs.

Printed in the United States
87094LV00001B/20/A